REDUCING ADOLESCENT RISK

To my daughter Adrienne and all young people making the
transition to adulthood.

REDUCING ADOLESCENT RISK

TOWARD AN INTEGRATED APPROACH

DANIEL ROMER, EDITOR

Annenberg Public Policy Center,
University of Pennsylvania

SAGE Publications
International Educational and Professional Publisher
Thousand Oaks ▪ London ▪ New Delhi

For information:

Sage Publications, Inc.
2455 Teller Road
Thousand Oaks, California 91320
E-mail: order@sagepub.com

Sage Publications Ltd.
6 Bonhill Street
London EC2A 4PU
United Kingdom

Sage Publications India Pvt. Ltd.
B-42, Panchsheel Enclave
Post Box 4109
New Delhi 110 017 India

Printed in the United States of America

Library of Congress Cataloging-in-Publication Data

Reducing adolescent risk: Toward an integrated approach /
Daniel Romer, editor.
    p. cm.
Papers presented at a conference held at the Adolescent Risk Communication
Institute of the University of Pennsylvania Annenberg Public Policy
Center in June 2002.
Includes bibliographical references and index.
ISBN 0-7619-2835-9 (hc) ISBN 0-7619-2836-7 (pb)
    1. Risk-taking (Psychology) in adolescence-Prevention-Congresses.
I. Romer, Daniel, 1946-RJ506.R57R43 2003
613´.0433—dc21

                                               2003002701

This book is printed on acid-free paper.

03   04   05   06   10   9   8   7   6   5   4   3   2   1

Acquisitions Editor:	James Brace-Thompson
Editorial Assistant:	Karen Ehrmann
Copy Editor:	Linda Gray
Production Editor:	Denise Santoyo
Typesetter:	C&M Digitals (P) Ltd.
Indexer:	Pamela Van Huss
Cover Designer:	Sandy Sauvajot

Contents

Acknowledgments

The Annenberg Public Policy Center (APPC) thanks the Annenberg Foundation and the Annenberg Foundation at Sunnylands Trust for their support of the conference on which this book is based. In addition, we thank the American Academy of Political and Social Science for cosponsoring the conference with the Annenberg Adolescent Risk Communication Institute of the University of Pennsylvania. Thanks also go to the seven session leaders of the conference who helped to organize their sessions and recruit panel members: Madelyn Gould, Mark Griffiths, John Jemmott, Lloyd Johnston, Douglas Kirby, Susan Millstein, and Paul Slovic. Although we were unable to include papers from all the panelists and session leaders, their participation produced a most stimulating and exciting meeting. The many attendees from government agencies and foundations (listed in Appendix B) were not only an excellent audience but also contributed greatly to the discussions. Kenneth Bollen of the University of North Carolina also consulted with us on the design of the causal modeling discussed in Chapter 1. Thanks also go to Linda Gray for her patience and dedication to editing the volume. Finally, we thank Belkys López and Nikki Dooner for their help in bringing this volume together and the following members of the APPC staff who helped to make the conference a success: Richard Cardona, Kyle Cassidy, Joshua Gesell, Deborah Porter, Carmen Renwick, and Debra Williams.

Preface

In January of 2001, the Annenberg Foundation provided an endowment to the Annenberg Public Policy Center (APPC) of the University of Pennsylvania to establish the Adolescent Risk Communication Institute (ARCI). The purpose of this new center is to synthesize what is known about effective strategies to reduce adolescent risk behavior and to encourage healthy youth development. In addition, ARCI was created to encourage new research that could lead to more effective strategies for healthy adolescent development and to communicate the findings to the policy community as well as to parents, youth, and persons who care for and educate young people.

As Kathleen Hall Jamieson, Director of the APPC, and Daniel Romer, Research Director of ARCI, considered how best to launch the new Institute, they considered it critical to recognize that the United States does not have a comprehensive youth development strategy. The schools are perhaps the most important venue for the training and development of the young. However, there has only recently been an attempt to fashion a nationwide strategy to promote the educational attainment of youth. The primary responsibility for the health and development of young people lies with the states. However, the states differ dramatically in programs and resources dedicated to young people's development and well-being. A diverse array of governmental departments take responsibility for youth development, but their programs have developed along separate paths with little common purpose.

Despite the fractured state of programming for youth, there is increased interest in developing more comprehensive strategies. The National Governors Association (NGA) has created a Youth Policy Network that is encouraging states to look for ways to integrate their youth-related programs. Seventeen states (including New York, California, and Massachusetts) have begun this process with help from the NGA as well as other national youth-oriented organizations (Ferber, Pittman, & Marshall, 2002). These efforts are increasingly looking for ways to involve schools, state agencies, and community-based organizations in a unified strategy to encourage positive youth development. In addition, policymakers look to the research community to provide guidance regarding the most effective approaches.

To achieve the goal of more coherent youth policy, the research community and federal agencies such as the Centers for Disease Control and Prevention and the Department of Education will be increasingly called on to identify strategies that can help states and the federal government create comprehensive programs.

Unfortunately, research-based recommendations for healthy development are usually focused on single outcomes with few comprehensive strategies. For example, recommendations from both *Healthy People* (U.S. Department of Health and Human Services, 2000b) and *Healthy Youth* (Fleming, Towey, & Jarosik, 2001) contain a plethora of worthy objectives spanning a wide range of youth outcomes, such as reduced drug, alcohol, and cigarette use; healthier approaches to sex; and reduced reliance on violent methods of problem solving. However, each is discussed as a separate problem with separate strategies.

Strategies to achieve healthy outcomes also rely heavily on the schools and medical providers to deliver health education programs. However, the federal government has recently embarked on a policy of increased emphasis on educational achievement to improve the academic readiness of the nation's youth. The No Child Left Behind program focuses on academic testing as early as third grade and imposes financial penalties on schools that fail to meet testing goals. Although the legislation concentrates heavily on poor and disadvantaged schools, the effects of this initiative will be felt across the educational spectrum. With this increased pressure on academic performance in schools, there will be even less room in the school day for health-related curricula. If they do not already, schools will soon lack the time in the school day to continue behavior-specific prevention curricula.

Another common strategy is the use of mass media campaigns to reach youth and parents regarding risky behavior. We now have major campaigns to discourage cigarette smoking, illicit drug use (especially marijuana), and childbirth before marriage. However, we often see messages that seem to ignore possible effects on other risk behaviors: for example, antismoking and drug messages that model young people's suicide behavior. There is also little recognition of the well-established pathway from cigarettes and alcohol to marijuana (see Hornik, this volume).

Despite evidence of comorbidity for major health risks, our interventions continue to be developed for single outcomes. So we asked, What do we know about interventions that might be able to reduce adolescent risk and increase resilience across behaviors?

To answer this question, we brought experts together from seven fields to discuss the pathways to risk behavior in their domain and possible strategies to reduce multiple risks. Our risk domains included traditional ones, such as tobacco, drugs, and alcohol as well as the prevention of risky sexual behavior. But we also included some relatively understudied domains, such as suicide and gambling. Indeed, gambling has not yet been recognized as a serious health threat to youth in the United States (National Research Council, 1999). However, we thought it would be helpful to learn more about this behavior because it might serve as a test case of the temptation to "reinvent the wheel" in developing interventions for this behavior. Indeed, if the past is any guide, the nation's approach to preventing the risks of this behavior in youth will be to develop a new set of interventions that compete with the other programs that currently take up time in the school curriculum and in medical care settings.

Suicide was selected not only because it is a leading cause of death among youth, but also because it is related to a range of conditions and behaviors that concern youth. Suicide is a major form of violent death that often involves firearms. It is also a major consequence of mental illness, especially depression, which is prevalent in youth and comorbid with many other adolescent risk behaviors (see Gould, this volume, and Alloy, Zhu, & Abramson, this volume). Hence, it was felt that a focus on this behavior would provide a useful lens through which to understand a range of youth behaviors that pose a serious risk to healthy youth development.

We invited researchers who study sexual risks not only because the problem is serious but also to gain a greater understanding of comprehensive strategies that might be effective for these risks. This field is fragmented by the division between the older and more established family-planning approaches to pregnancy prevention and the newer effort to reduce exposure to sexually transmitted diseases (STDs), especially HIV. In addition, there is a major split among policymakers about the best way to encourage safer sexual behavior in youth. Welfare reform legislation has emphasized "abstinence first" programs that on their face appear to encourage behavior that can reduce both pregnancy and STDs. However, it is not clear that such a strategy can be effective for all youth at all ages, just as a "Just Say No" approach has only limited success for other risk behaviors considered normative for adults but not for youth. Hence, we invited researchers from both fields to discuss what is known about sexual risks and potential intervention strategies that lead to comprehensive interventions.

Finally, we asked researchers who study risk perception and decision making in adolescents to review the state of the art in this field. Many intervention strategies presuppose that adolescents can be educated to make better decisions about risky activities. However, there remains considerable controversy within this field as to whether adolescents adequately perceive the risk of many harmful behaviors (e.g., tobacco use) and if they adequately integrate their understanding of risk into decisions about engaging in risky behavior. To the degree that adolescents are seen as rational actors, there is hope that they can be influenced to make adaptive decisions. At the same time, there are serious concerns that young people will become addicted, for example, to tobacco, before they adequately understand the risks of this activity.

The list of presenters at the conference is in Appendix A. In addition to the presenters, many representatives from federal agencies and foundations attended the meeting and contributed to the discussion and proceedings. Their names and affiliations are contained in Appendix B. The papers we include in this volume contain a wealth of references to the scholarly and policy literature; these are located at the end of the book.

OVERVIEW OF CHAPTER ORGANIZATION

Although the conference was organized around seven risk topics, we present many of the papers written for the conference according to the common themes that connect them, irrespective of the session in which they were presented. In the first chapter, Daniel Romer presents findings from a national survey of youth conducted by ARCI to inform the conference about potential relationships between the risk behaviors discussed at the meeting. The results of this analysis indicate not only that risk behaviors are related but that interventions to reduce this comorbidity may have a large effect across a wide range of behaviors. In addition, he shows that young people are aware of the co-occurrence of risk behavior and associate much of it with popular peers. These findings suggested that the ultimate aim of the conference, to identify comprehensive approaches to risk reduction, had considerable promise. However, simply telling young people not to engage in these behaviors is unlikely to be a successful strategy. Therefore, strategies that address the reasons for the appeal of risk behavior and that provide healthier alternatives will have greater chances for success.

Adolescents as Decision Makers

In Part I, Section A, we focus on the papers that addressed questions surrounding adolescents as decision makers. One enduring question concerning adolescents is whether they even consider the risks of their behavior before they engage in it. James Byrnes considers this and other questions regarding adolescent decision making and emphasizes the need to consider both the risky situations that adolescents find themselves in and their capacities for making good decisions in those situations. Laurence Steinberg proposes a definition of mature decision making and questions whether adolescents can fully master these skills. Daniel Lapsley addresses the question of whether young people are subject to belief in certain fables that encourage risky behavior. He takes a more optimistic tack by observing that adolescents are often protected from certain harmful conditions, such as depression, by the belief in optimistic fables. Hence, to the degree that adolescents believe in fables at all, the effects of these beliefs need not be harmful.

In Section B of Part I, Susan Millstein and Paul Slovic argue for the importance of affect in adolescent decision making. Millstein suggests that risk judgments may not have much influence on adolescents unless the risks reach a critical affective threshold. As a result, many risk judgments may be unrelated to behavior. Slovic explores the importance of the "affect heuristic" as a process that influences risk judgments and behaviors. Use of this heuristic encourages people to use their feelings toward a behavior rather than a reasoned analysis of risks as the basis for deciding to try the behavior. Advertising and promotion can create positive images of many risky behaviors likely to elicit favorable feelings. In addition, many of these behaviors are seen as popular and confer the appearance of adult status. As a result, young people are likely to give them a try. Unfortunately, the addictive properties of some risk behaviors can make this a hazardous strategy.

Other authors argue forcefully that many adolescents are sensitive to risk information and will moderate their behavior in line with risk perceptions under certain conditions. Martin Fishbein argues that risk judgments do affect intentions and that one can observe this relationship if one measures risk perceptions appropriately. He presents examples of sexual behavior that illustrate this relationship. In the realm of drugs and alcohol, Lloyd Johnston discusses the role of fads and other changes in popular culture that appear to induce widespread changes in drug use despite little or no change in personality predispositions or availability of drugs. He argues that perceptions of the risks of drugs have been a powerful mediator of these changes. These wider social influences also need to be understood to design effective interventions for the prevention of risk behavior in youth. In addition, he shows that some correlates of drug use (such as lack of attachment to school) may influence a wide range of drug use tendencies. Finally, Meg Gerrard, Frederick Gibbons, and Michelle Gano argue that risk perceptions are most likely to influence the behavior of adolescents who are willing to try a new behavior (but have not yet done so) and hence who are open to information about the consequences of those behaviors.

The authors in Section C of Part I present evidence that adolescents who approach complex decisions with more adaptive decision-making skills are more likely to make healthy choices than those whose decision-making skills are weak or simplistic. Myrna Shure reviews a long line of research that she pioneered to identify decision-making skills that can be taught in the primary grades and that lead to more adaptive behavior as children age. Kenneth Griffin argues that teaching these skills in combination with risk-specific information can be an effective strategy to insulate youth from risky peer influences. Andrew Parker and Baruch Fischhoff argue that basic decision-making skills are correlated with safer behavior across a range of risk domains, including substance use, unprotected sex, and delinquent behavior.

Geoffrey Fong and Peter Hall discuss the importance of sensitivity to delayed effects of risk behaviors and present evidence that young people who are taught to appreciate these delays will be more likely to persist in maintaining healthy behavior. Finally, Maria LaRusso and Robert Selman argue that school social environments are powerful influences on the decision maturity of middle school youth. Schools with chaotic and arbitrary discipline policies create cynicism regarding health advice and fail to provide credible guidance for youths who face challenges negotiating decisions about risky behavior.

Common Pathways and
Influences on Adolescent Risk Behavior

In Part II, we feature authors who focus on intervention strategies that exploit common pathways to risk behavior. In Section A of Part II, Anthony Biglan and Christine Cody review the findings of a project that synthesized what is known about multiple-problem youth. These youth follow developmental paths characterized by multiple risky behaviors, such as substance use, aggressive and antisocial behavior, and risky sexual behavior. These individuals account for a large proportion of the risk behavior engaged in by youth. However, these youth can be identified early (primarily by their aggressive tendencies in the elementary grades) and potentially helped to avoid some of the hazardous effects of their behavior. Herbert Severson, Judy Andrews, and Hill Walker also advocate early detection with the help of teachers who can be a valuable aid in identifying multiple-problem youth. Their research suggests that teachers can be trained to use objective assessment tools and that once identified, problem youth can be helped to find more adaptive ways of interacting with peers and teachers in school and other settings. Finally, Kenneth Winters, Gerald August, and Willa Leitten describe an intensive intervention currently under investigation to identify and help multiple-problem youth to avoid their likely maladaptive developmental paths.

In Section B of Part II, two chapters provide an overview of what is known about predispositions to engage in a range of risk behaviors. Caryn Lerman, Freda Patterson, and Alexandra Shields review the latest developments in genetics regarding addictive behaviors. Although they conclude that it is unlikely that there is a single gene for addiction, several traits are likely to be inherited that predispose persons to seek experiences that are addictive. They focus on sensation seeking and impulsiveness as paradigms of such traits. They also discuss some of the ethical issues that will arise once it becomes possible to identify risk-predisposing traits in children. Lewis Donohew and his coauthors review the extensive evidence for the role of sensation seeking as a trait that predisposes young people to seek risky experiences. He focuses on the implications of this relationship for the design of persuasive messages to discourage these outlets for sensation seekers.

Depression is a major risk factor for suicide and is itself an important mental health problem in adolescents. Lauren Alloy, Lin Zhu, and Lyn Abramson review recent research on the developmental precursors of depression and some potential interventions to prevent depression in young people. If successful, such interventions might also be able to help depressed persons overcome the need to abuse substances such as tobacco and alcohol.

Peers and the family, the focus of Section C of Part II, are important influences on adolescent risk behavior. Joseph Rodgers discusses the role of social contagion among teens as a mechanism for the spread of risky behaviors. The same mechanisms appear to underlie the social transmission of a range of risk behaviors, including tobacco use and sexual initiation. If these transmission processes could be postponed to even a little later in development, the reductions in risk behavior initiation could be sizable. Bonita Stanton and James Burns discuss the importance of including parents in interventions because their influence through mechanisms such as parental monitoring of behavior can affect a wide range of risk behaviors, including unprotected sex, violence, and drug use.

Mass media are an important influence on young people. In Section D of Part II, Barbara Delaney, from the Partnership for a Drug Free America, discusses the research strategies used to develop antidrug messages for the national campaigns that her organization has sponsored for over a decade. Joseph Cappella, Marco Yzer, and Martin Fishbein amplify the need to identify strong arguments that can persuade youth to avoid risk behavior and provide examples of some methods to accomplish this goal.

Perspectives From Different Risk Research Traditions

Part III provides perspectives on the challenges posed by several of the major risk behaviors discussed at the conference. In Section A of Part III, the first team of authors focuses on the relatively understudied behavior of problem gambling. Mark Griffiths summarizes the state of knowledge about this behavior from the perspective of the United Kingdom, where access to gambling by young people is less restricted than in the United States. As a result, it is possible to observe some of the potential abuses that greater access to gambling devices such as slot machines has on young people. This is particularly of concern because gambling restrictions in the United States have progressively been lifted to the point where access in venues such as the Internet is open to anyone. In addition, just as substance use can become addictive, there is evidence that gambling has the potential to induce the same type of dependencies on its frequent users. As we saw in the analysis of comorbidity among substance use and gambling in Chapter 1, gambling has many of the same precursors as substance use and may be able to be treated with some of the same strategies. Jeffrey Derevensky, Rina Gupta, Laurie Dickson, Karen Hardoon, and Anne-Elyse Deguire highlight the overlap in precursors and risk factors between problem gambling and other risk behaviors. They also suggest some ways of conceptualizing problem gambling within a risk-resilience framework. Marc Potenza discusses some of the potential interventions that might be tested to prevent youth addiction to gambling, and Rachel Volberg reviews some recent research concerning the prevalence of the behavior and some ways that states with fewer restrictions on gambling have attempted to shield youth from its effects.

The sessions devoted to sexual behavior at the conference, the focus of Section B of Part III, were perhaps the most contentious regarding appropriate strategies for prevention. Douglas Kirby provides an overview of the many intervention approaches to safer sexual behavior that have been tested. He concludes that whether one focuses on abstinence or safer sex as strategies, the important factor that seems to underlie successful interventions is increasing attachment to adults and peers who foster healthy norms for youth behavior. Across a wide range of interventions, attachment to adults in prosocial activities, such as community service, seems to have lasting impact on reducing risky sexual behavior.

Despite Kirby's optimistic assessment, the other authors find much that is problematic in current approaches to prevention in the sexual arena. Mignon Moore and Jeanne Brooks-Gunn review the research and find that programs with a comprehensive approach that includes access to contraception and information about a variety of options for sexual health are the most successful. In addition, they suggest that a focus on healthy youth development rather than on risk avoidance characterizes the successful programs. They also argue that the current emphasis on abstinence-first programs by the federal government places concerns about sexual morality above sexual health. Dennis Fortenberry argues that the emphasis on sexual risk stigmatizes a natural and important behavior in which youth will eventually be expected to engage. He argues that a middle ground in our search for effective strategies must be found that can encourage healthy regard for sex while also promoting greater safety in the way sexual relations are conducted.

Although suicide is the third leading cause of death in youth under age 25 and the second leading cause for college students, it remains an understudied problem in prevention research. In Section C of Part III, Madelyn Gould reviews what is known about the major precursors and influences on suicide. She also notes some of the important ways in which these precursors overlap with other risk behaviors. Furthermore, because mental disorders such as depression are major risk factors, the prevention of suicide dovetails with efforts to promote mental health and to reduce the stigma of seeking help for mental disorders.

David Brent discusses several intervention approaches for reducing adolescent suicide. He focuses on gun access as an important precursor to suicide. Nearly all the increase in youth suicide over the past 50 years has been related to increases in the use of firearms as a means of death. He discusses some ways in which removal of access to firearms for vulnerable youth may be able to save lives and avoid nonfatal injuries. Sean Joe discusses the problem of recent increases in suicide among African American youth. He argues that this phenomenon may be linked to changes in the status of African American youth that have led to greater tendencies for individuals to blame themselves rather than external conditions for failure.

Finally, in Section D of Part III, Robert Hornik reports some findings from the national evaluation of the United States antidrug campaign. He finds that the gateway hypothesis for tobacco and alcohol use as precursors to marijuana use is still quite viable. Very few youth begin to use marijuana without first smoking cigarettes or drinking alcohol. An effective strategy for reducing marijuana initiation could be reducing cigarette smoking. Similar effects should be observed from encouraging the safer use of alcohol.

Overarching Approaches and Recommendations for Future Research

In Part IV, we feature some of the presenters who focused on more global strategies for risk reduction. The approach that seeks to encourage engagement in positive activities and the creation of healthy environments (positive youth development) is discussed by Brian Flay as a strategy to reduce a range of risky behaviors. He argues that for such programs to succeed, they will need to change entire social units such as schools and communities. In addition, Jodie Roth and Jeanne Brooks-Gunn review the evidence concerning community-based programs for positive youth development. Their review finds that programs that were more successful in influencing multiple risk behaviors also increased attachment to the community and instilled positive norms for healthy behavior. Finally, Ralph DiClemente, Gina Wingood, and Richard Crosby survey recent developments in multilevel approaches that seek to change not only the individual but also higher levels of social connection, such as the family and community. They argue that such interventions will have greater endurance and success than ones that focus only on individual change.

In the last chapter, Kathleen Jamieson and Daniel Romer review the major implications of the conference proceedings for future research and policy development. They identify four major findings from the conference that should be pursued in future research to identify comprehensive intervention strategies and a unified policy for healthy youth development.

CHAPTER 1

Prospects for an Integrated Approach to Adolescent Risk Reduction

DANIEL ROMER

One of the concerns that motivated the Reducing Adolescent Risk Conference was the observation that prevention researchers frequently focus on only one or two risk behavior outcomes. In addition, they all too often fail to assess potential mediators of risk behavior that might help to explain covariation among risk behaviors. For example, smoking prevention researchers focus on reductions in smoking without assessing potential mediators of their intervention that might generalize to other risk behaviors that are comorbid with tobacco use. We will not be able to develop more comprehensive interventions until we develop better theory and measurement of potential causal pathways that underlie multiple risk behaviors. We know that many risk behaviors covary (and many conference presenters confirmed this). What is less clear is the basis for this covariation and whether it is amenable to intervention.

To help us begin to answer the mediation question, ARCI conducted a national survey of youth aged 14 to 22 in the spring of 2002.

The survey assessed the extent to which young people differ in sensation seeking and involvement in prosocial activities such as religion and community service. Each of these characteristics has been linked to a variety of risk behaviors, with sensation seeking increasing the likelihood of risky behavior (see Lerman, Patterson, & Shields, this volume, and Donohew et al., this volume) and prosocial activities reducing it (see Kirby, this volume, and Johnston, this volume). However, researchers have not examined the potential for these influences to affect a wide range of risk behaviors. We were interested to see therefore if the effects of either sensation seeking or prosocial activities were broad enough to influence a range of risk behaviors or were uniquely related to each risk behavior. To answer this question, we examined several risk behaviors, including tobacco, alcohol, and marijuana use; gambling; and failure to use seat belts while riding in cars. In addition, we assessed depressive symptoms and suicidal ideation, which are precursors to suicide.

We were also interested to see how young people perceive others who engage in risk behavior. If young people saw the behaviors as unrelated (whatever their actual co-occurrence), it might make sense to approach each risk behavior as a separate problem. However, if young people recognize that any one risky behavior is likely to be accompanied by other health-compromising behavior, then interventions that focus on only one at a time may be sending the wrong message about the importance of the other risks to health. On the other hand, if young people recognize that risks co-occur but believe that they do only among unpopular peers, then discouraging one risk behavior may be sufficient to reduce multiple risk behaviors. Hence, we asked our respondents about the prevalence of risk behavior among both popular and unpopular peers.

SAMPLE DESCRIPTION AND METHODOLOGY

Interviewing for the survey took place from May 8 to June 20, 2002. Youth between the ages of 14 and 22 were selected for interviewing using random-number telephone-dialing procedures. Households were screened for the presence of a targeted respondent. For youth under the age of 18, parents or guardians were asked for permission to interview their child. In households with more than one eligible youth, the one with the most recent birthday was selected for interviewing. Of the 8,517 households screened, approximately 19% had an eligible respondent. Of the eligible respondents (1,595), 900 youth completed the interview. Taking into account those households that could not be screened (but may have had an eligible respondent), the response rate was 49.9%.

The sample matched U.S. Bureau of the Census (2001) estimates within 1 percentage point for gender and within 2 points for region of the country and for gender by education level. The survey tended to over-represent Hispanic youth (21.1 vs. 14.5%) and to underrepresent white non-Hispanic (61.7 vs. 66.5%) and black non-Hispanic youth (10.7 vs. 14.2%). In view of the small discrepancies from national estimates, weights were not applied in any analyses.

RISK BEHAVIOR PROFILES

Respondents were asked whether they had ever drunk alcohol, smoked cigarettes, or smoked marijuana or hashish. They were also asked if they had ever gambled for money such as on the lottery. In addition, they were asked if they had ever failed to use a seat belt when riding in a car. If they reported ever having done any of the above, they were asked if they had done so in the past 30 days. For each of the substances, they were also asked how frequently they used the item in the past 30 days along a scale relevant for each substance.

The findings from these questions, shown in Table 1.1, indicate wide variation in risk behavior ranging from only 22.8% who never failed to wear a seatbelt to 64.4% who never smoked marijuana. Frequency of use in the past 30 days was scaled from a low score of 1 to either 4 or 5 gradations of high use. Failure to use seatbelts (43%) was the most frequent risk behavior, followed by use of alcohol (37%). Our estimates for engaging in gambling are probably low and attributable to our focus on the lottery. In later follow-up questions, we found higher percentages of youth reporting gambling activity when other forms of gambling were probed.

To determine respondents' experience of depressive symptoms and suicidal ideation, we asked, "During the past 12 months, did you ever feel so sad or hopeless for two weeks or more in a row that you stopped

Table 1.1   Distributions of Engagement in Various Risk Behaviors

Frequency	Risk Behavior				
	Alcohol (%)	Cigarettes (%)	Marijuana (%)	Gambling (%)	Nonuse of Seat Belts (%)
Never	24.4	48.8	64.4	58.0	22.8
Yes, but not in past 30 days	38.7	26.8	24.0	29.1	34.0
Past 30 days	36.9	24.4	11.6	12.9	43.2
Frequency					
1	8.6	5.3	3.6		
2	6.8	4.8	1.3		
3	6.8	8.4	2.9		
4	8.0	5.9	3.8		
5	6.8				

Table 1.2   Percentages of Respondents Who Reported Mental Health Problems

Response	Depression Symptom (%)	Suicidal Ideation (%)
No	77.2	92.9
Yes	22.8	7.1
No plan for suicide		3.7
Plan for suicide		3.4

doing your usual activities?" In addition, we asked if during the past 12 months, "you had ever seriously considered committing suicide?" and if so, "did you make a plan about how you would attempt suicide?"[1] Table 1.2 contains the rates of response to these questions. Nearly 23% of respondents reported experiencing the depressive symptom. In addition, about 7% said they had thought about committing suicide in the past 12 months, and about 3.4% claimed to have a plan to do so.

INFLUENCES ON RISK

We also asked respondents about various activities they engage in on a regular basis and if they were attracted to activities that involve high degrees of excitement. Among the activities that they might engage in regularly were religious attendance and community service. About 53% reported religious involvement, and about 39% reported engaging in some form of community service. Responses to these two items were correlated ($r = .22$, $p < .01$). Four items taken from the shortened form of the Sensation Seeking Scale (Hoyle, Stephenson, Palmgreen, Lorch, & Donohew, 2000) were used to identify persons with different degrees of attraction to exciting activities. The responses to these items, shown in Table 1.3, also tended to correlate with each other (alpha = .69).

ANALYSIS OF CO-OCCURRENCE

To study the interconnections between the risk behaviors and their potential relationships with the two sets of influences, we constructed the causal model shown in Figure 1.1. This model allowed each of the behaviors in Table 1.1 to load on the same risk factor. In addition, the model allowed the mental health indicators, depression and suicidal ideation, to load on a separate factor. Nevertheless, we allowed each risk factor to be related to the other, either because of influences on each from sensation seeking or

Table 1.3 Percentage of Responses to the Sensation-Seeking Items

Item	Strongly Agree (%)	Somewhat Agree (%)	Somewhat Disagree (%)	Strongly Disagree (%)
Like to explore strange places	32.9	38.3	10.8	17.0
Like to do frightening things	10.4	27.1	21.1	40.1
Like new and exciting experiences	15.6	32.7	24.0	27.2
Prefer friends who are exciting and unpredictable	30.1	40.7	15.0	12.4

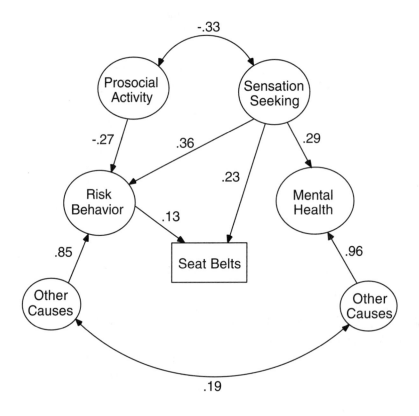

Figure 1.1 Model of Relations Between Risk Behaviors, Mental Health Indicators, and Potential Causal Influences on Them

NOTE: All path coefficients are standardized and significant at $p < .05$.

because of correlation between other common causes of the two risk factors.

We found that smoking (.73), drinking (.69), marijuana use (.68), and gambling (.47) loaded heavily on the risk behavior factor. However, failure to use seatbelts was only slightly related to this factor. Hence, we found that although many risk behaviors covary, some many not be very highly related to others (see Byrnes, this volume). Although mental health was separate from the risk behavior factor, sensation seeking influenced both risk factors. In addition, sensation seeking directly influenced nonuse of seatbelts. Other causes also influenced each risk factor, and these were correlated themselves ($r = .19$), indicating that the risk factors share influences apart from sensation seeking.

Engaging in prosocial activity was negatively related to sensation seeking, but even holding this relationship constant, prosocial activity tended to reduce risk behavior. We assumed that prosocial activity would not be related to mental health, and a separate analysis confirmed this.

The finding that each of the influences was related to many of the risk behaviors is not surprising because others have found such relationships before (see Johnston, this volume, for a demonstration of the same finding with a much expanded list of drugs). What this analysis does show however is that each influence's effect on risk behavior is mediated by a relatively simple factor structure. In the case of the risk behaviors, one underlying factor can account for all but one of the relationships between the influences and each risk behavior. The one exception is seat belt use, which does not appear to be mediated by the same factor that underlies the other risk behaviors.

Similarly for the mental health factor, all the relationships between sensation seeking and mental health risks were mediated by the underlying mental health factor. These findings indicate that interventions that can

alter the effects that sensation seeking has as a motivator for risky activity can potentially alter the effects on a wide range of risk behavior. Indeed, when we tested to see if the common factor underlying these four behaviors could account for all the relationships between the behaviors and sensation seeking, we found that there was no evidence of significant residual variation between use of cigarettes, alcohol, or marijuana; gambling; and sensation seeking.[2] In addition, interventions that can influence prosocial activity should be able to reduce engagement in the same set of risk behaviors. In total, prosocial activity and sensation seeking accounted for 27% of the variation in the factor producing comorbidity in the risk behaviors.

The analysis also suggests that interventions to reduce depressive symptoms may also be able to reduce dependence on potentially addictive behaviors. The correlation between the two risk factors is small when sensation seeking is controlled ($r = .19$), but this relationship may still be worth addressing, especially if it reflects attempts by depressed persons to medicate themselves in response to their depression. Although the causal direction is not fully understood, depression has long been recognized as comorbid with substance use (see Alloy, Zhu, & Abramson, this volume). Whatever the causal direction, however, efforts to treat depression in youth may have the beneficial effect of also reducing substance use and other thrill-seeking behaviors (such as gambling).

The finding that seat belt use is not mediated by the same factor that underlies the other risk behaviors does not argue against interventions that attempt to modify the effects of sensation seeking. It does suggest that even when risk behaviors are mediated by different factors, they may still be influenced by the same variables that affect other risk behaviors. As a result, despite the fact that seat belt use does not covary very highly with the other risk behaviors, an effective intervention to reduce the influence of sensation seeking on risky behavior could potentially also influence seat belt use.

The relationship between sensation seeking and depression is interesting as well. Here we have a relationship between two seemingly different predisposing conditions with sensation seekers appearing more likely to engage in suicidal ideation. Impulsiveness has been associated with elevated suicide risk in youth (see Gould, this volume). Perhaps impulsiveness is responsible for the comorbid relationship between the variables. In any case, these findings also suggest that interventions to reduce the harmful effects of sensation seeking may have beneficial effects on other risky conditions, such as suicidal ideation.

In summary, this analysis suggests that a focus on multiple risk behaviors and potential common pathways of influence on those behaviors can identify intervention strategies to reduce risks to healthy development across a multitude of risks. For example, although sensation seeking may well be a genetically determined trait (see Lerman, Patterson & Shields, this volume), there is no reason to rule out interventions that attempt to help sensation seekers find safer outlets for their sensation needs or to help them better understand the basis for their risky behavior preferences. Such interventions have the ability to reduce a wide range of risky practices and to encourage persons with sensation-seeking needs who are suicidal to seek care for their depressive symptoms. In addition, the analysis indicates that interventions to reduce depression may also help to reduce a range of other behaviors that have harmful consequences in themselves.

The results not only supported the goals of the conference but also suggest that future analyses of potential influences on risk behavior examine the ability of these variables to affect a wide range of behaviors

so that more comprehensive intervention strategies can be designed and tested.

RISK BEHAVIOR AND POPULARITY

Another question we posed to our respondents concerned their perceptions of co-occurrence of risk behaviors and the type of persons who are seen as engaging in the behaviors. We asked those surveyed to

> please think about popular young men (or women depending on the respondent's gender) in comparison to men (women) who are not popular. Would the popular person be more likely, about as likely, or less likely than the unpopular person to (a) smoke cigarettes, (b) smoke marijuana occasionally, (c) drink alcoholic beverages such as beer, wine, or liquor occasionally, or (d) gamble for money, such as playing the lottery or other games of chance?

The results shown in Figure 1.2 indicate that for the majority of respondents, engaging in these behaviors was not associated with unpopular peers. Indeed, for occasional alcohol use, the majority saw this as a popular thing to do. For the other behaviors, less than 40% saw the behavior as associated with unpopular peers.

We also looked at the co-occurrence of these perceived behaviors among popular peers and found that only about 27% of respondents did not see popular peers as engaging in at least one of the four behaviors (Table 1.4). In addition, about half saw popular peers as likely to engage in at least two of the behaviors. Hence, not only are the behaviors seen as likely to co-occur, but they are also associated with popularity.

These results suggest that young people are aware that risk behaviors are not exhibited as separate characteristics. Furthermore, the strategy of attacking one behavior at a

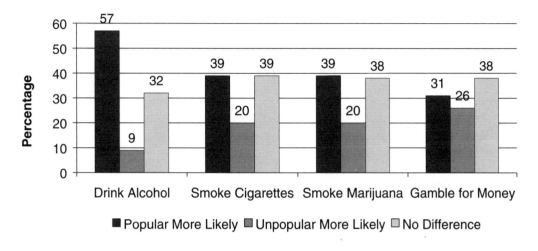

Figure 1.2   Percentage of Young Americans Who Link Certain Behaviors to Perceptions of Popularity

Table 1.4   Proportion of Respondents Saying That Popular Peers are Likely to Engage in Different Numbers of Four Risky Behaviors

Number of Behaviors	Percentage
None	26.5
At least one	73.5
At least two	50.6
At least three	31.5
All four	11.4

NOTE: Behaviors include smoking cigarettes, using marijuana, drinking alcohol, gambling for money.

time may not be very effective when the people who set the norms for this age group are likely to engage in more than one. We return to some suggested strategies for addressing this problem in the conclusion of the volume. However, these findings reinforce what we already know: Simply telling young people that many risk behaviors are harmful will not deter them from engaging in them. We will need a far more sophisticated approach to help young people make decisions about risky alternatives.

NOTES

1. For those respondents who said yes, we asked if they currently had this plan. For those few who said yes *(N = 4)*, we determined if they were in imminent danger of committing suicide and told them that we could connect them with a help line if they were not able to talk with anyone at their home.

2. The model provided an adequate fit to the data by several criteria, including a low root mean square error (.043) and a high comparative fit index (.993). We thank Kenneth Bollen for his advice and suggestions regarding the design and interpretation of this analysis.

Part I

ADOLESCENTS AS DECISION MAKERS

Section A

Differing Views of Adolescent Decision Making

CHAPTER 2

Changing Views on the Nature and Prevention of Adolescent Risk Taking

JAMES P. BYRNES

The phenomenon of adolescent risk taking has captured the attention of a number of highly productive scholars from a variety of disciplines (e.g., psychology, public health, communications, etc.). As result, the literature on this phenomenon is vast, diverse, and highly fragmented. From the standpoint of scientific progress, this state of affairs is problematic for two reasons: (a) The most fruitful areas of new research are difficult to discern, and (b) much of the work being done is duplicative across disciplines rather than progressive. In light of this situation, I offer my perspective on what we have learned about adolescent risk taking over the past 30 years and where we should be headed next. This perspective is based on my reviews of the literature on various kinds of risky behaviors (e.g., Byrnes, 1998; Byrnes, in press; Byrnes, Miller, & Schafer, 1999) and on comprehensive reviews written by others (e.g., DiClemente, Hansen, & Ponton, 1996b; Gerrard, Gibbons, Reis-Bergan, & Russell, 2000). My approach involves examining several early hypotheses about the nature of risk taking, its developmental course, and the best ways to reduce the level of unhealthy risk taking in adolescents. I will argue that these early views were reasonable when they were first proposed but should be reconsidered in light of recent developments in the field.

RETHINKING SOME EARLY PROPOSALS

Over the past 30 years, scientists and policymakers have made certain assumptions about risk taking that, in my opinion, need to be reconsidered in light of the accumulated evidence and the emergence of new perspectives. These assumptions include the following:

Assumption 1: Adolescents take risks because they lack knowledge. Numerous studies have shown that older adolescents are more likely than younger adolescents to engage in risky behaviors such as cigarette smoking, illicit drug use, driving while intoxicated, and unprotected sex (Byrnes, 1998; DiClemente et al., 1996b). Early on, it was assumed that adolescents engaged in these behaviors because they did not understand that their actions were risky (e.g., they did not know that cigarettes cause cancer or that unprotected sex leads to STDs or pregnancy). Instead of finding empirical support for this assumption, interventionists simply accepted the idea and created programs to increase adolescents' knowledge of the negative consequences of smoking, drug use, and so on. Unfortunately, knowledge-based interventions have been found to be uniformly ineffective across various domains (DiClemente et al., 1996b). Subsequent studies have also found that teens who engage in these behaviors tend to have as much or more knowledge than do teens who refrain from engaging in them (Gerrard et al., 2000).

These findings, of course, do not imply that adolescents know everything they need to know about the risks of unhealthy behaviors (e.g., smoking) or that they fully understand the negative consequences (e.g., what it would be like to battle lung cancer). For example, I am by no means agreeing with the claims of the tobacco industry that teens "know what they are getting into" when they start to smoke. I am merely saying that one cannot use a teen's level of knowledge to discriminate between teens who engage in risky behaviors and teens who do not. Risk takers and risk avoiders have similar levels of knowledge (superficial and inaccurate as it often is).

Assumption 2: Adolescents take risks because they think that they are invulnerable. One way to explain the lack of association between knowledge and risk taking is to assume that adolescents think the negative consequences associated with risky behaviors will happen to others but will not happen to them. In other words, adolescents think they are special or somehow protected from

harm. Two lines of evidence led to the common perception that adolescents think they are invulnerable. One consists of studies in which some teens respond "Yes" when asked if a behavior leads to a negative consequence (e.g., smoking causes cancer) but then respond "No" when asked if they personally will experience the negative consequence. The second line consists of studies on the phenomenon of adolescent egocentrism (Elkind, 1967). An important aspect of adolescent egocentrism is this sense of specialness.

The invulnerability assumption has been questioned recently for several reasons. Although a "No" response to questions about negative consequences could be interpreted as indicating that teens think they are invulnerable, it could also mean that they are simply willing to take a chance (Gerrard et al., 2000). Adults know that the next plane trip or car ride they take may be their last, but they are willing to take the chance and fly or drive anyway. Besides the ambiguity of the meaning of adolescent responses in such surveys, there are also the findings that (a) adolescents and adults seem to rate the likelihood of negative consequences similarly (Jacobs-Quadrel, Fischhoff, & Davis, 1993), (b) there has been no consistent or strong relationship between scores on adolescent egocentrism measures and risk taking (Cauffman & Steinberg, 2000b), and (c) many teens greatly *over*estimate their chance of death in the near future—they do not underestimate it (Fischhoff et al., 2000).

But again, it is important to be clear about what I am arguing and what I am not arguing. Scholars who advocate the invulnerability assumption need to show a strong covariance between invulnerability and engagement in risky behaviors (i.e., teens who believe they are invulnerable take the risk, whereas teens who believe they could be harmed avoid it). Although global measures of adolescent egocentrism show little consistent correlation with risky behaviors, more specific indicators of faulty perceptions do show correlations with risky behaviors (Fishbein, this volume; Millstein, this volume). Hence, such findings suggest that risk takers believe they are *less vulnerable* than their risk-avoiding peers, but these findings do not imply that teens believe they are *invulnerable*.

Assumption 3: All forms of risk taking are bad. In everyday language, the term *risk taking* has a certain connotation. Most people believe that it refers to highly dangerous activities such as skydiving (Boverie, Scheuffele, & Raymond, 1994). In my view, all behaviors are performed in contexts and all contexts contain uncertainty because of the inherent, probabilistic structure of the world (Byrnes, 1998; Byrnes et al., 1999). Because there are relatively few "sure things" in life, unintended negative consequences could follow from essentially any action that we perform. Hence, all actions are risky to some extent and there is no way to avoid taking risks.

Rather than assuming that risk taking always leads to problems and that risk aversion always leads to success, the more accurate perspective is that regular success follows from the *ability to discriminate between risks that should be taken and risks that should be avoided* (Byrnes & Miller, 1997). Sometimes people have to take risks to enhance their personal lives (e.g., get married even though marriages sometimes end in divorce) or improve their health (e.g., get surgery to remove a tumor even though some die as a result) or improve their financial well-being (e.g., take a higher-paying job in a new city even though things may not turn out as well as they hoped). The negative forms of risky behavior, then, are part of a larger universe of both health-promoting (positive) and health-compromising (negative) behaviors (see Flay, this volume, for a related line of argumentation).

Moreover, if adults in a society are charged with instilling competencies in children that they will need to be successful later in life, then it would seem that we should be helping the young learn how to discriminate between risks that should be taken and risks that should be avoided. Right now, most intervention efforts seem to be geared toward reducing a circumscribed list of unhealthy forms of risk taking (e.g., smoking, unprotected sex). Although this is certainly a worthwhile goal, the pervasiveness of both positive and negative risks in life suggests that we may be too restricted in our intervention efforts. In other words, we should be trying to instill health-promoting behaviors as well (Flay, this volume).

Assumption 4: Adolescents who take risks in one domain (e.g., smoking) usually take risks in others as well (gambling, sex, etc.); in other words, risk taking is a kind of cross-situational personality trait or syndrome that emerges in adolescence. The field of personality contains two kinds of scholars: (a) those who advocate the existence of traits (e.g., honesty) that emerge in all contexts that call for this trait and (b) those who suggest that behavior is much more situation specific (e.g., honest in one situation but dishonest in another). I tend to side with the latter perspective for two reasons. The first is that notions such as "trait" or "syndrome" are not very explanatory (Mischel, 1984). We do not want simply to know that people will behave in certain ways (in the set of situations listed on a personality questionnaire); we also want to know why they tend to behave that way (assuming that their self-reports are accurate). The more one gives serious consideration to the antecedent psychological factors that determine behaviors (e.g., beliefs, values, etc.), the less one tends to advocate cross-situational generality. As I'll argue later, people rarely have the same beliefs, values, and so on in different contexts. As such, there is no reason to expect them to act the same way in these contexts.

The second reason pertains to the fact that the literature on interrelations among risky behaviors reveals two contradictory patterns. On the one hand, many researchers have found generally low (near-zero) correlations between various measures of risk taking (Boverie et al., 1994; Byrnes, 1998; Heilizer & Cutter, 1971). On the other, many others have shown that behaviors such as regular smoking, binge drinking, illicit drug use, and unprotected sex are often moderately correlated (Biglan, this volume; Byrnes, 1998; Donovan, Jessor, & Costa, 1988; Flay, this volume; Johnston, this volume; Osgood, Johnston, O'Malley, & Bachman, 1988; Romer, this volume). Relatedly, some researchers have found single-factor solutions in factor analytic studies of risky behaviors (e.g., Donovan et al., 1988), whereas others have found anywhere from two to eight factors (e.g., Gullone, Moore, Moss, & Boyd, 2000; Jackson, Hourany, & Vidmar, 1972; Miller, Plant, Plant, & Duffy, 1995; Shaw, Wagner, Arnett, & Aber, 1992). If risk taking is a general disposition that emerges in all contexts, such multifactor solutions should not occur.

There are two ways to respond to these apparently contradictory findings. One way involves choosing sides and simply dismissing the findings from the other camp. The other, more productive approach (adopted here) would be to consider how scholars in both camps could be right. Careful analysis of the studies in this area suggests that the odds of finding correlations among risk-taking measures (and of finding single-factor solutions) can be increased by taking the following three steps in one's research:

1. Select subgroups of the population that are atypical in some respect.

2. Restrict the list of risky behaviors to daily smoking, regular binge drinking, illicit drug use, and regular unprotected sex.

3. Do not control for other "third variables" that could explain the apparent linkage between risky behaviors.

For example, one could follow the lead of Richard Jessor and colleagues by focusing on teens who engage in high levels of smoking and the like at very young ages (e.g., 12 or 13). These teens are atypical because most teens (> 70%) simply experiment with these behaviors (rather than engage in them on a regular basis) and also do so at later ages. Another approach would be to focus on the 5% to 6% of teens who are clinically depressed, suicidal, or problem gamblers (e.g., Gould, this volume; Griffiths, this volume). A third approach would be to select out teens who regularly engage in one of the Step 2 behaviors (e.g., smoking) and consider whether they also engage in the other three behaviors as well (e.g., Johnston, this volume).

Conversely, one could lower the odds of finding high correlations and single-factor solutions by expanding the range of risky behaviors beyond smoking, drinking, illicit drug use, and unprotected sex. Once behaviors such as seatbelt use, fast driving, trying out for a sport, and so on are added to the list, multiple factors always emerge. If respondents include both typical and atypical teens, correlations become lower as well. Finally, if one includes multiple predictors besides the risky behaviors (e.g., parent SES, achievement measures, aspirations, opportunities to take risks), some of the links between risky behaviors drop out because they are spurious. Note, however, that some the links between some problem behaviors remain after controls.

This analysis, if it is true, poses problems for theories that take one or the other side in the debate between syndrome theorists and situation-specific theorists. Syndrome theorists cannot explain why multiple factors emerge when one provides expanded lists of risky behaviors to representative samples; relatedly, situation-specific theorists cannot explain why behaviors such as smoking, drinking, illicit drug use, and unprotected sex repeatedly cluster in certain segments of the population. What is needed, then, is an integrative approach that can accommodate *both* sets of findings. Until such an approach takes hold, it would be a serious mistake to assume either that there is a syndrome of risky behaviors that have a common cause in all teens or that each instance of risk taking has a unique set of predictors. If nothing else, we could develop interventions based on an account that is only partially correct. Interventions work to the extent that they are based on an accurate causal story (regarding why teens smoke or drink, for example). When interventions are based on an inaccurate or partially correct causal story, they tend to have only modest or minimal effects.

Assumption 5: Risk-taking diminishes with age. If it is the case that (a) risk taking has both general and specific determinants, (b) all actions are risky to some extent, and (c) there are both positive and negative forms of risk taking, it follows that one would not necessarily predict age changes in absolute levels of risk taking between adolescence and adulthood. In my view, teens take risks in certain situations because these situations are conducive to taking risks. In other words, they are given the opportunity to take risks (e.g., they find themselves far from home and the person who drove them there is intoxicated) and many oblige (e.g., they accept the ride). Adults are also given many opportunities to take risks and they oblige as well (e.g., cheat on their taxes, drive too fast, tailgate, smoke cigarettes, call in sick when they are not sick, etc.). Thus, even if we were to find that the level of certain kinds of risks decreases between adolescence and adulthood (drinking in secluded parks on Friday nights with friends), this finding would not mean that the absolute level of risk taking has decreased. People may be taking different *kinds* of risks because the situations in which

they find themselves change. For example, why drink in hiding when you can drink in a bar when you are over 21? But even if contexts did not change with age, my review of the literature on behaviors such as smoking, drunk driving, and unprotected sex suggests that adults engage in these behaviors as often as teens (Byrnes, 1998). Hence, I do not think that the level of risk taking decreases between adolescence and adulthood.

Assumption 6: Males are always more likely to take risks than females. Just as problems with Assumptions 3 and 4 led to the conclusion that risk taking may not decrease with age, these problems also lead one to expect that gender differences in risk taking would vary by topic rather than be invariant across contexts (Byrnes, Miller, & Schafer, 1999). Although a meta-analysis of 150 studies on gender differences in risk taking that I conducted with colleagues did generate an average effect size of $d = .13$ (suggesting that males are slightly more prone to take risks than females), this average is entirely a function of the frequency with which researchers have investigated certain topics. If all studies on gender differences in risk taking examined risk taking while driving, our meta-analysis showed that the average would have been $d = .29$ instead of .13. Conversely, if all studies focused on risk taking using classic tasks from the heuristics and biases literature, the average would have been $d = .05$. Finally, if all studies focused on smoking in 20-year-olds or unprotected sex in adults over 20, the averages would have been $d = -.19$ and $-.11$, respectively, suggesting greater risk taking on the part of *females*. Thus, empirically, we know that males do not always take more risks than females. But theoretically, I argue that the size of the gender difference in risk taking is a function of the opportunities that present themselves to females and males. Males are more prone to take certain kinds of risks, and females are more prone to take others. We think that males are risk takers because they tend to take some of the prototypical risks that come to mind (see Assumption 3 and the everyday connotation of the term risk taking).

Assumption 7: Decision making can be improved simply by giving teenagers metacognitive insight into the nature of decision making. So far, my arguments have suggested that we have not properly diagnosed the problem of adolescent risk taking. In my view, we have wrongly attributed this problem to factors such as lack of knowledge or invulnerability and have wrongly assumed that (a) all risk taking is bad, (b) risk taking decreases with age, and (c) males are more likely to take risks than females. Even if we were to alter all these assumptions and discover the real reasons why teens take unhealthy risks (e.g., smoke cigarettes, use illicit drugs, engage in unprotected sex, etc.), we are only halfway there. It is one thing to properly diagnose a problem (e.g., rapid weight loss is due to liver cancer not diabetes), and it is quite another to figure out the best way to solve this problem (e.g., radiation? chemotherapy? surgery?).

At a basic level, interventions are designed either to instill something that is missing in the repertoire of participants (e.g., knowledge, values, strategies) or to eliminate something that is unproductive (e.g., self-defeating thoughts, bad habits). Several interventions to reduce unhealthy risk taking in teens are based on the idea that teens lack metacognitive insight into the nature of good decision making. In other words, if teens only knew how competent people make decisions (i.e., the things that competent people do and the things they avoid), teens would be able to make better decisions themselves. This part of the intervention reflects the diagnosis of the problem (that they are deficient in both their understanding of decision making and in identifying good strategies for making

decisions). I'm not sure this lack of insight is really the problem (but that is another story).

The second part of the intervention reflects beliefs about the best way to get this information across to adolescents. In many cases, school-based interventions of this sort organize material into courses that involve lectures, units on particular topics (e.g., unhelpful decision heuristics and how to avoid them), and tests. Children often learn the content of these courses (i.e., students can tell you what the representative heuristic is and why it causes problems), but there is no evidence that these courses reduce the level of unhealthy behaviors such as smoking or unprotected sex (Beyth-Marom, Fischhoff, Quadrel, & Furby, 1991; Byrnes, 1998).

Given the powerful effects of situation-specific influences on risk taking and what we know about the nature of effective instruction (Byrnes, 2001), there is little reason to think that such a "rule-of-thumb" approach would transfer to actual situations. Consider how admonitions such as "Eat 5 fruits or vegetables a day" tend not to alter the unhealthy eating habits of adults. In addition, some studies suggest that environmental feedback can sometimes have a stronger effect on choice of behavior than metacognitive insight (e.g., Berry & Broadbent, 1988; Byrnes, Miller, & Reynolds, 1999). In other words, if certain courses of action lead to success and others lead to failure, people show an increasing tendency to select the success-producing courses of action over time even though they may be completely unaware of this fact or of the basis for their choices. Hence, metacognitive insight may be neither necessary nor sufficient for high levels of decision-making success.

AN ALTERNATIVE PERSPECTIVE ON RISK TAKING AND INTERVENTION

So why, then, do adolescents take unhealthy risks and how can we reduce the level of unhealthy risk taking in this age group? Briefly, my perspective on these matters relies on a distinction borrowed from the criminology literature between the opportunity to take a risk and the propensity to do so (Gottfredson & Hirschi, 1990). More specifically, the claim is that people are likely to take risks if both of the following conditions are true: (a) They are given the *opportunity* to take a risk, and (b) they have the *propensity* to take that risk when given the opportunity. To illustrate, some teens report a low level of risk taking because they are closely monitored and restricted from doing so (e.g., strict parents, lack of access to cigarettes, alcohol, or sexual partners). Take away these restrictions (e.g., as when teens live away at college), however, and these same individuals engage in unhealthy behaviors with abandon. In contrast, there are teens who are regularly presented with opportunities to take risks but never do so.

This analysis implies that interventions to reduce the level of unhealthy behaviors in adolescence must take a two-pronged approach. First, measures need to be taken to reduce opportunities for teens to engage in behaviors such as cigarette smoking, underage drinking, or unprotected sex. However, given that we ultimately want teens to be self-regulated (i.e., exercise good judgment even when they are not monitored or supervised), interventions have to target the propensity to take risks as well. But here again, we need to return to the importance of having an accurate diagnosis or theory of the causes of risk taking. If lack of knowledge, perceived invulnerability, and lack of metacognitive insight are not the primary causes of risk taking, what other factors could be?

My current hypothesis reflects my own self-regulation model of decision making (Byrnes, 1998). This model suggests that when people make decisions in real-world contexts, their choices reflect (a) their beliefs about how one is supposed to behave in these situations (moral and conventional beliefs), (b) their values about what is important (including other people's opinions of you), (c) their beliefs about the likely consequences of actions carried out in that context (includes their risk perception), (d) their goals to pursue outcomes that elicit positive emotions and goals to avoid outcomes that elicit negative emotions, (e) their current state of mind (including fatigue, emotional arousal, mood, intoxication), (f) the degree to which they reflect on their options, (f) strategies for modifying or compensating for unhelpful states of mind or temperamental traits (e.g., impulsivity), and (g) their working memory capacity—that is, the processing space for entertaining the issues in (a) to (d) in consciousness. All these factors conspire together in a probabilistic fashion to determine who will take a risk in a particular situation and who will not. Which ones are operative in a given situation depends on the amount of working memory a person has, his or her prior experience, and the cues present in a situation.

CHAPTER 3

Is Decision Making the Right Framework for Research on Adolescent Risk Taking?

Laurence Steinberg

When my son, Benjamin, was 14, he and three of his friends decided to sneak out of the house where they were spending the night and visit one of their girlfriends at around 2 in the morning. When they arrived at the girl's house, they positioned themselves under her bedroom window and, using the time-tested method of many young lovers, threw pebbles against her windowpanes. Modern technology, unfortunately, has diminished the usefulness of this approach. The boys' pebble throwing set off the house's burglar alarm, which activated a siren and simultaneously sent a direct notification to the local police station, which dispatched a patrol car. When the siren went off, the boys ran down the street and right into the police car, which was heading to the girl's home. Instead of stopping and explaining their activity, Ben and his friends scattered and ran off in different directions throughout the neighborhood. One of the boys was caught by the police and taken back to his home, where his parents were awakened and the boy questioned.

I found out about this affair the following morning, when the girl's mother called our home to tell us what Ben had done. (Her daughter had identified the four boys.) It was especially embarrassing, because the girl's mother, in addition to being a fellow parent at our children's school, happens to be my wife's gynecologist. After his near brush with the local police, Ben had returned to the house out of which he had snuck, where he slept soundly until I awakened him with an angry telephone call, telling him to gather his clothes and wait for me in front of his friend's house. On our drive home, after delivering a long lecture about what he had done and about the dangers of running from armed police in the dark when they believe they may have interrupted a burglary, I paused. "What were you thinking?" I asked. "That's the problem, Dad," Ben replied. "I wasn't."

Ben's behavior and his insightful, albeit brief, analysis of it illustrate why the approach that social scientists have taken to the study of adolescent risk taking has yielded so little in the way of explaining the phenomenon. Cast within a decision-making framework, adolescent risk taking has been approached as if it were the product of a series of cognitions, involving the perception, appraisal, evaluation, and computation of the relative costs and benefits of alternative courses of action. Surely we would agree that what Ben and his friends did that night falls into the category of "risk taking" as most of us understand the phenomenon. But there was no evidence that Ben engaged in any of the processes, at least at a conscious level, that psychologists examine when they study adolescent risk taking. Had he paused for even a moment to perceive, appraise, evaluate, or compute the costs and benefits of sneaking out, trespassing, and running from the police, he probably would not have done any of these things. The problem isn't that Ben's thinking was deficient. The problem is that it was nonexistent.

Yet it is thinking that we continue to study when we attempt to explain risky behavior during adolescence. We study risk taking by giving individual adolescents questionnaires that ask them to tell us whether certain activities are risky or estimate the probability of various events or tell us what they would do in a hypothetical situation and describe how their behavior would change as a function of variations in levels of perceived risk. Under these conditions, adolescents look surprisingly similar to adults in the ways in which they process information. Indeed, my colleagues and I just finished a study in which, as a small part of it, we asked individuals between the ages of 11 and 24 to evaluate the riskiness, dangerousness, potential harmfulness, and relative costs of each of a series of genuinely risky activities, such as riding in a car with a drunk driver, having unprotected sex, or shoplifting (Cauffman, Steinberg, & Woolard, 2002). The 11- to 13-year-olds were more likely than any other age group to rate these activities as risky, scary, dangerous,

and more harmful than beneficial. After 13, however, there were no age differences in risk perception. In other words, 14-year-olds—individuals the same age as Ben when he and his friends took their risk—perceive the same amount of risk in things such as drunk driving, unprotected sex, or shoplifting as people 10 years older do. We didn't include wandering around the neighborhood at 2 in the morning, trespassing, and running away from the police on our questionnaire, but I would bet that, had we done so, we would not have found age differences in evaluations of these activities, either. And yet, something tells me that a group of 14-year-olds is probably more likely to do what Ben and his friends did than is a group of 24-year-olds. I am not sure what questionnaires like ours are capturing—we used a widely used measure developed by Benthin (Benthin, Slovic, & Severson 1993)—but whatever they are measuring doesn't seem to capture something very important about adolescent behavior.

If my son's nighttime exploits were typical of the situations under which adolescents take risks, as I think they are, it is fair to say that the conditions under which psychologists study risk taking bear little resemblance to the real world in which adolescents live. I say this for three reasons. First, psychologists study adolescent risk taking one adolescent at a time, yet most adolescent risk taking is a group phenomenon. Delinquency and criminal behavior, for example, are more likely to occur in groups during adolescence than they are during adulthood (Zimring, 1998). Drinking also is a group activity during adolescence; according to Add Health data, only 25% of adolescents who drink say they were alone the last time they used alcohol (Udry, 1998). Risky driving is a group activity in adolescence, and teenagers are more likely to drive in groups than are adults (Simpson, 1996). And by usual definition, sexual risk taking is an activity that involves more than one person at a time.

So the first mistake we make is studying adolescent risk taking as if it were an individual phenomenon when in reality it occurs in groups. The second problem is that psychologists study risk taking mainly by asking individuals to respond to hypothetical dilemmas, but in the real world, the risky, or potentially risky, situations in which adolescents find themselves are anything but hypothetical. The prospect of visiting a hypothetical girl from class cannot possibly carry the excitement about the possibility of surprising someone you have a crush on with a visit in the middle of the night. It is easier to put on a hypothetical condom during an act of hypothetical sex than it is to put on a real one when one is in the throes of passion and when one does not want to dampen the pleasurable feeling of sexual contact that everyone knows (but no one acknowledges) is diminished by using a condom. It is easier to just say no to a hypothetical beer than it is to a cold frosty one on a summer night. Shoplifting a CD from a music store seems like a much riskier proposition when posed in the abstract than when one is staring face-to-face at the actual CD whose music is blaring over the store's stereo system, where it suddenly doesn't seem so risky after all. And so on.

Finally, psychologists typically study risk taking under conditions designed to minimize emotional influences on decision making, yet most risk taking likely occurs under conditions of emotional arousal. Indeed, if any emotion is activated by the way we usually study risk taking, it is likely anxiety, because the procedures for studying risk taking often involve administering testlike stimuli to individuals in unfamiliar settings and under unfamiliar circumstances. This, I would assume, would lead to less risk taking than one would expect to see under non-anxiety-producing circumstances. Yet the emotion that serves as the backdrop for much adolescent risk taking is euphoria, either natural or drug induced. How many of our research subjects are in a state of euphoria when they complete our risk-taking questionnaires? How would their responses to these questionnaires differ if they were euphoric rather than anxious when they completed them?

I noted earlier the general absence of age differences in questionnaire studies of risk perception and risk assessment. Frankly, I have never been very surprised by the finding that adolescents' performance in paper-and-pencil studies of risky decision making is not that different from that of adults, especially if the adolescents are 15 or 16 years old and especially if the decision-making tasks are largely cognitive in nature. In a review of this literature that Elizabeth Cauffman and I published several years ago, we concluded that the sorts of reasoning abilities activated in most decision-making studies were fully developed, or nearly so, by 16, and that the growth curve mapping these abilities reached an asymptote at around this age (Steinberg & Cauffman, 1996). By the time they have reached 16, most adolescents reason about hypothetical dilemmas about as well as adults do.

So let's stipulate that by the middle of high school, adolescents and adults do not differ in the cognitive abilities underlying risk perception and appraisal. This, then, leaves us with a puzzle: If adolescents and adults do not differ in their capacity to perceive and appraise risk, why do adolescents take more risks than adults?

There are several answers to this question. The most frequently asserted one concerns the different values and priorities that adolescents and adults have. The argument here is that in evaluating risk, adolescents and adults use similar reasoning processes but draw on different data in reaching their conclusions (e.g., Jacobs-Quadrel, Fischhoff, & Davis, 1993). Thus, in the putative multivariate model that individuals use in deciding among alternative courses of action, some of which may be risky, adolescents and adults may put different variables into their mental regression equation and, even when they use the same variables, may attach different beta weights to them. It is therefore possible for adolescents and adults, in this framework, to evaluate the riskiness of a given act in the same way but to make different decisions about how to behave, either because they take into account different implications of their decision, because they weight the same implications differently, or because of some combination of the two. Thus, in assessing whether to try cocaine for the first time, both an adolescent and an adult might perceive the health risks of experimenting with the drug similarly but place different degrees of importance on health as a consideration. In addition, the adolescent may factor into account the possibility of rejection by his peers for refusing to try the drug, whereas this variable may not enter the adult's equation at all. Because adolescents and adults enter different variables into their calculus and because they weight these variables differently, they reach different conclusions about how to act.

I do not doubt that adolescents have different values and priorities than adults, but I don't believe that this is an especially useful way to think about developmental differences in risk taking, because it presumes that we can use a decision-making framework to model a phenomenon that is not really a decision. To say that Ben and his friends "decided" to sneak out is true only in the sense that their behavior was volitional. But there are many acts in which we engage that are volitional but that aren't best described as decisions. When I drive around suburban Philadelphia on a beautiful summer day with the top down on my convertible, I often lose myself in the moment and drive faster than the speed limit. I press on the accelerator willingly, but I would hardly describe my act to speed as a "decision." If

an officer were to pull me over and ask what I was thinking when I broke the speed limit, the honest answer would be Ben's answer to my question: "I wasn't."

It's like the bumper sticker: "Risk taking happens." Adolescents find themselves in situations that sometimes unfold in risky or dangerous ways, and they often fail to stop them from unfolding, either because they are not paying attention to what is happening, can't envision where the unfolding is leading, or are unable to extricate themselves from their circumstances. Beth Cauffman and I have argued that an awful lot of risk taking during adolescence is the product not of deficient thinking but of immature judgment. In our model, judgment refers to the complexity and sophistication of the process of individual decision making as it is affected by a range of cognitive, emotional, and social factors. We believe that *judgment* better captures the mix of cognitive and psychosocial processes of interest than does *decision making*, a term that traditionally has had a more purely cognitive flavor within the psychological literature.

In addition to being influenced by cognitive factors, judgment is influenced by three sets of psychosocial factors: responsibility (the capacity for autonomous behavior that is not unduly influenced by others), perspective (the capacity to place a decision within a temporal and social context), and temperance (the capacity to regulate one's impulses) (Steinberg & Cauffman, 1996). Unlike the literature on cognitive development, however, which suggests few age differences in reasoning beyond early adolescence, the literature on psychosocial development suggests that these sets of capacities continue to mature through middle adolescence and perhaps into late adolescence. As a consequence, adolescents' judgment is less mature than that of adults. In our view, therefore, adolescents take more risks than adults because they more are susceptible to peer pressure, more oriented to the present rather to the future, and less able to inhibit their impulses.

A study carried out by Beth Cauffman several years ago provided clear support for this view (Cauffman & Steinberg, 2000a). She had individuals ranging in age from preadolescence to middle adulthood complete a series of decision-making tasks in which they were asked about their likelihood of engaging in a mildly antisocial act, such as shoplifting, using an illicit drug, or deceiving one's employer under three conditions: if they were unlikely to get caught, if they were likely to get caught, or if they were not sure whether they would get caught. She also administered a battery of instruments designed to assess various aspects of responsibility, perspective, and temperance. Three main findings from this study support the notion that immaturity of judgment accounts for age differences in risk taking. First, adolescents made more antisocial decisions than adults (this is not the same as, but is akin to, the notion that adolescents take more risks than adults). Second, immature individuals, as indexed by their scores on measures of responsibility, perspective, and temperance, make more antisocial decisions than mature individuals. And third, age differences in decision making disappear once one controls for age differences in maturity. As predicted, then, adolescents exhibit worse judgment than adults—and presumably take more risks as a consequence—because they are less self-reliant, more shortsighted, and more impulsive.

These psychosocial liabilities are, I hypothesize, accentuated under conditions of high positive arousal—that is, under the conditions of euphoria that often develop when teenagers are with their friends in social situations. In other words, when adolescents are in this state, they become even more susceptible to coercion, more shortsighted, and more impulsive. Extant research on risk taking misses this, however. When we study decision making in the usual laboratory paradigms, we construct a social and emotional context that removes peers, dampens individuals' emotional arousal, and permits individuals to be more circumspect (Cauffman & Steinberg, 2000b).

The logical implication of this conclusion is to try to find ways of studying adolescent risk taking under the social and emotional conditions that more closely approximate the real world. This has proven enormously difficult to do. One of my current graduate students, Margo Gardner, has recently completed a study in which she attempted to do this, at least a little. In this study, she presented a sample of individuals between the ages of 13 and 22 with a series of tasks designed to assess risk taking and the psychosocial components hypothesized to affect judgment. In a computer-administered risk-taking task, subjects were given the opportunity to take chances while driving a car. The game simulates the situation in which one is approaching an intersection, sees a traffic light turn yellow, and tries to decide whether to stop or proceed through the intersection. In the task, a moving car is on the screen, and a yellow traffic light appears, signaling that at some point soon, a wall will appear and the car will crash. Loud music is playing in the background. As soon as the yellow light appears, participants must decide whether to keep driving or apply the brakes. Participants are told that the longer they drive, the more points they earn but that if the car crashes into the wall, all the points that have been accumulated are lost. The amount of time that elapses between the appearance of the light and the appearance of the wall is varied across trials, so there is no way to anticipate when the car will crash. Individuals who are more inclined to take risks in this game drive the car longer than those who are more risk averse. Performance on this task was correlated with responses to the questionnaire measure of antisocial decision making used by Cauffman in her study, such that individuals who took more chances in the driving game were more likely to say they would commit an antisocial act if they believed they would not be caught.

The added twist in Gardner's study was that individuals were asked to come to the lab under one of two conditions: either with two of their friends or alone. When playing the driving game, therefore, some individuals played it alone, whereas others had their friends looking over their shoulder, giving them advice on what to do. The data indicate that individuals at all the ages we have studied take more chances when they are with their friends than when they are alone, paralleling findings on the links between vehicle occupancy and automobile accidents in adolescence. The effect of being in a group on task performance did not vary as a function of age, but this may be because the age range in the study is very constricted. We need to replicate this experiment with adults who are older to see if the group effect still holds. Our hypothesis is that the group effect will be weaker among adults than adolescents, but even if the group effect is seen among older individuals, it may nevertheless be important in understanding adolescent risk taking, because as I noted earlier, in the real world, adolescents are more likely to drive in groups than are adults.

I should also note that we did not find the same group effect for two other tasks employed in this study: a delayed discounting task (in which individuals are asked to choose between a larger reward given sometime in the future and a smaller reward given immediately) and a gambling task (in which individuals choose between a large reward with a low probability of attainment and a small reward with a higher probability of attainment). Group administration had no effect whatsoever on performance in the delayed discounting task. And in the gambling

task, contrary to prediction, we found that the group effect was more powerful among the older participants than the younger ones. My suspicion is that the sort of group effect hypothesized to operate in adolescence is operative mainly in tasks in which adolescents get excited and "lost in the moment," such as our driving task. When the task starts to look too much like a decision-making task (as I believe our gambling and discounting tasks did), we may miss what I believe is distinctive about adolescent risk taking, which is not, as I have suggested, best thought of as a decision-making process.

There has been a flurry of interest in the last several years in linking adolescent risk taking with emerging results from studies of brain maturation. Much of the discussion of this in the popular media has focused on the discovery that areas of the prefrontal cortex involved in executive functioning are still undergoing significant maturation in middle and late adolescence, in the form of myelination and synaptic pruning (Huttenlocher, 1994; Spear, 2000). This maturation ostensibly has implications for the development of capabilities such as planning, goal setting, and decision making. (I say "ostensibly" because no studies have linked changes in brain structure and function in adolescence with changes in cognition or behavior.) However, in light of the findings from the decision-making research I have discussed, it does not make a great deal of sense to search for the biological underpinnings of adolescent risk taking in the part of the brain primarily associated with decision making, because we do not see great age differences in this realm of cognition. It strikes me that what we should be looking at, to the extent that we want to link brain maturation with risk taking, are brain systems implicated in psychosocial development, not straight cognitive development. This is, in fact, what my colleagues and I are planning in connection with some work we are doing on the development of culpability, or blameworthiness, during adolescence. More specifically, we are interested in understanding the neurobiological and neuropsychological underpinnings of such phenomena as susceptibility to peer pressure, inhibitory control, and future orientation.

I do not believe that the decision-making framework that has guided the study of adolescent risk taking for the past decade has proven as useful as we might have hoped. As I have suggested, although some of the risks that adolescents take may be best thought of as decisions, many of them—perhaps even most—are not. I believe it is time to reassess the utility of the decision-making framework and think carefully about alternative conceptualizations of risk taking that emphasize psychosocial differences between adolescents and adults and the implications of these differences for the development of mature judgment.

I am hesitant to make explicit recommendations, based on the ideas advanced here, about the ways we might intervene to reduce risk taking by adolescents. To the extent that adolescent risk taking has its origins in immature psychosocial development, much of which is normative, there is probably very little we can do with respect to intervention that will magically stimulate the growth of emotional and social maturity. It would seem to me that rather than attempting to change the way that adolescents perceive, appraise, and evaluate risk, a more profitable strategy might focus on limiting opportunities for immature judgment to have harmful consequences. Thus, strategies such as raising the price of cigarettes, more vigilantly enforcing laws governing the sale of alcohol, expanding access to mental health and contraceptive services, and raising the driving age would likely be more effective in limiting adolescent smoking, substance abuse, suicide, pregnancy, and automobile fatalities than strategies aimed at making adolescents wiser, less impulsive, or less shortsighted. Some things just take time to develop, and mature judgment is probably one of them.

CHAPTER 4

The Two Faces of Adolescent Invulnerability

Daniel K. Lapsley

The onset of adolescence is associated with a dramatic increase in health-compromising behavior, including the use of tobacco, alcohol, and controlled substances; unprotected sexual activity; and numerous other "reckless" behaviors (Arnett, 1992). Moreover, it is widely believed, in both the popular and theoretical literature, that adolescents engage in risk behaviors partly because of their greater sense of felt invulnerability to injury, harm, and danger. According to the received view, there is something about the developmental status of adolescents that disposes them to feelings of greater invulnerability, which, in turn, underwrites their tendency to engage in patterns of "risk-taking" behavior. When put this way, adolescent invulnerability is considered a psychosocial risk factor that warrants intervention.

Hence, the received view makes at least three claims: (a) that the sense of invulnerability has a developmental source, (b) that adolescents engage in risk behaviors because of their greater sense of felt invulnerability, and (c) that invulnerability is a psychosocial risk factor that should be the target of intervention. Each of these claims is controversial.

The claim that invulnerability has a developmental source, or is otherwise linked to the developmental status of adolescents, is contested by research in the risk perception and decision-making literature (e.g., Beyth-Marom, Austin, Fischoff, Palmgren, & Jacobs-Quadrel, 1993; Cohn, MacFarlane, Imai, & Yanez, 1995; Jacobs-Quadrel, Fischhoff, & Davis, 1993; Whalen et al., 1994). This research shows that teenagers and adults do not appear to differ greatly in how they appraise risk, with both groups tending to "rely on similar, moderately biased psychological processes" that lead them to attribute more risky possibilities to target others than to the self (Jacobs-Quadrel et al., 1993, p. 112). Hence, these data do not support the claims regarding the singularly invulnerable adolescent. The claim that greater felt invulnerability predicts engagement in risk behaviors is not well established and is otherwise contradicted by research that shows that risk behavior is compatible with perceptions of vulnerability (e.g., Gerrard, Gibbons, Benthin, & Hessling, 1996). The claim that felt invulnerability should be the target of intervention in order to reduce exposure to health-compromising hazards is premature in the absence of a better theoretical understanding of the function of invulnerability in normal adolescent development and in light of research on allied constructs that suggest that self-enhancing ideation, including perceptions of invulnerability, is an important moderator of stress and otherwise serves broad adaptational purposes.

In this chapter, I would like to explore each of these claims about adolescent invulnerability and its relationship to risk behavior. I will argue that felt invulnerability has a developmental source that has not been adequately considered in adolescent health psychology. Moreover, I will argue that the traditional assessment of invulnerability in terms of risk perception (or "optimism bias") does not exhaust our methodological options. To this end, I will describe a new assessment strategy and report on preliminary studies that document the "two faces" of adolescent invulnerability—that is, its role in predicting both risk behaviors and positive developmental outcomes. I will conclude with some implications of these data for health promotion and risk reduction intervention.

DEVELOPMENTAL SOURCES

Peterson (1996) argued that the promise of health psychology in contributing to the current strong emphasis on health promotion and prevention cannot be fully realized without increased attention to the role of developmental processes in shaping health behaviors. A developmental approach would help identify, for example, "critical developmental junctures of vulnerability to health risks and receptivity toward health interventions" (p. 155). Within health psychology, adolescent risk taking is more often attributed to faulty decision making (Furby & Beyth-Marom, 1992) or unrealistic optimism

(Weinstein, 1993), which is itself understood as an "error in judgment" (Weinstein, 1980, p. 806). Is there a developmental source for these errors of judgment and decision making? The theory of adolescent egocentrism has been frequently invoked as a possible framework for understanding the developmental components of faulty risk perception and risk-taking behavior (Greene, Rubin, Walters, & Hale, 1996).

According to Elkind (1967) the transition to formal operations is accompanied by a tendency to assimilate social information to self-regarding ideation, resulting in a peculiar variety of cognitive egocentrism. According to this view, a young adolescent fails to differentiate what is the object of his or her own concern (e.g., the self) from the concerns and preoccupations of others, assuming, egocentrically, that others share one's own preoccupation with the self. One consequence of cognitive egocentrism is the tendency to construct *personal fables,* which are modes of self-understanding that include themes of *invulnerability* (the self is incapable of being harmed or injured), *omnipotence* (viewing the self as a source of special authority or influence), or *personal uniqueness* (the perspective of the self is so special it cannot be understood, "No one understands me!"). This tendency to construct personal fables is traditionally invoked to account for reckless behavior in adolescents and for their seeming disregard for the dangerous consequences of their behavior.

Elkind (1967) suggested, for example, that personal fable ideation might help us understand teenagers who risk pregnancy by engaging in unprotected sex ("their personal fable convinces them that pregnancy will happen to others but never to them," p. 1032). Similarly, Arnett (1992; also, Greene et al. 2000) explicitly argues that personal fable ideation ("cognitive egocentrism"), along with sensation seeking, is implicated in a variety of reckless teenage activities, including drunk driving, driving at high speeds, engaging in unprotected sex, use of illegal substances, and other delinquent behaviors. Personal fable ideation has also been treated as "negative cognition" that predicts anxiety and depression (Garber, Weiss, & Shanley, 1993). Clearly, then, according to this traditional view, the personal fable is a lamentable feature of adolescent development. It is a sign of cognitive immaturity that has the untoward effect of impairing the judgment of adolescents in critical situations.

A number of studies purport to demonstrate a relationship between cognitive egocentrism and adolescent risk taking (Arnett, 1990a, 1990b; Greene, Rubin, & Hale, 1995; Greene et al., 2000; Greene et al., 1996), mostly by showing that personal fable tendencies (measured in various ways) are correlated with risk behaviors. Yet there are both theoretical (Blasi & Hoeffel, 1974; Lapsley, 1985, 1993; Lapsley & Murphy, 1985) and empirical (Lapsley, Milstead, Quintana, Flannery, & Buss, 1986; also, Dolcini et al., 1989) grounds for doubting that the link between personal fable ideation and risk behaviors can be safely traced to cognitive egocentrism as its developmental source. Moreover, in studies of risk perception, it is now well established that the "invulnerability fable" is not unique to adolescents (Millstein, 1993). For example, both adults (Jacobs-Quadrel et al., 1993; Weinstein, 1987) and children (Whalen et al., 1994) report evidence of an optimism bias when asked to estimate one's vulnerability to health and environmental hazards, findings often considered at odds with the theory of adolescent egocentrism.

Hence, adolescent egocentrism is not a good candidate for explaining the emergence of personal fable ideation or for providing the developmental link between felt invulnerability and adolescent risk behaviors. An alternative candidate views personal fable ideation not as an outcome of cognitive egocentrism but, rather, as an adaptive response to the demands of adolescent ego development (Lapsley, 1993; Lapsley & Rice, 1988). According to this view, an inflated sense of personal uniqueness, omnipotence, and invulnerability is an attempt by the adolescent to maintain the boundaries, integrity, and cohesiveness of the self as the adolescent wrestles with the second phase of separation-individuation (e.g., Blos, 1962). As such, personal fable ideation has little to do with the differentiation errors of formal operations but is instead a defensive or compensatory response, fueled by an upsurge of narcissism, that allows the adolescent to ward off mourning reactions, feelings of depletion, self-image vulnerabilities, and threats to self-esteem. It may also facilitate the taking of appropriate risks, motivate psychological separation from parents, and provide the inner resources for adolescents to explore new identities, roles, and tasks (Bjorklund & Green, 1992).

The "two faces" of personal fable ideation—that is, its dual role in predicting both risk behaviors and adaptive outcomes—was recently shown by Lapsley and Flannery (2002). In this study, 561 early and middle adolescents responded to the New Personal Fable Scale, which yields assessments of felt invulnerability, omnipotence, and personal uniqueness. They also responded to indices of internalizing symptoms (depression, suicidal ideation), health risks (smoking, drinking, various controlled substances), delinquent behavior (fighting, vandalism, stealing), and positive mental health (self-worth, mastery coping, superior adjustment). The results showed that the three personal fables had a differential relationship to risk behaviors and adjustment. The omnipotence fable, for example, was consistently associated with positive adaptational outcomes. It was a strong predictor of self-worth, mastery coping, and superior adjustment. Indeed, the correlation between omnipotence and mastery coping got significantly stronger with age. Moreover, omnipotence strongly counterindicated depressive affect and suicidal ideation. In contrast, the personal uniqueness fable was strongly and positively correlated with internalizing symptoms and had few redeeming qualities. Hence, the fables of omnipotence and personal uniqueness had uniformly positive and negative implications for mental health, respectively.

But the invulnerability fable cut in both directions. It was, as long suspected, a strong predictor of risk behaviors, including the use of tobacco, beer, and other controlled substances, at all ages. Moreover, there was a significant increase in reported invulnerability from early to middle adolescence, a shift that also corresponded to increases in reported delinquent acts (although the bivariate relationship between invulnerability and risk behaviors did not increase with age). However, invulnerability also predicted (along with the omnipotence fable) selfworth, mastery coping, and superior adjustment. Hence, these data would suggest that felt invulnerability presents two faces: It is a risk factor with respect to externalizing, health-compromising behavior; it is also associated with adaptive aspects of adolescent mental health.

FOUR IMPLICATIONS

Dual Functions. The fact that invulnerability (and omnipotence) predicted numerous aspects of positive adjustment is congruent with the theoretical claim that these are defensive or compensatory mechanisms that support adaptive functioning as the adolescent wrestles with normative developmental challenges. Indeed, that invulnerability is also positively associated with risk behaviors is perhaps not surprising in light of claims that engaging in risk behaviors may well serve

normal psychological goals in adolescence. According to Jessor (1992), for example, a large class of risk behaviors is characteristic of normal psychosocial development. Engaging in risk behaviors often serves important personal and social functions, such as consolidating peer acceptance, affirming maturity and independence, and warding off stress, frustration, and anxiety. For many adolescents, risk behavior provides an opportunity to solidify a friendship, separate from parents, and experience autonomy. Hence, in his view, such behaviors, far from being irrational or psychopathological, are instead "functional, purposive, instrumental and goal-directed, and . . . the goals involved are often those that are central in normal adolescent development (Jessor, 1992, p. 378). The invulnerability bias may well be at the service of these normative developmental goals.

A Singular Construct? I noted earlier that there is little reason to regard personal fable ideation as an outcome of cognitive egocentrism. It is also time to reject the notion that personal fable ideation is a unitary construct. There has been a tendency in previous research to treat *the* personal fable as if it were a unidimensional construct with straightforward implications (invariably negative) for adolescent adjustment. This view is no longer tenable. It is now clear that personal fable ideation is a multidimensional construct, with differentiated relationships with risk behavior and indices of adjustment. This was clearly evident in the findings reported above (see Lapsley & Flannery, 2002). A similar pattern was noted by Goossens, Beyers, Emmen, and van Aken (2002). In a series of studies involving over 1,400 adolescents, Goossens et al. (2002, p. 209) reported that the three personal fables do not load on a common underlying factor and that the three fables show a differentiated pattern of association with indicators of mental health and of separation-individuation.

Fables and Illusions. Rather than a singular construct, the various personal fables may well be part of a family of "positive illusions" that have been linked to psychological and physical well-being (Taylor & Brown, 1988; Taylor, Kemeny, Reed, Bower, & Gruenewald, 2000). Research has identified, for example, three cognitive illusions that appear to be consistently related to positive adaptation. Hence, individuals who demonstrate unrealistically positive self-evaluations, exaggerated perceptions of control or mastery, and unrealistic optimism (which is how invulnerability is regarded within the health psychology literature) tend to show better adaptation to psychosocial stressors, trauma, and risk than do individuals who are more accurate in their self-perceptions. Positive illusions are related to marital and relational satisfaction (Fowers, Lyons, & Montel, 1996; Murray, Holmes, & Griffin, 1996). They counterindicate depressive symptoms (Alloy & Clements, 1992). They are associated with a wide range of positive criteria of mental health, including "positive self-regard, the ability to care for and about other people, the capacity for creative and productive work and the ability to effectively manage stress" (Taylor & Gollwitzer, 1995, p. 213).

Under this interpretation, then, having an exaggerated sense of one's influence, authority, or power ("omnipotence") or an exaggerated perception of one's ability to resist injury or harm ("invulnerability") is just the sort of self-enhancing bias that may characterize the thinking of many individuals, not just adolescents. Although this literature makes no developmental claims, it does underscore the fact that "illusions" and "fables" are often in the service of cognitive adaptation, including, presumably, adaptation to the developmental challenges common

to adolescence. Of course, illusions and fables may also incur costs (Lapsley & Flannery, 2002; Robins & Beer, 2001).

Assessment. It is now clear that the current conceptualization of personal fable ideation is a long way from its source in the egocentrism of Piagetian cognitive development. As we have seen, the "new look" views personal fable ideation as a plural construct, conceptually related to other forms of narcissistic illusions, with differentiated relationships to separation-individuation and to risk behaviors, mental health, and adjustment. This change in the theoretical status of the construct calls for new forms of assessment of each variety of personal fable ideation. Although we have derived new scales to assess personal uniqueness (Duggan, Lapsley, & Norman, 2000) and omnipotence (Lapsley, 2000), most of our efforts have been directed toward development of the Adolescent Invulnerability Scale (AIS), given the prominence of invulnerability as an explanation of adolescent risk behavior. In the next section, I report preliminary research using the AIS that documents the "two faces" of invulnerability—that is, its association with certain risk behaviors and also its positive relationship to adaptive mental health.

THE ADOLESCENT INVULNERABILITY SCALE

Duggan et al. (2000) administered the AIS and a measure of delinquent risk behaviors (e.g., fighting, stealing, vandalism; Rowe, 1985) to a sample of 228 late adolescents. Exploratory factor analysis of the AIS resulted in two factors. One factor appeared to represent an invulnerability to external danger and was therefore labeled "danger invulnerability." The second factor appeared to represent an invulnerability to psychological distress and was therefore labeled "psychological invulnerability." Both subscales were significantly and positively correlated with risk behaviors. In a second study of early adolescents, danger and general invulnerability factors were joined by a third factor that reflected a belief that gossip, the opinion of others, and what "other people say" has no effect and cannot hurt the self. This "interpersonal invulnerability" was not evident in the previous study of older adolescents, and its presence in this sample of middle school students perhaps reflects the greater peer focus of younger teens.

As expected, the three invulnerability factors also showed a differential pattern of correlation with risk behaviors and indices of adjustment. For example, depressive symptoms were counterindicated by interpersonal invulnerability, but not by the other invulnerability factors. Use of substances (alcohol, tobacco, drugs) was more strongly related to danger invulnerability than to the other invulnerability factors. And general invulnerability more strongly predicted delinquent behavior than did general and interpersonal invulnerability, although these factors were also significant predictors as well. Clearly, then, the three dimensions of invulnerability have different implications for understanding adolescent behavior and adjustment: Danger invulnerability is more uniformly predictive of drinking, drug use, and smoking. General invulnerability is more strongly predictive of general delinquent or reckless behavior. Interpersonal invulnerability counterindicates depressive symptoms.

Not only is invulnerability not a unidimensional construct, it also does not function uniformly as a risk factor for poor adaptation in early adolescence. This is evident in the fact that at least one invulnerability factor (interpersonal invulnerability) counterindicates depressive symptoms. It is also evident in the fact that all three invulnerability factors were positively associated

with mastery coping. Clearly, then, felt invulnerability is not a unidimensional construct with uniform implications for health and adjustment. Although danger and general invulnerability are each linked with certain risk behaviors, it would be inappropriate to conclude that adolescent invulnerability invariably menaces the adjustment of teenagers.

IMPLICATIONS FOR HEALTH PROMOTION

It is said that adolescents engage in all sorts of foolish, reckless, even dangerous, behavior as a result of their felt invulnerability to negative consequences. The implication is that health promotion would be served if adolescent invulnerability were to be undermined, perhaps by making salient the risks that attend such behavior. But it is now clear that the invulnerability construct will frustrate such straightforward conclusions. Although there is certainly evidence that felt invulnerability predicts both delinquent and health-compromising behaviors, there is also reason to believe that invulnerability, and other forms of personal fable ideation, have adaptive functions as well. Consequently, it is by no means clear that undermining an adolescent's sense of invulnerability is desirable if this self-enhancing illusion contributes to psychosocial resilience in the face of normative developmental challenges.

Even if health promotion campaigns against adolescent invulnerability are desirable, these campaigns may well require precise targeting in order to effect desired outcomes. For example, interventions aimed at reducing the incidence of adolescents' use of tobacco, alcohol, and drugs would be better served to target "danger invulnerability" rather than other forms. In contrast, interpersonal invulnerability should not be targeted at all and, indeed, may well have to be mobilized as a psychosocial resource to reduce the incidence of internalizing symptomatology in early adolescence. Invulnerability is not a unidimensional construct, nor does it have uniform implications for health promotion.

Moreover, the effectiveness of health promotion and risk reduction interventions will hinge on how sensitive they are to "critical developmental junctures" (Peterson, 1996, p. 155) that adolescents face. One theme of this chapter is that felt invulnerability has a developmental source. It is a concomitant of normative separation-individuation, and its emergence underwrites positive developmental goals. Indeed, making friends, falling in love, trying out identity stances, experimenting with autonomy, exploring emotional reactions, testing ideological limits—these are normative experiences that are critical to adolescent ego development, and safe passage through this developmental juncture is not without risk. Consequently, it is here, at this juncture, facing up to these challenges, that a measure of felt invulnerability has adaptational advantages. Yet many adolescents will attempt to realize these normative developmental goals in the context of risk behavior, and hence, felt invulnerability will also underwrite a wide range of health-compromising behavior as well. But it is critical to note that adolescents will engage in risk behavior not so much because they are unaware of the risks but because of their perception of its benefits (Goldberg, Halpern-Felsher, & Millstein, 2002). The desire to realize important developmental goals trumps risk assessment. Indeed, as Jessor (1992) noted, risk behavior will seem attractive to adolescents as a means of realizing developmental goals so long as adequate alternatives are unavailing. One might conclude, then, that the enemy of health promotion is not felt invulnerability per se but, rather, inadequate alternatives for adolescents to achieve developmental goals.

Part I

Section B

Affect, Risk Perception, and Behavior

CHAPTER 5

Risk Perception

Construct Development, Links to
Theory, Correlates, and Manifestations

SUSAN G. MILLSTEIN

WHAT IS RISK PERCEPTION?

The term *risk perception,* and what we mean by risk perception, generates much diversity (one might say confusion) in thinking. Thinking and research about the construct has tended to be isolated within individual disciplines, and we see little cross-disciplinary fertilization. It has been measured in such diverse ways that it is virtually impossible to compare findings across studies, let alone across different disciplinary literatures.

We can examine the content of individuals' risk and vulnerability beliefs, identifying those things that worry or concern them, as well as the degree of anxiety generated by these concerns. We can observe whether people recognize the risks inherent in a given situation, or we can look at how accurately someone judges a specific risk. Risk judgments may focus on situations (e.g., "Is having unprotected sex dangerous?") or on their potential outcomes (e.g., "What is the chance that you will get an STD?"). Personal risk can be viewed in absolute terms (e.g.,

"What is your chance . . . ?") or relative terms (e.g., "How does your risk compare with other risks?"). For any given individual, we can also examine his or her relative ranking of the importance of various "risks" to assess that person's risk perceptions (Millstein & Halpern-Felsher, 2002b).

Others have commented on the problems associated with the diversity in measurement of the constructs, as well as problems associated with the use of specific measures (van der Pligt, 1998; Van der Velde, Hooykaas, & van der Pligt, 1996). Some have suggested that uniform measures be developed and used to increase comparability across studies. However, it is unlikely that developing a single measure will help us answer the questions of most importance.

There is value in viewing the notion of risk perception from different angles and perspectives. Doing so not only allows us to convey the richness and multidimensional nature of the construct but also lets us think beyond traditional paradigms. The variations in how we conceptualize risk and vulnerability may have something important to tell us about individuals' perceptions of them. But just as each of the blind men describing the elephant they are touching describes a different part of the creature (and thus paints a particular portrait of the beast), scholars also focus on different facets of the construct. Similarly, there are layers involved in perceiving risk, ranging from general knowledge that something may be risky to a deeper, more fundamental sense of one's vulnerability. So why should we think that one measure of risk perception could capture both of these levels? And why would we think that each level would have the same relationship to behavior?

WHAT SHOULD WE BE ASKING ABOUT RISK PERCEPTION?

Perceptions of risk play a central role in most theoretical models of health and risk behavior, such as social cognitive theory (Bandura, 1994), protection motivation theory (Maddux & Rogers, 1983), the health belief model (Rosenstock, 1974), the theory of reasoned action (Fishbein & Ajzen, 1975), the theory of planned behavior (Ajzen, 1985), self-regulation theory (Kanfer, 1970), and subjective culture and interpersonal relations theory (Triandis, 1977). Perspectives on behavior from behavioral decision theory also emphasize the importance of perceived risk (Beyth-Marom & Fischhoff, 1997). Among those who work with adolescents, risk perception has been seen as having a fundamental impact on adolescent risk behavior and, as such, has been incorporated into a multitude of educational and intervention programs (Beyth-Marom, Austin, Fischhoff, Palmgren, & Jacobs-Quadrel, 1993).

Despite the recognized significance of risk perception and its widespread application in interventions, few conceptual models for understanding the construct exist. We have failed to devote sufficient time to asking how

people go about assessing their personal risk for negative outcomes and what kinds of processes people use in coming to these assessments. Answers to these questions will bring us much closer to understanding how perceptions of risk relate to behavior and will also help us identify points in the process where interventions may be needed or helpful.

A Process Model of Risk Perception

To begin, it may be useful to think about risk perception in terms of general sequencing or temporal phases. I would like to suggest that, at a minimum, risk perception involves three phases, the first reflecting attentional processes and the second two involving appraisal processes.

Attention Phase[1]

Before making any judgments about risk, cues are necessary to set the later appraisal processes in motion. These cues serve to get something on our radar screen—to tell us that something is worth our attention. Consider, for example, what occurs when we go to a large party. There is a lot going on. As we take in these external stimuli, we notice some aspects of the situation but not others.

I suspect that many of the things we think adolescents should attend to are simply not on their radar screen. If we think about attentional processes in general, it may help us understand why this may be the case. We know that attentional capacity grows during adolescence and that the influence of distraction plays a smaller role than it does in childhood (Hamilton, 1983). But to get a potential risk on the radar screen, individuals also need some basis on which to notice it. To some degree, this requires cognitive knowledge about potential risks in the world. If you were at a party and someone offered you a drink, would you be thinking that something could have been slipped in the drink? If

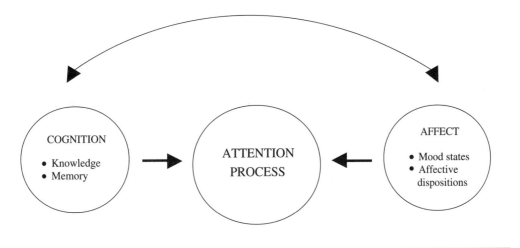

Figure 5.1   A Process Model of Risk Perception—Attention Phase

you had never heard of date rape drugs, perhaps not. Another source from which we gain information is the situation itself. Our memory of similar situations helps us define the kind of situation we are in and directs our attention toward, or away from, various aspects of the situation. In both of these arenas, adolescents are likely to have less to draw on than adults. Even when attentional capacity is adequate, limitations in adolescents' cognitive knowledge base as well as their lack of experience with different types of situations are likely to have important effects on the focus of their attention. These attentional deficits may be one of the important stumbling blocks in adolescents' abilities to judge risks in real-life situations.

Affective states also play a role in attention. Transient mood states influence attention and the degree to which individuals are likely to notice potential risks. We tend to notice and recall those aspects of situations that are congruent with our current mood state. So the happy adolescent who is having fun may be more likely to attend to the positive aspects of the situation, such as the attractive girl at the other end of the room, than to the negative aspects, such as the potential for harm.

Affective dispositions are also important. For example, heightened sensitivity and vigilance to threat cues in one's environment are characteristic among people who have high levels of dispositional (trait) anxiety (see Eysenck, 1992; Stober, 1997). Other individual differences in attentional style, such as locus of control, repression-sensitization, need for stimulation, and self-monitoring are also important (see Fiske & Taylor, 1984).

The attention phase of risk perception involves a number of different dimensions. Specifically, I am arguing that the process of detecting a potentially risky signal involves both cognitive and affective processing systems, both of which can be influenced by situational as well as dispositional factors (Figure 5.1). As I will suggest in a moment, perceiving risks at any level involves all these dimensions.

Appraisal Phase

Once a signal has been detected, some kind of appraisal processes is likely to be invoked (see Figure 5.2). Whereas the attention phase serves to focus us, the appraisal phase involves the interpretation of what it is we have noticed. During the appraisal phase,

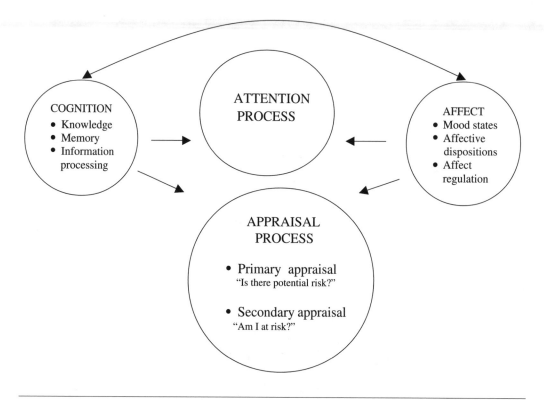

Figure 5.2   A Process Model of Risk Perception—Attention and Appraisal Phases

one makes meaning of the environmental cues that have been detected. In the appraisal phase, we are likely to be addressing questions such as, "Is there risk in this situation?" "Is this behavior risky?" "Could something bad happen if I take this chance?" Although individuals may be consciously aware of these appraisals, they may also be subject to more automatic cognitive and emotional processing.

In my view, the appraisal process takes place at two levels, one oriented toward generalized and hypothetical risk judgments ("What is possible?") and the other focused on personal judgments of risk for oneself ("What is probable?"). At both levels, cognitive as well as affective processes are likely to be involved.

Primary Appraisal. If the aim of the primary appraisal phase is to determine whether there is potential for harm, what kinds of cognitive tasks might be involved? To the degree that judging risks involves assessing the causal linkage between antecedents and consequences, the task requires that the individual not only attend to relevant correlational evidence but also that he or she has the ability to process a large array of data (e.g., processing information about all possible combinations of antecedents and outcomes). This process also requires metacognitive skills to integrate new information relevant to one's own theories about causal relationships. Cognitively, both analytic and heuristic processing strategies are likely to operate during the primary appraisal phase. It is from the cognitive side of the primary appraisal process that much of the work on risk perception has emerged. For example, a fairly sizable literature on heuristic processes exists. Although some researchers are exploring these cognitive processes within adolescent populations (Jacobs & Potenza, 1991; Reyna & Ellis, 1994), most of this work has been conducted with adults.

Affective processes influence cognitive processing during the primary appraisal phase. Mood states, such as positive affect, have substantial and pervasive effects on the kinds of processes used, with positive mood favoring more efficient, heuristic processing (Isen, 2001; Roesch, 1999) and negative mood associated with the use of more detail-oriented, narrowly focused processing strategies. Affective dispositions such as trait anxiety may also influence the cognitive appraisal of risks by decreasing tolerance for risk. Optimism may also play a role; those who think that good things usually come their way may be less likely to view themselves, even theoretically, as being at risk (see Scheier & Carver, 1985). These "trait" and "state" measures, of course, have a relationship with each other as well. For example, extraverts experience more positive moods than do introverts (see Roesch, 1999).

There are also affective consequences of cognitive appraisals. To the extent that there is a perception of possible risk, feelings of concern or worry may emerge. These may be tempered or fueled by perceptions of the seriousness of the risk, coupled with perceptions about the extent to which the risk can be controlled. Seriousness and controllability form what is called the "dread" factor (see Slovick, 1987).

Although affect clearly plays a role during primary appraisal, I see this phase as being more cognitive than affective in nature. It is similar to what Epstein (1994) describes as "rational" information processing. Affect may influence our cognitive processing style, and we may have affective responses to our cognitive appraisals, but during this phase I see the cognitive processes as providing the steam behind the engine, so to speak. Even when we phrase questions in a manner designed to elicit personal risk assessments (e.g., "What is the chance that you will get an STD"?), we are probably still tapping into this cognitive primary appraisal process. I may feel dread at the idea of acquiring a life-threatening illness, but the dread remains theoretical, cognitive, and distal at this level. As I will argue later, most of what we measure in risk perception and risk behavior research is at the level of primary appraisal.

Secondary Appraisal. If the conclusion produced by my primary appraisal is that there is no risk, I need go no further. But if I acknowledge that there is a potential risk for me, the appraisal process takes on a far more affective tone, similar to what Epstein (1994) would describe as "experiential" processing. At the level of secondary appraisal, the question of whether there is a potential risk moves from a theoretical level ("Is it possible that I am at risk"?) to a far more personal and immediate level ("Am I truly at risk?"). At this secondary appraisal level, fundamental feelings of vulnerability can emerge, and we can begin to understand the meaning of risk to individuals. At this level, the question, "Am I at risk?" becomes meaningful.

Emotional distress in response to anticipated threats is a natural human response. Of course, there are likely to be significant individual differences in both the degree of distress experienced as well as in the level of tolerance one has for it. Some are hypersensitive to perceived threat; an extreme example would be people suffering from posttraumatic stress dysfunction. Others seem to feel distress less acutely. Other corresponding dispositional dimensions, such as seeing the world as a safe or as a threatening place, may play a role.

To the degree that threat is perceived, emotional regulation processes are likely to emerge (see Gross, 1999). As children mature, they are increasingly able to use a variety of effective regulatory strategies, such as distraction, cognitive blunting, sensitization, and cognitive reappraisal (see Saarni, Mumme, & Campos, 1998). One way that cognitive reappraisal might take place is via social comparison processes. Individuals compare themselves with others along many dimensions, including risk status. One of the strategies people use to maintain a self-perception of low risk on the comparative scale is to change the reference group with which they compare themselves (see Perloff & Fetzer, 1986; Taylor, Lichtman, & Wood, 1984). We would expect the importance of reference groups in relative risk assessment to be quite salient during adolescence, a time when social normative factors and comparisons of self with others become paramount (Harter, 1990).

Another way that cognitive reappraisal can reduce emotional distress focuses on how individuals view the actions they themselves might take to reduce risk. These perceptions of risk-reducing behaviors or strategies can be used to rationalize the view of oneself as having a lower risk status. Thus, for example, adolescents may acknowledge that having unprotected sex increases the chances of getting a sexually transmitted disease (STD) but see themselves as being at less risk because they are having sex only with partners who are "clean."

I believe that at this secondary appraisal level, fundamental feelings of vulnerability can emerge and cognitive strategies for managing and regulating these affective consequences operate. Both feelings of vulnerability and invulnerability may emerge during secondary appraisal because it is here that one may experience the most basic feelings of vulnerability. But it is also here that one can use cognitive skills and emotional coping strategies to make it all go away. Most of us emerge from this appraisal process with a healthy dose of positive illusions. We could not live without them.

It is interesting to speculate about how developmental processes intersect here. Most often, development is viewed as enhancing risk judgment. Adolescents, for example, are seen as having little awareness of or concern about risk. Although this view persists in popular culture and many academic avenues, research does not support the view of the "invulnerable adolescent" (Millstein & Halpern-Felsher, 2002a; Fischhoff et al., 2000; Jacobs-Quadrel, Fischhoff, & Davis, 1993). An alternative view is that as we age, we become more and more skilled at kidding ourselves. Our cognitive processes allow us to engage in very sophisticated self-serving biases, and our efforts at regulating unpleasant emotions are well tuned. So perhaps it is the adults who have the more positive illusions.

DOES RISK PERCEPTION INFLUENCE RISK BEHAVIOR?

Despite a plethora of studies on adolescent risk behavior, we currently have few answers about how risk perceptions influence adolescent behavior. Although it is beyond the scope of this chapter to describe all the reasons why this might be the case, two have particular relevance to the topic of this chapter.

Earlier, I speculated that most of our attempts to measure perceived risk remain at the primary appraisal level and fail to tap into the deeper meaning of risk to the individual. The failure to deal with risk perception at the level of most meaning may explain why its relationship to behavior remains unclear. Yet measuring perceptions at this level is likely to be quite challenging. I suspect that good measurement of perceived risk at the secondary appraisal level requires that we be in the situation prompting the appraisal or, at a minimum, be able to psychologically transport ourselves there. This would involve more than simply imagining oneself in a situation, because imaginative processes can remain at a cognitive level. It also involves experiencing the noncognitive aspects of that situation, including somatic sensations and affective states.

Research on adolescent decision making forecasts the challenges we face. In studies on adolescent decision making, hypothetical scenarios make it possible to examine decisions (e.g., sexual ones) that would be difficult to study in vivo. But there are concerns about how well performance in hypothetical scenarios reflects decision making in real situations (e.g., see Beyth-Marom & Fischhoff, 1997; Tester, Gardner, & Wilfong, 1987), particularly in sensitive, emotion-arousing areas. The same concerns appear valid for assessments of risk.

Real-world studies have ecological validity (the decisions are salient, contextually accurate, and have real consequences), but their use of highly selected samples and decisions limits our ability to generalize from them. It is difficult to identify situations in which people will, within some reasonable length of time, make decisions that can be studied.

Laboratory-based studies offer investigators control as well as the ability to look for generalizable processes. Samples can be selected that offer greater generalizability, and subjects can be studied in close temporal proximity to the decisions they make. But these studies often lack ecological validity. Even if the decision tasks are salient, when carried out in laboratory settings they may generate unrepresentative behavior due to participants' knowledge that they are being studied, due to contextual differences between the real world and the laboratory (such as the absence of social pressures and social supports), or both (Beyth-Marom & Fischhoff, 1997). Comparisons of adults' decision making in laboratory simulations with decision making in the real world have provided evidence that the results from the two may not be comparable and can lead to very different conclusions about basic decision processes (Ebbesen & Konecni 1980).

As a result, there has been a call for efforts to create more realistic, "real-world" simulations that would offer the advantages of laboratory research while maintaining salience and ecological validity (Ebbesen & Konecni, 1980). In such a paradigm, we would create study environments that mimic the kinds of emotionally arousing situations in which judgments about risk are typically made. Such simulations could be enormously useful in allowing us to observe the risk perception processes more closely.

The notion that scholars have missed the mark becomes salient when we examine how we have applied the models we use to think about the perception-behavior link. Among the more popular models for explaining why adolescents engage in risk behaviors are those based on subjective expected utility (Edwards, 1954) and its variants, including behavioral decision theory. These models view perceptions of risk as important, to be sure, but also posit an important role for perceptions of reward and benefits. Indeed, the balance between perceived risks and benefits is viewed as providing the motivation for engaging in a particular action. Studies that have included perceived benefits show them to be important predictors of behavior (Christiansen, Smith, Roehling, & Goldman, 1989; Goldberg, Halpern-Felsher, & Millstein, in press; Kelly & Kalichman, 1988; Parsons, Halkitis, Bimbi, & Borkowski, 2000; Smith, Goldman, Greenbaum, & Christiansen, 1995; also see Benthin, Slovic, & Severson, 1993). Importantly, they appear to become far more meaningful to adolescents as they mature and gain experience. Yet we tend to ignore the benefits in most research that has looked at the role of risk perception and adolescent behavior, and we have not considered them seriously in interventions designed to influence adolescent behavior.

WHERE TO GO FROM HERE?

I have speculated about some of the processes that may be involved in how individuals' attend to and appraise risk. I have argued that risk perception can be considered in terms of different phases or levels of processing, each of which represents a set of processes that involve both cognitive and affective components, which themselves interact in a reciprocal fashion. For simplicity, I have presented the model as reflecting a series of sequential phases. However, it is likely that the appraisal phases operate simultaneously, or nearly so. For example, early in the risk appraisal process, neurally mediated affective appraisals take place (see Damasio, 1994). These are probably closer to what I describe as part of the secondary appraisal processes in that they are closer to the "feeling" side of risk appraisal.

I have not elaborated on how such a model might explain decisions to engage in risky behaviors, but it is certain that it would be a more complex one. For example, some of the relatively "simple" relationships that I described concerning the effects of mood on risk perception become more complex when we move to explaining behavior. Although positive moods are associated with expectations of positive outcomes, in some contexts (e.g., higher-risk situations) positive affect is associated with greater sensitivity to potential losses and with more conservative decision making (Isen, 2001). I have also presented a more simplified picture of emotion than exists, because different emotions with the same valence (e.g., fear and anger) appear to have different effects on risk judgment (see Lerner & Keltner, 2000). Furthermore, when we move from perceptions to decisions, we would also need to consider additional factors, such as the effects of anticipated emotions— for example, disappointment and regret (Zeelenberg, van Dijk, Manstead, & van der

Pligt, 2000; also see Lowenstein, Weber, Hsee, & Welch, 2001).

I am not the first to suggest that what is needed in risk perception research is more theory (Wahlberg, 2001), nor am I the first to suggest that integrating diverse disciplinary approaches is important. Furthermore, although I have attempted to provide a conceptual context for bringing together some of what we know about risk perception, I am not suggesting that these ideas constitute a comprehensive model for explaining the ways in which people attend to and appraise risk.

A comprehensive theory of risk perception would draw on a number of additional theoretical and research areas. For example, I have made no mention of developmental theories concerning adolescents' perceptions of invulnerability. These theories posit that adolescents hold an exaggerated sense of uniqueness and believe in a "personal fable"—the view that one is special and in some way immune to the natural laws that pertain to others. The origins of these beliefs were originally thought to be cognitive (e.g., Elkind, 1967; Elkind, 1978), but recent reformulations that appear to be more promising than the original conceptualizations relocate the origins of adolescent egocentrism in social-cognitive and ego development (Lapsley, 1993; Lapsley, FitzGerald, Rice, & Jackson, 1989; Lapsley & Murphy, 1985).

There is also exciting work emerging from the neurosciences, ranging from research on brain development and capacity in adolescence (see Spear, 2000) to affective neuroscience (see Damasio, 1994; Davidson, 1998). Cross-cultural studies on risk perception are leading to cultural theories of both the cognitive and affective components of risk perception (Rippl, 2002; Weber & Hsee, 2000). There is also more to be gleaned from some of the traditional areas in which risk perception has been studied.

My final comment concerns the need for developmentally based research on adolescents. Most of the research I have cited here has been carried out with adults. For example, although we know that emotion has powerful effects on adults' perceptions of risk (Isen, 2001; Nygren, Isen, Taylor, & Dulin, 1996), little is known about how specific emotional states influence adolescents' perceptions, including their perceptions of risk. Are there developmental differences in the effects of emotion on judgment? For example, does fear play a more important role in adults' risk judgments than it does in adolescents'? An even more basic question is whether adolescents experience emotion in ways similar to adults. How does brain development influence affective expression during adolescence? These are but a few of the questions we might want to consider as we move into the next generation of research on adolescent risk perception.

NOTE

1. I am using the term *attention* broadly, to include the process of encoding information (i.e., the taking in and organization of stimuli) as well as what is being encoded and retrieved from long-term memory.

CHAPTER 6

Affect, Analysis, Adolescence, and Risk

PAUL SLOVIC

An insightful paper written for this conference by Laurence Steinberg argues that we should not view adolescent risk taking "as if it were the product of a series of cognitions, involving the perception, appraisal, evaluation, and computation of the relative costs and benefits of alternative courses of action" (Steinberg, this volume, p. 19). In Steinberg's view, "decision making" is not the right framework for understanding, studying, or intervening in adolescent risk taking.

Although much of my research has been squarely in the decision tradition that Steinberg criticizes, my more recent studies have led me to a position quite similar to his. In this chapter, I briefly outline my position as it applies specifically to adolescent smoking and then speculate a bit on its relevance for understanding other adolescent risk-taking behaviors.

CIGARETTE SMOKERS: RATIONAL ACTORS OR RATIONAL FOOLS?

As I have indicated in work published recently, I take issue with the view of smoking

as rational decision making propounded most vigorously by Kip Viscusi (see, e.g., Slovic, 2001; Viscusi, 1992, 2002). Viscusi argues that young people not only know the risks of smoking, they overestimate them. When they "decide" to smoke, they do so, says Viscusi, on the basis of rational evaluation of the known risks and benefits.

My research leads me to a different view, similar to Steinberg's. This research and that of many other psychologists and cognitive neuroscientists, points to imagery and affect—not analysis—as the motivating factors in smoking decisions (Slovic, 2001; Slovic, Finucane, Peters, & MacGregor, 2002).

Simply put, I find that many adolescents do not adequately understand and appreciate the risks that smoking entails. Beginning smokers give little conscious thought to risk. They are lured into the behavior by the prospects of fun, excitement, and adventure. Most begin to think of risk only after they have started to smoke regularly, become addicted, and gained what to them is new information and appreciation of smoking's health risks. They then wish they had never begun to smoke. Cigarette advertising and promotion are designed to play a key role in this process by exposing young people to massive amounts of positive imagery associated with smoking. Research in psychology and cognitive neuroscience as well as marketing studies done for and by the tobacco industry demonstrate how powerful such imagery can be in suppressing perception of risk and manipulating behavior (Finucane, Alhakami, Slovic, & Johnson, 2000; Slovic et al., 2002).

More generally, the vast majority of risk decisions are motivated by affect rather than by analysis of quantitative statistical facts. Affect is a subtle form of emotion, defined by positive (like) or negative (dislike) evaluative feelings toward an external stimulus (such as a cigarette, or the act of smoking, or images of cigarettes and smoking). Such evaluations occur rapidly and automatically in people (Epstein, 1994; Zajonc, 1980). Although reasoned, deliberative analysis is certainly important, reliance on affect and emotion (known as "experiential thinking") is a quicker and easier way to navigate in a complex, uncertain, and dangerous world and is greatly relied on in decision making.

Marketing and advertising specialists have long exploited the power of affect. A considerable variety of cigarette advertising and other promotions have been designed to associate positive imagery and positive affect with the act of smoking (U.S. Department of Health and Human Services, 1994). In addition to advertising and marketing manipulations of imagery and affect, the affective cues emanating from the social environment are also powerful influences on smoking behavior. Having a good time with friends and avoiding the risk of peer disapproval are examples of social factors in which affect (experiential thinking) probably dominates any tendency for analytic or deliberative thinking.

Experiential thinking served human beings well during the long course of evolution when survival required fast action in the face of visible, imminent, known threats—such as a menacing animal. Such thinking did not evolve to protect us against threats from latent carcinogens, such as cigarette smoke. Experience with smoking is misleading. Smokers appear healthy, happy, and active, even more so in cigarette ads. There is no evidence to show that adolescents, or others who start smoking, have realistic knowledge of what it is like for a smoker to experience lung cancer, chronic obstructive pulmonary disease, congestive heart failure, or any other of the fates awaiting smokers that many would consider "worse than death."

Experiential thinking also fails to grasp the cumulative nature of smoking risk. Cigarette smoking is a behavior that takes place one cigarette at a time. A person smoking one pack of cigarettes every day for 40 years consumes about 300,000 cigarettes, and the risk accumulates very slowly with each one. Research shows that young smokers, as cumulative risk takers, believe they can get away with some amount of smoking before the risk takes hold. In short, many young smokers tend to believe that smoking the "very next cigarette" poses little or no risk to their health or that smoking for only a few years poses negligible risk (Slovic, 2000). These young people expect to smoke occasionally for a short while and then quit before any real harm occurs to them. The problem is nicotine addiction—another factor not adequately appreciated by the experiential mode of thinking. As Loewenstein (2001) and others have demonstrated, the powerful visceral cravings characteristic of addiction are difficult, if not impossible, to appreciate unless you are in their grip. The "experience" of these cravings is impossible to predict or even to remember accurately. As a result, young smokers end up smoking more cigarettes, over a longer time period, than they ever anticipated (Benowitz, 2001; Jarvis, McIntyre, & Bates, 2002).

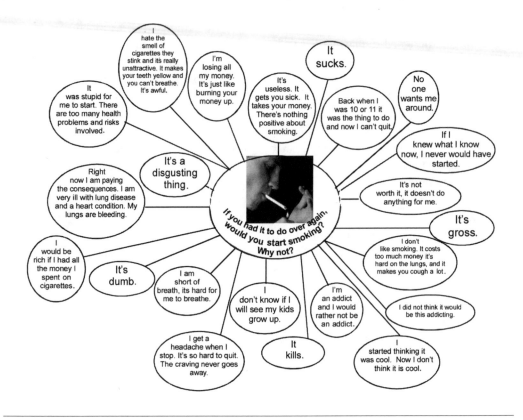

Figure 6.1 A Picture of Misery: Smokers Who Would Not Do It Over Again Answer the Question "Why Not?"

SOURCE: Unpublished data (Weinstein & Slovic, 2001).

Reliance on "risk as feelings" misleads in other ways. Positive feelings of benefit suppress feelings of risk (Finucane et al., 2000). Lack of analytic thinking causes scientific or statistical warnings to be ignored or undervalued (Slovic, 2001).

For those whose reliance on experiential thinking leads to regular smoking, the "experience" of smoking seems to change. When asked, "If you had it to do over again, would you start smoking?" more than 80% of current smokers, both young and old alike, answer "no." Moreover, the more they feel addicted to cigarettes, the longer they have been smoking, and the more cigarettes they are smoking per day, the more likely they are

to say "no" (Slovic, 2001). When those who answer "no" to the "Would you begin again?" question are asked "Why not?" their answers display what McIntyre (2002) has termed "a picture of misery." Figure 6.1 displays a selection of answers that Neil Weinstein and I received recently to the "Why not?" question (Weinstein & Slovic, 2001). McIntyre presents similar data. The answers show clearly the disgust and unhappiness that smokers feel about the behavior they are performing.

These findings strongly repudiate the model of informed rational choice put forth by Viscusi (1992, 2002). The overwhelming regret and dissatisfaction associated with the decision to smoke paints a portrait of individuals who are unable to control a behavior they have belatedly come to recognize as harmful. By failing to appreciate the severe and cumulative consequences that can follow from this harmful addictive behavior, young smokers clearly underestimate the risks they face when they begin to smoke. Their experiential system serves them rationally in meeting short-term goals (having fun at a party). It fails them in meeting longer-term goals (health and longevity), turning the "rational actor" into the "rational fool."

Implications

This experiential analysis has a number of implications for interventions to reduce adolescent smoking. To the extent that this account also generalizes to other adolescent risk behaviors, it has implications there as well.

Let's start with smoking.

Ban Advertising. The affect/experiential thinking account shows the need to ban tobacco advertising and promotion. Tobacco marketers have understood the importance of imagery and affect for decades. They have hired sophisticated researchers to do focus groups and surveys designed to help them understand and exploit "smoker psychology," and the results of these studies have guided marketing and promotional activities that now exceed $10 billion per year in the United States. Companies learned that it is image and affect that manipulate the behaviors of their target audiences. Thus, tobacco advertising has virtually no informational value, and what little informational content it does have (e.g., "light," "low tar") has been found to be misleading. Positive imagery in advertising creates the wrong impression of the "smoking experience." Through the workings of the affect heuristic, it likely depresses the perception of smoking risks.

The repetitive exposure to smoking and cigarette brands through advertising likely creates positive affect by means of what is known as "the mere exposure effect" (Bornstein, 1989; Zajonc, 1980). As studies using subliminal images show, the influence of affective imagery is powerful, manipulative, and not under conscious control (Winkielman, Zajonc, & Schwarz, 1997). Thus, people, young and old alike, are unaware of these effects and are poorly equipped to defend against them.

Related implications are that antitobacco messages should be designed with the same skill and appreciation of affect that pro-tobacco messages have exhibited. In addition, promotional activities such as giving people cigarettes or clothing with brand logos and the like should be prohibited. We know that such "endowments" manipulate affect and preference (Knetsch, 1989).

Create Experiential Knowledge. We also know that health statistics, designed to engage the analytic mind, have less impact on youths than do experiential knowledge and imagery. The problem is that valid experience is hard for young people to acquire. Adolescents need opportunities to meet and learn from people who are caught in the grip of nicotine addiction and from people who are suffering from tobacco-induced illnesses. They need to become familiar with the misery and feelings of self-loathing being experienced by regular smokers.

Time and risk are hard to understand experientially (Ainslie & Haslam, 1992; Loewenstein & Elster, 1992). Research should be undertaken to help people deal with cumulative risk—risk that increases very slowly but surely over thousands of repeated acts. Similarly, we need to better educate about the difference between dying at age 55 and dying at 70 or 80 for young people whose minds, from a temporal distance, see 55, 70, and 80 as basically the same.

Apply This Account to Other Adolescent Risk Behaviors. It remains to be determined how this affect/experiential account generalizes to other risk problems faced by youths: gambling, drinking, depression, suicide, drugs, and sex.

Clearly, the visceral forces that so strongly affect smoking play a role in "decisions" about drugs, sex, and alcohol. Whether gambling creates addiction similar to nicotine and other drugs is unclear, but recent studies of brain activity suggest that there may be a common brain response to a wide range of behaviors that show addictive qualities (see, e.g., Holden, 2001).

Advertising is less an issue for these other risk behaviors than it is for smoking, but the need to provide experiential "wisdom" is no less important. The proper way to do so will obviously vary with the particular problem behavior. Drugs and alcohol and perhaps gambling may also be seen as less desirable if young people understand how it "feels" to be addicted to them.

The main message here is that, although statistical and other health science messages are important, we cannot depend on them. We have to learn to play "the affect game," building images and feelings that promote healthful behavior and block destructive risk taking.

CHAPTER 7

Toward an Understanding of the Role of Perceived Risk in HIV Prevention Research

MARTIN FISHBEIN

Both the health belief model (Becker, 1974; Rosenstock, Strecher, & Becker, 1994) and protection motivation theory (Rogers, 1975, 1983) predict that people are unlikely to even consider performing a health-protective behavior unless they feel personally susceptible to a severe and serious illness. As a result, many attempts to develop interventions to prevent the spread of HIV and other STDs have begun with the assumption that people first must be made aware that they are personally susceptible to, or at high risk for, acquiring and/or transmitting HIV. However, at least in the HIV arena, there is little evidence that perceived risk of acquiring HIV is related to any HIV-protective behavior (see e.g., Gerrard, Gibbons, & Bushman, 1996). Thus, it is important to understand the meaning of perceived risk in the context of HIV prevention. In this chapter, I will consider different measures of perceived risk and their relationships to AIDS-protective behaviors.

Perhaps the most common measure of perceived risk in the HIV arena has been a general question such as, "How likely do you think it is that you will get AIDS? Would you say: Extremely Likely, Somewhat Likely, Somewhat Unlikely, or Extremely Unlikely?" Responses to this question are then used to predict AIDS-protective behaviors, such as condom use and the sharing and cleaning of drug injection paraphernalia. For example, in the CDC AIDS Community Demonstration Projects (CDC AIDS Community Demonstration Projects Research Group, 1999), respondents were asked this question as well as ones such as the following: "When you have vaginal sex with your main partner, how often do you use a condom? Would you say: Always, Almost Always, Sometimes, Almost Never, or Never?"

Figure 7.1 shows the relationship between self-perceived risk and the frequency of (a) condom use for vaginal sex with one's main partner, (b) condom use for vaginal sex with one's occasional partners, and (c) using bleach to clean one's needle and syringe when sharing. It can be seen that in contrast to the expectations of the health belief model

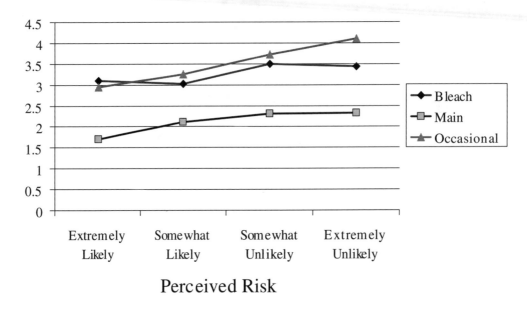

Figure 7.1   Frequency of Behavior (*Always*–5, *Never*–1) as a Function of Perceived Risk

(HBM) and protection motivation theory (PMT), there is actually a negative relationship between perceived risk and HIV-protective behaviors. That is, those at highest self-perceived risk are least likely to report condom use or bleaching.

In retrospect, this should not come as a great surprise. Indeed, it makes perfectly good sense that those who are engaging in HIV risk behaviors (i.e., who engage in unprotected sex or share unsterilized needles) would be most likely to perceive that they are at risk for acquiring HIV. Clearly then, to the extent that measures of perceived risk of acquiring HIV accurately reflect the degree to which a person is (or has been) engaging in AIDS risk-related behaviors, these measures should not be expected to be positively related to current or past protective behaviors. It follows that it is inappropriate to test either the HBM or PMT using past or current behavior.

However, both the HBM and PMT would predict that perceived risk should predict future behavior or, at least, one's intentions to engage in safer behaviors in the future. That is, according to these theories, the more one recognizes that he or she is at personal risk for acquiring a severe and serious illness, the more likely one should be to intend to, and to actually, engage in protective behaviors in the future. The AIDS Community Demonstration Project (ACDP) also obtained measures of respondents' intentions to use condoms and, for those who shared needles, measures of their intentions to use bleach to sterilize their syringes and needles when sharing. For example, respondents were asked, "How likely is it that, in the next 3 months, you will always use a condom for vaginal sex with your main partner? Would you say: Extremely Likely, Quite Likely, Slightly Likely, Neither Likely nor Unlikely, Slightly Unlikely, Quite Unlikely, or Extremely Unlikely?"

Table 7.1   Correlations of Risk With Behavior and Intention

Behavior	N	Risk With Behavior	Risk With Intention
Bleach	427	−.15*	−.13*
Condom use with main partner	1,032	−.11*	−.05
Condom use with occasional partner	1,056	−.34*	−.28*

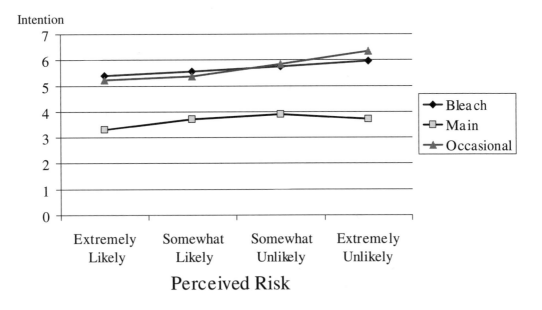

Figure 7.2   Strength of Intentions (*Extremely Likely*–7, *Unlikely*–1) as a Function of Perceived Risk

Figure 7.2 shows the relationships between perceived risk and intentions to engage in AIDS-preventive behaviors. Once again, in contrast to the predictions of the HBM and PMT, there is a negative relationship between perceived risk and intentions to engage in health-protective behaviors in the future; the greater the perceived risk, the less likely people are to intend to engage in HIV prevention. Although this finding may initially appear surprising, in retrospect, it, like the relationship between perceived risk and past or current behavior, is quite predictable. Research has long shown that one of the best predictors of future behavior is past behavior. Thus, one would expect a high correlation between past behavior and intentions to perform that behavior in the future. Consistent with this, future HIV-protective intentions are highly correlated with past behavior (for using bleach, $r = .57$; for always using condoms with one's main partner, $r = .76$; and for always using condoms with occasional partners, $r = .75$). Given these high past behavior and future intention correlations, it follows that one will find the same relationship between perceived risk and intention as that found between perceived risk and past behavior. Table 7.1 summarizes the above by presenting the correlations between perceived risk and both past behavior and future intentions. Clearly, if one is trying to develop a prevention program, there seems to be little reason to increase people's perceptions that they are at risk for a given illness. Indeed, the current findings suggest that such a strategy may actually decrease the likelihood that one will engage in protective behaviors.

To explain this lack of relationship between perceived risk and HIV-protective behaviors, several authors have raised questions about the measurement of perceived risk (e.g., Poppen & Reisen, 1997; Weinstein & Nicolich, 1993). For example, Reisen and Poppen (1999) suggested the use of a specific (i.e., partner-based) risk measure (i.e., "How likely is that you will contract AIDS from your current partner?") instead of a global risk measure ("How likely is it that you will contract AIDS in the future?"). They argued that one's own risk perceptions and behaviors can vary with the perceptions of whether one's partner is high or low risk. However, a closer inspection of the research conducted with the partner-specific risk measure suggests a floor effect; people tend to perceive that it is highly unlikely that they will acquire HIV from their current partners (Reisen & Poppen, 1999).

In a somewhat different approach, Rosenstock et al. (1994) suggested that measures of risk have behavioral anchors. They argued that rather than simply assessing the likelihood that one will "get" AIDS (or some other disease) in general or from a specific partner, the risk question should be tied to a specific behavior. Consistent with this, the ACDP also asked questions such as, "How likely do you think it is that you could get AIDS by having vaginal sex with your main partner without using a condom? Would you say Extremely Likely, Quite Likely, Slightly Likely, Neither Likely nor Unlikely, Slightly Unlikely, Quite Unlikely, or Extremely Unlikely?"

Behavior	N	G Risk With S Risk
Behavior	426	.15*
Condom use with main partner	1,033	.34*
Condom use with occasional partner	1,056	.09*

Table 7.2 Relationships Between "General" and "Specific" Risk

Rather than having a floor effect (i.e., rather than finding that most people felt it was unlikely they could get AIDS from their main or occasional partners), practically everyone was uncertain or believed it was likely they could get AIDS if they had unprotected sex with an occasional partner, and there were at least some who believed they could get AIDS from unprotected sex with their regular partner. Similar to the findings concerning unprotected sex with an occasional partner, almost all injecting drug users believed they could get AIDS if they shared injection equipment without bleaching. Interestingly, as can be seen in Table 7.2, there is a slight positive relationship between the general risk measure and the measures of specific behavioral risk. That is, the more one believes that in general, he or she is at risk for acquiring HIV/AIDS, the more certain one is that unprotected sex and failure to bleach will lead to AIDS. Note, however, that this is merely correlational data, and thus one could just as well suggest that the more certain one is that unprotected sex and failure to bleach will lead to AIDS, the more likely one is to perceive that they are at risk for AIDS.

Figure 7.3 shows the relationship between behavior-specific perceived risk vis-à-vis not bleaching and both the frequency of bleaching and intentions to bleach in the future. In contrast to the findings with respect to general risk, but consistent with the HBM and PMT, we now find a positive relationship between

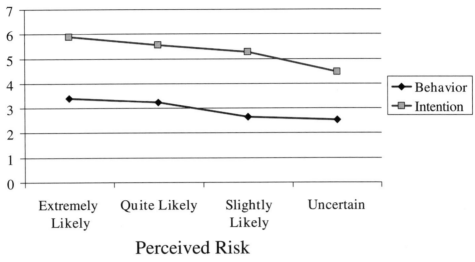

Intention (1-7)

Behavior (1-5)

Perceived Risk

Figure 7.3   Bleaching Intentions and Behavior as a Function of Behavior-Specific Perceived Risk

Table 7.3   Correlations of "Specific Risk" With Behavior and Intention

Behavior	N	Risk With Behavior	Risk With Intention
Bleach	429	.28*	.24*
Condom use with main partner	1,070	.27*	.30*
Condom use with occasional partner	1,094	.19*	.24*

perceived risk and both of these measures. Figures 7.4 and 7.5 present similar findings for condom use for vaginal sex with occasional and main partners, respectively. In other words, the more people believe that they could acquire HIV if they don't always use a condom with either an occasional or main partner, the more likely they are to intend to use, and to actually use, condoms. Table 7.3 presents the correlations between each of the behavior-specific risk measures and both intention and current (or past) behavior.

Very similar results have been obtained by Ellen et al. (2002) and Fishbein and Jarvis (2000). For example, Fishbein and Jarvis (2000) found that the stronger one's belief that unprotected sex with a main or an occasional partner puts one at risk for HIV, the more likely one is to always use a condom with that partner. Similarly, Ellen et al. (2002) observed a zero-order correlation of .33 (*p* < .001) between the perceived risk of getting HIV from engaging in unprotected sex with a main partner and intentions to use condoms with that partner.

Given these positive relationships between behavior-specific measures of risk and behavioral intentions, it seems reasonable to ask why the behavior-specific risk measures are

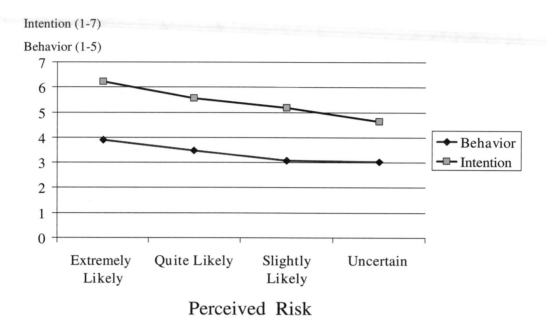

Figure 7.4   Condom Use With Occasional Partner: Intention and Behavior as a Function of Behavior-Specific Perceived Risk

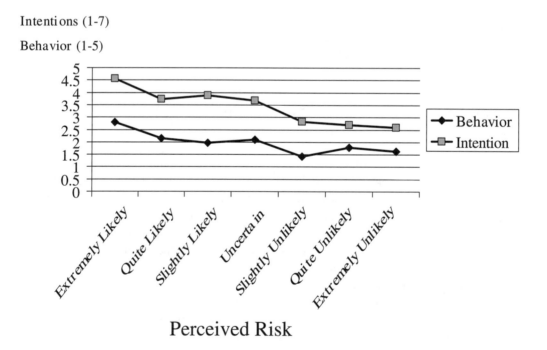

Figure 7.5   Condom Use With Main Partner: Intention and Behavior as a Function of Behavior-Specific Perceived Risk

associated with health-protective behaviors, whereas the more general risk measure is not. The answer is relatively simple. Whereas the general risk measure is largely a reflection of past (or current) behavior, the specific risk measure is what Bandura (1986, 1997) called an "outcome expectancy" and what Fishbein and Ajzen (1975; Ajzen & Fishbein, 1980) labeled a "behavioral belief." Thus, consistent with expectancy value models of attitude (see e.g., Fishbein, 1963), behavior-specific "risks" (or outcome expectancies) are important determinants of one's attitude toward the behavior in question. That is, the more one believes that "my not using a condom" will lead to negative outcomes and/or prevent positive outcomes, the more negative will be one's attitude toward "my not using a condom." And as has often been shown, these attitudes toward performing (or not performing) a specific behavior are important determinants of intentions to perform (or not perform) that behavior (see, e.g., Ajzen & Fishbein, 1980; Fishbein & Ajzen, 1975).

Generally speaking then, behavior-specific "risk" measures or outcome expectancies are theoretically linked to attitudes that in turn are theoretically linked to intentions and behaviors. To put this somewhat differently,

behavior-specific risk measures are what Petraitis, Flay, and Miller (1995) have called "proximal" determinants of behavior. It is important to recognize however that a behavior-specific risk is only one of many possible outcome expectancies associated with "my not using a condom." Thus, although one would expect a correlation between behavior-specific risk and attitude, the strength of the association can vary considerably. In contrast to this proximal role of behavior-specific risk measures, more general risk measures can best be seen as having a "distal" influence on attitude, intention, and behavior. As Petraitis et al. (1995) and Fishbein (2000) have pointed out, although "distal" variables are useful in helping one understand the determinants of specific beliefs, they have no necessary connection to attitude, intention, or behavior. Distal variables may or may not affect behavior. More specifically, distal variables are assumed to influence a particular behavior only to the extent that they influence the more proximal determinants of that behavior. Clearly, if one is going to better understand the role of perceived risk as a factor influencing intentions and behavior, the time has come to move away from more general risk measures to behavior-specific measures (or outcome expectancies).

CHAPTER 8

Alcohol and Illicit Drugs
The Role of Risk Perceptions

Lloyd D. Johnston

The general domain of behaviors to which this chapter is addressed is the use of licit and illicit drugs.[1] It might also be called substance use or, more commonly but less precisely, substance abuse.

I will begin with a consideration of what might distinguish this domain of behaviors from most or all other risk behaviors being dealt with in the Reducing Adolescent Risk Conference—namely, suicide, gambling, pregnancy, HIV/STD, and tobacco use. My focus will then turn to a consideration of the degree to which these various substance-using behaviors are part of larger, overarching constructs versus the degree to which they are unrelated behaviors. That will be followed by a discussion of what I and my colleagues on the Monitoring the Future study have learned about the importance of risk perceptions with regard to substance use and whether they are important determinants of substance use.

BOUNDARIES AND DEFINITIONS

Perhaps more than any of the other risk areas, substance abuse comprises a wide array of specific behaviors—namely use of each of many substances—which provides the opportunity to study multiple instances of the behaviors and also variations among them. For the most part, the substances usually encompassed in this domain are psychoactive substances and include alcohol in its various forms, tobacco, a large and ever-growing list of illegal drugs (marijuana, cocaine, hallucinogens, heroin, ecstasy, etc.), and legally controlled psychotherapeutic drugs (stimulants, sedatives, tranquilizers, and some narcotic drugs other than heroin). A number of legal substances commonly used for their psychoactive effects may be included in this domain of behavior. Alcohol and tobacco have long been considered part of the domain, as well as inhalants. Nearly all inhalants are legal products that are not even manufactured as psychoactive substances but are often used for that purpose by adolescents—in particular younger ones. Indeed, inhalants are the only class of drugs defined by their mode of administration rather than by their pharmacological properties.

The domain might be defined to include noncontrolled (or "over-the-counter") drugs taken for their effects on wakefulness, energy level, sleep, and hunger. Although the inclusion of this last set may seem less intuitively obvious, these substances are taken for their psychoactive effects and can have deleterious effects on the users. In addition, as we will see below, their use actually is correlated with the use of the other psychoactive substances listed above. Including over-the-counter drugs in the domain may help us to parse out some of the underlying causes of substance abuse behaviors, I would argue, since their use is not illicit or deviant, as is the use of many of the other substances just listed.

The domain of substance use might even be stretched to include the use of some nonpsychoactive performance-enhancing or physique-enhancing substances, such as steroids. Characteristics that steroids share with most of the drugs just listed are that they are controlled substances, are sold illegally, and can have serious adverse consequences. Generally, they are not used for their psychoactive effects, however, although they may have some.

In sum, the constellation of behaviors encompassed by the definition of substance use is potentially quite broad. What is included in or excluded from the definition may partly depend on the degree to which these different behaviors have common motives for use, common status in society, or some degree of positive correlation with the other behaviors included in the domain. Insofar as there is a pattern of intercorrelation among them, studying them conjointly may provide an understanding of what underlies and influences them.

DISTINGUISHING CHARACTERISTICS OF THIS AREA

What makes the substance use domain of behavior potentially useful for gaining a

general understanding of the dynamics of risk behavior? For one, this multitude of substances provides *multiple opportunities* to examine how each relates to specific other factors in the intrapersonal and interpersonal spheres. So, for example, we can look at how certain attitudes or beliefs (e.g., perceived risk) relate to behavior not just for one drug but for many. Seizing these opportunities creates potential for determining the extent to which certain associations replicate both across substances and across time.

Because data on youth substance use have been systematically collected over a long time period and in a consistent manner across both time and drugs, researchers possess the *capacity* to study a number of these instances. There are several time-series studies in the substance use field, including the National Household Survey on Drug Abuse (NHSDA), Monitoring the Future (MTF), and more recently, the Youth Risk Behavior Study (YRBS). Of these, MTF has the most surrounding attitudinal, belief, and experiential measures, and YRBS the least (by design). YRBS, on the other hand, contains the broadest array of youth risk behaviors.

Furthermore, various drugs have been introduced into the general population at different points in time. These diverse time periods make it easier to separate the sequelae of intrapersonal and interpersonal events related to each drug and to determine how robust they are across different historical contexts.

Clearly, the various substances differ in the probability, nature, and severity of their adverse consequences. Of special importance, they also vary in length of time between initiation of the behavior and the likely occurrence of those adverse outcomes. For example, cigarettes primarily carry very long-term risks, cocaine quite serious intermediate-term risks, and PCP (phencyclidine) very immediate and severe short-term risks. Such differences make it possible to examine variations in risk perceptions that may relate to the time horizon of the risk. I have argued elsewhere (Johnston, 1991b) that the lag time in the occurrence of the adverse consequences is an important determinant of how long it will take for a natural corrective cycle to set in—one in which use of the drug eventually begins to recede.

The drugs differ even in how certain it is that various consequences even exist. There is little disagreement that particular sexually transmitted diseases (STDs) have specific adverse outcomes, but there is considerable disagreement, even among scientists, about whether marijuana use is dependence producing or whether its use contributes to the likelihood that a person will advance to the use of other illicit drugs.

A final distinguishing characteristic of this domain of behaviors is that taking psycho-active substances can have direct chemical effects on the neurological reinforcement systems. Those effects can lead to lasting alterations of those systems, thus giving rise to dependence or addiction. Whether some other risk behaviors—such as gambling, overeating, and certain sexual behaviors—have similar effects is an important question.

THE STRUCTURE OF ASSOCIATIONS AMONG DRUG-USING BEHAVIORS

It is a long-established fact that a great many of the various drug-taking behaviors in this domain tend to be highly intercorrelated (see Akers, 1984; Elliott & Huizinga, 1984; Johnston, 1973; Kandel, 1975; Yamaguchi & Kandel, 1984). Indeed, Kandel and her colleagues have established empirically that there tend to be fairly regular stages of involvement in various substances that fit rather well with Gutman scaling (Yamaguchi & Kandel, 1984). Either tobacco or alcohol usually comes first in the sequence; then the

other of those two; then marijuana; then any of a number of the other illicit (so-called harder) drugs. Our own analyses tend to confirm those regularities. They have additionally suggested that the use of some of the drugs in the last category that are considered among the most dangerous (such as crack or heroin) is usually preceded by use of some of the others in that group considered as less dangerous (such as amphetamines, tranquilizers, or LSD). We also find that inhalants tend to be another early-stage drug class in addition to alcohol and tobacco. Indeed, there is a fairly strong correlation between the degree to which each drug is seen as dangerous and the percentage of the youth population that uses it (Johnston, O'Malley, & Bachman, 2001).

Based on a new analysis of MTF data, Table 8.1 presents measures of pairwise associations among usage measures for nearly all the substances discussed so far, except the over-the-counter drugs, based on data from the 12th-grade students surveyed in 2001.[2] The use of most drugs is represented in the analysis by the self-reported frequency of use during the 12-month period preceding the survey. (Frequency of use for alcohol and cigarettes are measured in the prior 30-day interval, because these behaviors are so much more prevalent than the others.) Both product-moment correlations and gamma statistics were run, but only the gammas are shown in the table. The gamma statistic (Goodman & Kruskal, 1979) is a nonparametric statistic indicating the degree of ordinal association between two variables. It ranges from +1 to −1, with 0 indicating no association, much like a Pearson product-moment correlation. What Table 8.2 shows is the very high degree of association among all these disparate drug-using behaviors—even including the use of steroids and inhalants. Indeed, the Pearson product-moment correlations among them (not shown) all were significant at below the

(text continues on page 62)

Table 8.1 Associations Among the Different Substances (and Dangerous Driving)

	1. FREQ. CIGS SMKD/30	2. FREQ. DRNK/30 DAY	3. 5+DRK ROW/LST 2WK	4. FREQ. MARIJ/12 MO	5. FREQ. LSD/12 MO	6. FREQ. OTH PSYD/12 MO	7. FREQ. COKE/12 MO	8. FREQ. CRACK/12 MO	9. FREQ. AMPH/12 MO	10. FREQ. ICE/12 MO	11. FREQ. BRBT/12 MO
2. FREQ. DRINK/ 30 DAY	0.59										
3. 5+DRINKS ROW/LST 2WK	0.61	0.92									
4. FREQ. MARIJ/ 12 MO	0.63	0.62	0.62								
5. FREQ. LSD/ 12 MO	0.68	0.64	0.65	0.87							
6. FREQ. OTH PSYD/ 12 MO	0.68	0.67	0.68	0.88	0.94						
7. FREQ. COKE/ 12 MO	0.71	0.68	0.70	0.87	0.90	0.90					
8. FREQ. CRACK/ 12 MO	0.72	0.71	0.74	0.83	0.89	0.91	0.98				
9. FREQ. AMPH/ 12 MO	0.59	0.55	0.57	0.65	0.81	0.81	0.82	0.83			
10. FREQ. ICE/ 12 MO	0.71	0.51	0.56	0.80	0.91	0.87	0.94	0.92	0.85		
11. FREQ. BRBT/ 12 MO	0.60	0.59	0.60	0.72	0.84	0.83	0.84	0.86	0.87	0.85	
12. FREQ. TRQL/ 12 MO	0.63	0.61	0.62	0.75	0.85	0.86	0.85	0.86	0.86	0.88	0.92
13. FREQ. HEROIN/ 12 MO	0.65	0.67	0.69	0.81	0.91	0.91	0.94	0.96	0.85	0.95	0.85
14. FREQ. OTH NARC/ 12 MO	0.65	0.63	0.64	0.80	0.89	0.88	0.87	0.86	0.83	0.87	0.87
15. FREQ. INHAL/ 12 MO	0.61	0.54	0.55	0.64	0.75	0.75	0.80	0.76	0.67	0.83	0.73
16. FREQ. STEROIDS/ 12 MO	0.42	0.63	0.69	0.38	0.50	0.30	0.58	0.82	0.72	0.41	0.63
17. ANY ILLICIT INDEX	0.61	0.61	0.61	0.96	0.92	0.94	0.93	0.91	0.72	0.82	0.87
18. ANY ILLICIT OTHER THAN MJ	0.63	0.60	0.62	0.78	0.95	0.95	0.95	0.94	0.83	0.88	0.94
19. FREQ. ACCDNTS/12 MO	0.24	0.24	0.24	0.25	0.29	0.36	0.40	0.36	0.30	0.33	0.32
20. FREQ. TICKETS/ 12 MO	0.31	0.33	0.37	0.33	0.38	0.47	0.41	0.42	0.31	0.08	0.38

(Continued)

Table 8.1 (*Continued*)

	12. FREQ. TRQL/ 12 MO	13. FREQ. HEROIN/ 12 MO	14. FREQ. OTH NARC/ 12 MO	15. FREQ. INHL/ 12 MO	16. FREQ. STER/ 12 MO	17. ANY ILLICIT INDEX	18. OTHER THAN MJ INDEX	19. FREQ. ACCIDNTS/ 12 MO
2. FREQ. DRINK/ 30 DAY								
3. 5+DRINKS ROW/LST 2WK								
4. FREQ. MARIJ/ 12 MO								
5. FREQ. LSD/ 12 MO								
6. FREQ. OTH PSYD/ 12 MO								
7. FREQ. COKE/ 12 MO								
8. FREQ. CRACK/ 12 MO								
9. FREQ. AMPH/ 12 MO								
10. FREQ. ICE/ 12 MO								
11. FREQ. BRBT/ 12 MO								
12. FREQ. TRQL/ 12 MO								
13. FREQ. HEROIN/ 12 MO	0.88							
14. FREQ. OTH NARC/ 12 MO	0.88	0.91						
15. FREQ. INHAL/ 12 MO	0.75	0.75	0.75					
16. FREQ. STEROIDS/ 12 MO	0.67	0.66	0.69	0.57				
17. ANY ILLICIT INDEX	0.88	0.93	0.91	0.68	0.48			
18. ANY ILLICIT OTHER THAN MJ	0.94	0.95	0.95	0.75	0.60	n/a		
19. FREQ. ACCDNTS/12 MO	0.34	0.44	0.37	0.25	0.27	0.25	0.31	
20. FREQ. TICKETS/12 MO	0.39	0.34	0.40	0.30	0.43	0.32	0.35	0.47

Table 8.2   Associations Between Use of Over-the-Counter Drugs and Other Substances

	1. FREQ. MJ/LAST 12MO	2. ILLICIT OTH THAN MJ	3. FREQ. CIGS SMKD/30 DAY	4. FREQ. ALC/30 DAY	5. 5+DRNK /LAST 2 WK	6. FREQ. DIET PILLS/ 12 MO	7. FREQ. STA-AWAKE/ 12 MO
2. ANY ILLICITS OTHER THAN MJ	0.75						
3. FREQ. CIGS SMKD/ 30 DAY	0.60	0.60					
4. FREQ. ALC/ 30 DAY	0.62	0.62	0.55				
5. 5+DRNK / LAST 2 WK	0.64	0.67	0.57	0.92			
6. FREQ. DIET PILLS/ 12 MO	0.29	0.45	0.43	0.31	0.27		
7. FREQ. STA-AWAKE/ 12 MO	0.49	0.63	0.49	0.48	0.54	0.66	
8. FREQ. LOOK-A-LIKE/ 12 MO	0.51	0.73	0.50	0.50	0.58	0.67	0.82

61

.0001 level, with the exception of a few of the associations related to steroid use.[3]

Less obvious to include in this domain of behavior, perhaps, is the use of over-the-counter drugs for functional reasons such as losing weight or staying awake. But these behaviors also turn out to be correlated with the use of licit and illicit psychoactive drugs (see Table 8.2[4]). For example, of those high school seniors in the class of 2000 who were surveyed in the MTF study, only 9% of those who never used an illicit drug reported diet pill use. This compares with 14% of those who had ever used marijuana but no other illicit drug and 35% of those who had ever used an illicit drug other than marijuana. We (Osgood, Johnston, O'Malley, & Bachman, 1988) and others have argued that a propensity toward deviance explains much of the variance in individual substance use measures, as will be discussed below. But the connection found with the over-the-counter drugs raises the question of whether there might be another underlying construct, such as a propensity to use psychoactive chemicals of all kinds to alter mood.

In fact, in the early years of the MTF study, we even included the use of beverages containing caffeine (colas, coffee, and tea) to test that hypothesis, and we found some degree of positive association between the use of even these very common and traditionally licit substances and the degree of involvement with illicit drugs (e.g., Bachman, Johnston, & O'Malley, 1984).

THE STRUCTURE OF ASSOCIATIONS WITH OTHER RISK BEHAVIORS

As alluded to earlier, there is a substantial literature showing that both licit and illicit drug use are largely explainable in terms of a more general propensity toward deviance of any kind. Some years ago the Jessors and their colleagues (Donovan & Jessor, 1985; Jessor & Jessor, 1977) described the more general domain as "problem behaviors." They posited that a variety of deviant behaviors form what they describe as a syndrome caused by a general latent variable they label as "unconventionality." Even earlier, Johnston (1973), working with a national sample of young males, found that the use of all psychoactive drugs, both legal and illegal, was strongly correlated with an index of non-drug-related forms of delinquency. He also concluded from panel analyses that involvement in drugs short of addiction did not seem to increase such delinquency; in other words, the use of drugs appeared to be simply another (perhaps age-graded) manifestation of a more general deviant behavioral pattern.[5]

Osgood et al. (1988) again demonstrated, using panel data from national samples in the MTF study, that drug use is strongly inter-correlated with non-drug-related forms of deviance, including specific criminal behaviors and dangerous driving. They concluded,

> A relatively stable general involvement in deviance accounted for virtually all association between different types of deviance, but the stability of each behavior could only be explained by equally important and stable specific influences. Thus, theories that treat different deviant behaviors as alternative manifestations of a single general tendency can account for some, but far from all, of the meaningful variance in these behaviors. (p. 81)

I believe this is a particularly important finding for the present volume. It means that each individual behavior in the larger domain of risk behaviors, whether defined in terms of deviance or risk taking or sensation seeking (to take the three most commonly used cross-cutting constructs), likely has many specific determinants that do not act on the other behaviors in the domain.

Of course, there very likely *are* a number of common determinants, both intrapersonal and interpersonal (subjects to which I will return later), but there are important behavior-specific determinants, as well. Some of those behavior-specific determinants may have *parallel* determinants for other behaviors, but not necessarily the *same* determinants. The particular example I can offer regards the perceived level of risk associated with engaging in the behavior. Perceived risk of pregnancy may influence sexual behavior just as perceived risk of marijuana use may influence marijuana use, but neither belief may influence the behavior in the other domain. Surely one important goal of this conference is to determine the extent to which the various risk behaviors may have parallel determinants across domains.

Within the general category of potential *parallel determinants,* I might place perceived risk, personal disapproval, perceived peer norms, perceived role model behavior (among public, family, and peer role models), and so on—all specific to the particular behavior in question. Among the *common determinants,* I might put propensity toward deviance (or unconventional behavior), sensation seeking, risk taking, involvement in a deviant peer subgroup, strong family bonds, adjustment and academic success at school, religiosity, and so on. Table 8.3 shows how several of these potential common determinants relate to both the full set of drugs given in Table 8.1 and to two measures of dangerous driving, again using the gamma statistic to measure the degree of association among 12th graders in 2001.[6]

Drug use may be related to a number of other high-risk adolescent behaviors for any of several reasons. Perhaps the most obvious is the one that we have been discussing: These behaviors may all have some common determinants in the intrapersonal or interpersonal spheres. (That they have parallel determinants would not necessarily lead to any intercorrelation among them unless

those parallel determinants—for instance, the degree of danger associated with each—are themselves correlated.)

Another likely source of intercorrelation among many of the risk behaviors may be causal linkages among them. For example, use of many of the drugs discussed here can impair both physical and cognitive performance, as well as judgment, in other domains of behavior. Many psychoactive drugs impair motor and cognitive performance, often with tragic results when combined with driving, swimming, or engaging in some other behavior requiring adept performance or sober judgment. A drunk teen may be less cognizant of his or her performance limitations when under the influence, for example, and insist on driving a car—a judgment he or she may not think wise when sober. Or youngsters high on marijuana or other drugs may decide to have sexual intercourse—which they may not have done had they been sober—and furthermore, they may do so without protection against either pregnancy or STDs. Indeed, the impairment of performance or judgment with regard to some of these other behaviors is one of the risks associated with most kinds of substance use.

There are many known risk and protective factors for the various types of substance use, and I will not try to review that very large literature here. (A review of that literature may be found in Johnston, O'Malley, Schulenberg, & Bachman, 2001, pp. 67-74.) Some of the strongest risk and protective factors are captured in the variables given in Table 8.3; it should be noted that all have to do with the young person's degree of attachment to adult-run institutions traditionally charged with the education and socialization of youth—family, school, and church. The four variables are religiosity, number of days of school cut in the prior four weeks, academic grades, and average number of evenings out of the parental home per week for fun and recreation. (Religiosity is based

Table 8.3 Associations Between Selected Risk Factors and Use of Different Substances (and Dangerous Driving)

	1. RELIGIOUS COMMITMENT	2. FREQ. DAYS/ 4 WK CUT SCHOOL	3. HS GRADE/ D=1	4. FREQ./ AV WK GO OUT
2. FREQ. DAYS/4WK CUT SCHOOL	-0.16			
3. HS GRADE/D=1	0.11	-0.22		
4. FREQ./AV WK GO OUT	-0.07	0.24	-0.06	
5. FREQ. CIGS SMKD/30 DAY	-0.22	0.31	-0.24	0.31
6. FREQ. DRNK/ 30 DAY	-0.23	0.38	-0.13	0.35
7. 5+DRNK ROW/LST 2WK	-0.23	0.41	-0.17	0.39
8. FREQ. MARIJ/ 12 MO	-0.28	0.40	-0.23	0.34
9. FREQ. LSD/ 12 MO	-0.40	0.44	-0.29	0.44
10. FREQ. OTH PSYD/ 12 MO	-0.34	0.50	-0.27	0.45
11. FREQ. COKE/ 12 MO	-0.29	0.48	-0.31	0.47
12. FREQ. CRACK/ 12 MO	-0.30	0.54	-0.38	0.52
13. FREQ. AMPH/ 12 MO	-0.23	0.37	-0.25	0.35
14. FREQ. ICE/ 12 MO	-0.47	0.41	-0.37	0.47
15. FREQ. BRBT/ 12 MO	-0.25	0.40	-0.19	0.34
16. FREQ. TRQL/ 12 MO	-0.29	0.45	-0.21	0.42
17. FREQ. HEROIN/ 12 MO	-0.28	0.55	-0.27	0.46
18. FREQ. OTH NARC/ 12 MO	-0.30	0.44	-0.25	0.45
19. FREQ. INHAL/ 12 MO	-0.20	0.37	-0.22	0.36
20. FREQ. STEROIDS/ 12 MO	0.10	0.35	-0.24	0.25
21. ANY ILLICIT INDEX	-0.27	0.39	-0.21	0.33
22. ANY ILLICIT OTHER THAN MJ	-0.31	0.41	-0.21	0.37
23. FREQ. TICKETS/ 12 MO	-0.08	0.28	-0.08	0.23
24. FREQ. ACCIDENTS/12 MO	-0.06	0.16	-0.05	0.16

on the mean of two variables—frequency of church attendance and rated importance of religion in the respondent's life.) There has proven to be a considerable robustness across time in these and many other risk and protective factors, as is documented for a 21-year period in Brown, Schulenberg, Bachman, O'Malley, and Johnston (2001).

THE ROLE OF RISK PERCEPTIONS

For the remainder of this chapter, I would like to focus primarily on what we have learned about the nature and role of risk perception in determining substance-using behaviors, while taking advantage of some of the long-term data we have from the MTF study. The 27-year period that the study now spans provides a number of instances of inflections

in perceived risk related to the various drugs and in the use of the substances themselves. It also encompasses a number of historical events that may be linked to some of the changes we have seen. I will begin, however, by listing several findings about this domain of behavior that help to set the stage for this discussion.

Substance-Using Behaviors Have Proven to be Quite Malleable

Nearly all substance-using behaviors have changed substantially over time in their prevalence and frequency levels, more so than a number of other risky behaviors such as delinquency, for example (Johnston, O'Malley, & Bachman, 2001). These changes suggest that the behaviors can be, and have been, influenced substantially by

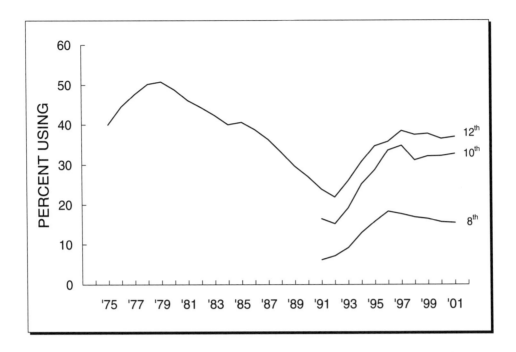

Figure 8.1   Trends in Annual Prevalence of Marijuana: Three Populations

social influences. I emphasize this point because one often hears, particularly by critics of the nation's strategy for dealing with drug use, that the war on drugs has been lost. That conclusion can lead to a sense of impotence in dealing with the drug problem(s) that is simply not justified, whatever the merits of the particular policies in place at any given time. Very appreciable progress in reducing youth substance use has been made in certain historical periods, which means that it could be made again.

Figures 8.1 and 8.2 show the trend lines over the past quarter century for marijuana, by far the most prevalent of the illicit drugs, and for an index of use of any of the other illicit drugs, regardless of specific type. Both measures have shown very considerable variation over the decades. Variability is even greater when looked at by individual substance, which relates to the next point.

Trends and Influences Have Been, to a Considerable Degree, Drug Specific

The index of using any of the illicit drugs other than marijuana might be thought of as measuring the proportion of the youth population willing to entertain the idea of violating general social norms regarding illicit drug use beyond the use of marijuana. Although there is considerable cross-time variability in this condition, as is illustrated in Figure 8.2, there is far more variability in the use of the specific individual substances that make up the index. See Figures 8.3 and 8.4 for some concrete examples of their differing cross-time profiles of use.

This high degree of variability strongly suggests that many of the influences driving these drug-using behaviors are substance specific. I have argued elsewhere that key among these substance-specific factors are (a) young peoples' awareness of the psychoactive potential of the drug, (b) their access to the drug, (c) the alleged

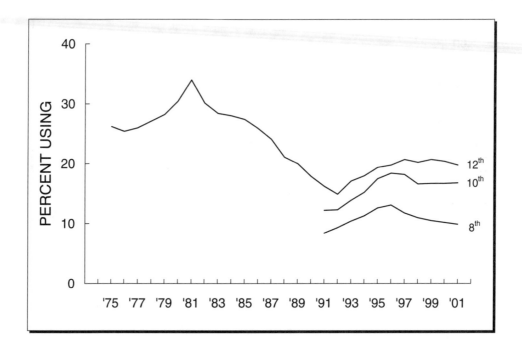

Figure 8.2   Trends in Annual Prevalence of Any Illicit Drug Other Than Marijuana: Three Populations

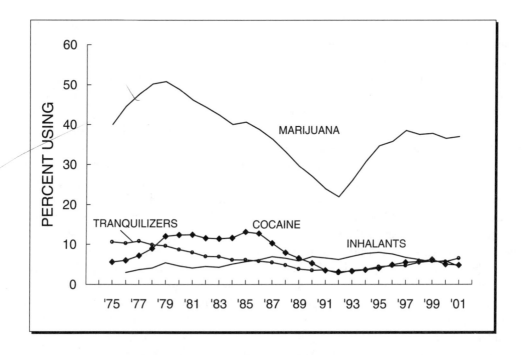

Figure 8.3   Trends in Annual Prevalence of Various Illicit Drugs: 12th Graders

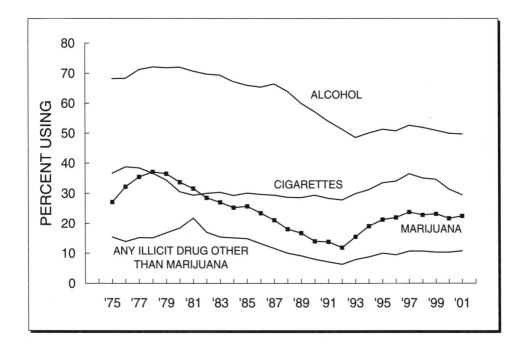

Figure 8.4   Trends in 30-Day Prevalence of Various Drugs: 12th Graders

benefits of use, (d) the degree to which using the drug is seen as deviant both in the larger society and the peer group, and (e) the perceived risks of use (Johnston, 1991b). Awareness, access, and alleged benefits (a very broad category) can all be seen as factors encouraging use, whereas social norms and perceived risk can be seen as controlling factors. (Remember, I am attempting here to distinguish among drugs in their population trends. Obviously, many other such factors contribute to the individual's susceptibility or risk proneness.)

Changes in Both Initiation and Quitting Rates Have Been Associated With Changes in Perceived Risk

My colleagues and I have written for some time about the association between perceived risk and the use of various drugs. We have tried to demonstrate that trends in perceived risk have played an important role in the decline of marijuana use in the

1980s (Bachman et al., 1988; Johnston, 1991a; Johnston, O'Malley, & Bachman, 2001, and prior volumes in that series), the decline of cocaine use in the late 1980s (Bachman, Johnston, & O'Malley, 1990; Johnston, O'Malley, & Bachman, 2001, and prior volumes), and the increases in marijuana use in the 1990s (Bachman et al., 1998; Johnston, O'Malley, & Bachman, 2001, and prior volumes).

In fact, there are many examples of covariation across time between the use of a drug and perceived risk of its use, as measured by the proportion of respondents who see great risk of harm to the user (associated with experimental, occasional, or regular use). Indeed, in a number of cases, shifts in perceived risk have preceded inflections in actual use by a year, helping to address the concern that they may both be just different sides of the same coin. These relationships may be seen most easily in our annual overview document (Johnston, O'Malley, & Bachman, 2002). However, for illustration

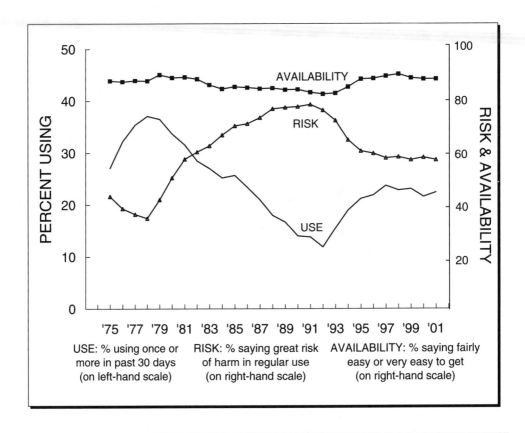

USE: % using once or
more in past 30 days
(on left-hand scale)

RISK: % saying great risk
of harm in regular use
(on right-hand scale)

AVAILABILITY: % saying fairly
easy or very easy to get
(on right-hand scale)

Figure 8.5   Marijuana: Trends in Perceived Availability, Perceived Risk of Regular Use, and
Prevalence of Use in Past 30 Days for 12th Graders

purposes, I will focus here on just a few relationships that make the point.

Marijuana use and risk are charted, along with availability, in Figure 8.5, and a similar chart is shown for cocaine in Figure 8.6. The marijuana figure shows that use moved inversely with perceived risk over the 25-year interval, and in fact, perceived risk started to drop in 1991, a year before use started to increase. Other instances of perceived risk being a leading indicator of change in use have also been reported for crack, amphetamines, and heroin (Johnston et al., 2002).

Cocaine offers another interesting example of the role of perceived risk in influencing drug use. Figure 8.6 shows the strong inverse covariance across time between use

and perceived risk of experimental use. The most noteworthy interval in the 25-year span is the period following 1986. That was the year that Len Bias, a first-round draft pick in the NBA, died of what was initially reported to be his first experience with cocaine. That year, an alarmist concern regarding crack reached a crescendo in the media and among elected officials. It is clear from Figure 8.6 that there was a very sharp increase in the perceived risk of cocaine by 1987, and associated with it was the beginning of what became a dramatic drop over the next few years in the prevalence of use among 12th graders. (Use declined by roughly 75%.)

Figure 8.7 presents somewhat more detailed information on the perceived risk of

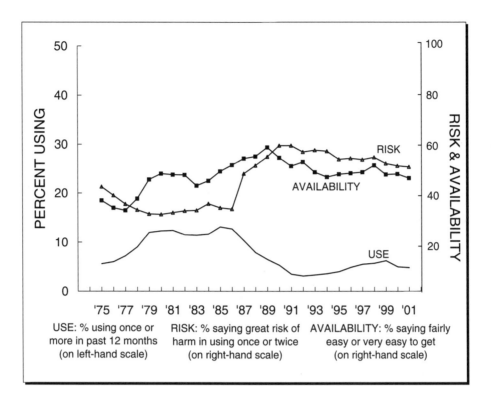

Figure 8.6 Cocaine: Trends in Perceived Availability, Perceived Risk of Trying, and Prevalence of Use in Past Year for 12th Graders

cocaine. It shows trends separately for the proportions saying that there is "great risk" involved in experimental use, occasional use, and regular use. The figure reveals an upward drift in the early 1980s in the proportion of high school seniors seeing great risk in regular cocaine use (but not in experimental use). The fact that use was not moving as expected in the presence of an increase in perceived risk surprised us and led us to the hypothesis that it is the risk associated with the type of use that seniors contemplate for themselves that matters. Given rather long lag time on average between the times people first use cocaine and become regular users, it seemed likely that young people viewed themselves as likely to be light or, at most, occasional users.

That hypothesis prompted us to add the question on perceived risk of occasional use to the 1986 survey—and none too soon, because that measure moved up sharply the year after it was introduced. And the hypothesis was confirmed, insofar as use finally began to drop when occasional and experimental use came to be seen as more dangerous. It seems likely that the Len Bias episode played an important role in modifying these beliefs, because he was, after all, a young person in peak physical condition who apparently was struck down by his first experience with cocaine. (It was revealed only later that this had not been his first encounter with the drug, an account that did not play nearly as widely as the original story.)

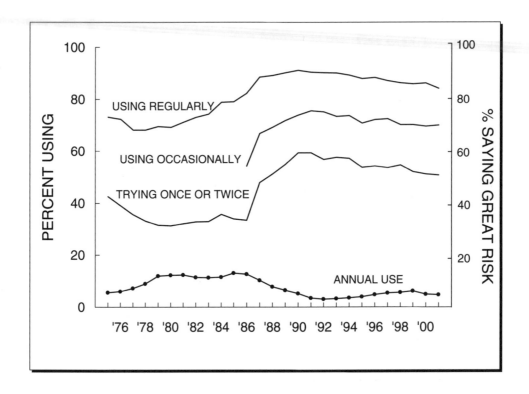

Figure 8.7   Cocaine: Trends in Annual Prevalence and in Perceived Risk of
Different Levels of Use

There are two other points to consider on the cocaine story. Crack cocaine was coming onto the scene roughly from 1983 through 1986, and it very rapidly got a reputation—widely reported in the media—as an extremely addictive and dangerous drug. I think it very likely that this rapid negative assessment of the drug kept the prevalence rate of crack cocaine low. Its annual prevalence among high school seniors in 1996 (almost surely the peak year) was only 4.1%, and that statistic fell steadily to 1.5% by 1991.

I also think it likely that, because of the similarities between the two drugs, crack's bad reputation rubbed off on another smokable crystalline stimulant drug that emerged just a few years later—namely, crystal methamphetamine or "ice." The annual prevalence for ice among high school seniors stayed between 1.3% when it was first measured in 1990 and 1.8% in 1994. After 1994, both ice and crack use began to rise, quite possibly because a newer generation of teens had replaced the earlier one that had "learned" how dangerous these drugs are, and with that generational replacement came what I have termed "generational forgetting" of the dangers of drugs.

The hypothesis I am suggesting is that living through a period when the dangers of a drug (whether valid or not) become widely accepted, influences the individual's belief about those dangers and, to some degree, inoculates him or her against use. Other drugs for which I think this has happened are LSD in the early 1970s and PCP in the late 1970s. LSD came to be seen as dangerous in part because it was widely known that users could have uncontrolled flashbacks, and in part because some scientists alleged that it could cause brain shrinkage and damage chromosomes. (Both of the latter beliefs were eventually debunked.) PCP, which had an annual prevalence of 7% among high school seniors when we first measured it in 1979, rapidly gained a reputation for causing users to do dangerous and aggressive things, and its use dropped rapidly—to 2.2% within just 3 years. Growing up without learning about those dangers leaves the replacement generation vulnerable to the lures of the very same drugs that fell from popularity in an earlier time period.

To generalize this point, I have hypothesized that a similar learning, and subsequent generational forgetting, of the dangers of HIV may explain the fallback in protective practices among gay men. Whether a similar dynamic might work for other risk behaviors, such as gambling, is less clear to me.

To finish this discussion of the role of perceived risk, let me note that disapproval of a drug usually moves inversely and synchronously with use; in a number of the cases cited above, where perceived risk was a leading indicator of changes in use, it was also a leading indicator of changes in disapproval. Clearly, other factors can influence disapproval, but our hypothesis is that beliefs about a drug's danger level play an important role in influencing personal disapproval and, quite likely, in influencing eventual peer disapproval.

Changes in Perceived Risk and Use Have Been Associated With Possible Explanatory Historical Events in a Number of Cases

Deducing causation from time-associated events in history is a dangerous business, of course, but still, a number of time links are worth consideration. My theory of popular drug epidemics suggests that the experiences of role models (particularly among role model groups favored by teens, such as professional athletes, actors and actresses, and rock musicians) can have a modeling influence on teen behavior, including drug use. Likewise, "unfortunate role models" are those in these same groups who come to a bad end because of their drug use, and they can provide vicarious learning for teens about the dangers of drugs.

Len Bias was such an unfortunate role model, I would contend. Periods of high prevalence of drug use, such as the late 1970s, led to the early deaths of several performers (particularly rock musicians) due to drug use, which may well have contributed to the downturn in the use of most drugs in the 1980s. Another unfortunate role model, with a twist, may have been Lyle Alzado, a professional football player who believed his terminal brain tumor was caused by steroid use and who set out in advance of his death to get that word out to young people. In an MTF occasional paper written in 1991 (and published 2 years later), we predicted that his actions may well influence young people's views about the dangers of steroids (Johnston, O'Malley, Bachman, & Schulenberg, 1993), and the 1992 survey data showed a highly significant 5-percentage-point jump in perceived risk for steroids in all three grade levels surveyed. (Use fell some that year among 12th graders, but not among 8th and 10th graders.)

Mark McGwire may well have been an unintentional role model for steroid use in 1998, the year he hit his home run record, when it became known through the press that he had been using androstenedione, a legal over-the-counter steroid precursor. In the 1999 MTF survey, we saw a sharp increase in reported steroid use among 8th and 10th graders and a highly significant 6-percentage-point drop in perceived risk for trying steroids among 12th graders (the only ones being asked the risk questions).[7]

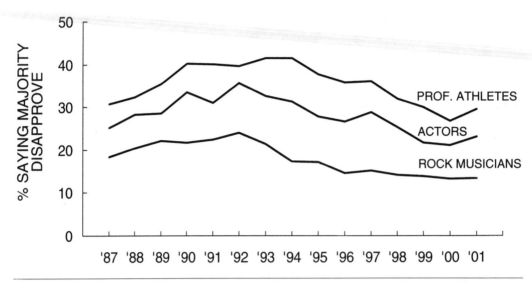

Figure 8.8 Percentage Who Think a Majority of Each Role Model Group Strongly Disapproves of Drug Use: 12th Graders

Role modeling may well have played a role in drug use increase in the early to mid-1990s. Using a set of questions about the students' perceptions of several role model groups (athletes, actors, and rock musicians), we found that during that historical period, there was an increase in the proportions of who thought that these groups used drugs themselves and students approved of their use (see Figure 8.8).

One other historical connection worthy of particular mention deals with the intentional use of advertising to change perceptions of risk. After watching inhalant use rise for nearly two decades, I urged the Partnership for a Drug-Free America to consider a campaign dealing with that class of drugs. They did so, launching their campaign in 1995. In the 1996 MTF survey, there was a 5- to 6-percentage-point increase in perceived risk of trying inhalants in the two grades in

which it was measured (8th and 10th). A turnaround in inhalant use began in 1996 (a year in which practically no other drug was trending down), and it continued at least through 2001. Coincidence? Perhaps, but little else happened during that period that would seem to offer alternative explanation for what happened to perceived risk and use relevant to inhalants.

Ecstasy may provide the next case to test the theory. I have said previously that ecstasy use won't turn around until young people come to see it as dangerous. There is evidence that such a change began to occur in 2001, as perceived risk for ecstasy jumped and the rate of increase slowed (Johnston et al., 2002). We think that an outright turnaround has not yet begun, in part because the drug is still diffusing to communities in which it was not previously available. But as saturation occurs and perceived risk continues to grow (a new media campaign dealing with ecstasy is now underway), I predict that we will see a turnaround in the use of that drug as well.[8]

In fact, I have attempted in my public statements and writings (e.g., Johnston, 1991b) to convey the notion that a natural corrective cycle applies to almost any drug that has come along and that is likely to come along. Because at first the dangers of the drug go unrecognized and only its alleged benefits are touted, young people are naive and begin to use it. Only when the adverse consequences become painfully obvious do young people become convinced that they should avoid that drug. One strategy for public health education could be to help young people generalize from the past—to help them realize that virtually all new drugs are likely to have adverse consequences—and help them avoid learning the hard way what those consequences are. In other words, promote among young people a more generalized risk perception or belief about psychoactive drugs. I use cocaine as an example from the past (in the early years of the cocaine epidemic, even the experts did not think it was addictive or deadly) and ecstasy as an example in the present, for which the cycle is still playing out. It is not an easy prevention message to sell, but I believe it holds the kernel of a promising idea.

NOTES

1. For the purposes of this conference, one of the licit drugs (tobacco) is being treated separately, as well, but I will include tobacco use here in talking about the larger domain of which it clearly is a part.

2. Most cells are based on about 12,500 cases, although a few drugs are contained on only a subset of the six questionnaire forms, yielding smaller Ns. All cells are based on at least 3,500 cases, however, with only one exception—that between steroids and ice, which has 1,750 cases.

3. Steroid use is contained in only two questionnaire forms (3,600 respondents). Even then, the only correlation involving steroid use that was not found to be significant at the .05 level was that between steroids and ice. It is based on the fewest cases of any cell, although it still had a gamma of .41.

4. Table 8.2 contains data from a single questionnaire form, resulting in an N of about 2,000 cases. Questions are asked about the use of over-the-counter stay-awake pills (such as No-Doz, Vivarin, Wake, and Caffediine), diet pills (such as Dietac, Dexatrim, and Prolamine), and the look-alike/sound-alike stimulants (nonprescription—often mail-order drugs—described at some length in the actual question).

5. He also showed that quite a different syndrome of attitudes and behaviors that defined an ideologically alienated subculture at the time—the "counterculture"—was also related to the use of a subset of the drugs, but it was not correlated with delinquency. I do not pursue that finding further here, because it does not seem central to the issues before the conference, except insofar as it illustrates that drug use can be an integral part of a more general lifestyle that may involve other high-risk behaviors.

6. Here again the Pearson product-moment correlations (not shown) were nearly all highly significant *(p < .0001)*, with the exception of some cells for

steroid use. For steroids, only the correlations with cutting school and evenings out were significant.

7. Perceived risk fell another 4 percentage points the next year.

8. Since the conference and the writing of the draft for this chapter, the 2002 MTF results have become available, and ecstasy use declined in all three grades, as perceived risk continued to increase sharply.

CHAPTER 9

Adolescents' Risk Perceptions and Behavioral Willingness

Implications for Intervention

MEG GERRARD
FREDERICK X. GIBBONS
MICHELLE L. GANO

Virtually all health behavior theories hypothesize that precautionary behaviors are partly a function of perceptions of vulnerability to the negative consequences that would result if one did not take preventive action—for example, not getting a flu shot or not having a mammogram (Health Belief Model—Hochbaum, 1958; Rosenstock, 1966, 1974; Protection Motivation Theory—Maddux & Rogers, 1983; Rogers, 1975; Precaution Adoption Process—Weinstein, 1988). Likewise, it is widely accepted that risk perceptions are antecedent to various health risk behaviors, especially among adolescents (Hawkins, Catalano, & Miller, 1992). In addition, these theories also assume that risk perceptions promote healthy and precautionary behavior through a thoughtful and reasoned (although not necessarily rational) process mediated by intentions. For example, it is assumed that if a person believes that neglecting a precautionary behavior, such as failing to wear a seat belt, will increase the likelihood or severity of a negative event or injury, he or she is more likely to intend to take that precaution. Similarly, if a person has decided he or she can drink and drive without having an accident, that individual will be more inclined to do so. Our research suggests, however, that the assumption that reasoned thought or intentions *necessarily* precede risky and precautionary behavior is not accurate, especially among adolescents.

NONINTENTIONAL BUT VOLITIONAL RISK BEHAVIOR

When we ask young adolescents (ages 11–15) in our studies if they intend to drink, smoke, or use substances any time in the next year, the vast majority say no. Nonetheless, a significant percentage of these "nonintenders" will report a year later that they have, in fact, used one or more substances. For example, in one of our studies of rural adolescents, one third of 16-year-olds indicated they had never drunk alcohol and had no intention of drinking (i.e., they responded with a 1, labeled *never*, on a 7-point scale to the question "How often do you think that you will drink alcohol in the next year?"). One year later, however, 20% of this group of "nonintenders" indicated they had imbibed (Gibbons & Gerrard, 1995; Gibbons, Gerrard, Blanton, & Russell, 1998). Similarly, 44% indicated they had no intention or expectation at all of driving after drinking in the next year (i.e., they provided a 1, or *definitely not* on each of three separate intention and expectation questions), and yet a year later, 28% of these nonintenders reported that they had driven after drinking.

We do not believe that these young people were lying or even responding in a socially desirable manner. We believe that they actually had no intention of engaging in these behaviors—quite possibly right up until the time they actually did them. Their risky behavior was not planned or intentional; instead, it was a reaction to a social situation they encountered, in which there was an *opportunity* to do something risky. This distinction between behavior that is reasoned or planned and behavior that is reactive is at the heart of our research on the prototype/willingness model of adolescent risk behavior. This chapter focuses on research on the relation between perceptions of vulnerability and one component of the model, behavioral willingness, and the implications of this research for interventions with adolescents. For a more complete discussion of the prototype/willingness model, see Gerrard, Gibbons, Reis-Bergan et al. (2002); Gibbons and Gerrard (1995, 1997); and Gibbons, Gerrard, and Lane (in press).

Behavioral Willingness

We view health risk behaviors among adolescents as primarily "social events"; they are almost always done in the presence of, and sometimes for the benefit of, friends and peers. A basic assumption of the model is that there are two paths to risk behavior. One is the reasoned or intentional path, as outlined in expected utility theories, and the theories of reasoned action and planned behavior (see Salovey, Rothman, & Rodin, 1998). It reflects the fact that for some adolescents, risk behavior is planned or intentional. These young people have thought about the behavior and made a conscious decision one way or the other—either to do it or not to do it (Gerrard, Gibbons, Reis-Bergan, et al., 2002).

The second path to risk in the prototype/willingness model is the social reaction path. Adolescents who follow this route have not thought much about the risky behavior or its consequences and, indeed, may have *avoided* such consideration (Gibbons, Gerrard, Ouellette, & Burzette, 1998). A fair number of these adolescents have no intention of engaging in a specific risk behavior prior to the time they do so. More important, they also have not made a decision *not* to engage in the behavior. In short, they are ambivalent—they might be willing to use substances, drive recklessly, or have unprotected sex under some circumstances, but they have no specific plans to do so.

The prototype/willingness model maintains that the social reaction path to behavior proceeds through an additional proximal antecedent, which is unique to the model—behavioral willingness. Behavioral willingness is an openness to risk opportunity—a recognition that one might engage in a risky behavior in some circumstances. It is associated with risk behavior independent of intentions to engage in it and has been shown to add significantly to the variance in adolescent substance use and risky sex that is explained by intentions (see Gibbons & Gerrard, 1997; Gibbons, Gerrard, & Lane, in press). Thus, intentions and willingness both predict adolescent risk behavior, and they do so independently, as well as in concert (Gibbons, Gerrard, Blanton, et al., 1998). Moreover, willingness has been shown to be a better predictor of younger adolescents' (ages 13–17) risky behavior than are intentions (Gibbons, Gerrard, & Lane, in press; Reis-Bergan, Gibbons, & Gerrard, 2003).

HOW DO ADOLESCENTS' RISK PERCEPTIONS AFFECT SUBSEQUENT BEHAVIOR?

Risk perception is typically conceptualized as a cognitive construct—that is, an estimate of the likelihood of a negative event happening—rather than as an affective construct. Thus, it is logical to assume that the relation between these perceptions and intentions can be characterized as thoughtful and planful. In other words, if people see themselves as vulnerable to skin cancer, this perception should lead to intentions to engage in protective behaviors against ultraviolet rays such as using sunscreen (Jackson & Aiken, 2000). In fact, the relation between risk perceptions and intentions *to engage in healthy behaviors* has been demonstrated repeatedly in adults. For example, perceptions of vulnerability are positively related to plans to quit smoking (Klesges et al. 1988). The prototype/willingness model, however, raises the question of whether intentions mediate the relation between risk perceptions and *risk behavior,* especially among adolescents. More specifically, it suggests that because adolescent risk behavior is often not intentional, the link between risk perceptions and behavior is not likely to be thoughtful and planful and, thus, is not likely to be mediated by intentions.

College Students and Unprotected Sex

This hypothesis was addressed in a recent study of the relations between college students' perceptions of the consequences of sex without a condom, their intentions and willingness to have sex without condoms, and their subsequent sexual behavior (Thornton, Gibbons, & Gerrard, 2002, Study 3). This study was part of a panel study of 496 college students who were surveyed about their pregnancy risk behavior, willingness and intentions to have unprotected sex, and perceptions of vulnerability to unplanned pregnancy during the second semester of their freshman year (Time 1) and approximately 6 months (Time 2) and 1 year (Time 3) later. Willingness to engage in unprotected sex was assessed, as it is typically, by asking participants to imagine themselves in a hypothetical "risk-conducive" situation. In this case, that scenario involved imagining being with a date who wanted to have sex, even though no means of contraception was available. The students then indicated how willing they would be to engage in a series of actions, ranging from low risk (not have sex), to high risk (go ahead and have sex without contraception). Consistent with the prototype/willingness model, risk perceptions were assessed with a hypothetical question—that is, risk conditional on participation in the behavior. Specifically, participants were asked to indicate the likelihood that they would have an unintended pregnancy *if they were* to have unprotected sex several times a month (see Aiken, Gerend, & Jackson, 2001). Thus, neither of these variables required that the participants assume personal responsibility for being in the situation or for engaging in the risk behavior. (Reduced perceptions of responsibility are an important component of willingness; see below.)

As expected, analyses revealed that Time 2 willingness and intentions independently predicted unprotected sex 6 months later (at Time 3). In addition, analyses also demonstrated that risk perceptions predicted willingness, but not intentions. Thus, the relation between Time 1 risk perceptions and Time 3 risk behavior was mediated by Time 2 willingness, but not by Time 2 intentions. It should also be noted that because it controlled for prior behavior, this study provided a relatively conservative test of the relation between risk perceptions and subsequent behavior (at Time 1).

African American Adolescents and Substance Use

A second study of the role of willingness as a mediator of the relation between risk perceptions and risk behavior was conducted with African American adolescents (Gerrard, Gibbons, Vande Lune, Pexa, & Gano, 2002). This study analyzed data from the Family and Community Health Study (FACHS), a panel study of 897 African American families from Iowa and Georgia, all of whom had a target child between the ages of 10 and 11 at the first wave of data collection (for additional information about the sample and procedures, see Brody et al., 2001; Gibbons, Lane, Gerrard, Pomery, & Lautrup, 2002; Wills, Gibbons, Gerrard, & Brody, 2000). This study employed structural equation modeling to examine the relation between substance use risk perceptions, willingness to use substances, and the subsequent substance use of older siblings of the target children ($N = 298$; mean age = 13 at Time 1, 15 at Time 2). Willingness to use substances was assessed with three sets of items, one set each for smoking, drinking, and use of other substances (see also Gerrard, Gibbons, Zhao, Russell, & Reis-Bergan, 1999; Gibbons, Gerrard, Blanton, et al., 1998). For example, willingness to smoke was assessed by first asking the adolescents to "Suppose you were with a group of friends and some of them were smoking. . . . You could have some cigarettes if you wanted. How willing would you be to: a) smoke a cigarette, b) smoke more than one cigarette, c) not

smoke any cigarettes?" (item reversed). Substance use was measured at Time 2 by asking, "In the past 12 months, how often have you smoked cigarettes . . . drunk alcohol . . . drunk a lot of alcohol (3 or more drinks at one time) . . . used illegal drugs?" This study also compared the predictive validity of two different measures of risk perceptions: conditional (e.g., "If you smoked, do you think that in the future you would get a sickness that comes from smoking, like cancer?") and comparative conditional (e.g., "Compared to other kids your age who smoke, how likely is it that you would get a sickness . . . if you smoked?"). Because the comparative estimates did not predict willingness or subsequent behavior, this construct will not be discussed further here.

Although there was not a lot of substance use at Time 1, consistent with previous findings (Gibbons, Gerrard, Ouellette, et al., 1998), Time 1 willingness was a significant predictor of Time 2 use (2 years later). In addition (and also as expected), risk perceptions were directly (and negatively) associated with willingness. Finally, Time 1 risk perceptions were also indirectly (again, negatively) associated with Time 2 use through willingness, replicating the earlier finding that perceived vulnerability predicts subsequent behavior through behavioral willingness (see also Cleveland, Gibbons, Gerrard, & Pomery, under review). The study also assessed the impact of parental communications about substance use, risk-taking tendency, and friends' use of substances on risk perceptions, willingness, and subsequent use. The results revealed that the entire effect of parental communication on willingness and use was mediated by its effect on risk perceptions—parental communication about substances was associated with increased risk perceptions, which in turn, were associated with less willingness and, subsequently, with less substance use almost 2 years later.

WILLINGNESS, INTENTIONS, AND CONTEMPLATION OF CONSEQUENCES

According to the prototype/willingness model, willingness is distinguished from behavioral intention in two primary ways. First, willingness is less thoughtful. Unlike intentions, which involve consideration and evaluation of the potential outcomes associated with a particular behavior (Fishbein & Ajzen, 1975), willingness to engage in a risk behavior is a reaction to a risk-conducive situation and, therefore, involves relatively little precontemplation or consideration of the behavior of the potential negative consequences associated with it. Evidence of this comes from a recent study that demonstrated that contemplation of the positive social consequences of being "a nondrinker" was associated with less subsequent drinking (Gerrard, Gibbons, Reis-Bergan et al., 2002). Contemplation of the (largely negative) social consequences of drinking, however, was not associated with willingness or subsequent consumption. In other words, thinking about the benefits of abstaining (a healthy behavior) inhibited alcohol consumption, whereas thinking about the social disadvantages of drinking was not related to willingness or subsequent consumption.

The second distinction between willingness and intention is that willingness involves less internal attribution of responsibility for the behavior or its attendant consequences. Intention, by definition, implies some commitment to an action—it is a plan to act or even a goal state (Ajzen, 1985). People who have an intention "consider the implications of their actions before they decide to engage or not engage in a given behavior " (Ajzen & Fishbein, 1980, p. 5). Thus, adolescents who have made a conscious decision to drink (which they acknowledge) are not likely to deny responsibility for their actions (they may not accept *full* responsibility, but they

can't deny it either). In contrast, an adolescent who is willing to drink, but not intending to do so, has much less commitment to the behavior and is less likely to accept responsibility for it and its consequences ("It's not really my fault—I didn't intend to drink that much.").

This type of reasoning (or rationalizing) is not uncommon among young people who drive after drinking—they did not intend to drink enough to need a ride home and therefore did not arrange for one. Another example can be found in the research on unplanned sexual intercourse (Zabin, Stark, & Emerson, 1991). Many adolescents do not intend to have intercourse, especially early in a relationship, but find themselves in circumstances in which they end up doing so. Effective contraception and condom use require planning, but because their sexual behavior was not planned, these adolescents often fail to protect themselves (Gerrard, 1982, 1987). That being the case, even though they may not engage in as much sexual behavior as those who intend to have sex, they may be at higher risk of unplanned pregnancy. In short, for some adolescents, being willing to engage in a risk behavior may actually be more dangerous than intending to engage. Adolescents who are willing, but not intending, do not feel the need to think about consequences and may actually avoid such thoughts because they do not plan to take a risk.

SUMMARY

The effects of risk estimates on subsequent behavior in these studies provide support for the hypothesis that risk perceptions *can* motivate precautionary behavior and inhibit risk behavior. However, although most prior investigations of this relation have looked for a direct link, these findings suggest that this relation is not direct but, instead, is mediated by willingness. More specifically, perceived risk inhibits willingness, and willingness is associated with behavior. Furthermore, these studies suggest that previous conflicting findings regarding the relation between risk perceptions and behavior may be explained by failure to account for the fact that risk perceptions inhibit willingness to take advantage of risk opportunities more than they inhibit intentions to engage in risk behavior.

IMPLICATIONS FOR PREVENTIVE INTERVENTIONS

Changing Behavioral Willingness

Traditionally, preventive interventions have focused on dangers to health (and to a lesser extent, legal consequences), in an attempt to alter risk perceptions, and in so doing, decrease or prevent risk behavior. One problem with this approach is that many adolescents do not feel vulnerable to these potential consequences, *because* they are not intending to engage in the risk behavior. Our data suggest an alternative approach—one designed to counteract this tendency by facilitating adolescents' contemplation of the behavior, as well as its consequences, *and* what they might do if and when they find themselves in a risk-conducive situation. Central to this approach is the assumption that it is necessary to do this *before* the adolescents get in these situations—when they first report some willingness to engage but before they have formed intentions to do so. As suggested earlier, willingness and risk behavior are, in part, a reflection of a tendency to avoid consideration of consequences (Gerrard, Gibbons, Reis-Bergan et al., 2002; Gibbons, Gerrard, Ouellette, et al., 1998). Thus, thinking ahead of time about these risk-conducive situations should reduce willingness. Admittedly, this kind of approach will not have much impact

on those adolescents who are "intenders," the small but significant number who have already made a decision to engage. Because intentions involve some premeditation and planning, this group is less likely to respond to efforts to get them to think about risk-conducive situations and potential responses to them. The group that interventions are most likely to influence is made up of those in the middle, the adolescents who have little or no intention to engage in risk behavior but who have some willingness to do so (typically about 20% to 30% of adolescents, depending on age and the behavior involved; Gibbons, Lane, Gerrard, Eggleston, & Reis-Bergan, 2003).

These adolescents are a logical group to target. On the one hand, they are clearly at risk. Precautions, such as carrying condoms, assigning a designated driver, or even avoiding certain risk opportunities, require some acknowledgment of a tendency to engage in the behavior (Gerrard, 1987; Weinstein, 1988), and they aren't doing that ("I am not intending to have sex tonight, so why should I do something potentially embarrassing like carry a condom?"). As mentioned earlier, these young people maintain that they have no plans, intentions, or even expectations to engage in a risk behavior, but they will acknowledge their willingness to do so under certain circumstances. Thus, the relation between willingness and subsequent risk behavior suggests that it would be productive to prepare adolescents to recognize and anticipate the kinds of risk-conducive situations in which they are likely to find themselves in the future—whether they sought these situations or not—so that their resistance to these situations can be bolstered (Gibbons, Gerrard, & Lane, in press).

Finally, unlike most refusal efficacy approaches, we suggest that interventions should not suggest to adolescents that their risk behavior is largely a reaction to influence attempts from others. Such programs do not fully acknowledge that many adolescents have some interest or curiosity about the behavior and are willing to do it. Moreover, these programs can backfire (Donaldson, Graham, Piccinin, & Hansen, 1997; Donaldson et al., 1996; Donaldson, Thomas, Graham, Au, & Hansen, 2000). One reason for this is that they can cause reactance among some adolescents ("intenders") who do not like the implication that their behavior is not self-determined. Instead, it may be more productive to help them acknowledge a normal level of curiosity and interest in the behaviors—that is, some willingness rather than arousing reactance by suggesting that their (risky) behavior is actually determined more by their peers than by themselves (Gibbons, Gerrard, & Pomery, in press).

Reasons for Optimism

Our research has demonstrated that cognitions, such as perceptions of vulnerability and willingness, are malleable (Gibbons, Lane et al., 2002)—more so than many other antecedents of adolescents risk behavior (e.g., peer use, socioeconomic status). Thus, they appear to be more viable targets for intervention (Conner & Norman, 1996; see also Hawkins et al., 1992). Previous research on the prototype/willingness model suggests that parents can play a very active role in forming a base of risk and nonrisk cognitions that set the stage for a child's eventual behavior (Blanton, Gibbons, Gerrard, Conger, & Smith, 1997; Gerrard et al., 1999; Gibbons, Gerrard, Cleveland, Wills, & Brody, 2003; Ouellette, Gerrard, Gibbons, & Reis-Bergan, 1999). More specifically, parents can have positive effects on their children's risk behavior by fostering the formation of risk perceptions, by preparing their children to deal with the internal motivation to engage in risk behaviors as well as peer pressure, and by decreasing willingness.

Part I

Section C

Problem-Solving Approaches

A Problem-Solving Approach to Preventing Early High-Risk Behaviors in Children and Preteens

MYRNA B. SHURE

In the early 1960s, when my colleague George Spivack was a researcher and the clinical director at a residential treatment center in Devon, Pennsylvania, one of his charges, a 15-year-old predelinquent boy headed down the railroad tracks toward the city at 2:00 a.m. on a Sunday. Summoned to rescue him, Spivack, in disbelief, grabbed him to safety, and asked him why he was doing this. "I need to go shopping," the boy replied meekly. With stores being closed on Sundays in those days, Spivack then asked, "Don't you know the stores aren't open on Sundays?" "I didn't think of that," answered the boy. Trying to stay calm, Spivack then asked, "Don't you know walking down railroad tracks is dangerous?" "No, I didn't think of that," the boy repeated. Now exasperated, George asked one more question— "Don't you know you'll get in trouble for going AWOL!?" For the third time, the boy murmured, "No, I didn't think of that." Believing at the time that youngsters who behave this way might have an unconscious

or even conscious desire to get into trouble, Spivack began pondering about what the boy kept saying—"I didn't think of that." Perhaps, thought Spivack, this boy was telling the truth. Perhaps he really didn't think about his actions and their consequences. Perhaps he didn't know how.

This and other experiences as a clinician led George Spivack the researcher to test a new theoretical position about why youngsters behave as they do. With his colleague Murray Levine, Spivack tested the theory that youngsters who behave differently may think differently about their interpersonal worlds. They tested whether there is a set of interpersonal cognitive problem-solving skills that mediate behavior. Spivack and Levine identified two such skills in adolescents, ages 15 to 18: The first, *means-ends thinking,* includes a spontaneous tendency to plan sequenced steps toward a stated goal (e.g., making new friends), the recognition of potential obstacles that could interfere, and appreciation that it takes time to reach the goal (a form of nonimpulsive thinking). The second skill was the *weighing of pros and cons of choices*, such as whether to go to a party the night before an exam. Spivack and Levine found that regardless of IQ, the residential treatment boys were less competent than normal comparison groups in both of these skills. On the basis of this initial research conducted in the 1960s (see Spivack & Shure, 1974), Spivack refined his theoretical position that formed the springboard for our research when I joined him in 1968.

I begin this chapter with Spivack's cognitive theory of behavioral mediation, followed by our early correlational research, which identified specific skills that related to specific behaviors in children ages 4 through 12. Once the cognitive skills and associated behaviors were identified, I created interventions to test Spivack's behavioral mediation theory. In the rest of the chapter, I describe the interventions, touch on the highlights of our research and that of others, and, finally, discuss some implications for prevention of later, serious risk behaviors such as unsafe sex and drug abuse.

THEORETICAL BASIS FOR A COGNITIVE APPROACH TO PREVENTION OF HIGH-RISK BEHAVIORS

Highlights of Spivack's theory behind the problem-solving approach to behavior (described in full in Spivack, Platt, & Shure, 1976) include the following:

- A key and common element of any theory of social adjustment of psychopathology is the quality of social relationships and capacity to cope with interpersonal problems. Experiencing interpersonal problems is viewed as a natural consequence of being human, because satisfactory social relationships are central to human development.

- To appreciate fully the efficiency with which a person navigates a problem, it is necessary to understand how well he or she recognizes and thinks through the interpersonal situation. It is *how* one thinks that is crucial if one is to understand the likelihood of successful adjustment in the long run.

EARLY CORRELATIONAL RESEARCH: INTERPERSONAL COGNITIVE SKILLS AND BEHAVIORS

In Nine- to Twelve-Year-Olds

To learn whether the two identified cognitive skills associated with behaviors in teens would be associated with behaviors in slightly younger children, we compared the interpersonal cognitive skills of 9- to 12-year-olds in a school for diagnostically disturbed juveniles with peers in regular public schools (Shure & Spivack, 1972). Although the *weighing of pros and cons* did not distinguish these two groups, *means-ends thinking* did. For example, when asked how someone his age can make new friends, a behaviorally competent child will not only imagine the steps to achieve the goal (e.g., "Show them how to play basketball") but will also recognize potential obstacles (e.g., "They don't like basketball"). This child might respond to such an obstacle by asking a potential new friend, "What do you like?" (*a new step*). Then describing himself as one example of how one makes a new friend, "If he likes hockey, I could learn how to play hockey." The child might add, "Three months later (*statement of time*) he might see me practicing and ask me to teach him how to shoot pucks" (*another new step*). We then tested a more homogeneous sample of normal public school fifth graders. We found that youngsters who were deficient in means-ends thinking were more likely to display impulsive behaviors such as physical and verbal aggression, inability to wait and cope with frustration, less tendency to show empathy or sympathy to peers in distress, had poor peer relations, and also, were more socially withdrawn (Shure, 1984). Relationships of this cognitive skill to behaviors have also been found in homogeneous groups in institutionalized settings (Higgens & Thies, 1981).

In my 1984 research, I found two new cognitive skills to be associated with impulsive and withdrawn behaviors in this age group, as well as with positive, prosocial behaviors. One skill, *alternative solution thinking,* is the ability to think of different ways to solve an interpersonal problem. Instead of connecting sequenced plans to make friends, a child could say, "She could have a party and invite lots of kids," or "She could get another kid to say nice things about her," or "She could ask her to play video games with her," and so on. The second skill, *consequential thinking,* is the ability to anticipate a variety of possibilities as to what might happen next if a particular solution were carried out. Behaviorally adjusted children could think of more solutions and consequences than their behaviorally aberrant classmates. If, for example, a girl bribes another to be her friend, "The girl might lose respect for her," or "The girl might take the bribe and then not show up," or "She might get a bad reputation," and so on. Spivack and I now dubbed the identified cognitive skills associated with interpersonal competence and social adjustment as interpersonal cognitive problem solving, or ICPS.

ICPS In Younger Children

With age-appropriate scenarios such as wanting a toy another child has or keeping mom from being angry after having damaged property important to her (e.g., a flowerpot), ICPS-competent children could be distinguished from their less competent peers by their ability to give more *alternative solutions* to problems and *consequences* to acts as early as age 4. Like the older children, high "ICPS-ers" were less likely to show impulsive and inhibited behaviors, were more cooperative, better liked, and showed more empathy. These findings held for low-income African American preschoolers (Shure, Spivack, & Jaeger, 1971; replicated by Dimson, 1992; Schiller, 1978, as well as in middle-income groups (Arend, Gove, & Sroufe, 1979) and in slightly older children ages 6 to 8 (Johnson, Yu, & Roopnarine, 1980).

Risk and Protective Factors: The ICPS Link

As early as preschool (Parker & Asher, 1987) and escalating in the preteen and teenage years, Botvin, Malgady, Griffin, Scheier, and Epstein (1998); Eron and Heusman (1984); and Hawkins, Catalano, and Miller (1992) have found antisocial behaviors, poor impulse control (including inability to cope with frustration and delay gratification) poor peer relations, and lack of empathy to be early high-risk behaviors that predict subsequent delinquency, substance abuse, unsafe sex, poor academic achievement, school dropout, and some forms of psychopathology. In addition, Rubin and Mills (1988) suggest that early social withdrawal predicts more internalized problems such as depression, perhaps suicide. Importantly, these impulsive and inhibited behaviors are the same ones associated with the measured ICPS skills. By adolescence, ICPS skill deficiencies are clearly evident in delinquents (see Spivack et al., 1976), substance abusers (Botvin et al., 1998), and girls who practice unsafe sex (Flaherty, Marecek, Olsen, & Wilcove, 1983; Steinlauf, 1979). By enhancing ICPS skills, the ultimate goal is increasing the probability of preventing the later, more serious problems by nipping their behavioral predictors in the bud very early in life.

ICPS INTERVENTIONS

The assumption drawn from our correlational research reported above is that individuals showing early high-risk behaviors suffer from an ICPS deficiency that gets them into difficulty with others. Whether availability of identified ICPS skills is an antecedent condition to adjustment cannot, however, be ascertained from correlational studies alone. As a result, an intervention was created to investigate a link between ICPS ability and behavioral adjustment. By experimentally altering ICPS skills, then observing changes in the child's display of their associated behaviors, the critical question was whether those who would most improve in the trained ICPS skills would be the same youngsters who would most improve in the measured overt behaviors. If such a link would occur, and also be independent of general IQ, we would have a new approach to primary prevention of early high-risk behaviors in children. We began our interventions in schools with very young children—in preschools and kindergartens.

ICPS in School

Originally called *interpersonal cognitive problem solving* (ICPS), now called *I can problem solve* (also ICPS), the goal was to teach children *how* to think, not what to think, in ways that would help them successfully resolve interpersonal problems with peers and adults. Our first intervention was conducted in federally funded day care, with 4-year-olds (see Spivack & Shure, 1974). The revised training manual for preschool (Shure, 1992a) consists of daily 20-minute games and exercises through which teachers and children interact in small groups over a period of about 3 months. With the concepts taught in kindergarten and the primary grades (up to Grade 2) being essentially the same as for preschool, and more sophisticated concepts

for the older children (Shure, 1992b), basic word concepts are taught that help set the stage for later problem-solving thinking. The words *is* and *not* and *might* and *maybe* are taught in game form to help children later think about whether an idea *is* or is *not* a good one in light of what *might* happen next (consequential thinking). Words such as *same* and *different* are taught so children can later think, for example, that hitting can hurt someone and then to think of a *different* way to solve the problem (alternative solution thinking). Through pictures, puppets, and role plays, subsequent games focus on recognition and awareness of the children's own and other people's feelings, building empathy that could enrich the range and quality of solution and consequential thinking. Children are never told specific solutions or consequences. Rather, they are encouraged to generate their own ideas and then to think about how people might feel and what they might do as a result.

In addition to the formal lesson-games, teachers and their aides are trained to use a problem-solving approach when actual problems arise. Instead of commanding, suggesting, or even explaining, children are guided to think for themselves about what and what not to do, and why. With a technique we call "ICPS dialoguing," teachers learn to ask questions such as these: "What's the problem?" "How do you think (Peter) *might* feel when you (grab the truck)?" "What happened when you did that?" "How do you feel about that?" "Can you think of a *different* way to solve this problem so you both won't feel (mad) and (he won't hit you)"? By engaging children in the process of thinking about their own and other's feelings, potential consequences of an act, and solutions to the problem, ICPS dialoguing helps them associate how they think with what they do and how they behave.

Implemented in third- to sixth-grade grade classrooms, three times a week over a 4-month period (often during health or language arts periods), the overall approach to ICPS in the intermediate elementary grades (Shure, 1992c) is the same as that for younger children. In addition to empathy building, and the solution and consequential-thinking skills taught with age-appropriate problem situations, more complex skills are introduced, such as (a) recognition of why people *might* do what they do (e.g., bully others); (b) skills to avoid coming to hasty, often false conclusions about why people do what they do; and (c) means-ends thinking. Again, ICPS dialoguing is integrated into the school day.

ICPS at Home

Because we were interested in learning whether parents could become effective training agents, we took ICPS into the home. Designed for children ages 4 through 6 (Shure, 1996; Shure & Spivack, 1978) and now available in workbook form (Shure, 2000), the concepts are the same as those used by teachers of this age group. In problem situations relevant to families (e.g., a child won't clean his room or go to bed on time, squabbles with sibs or friends, interrupts on the phone), parents are helped to (a) think about their own feelings and become sensitive to those of their child, (b) find out how their child views the problem, and (c) engage their child in the process of thinking about the problem through ICPS dialoguing.

INTERVENTION RESEARCH IMPACT

The major findings of our ICPS research, conducted with low-income African American youngsters, reported in Shure (1999) are as follows:

• Independent of IQ, alternative solution and consequential-thinking skills improved in the trained ICPS groups compared with comparable controls from preschool through Grade 6, as did means-ends thinking measured in Grades 5 and 6. In addition, standardized achievement test scores (Grades 1 to 5) increased in language arts, reading, math, and social studies.

• Also from preschool through Grade 6, both positive prosocial behaviors and negative aggressive and other impulsive behaviors improved as well as social withdrawal, with all behavior gains lasting as long as 4 years later. In all age groups studied, decreases in impulsive and disruptive behaviors were most evident in children who most improved in the trained ICPS skills (the direct link), suggesting the behavior gains were a function of the ICPS interventions.

• Parents could be as effective agents of ICPS training as teachers. Children trained by their mothers who most improved were those whose mothers best learned how to apply a problem-solving approach to discipline when real problems came up at home (ICPS dialoguing). Importantly, the improved behaviors of children trained at home generalized to the school, and the reverse, suggesting that the benefits of acquiring ICPS mediating skills are not situation specific.

Our research is now supported in both low- and middle-income levels across ethnic groups and across ages from preschool through Grade 6 (summarized in Denham & Almeida, 1987). ICPS has also been successful with special-needs youngsters, including those with attention deficit hyperactivity disorder, or ADHD (reported in detail in Aberson & Shure, 2002; Shure, 1999).

SOCIAL PERSPECTIVE TAKING AS MEDIATORS OF BEHAVIOR

Although related to prosocial behavior at pretest in fifth graders, change in ability to see other people's points of view, including sensitivity to their feelings, did not directly link with change in behavior. However, improved multiple perspective taking did accompany increased ICPS skills, which in turn directly linked to behavior change (Shure, 1984). These results suggest that ability to appreciate others' points of view and emotional sensitivity in a problem situation may play a part in the process of thinking through plans or solutions, but alone, this ability is not a sufficient mediator of social adjustment. If, for example, I am aware that I did something to provoke another's anger but do not know what to do to relieve that person's anger, the problem will not be solved. I may continue to feel anxiety that could in turn affect my behavior—especially if problem after problem remains unresolved.

Spivack and I do agree with Selman (1980) that competence in perspective taking is related to competence in conflict resolution. My sensitivity to the other person's anger may enrich my ability to select a solution that requires appreciation of the person's point of view rather than a solution that considers my needs alone. I may also be better able to evaluate my solution because of greater sensitivity of how my actions might affect others—and then, if need be, stretch my thinking for a solution that would meet the other person's needs without sacrificing my own. In young children, some support for evidence of this conjecture is provided by a study of preschoolers (in Shure, 1982) and in second graders (Hudson, Peyton, & Brion-Meisels, 1976).

IMPLICATIONS OF ICPS FOR PREVENTION OF MORE SERIOUS DISTAL OUTCOMES

Although we have direct evidence that enhancement of ICPS skills does indeed reduce and prevent early high-risk behaviors that predict later, more serious outcomes, we do not have direct evidence that ICPS skills learned early in life actually do prevent those later outcomes. We can, however, speculate about how ICPS skills developed as early as preschool can help youngsters prepare for their teen years and avoid later problems such as unsafe sex, smoking, alcohol, drug abuse, and being the victim, or the perpetrator, of violence.

Regarding unsafe sex and unwanted pregnancy, it is interesting that Lonczak, Abbott, Hawkins, Kosterman, and Catalano (2002) found that their interventions, which included ICPS in elementary school, significantly reduced the likelihood that females would experience unwanted pregnancy many years later, at age 21. It is important that Flaherty et al. (1983) and Steinlauf (1979) found that compared with teenage girls who did not engage in sexual activities or who used contraceptives, those who engaged in unsafe sex were less able to solve interpersonal problems that had nothing to do with pregnancy. If these girls could not make plans and think of solutions for the everyday problems of their lives—how to make friends or entice a reluctant friend to go to a movie—they would likely be equally unprepared to cope with problems of this magnitude. In today's world, in which unsafe sex can result in contracting sexually transmitted diseases such as herpes or HIV-AIDS, behaviors enhanced by ICPS skills earlier in life such as delay of immediate gratification are now as critical for boys as for girls.

As for cigarettes, alcohol, and drugs, familiar slogans such as "Just say no," and "Just don't do it" make the problem sound simple when it is not. Not only do slogans such as these simply tell youngsters what to do (no doubt falling on many deaf ears), but they do nothing to stimulate them to think about why they should or shouldn't engage in those activities. And importantly, they don't help anyone think about what to do instead. Selman (2002; LaRusso & Selman, this volume) found that many teens do, in fact, know the dangers of smoking, drinking, and drugs, and I learned that some youngsters have those facts as early as age 8 (Shure, 2001). But when pressured by peers, do they know how to resist? To Selman (2002), "Just say no" is a lower-level tactic for adolescents because it does "not involve any discussion with or explanation to others who might be viewed as pressuring them" (p. 26). Even some of the preteens I interviewed were capable of Selman's highest level of strategy, such as "offering resistance to pressure by trying to convince others of the risks involved" (p. 26), evidenced by creating means-ends stories in which the protagonist ends up resisting pressure to smoke cigarettes.

Selman (2002) also notes that "Prevention efforts need to take into account the adolescent's developing capacity to think more abstractly and to differentiate among degrees of risk in order to be taken seriously by middle school students" (p. 21). He adds that "it is especially important that school-based prevention efforts provide a space for genuine conversation where students can grapple with the conflicting messages and pressures they have around risks" (p. 21). Many teens have told me they do their homework in health classes while the teachers drone on about why they shouldn't drink, smoke, or try drugs. One ninth grader told a newspaper reporter, "They should get the kids into small groups and let us talk and listen to each other." We believe that developing the skills to think, to listen, and to talk about these things earlier in life will give them the ability to do just that.

Finally, research is now showing that children who are the victims of bullies may later *become* bullies (e.g., Dwyer, Osher, & Warger, 1998). One 8-year-old showed his ICPS skills by responding to classmates who called him "bacon" because he was fat with, "Yeah, and I sizzle, I sizzle." Today, 4 years

later, this boy is very popular and is doing well in school, a very different outcome from those who build up anger and resentment and later explode.

SUMMARY AND CONCLUSIONS

Our research and that of others (summarized in Denham & Almeida, 1987) support Spivack's theory that ICPS skills do indeed mediate overt behaviors at various age levels and in various income and ethnic groups. As early as age 4, and regardless of IQ, youngsters who behave differently do think differently. Children who display impulsive, aggressive behaviors think more about "now" without consideration for their own or other's feelings, for the consequences of their acts, or for different ways to solve a problem. These youngsters often have difficulty making friends and are unaware of, or unconcerned about, others in distress. We know that as early as preschool, genuine concern for others in distress does exist and can be trained. Furthermore, lack of this kind of genuine empathy early in life, along with other ICPS skill deficiencies and their accompanying behavioral maladaption, can predict violence (a form of hurting others), substance abuse (a form of hurting oneself), and other forms of psychological dysfunction. Because withdrawn children are also poor problem solvers and at risk for later depression, it is critical that they not fall through the cracks and go unnoticed because their behavior is less visible. With unattended high-risk behaviors increasing as children move through the elementary grades, peaking in Grades 4 and 5 (Spivack, Cianci, Quercetti, & Bogaslav, 1980), it appears that the impact of ICPS intervention has potential to reverse that trend.

With the emphasis today on academic achievement, and the premise that kids who achieve better, behave better, I was pleased to see Flay's (this volume) plea to focus also on the reverse—that improved behavior might lead to improved school performance. Our research supports the latter. It appears that because trained children also improved academically, regardless of actual IQ, less stress fostered by ICPS and other social-emotional interventions allows children to concentrate better on the task-oriented demands of the classroom and, subsequently, do better in school. I was also pleased to see his argument that prevention programs need to start in elementary school, *before* serious problem behaviors are seen. Our research supports the notion that perhaps it is optimal to begin even before that—in preschool.

In conclusion, it is quite possible that by thinking of their own ideas, children feel pride, instead of anger and frustration. They are more likely to carry out their own idea than one demanded, suggested, or even explained by an adult. By giving them the skills and the freedom to use them, children as early as age 4 will feel pride in making decisions that will have positive, not negative, consequences. And by thinking about how to solve problems that are important to them when they are young, they will be more likely to think about and solve problems they will face when they reach their preteen and teenage years, and beyond.

CHAPTER 11

Contemporary School-Based Prevention Approaches and the Perceived Risks and Benefits of Substance Use

KENNETH W. GRIFFIN

Adolescent substance use is an important problem facing society today. National surveys indicate that adolescents often begin to use alcohol, tobacco, and other drugs during the middle school years and that rates of drug use typically increase over the course of adolescence. In fact, most young people report engaging in the use of one or more substances by the time they are in secondary school. According to the Monitoring the Future study (Johnston, O'Malley, & Bachman, 2000), alcohol and tobacco are the most commonly used substances by teenagers, with about one in three 12th graders reporting drunkenness, binge drinking (i.e., five or more drinks in a row), or smoking cigarettes in the past month. Additional findings indicate that almost half of high school students report using marijuana in their lifetimes and more than one fourth report using marijuana in the past month. There is also evidence that the initiation of drug use among young people is now occurring at earlier ages than in the past. The Youth Risk Behavior Surveillance Survey (Kann et al., 2000) surveyed over 16,000 youth and found that 9th graders were significantly more likely than students in the 12th grade to report smoking a whole cigarette, having tried alcohol, or using marijuana before 13 years of age. These data are important because there are a variety of potentially serious social, psychological, health, and legal consequences of adolescent drug use and abuse, including later more serious drug involvement, violent and delinquent behavior, poor physical health, and mental health problems (Ellickson, Tucker, & Klein, 2001; Griffin, Botvin, Scheier, & Nichols, 2002; Newcomb & Bentler, 1988).

CONTEMPORARY APPROACHES TO DRUG ABUSE PREVENTION

In response to the problem of adolescent drug abuse, primary prevention programs aimed at reducing gateway substance use (i.e., alcohol, cigarettes, and marijuana) have been developed and tested in a series of school and community-based prevention trials (Botvin & Griffin, 1999; Hansen, 1992). Schools provide natural settings for conducting primary prevention efforts, and evaluation studies indicate that several school-based approaches are effective (Bangert-Drowns, 1988; Tobler & Stratton, 1997). The most effective research-based approaches to the prevention of adolescent drug abuse are derived from psychosocial theories and focus primarily on risk and protective factors associated with the initiation and early stages of drug use (Hawkins, Catalano, & Miller, 1992; Petraitis, Flay, & Miller, 1995).

Contemporary prevention approaches for adolescent drug abuse that have been shown to be effective in school settings include those that focus on (a) social resistance training, (b) normative education, (c) competence enhancement, or (d) some combination of these approaches. These prevention approaches have different assumptions about the motivational factors that contribute to drug use, including the perceived risks and benefits of substance use.

Social Resistance Approaches. A variety of social influences, including the direct modeling of drug use behavior and social pressure from peers, contribute to experimentation with substance use. Other important social influences include persuasive advertising appeals and media portrayals encouraging alcohol, tobacco, and other drug use. Social resistance approaches to adolescent drug prevention focus extensively on teaching young people how to recognize and resist pressures to use drugs, ways to avoid high-risk situations in which they are likely to experience pressure to smoke, drink, or use drugs, as well as skills training in ways to handle social pressure in these and other situations. A basic assumption of the social resistance approach

is that adolescents do not want to use drugs but lack the skills to turn down drug offers and are not adequately prepared to resist pro-drug influences in the media. This approach makes no specific assumptions regarding how young people perceive the risks or benefits of substance .use. However, to the extent that resistance skills training presents pro-drug influences as ubiquitous, this approach may imply to young people that substance use itself is ubiquitous and therefore normative.

Normative Education Approaches. Most adolescents overestimate the prevalence of drug use among peers and adults. Therefore, providing accurate information regarding actual rates of use typically reduces the perception that drug use is common and normative behavior. This component of contemporary prevention programs has been termed "normative education." Normative education teaches young people that most young people and most adults in fact do not use drugs and that those who do are not engaging in normative behavior. Changing normative expectations can be accomplished using a variety of teaching methods, such as surveying students regarding perceived prevalence rates of substance use and providing feedback about actual rates of use, by having students conduct their own surveys of substance use among their peers and providing the results to the class, or simply by asking students to estimate how many teenagers and how many adults smoke, drink, or use drugs and then providing the correct statistical information from national or regional survey data. The normative education approach assumes that young people may perceive an important social benefit to drug use to the extent that engaging in this behavior is viewed as normative and will help them to "fit in."

Competence Enhancement Approaches. According to competence enhancement approaches, drug use is conceptualized as a socially learned and functional behavior that is the result of interplay between social and personal factors (Botvin, 2000). In addition to recognizing the importance of social learning processes such as modeling, imitation, and reinforcement, competence enhancement approaches aim to enhance a young person's overall repertoire of social and personal skills. These may include decision-making and problem-solving skills, cognitive skills for resisting interpersonal and media influences, skills for enhancing self-esteem (goal setting and self-directed behavior change techniques), adaptive coping strategies for dealing with stress and anxiety, and general social and assertiveness skills. Competence enhancement programs are most effective when they teach these basic skills and include behavioral rehearsals of scenarios in which students practice these skills in situations directly related to alcohol, tobacco, and other drug use. Thus, this type of program teaches adolescents a repertoire of skills that they can use to deal with many of the challenges confronting them in their everyday lives, including but not limited to drug use. The competence enhancement approach assumes that adolescents with poor personal and social skills are not only more susceptible to influences that promote drug use but also may be motivated to use drugs as an alternative to more adaptive coping strategies (Botvin, 2000). From the perspective of adolescents with poor competence skills, drug use may be viewed as a valid, alternative way to establish an identity, enhance the way others view them, or enhance the way they view themselves—all potential perceived benefits of engaging in drug use.

ADDRESSING THE PERCEIVED RISKS AND BENEFITS OF SUBSTANCE USE

The various approaches to school-based drug abuse prevention differ in their assumptions regarding whether young people want to use drugs and why. Whereas the social influence approach assumes that young people don't want to use drugs, the normative education and competence enhancement approaches recognize that adolescents may want to use drugs because it serves some function or purpose in their lives and can help them achieve important developmental goals such as "fitting in" with peers, establishing an identity, or attracting attention from others. Because it assumes that young people don't want to use drugs, the social influence approach is limited in focus and does not address a number of important etiological factors shown to be important in the development of adolescent substance use. In particular, social resistance approaches may not directly address the perceived benefits (or risks) of substance use.

The normative education approach is based on a fairly limited set of assumptions regarding the causes of adolescent substance use; however, these assumptions are closely related to the perception of risks and, in particular, the perceived benefits of substance use. If young people tend to initially believe that everyone else is using drugs and that it is normative to do so, giving them accurate information about the prevalence of substance use can reduce one of the major perceived benefits of engaging in substance use, that is, being like everyone else. Furthermore, if a young person comes to believe that one reason most people don't do drugs is that it is harmful, then changing perceived norms may also increase the perceived risk of engaging in drug use.

Unlike the social resistance training approach, competence enhancement approaches recognize that some adolescents want to smoke, drink, or use drugs not because they are yielding to peer pressure but because substance use has some instrumental value; it may, for example, help them deal with anxiety, low self-esteem, or a lack of comfort in social situations. By teaching cognitive and behavioral skills that can help youth deal with these issues in more adaptive ways, competence enhancement approaches may reduce these perceived benefits of engaging in drug use. Taken together, two of the three effective approaches (normative education and competence enhancement) may be effective to the extent that they reduce the perceived benefits of substance use rather than by specifically increasing the perceived risks of use. This notion is surprising given the fact that perceived risk is closely associated with adolescent drug use. The Monitoring the Future study has shown that changes in the perceived risk of drug use over time correspond directly to changes in prevalence rates among adolescents. Historically, as the perceived risk of drug use increases among adolescents, the prevalence of drug use decreases. However, most contemporary school-based prevention approaches do not emphasize the long-term negative consequences of drug use, nor do they typically include traditional fear appeals as a means of increasing perceived risk. More research is needed on ways to provide the right information so that young people can adequately understand the risks of drug use so that school-based prevention programs can effectively increase the perceived risk of drug use in addition to disconfirming the perceived benefits of use.

AN ARGUMENT FOR MULTICOMPONENT PREVENTION PROGRAMS

School-based prevention programs that include content from all three contemporary approaches—social resistance, normative education, and competence enhancement— are likely to be more effective than any one of the approaches alone. Furthermore, this multicomponent, combined approach may have relevance for a variety of problem behavior

outcomes in addition to adolescent substance use. The following are some reasons why multicomponent approaches to adolescent drug abuse prevention are likely to be most effective:

1. *Social resistance programs may be ineffective in the absence of conservative social norms against drug use.* If the perceived norm is to use drugs, adolescents will be less likely to resist offers of drugs (Donaldson et al., 1996). This suggests that correcting normative expectations and attempting to create or reinforce conservative beliefs about the prevalence and acceptability of drug use is of central importance to the success of resistance skills training programs. Normative education may also reduce the unintended message inherent in resistance skills training that pro-drug influences—and therefore drug use itself—are ubiquitous in society.

2. *Social resistance programs are likely to be ineffective for adolescents predisposed to risk taking.* Because social resistance skills prevention programs assume that young people do not want to use drugs (and do not address the perceived benefits of substance use among youth), they are likely to be ineffective for young people predisposed to risk-taking behavior, who may see substance use as an attractive option. To the extent that some risk taking is normative during adolescent development, resistance skills training by itself may fail to have an impact on a large proportion of young people.

3. *Competence enhancement prevention programs that include applications to situations directly related to tobacco, alcohol, and drug use are most effective, relative to competence enhancement programs with no drug content.* Competence enhancement programs teach adolescents a repertoire of skills that they can use to deal with many of the challenges confronting them in their everyday

lives, and therefore contrasts markedly with resistance skills training approaches, which are designed to teach students information and skills relating solely to the domain of drug use. However, as part of teaching generic skills for coping with life that will have broad application, it is crucial to specifically include how to apply social and personal skills to situations related to the initiation of drug use. This suggests that social resistance training is of central importance to the success of competence enhancement approaches. In fact, some evidence suggests that generic-skills training approaches are effective only if they also contain domain-specific material (Caplan et al., 1992).

4. Etiology literature indicates that drug use and abuse have a complex set of determinants. These may include a variety of cognitive, attitudinal, social, personality, pharmacological, and developmental factors that serve to promote the initiation and maintenance of substance use. Given this, it seems logical that the most effective prevention strategy would be one that is comprehensive, targeting a broad array of etiologic determinants.

APPLICATION TO RISK BEHAVIORS OTHER THAN SUBSTANCE USE

In addition to preventing drug abuse, multicomponent prevention programs that enhance social and personal competence skills may be a useful prevention approach for other negative behaviors during adolescence. Indeed, several previous studies have shown that young people with good competence skills have lower rates not only of substance use but also of depression, delinquency, aggression, and other problem behaviors and that skills training programs that promote social and personal competence

can effectively prevent these behaviors and promote school success (Dalley, Bolocofsky, & Karlin, 1994, Frey, Hirschstein, & Guzzo, 2000; Weissberg, Barton, & Shriver, 1997; Zins, Elias, Greenberg, & Weissberg, 2000). In particular, competence enhancement may be a useful approach to preventing youth violence and aggression. Like drug abuse, interpersonal violence is a major public health problem that contributes to morbidity and mortality rates among youth (Koop & Lundberg, 1992). Programs to prevent violence and aggression have traditionally been developed and implemented independently of adolescent drug abuse prevention programs. However, because substance use and interpersonal violence share similar etiological factors related to peer social influences and poor social and personal skills, a common prevention approach may be able to address the underlying determinants of both behaviors and possibly others.

SUMMARY

The initiation of substance use often occurs during early adolescence, a key period during which young people face a variety of new challenges and developmental goals. Contemporary school-based drug prevention typically includes a focus on (a) social resistance training, (b) normative education, (c) competence enhancement, or (d) some combination of these approaches. Each approach has different assumptions about the motivational factors that contribute to adolescent substance use, including the perceived risks and benefits of use. Social resistance approaches assume that young people do not want to use drugs but lack the skills to resist drug offers. Normative education and competence enhancement approaches assume that adolescents may want to use drugs because they perceive significant benefits to doing so, such as "fitting in" or achieving other important developmental goals. These prevention approaches differ in the extent to which they address the perceived risks and benefits of substance use. Addressing the perceived benefits of substance use appears to be an important component of effective prevention programs. Furthermore, social resistance, normative education, and competence enhancement approaches are likely to have a synergistic effect when combined. Multicomponent programs (social resistance, normative education, and competence enhancement) have effects that are more than simply additive and may be able to address multiple-problem behavior outcomes in addition to alcohol, tobacco, and drug use, particularly if students are taught to apply new skills to each problem behavior outcome. Multicomponent prevention programs are not only more likely to prevent adolescent substance use but may have broad application to other adolescent risk behaviors.

CHAPTER 12

Decision-Making Competence and Risk Behavior[1]

ANDREW M. PARKER
BARUCH FISCHHOFF

During adolescence, many teens face the need to make their own important decisions for the first time. Often, these decisions concern risky behaviors involving drugs and alcohol, crime, sex, and contraception. Because the stakes riding on these decisions are increasing, development of decision-making skills is especially crucial during this period.

Past research on decision making has shown systematic departures from rational choice, with both teens and adults. These departures include inappropriate attention to "sunk costs," susceptibility to the way a question is framed, overconfidence, and many other well-documented effects (e.g., Kahneman, Slovic & Tversky, 1982). This research has been primarily experimental, focusing on general cognitive processes (Lopes, 1987). As a consequence, little attention has been given to individual differences in decision making. Nevertheless, individual performance on these tasks often varies widely. Some people simply do better than others.

To the extent that this variability correlates across tasks, it may represent one or more underlying competencies. Furthermore, to the extent that these experimental tasks capture essential elements of real-world decision making, susceptibility to these performance problems may be reflected in real-world behavior. Collaboration with an ongoing longitudinal study gave us the opportunity to examine these possibilities. We compiled a set of tasks designed to assess different aspects of decision-making competence and compared performance on them with measures of intelligence, cognitive style, social environment, and most important, risk behavior.

TOWARD A MEASURE OF DECISION-MAKING COMPETENCE

Research in behavioral decision making has documented many clear departures from optimal decision making. These departures occur at many different points in the decision-making process. In selecting tasks, we sought to represent a cross section of these processes, including five general skills necessary for competent decision making: structuring a decision situation, assessing beliefs and values, integrating these components, and having a metacognitive understanding of one's own decision-making processes (Edwards, 1954; Raiffa, 1968). The following paragraphs step through each of these five skills, and where appropriate propose specific tasks (noted in italics) to address each skill.

Decision structuring involves extracting structure from decision situations. Such tasks are necessarily open-ended and were beyond the technical constraints of our study.

Belief assessment involves determining the likelihood of potential outcomes (Fischhoff & Beyth-Marom, 1983). We represented these skills with a task asking respondents to assess the chance of various events occurring to them during a specified time period. For example, "What is the percentage chance that you will be arrested, whether rightly or wrongly, at least once in the next year?" *Consistency in risk perception* reflects the logical consistencies to responses on related items (e.g., the answer to the preceding question should be less than or equal to the response to a later question, with the time frame, "between now and when you turn 30?").

Value assessment involves determining the personal value of potential outcomes. In decision theory, values are a matter of personal preference and, hence, cannot be evaluated for their appropriateness. However, values can be judged in terms of their internal consistency. Our first value-related task, *resistance to framing*, measures people's resistance to ostensibly irrelevant changes in the wording of questions. For example, one pair of problems presents a type of condom with either a 95% success rate or a 5% failure rate for preventing AIDS transmission.

Respondents see both problems, and their judgments of efficacy are evaluated for consistency.

The second values-related task, *resistance to sunk costs,* assesses the ability to ignore resources that have already been sunk into a course of action. One such question asks,

> You and your friend have driven half way to a resort. To get a lower price, you have put down a $100 deposit for the weekend there. Even if you cancel, you cannot get the $100 back. Both you and your friend feel sick. You both feel that you both would have a much better weekend at home. Your friend says it is "too bad" you have paid the deposit because you both would much rather spend the time at home, but you can't afford to waste $100. You agree. Do you drive on or turn back? (Adapted from Dawes, 1988)

The rational choice would be to turn back (because decisions about future actions should depend only on future consequences).

The third value-related task, *path independence,* uses choices among gambles to assess individuals' adherence to the rational-choice axiom of path independence (which states that a decision should be based solely on the value and probability of final outcomes rather than on the path one takes to those outcomes). For example, a respondent's choice, when presented with a sure $50 and a coin flip which pays $100 for heads (vs. $0 for tails), should not depend on whether a previous flip came up heads. Pairs of these problems are used to measure consistency with path independence.

Finally, *recognizing social norms* measures individuals' understanding of peer social norms (one reasonable input to personal valuation). Respondents are presented with a set of socially undesirable behaviors (e.g., use your fists to resolve a conflict) and asked (a) whether it is sometimes OK to do each behavior and (b) how many "out of 100 people your age" would say it is sometimes OK. Responses on (b) are compared with norms created using (a).

Integration processes combine beliefs and values into coherent decisions. One component ability is executing a desired decision strategy. *Applying decision rules* poses choices among options (e.g., different styles of Walkman) varying on defined attributes (e.g., radio sound and battery life). Respondents are presented with a decision rule and asked to apply it. Responses are evaluated for accuracy.

Metacognition, the understanding and regulation of one's own decision making, operates on all component processes. One metacognitive skill is having an accurate understanding of the limitations of one's own knowledge. Here, respondents are presented with a set of statements (e.g., smoking marijuana improves a person's driving ability). For each statement, respondents are asked to judge (a) whether the statement is true or false and (b) how certain they are (from 50% to 100%) that they made the right true-or-false choice. |*Under/overconfidence*| (the absolute difference between a respondent's average confidence and the percentage of correct true-or-false answers) measures the appropriateness of individuals' confidence in their knowledge.

We administered these seven tasks as a test battery. To the extent that they tap common constructs of decision-making competence (DMC), they should (a) correlate positively with each other, (b) conform to a coherent factor structure, and (c) correlate sensibly with other aspects of teens' lives.

CEDAR STUDY

The Center for Education and Drug Abuse Research (CEDAR) is an NIH-funded research center focused on the etiology of substance abuse. CEDAR's large collection of social, economic, physical, psychological, and behavioral measures provides a unique opportunity to compare traditional laboratory tasks with important real-world correlates.

CEDAR's sampling design distinguishes between low- and high-average risk teens (LAR and HAR, respectively). If a teen's father has a history of substance use disorder, the teen is labeled HAR; otherwise, he or she is labeled LAR. The HAR teens are a convenience sample identified through clinical sources, such as drug treatment centers. The LAR teens are a representative sample of Pittsburgh-area youths (excluding HAR-eligible teens). The CEDAR sample is half LAR and half HAR. At the baseline assessment, respondents are 10 to 12 years old, with additional assessments every 2 to 3 years.

The current data were collected from 110 respondents in the fourth assessment wave. Because females were added to CEDAR after it had begun, few had reached the fourth assessment, so our entire sample was male. At the end of the assessment visit, each respondent completed an additional packet with the decision-making questionnaires, which generally took about an hour.

Results

We expected to see positive correlations among the different types of decision-making performance.[2] As seen in Table 12.1, most intertask correlations are, indeed, positive. A principal-components exploratory factor analysis revealed a single factor accounting for 25.1% of the variance in task performance. All factor loadings were positive, with particularly large ones for resistance to framing, applying decision rules, and |under/overconfidence| (see the last column of Table 12.1). We focus here on factor scores from this model, labeled DMC.

Table 12.2 displays correlations between DMC and a set of relevant CEDAR measures.

Table 12.1 Intercorrelations Among Factor Scores for the Seven Decision-Making Competence (DMC) Measures and Factor Loadings From Principal Component Analysis

	Correlations						
DMC Measure	Risk Perception	Framing	Sunk Costs	Path Independence	Social Norms	Decision Rules	Factor Loadings[a]
Consistency in risk perception	1						.29
Resistance to framing	.22*	1					.67
Resistance to sunk costs	.15	.02	1				.39
Path independence	−.05	.05	.21	1			.31
Recognizing social norms	.18*	.16	.23**	.03	1		.44
Applying decision rules	.12	.24**	.03	.06	.08	1	.63
|Under/ overconfidence|	−.01	.31***	−.05	.17*	.05	.35**	.62

a. Using a forced single-factor model from a principal-components exploratory factor analysis
*One-sided $p < .05$; **$p < .01$; *** $< .001$

To the extent that DMC reflects cognitive abilities, it should be correlated with other measures of cognitive ability. Those correlations might reflect the influence of those abilities on DMC or some common higher-order influences (e.g., Jensen, 1998). The first two rows show strong positive correlations between DMC and two common measures of cognitive ability, the Vocabulary subscale of the Wechsler Intelligence Scale for Children—Revised (WISC—R; Wechsler, 1972) and a composite measure of executive cognitive functioning (ECF; Giancola, Martin, Tarter, Pelham, & Moss, 1996). Both correlations diminish, but remain significant, when controlling for the other cognitive ability measure. Given these relationships, columns 3 to 5 in the table provide semi-partial correlations, controlling for these measures of cognitive ability, first individually and then together. The remaining rows of the table show the results of testing for other anticipated correlations with DMC.

In terms of cognitive style, DMC was correlated with several measures of constructive and introspective cognitive styles (Stanovich & West, 2000). Polarized Thinking, a subscale of the Constructive Thinking Inventory (CTI; Epstein & Meier, 1989), represents a tendency to think in black-and-white terms. As expected, DMC was negatively correlated with Polarized Thinking. It was also positively correlated with two measures of self-awareness: Self-Consciousness (concern for how others view oneself; Fenigstein, Scheier, & Buss, 1975) and Self-Monitoring (analyzing one's own behavior in terms of social or situational factors; Snyder, 1974). DMC was also correlated with Behavioral Coping (also from the CTI), which measures whether individuals endorse good problem-solving skills, thus providing an attitudinal measure of what DMC tries to measure behaviorally. Except with Self-Consciousness, these correlations remained significant after controlling for cognitive ability.

Table 12.2 Decision-Making Competence (DMC), Correlated With the CEDAR Variables, Controlling for Cognitive Ability

DMC Correlated With	Pearson r	Semipartial Correlation, Controlling for		
		Vocabulary	ECF[a]	Vocabulary & ECF
Cognitive ability				
Vocabulary	.50***	—	.28***	—
Executive cognitive functioning	.48***	.26***	—	—
Cognitive style				
Polarized thinking	−.34***	−.20*	−.24**	−.19*
Self-consciousness	.20*	.14	.05	.11
Self-monitoring	.24*	.29**	.30**	.32***
Behavioral coping	.32***	.27**	.28**	.26**
Risk behavior				
Antisocial disorders	−.19*	−.18*	−.05	−.09
Externalizing behavior	−.32**	−.28**	−.18*	−.20*
Delinquency	−.29**	−.28**	−.18*	−.21*
ln[b] (lifetime no. of drinks)	−.18*	−.22*	−.15	−.18*
ln (lifetime marijuana use)	−.25***	−.30***	−.20*	−.25**
ln (no. times had sex)	−.24*	−.30**	−.21*	−.27**
ln (no. sexual partners)	−.30**	−.33***	−.29**	−.31**
Social and family influences				
Risk status (HAR = 1; LAR = 0)	−.35***	−.27**	−.23**	−.21*
Socioeconomic status	.35***	.20*	.21*	.15*
Positive peer environment	.33***	.35***	.32***	.35***

a. ECF = executive cognitive functioning
b. ln = logarithm
*One-sided $p < .05$; **$p < .01$; ***$p < .001$

Decisions to engage in risky behavior need not be irrational, if they follow from beliefs and values in an orderly fashion. However, they may be poor choices in a society for which they are proscribed, for the protection of the individual or the society. As a result, we expected negative correlations between DMC and risk behavior (Dryfoos, 1990; Jessor & Jessor, 1977).

CEDAR's mix of low- and high-risk populations provides the statistical power to detect relationships between risk status and other behaviors (while complicating the inference of population incidence). The third section of Table 12.2 has seven measures of risk behavior, measured between ages 10 and 16. These include clinical diagnoses, individual self-reports, and parental reports. The first measure records whether the teen has ever been diagnosed with oppositional-defiant disorder or conduct disorder (Endicott & Spitzer, 1978). Externalizing Behavior (from the Child Behavior Checklist, Achenbach & Edelbrock, 1983) reflects aggression and directing anger outward. Delinquency is a subscale of Externalizing Behavior. CEDAR collects extensive data on substance use, from which the following two measures are derived: the natural logarithms of estimated lifetime number of alcoholic drinks and episodes of marijuana use through age 16 (Skinner, 1982). Finally, sexual activity was measured at the 16-year-old assessment by self-reports of the number of sexual acts and sexual partners in the previous 12 months. DMC correlates negatively with each. These correlations are strongest for Externalizing Behavior, Delinquency, marijuana use, and number of sexual partners. They remain significant when controlling for Vocabulary, and, to a lesser extent, with ECF.

The final section of Table 12.2 shows significant correlations between DMC and having a positive family and social environment. They include a negative correlation with risk status (coded 1 if the teen is HAR, 0 if LAR) and positive correlations with both socioeconomic status (SES; Hollingshead, 1975) and a positive peer environment (Tarter, 1991). Again, controlling for cognitive ability reduces the correlations (more for risk status and SES than for peer environment), but the relationships remain significant.

CONCLUSIONS

Using a collection of decision-making tasks developed primarily in experimental research, we identified a unitary measure, reflecting an underlying construct of decision-making competence. This measure of "good" decision making correlates strongly in the predicted directions with many different aspects of the CEDAR teens' lives. In particular, better DMC predicts less risky behavior, even when controlling for two measures of cognitive ability. Furthermore, in analyses not reported here, DMC appears to be a stronger correlate of such behavior than either Vocabulary or ECF by itself.

Although the current analysis does not allow causal inferences, it is not difficult to hypothesize such links. A supportive family and social environment (reflected by risk status and positive peer environment) could provide models of good decision-making processes and lead a young person down more constructive life paths. DMC, in turn, could influence decisions to engage in risk behaviors. The relationships between such complex constructs are presumably more complex, but the results do suggest the importance of further investigation.

To the extent that DMC represents a set of trainable skills rather than a trait, educating teens about good decision making may facilitate reducing risk behaviors (Beyth-Marom & Fischhoff, 1997; Fischhoff, 1992; Hammond, Keeney, & Raiffa, 1998). Indeed, training has apparently improved performance on several specific decision-making tasks (e.g., Hammond et al., 1998; Lichtenstein & Fischhoff, 1980).

Although these analyses focus on *relative* competence, they might be extended to considering issues of *absolute* competence, of the sort central to many legal and medical decisions, such as teens' ability to stand trial or right to make health care and reproductive decisions (Gardner, Scherer, & Tester, 1989). Many of the HAR teens have made life choices that might be seen as demonstrating insufficient absolute competence. Establishing acceptable benchmarks would be a nontrivial requirement for a measure of absolute competence.

In summary, these results suggest that good decision making consists of a set of interrelated skills related to other abilities, behaviors, and experiences. In particular, the quality of a teen's decision-making processes may be an important factor in his or her risk behavior. This research supports the nomological validity of the "traditional" behavioral decision-making tasks, from which the present set of measures was derived. Tasks that proved central here, specifically resistance to framing, applying decision rules, and |under/overconfidence|, may be particularly promising for future investigation.

NOTES

1. A full description of this research is available in Parker and Fischhoff (2002).

2. All the decision-making competence measures are coded such that higher scores represent better performance.

CHAPTER 13

Time Perspective

A Potentially Important Construct
for Decreasing Health Risk Behaviors
Among Adolescents

GEOFFREY T. FONG
PETER A. HALL

There are few endeavors as humbling as trying to change people's health behaviors. It is difficult at best to achieve even moderate gains in many health domains, and initial successes often give way to very high rates of relapse just a few weeks or months after a seemingly successful intervention (e.g., Brownell, Marlatt, Lichtenstein, & Wilson, 1986).

In this chapter, we briefly outline one possible approach for understanding the difficulty that adolescents (and people in general) have both in reducing their health risk behaviors and in adopting health-protective behaviors. Our approach focuses on the *temporal asymmetry* between costs and benefits related to health behaviors that lead individuals to fail to appreciate the importance of adopting and maintaining health-protective behaviors at the time of decision making.

We make three general points in this chapter. First, we outline the difficulties that an individual encounters when making judgments about health behavior in a temporal context—particularly when it involves addictive substances such as tobacco—and suggest a way of understanding how those difficulties may lead individuals—notably adolescents and young adults—to failure to engage in health-protective behavior. Second, we briefly review research we have conducted

AUTHORS' NOTE: Preparation of this chapter was supported by Grant R01 CA90955 from the National Cancer Institute of the United States and grants from the Centre for Behavioural Research and Program Evaluation of the National Cancer Institute of Canada, the Canadian Tobacco Control Research Initiative, Social Sciences and Humanities Research Council of Canada, the Canadian Institutes for Health Research, and the Lyle S. Hallman Institute Fund. We thank Tara Elton, Carrie Lynn Choy, Cathleen McDonald, Karen Choi, Alexandra Lin Marie Fong, and Kiara Fong for their assistance.

demonstrating that individual differences in the extent to which people think about the long-term consequences of their actions are correlated with their likelihood of engaging in health-protective and health-risk behavior. Third, we briefly describe a recent intervention trial that we have conducted suggesting that the relationship between time perspective (long-term vs. short-term) and health behavior is causal in nature. This research is, we believe, the first experimental evidence that intervention material that explicitly links current health behaviors with long-term consequences can enhance the effectiveness of such interventions. We suggest that this intervention strategy has the potential to enhance intervention effectiveness across different domains of health-risk behavior.

THE IMPORTANCE OF TIME PERSPECTIVE: LINKING CURRENT ACTION TO LATER OUTCOMES

In industrialized nations such as Canada and the United States, most of today's major life-threatening diseases are chronic rather than infectious in nature. Many of these chronic diseases could be prevented through the alteration of just a few behavioral patterns: poor diet, smoking, lack of exercise, substance abuse, and maladaptive responses to stress (LaLonde Commission of Canada, 1974; U.S. Surgeon General, 1979). Importantly, the prevention of chronic diseases requires action many years, or even decades, before any symptoms of the disease develop. Only through the recognition that one's current actions are linked to the future likelihood of disease is it possible to regulate one's own behavior to reduce one's risk.

Smoking behavior provides an illustrative example. For the habitual smoker, lighting up the next cigarette is potentially associated with a variety of immediate benefits, including feelings of well-being, avoidance of withdrawal symptoms, and improved concentration. Depending on the composition of one's social network, lighting up might also win acceptance from one's peers and improve one's sense of self-worth through feelings of belonging within the group. Indeed, there is strong evidence that youth smoke because they hope to convey a positive image to themselves and to other people (Barton, Chassin, Presson, & Sherman, 1982; Belk, Mayer, & Driscoll, 1984). In contrast to a multitude of immediate benefits, there are few immediate costs, and those consequences that might be perceived by others as costs (e.g., risks that a junior high school student might be punished for breaking the rules) might be perceived by the young smoker as a benefit (e.g., independence, autonomy, risk taking).

In the long term, however, the balance of costs and benefits becomes reversed. Although presumably there are few long-term benefits associated with smoking, the long-term health consequences are devastating: Approximately half of all chronic smokers will die prematurely, with an average loss of life expectancy of 15 years (e.g., Doll, Peto, Wheatley, Gray, & Sutherland, 1994). Given the positive valence of the short-term contingencies associated with smoking and the strong negative valence of the long-term contingencies, temporal focus should have a powerful impact on decisions about smoking behavior.

The same temporal issues figure prominently in virtually all health behaviors, including engaging in regular physical activity, adhering to a medical regimen, and maintaining a healthy diet. Each of these behaviors is associated with a characteristic set of contingencies whose valence changes dramatically depending on the temporal frame. Each behavior is associated with many costs in the short-term (e.g., inconvenience, discomfort, loss of pleasure) and with few benefits. In the long-term, many benefits emerge (e.g., longer life span, improved functional status, decreased risk for disease), and costs are minimal. Attention to long-term contingencies, then, should motivate health behavior performance, and attention to short-term contingencies should "de-motivate" health behavior performance.

THE IMPORTANCE OF CONSIDERING LONG- VERSUS SHORT-TERM CONSEQUENCES

In recent years, decision researchers have begun to address the vexing problem of how to understand the persistence of self-defeating behaviors—those that are not in the best interest of the individual, even when the individual himself or herself recognizes that the behavior is unwise. Perhaps the prototypic example is addictive behavior. Why do people continue to intake substances that are well-known to be self-destructive when, in many cases, the self-destructive nature of those substances is well-known to users themselves? In addressing this issue, researchers have suggested that it is necessary to take into account the *time course* of the costs and benefits of a behavior (Ainslie, 1975). Research on choices and judgments that have a time element to them (known as "intertemporal choice") shows that costs and benefits that occur in the short term are more likely to loom larger—that is, carry more weight—than costs and benefits that occur in the long term (Loewenstein & Elster, 1992). Decision models that view decisions as resulting from static, time-invariant processes have difficulty explaining health behaviors such as smoking (or quitting) driven by different time courses of costs and benefits. In contrast, newer models of intertemporal choice capture the dynamic process of decision making, and the research emanating from those models shows quite clearly that people can readily engage in

behaviors without full knowledge and information about the future consequences, thereby suggesting that any appropriate account of smoking behavior must take into account the fact that short-term benefits loom much larger than long-term costs and consequences.

Because of this asymmetry between the short-term and long-term aspects of smoking, health-protective messages, such as warning labels, ad campaigns, and other public health information programs, are at a distinct disadvantage in attempting to inform the public about the long-term negative consequences of smoking compared with the sheer power and magnitude of the attractive aspects of smoking in the short term. Because of this, it is *even more important* that warning labels (and other public health messages that provide information about smoking) be equipped with the ability to convey their messages vividly (see Strahan et al., 2002).

THE IMPORTANCE OF CONSIDERING THE EFFECTS OF ADDICTION IN SMOKING-RELATED DECISION MAKING, JUDGMENTS, AND BEHAVIORS

The second problem with how young people think about smoking is that those who smoke, or who are considering smoking, may underappreciate the addictive power of nicotine. Many researchers have commented on how addictive behavior differs in systematic ways from the rational model. Some suggest that the costs of addiction are hidden from the initial user, and thus, any kind of decision process that occurs in the initial stages of smoking—even if the decision maker has resolute intentions to make decisions on whether or not to smoke in a cold, calm, and rational way—is not sufficiently informed about the actual future costs. The rules we use to predict normal, nonaddictive behaviors are inadequate to predict our behavior regarding addictive substances.

Loewenstein (1996) points out that people have a strong tendency to underestimate the power of "visceral factors" in guiding their judgments, decisions, and behaviors. Examples of visceral factors are drive states such as hunger, thirst, and sexual desire, and emotions, pain, and craving for addictive drugs. Loewenstein suggests that these visceral factors have a disproportionate effect on behavior—a disproportionate effect that is often surprising to people when they encounter their effect and one that is not salient, recognized, remembered, or anticipated to even those same people when they are not being driven by those visceral factors. As applied to smoking, Loewenstein's model suggests that beginning smokers are very unlikely to have much, if any, appreciation for the power and magnitude of the effects of nicotine addiction.

Unfortunately, nicotine dependence can occur very quickly. Tolerance can begin with the first cigarette, and symptoms of dependence can follow shortly thereafter. In a study of 681 Grade 7 students, DiFranza et al. (2000) found, in a prospective, longitudinal study that 22% of those 95 students who had initiated occasional smoking reported a symptom of nicotine dependence within 4 weeks of initiating monthly smoking. One or more symptoms were reported by 60 of these 95 students (63%). Of the 60 students who reported one or more symptoms, 62% of them reported experiencing their first symptom before smoking daily or began smoking daily only when they experienced their first symptom. In an extensive review of the literature on adolescent nicotine dependence, withdrawal, and related physical symptoms, reviewing studies from national surveys, school-based surveys, and smoking cessation studies, Colby, Tiffany, Shiffman, and Niaura (2000) reported that,

overall, 20% to 60% of adolescent smokers are dependent on nicotine. Two thirds or more of adolescent smokers report experiencing withdrawal symptoms during attempts to quit or reduce their smoking.

This research on the power of nicotine addiction provides an important context to understanding young people's perceptions of their own risks regarding the health consequences of smoking. Young people may believe wholeheartedly that smoking is dangerous, but they may not believe that the risks pertain to them because *they aren't going to become addicted*. They believe that they will be able to quit, thereby avoiding the long-term health threats that would befall those who continue to smoke. But these beliefs are far too optimistic. According to research cited in the Surgeon General's 1994 report (U.S. Department of Health and Human Services, 1994), among high school smokers, only 5% expect to be smoking 5 years after graduation, yet 75% will still be smoking. Adolescent smokers do not anticipate that they will have difficulty quitting in the future. Yet more than half of smoking adolescents report attempting to quit each year, and among those who smoke 10 or more cigarettes per day, fewer than 20% report being successful for even 1 month. Most adolescents who are addicted to nicotine want to quit smoking, but are unable to do so.

TIME PERSPECTIVE AND HEALTH BEHAVIOR

Our initial efforts to understand the relationship between time perspective and health behavior resulted in the development of an individual difference measure. Our *Time Perspective Questionnaire* (TPQ; see Appendix) consists of 13 items that ask respondents to describe themselves with reference to statements about their valuation of short- versus long-term outcomes (e.g., "living for the moment is more important than planning for the future"), and the influence of these long-term outcomes on their decision making processes ("I have a defined set of long-term goals that I think about when I make decisions in my life"). The TPQ has good reliability (Hall & Fong, 1997), including high internal consistency ($\alpha > .80$) and good test-retest reliability ($r > .80$ over 4- and 10-week periods).

With regard to validity, we found that university students that had a *long-term time perspective,* as measured by the TPQ, were less likely to engage in health-damaging behaviors (e.g., alcohol consumption, smoking) and more likely to engage in health-protective behaviors (flossing, eating low-fat foods, and using seat belts) than were students that were identified by the TPQ as having a *short-term time perspective,* even when statistically controlling for the influences of potentially similar constructs such as impulsivity (Hall & Fong, 1997). The predictive power (about $r = .21$) is reasonable given that correlations between domain-general, self-report measures of personality and health risk behaviors rarely exceed .20 (e.g., Cooper, Agocha, & Sheldon, 2000; Zuckerman & Kuhlman, 2000).

We have also demonstrated the predictive power of the TPQ in other populations. In the North American Student Smoking Survey (NASSS; Fong et al., 2002) of over 12,000 high school students across Canada and the United States, we found that an index of just two items from the original TPQ, modified for this younger group of respondents ("I have a good idea of what my long-term goals in life are," and "I spend a lot of time thinking about how what I do today will affect my life in the future"), was correlated with (a) whether students were smokers and (b) among students who had never tried smoking, whether they were likely to initiate in the future (measured by Pierce, Choi,

Gilpin, Farkas, & Merritt's, [1996] measure of susceptibility to future smoking) at about the same level as the 4-item measure of sensation seeking (Hoyle, Stephenson, Palmgreen, Lorch, & Donohew, 2002) when both were entered in the regression equation. Thus, the predictive power of the TPQ, coupled with the discriminant validity vis-à-vis impulsivity and sensation seeking, demonstrates that time perspective is a valuable construct in predicting and understanding health-protective and health-damaging behavior among adolescents and young adults.

THE ROLE OF TIME PERSPECTIVE IN HEALTH BEHAVIOR INTERVENTIONS

Many existing health interventions implicitly incorporate elements of time perspective and long-term orientation into their materials. Virtually all health interventions describe the long-term consequences of failing to engage in health-protective behavior. Anti-smoking interventions highlight the fact that smoking increases the likelihood of cancer and cardiovascular diseases (a vivid example of this strategy in the policy domain is the introduction of graphic warning labels on Canadian tobacco packages in December 2000). Interventions designed to prevent or reduce alcohol and drug use describe the adverse long-term consequences of use, even as they also describe the potential negative short-term consequences (e.g., consequences of binging, increased likelihood of motor vehicle accidents).

In nearly all health interventions, then, long-term health consequences are made salient. Some interventions take additional steps to explicitly connect those consequences with current behavior. For example, in the "Be Proud! Be Responsible!" behavioral intervention for reducing HIV-risk sexual behavior among minority youth (e.g., Jemmott, Jemmott, & Fong, 1998; Jemmott, Jemmott, Fong, & McCaffree, 1999), Module 1 contains an exercise that focuses participants' attention on how being infected with HIV or another sexually transmitted disease (STD) would adversely affect their hopes and dreams for their future. The rest of the intervention focuses on how participants can engage in protective behaviors *now* in order to avoid the long-term consequences of HIV/STD infection.

FROM CORRELATION TO CAUSE: INITIAL EVIDENCE IN THE DOMAIN OF EXERCISE

The correlational evidence that we and others (Keough, Zimbardo, & Boyd, 1999; Strathman, Gleicher, Boninger, & Edwards, 1994) have gathered suggests that time perspective—thinking about the future, and in particular the consequences of present behaviors for future outcomes—is related to health behavior. We have also noted that most health behavior interventions include material that highlights the adverse future consequences of continuing to engage in health-risk behavior, and some are more explicit in linking current behavior to future consequences. Yet to our knowledge, no research has specifically tested whether such material designed to increase future time perspective per se can be used to improve the effectiveness of a health intervention.

To begin to address the important issue of whether time perspective is *causally* associated with health behavior, we first developed a standard goal-setting intervention designed to increase exercise behavior among university undergraduates, taking principles and material from a number of existing exercise interventions, notably Sallis's curriculum for increasing exercise among undergraduates (Sallis et al., 1999). We then developed a time perspective module (Hall & Fong, 2001), which included activities and discussions designed to enhance salience of long-term contingencies associated with exercise and to reinforce the connectedness between current behaviors and later outcomes.

Two intervention trials were conducted to evaluate the efficacy of our time perspective intervention—a pilot study involving a small sample ($N = 18$) and a second, larger trial ($N = 81$)—each of which randomized undergraduates enrolled in exercise classes at the University of Waterloo to one of three conditions: (a) goal-setting control intervention, (b) time perspective intervention, and (c) no-treatment control. In the pilot study, we found that, controlling for pre-intervention physical activity levels, time perspective participants reported increased levels of physical activity relative to the two other groups at post-intervention, and relative to the no-treatment group at 10-week follow up. The second, larger trial replicated some of the effects of the pilot study (Hall & Fong, 2003). Together, these studies provide tentative initial evidence that the effects of health behavior interventions may be enhanced through the addition of a time perspective component.

CONCLUSION

In summary, research efforts to understand risky health behaviors and reduce their prevalence may benefit from a more explicit appreciation of temporal influences on adolescents' thought processes and behavior patterns. As a psychological construct, time perspective is capable of explaining a variety of risk-related phenomena across a broad range of behavioral domains, including why adolescents engage in risky health behaviors, why they have difficulty stopping such behaviors, and what we as researchers and public health professionals can do to help.

Appendix

Time Perspective Questionnaire[a]

For each of the statements below, indicate your level of agreement or disagreement by using the following scale:

1	2	3	4	5	6	7
Disagree very strongly	Disagree strongly	Disagree	Neutral	Agree	Agree strongly	Agree very strongly

1. I have a defined set of long-term goals that I think about when I make decisions in my life.
2. *Living for the moment is more important than planning for the future.
3. I have a good sense of what my long-term priorities are in life.
4. *I spend a lot more time thinking about today than thinking about the future.
5. *Short-term goals are more important to me than long-term goals.
6. People who know me would describe me as a person who plans for the future.
7. *I often try to do things that are good for me at the time, even if they are not good for me in the long run.
8. *It's really difficult to predict what will happen in the future, so it's more important to focus on today.
9. *Living in the here-and-now is better than living for the future.
10. I consider the long-term consequences of an action before I do it.
11. *Many people are disappointed in life because they sacrificed their daily enjoyment for a better future that never came.
12. I spend a great deal of time thinking about how my present actions will have an impact on my life later on.
13. *"Eat, drink, and be merry, for tomorrow we die" is a good philosophy to follow in life.

NOTE: Items marked with an asterisk are reverse-scored so that higher totals on the TPQ scale reflect higher levels of long-term time perspective.

a. This version of the TPQ has been used in research involving university students. We have revised the TPQ for use with younger age groups, and the revision is available from the authors.

CHAPTER 14

The Influence of School Atmosphere and Development on Adolescents' Perceptions of Risk and Prevention

Cynicism Versus Skepticism

Maria D. LaRusso
Robert L. Selman

Year after year, reports on the prevalence of adolescent risky behavior (e.g., illicit drug use, smoking and drinking, unprotected sexual activity, etc.) often read like a roller-coaster of hope and despair, steeply up one year, slightly down the next, only to quickly rise again with the appearance of a new street drug (Johnston, 2002). What lies behind these numbers? What is a reasonable set of expectations for the reduction of certain risky behaviors without the likelihood that dips in one will simply be offset by peaks in another? How does the developing adolescent interpret these risks and the efforts of adults to prevent them?

Variations in adolescent beliefs about health risks and prevention efforts are, to a large extent, a function of differences in individual interpretations of risk based on each adolescent's social or cultural experiences and knowledge (Burton, Obeidallah & Allison, 1996; Lightfoot, 1997; Ponton, 1997). However, we have found in our research that, especially during early adolescence, variations in beliefs are also based on important developmental differences in adolescents' interpretation of risks, relationships, and prevention messages (Selman & Adalbjarnardottir, 2000). Here, we will consider the influence of both contextual and

AUTHORS' NOTE: Partial support for this work was provided by the Robert Wood Johnson Foundation. The authors would also like to thank Lynn H. Schultz for her collaboration on this research.

Table 14.1 Sample Rel-Q Question Measuring Students' General Beliefs About Relationships Between Students and Teachers

	Poor	OK	Good	Excellent
A good teacher				
a. Does not yell	❑	❑	❑	❑
b. Keeps the class quiet	❑	❑	❑	❑
c. Lets the students help make some decisions	❑	❑	❑	❑
d. Listens to students' ideas	❑	❑	❑	❑

Write the letter (a, b, c, or d) of the choice that you think is the best in this blank _____

SOURCE: Schultz and Selman (2002).

developmental factors, using as a case study an evaluation we conducted for a Middle Grades Drug Prevention and School Safety grant.

In the fall of 1999, the U.S. Department of Education, Office of Safe and Drug Free Schools Programs, awarded a 3-year grant to an urban public school district in the northeast to build a comprehensive approach to risk prevention and intervention among the district's middle-grades students, specifically in the areas of violence and substance abuse. Data collection focused on a cohort of students followed from 6th through 8th grades (41% European American, 22% African American, 13% other Black, 15% Latino, 8% Asian American). We collected quantitative data using a cluster of risks surveys and questionnaires. We also collected qualitative data at four schools selected from the 15 district schools for more intensive study. In each of these schools, multiple focus group sessions were conducted to explore students' experiences of health risks such as fighting, smoking, and drinking in the context of their social relationships and their experiences of prevention and intervention efforts in their schools, including formal programs, teacher responses to incidents of violence, harassment, and rule violations, as well as schoolwide policies and disciplinary actions.

We also administered the Relationship Questionnaire (Rel-Q), a multiple-choice "developmental" questionnaire designed by our research group to assess the maturity of children's and adolescents' interpretations of their relationships with both adults and peers (Schultz, Barr, & Selman, 2001; Schultz & Selman, 2002). The questionnaire presents students with brief "item responses" to sentence stems or dilemmas and asks them to rate each item on a 4-point scale indicating whether the response is poor, OK, good, or excellent. Then, after rating each item, they are asked to select the response they think is the "best choice." For example, the sentence stem and item responses in Table 14.1 focus on students' general beliefs about relationships between students and teachers.

According to our developmental coding of the questionnaire, students who select items c or d as their best choice or rank them as good or excellent choices are given higher scores than students who select a or b as their best choice or rank these among the good or excellent options. This is because our research suggests that, in general, younger (elementary school) children "naturally" gravitate toward unilateral answers like a and b and earn lower scores than middle school children who tend to attribute greater value to choices like c and d that imply reciprocity (Schultz et al., 2001; Schultz & Selman, 2002).

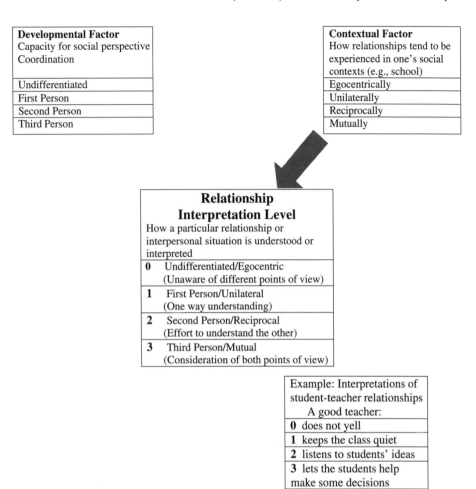

Developmental Factor
Capacity for social perspective Coordination

| Undifferentiated |
| First Person |
| Second Person |
| Third Person |

Contextual Factor
How relationships tend to be experienced in one's social contexts (e.g., school)

| Egocentrically |
| Unilaterally |
| Reciprocally |
| Mutually |

Relationship Interpretation Level

How a particular relationship or interpersonal situation is understood or interpreted

0	Undifferentiated/Egocentric (Unaware of different points of view)
1	First Person/Unilateral (One way understanding)
2	Second Person/Reciprocal (Effort to understand the other)
3	Third Person/Mutual (Consideration of both points of view)

Example: Interpretations of student-teacher relationships A good teacher:
0 does not yell
1 keeps the class quiet
2 listens to students' ideas
3 lets the students help make some decisions

Figure 14.1   Levels of Relationship Interpretation

The theoretical basis for the scoring of the Relationship Questionnaire is a developmental framework that focuses on the increasing capacity with age to coordinate the points of view of the self and others and the application of that capacity in real-life contexts (Selman, 1980; Selman, in press). Figure 14.1 depicts the theoretical framework that guides the assessment. Although it provides a general sense of a developmental progression, the figure should not be interpreted as suggesting that individuals follow a pure, linear pathway through these levels of relationship

interpretations. Although *developmental factors* (left side of the figure), such as the capacity to engage in higher-level perspective coordination, do tend to emerge with age, *contextual factors* (right side of the figure), such as school atmosphere, often interact with developmental competencies to determine the actual level at which individuals experience and interpret the meaning of risks and relationships in specific moments.

For example, an adolescent who has the capacity to take a "third-person" perspective may still interpret relationships as primarily

Table 14.2   Rel-Q Scores, Free-Lunch Status, Students' Perceptions of School Safety, and Adolescent Risks Engaged in During the Past 6 Months, Based on Self-Reports From 7th-Grade Students in the Four Focus Schools

	School A	School B	School C	School D
Level of relationship interpretation				
Average relationship questionnaire score	1.84	1.96	2.07	2.13
Socioeconomic status				
Receive free lunch	75%	72%	24%	15%
Perceptions of school atmosphere				
Do not feel safe in their school	32%	32%	18%	20%
Adolescent risks during past 6 months				
Bullied other kids	58%	36%	36%	16%
Smoked cigarettes	27%	20%	9%	5%
Forced/pressured someone to have sex	27%	9%	0%	0%

unilateral if he or she has many one-way relationships or is negotiating with others in what the adolescent perceives as an authoritarian environment (e.g., in which teachers actually do yell a lot).

Thus, the mean Rel-Q score for an aggregate group of students in a school can also provide information about the overall quality of the students' relationships with the teachers and other students, or what we would call the "social health" of the school. In empirical studies, average Rel-Q scores ranged from 1.8 (*SD* = .36) in Grade 4 to 2.10 (*SD* = .38) in Grade 8 to 2.40 (*SD* = .40) in Grade 12. When a school has students with Rel-Q scores that are, on average, lower than typical for their grade, it may indicate that the school environment is not supporting the development of students' most mature social interpretations as well as it could.

In the Middle Grades study, we found large variation in mean Rel-Q scores across individual schools. When the cohort students were in the 7th grade, the average Rel-Q score for students in the district was 2.04, but across the four individual focus group schools, mean scores ranged from 1.84 to 2.13 (see Table 14.2). This range is equivalent to a 4-year span of development. The lowest mean Rel-Q score (1.84) for a school in this district approximates what would be considered typical for 4th-grade students, while the highest mean Rel-Q score for a school, 2.13, is roughly equivalent to the norm for students in 8th grade. Because all these students were in the 7th grade, the responses of the students in Schools C and D seem developmentally advanced, on average, whereas in Schools A and B, the students' responses appear to be developmentally behind. Our analysis of school differences in Rel-Q scores prompted a closer examination of school differences in other sources of survey data (Table 14.2).

Social class and student perception of school safety are among the indicators that parallel the differences in the mean Rel-Q scores for the schools. The schools with higher percentages of students who report that they do not feel safe (e.g., schools A and B) are the same ones that have lower relationship interpretation scores. In contrast, the schools with the higher Rel-Q scores have a smaller percentage of students who receive free lunch and a smaller percentage of students who report not feeling safe in their school. There is a similar pattern in some of the adolescent risks with the percentage of students who report engaging in these risks inversely related to the mean level of relationship interpretation scores.

Although our evidence cannot identify the causal connections within these patterns, it suggests that Rel-Q scores may serve as an important indicator of school health (through comparisons of aggregate scores across schools) as well as a measure of individual differences in adolescents' relationship maturity. In other words, it is not a matter of whether Rel-Q findings can be explained by either the level of competence the students bring to the school or the influence of the school's atmosphere on them. Rather, the Rel-Q might best serve as a rough indicator of the intertwining forces of individual development and school culture on the interpersonal communication within the school and its interpretation by the students.

The focus group data, in particular, provide a way to untangle these two strands of influence on Rel-Q scores. For instance, although it was not an intended topic for our focus group sessions, student-teacher relationships were mentioned frequently by students and their depictions varied widely across the schools. At School A, the school with the lowest mean Rel-Q score, stories and comments regarding teachers' poor treatment of students were offered throughout discussions that were focused on risk behaviors and peer relationships. Below are some sample comments from a focus group on bullying, in which students frequently shifted the conversation from peer interactions to their experiences of teachers bullying students.

> Can I say something? Some teachers harass kids . . .
>
> Certain teachers don't listen to people.
>
> Teachers tell you to shut up.
>
> They call us dumb.

When students report that their teachers don't listen to them, tell them to shut up, and call them names, it should not be not surprising that they would have lower Rel-Q scores than their peers who are not offering similar reports about teachers in their school. Take, for example, the earlier question from the Rel-Q that focuses on the students' general beliefs about relationships between students and teachers: The most popular answer among the middle-grade students at School A was "Does not yell."

In contrast, "Listens to student ideas" was the most popular choice among students in School D, the school with the highest mean Rel-Q scores. In this school, students seemed to have more positive experiences of teacher-student relationships allowing them to have a wider perspective on what it can mean to be a good teacher. As one of the students from this school reported,

> You can tell that they respect you. They don't put you down just 'cause you are younger than them. Like some teachers you can just tell how the way they act. Like they don't say, "I'm the teacher and you are the student. You always listen to me." Like they actually listen to your opinion, like in class and you raise your hand and point out something when they are wrong or you have a different opinion than them, and they actually respect that. And then I think it would make me more comfortable to talk to those teachers, because I know that they have more respect for me than maybe other teachers do.

Students at this school do not suggest that all their teachers listen, but they have had enough experiences with teachers who value their opinions that most of them would define a good teacher as one who "listens to student ideas." It is likely that these students' high Rel-Q scores were, at least in part, nurtured by the climate of respect and trust they have encountered in their school (see also Bryk & Schneider, 2002; Meier, 2002). In contrast, students in School A describe one-way, unilateral power-based relationships with teachers, creating a context in which relationships are experienced and understood at a level that is typically below the developmental capacity of students at this age and probably below the capacity of most of the 7th-grade students in this school.

The primary issues that seemed to differentiate between the schools whose students appeared to be developmentally behind and those ahead were the students' perceptions of the level of trust and respect they experienced in their relationships with both peers and adults and their perceptions of the amount of fairness and care underlying the school rules and policies intended to protect them from risks. For example, in the two schools with the lower mean relationship interpretation scores, students reported a large degree of hostility, bullying, and harassment among peers and complained of their schools being inconsistent or ineffective in helping students deal with these problems.

> I think it's everywhere. Every school has like a bully or some kids that are being harassed. Some schools have different ways of solving it. . . . I don't really like the way that this school solves problems, 'cause they wait until . . . an action, like if someone hits you . . .

Although students learned to identify bullying behavior from prevention programs in school, they still felt unequipped to protect themselves in a climate in which hostile interactions between students were often tolerated (see also National Center for Educational Statistics, 1995, cited in Pelligrini, 2001; Olweus, 1993). Consequently, the students conclude that the adults "really don't care." In such an environment, we would expect the students to be less inclined to interpret relationships at levels that are based on reciprocity and trust.

Although such inconsistent or indifferent responses to school social problems leave students feeling abandoned, perhaps paradoxically, students also identify punitive and intolerant school practices as lacking in care (see also Ayers, Dohrn, & Ayers, 2001; Skiba & Noam, 2001). For example, students in the focus groups interpreted "zero tolerance" policies as contributing to a school climate of mistrust. They indicated that these policies communicate that the school expects that students will be violent, carry weapons, or use drugs and that when and if a student indeed does mess up, the student will be expelled from the school community rather than offered help to address whatever problems may be underlying the behavior.

> You'd get kicked out, one strike and you're out, at least I think that's what would happen with zero tolerance. I don't think that's the best thing because then the kid's going to still keep having problems and drinking, and he'll just bring those problems to the next school, and just keep getting kicked out of school.

These school practices and policies lead students to question whether school officials really care about protecting students from risks or whether they just care about protecting the school's reputation.

Similarly, students found several other prevention policies to be inconsistent or hypocritical in their supposed intention to protect youth. For example, some adolescents proclaimed that school officials care about fighting only when it occurs on school property, explaining that when students fight off school grounds, the school will claim to have no responsibility for addressing these incidences of violence between students. And at a historical moment when regulatory policies prohibiting the purchase of cigarettes by minors are being powerfully enforced, some students wryly observed that police monitor convenience stores but do not react when kids openly smoke on street corners. Initially, they concluded that if an activity is not illegal, it cannot really be that bad for you. But when we probed further, we reached what seemed to be the deeper personal issue for these adolescents: whether those in authority (policymakers, school officials) truly care about youth or whether they are just trying to cover themselves.

In general, the students' critiques of prevention policies and their schools' social environment reflected their increasing capacity to think critically and understand multiple perspectives. However, the school's social atmosphere seemed to play a large part in determining whether this more mature understanding of relationships was marked by a cautious trust we would call "adolescent skepticism," or by a rigid mistrust we would call "adolescent cynicism." In the school with the highest relationship interpretation scores, students were critical of the policies in their school but, at the same time, they described an overall climate of respect and trust among students and teachers. As one student stated,

> The school does not want to have to deal with suspended people or deal with things that look bad on their record. I think that a lot of teachers, especially at this school, are really great because they really care about you. But the school's policies, in general, I don't think they represent, because the teachers care about us.

Students in this school not only demonstrated an ability to consider different points

of view but also differentiated between schoolwide approaches to managing student behavior and the orientation of individual teachers, revealing an openness to trust others despite skeptical interpretations of the overall level of trustworthiness and care in their environment.

In contrast, students in the school with the lowest relationship interpretation scores appeared more cynical, responding to many examples of untrustworthiness in their schools with a self-protective orientation of distrust for everyone. These students offered multiple examples of teachers verbally harassing and threatening students and recalled an often-cited story of a student being physically assaulted by a substitute teacher who was then hired for a permanent teaching position the following year. They interpreted this as meaning that the administration did not care about them. When asked what they learned from this experience, the group concluded, "*Don't trust anyone.*"

When adolescents become capable, developmentally, of taking a third-person perspective on relationships with others (upper left side of Figure 14.1) but are in contexts in which they experience relationships as primarily unilateral (upper right side of the figure), they are vulnerable to developing cynical attitudes about practices and policies directed toward them. In particular, these cynical attitudes reflect the adolescent's lack (or loss) of faith in the expectation that relationships will be based on mutual trust and caring. Thus, they interpret policymakers, school administrators, and teachers as caring only about themselves and approach future interactions in their school with distrust.

Although it is probable that the students in the lower socioeconomic status (SES) schools also bring in more problem behavior, our qualitative data do not support the notion that the difficult environment in those schools was created solely by the students. Students' perceptions of school atmosphere were informed by much more than the behavior of their peers. In fact, students seemed to expect a certain amount of difficulty with peers ("It's everywhere. Every school has like a bully or some kids that are being harassed."), but the lack of concern they perceived in the adult responses and policies of the school appeared to be the greatest source of their indignation. And it was conversations about abuse and neglect by teachers and school administration that ended with students in the lowest SES school concluding that they should no longer "trust anyone." Although it is true that some schools may have more difficult students, when teachers and schools respond to students in unilateral ways, they are contributing to the perpetuation of an unhealthy school atmosphere rather than providing an opportunity for the students to both experience and develop faith in the reciprocity of relationships.

If social development and social experiences of early adolescence create opportunities and vulnerabilities for the emergence of skeptical or cynical orientations toward risks and relationships, what might be the implications for these adolescents' interpretations of prevention messages? In the focus groups, we found middle school students to be highly attuned to inconsistencies in messages about risks; hypocrisies embedded in the words and the practices of adults, schools, and society; and ambiguities not addressed in school-based prevention programs. As students grappled with these issues, their reactions ranged from confusion and sarcastic amusement to mistrust and outrage at the messages they receive from the adult world about adolescent risks. These themes cut across categories of risks (i.e., drinking, smoking, etc.) and encompassed attitudes that ranged from a dismissive cynicism to a healthy skepticism.

Student: Miss S. tells us not to smoke sometimes. But then she smokes, she smells like smoke.

Facilitator: When they tell you not to smoke or drink, what are they saying?

Student: They are just saying it because they have to.

Facilitator: You don't think that they mean it?

Student: No, I don't think they care. But that's all they ever tell us.

Student: I think people have to be real dumb to tell us not to smoke and then they smoke.

Student: I just don't listen because they're a bad example.

Many students struggled to make sense of what they perceived to be inconsistencies between adult messages about smoking and adult behavior. In particular, in School A where the above session was conducted and where 27% of the 7th graders reported smoking, the students questioned the authenticity of adults' words, suggesting that adults were merely regurgitating a message they were expected to endorse while ultimately not caring what kids do. The students appear cynical because they begin from a place of distrust, doubting the sincerity of the adults delivering the prevention messages without considering alternative explanations that could make space for both good intentions and contradictory behavior. Instead, these students dismiss the message because they don't trust the source.

In contrast, at School B where 20% of students report smoking, we saw a mix of cynical and skeptical attitudes.

Facilitator: So what does it mean if adults tell you that you shouldn't smoke but they do?

Student: Hypocrites!

Student: I know. They're telling us not to, but they do it themselves. It's like what influence is that?

Student: My dad's a hypocrite. My mom's a hypocrite because she tells me not to smoke but then she does it herself.

Student: [But] the parents who smoked, then quit and tell their little kids not to smoke, it's because they want their kids to know-(interrupted)

Student: How much trouble they went through to try to quit.

Student: Some parents don't want you to smoke because they might have a problem and they can't stop and it's like a need that they have to do. But they don't want you to end up like them, so that's probably why even if they smoke, they're telling you not to.

In this group, some students seemed to understand the challenge of breaking addictions like smoking and, thus, see adults who smoke as suffering and genuinely interested in protecting kids from the harm of cigarettes. Although some of these students identified the adults' behavior as hypocritical, others attempted to understand the inconsistencies in what the adults say and do. What makes these students' attitudes skeptical rather than cynical is that they are cautious and questioning rather than simply assuming that adults are operating from a position of self-interest and without good intentions.

Adolescents are also more likely to react with cynicism when prevention programs lack the complexity necessary to match their increasing capacity to see things from multiple perspectives. For example, students described many prevention programs as promoting "black and white" perspectives and encouraging complete avoidance of risks rather than engaging students in honest discussions that acknowledge possibilities, such as drinking in moderation. Some students pointed out paradoxes such as drinking wine and smoking marijuana being understood both as health risks and as health enhancments or therapy for some illnesses. Others spoke at length about cultural meanings and individual differences in vulnerability,

explaining, for example, how some people can manage alcohol better than others. In addition, adolescents report that the prevention messages from the school often compete with other perspectives they perceive to be less rigid and more trustworthy. The following excerpts are from a focus group at the school with the highest relationship interpretation scores where students expressed frustration with what they considered overly simplified prevention messages.

> But another thing about the school, about why you do not trust it, is because when you get into the [drug and alcohol] program you cannot do anything without it being bad.

> School kind of verges on "oh my God, it is a sin." They really take it way out of proportion, how bad it is. My friends, my parents and I all kind of think that [drinking] is good or OK in moderation, but too much is bad. Much less drastic.

> I definitely listen to my parents. I feel like, at times, my peers can have their own opinions that I do not necessarily believe or think come from a lot of experience, so I do not necessarily listen to my peers. And then I feel like the school is always like "it is evil . . ." and . . . totally exaggerates it and so I do not want to listen to the school. So it just leaves my parents and my poor judgment.

When adolescents are capable of understanding risks more complexly, they are likely to reject prevention messages that sound too much like rigid, unilateral directives. The unintended consequence of such well-meaning prevention efforts is that student trust is lost and messages from the school are quickly dismissed, even in schools where relationship interpretation scores are high and teachers are described as caring. Thus, context matters not only in terms of general social atmosphere, but also in the context of specific communications.

In sum, adolescents' perceptions of risk and prevention are largely determined by a complex interplay of development and context. We would not expect all early adolescents at, say, 12 or 13 to be at the same level of maturity (Freud, 1981); however, individual differences in development do not provide a sufficient explanation for the variation. We must also examine the social contexts in which middle school students are developing. In particular, when youth this age become capable of a more sophisticated understanding of social worlds but are schooled in environments that they feel are authoritarian, unsafe, or uncaring, they are likely to continue formulating less mature interpretations of relationships and social situations (and reasonably so). For these adolescents, the increasing complexity in their understanding becomes muddled in the development of a cynical mistrust of relationships. Similarly, if prevention messages are delivered in untrustworthy contexts or by distrusted sources, or if the messages lack the complexity needed to satisfy the deeper understanding of maturing adolescents, they will hear such messages with a cynical and, hence, unreceptive ear.

On the other hand, the developmental shifts of early adolescence also provide a necessary foundation for building healthy skepticism. Unlike adolescent cynicism, adolescent skepticism should not be heard negatively, because it is exercised by individuals who, in the process of learning to take a third-person perspective, become naturally more cautious and questioning in their attempts to understand the complicated world around them. Rather than fighting the inevitability of adolescent skepticism, prevention specialists might consider ways to both promote and harness it for the benefit of youth. First, where cynicism exists, skepticism should be the near-term goal. This work requires attention to the social environment in which prevention efforts are implemented so that those efforts will be appreciated and trusted by young adolescents as they increasingly question the intentions and authenticity of adults. Second, a prevention approach that builds on adolescents' growing capacities to understand and coordinate multiple perspectives will not fight or resist skeptical reactions but will bring the mixed messages and varied meanings of risks into the conversation, inviting adolescents to challenge, debate, and protest rather than disengage. By encouraging students to use their ability to think critically, we help them to avoid both the hopelessness and apathy of cynicism and the vulnerability that comes with a naive optimism. Armed instead with a cautious skepticism, adolescents can face the future with confidence in their ability to make choices based on realistic and careful interpretations of the risks and opportunities in their lives.

Part II

COMMON PATHWAYS
AND INFLUENCES
ON ADOLESCENT RISK
BEHAVIOR

Section A

Multiple-Problem Youth

CHAPTER 15

Preventing Multiple Problem Behaviors in Adolescence

ANTHONY BIGLAN
CHRISTINE CODY

One of the most consistent findings in studies of adolescent problem behavior is that problems are interrelated. For example, the same youth who engage in delinquent behavior are the ones more likely to smoke, drink alcohol in excess, use other drugs, engage in high-risk sexual behavior, drop out of school, or attempt suicide. The relationships are by no means inevitable, but they are large enough and consistent enough to justify a focus on the factors that influence the development of multiple problems and on the interventions that are likely to reduce the number of youth with these problems.

Over the course of the 2000–2001 academic year, the Robert Wood Johnson Foundation and a consortium of National Institutes of Health agencies funded a project at the Center for Advanced Study in the Behavioral Sciences (CASBS) that synthesized what we know about multiproblem youth. This chapter summarizes the work of the CASBS team. A more detailed account of our findings is forthcoming (Biglan et al., in press).

THE INTERRELATIONSHIPS AMONG PROBLEM BEHAVIORS

Numerous researchers have found that adolescents with one problem behavior (such as smoking cigarettes) also have others (e.g., violence or high-risk sexual behavior). Links exist between delinquency and high-risk sexual behavior (Biglan et al., 1990), antisocial behavior and illicit drug use (Elliot, Huizinga, & Menard, 1989; Robins & McEvoy, 1990), and behavioral problems and alcohol consumption (Hanna, Hsiao-ye, DuFour, & Whitmore, 2000). Annual surveys conducted by government agencies such as the Substance Abuse and Mental Health Services Administration (1999), National Institute on Alcohol Abuse & Alcoholism (1996), and the National Highway Traffic Safety Administration (2001) indicate that alcohol use by youth is related to serious conduct problems, including drunk driving, homicide, other violent crimes, and risky sexual behavior.

One way of gauging the importance of a focus on multiproblem youth is to look at the proportion of all problems for which they account. In an analysis of National Household Survey data, the CASBS team looked at the 12- to 20-year-olds who reported engaging in none, one, or two or more of the following problems: serious antisocial behavior, smoking, alcohol misuse, illegal drug use, and high-risk sexual behavior. Only 18% of young people had two or more of these problems, but those individuals accounted for 65% of drunk driving, 88% of violent arrests, 72% of all arrests, 87% of the health problems related to drug use, and 75% of improper needle use among drug abusers (U.S. Department of Health and Human Services, 2000b).

THE SOCIAL COSTS OF ADOLESCENT PROBLEM BEHAVIOR

Ted Miller of the CASBS team analyzed the costs of multiproblem youth. To do so, he reviewed existing evidence from cost analyses of individual problem behaviors and examined what proportion of each problem was likely attributable to youth with multiproblem behaviors. The behaviors included in his analysis were juvenile crime, cigarette smoking, binge drinking, cocaine or heroin abuse, high-risk sexual behavior, suicide acts, and dropping out of school. He compiled an estimate for the costs incurred in 1998 by each behavior. These included long-term costs of these behaviors, such as the continuing costs of permanent injury to a crime victim. However, it did not account for the long-term costs of youthful cigarette smoking, which are enormous (Centers for Disease Control and Prevention, 2002a).

The estimate of the total cost of multiproblem behavior in 1998 for the United States was $422 billion. The two most costly were antisocial behavior ($165 billion) and dropping out of school ($141 billion).

INFLUENCES ON THE DEVELOPMENT OF MULTIPLE PROBLEMS

Research over the last 40 years has provided much greater understanding of the factors that influence young people. Here, we will briefly summarize factors—from the prenatal period through adolescence—shown to influence problem behavior in adolescence.

Prenatal factors that contribute to problems in adolescence include maternal nutrition and substance use. For example, male children of mothers who smoked during pregnancy display a higher incidence of criminal and conduct problems than do children of nonsmoking mothers (Brennan, Grekin, & Mednick, 1999; Gibson, Piquero, & Tibbetts, 2000; Wakschlag et al., 1997). Raine, Brennan, and Mednik (1994) found that children of mothers who had birth complications (e.g., forceps extraction, breech delivery, umbilical cord prolapse, preeclampsia, long birth duration) or experienced maternal stress about having a child were likely to commit crimes in adolescence. Similarly, genetic factors appear to contribute to antisocial behavior. For example, Reiss (2000) examined the correlation between parenting behavior and child outcome for both biologically related and biologically unrelated mother-child pairs. He found that genetic influences could almost entirely explain the relationship between harsh parenting and antisocial outcome in adolescence.

Converging evidence suggests that, through their effect on parent-child—and particularly early maternal-child—interactions, all of the just-cited factors may lead to problem behavior. All appear to involve the infant's being fussy and difficult to console. This makes it less likely that the mother and infant will develop synchronous and comforting interactions that lay the groundwork for shaping the child's cooperative, prosocial behavior. Instead, patterns of aggressive and uncooperative behavior on the part of the child and coercive reactions on the part of the parent may develop. These patterns of coercive interaction have been shown to contribute to the further development of aggressive behavior (Patterson, Reid, & Dishion, 1992).

Such aggressive behavior appears to be the single most important predictor of the development of diverse problems in adolescence. When children enter elementary school, aggressive and uncooperative behavior contributes to academic failure and peer rejection. Aggressive and socially rejected children are significantly more likely to engage in delinquency in adolescence (Patterson, DeBaryshe, & Ramsey, 1989).

A key pathway through which aggressive elementary school children become adolescents with multiple problems is their association with deviant peers. From initial experimentation with cigarettes (Friedman, Lichtenstein, & Biglan, 1985) to engagement in criminal acts (Patterson et al., 1992), adolescent problem behavior is a social activity. Dishion and his colleagues (Dishion, Eddy, Haas, Li, & Spracklen, 1997) have recently shown that one of the mechanisms of this influence is straightforward positive reinforcement of talk of deviant behavior—which presumably accompanies approval of the behaviors themselves.

Concerns About
Stigmatizing Multiproblem Youth

One concern sometimes raised in discussions of multiproblem youth is that, by stigmatizing young people with problems, we will increase the punitive and unproductive ways in which they are treated. Our response is that at-risk youth are already regarded in punitive and stigmatizing ways. Consider the policies currently in place that track young people into "opportunity schools" and the policies that increasingly try juvenile offenders

as adults and require mandatory minimum sentences. Articulating the extent and cost of youth with multiple problems may prompt an already too punitive society to further punishment, but it can also be the occasion to point to the inadequate and harmful nature of current practices and to describe more effective interventions that have recently been identified. There are interventions all along the course of development that can help young people develop the skills and interests they need to avoid multiple problems and lead productive and satisfying lives. Let us briefly review some of them.

PREVENTION OF
ADOLESCENT PROBLEMS
THROUGH PREADOLESCENT
INTERVENTIONS

Interventions for the
Prenatal, Perinatal, and
Early Childhood Periods

Three programs that target this period of development are the Nurse Visitation Program (Olds et al., 1998), the Syracuse Family Development Research Program (Lally, Mangione, Honig, & Wittner, 1988), and the Perry Preschool Project (Clarke & Campbell, 1998; Yoshikawa, 1995). Each has shown encouraging results.

The Nurse Visitation Program, developed by David Olds and colleagues, focused mostly on white (89%), unmarried (62%), and low socioeconomic status women (61%). It consisted of home visits by nurses during the young mother's pregnancy and the first 2 years of the child's life. The nurses befriended the mother and supported her in making health and behavior changes, such as quitting smoking and getting a job. The randomized trial evaluating the program showed that these mothers reported fewer sexual partners, fewer cigarettes smoked per day, and fewer days on which they had consumed alcohol in the past 6 months. As adolescents, the children of mothers who were poor and unmarried had significantly fewer arrests, fewer convictions, and fewer probation violations than did the offspring of poor unmarried women who did not receive nurse visitation. A later randomized trial among African American women (Kitzman et al., 2000) achieved results similar to those of the initial study.

Interventions for School-Aged Children

The Good Behavior Game has been in use in schools around the world since its development in the 1960s by Barrish, Saunders, and Wolf (1969). The classroom is divided into two or more groups and groups earn free time and other rewards for brief periods of on-task and cooperative behavior. Embry (2000) reviewed 13 evaluations of the program and concluded that the game can reduce aggressive and uncooperative behavior and increase cooperative behavior across diverse socioeconomic and ethnic groups. Kellam, Ling, Merisca, Brown, and Ialongo (1998) evaluated the program in a randomized trial involving first grade students in 19 Baltimore elementary schools. The game reduced aggressive behavior in 1st grade (Dolan et al., 1993) and boys' aggression remained lower even in 6th grade (Kellam, Mayer, Rebok, & Hawkins, 1998). Boys who received the intervention were significantly less likely to be smoking at age 14 (Kellam & Anthony, 1998).

These results are not isolated. Other programs shown to prevent the development of problem behavior among aggressive elementary school students include the Montreal Longitudinal Experimental Study (Tremblay, Pagani-Kurtz, Masse, Vitaro, & Pihl, 1995), the Seattle Social Development Program (Hawkins, von Cleve, & Catalano, 1991),

and LIFT (Linking the Interests of Families and Teachers).

Researchers at the Oregon Social Learning Center developed LIFT (Reid, Eddy, Fetrow, & Stoolmiller, 1999). Targeting 1st- and 5th-grade students ($N = 671$), LIFT consisted of the Good Behavior Game, parenting skills training, and increased contact between parents and teachers, via the phone. Reid and colleagues evaluated LIFT in a randomized trial in which they assigned schools to receive or not to receive the program. Fifth-grade children who had been involved in the program had less association with deviant peers, lower likelihood of a first arrest, and less initiation of alcohol and marijuana use than did 5th graders who did not receive the program (Eddy, Reid, & Fetrow, 2000).

UNIVERSAL PREVENTION PRACTICES TARGETING ADOLESCENTS

A universal program is one designed to reach all members of the population, as opposed to only those who are at risk. The programs often reach the adolescents through schools, but some successful programs have worked with adolescents and their families.

Family-Focused Interventions

Preparing for the Drug Free Years (PDFY; Haggerty, Kosterman, Catalano, & Hawkins, 1999) and the Iowa Strengthening Families Program (ISFP) are two promising programs. PDFY works mostly with parents, but ISFP consists of seven sessions during which parents and children learn new skills for communication and for dealing with emotions. Spoth and colleagues evaluated both programs in a randomized, controlled trial involving 33 mostly white, dual-parent families in Iowa (Spoth, Redmond, & Shin, 2000, 2001). ISFP had a significant impact in reducing youths' use of tobacco, alcohol, and other drugs. Among control youngsters, 19.1% reported having ever been drunk at a 2-year follow up, whereas only 9.8% of the ISFP young people did so. PDFY also led to significantly lower rates of initiation of substance use.

School-Based Programs

Within the schools, researchers have developed classroom-based curricula to prevent substance use. A recent meta-analysis by Tobler and colleagues (Tobler et al., in press) indicated that the most widely known approach, Drug Abuse Resistance Education (DARE), has not shown significant effects in the 16 years since its creation. Life Skills Training (LST), developed by Botvin and colleagues (Botvin, Baker, Dusenbury, Botvin, & Diaz, 1995), has been more successful. LST is a 20-session, 7th-grade curriculum that has booster sessions in 8th grade. It includes, among other things, activities designed to enhance awareness of social influence to use substances and training in social skills, for resisting influences, and for coping with stress. It has shown positive results on drug use among 12th-grade students who received this social skills training as early as the 8th grade (Botvin et al., 1995). However, a significant finding stresses the importance of implementing programs such as this with fidelity. Botvin and colleagues (Baker, Dusenbury, Tortu, & Botvin, 1990) found no benefit of LST when it is delivered inadequately.

Policies to Affect Adolescent Problem Behaviors

Many educators have overlooked the capacity of policy to prevent problems. For example, if there were laws in place affecting price, availability, and opportunity for alcohol, it could reduce binge drinking even without the family and school interventions. It is also important to restrict advertising that targets youth (Biglan, 2001).

INTERVENTIONS TARGETING ADOLESCENTS WITH BEHAVIOR PROBLEMS

Interventions for Delinquency and Antisocial Behavior

An exemplary program is Multidimensional Treatment Foster Care (Chamberlain, 1994), which focuses on adolescents who are repeat offenders, targeting family and peer risk factors that can lead to an increase in multiple-problem behaviors. The program places the adolescents in foster homes with parents trained in behavior management and at the same time trains the biological parents to better equip them for the time when adolescents return to their home. A randomized controlled trial indicated that the program reduces recidivism (Chamberlain & Reid, 1998). In addition, cost analysis has found the program to be more cost-effective than incarceration (Aos, Phipps, Barnoski, & Lieb, 2001).

Multidimensional Family Therapy addresses multiple factors that can affect use of drugs or other antisocial behavior. Therapists teach life skills to adolescents and work to improve relationships between parents and children as well as between parents and outside agencies. Families receive up to 25 individualized treatment sessions over a 3- or 4-month period (Hogue, Liddle, Becker, & Johnson-Leckron, 2002). Evaluations of the program involving randomized controlled trials show that it has some promise for reducing drug use, but these evaluations have not sufficiently established its effectiveness in prevention.

The juvenile justice system has long been involved with youth intervention, particularly with incarceration, youth diversion programs, and intensive probation, parole, or both. There is some evidence that behavioral skills training provided to delinquents in these contexts can have value (Lipsey, 1998). However, our society makes far greater use of punishment than the evidence merits. For example, boot camps have become popular recently, but evidence indicates that they have no benefit (Aos et al., 2001). In general, incarceration should be evaluated in light of the evidence that it reduces participation both in the workforce and in committed relationships, thereby contributing to continued involvement in crime in adulthood (Sampson & Laub, 1994).

COMPREHENSIVE COMMUNITY AND STATEWIDE INTERVENTIONS

Community Interventions

Community interventions could reach a wide range of ages and target numerous behavioral problems. However, to date, the most evaluated community interventions have focused on the prevention of substance use. For example, Project SixTeen (Biglan, Ary, Duncan, Black, & Smolkowski, 2000) targeted tobacco use, and Project Northland (Perry et al., 1993), Communities Mobilizing for Change on Alcohol (Wagenaar & Toomey, 2000), and the Saving Lives Project (Hingson, Heeren, & Winter, 1996) focused on alcohol use among adolescents. The Community Trials Project (Holder et al., 1997) sought to reduce alcohol-related problems among all ages, and the Midwestern Prevention Program (Pentz, Dwyer, et al., 1989; Pentz, MacKinnon, et al., 1989) concentrated on adolescents only, but across a wide range of substance use.

Each of these programs has shown some success when evaluated in a randomized trial. These promising results indicate the possibility

of additional wide-range targets across all ages of development. It is time to evaluate community interventions designed to affect antisocial behavior among adolescents.

Statewide Campaigns

Statewide efforts tend more to the implementation of policies and, although initially focused only on alcohol use, have recently included tobacco regulation, particularly in California, Massachusetts, Arizona, Oregon, and Florida (Chaloupka, Grossman, & Tauras, 1997). States could consider this same kind of effort in prevention of other high-risk behaviors.

REALIZING THE PROMISE OF THESE INTERVENTIONS

The evidence briefly reviewed here and covered more comprehensively by Biglan et al. (in press) indicates that, throughout development, there are programs and policies able to prevent young people from developing multiple problems. As research accumulates, we can be confident that available interventions will grow in number and strengthen in efficacy.

Yet the true promise of all this knowledge will come when these interventions are widely implemented with careful attention to ensuring that they have the effects that existing evidence suggests are possible. The CASBS team convened a meeting of experts who developed recommendations on how communities could realize the promise of these interventions. We summarize them here.

• *Develop a shared vision among community organizations.* Communities with a shared vision of what they want child rearing to be like are more likely to mobilize the resources to bring about improvements (Roussos & Fawcett, 2000). That vision can specify the outcomes that the community most desires for its young people, the outcomes that most need attention, risk and protective factors that need modification, and the interventions that need to be implemented to bring about improvement. Although research on how to achieve these partnerships is limited, there are useful guides that provide the basis for further evaluation of strategies (Roussos & Fawcett, 2000).

- *Ongoing assessment of child and adolescent well-being.* Just as we monitor economic performance, we need to develop a system for monitoring the well-being of children and adolescents. Such systems will focus communities on the more important problems, provide the basis for advocacy about what needs to be done (e.g., Kingsley, 1998), and allow them to evaluate their efforts. Over time, the widespread use of such systems will foster the selection of more, and more effective, child-rearing practices, as those associated with improvements are retained and those that appear to be of no value are abandoned or modified. There has been considerable progress in articulating what such systems might look like and how to achieve them (Kingsley, 1998; Mrazek & Biglan, 2002). The cost of obtaining, organizing, and making data available on youth well-being is decreasing. The CASBS meeting concluded that it is not too early to establish a national goal of helping communities establish such monitoring systems.

- *Empirically supported interventions across the life span and across multiple levels of influence.* The studies cited earlier testify that throughout young people's development, we can do something to prevent problems and promote success. Interventions can target families, peer groups, schools, neighborhoods, and communities. We need policies at the federal and state levels to foster the adoption and implementation of programs and policies shown to make a difference. Knowing that even the best studies with the most successful outcomes do not guarantee success in a new setting, those policies also require ongoing monitoring of outcomes.

- *The innovating and evaluating society.* Our society is evolving toward more frequent and systematic use of science to assess the effects of policies and programs. It is doing so because of mounting evidence—such as that noted here—that careful scientific research can contribute to the improvement of many lives and the avoidance of many costs. Recognition of this evolutionary process may further accelerate our progress. To the extent that each community begins to demand that the outcomes for its youth be carefully measured and the importance of its child-rearing practices understood, we will achieve a society in which far fewer young people suffer and many more lead happy and productive lives.

CHAPTER 16

Screening and Early Intervention for Antisocial Youth Within School Settings as a Strategy for Reducing Substance Use

HERBERT H. SEVERSON
JUDY A. ANDREWS
HILL M. WALKER

Substance use by adolescents has become a major social problem in the United States over the past three decades. Despite growing efforts to curb substance use among teens, there has been little change in prevalence rates over the years, and in some cases, use has actually increased. For example, the proportion of 8th graders reporting use of any illicit drug in the last 12 months has almost doubled since 1991, from 11% to 21%. Since 1992, the proportion reporting use of any illicit drugs in the past year has risen by nearly two thirds among 10th graders, from 20% to 39% (Johnston, O'Malley, & Bachmann, 1995). Rates of tobacco and alcohol use among youth are also exceedingly high. According to the most recently published results of the Youth Risk Behavior Survey (YRBS), nationwide, 70.4% of students had tried cigarette smoking (including those who had taken only one or two puffs), and in 1999, 34.8% of high school students had smoked cigarettes during the past 30 days (Centers for Disease Control and Prevention [CDC], 2000). In addition, 50% had drunk alcohol during the past 30 days (CDC, 2000). These figures, already alarming, probably do not accurately reflect the scope of the problem because they fail to assess alcohol, tobacco, and drug use among teenagers

---

AUTHORS' NOTE: The authors are grateful for the assistance of Missy Peterson with the data analysis and Katie Clawson in preparing this manuscript. This research was supported in part by Grant #5 R01 DA10767–02 from the National Institutes of Health, National Institute on Drug Abuse.

not attending school, a population in which these behaviors are significantly higher.

The leading causes of mortality and morbidity among youth can be traced to a relatively small number of preventable health-risk behaviors that are often initiated during youth and may extend into adulthood (Kolbe, Kann, & Collins, 1993). Surveys of drug use confirm not only that drugs are being used but also that the age of initial use for most drugs is at the elementary school level. Studies of cigarette, chewing tobacco, and marijuana use report experimentation in 4th and 5th grades. This early experience with drug use is related to subsequent regular use and abuse (Severson, 1984). It has been shown repeatedly that initiation of alcohol and drug use at an early age is one of the strongest predictors of later substance abuse (Grant & Dawson, 1997; Robins & Przybeck, 1985). Early drug use has been related to a wide range of antisocial behaviors and subsequent school failure (Donovan & Jessor, 1978). Substance use by adolescents often occurs in the context of other behaviors, such as delinquency (Donovan & Jessor, 1978), school failure (Hundleby, Carpenter, Ross, & Mercer, 1982), and high-risk sexual behavior (Biglan et al., 1990), as well as low self-esteem (Bry, McKeon, & Padina, 1982). Indeed, the number of problems a youth experiences (e.g., poor relationships with parents or peers, psychopathology, low grades in school) increases the risk of concurrent and later drug use (Newcomb, Maddahian, & Bentler, 1986).

The school setting provides an important context for accessing and identifying children and youth who suffer from risk exposure (poverty, parental abuse and neglect, chaotic family situations, neighborhood crime) in their daily lives. Recent longitudinal, intervention research shows that systematic early intervention involving the child, peers, teachers, and caregivers is instrumental in facilitating bonding, engagement, and attachment to the process of schooling. These factors, in turn, are strongly associated with school success, which serves as a protective factor against destructive outcomes in adolescence, including violent delinquent acts, heavy drinking, sexually transmitted diseases, multiple sex partners, disciplinary episodes at school, and school dropout (Hawkins, Catalano, Kosterman, Abbott, & Hill, 1999). School success depends heavily on being able to negotiate the legitimate demands of schooling and forge effective social relationships with other students and adults in the school.

Students arriving in school are required to make two major social-behavioral adjustments: (a) responding to the behavioral expectations of peers and learning how to make and sustain friendships and (b) adjusting to the academic and behavioral expectations of teachers. Failure in either of these critical adjustment areas can lead to school failure, peer rejection, and/or development of problematic behavior patterns (Walker, Colvin, & Ramsey, 1995). Failure in both adjustments may lead to impairments in a youth's overall quality of life. These outcomes are often predictive of later serious problems, such as school failure or school dropout, substance use, and delinquency (Loeber & Farrington, 1998). Universal screening procedures can be used to identify vulnerable children in the early elementary grades who are at risk for these academic, emotional, and behavioral difficulties (Walker & Severson, 1990; Walker, Severson, & Feil, 1995). Reliable, valid, and cost-efficient instruments and procedures for this purpose have been developed for both social-behavioral (Severson & Walker, 2002) and academic (Daly, Duhon, & Witt, 2002) domains. The judgments of classroom teachers are critically important sources of information in this regard.

Teachers are an underutilized resource with the potential to assist appropriately in the evaluation and referral of at-risk students for specialized services. Analysis of existing school practices indicate that students whose behavior problems are externalizing in nature (i.e., exhibiting noncompliant, aggressive, or disruptive behavior or defiance toward teachers) have the highest likelihood of referral by their teachers for specialized services (Grosenick, 1981; Noel, 1982; Walker & Severson, 1990). Students with internalizing problems (depression, social isolation, avoidance, and school phobia), on the other hand, are rarely referred by teachers for their behavioral problems even though such students are at risk for serious long-term development of social and emotional problems (Horne & Packard, 1985; Parker & Asher, 1987; Robins, 1966). Evidence also indicates that externalizing students with moderate to severe degrees of adjustment impairment are also referred at much lower rates than prevalence in the school population would indicate (Kauffman, 1999; Walker et al., 1988). Unfortunately, students at risk for serious behavior problems, of either an externalizing and internalizing nature, will continue to be substantially underidentified and underserved as long as we rely on the current system of idiosyncratic teacher referrals alone to initiate the referral process.

Some authors have suggested that teacher judgments of child behavior and performance can provide the strongest empirical data and information base for making screening decisions regarding behavior disorders (Gerber & Semmel, 1984; Greenwood, Walker, Todd, & Hops, 1979; Gresham, 1986). Gerber and Semmel (1984) argued convincingly, for example, that the classroom teacher is perhaps the best, most knowledgeable, and most accurate judge of whether a pupil can benefit from instruction in the regular classroom. In a notably radical departure from common practice and thinking, they suggested that traditional psychometric procedures conducted by school

psychologists should be validated against teacher judgment. Similarly, Forness and Kavale (1996) have advocated for a more instrumental role of the classroom teacher in the screening and identification of school-age children who are at high risk for the development of more serious behavior problems. Jackson, Reid, Patterson, Schaughency, and Ray (1990) found that classroom teachers, when using a structured teacher rating form, were more accurate compared with both mothers' and fathers' Child Behavior Checklist (CBCL) externalizing scores in predicting a boy's arrest frequencies in early adolescence. In an important recently reported study, Loeber and his colleagues found that teacher appraisals of child behavior were more accurate than those of either parents or peers (Loeber, Green, Lahey, Frick, & McBurnett, 2000). In the face of this evidence, we firmly believe that the classroom teacher should be an indispensable component of any school-based screening-identification process for detecting at-risk youth who may be on a path to substance use and abuse. The key is for teachers to be provided a standardized and systematic procedure for screening and not depend on idiosyncratic criteria left to individual teacher determination.

Externalizing symptoms are regarded by many as the single best predictor of risk status for future conduct disorder and antisocial behavior (Loeber, 1991; Lynam, 1996; Moffitt, 1993; Patterson, 1993; Yoshikawa, 1994). It has been suggested that even in nonclinic populations of children as young as 4 and 5 years, 50% or more of those with troublesome, externalizing symptoms will later develop persistent conduct problems (Campbell, 1995; Coie, 1996; Reid, 1993; Reid & Patterson, 1991). Since externalizing behavior problems in childhood are associated with increased risk for multiple, serious negative health and psychosocial outcomes in adolescence and adulthood (Bennett et al.,

1999) and given the increasing evidence for the effectiveness of preventive interventions (Kazdin, 1987; Offord, 1987), there is a strong need for accurate, cost-effective methods of identifying children at an early age who meet this high-risk profile. Schools provide a convenient and readily accessible setting for realizing this goal.

TEACHER RATINGS OF BEHAVIOR AS A PREDICTOR OF SMOKING

Herein, we describe the procedures and results of a longitudinal study in which we examined the prospective relationship between teacher ratings of overt and covert aggressive child behavior, prosocial behavior, teacher- and peer-preferred social behavior, and school adjustment to subsequent initiation of smoking. Teacher ratings were obtained when participants were in the 4th and 5th grades, and smoking initiation was assessed when students were in the 7th and 8th grades.

A representative sample of 1,075 children in the 1st through 5th grades were recruited from 15 elementary schools in one school district in western Oregon to participate in the Oregon Youth Substance Use Study. Data presented here are from 319 children who were enrolled in the 3rd or 4th grade at the time of the first assessment.

At the first assessment (T1), teachers reported on children's behavior using the Children's Social Behavior Scale for Teachers (Crick, 1996). This scale consists of three subscales: Overt Aggressive Behavior (alpha = .90; mean = 1.26; SD = 2.33), Relational Aggressive Behavior (alpha = .93; mean = 5.46; SD = 5.66), and Pro-Social Behavior (alpha = .93; mean = 5.11; SD = 3.86). Teachers reported on children's social skills using the Walker-McConnell Scale of Social Competence and School Adjustment (Walker & McConnell,

1995). This scale also consists of three subscales: Teacher-Preferred Behavior (alpha = .91; mean = 22.53; SD = 5.66), Peer-Preferred Behavior (alpha = .94; mean = 28.49; SD = 5.99), and School Adjustment Behavior (alpha = .96; mean = 36.76; SD = 8.33). At first and fourth assessment, students reported if they tried cigarettes using the following item: "Have you ever tried a cigarette/cigar"?

At the third assessment, parents reported on the antisocial behavior of their child's friends using an adaptation of items from the Delinquent subscale of the Child Behavior Checklist (alpha = .76; mean = 1.65; SD = 1.90; Achenbach, 1991).

At T1, 4.9% of 4th graders and 5.1% of 5th graders had tried cigarettes. By T4, 20.4% of the 7th graders and 24.8% of the 8th graders had tried cigarettes. We predicted the initiation of cigarette use between T1 and T4 from teachers' ratings of children's behavior across the six subscales—overt aggression, relational aggression, prosocial behavior, teacher-preferred behavior, peer-preferred behavior, and school adjustment. Analyses predicted trying smoking at T4, controlling for trying at T1, age, and gender. To assess differential prediction as a function of age and gender, we included interactions between each teacher variable, age, and gender.

As shown in Table 16.1, for both genders, overt aggression significantly predicted initiation of cigarette use between T1 and T4. Gender interacted with teacher-preferred behavior and school adjustment. For males, teacher-preferred behavior marginally predicted initiation of smoking, and school adjustment significantly predicted initiation of smoking. For females, these teacher-rated behaviors did not predict initiation of smoking.

We dichotomized our predictors to identify those children who were most at risk in terms of their overt aggression and lower social skills. For overt aggression, the cutting

Table 16.1 Prediction of Trying Cigarettes at T4 From Teachers' Rating of Behavior at T1

Variable	Odds Ratio	95% Confidence Interval
Try at T1	93.89***	11.17, 789.07
Grade	1.70	0.91, 2.16
Gender	2.40	0.12, 47.26
Teacher preferred	1.12[a]	0.99, 1.27
School adjustment	0.90**	1.04, 1.19
Overt aggression	1.26**	1.07, 1.50
Gender × Teacher Preferred	0.85*,[b]	1.03, 1.36
Gender × School Adjustment	1.12*	1.02, 1.22

NOTE: Because boys are coded as 0, and females as 1, simple slopes are for boys
a. $p < .10$
b. Reciprocal of odds ratio = 1.18
*$p < .05$; **$p < .01$; ***$p < .001$

point was at the 85th percentile, whereas for teacher-preferred behavior and school adjustment, the cutting point was at the 20th percentile. Data were reanalyzed using multivariate logistic regression. Results showed that both girls and boys rated as high in overt aggression were three times as likely to start smoking (odds ratio [OR] = 3.21; 95% confidence interval [CI] = 1.18, 8.67). Boys who did not display appropriate levels of school adjustment were four times as likely to smoke (reciprocal of OR = 4.05; 95% CI = 1.46, 11.26), and girls who displayed lower levels of teacher-preferred behavior were three times more likely to smoke (reciprocal of OR = 3.11; 95% CI = 1.05, 9.26). Thus, both boys and girls who were identified by their teachers in the 4th and 5th grades as overtly aggressive or as displaying poor social skills were more likely to initiate smoking sometime during the next 3 years.

Based on Patterson and Dishion's (Dishion, 1990; Patterson, Reid, & Dishion, 1992) model of the development of antisocial behavior patterns, we hypothesized that association with deviant peers explains the relationship between early, teacher-identified aggressive behavior and poor social skills, and subsequent initiation of cigarette use. Although trying cigarettes ($r = .25$), overt

aggression ($r = .27$), teacher-preferred behavior ($r = -.21$), and school adjustment ($r = -.26$) were related to parent's rating of friend's delinquency at T3 and friend's delinquency was related to trying at T4 ($r = .25$), friends' delinquency did not mediate the effect of early teacher-rated behavior on subsequent smoking. However, with all four predictors in the equation, friends' delinquency remained a significant independent predictor of initiation of cigarette use by T4 (OR = 1.31; 95% CI = 1.11, 1.54; $p < .01$).

IMPLICATION OF STUDY RESULTS

This longitudinal study confirms the role of early overt aggression, poor social skills, and weak school adjustment in the elementary grades as predictors for initiation of tobacco use in the middle school grades. A brief measure of overt aggression predicted subsequent tobacco use for both boys and girls. The role of overt aggression in predicting other problem behaviors has been well established, and this behavior profile can be rated reliably by teachers as early as preschool (Severson & Walker, 2002). However, the role of overt aggression has been less well established for females. In addition to aggression, factors such as adjustment to the expectations of teachers and teacher-preferred social skills, such as being attentive and engaging in academic tasks, appear to play a significant role in predicting the smoking initiation, particularly for males.

Teacher ratings can provide a cost-effective way of identifying children exhibiting antisocial or aggressive behavior as well as internalizing children who are socially withdrawn (Severson & Walker, 2002). Walker and Severson (1990) have provided a systematic method for using teacher judgment in a multiple-gating system to provide for the screening of all students for behavior disorders in the elementary grades. When teacher judgments are structured and solicited in the right context, they can be highly accurate and extremely useful (Severson & Walker, 2002). Other researchers with at-risk child and youth populations have expressed similar observations about the value of teacher judgments. As noted earlier, Jackson et al. (1990) found that classroom teachers, when using a structured teacher rating form, were more accurate compared with both mothers' and fathers' CBCL externalizing scores in predicting a boy's arrest frequencies in early adolescence. Dishion and Patterson (1993) also advocate the use of teacher ratings as a first step in the screening for antisocial behaviors.

Models of social aggression and the development of delinquent behavior have postulated that children who display high rates of aggressive behavior in the early elementary grades tend to be rejected by most of their peers and often gravitate toward friends who are similarly rejected. When this happens, their risk status for felony offending tends to accelerate markedly (Patterson et al., 1992). As shown here, the participating parents' reports of their child's association with "delinquent friends" contributed independently to their smoking initiation. The combination of early, overt aggressive behavior as

reported by the teacher and association with delinquent peers as reported by the parents could provide more confidence and accuracy in targeting a child as being at higher risk for tobacco and other drug use.

In addition to providing a readily accessible child-youth population that affords the implementation of sensitive, multiple-gating, screening-identification procedures, schools also provide an excellent context for the combined or integrated use of universal and selected intervention approaches (Walker et al., 1996). Universal interventions are typically applied in schools to achieve primary prevention goals or outcomes, whereas selected interventions address the needs of more severely involved students and achieve secondary or tertiary prevention. Public health approaches to the prevention of smoking have successfully delivered antismoking curricula through universal intervention approaches that target all students in a classroom or school. The Second Step Program, developed by the Committee for Children, teaches four target skills to all students in Grades K–9 for the purpose of preventing violence and is an example of an effective intervention approach for use on a schoolwide basis. The Second Step skills are (a) anger management, (b) conflict resolution, (c) impulse control, and (d) empathy. This universal intervention has been proven effective in changing students' attitudes and behavior (Committee for Children, 1992) and is an exemplar of the increasing use of universal interventions in schools for the purpose of achieving primary prevention goals and outcomes.

Selected interventions are generally required to adequately address the needs and problems of more severely at-risk student populations. When selected interventions are combined with the effective use of universal screening procedures having multiple-gating features, at-risk children and youth can be targeted and served very effectively within the context of schooling. The use of targeted interventions that focus on high-risk children and youth early in their school careers is an approach that offers substantial advantages (Institute of Medicine, 1994; Tolan, Gucera, & Kendall, 1995). Targeted interventions, for example, have the potential to increase coverage and population impact when compared with universal intervention programs; this approach is more efficient because only children in need receive the intervention. However, the success of targeted interventions depends heavily on having in place an accurate method of identifying children exhibiting high-risk behaviors. When such children are correctly identified and diagnosed, the impact of the intervention is enhanced. False-negative classification errors deny children the opportunity to receive the intervention that may benefit them. False-positive errors result in wasted resources, expose children to unnecessary programs, and risk the negative effects of labeling (McConaughy, 1993). As shown here, children targeted for smoking prevention programs could be those who were high in overt aggression and displayed poor social skills, as measured by school adjustment and teacher-preferred behavior.

Two of the authors have been involved in a long-term effort to develop, test, and validate a targeted approach to the prevention of emerging antisocial behavior patterns among at-risk children in Grades K–2. This selected intervention program was developed initially through a 4-year federal grant and is called First Step to Success (Walker et al., 1998). First Step involves the target child, peers, the teacher, and parents in a coordinated, 3-month intervention designed to foster school readiness skills at home and to teach and develop an adaptive behavior pattern at school for ensuring school success.

The First Step intervention has been included in a number of recent, national reviews of effective, early intervention programs (e.g., Greenberg, Domitrovich, & Bumbarger, 1999; Leff, Power, Manz, Costigan, & Nabors, 2001).

In sum, there is increasing evidence for high interrelationships between multiple problem behaviors of youth (Brener & Collins, 1998), and it appears that overt aggression exhibited early in a child's school career may be a strong predictor of the initiation of later smoking. Teachers can provide accurate assessments of overt aggression and social skills for students in their classes and using standardized assessments and rating measures that have been developed for this purpose can enhance their contributions further. A number of interventions designed to reduce aggressive antisocial behaviors in young children are now available, and many have strong empirical evidence for their efficacy from published randomized trials (Metzler, Eddy, & Taylor, 2002). Schools have the ability, and demonstrated interest, in adopting classwide and schoolwide universal interventions that not only can achieve primary prevention outcomes for marginally at-risk students but can also create a context in which selected interventions for targeted students can be more effective. The use of selected interventions could ameliorate or significantly reduce a child's overt aggression before it escalates into a more serious set of behavior problems. Early targeted interventions in school that involve the most important social agents in a child's life (i.e., parents, peers, and teachers) could provide cost-effective ways to reduce antisocial behavior, prevent the escalation of school-related problem behaviors, and provide an effective early intervention to prevent or reduce tobacco use.

CHAPTER 17

Preventive Interventions for Externalizing Disorders in Adolescents

KEN C. WINTERS
GERALD AUGUST
WILLA LEITTEN

Adolescent externalizing disorders refer to the cluster of highly co-occurring behaviors and disorders that include conduct disorders, oppositional defiant disorders, attention deficit hyperactivity disorder (ADHD), substance use disorders, and more recent to the literature, problem gambling.[1] Externalizing disorders are likely influenced by several personal (e.g., personality, attitudes, values) and environmental (e.g., peers, parenting practices, intervention or treatment experiences) factors (Crowley & Riggs, 1995). The emerging discipline of developmental psychopathology provides a conceptual framework applicable to the study of the etiology, prevention, and treatment of externalizing disorders of youth (Clark & Winters, in press). Developmental psychopathology is a macroparadigm that emphasizes the contrast between normal and atypical development. This conceptualization allows for qualitative changes in functioning over time and the influence by mediator and moderator variables at varying developmental stages from adolescence to young adulthood.

In the past, preventive interventions for youth with externalizing disorders, many of which have focused on substance abuse, were designed as one-size-fits-all. The disappointing results have drawn attention to the complexity and multiplicity of the risk factors involved. To prevent the onset, maintenance, and course of externalizing behaviors among adolescents, a prevention framework must include strategies crafted to respond to the unique risk profiles of various subgroups of the population. Consequently, prevention efforts initiated early in a child's life, adjusted with emerging developmental tasks, and sustained over time are the best possible tools available today.

EARLY-STARTER PATHWAY
TO EXTERNALIZING DISORDERS

One developmental pathway to externalizing disorders discussed in the literature is defined by early signs of aggression. The likelihood of early aggression is increased by deficits within the child and harmful influences in the family, peer group, school, and community (Dobkin, Tremblay, Masse, & Vitaro, 1995; Hawkins, Catalano, & Miller, 1992; Kellam, Brown, Rubin, & Ensminger, 1983; Shedler & Block, 1990). The result is a progression of disruptive behavior and failed skill acquisition. In time, this leads to academic failure, peer rejection, and alienation from school, which escalates to more serious conduct problems (Elliott, Huizinga, & Menard, 1989). This pathway has been labeled the "early-starter" model of antisocial behavior (Patterson, 1986; Patterson, DeBaryshe, & Ramsey, 1989).

Research has shown that the overwhelming majority of early aggressive children will continue to engage in antisocial behavior of one sort or another at every stage of life (Moffitt, 1993). The pattern of stability across time is matched only by its cross-situational consistency. These adolescents are at risk for drug abuse and are in jeopardy of experiencing unstable employment, homelessness, vehicular accidents, multiple and unstable relationships, domestic violence, child abuse, and psychiatric disorders (Caspi, Elder, & Bem, 1987). Because these youth engage in antisocial behaviors and in other adultlike behaviors at an early age when their peers yearn for such adult privileges, they may come to serve as temporary role models (see Finnegan, 1990). During the adolescent years, early starters often coalesce into groups, which then function as magnets, drawing in other teens who have no preexisting risk factors but who are nevertheless attracted to the adultlike status of their early-starter peers. In time, these formerly prosocial teens may join the adolescent drug culture. Because the cost to society resulting from the antisocial actions of early starters is high, with cost magnified by the contagion influence on their peers, there is compelling evidence to target early starters for a prevention response.

PREVENTIVE
INTERVENTION TARGETS

Over the course of development, all children are challenged by stage-salient tasks, which provide opportunities for them to develop emotional, cognitive, and social competencies necessary for healthy adjustment. During the early- and middle-childhood years, these developmental tasks fall into three primary domains: (a) tasks requiring emotional regulation, (b) tasks involving adaptive prosocial peer affiliation, and (c) tasks requiring literacy acquisition, achievement motivation, and positive attitudes toward education. For the child, the key to successful competence acquisition is support, guidance, and instruction provided by primary caregivers. Aggressive children on the early-starter pathway are inclined to use antisocial solutions in each of these domains. However, a child's level of competence or deficit in these task domains does not develop in a vacuum. Parents of aggressive children often contribute to their child's poor adjustment by virtue of their own aberrant personality characteristics (e.g., authoritarian parenting style). This style of parenting combined with a child's difficult temperament or aversive behavior sets in motion a process of reciprocal coercion.

The development of effective preventive interventions requires the identification of key deficits and assets associated with risk and protection from future externalizing disorders. Whereas the healthy developing child achieves competence in predictable sequences, the early-starter child readily demonstrates deficiencies in attempts to reach this competence. In what follows, the intended changes of a preventive intervention aimed at early starters are specified. The primary focus is on child and family factors.

CHILD-FOCUSED TARGETS

Emotional Regulation

Youth in the early-starter group are, from infancy, prone to respond to stressful situations with high levels of negative emotionality. They express negative emotions without awareness either of their feeling states or those of others, thereby reducing the chances of regulating expressions in an appropriate fashion (Eisenberg et al., 1997). As a consequence of negative emotionality as well as caregiving relationships characterized by unpredictability, hostility, nonresponsiveness, or some combination of all three, the early-starter child's emotional reactions to social demands are likely to be ineffective. This pattern of poor social behavior often takes the form of aggression, which leads to negative reactions from the child's caregiver and a further strengthening in the child that antisocial strategies are his or her only coping options (Lochman & Dodge, 1994).

The goal of the intervention is to sort out the difficulties with emotional regulation. Strategies should enhance the child's ability to (a) recognize internal and external cues signifying emotional states, (b) assign and monitor appropriate labels, (c) learn appropriate verbal expression skills, (d) understand the causes and meanings of the emotions of others, and (e) develop skills for impulse and anger control.

Prosocial Peer Affiliation

Early-starters are deficient in social skills. Over time, egocentric, nonconforming,

oppositional, and hostile behaviors emerge, setting off a cascade of negative peer interactions. These negative interactions result in disapproval, ostracism, rejection, and victimization by peers. As a consequence, opportunities for the development of cooperation and negotiation skills, aggression control, and perspective-taking abilities are diminished (Ladd & Asher, 1985).

The intervention goal is to assist with problems in prosocial peer affiliation. Intervention strategies should seek to teach behavioral social skills that (a) facilitate peer acceptance and making friendships, (b) encourage the use of effective communication exchanges, and (c) teach alternatives to aggression.

School Adjustment

Aggressive children are often academically delayed and lack the behavior control and motivation to experience academic success (Moffitt, 1993). Collectively, poor learning skills, attention capacity, and motivation impair daily school performance, behavior, and academic achievement. These disruptive and nonconforming behaviors have a further negative impact. The behavior leads teachers to have negative attributions and low expectations for the child. The result is a poor bond to school, expressed in terms of decreased compliance, lack of adherence to rules, alienation from school, and increased risk for academic failure (Hawkins, Doveck, & Lishner, 1988).

The intervention goal is to increase the student's academic success by applying instructional methods and curricula to improve basic learning skills, using techniques to help with on-task behavior and attention, providing incentives to enhance interest and motivation, and working to cultivate positive attitudes toward school.

PARENT-FOCUSED TARGETS

Behavioral Control

Parents of early starters provide inconsistent and power-assertive discipline methods (Patterson, 1982), monitor their children's activities less often (Haapasalo & Tremblay, 1994; Patterson et al., 1989), and use harsh and negative communication with their children. Over time, these aversive interactions are played out, escalating into intense and aggressive confrontations. The children's use of coercive techniques may crystallize in time, thus affecting interactions with teachers and peers and lead to annoyance and rejection (Snyder, 1991).

The intervention goal is to teach and train parents to improve the management of their child's behavior. To achieve this goal, parents need to acknowledge the child's positive behavior and reward compliance, communicate clear expectations and consequences, employ consistent and nonviolent techniques to increase appropriate and decrease inappropriate behaviors, monitor and supervise their children, and provide encouragement and praise.

Emotional Relatedness

In addition to deficiencies in behavior management, parents of early starters often do not display affection and are insensitive to their child's emotional states. When these relationships are characterized by unpredictability and unresponsiveness, children react with anxiety, frustration, anger, or ambivalence that may become a pattern of expectations with others (Greenberg, Kusche, & Speltz, 1990). For the aggressive child, such working models may include the child's expectations that the world is unsafe and others are not to be trusted (Greenberg, Speltz, & Deklyen, 1993).

The intervention goal is to help repair deficiencies in emotional relatedness between the parent and child. Intervention strategies should encourage parents to provide sensitive and supportive responses in times of emotional distress, model effective communication, and use planning, negotiation, and guidance.

Involvement in Schooling

When parents are involved in schooling, children show improved grades, test scores, academic work, attitudes toward school, self-esteem, and participation (Christenson, Hurley, Sheridan, & Fenstermacher, 1997). In contrast, parents of early starters often harbor cynical attitudes toward educators and the likelihood of their child's school success. Likewise, educators often hold tacit beliefs that families of aggressive children are not invested in their children's education. Sometimes, as a result of their own educational limitations and negative school experiences, parents may discount academic objectives and show skepticism regarding the value of education. Ultimately, they may fail to stimulate their child's intellectual curiosity or be aware of their child's classroom efforts or successes.

The intervention goal is for the parents to show a level of interest in their child's education, reward and encourage academic effort, and assist the child in managing academic and classroom difficulties as they arise. To enhance parental involvement in school, strategies should seek to increase contact between homes and schools, review and monitor homework, and participate in parent-initiated educational activities.

AN EXAMPLE OF AN INDICATED PREVENTIVE INTERVENTION: EARLY RISERS "SKILLS FOR SUCCESS" PROGRAM

The Early Risers Program is a comprehensive preventive intervention that targets both risk and protective factors pertinent to the early-starter pathway over time and across community, school, peers, families, and child systems. The program conforms to a developmental-psychopathology-ecological perspective on the prevention of externalizing disorders (see Tarter et al., 1999). The developmental-psychopathology approach incorporates the effects that the child and environmental risk factors have on normal developmental tasks of childhood and the potential impact of these risks on the development of a disorder over time. The ecological perspective emphasizes the multiple contextual influences that affect child development, including peer affiliations; family relationships; and neighborhood, school, and community influences, as well as cultural values and belief systems. The program is designed to select candidate children by virtue of those who show early aggressive behavior patterns (e.g., bullying, teasing, frequent physical fighting), but the selection criteria could be organized around other risk behaviors as well (e.g., school adjustment problems). The program's package of intervention activities attempts to interrupt the early-starter pathway by positively modifying both developmental and ecological factors that challenge key child and parent competencies. As a result, both child and parent are better prepared to cope with risk factors that emerge. A summary of the program's main features follows.

The first step in securing an intervention in any particular community setting is establishing a collaborative partnership to provide administrative direction and oversight of the program. Ideally, the collaborative is represented by key community sectors, which may include (a) one or more local child or family service agencies, (b) the public education system, and (c) a consulting research-based structure. The explicit mission of the collaborative is to develop culturally competent, family-centered systems of care

that provide a wide array of educational, health, and social services for families of at-risk children.

The Early Risers "Skills for Success" intervention model includes two complementary components, CORE and FLEX, which when delivered in tandem form a comprehensive and coordinated package of intervention actions. CORE consists of evidence-based technology of change procedures, informed by social development theory, which seeks to ameliorate *child-level* risk by building strengths in key developmental competencies within schools, as well as peer and family systems. CORE can be implemented continuously for 2 or more years following the kindergarten year and includes (a) a 6-week Summer School experience, (b) a Monitoring and Mentoring School Consultation Program during the regular school year, (c) an evening Family Program that offers concurrent parent and child education and skills training groups, and (d) an optional after-school program (for urban participants).

FLEX is a proactive-type family education, support, and empowerment intervention individually tailored to address unique sources of *parent* and *family* needs. The FLEX component includes a deliberate process of family and child need assessment and asset appraisal, initiates further asset building through strategic goal setting, and accesses formal and informal community resources through a negotiated contract with the participant. The underlying goal of FLEX is to empower families to remedy the personal and contextual conditions that create stress in their lives and negatively affect their capacity as parents to nurture and support their child's healthy development. Ultimately, the goal of FLEX is to increase parent investment in their child's healthy development by promoting competence in three dimensions of parenting practice—namely, behavioral control, emotional relatedness, and involvement in education and schooling.

The Early Risers Program was designed to function as an integrated services model that uses existing programs in a community. Although it identifies candidate youth in the school setting (with a standardized test of aggression), the model includes intensive involvement from several youth-serving organizations in the community, including the local YMCAs, YWCAs, and mental health centers. Operational integration is enhanced by the program's family advocates who serve as the primary intervention agents by providing coordination and direct service across CORE and FLEX intervention components. Ideally, family advocates are recruited from the same communities that serve program participants. As such, they are knowledgeable about cultural norms and local informal resources and have access to their agencies' programs. They also have established lines of referral to health care systems in the community as well as in-service opportunities and staff consultation that provide valuable resources for the program. In this key role, the family advocates can marshal resources and services that are effective for leveraging change.

Future directions include examination of the unique aspects of community-delivered prevention trials that contribute to program acceptability and sustainability, as well as other aspects of program dynamics that affect outcome. Ultimately, an evaluation of the program's effectiveness in preventing the onset and continuation of drug use as these high-risk children enter adolescence is obligatory.

SUMMARY AND CONCLUDING THOUGHTS

To effectively combat the pernicious effects of externalizing disorders, major leaders in the field have called for the adoption of a perspective where prevention is positioned at the forefront of a comprehensive spectrum of mental health services. If prevention is to fulfill its promise, innovative programs must first be tested under rigorous, controlled trials. Once their efficiency has been verified, these programs then need to be transported to community settings and tested under real-life conditions. Last, once proven to be effective, program developers must package their programs for wide-scale dissemination to the general public.

Early Risers is undergoing an extensive evaluation. Prior to the main evaluation in which we look at the behavioral outcomes of the youth who participate in the program as they enter into the drug-using years, we are undertaking a process evaluation. One major aim of this evaluation is to determine the extent to which a multi-component program such as Early Risers can be assimilated into the community. For example, we are examining the extent to which assimilation depends on the requirement that local stakeholders are requested both to assume some ownership of the program and to identify funding streams that will support the deployment of the family advocates. We are also exploring the extent to which competing responsibilities at the county level and conflicting priorities at the school level are impediments to program implementation and community integration.

Given that recruitment, active participation, and retention of program participants are all challenges, a second goal of the evaluation is to identify factors that enhance motivation for participation in a time-intensive prevention program such as Early Risers. Early results from a survey of participating families have highlighted the importance of several external reinforcements that we have built into the program that appear to encourage program satisfaction and that help to establish bonds with the program and staff. These reinforcements include provisions for transportation, holiday celebrations, and a summer program that focuses on recreational activities.

We hope that comprehensive prevention programs can be exported for large-scale implementation. A demonstration of their success should convince communities of their cost and social benefits.

NOTE

1. Estimates of many of these externalizing disorders have benefited from several epidemiological studies. Although age, gender, and sampling strategies, among other factors, naturally affect population estimates across studies, the epidemiological literature has fairly consistently reported population rates among youth for ADHD and conduct disorders to be approximately 2% to 5% and 2% to 4%, respectively (Clark & Winters, in press). However, studies of youth problem or pathological gambling rates are not as plentiful and have not benefited from sophisticated research designs (e.g., absence of rigorous diagnostic measures). Nevertheless, extant studies largely based on screening tools have yielded provocatively high rates, ranging from 1% to 9% past year (median = 6%) (National Research Council, 1999).

Part II

Section B

Personality and Other Predispositions

CHAPTER 18

Genetic Basis of Substance Use and Dependence

Implications for Prevention in High-Risk Youth

CARYN LERMAN
FREDA PATTERSON
ALEXANDRA SHIELDS

Adolescent tobacco, alcohol, and illicit drug use are widely recognized as major public health problems (Windle & Windle, 1999). According to recent data, 64% of adolescents reported ever having smoked cigarettes, 79% reported ever having consumed alcoholic beverages, and 26% reported having used illicit drugs in the last month (Centers for Disease Control and Prevention [CDC], 2002d; Johnston, O'Malley, & Bachman, 2002; Substance Abuse and Mental Health Services Administration [SAMHSA], 2001). After increasing steadily in the 1990s, rates of tobacco and alcohol use have recently leveled off or declined; however, rates of usage of most illicit drugs have continued to climb (CDC, 2002d; Johnston et al., 2002).

With regard to adolescent tobacco use, recent data suggest that a substantial proportion of young people are at risk for becoming addicted smokers. In a recent survey, 28% of adolescents reported having smoked on at least 1 day in the past month, and 14% reported having smoked on at least 20 of the last 30 days (CDC, 2002d). Among high school seniors who indicated that they currently smoked, 29% reported symptoms that met the *DSM-III-R* (*Diagnostic and Statistical Manual of Mental Disorders*, 3rd ed., rev.; American Psychiatric Association [APA], 1987) criteria for nicotine dependence (Stanton, 1995). Moreover, over half of adolescents said they experienced withdrawal symptoms following an attempt to quit, and 70% regretted ever having started smoking (CDC, 1998c; Colby, Tiffany, Shiffman, & Niaura, 2000). These data suggest that patterns of early use among adolescents may develop into lifelong nicotine addiction.

Alcohol use and abuse are also highly prevalent among adolescents. In the 1997 Youth Risk Behavior Survey (YRBS), 51% of high school students reported having had at least one drink in the last month, and 33% reported binge drinking (having five or more drinks) on at least one occasion in the last month (CDC, 1998d). Symptoms of alcohol dependence (i.e., tolerance, withdrawal, drinking more or longer than intended) were also prevalent in this age group, with 12% reporting some or all these symptoms before leaving high school (Chung, Martin, Armstrong, & Labouvie, 2002).

Rates of illicit drug use by adolescents in the previous month were reported to be higher than for any other age group (SAMHSA, 2001) and have increased among older high school students (10th and 12th graders) (Johnston et al., 2002; SAMHSA, 2001). Marijuana is the most commonly used illicit drug with prevalence rates ranging from 1.1% to13.7% (SAMHSA, 2001). Over half of adolescents who smoked marijuana in the last month stated they "wanted to cut down," but almost 40% said they had built up a tolerance to the drug (SAMHSA, 2001; Weinberg, Rahdert, Colliver, & Glantz, 1998). Ecstasy use has increased by 5% since 1996 in this age group, whereas use of inhalants and cocaine has decreased slightly in recent years (Johnston et al., 2002).

To develop and implement more effective programs for adolescent substance abuse prevention, a greater understanding of the determinants of these behaviors is needed. Although much has been learned about the social and environmental factors that promote substance use in this group, less is known about the biological determinants. Advances in the field of genetics are beginning to fill this gap in our knowledge. Several converging lines of research have provided consistent support for heritable influences on adolescent substance use and dependence.

This chapter summarizes the evidence for the role of genetic factors in substance abuse and describes how insights from this line of research might be applied to the design and implementation of novel approaches to prevent substance use and dependence among high-risk youth.

We begin by presenting a bio-behavioral model of adolescent substance use, an overarching framework for integrating research on genetics, personality, and substance use patterns. Following a brief introduction to the methods used in genetics research, we summarize briefly the evidence for genetic influences on tobacco use, alcohol use, and use of illicit drugs. We then present evidence for the mediating role of heritable personality traits involving sensation seeking and impulse control. Finally, we explore how this new knowledge might be used to develop better prevention approaches and the challenges inherent in applying these findings to adolescent populations.

BIO-BEHAVIORAL MODEL OF ADOLESCENT SUBSTANCE USE

A bio-behavioral model of adolescent substance abuse is proposed as an overarching conceptual framework for understanding the bio-behavioral mechanisms by which genetic factors may contribute to substance use in adolescents. This model is an extension and integration of the biosocial model (Zuckerman & Kuhlman, 2000) and the bio-behavioral model of tobacco use (Lerman & Niaura, in press). As illustrated in Figure 18.1, there are three basic tenets of this model.

First, there are multiple biological pathways by which genetic factors may influence adolescent substance use. Genetic variation, together with early environment, contributes to brain structure and function. Some genetic variants (referred to as "alleles") give rise to

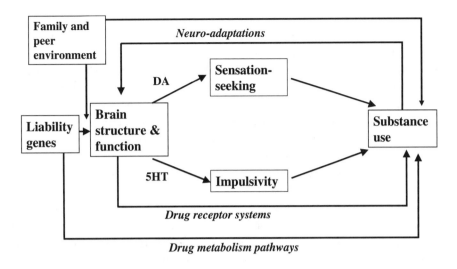

Figure 18.1   Bio-Behavioral Model of Adolescent Substance Use

perturbations in neurotransmitter pathways. Evidence presented later suggests that the neurotransmitter pathways most relevant to substance use are those that regulate the brain's reward mechanism (i.e., dopamine [DA]) and modulate the organism's capacity for impulse control (i.e., serotonin [5HT]). Genetic variation also determines the expression and function of neural receptor systems that determine the positive and negative reinforcing effects of specific substances of abuse. Although variation in the dopamine and serotonin pathways may increase the vulnerability to substance abuse in general, differences in drug-specific receptor systems may drive the choice of specific substances of abuse (i.e., nicotine versus alcohol). The pleasurable and aversive effects of specific drugs of abuse are also mediated by genetically determined individual differences in the capacity to activate and eliminate drugs.

Adaptive theories of substance abuse posit that drug use is motivated, in part, by attempts to correct or "self-medicate" these inherited deficits in neurotransmitter and receptor systems (Bardo, Donohew, & Harrington 1996). Chronic use, in turn, produces neuroadaptive changes that sustain continued use and promote dependence (Dackis & O'Brien, 2001).

A second premise of this model is that these neurobiological influences on substance use risk are mediated, in part, by individual differences in temperament or personality, particularly traits involving sensation seeking and impulsivity (Zuckerman & Kuhlman, 2000). Both traits have been shown to have a significant heritable component (Eaves & Eysenck, 1975; Koopmans, Boomsma, Heath, & van Doornen, 1995). Although complex behavioral traits such as these are thought to be oligogenic (arising from the interactions of multiple genes), evidence presented later suggests that the dopamine pathway may be relatively more important in determining levels of sensation-seeking trait, whereas the serotonin system may play a greater role in impulse control.

Third, this model suggests that sensation seeking and impulsivity influence substance use. Abundant animal and human data have shown that organisms high in sensation-seeking trait are more likely to self-administer drugs of abuse and to experience greater reinforcing effects from these drugs (Dellu, Piazza, Mayo, Le Moal, & Simon, 1996; Laviola, Adriani, Terranova, & Gerra, 1999). This propensity is most likely to lead to problematic patterns of substance abuse in individuals who have deficits in impulse control or those who discount the negative consequences of substance use (Mitchell, 1999; Petry & Casarella, 1999). In addition to these direct effects, these personality traits may also increase substance abuse risk indirectly by facilitating exposure to particular environmental influences (Plomin, DeFries, & Loehlin, 1977). For example, a high sensation-seeking adolescent may be more likely to elicit particular parenting patterns and to choose peers who are more rebellious. These environmental influences, in turn, would promote substance use.

The bio-behavioral model is presented as a framework to explain the pathways by which genetic influences may affect adolescent substance use. However, it is clear that genetic predisposition is moderated by key psychological, sociocultural, and environmental influences that are not under genetic control (Heath & Martin, 1988; Kendler, 2001). Although a review of these nongenetic effects is beyond the scope of this chapter, the final section addresses how novel prevention approaches may prevent substance use in high-risk adolescents.

OVERVIEW OF GENETIC MODELS

Research using both animal and human models is advancing our understanding of the role of genetic factors in substance use. Animal models of drug addiction can manipulate genetic factors using selective breeding or "knock-outs" (e.g., mice lacking a critical gene) to explore general and specific genetic effects on behavioral responses to drugs and propensity to self-administer drugs. As reviewed by Crabbe (2002), this line of research has generated important knowledge about the role of genetic factors in initial sensitivity to drugs, neuroadaptive changes from chronic exposure, withdrawal syndromes, and reinforcing effects. Of particular relevance to adolescent substance use, animal research is elucidating how the adolescent brain may be especially vulnerable to the stimulating effects of both novel environment and drugs of abuse (Laviola et al., 1999). This work suggests that adolescence is a critical period during which exposure to drugs may interfere with more adaptive coping strategies and produce lifelong behavioral substance abuse patterns.

In humans, twin models have been used to explore the relative contribution of genetic and environmental factors to substance use and dependence. This is accomplished by comparing concordance rates for a particular trait in monozygotic twins, who share all their genes in common, with those for dizygotic twins, who share roughly 50% of their genes (Kendler, 2001). As described in greater detail below, this methodology has been used to study the role of heritable factors for smoking, alcohol use, and use of illicit drugs.

Once a particular behavioral trait (also referred to as a "phenotype") has been established as heritable, molecular genetic approaches are used to identify the specific genetic variants that may be responsible. One such approach identifies candidate genes based on neurobiological or biochemical pathways (e.g., dopamine or serotonin genes) and uses a case-control study design to compare the frequency of genetic variants (alleles) in these pathways among persons with and without the phenotype (e.g., nicotine dependent persons versus nondependent persons) (Lerman & Berrettini, in press; Sullivan, Eaves, Kendler, & Neale, 2001). Several studies employing the candidate gene approach to investigate substance abuse genes are described later. The role of specific genetic variants can also be investigated using family-based designs that examine allele sharing or allele transmission for candidate genes within families (Spielman & Ewens, 1996). This latter approach controls for potential bias due to ethnic admixture but has less statistical power and is more costly to implement.

In contrast to these hypothesis-driven approaches, genetic linkage analysis can be used to search for as yet unidentified genetic variants that may be linked with substance use phenotypes. This approach uses families or relative pairs (e.g., sibling pairs) and looks for linkage with anonymous markers across the genome. Because the effect sizes of any individual gene conferring susceptibility to a behavioral trait are expected to be small (Comings et al., 2001), this approach requires a large number of family members. As described later, the results of such studies are beginning to reveal regions of interest in the genome; however, it is likely to take several years before specific loci are identified and validated as important in substance use and dependence.

Next, we summarize the literature on the heritability and specific genetic effects for tobacco use, alcohol use, and use of illicit drugs. Although most of these studies used adult populations, we highlight investigations that included adolescent participants. The results of both adolescent and adult studies provide insights into the bio-behavioral basis of substance use and its relevance to prevention in high-risk youth.

Genetic Contributions to Tobacco Use

Abundant data from twin studies provide evidence for the heritability of cigarette smoking. Using the Australian twin registry, Heath and Martin (1993) found that inherited factors accounted for 53% of the variance in smoking initiation. More recent data suggest that the heritability of a diagnosis of nicotine dependence is even higher (Kendler et al., 1999). Sullivan and Kendler (1999) summarized data from a large number of twin studies indicating that additive genetic effects account for 56% of the variance in smoking initiation and 67% of the variance in nicotine dependence. Significant genetic influences have also been documented for age at smoking onset (Heath, Kirk, Meyer, & Martin, 1999) and for smoking persistence (Madden et al., 1999).

Genes in the dopamine pathway have been studied most extensively with respect to tobacco use and addiction. It is speculated that individuals with low-activity genetic variants may experience greater reinforcement from nicotine because of its dopamine-stimulating effects. In support of this hypothesis are three studies showing a higher prevalence of the more rare A1 or B1 allele of the Dopamine 2 receptor (DRD2) gene among smokers than among nonsmokers (Comings et al., 1996; Noble et al., 1994; Spitz et al., 1998). However, a small family-based analysis did not provide evidence for significant linkage of smoking to the DRD2 locus (Bierut et al., 2000).

In a case-control study of smokers and nonsmokers, Lerman and colleagues (Lerman et al., 1999) found that DRD2 interacted with the dopamine transporter (DAT) gene in its effects on smoking behavior. The DAT polymorphism is of particular interest because the 9-repeat allele has been associated with a 22% reduction in dopamine transporter protein (Heinz et al., 2000). Because a reduction in dopamine transporter level would result in less clearance and greater bio-availability of dopamine, it is speculated that individuals who have the 9-repeat may have less need to use nicotine to stimulate dopamine activity. The association of the DAT gene with smoking behavior has been supported in one study (Sabol et al., 1999) but not replicated in two other studies (Jorm et al., 2000; Vandenbergh et al., in press). Thus, the role of DAT in smoking behavior remains unclear.

The serotonin pathway is also under investigation in genetic studies of smoking behavior. Candidate polymorphisms (genetic variants) include those in genes involved in serotonin biosynthesis (e.g., tryptophan hydroxylase [TPH]) and serotonin reuptake (serotonin transporter, [5HTTLPR]). Two recent studies have shown that individuals who are homozygous for the more rare A allele of TPH are more likely to initiate smoking and to start smoking at an earlier age (Lerman et al., 2001; Sullivan et al., 2001). Although the 5HTTLPR was not associated with smoking status (Lerman et al., 1998), there is evidence that this polymorphism modifies the effect of anxiety-related traits on smoking behavior (Lerman et al., 2000).

Although genes in the dopamine and serotonin pathways may have generalized effects on risk for substance abuse, genes that regulate nicotine metabolism should be specifically relevant to smoking behavior. One hypothesis is that slower metabolizers of nicotine may be less prone to initiate smoking because they may experience more aversive effects (Pianezza, Sellers, & Tyndale, 1998). Once smoking is initiated, slower metabolizers may require fewer cigarettes to maintain nicotine titers at an optimal level (Benowitz, Perez-Stable, Herrera, & Jacob, 2002). Initial support for this premise was provided in a study of the P450 CYP2A6 gene, which encodes the key enzyme involved in metabolism of nicotine to inactive cotinine (Pianezza et al., 1998). Unfortunately, however, later studies did not support this finding and suggested that the CYP2A6 variant is much more rare than originally reported (London, Idle, Daly, & Coetzee, 1999; Sabol & Hamer, 1999).

Although genes regulating nicotine receptor function would be prime candidates for smoking risk, data on *functional* genetic variation in humans are not yet available. In two recent studies of the B2 nicotinic receptor, several single neucleotide polymorphisms (of unknown functional significance) were identified, but none were associated with smoking behavior (Lueders et al., 2002; Silverman, Raj, Mucci, & Hathaway, 2001).

As mentioned earlier, linkage analysis approaches can also be used to scan the genome for regions that may harbor nicotine dependence susceptibility genes. However, there are a limited number of reports using this approach. Straub and colleagues (Straub et al., 1999) performed a complete genomic scan to search for loci that may confer susceptibility to nicotine dependence. Using a sample of affected sibling pairs, linkage analysis provided preliminary evidence for linkage to regions on Chromosomes 2, 4, 10, 16, 17, and 18. However, these results were not statistically significant, and the sample size in this study (130 families) may not have been large enough to identify genes with small effects. Two other studies used families from the Collaborative Study on the Genetics of Alcoholism (COGA) and reported evidence for linkage of smoking behavior to Chromosomes 5 (Duggirala, Almasy, & Blangero, 1999), 6, and 9 (Bergen, Korczak, Weissbecker, & Goldstein, 1999). Notably, the regions identified in the different studies do not overlap. This may be attributable to the fact that regions identified in the COGA sample may harbor loci predisposing to addiction to both alcohol and smoking.

Genetic Contributions to Alcohol Use

As with tobacco, twin studies of alcohol use provide consistent evidence for significant genetic effects. Estimates for the proportion of variance accounted for by genetic factors range from about 30% to 70%, depending on whether the studies used population-based or treatment samples (Kendler, Gardner, Neale, & Prescott, 2001) and on the specific phenotype examined (van den Bree, Johnson, Neale, Svikis, et al., 1998). A study of over 1,500 twin pairs, 20 to 30 years old, reported that 47% of the variance in use (vs. abstinence) in males was attributable to genetic factors, with 48% of the variance due to shared environment (and the remainder due to individual environmental effects) (Heath & Martin, 1988). The comparable figures for females were 35% and 32%, respectively. Heritability estimates in other studies ranged from about 50% for alcohol dependence to 73% for early age of onset alcohol problems (McGue et al., 1992; Pickens & Svikis, 1991; Prescott & Kendler, 1999). Physical symptoms of alcohol dependence also appear to have a significant heritable component (e.g., binge drinking, withdrawal), although the potential behavioral consequences appear to be less heritable (e.g., job trouble, arrests) (Slutske et al., 1999). Of particular relevance to the biobehavioral model of substance abuse, there is evidence for shared genetic influences for tobacco and alcohol consumption (Swan, Carmelli, & Cardon, 1996).

The search for specific genetic effects on alcohol use has led to genes in key neurotransmitter pathways and genes that influence the metabolism of alcohol. Once again, the dopamine pathway has been a central focus of this research. An initial study relating the DRD2 A1 allele to alcoholism attracted a great deal of attention (Blum et al., 1990); however, several studies failed to replicate this initial result (Bolos et al., 1990; Cook et al., 1996). Noble (1993) reviewed nine independent studies including 491 alcoholics and 495 controls. Across these studies, the more rare A1 allele of the DRD2 gene was carried by 43% of alcoholics, compared with 25% of nonalcoholic controls. When only severe alcoholics were examined, the prevalence of the A1 allele was 56%. Hill and colleagues (Hill, Zezza, Wipprecht, Xu, & Neiswanger, 1999) used the more conservative family-based approach to test for linkage between DRD2 and alcoholism. Although an overall association with alcoholism was not supported, there was evidence for linkage when only severe cases were examined. Studies examining other genes within the dopamine pathway for association with alcoholism have yielded mostly negative results (Parsian, Chakraverty, Fisher, & Cloninger, 1997).

Genes in the serotonin pathway are also plausible candidates for alcohol dependence because of the effects of alcohol on brain serotonin levels (Lesch & Merschdorf, 2000). The low activity S allele of the serotonin transporter gene (5HTTLPR) has been linked with alcoholism in one family-based study (Lichtermann et al., 2000). Although the prevalence of this variant has not been found to differ significantly in case-control studies comparing alcoholics and nonalcoholics, there is evidence that it increases risk for particular alcoholism subtypes, including binge drinking (Matsushita et al., 2001) and early-onset alcoholism with violent features (Hallikainen et al., 1999). Similarly, the TPH gene has been linked with alcoholism with comorbid impulse control problems, such as antisocial behavior or suicidal tendencies (Ishiguro et al., 1999; Nielsen et al., 1998).

The most consistent evidence for genetic effects on alcoholism has been generated from studies of genes that regulate the metabolism of alcohol. Alcohol is converted to its major metabolite acetaldehyde by the enzyme alcohol dehydrogenase (ADH). Decreased metabolism results in more aversive effects of alcohol consumption, such as flushing and toxicity. A reduced activity allele of the ADH2 gene (ADH2*2) is found more commonly in Asian populations and has been shown to be protective for alcohol dependence in Chinese (Chen et al., 1999) and European (Borras et al., 2000) populations. There is some evidence that the genetic effect is stronger for males than for females (Whitfield et al., 1998). The reduced activity allele of ADH2 is also found more commonly in Ashkenazi Jewish populations and has been associated with reduced alcohol consumption among Jewish college students (Shea, Wall, Carr, & Li, 2001).

The opioid system has also been implicated in the reinforcing effects of alcohol, as well as other drugs of abuse (see next section). With respect to alcoholism, the results of initial studies have been mixed. Two studies have suggested that variants of the mu-opioid receptor gene may be associated with a general liability to substance dependence, including alcohol (Kranzler, Gelernter, O'Malley, Hernandez-Avila, & Kaufman, 1998; Schinka et al., 2002). However, another larger study did not find significant differences in allele frequencies in dependent and nondependent individuals (Gelernter, Kranzler, & Cubells, 1999).

Genetic Contributions to Illicit Substance Use

The Harvard Twin study is one of the most extensive investigations of the role of heritable factors in drug use (Tsuang, Bar, Harley, & Lyons, 2001; Tsuang et al., 1999). Summarizing the results from 8,000 twin pairs, Tsuang and colleagues reported heritability estimates ranging from .38 for sedative drugs to .44 for stimulant drugs. Interestingly, the variance in illicit drug use attributed to shared environmental influences tended to be much smaller than that due to individual environmental effects (Tsuang et al., 2001). Somewhat higher estimates for heritability were generated from a study of twins ascertained through alcohol and drug programs, who thus exhibited more severe forms of substance abuse disorders (van den Bree, Johnson, Neale, &

Pickens, 1998). Among males, heritability estimates for substance dependence were 58% for sedatives, 57% for opiates, 74% for cocaine, 78% for stimulants, and 68% for marijuana. With the exception of dependence on stimulants, estimates were significantly lower for females. In general, the genetic variance appeared to be greater for heavy use or abuse than for ever using (Kendler & Prescott, 1998).

Of particular relevance to youth substance abuse, the transitions in drug use have been shown to have a significant heritable component. For example, genetic variance for the transition from never to ever using was reported to be 44% for marijuana, 61% for amphetamine, and 54% for cocaine (Tsuang et al., 1999). For the transition to regular use, the comparable figures were 30%, 39%, and 34%. As was shown for tobacco and alcohol, there was evidence for common genetic variance underlying dependence on alcohol and illicit drugs (Pickens, Svikis, McGue, & LaBuda, 1995; Tsuang et al., 2001).

Because many illicit drugs increase levels of dopamine (Dackis & O'Brien, 2001; Kuhar, Ritz, & Boja, 1991), initial genetic investigations have focused on this pathway. Uhl and colleagues (Uhl, Blum, Noble, & Smith, 1993) summarized data from nine studies of mixed groups of substance abusers and reported a twofold increase in risk in individuals who have at least one copy of the DRD2 A1 allele. The risk ratio was nearly threefold for more severe substance abuse. A high-activity allele of the catechol-o-methyltransferase gene, which codes for a dopamine-metabolizing enzyme, has also been associated with polysubstance abuse (Vandenbergh, Rodriguez, Miller, Uhl, & Lachman, 1997).

Other studies have investigated genetic effects on specific forms of illicit substance dependence. With regard to cocaine, there is preliminary evidence for a modest association of cocaine dependence with the DRD3 gene (Comings et al., 1999) and for a relationship of cocaine-induced paranoia with the 9-allele of the dopamine transporter (DAT) gene and with a reduced-activity variant of the dopamine beta hydroxylase gene (Cubells et al., 2000; Gelernter, Kranzler, Satel, & Rao, 1994). Case-control and family-based studies have provided inconsistent evidence for an association of heroin addiction with the dopamine D4 (DRD4) receptor gene, including one positive study (Kotler et al., 1997) and two negative studies (Franke et al., 2000; Li, Zhu, et al., 2000). Of relevance to the bio-behavioral model, Duaux and colleagues (Duaux et al., 1998) found that heroin addicts who were also high on sensation seeking were significantly more likely to have a DRD3 polymorphism.

The serotonin and opioid systems play an important role in the subjective euphorant effects of cocaine and illicit drugs. The high-activity variant of the serotonin transporter (5HTTLPR) was found to have a modest association with cocaine dependence in one study (Patkar et al., 2001), whereas the serotonin receptor 5HT1B was unrelated to cocaine dependence in another population (Cigler et al., 2001). A genetic variant of the mu-opioid receptor has been associated with heroin addiction in a Chinese population (Shi et al., 2002). However, the results of other investigations in this area have been inconsistent (Gelernter et al., 1999; Schinka et al., 2002).

Although little attention has been devoted to the genetic basis of marijuana dependence, there is preliminary evidence for an association of a polymorphism in the canaboid receptor gene (CNR1) with canaboid dependence (Comings et al., 1997). Interestingly, this gene has also been associated with a deficit in brain-evoked potentials (p300) that is thought to be a liability marker for substance abuse and mental illness (Johnson et al., 1997).

As an alternative to the candidate gene approach, Uhl, Liu, Walther, Hess, and Naiman (2001) used genomic scans to identify markers associated with a *DSM-IV* (*Diagnostic and Statistical Manual of Mental Disorders*, 4th ed.; APA, 1994) substance abuse diagnosis (various forms combined). Among the positive markers identified were loci for brain-derived neurotropic factor (BDNF) and alcohol dehydrogenase (ADH), two loci with relevance to biological pathways for susceptibility to drug and alcohol dependence. As additional genome scans are completed, regions that may harbor susceptibility genes for substance dependence will likely be identified.

Mediating Role of Personality Traits

As suggested by the bio-behavioral model, these genetic influences on substance use are mediated, in part, by heritable personality traits. Although a number of personality traits (e.g., neuroticism, conscientiousness) may be relevant to substance use, the bulk of evidence supports the importance of sensation seeking and impulsivity (Zuckerman & Kuhlman, 2000).

Genetic Influences on Sensation Seeking and Impulsivity

Earlier conceptions of the biological basis of personality focused on extraversion, an enduring trait characterized by craving for stimulation, impulsivity, and a need for social interaction (Eaves & Eysenck, 1975). Studies of twins reared together and those reared apart suggested that as much as half the variance in extraversion was attributable to genetic influences (Plomin, 1990). Sensation-seeking trait, characterized by boredom susceptibility, thrill and experience seeking, and disinhibition (impulsivity), has also been shown to be influenced significantly by heritable factors (Fulker,

Eysenck, & Zuckerman, 1980). Studies of both adolescent twins and adult twins have documented heritability estimates in the range of 34% to 68% for the different dimensions of sensation seeking (Eysenck & Fulker, 1983; Koopmans et al., 1995). There is also evidence that genetic influences on these traits are strongest in adolescence and diminish over time (Viken, Rose, Kaprio, & Koskenvuo, 1994).

Evidence from animal models suggest that inherited susceptibility to sensation seeking may be expressed biologically in a deficient dopamine system (Bardo et al., 1996; Laviola et al., 1999). Molecular genetic studies in humans provide additional support for this view. Such studies have reported associations of sensation seeking or correlated traits (e.g., novelty seeking, extraversion) with a polymorphism in the dopamine D4 (DRD4) gene (Benjamin et al., 1996; Okuyama et al., 2000). In a study of 119 adolescent boys, Noble et al. (1998) found that novelty-seeking scores were associated with variants in the DRD2 and DRD4 genes. However, these findings have not been replicated in all cases (Vandenbergh, Zonderman, Wang, Uhl, & Costa, 1997).

By contrast, the weight of the evidence for specific genetic influences on impulsive behavior is from studies of genes in the serotonin pathway. This is biologically plausible, because the serotonin system plays an important role in behavioral inhibition as well as uninhibited aggression (Lesch & Merschdorf, 2000). Several studies have reported a higher prevalence of the more rare allele of the TPH gene with impulsivity or behaviors involving poor impulse control (e.g., suicide, aggressive behavior) (Evans et al., 2000; Manuck et al., 1999; Roy et al., 2001). The serotonin transporter gene (5HTTLPR) has also been linked with suicide attempts in normal and alcohol-dependent groups (Gorwood, Philippe, Ades, Hamon, & Boni, 2000; Preuss, Koller, Soyka, & Bondy, 2001).

Sensation Seeking, Impulsivity, and Substance Use

Several converging lines of evidence suggest that high sensation seekers have a greater risk of substance abuse. In a large community sample of adolescents, high sensation seekers were twice as likely as low sensation seekers to be smokers (Kopstein, Crum, Celentano, & Martin, 2001). Similarly, in a prospective study of over 250 high school students, sensation seeking predicted the progression to regular cigarette smoking (Skara, Sussman, & Dent, 2001). The related trait of novelty seeking has also been shown to correlate with tobacco use patterns in a large sample of 9th graders (Audrain et al., in press). The risk associated with sensation-seeking personality traits has also been supported by studies examining use of alcohol and illicit drugs among adolescents and young adults (Kosten, Ball, & Rounsaville, 1994; Zuckerman & Kuhlman, 2000).

An increased risk for tobacco and other substance dependence among high sensation seekers appears to be attributable, in part, to neurochemical factors that enhance the rewarding properties of drug use (Laviola et al., 1999; Perkins, Gerlach, Broge, Grobe, & Wilson, 2000). For example, rat strains that are highly responsive to novelty learn to self-administer drugs more quickly than do low-responder rats (Dellu et al., 1996). Likewise, in humans, high novelty-seeking nonsmokers exhibit stronger subjective and physiological responses to nicotine than do low novelty seekers (Perkins et al., 2000). Alternatively, sensation-seeking personality traits may increase liability to smoking by increasing receptivity to the highly stimulating tobacco industry marketing campaigns (Audrain et al., in press) or by prompting affiliation with peer groups that support substance use (Donohue, Van Hasselt, Hersen, & Perrin, 1999).

Impulsive personality tendencies may further increase liability for substance use by minimizing behavioral control in an environment where drugs are highly accessible. In a study of over 3,000 college students, "impulsive sensation-seeking" was associated with a general risk-taking attitude, as well as with use of tobacco, alcohol, and illicit drugs (Zuckerman & Kuhlman, 2000). Other data suggest that drug users may be more prone to value immediate rewards over long-term rewards, suggesting a specific cognitive bias in impulsive individuals that promotes continued substance use (Mitchell, 1999; Petry & Casarella, 1999).

The research just described provides strong support for specific genetic effects on sensation seeking and impulsivity and for the effects of these traits on liability to substance abuse. Surprisingly, however, the mediation hypothesis has not yet been tested directly. Additional research is needed to test whether these traits are statistical mediators of the effects of specific genes on substance abuse and to determine the proportion of the mediated variance accounted for by these variables.

KEY FINDINGS FROM RESEARCH ON GENETICS, PERSONALITY, AND SUBSTANCE USE

- *There is no "gene for addiction."* Although heritable factors are clearly important in substance abuse and dependence, such effects involve a complex interaction between multiple genes in different biological pathways. Some genetic variants may result in a more generalized predisposition to substance use and dependence, whereas other variants may influence risk for dependence on specific substances. These genetic effects interact with environmental factors, and any individual genetic variant is likely to account for only a small proportion of the overall variance in a substance use behavior.

- *Findings on the effects of specific genetic variants are not consistent.* The use of different study designs and methods of subject ascertainment, the focus on polymorphisms of unknown functional significance, and ethnic admixture have resulted in inconsistent findings in this field. Very large studies, using both population-based and family-based designs, are needed to validate specific genetic effects and to identify the set or sets of genetic variants that predispose to general addiction potential and dependence on specific substances.

- *Genetic effects on substance abuse are mediated by personality traits, particularly those involving the drive for sensation/novelty and deficits in impulse control.* Individuals exhibiting these traits may be more prone to drug use, and as such, these traits may serve as liability markers for susceptibility to substance use and dependence. Whether these trait markers provide greater predictive value than the underlying genetic markers remains to be determined.

- *A complete understanding of specific genetic influences on substance dependence will reveal only part of the picture.* On average, genetic influences account for roughly half the variance in specific substance use behaviors. Such effects occur in the context of complex socioenvironmental and psychological influences. Even the best panel of genetic tests to identify individuals predisposed to substance abuse will have low sensitivity and specificity unless nongenetic influences are incorporated into the model. Increased understanding of the role of genetic factors in addiction will never diminish the importance of behavioral and social influences.

IMPLICATIONS FOR PREVENTION: PUBLIC HEALTH APPROACHES

The reviewed literature suggests that genetic predisposition to substance abuse is mediated, in part, by individual differences in sensation seeking. Thus, broad-based prevention programs designed to meet the needs of this high-risk group may be most effective in reducing liability to substance use. One excellent example of this approach is from the work of Donohew, Palmgreen, and colleagues on mass media interventions to prevent cocaine and marijuana use (Donohew, Palmgreen, & Lorch, 1994; Everett & Palmgreen, 1995; Palmgreen et al., 1991). In a series of studies, this group developed and evaluated public service announcements (PSAs) targeted to high versus low sensation seekers. The high sensation value PSAs used fast-paced edits, intense music and sound, and vivid scenes designed to generate sensory and affective responses. Alternative adventurous activities were also featured in the high sensation value PSAs. By contrast, the low sensation value PSAs were slower, had softer music, used less novel stimulation, and had themes emphasizing resistance to peers. In both forced exposure and naturalistic viewing experiments, high sensation seekers exhibited greater attention to and recall of PSAs that were high in sensation value compared with those low in sensation value. They also perceived these PSAs as more effective and expressed stronger behavioral intentions to call a hot line for educational information.

This work has also been validated in a field study in which the high sensation value PSAs were disseminated in a 5-month television antidrug campaign. This campaign was shown to be effective in reaching the high sensation seeker target audience and prompting them to call a drug abuse hot line (Palmgreen et al., 1995). Furthermore, Palmgreen and colleagues (Palmgreen, Donohew, Lorch, Hoyle, & Stephenson, 2002) were able to document a significant decrease in drug use among high sensation seekers that lasted for at least several months after the campaign. Among low sensation

seekers, there appeared to be no effect of the campaign. This is important, because it suggests that the dissemination of public health interventions targeted to high sensation seekers can have significant benefits for this high-risk group while at the same time potentially reinforcing not engaging in the behavior in the low-risk group.

The bio-behavioral model and relevant literature also suggest that adolescent substance use prevention programs should substitute alternative rewards, particularly those that may stimulate biological pathways that regulate the brain's reward mechanism (Bardo et al., 1996). Because high sensation seekers are more likely than low sensation seekers to engage in action-adventure activities, prevention approaches that incorporate these activities as alternative reinforcers may be most effective (D'Silva, Harrington, Palmgreen, Donohew, & Lorch, 2001). Programs that incorporate physical and social activities that involve exposure to novel situations might be most successful. Consistent with this suggestion, tobacco use risk is significantly lower among high school students who engage in sports (Nattiv & Puffer, 1991; Ussher, Taylor, West, & McEwen, 2000). However, to our knowledge, the impact of incorporating highly novel alternate reinforcers into adolescent substance abuse prevention programs has not yet been systematically tested. Other prevention approaches suggested by this research are interventions to enhance behavioral control and reduce impulsive behavior. Although such approaches are used in cognitive-behavior therapy for adolescents with behavioral problems, we are not aware of substance abuse prevention programs that have specifically tested these components.

The enormous toll that substance abuse takes on America's youth may also lead prevention experts to consider ways that individual genetic risk information might be used to identify high-risk subgroups that might benefit from more intensive or tailored prevention approaches. For example, a future scenario might entail identifying a subset of adolescents that has addiction risk-conferring genotypes and developing an intensive intervention aimed at this cohort. Such an application of this new knowledge, however, is fraught with ethical complexities, some of which may be resolved by future research and others that are apt to persist. Although it may take years to realize the full benefit of current research on adolescent substance abuse, it is not too soon to consider the challenges inherent in making use of this new knowledge. These issues are discussed in the final section of this chapter.

IMPLICATIONS FOR PREVENTION: INDIVIDUALIZED RISK COMMUNICATION

Perceptions of vulnerability to addiction have generally been underestimated by the adolescent population (Jamieson & Romer, 2001; Johnston et al., 2002). Despite acknowledging that nicotine is an addictive chemical, a large proportion (62%) of adolescents who smoke cigarettes reported that quitting smoking was either easy or manageable for most people if they tried hard enough (Jamieson & Romer, 2001). Likewise, data from the 2002 Legacy Tracking Survey indicate that among current smokers ages 12 to 18, 60% reported that they would definitely be able to quit smoking if they wanted to, and 28% said they probably would be able to quit (American Legacy Foundation, 2002). These figures are of particular concern, because perceptions of invulnerability to addiction predict subsequent smoking behavior. In a longitudinal study of 965 adolescents, those who felt that they could quit at anytime were almost twice as likely to become established smokers, compared with adolescents who were less confident in their

ability to quit (Choi, Ahluwalia, Harris, & Okuyemi, 2002).

It is tempting to consider whether individualized feedback about genetic susceptibility to addiction could overcome adolescents' perceptions of invulnerability and reduce the chances of substance use or the transition to substance dependence. Although intriguing, data from research on genetic testing for disease susceptibility do not provide strong support for an effect of genetic risk communication on health-protective behaviors (Marteau & Lerman, 2001). With regard to cigarette smoking, Lerman and colleagues (Lerman et al., 1997) conducted a clinical trial to determine whether feedback regarding genetic susceptibility to lung cancer would motivate smoking cessation in an adult population. The results showed that such information did have beneficial effects on risk perceptions and the perceived benefits of quitting smoking; however, there was no significant effect on smoking behavior. Whether or not communication of genetic risk for addiction to adolescents would have a significant impact on relevant attitudes and behavior is an open empirical question.

CHALLENGES INHERENT IN MAKING USE OF NEW KNOWLEDGE ABOUT GENETIC RISK FOR SUBSTANCE USE

Despite the rapid pace of new knowledge about the role of genetics in complex diseases and behavior, we are still a long way off from the promised world of individualized prevention and treatment (Collins, 1999; van Ommen, Bakker, & Dunnen, 1999). Most currently available genetic tests are for rare diseases. In a recent survey of a major Web-accessible database (www.genetests.org), only 423 of the 751 tests listed for inherited diseases or conditions were available for clinical use, and only 51 of these affected more than 1 in 2,000 people (Yoon et al., 2001). There are several forces at play, however, that may lead to wider use of genetic testing in public health programs and prevention efforts related to adolescent substance abuse. These include the enormous toll of adolescent substance abuse and the commercial potential of large-scale genetic screening for common traits (Clark, 1995). Issues that must be considered prior to the application of genetic testing for adolescent substance abuse risk, at an individual or a population level, are discussed next.

Limitations of Knowledge

Although great advances in understanding the role of genetic factors in addiction have been made, we currently lack a complete understanding of pertinent gene-gene and gene-environment interactions. This limits our ability to estimate the penetrance of specific genetic effects (i.e., the proportion of adolescents with addiction susceptibility genotypes who will actually become substance abusers) and to provide accurate individualized risk information. These uncertainties are compounded by a lack of knowledge about the benefits of early interventions for those at risk (Welch & Burke, 1998) and by physicians' difficulties communicating probabilistic information (Hofman et al., 1993). Research to address these issues is urgently needed prior to the integration of genetic information into the clinical or public health domains.

Pleiotropic Effects of Substance Abuse Susceptibility Genes

Pleiotropy refers to the fact that many of the genetic variants associated with complex traits such as addiction are also associated with other conditions. For example, the tryptophan hydroxylase (TPH) gene that has been implicated in smoking initiation (Lerman et al., 2001; Sullivan et al., 2001) has also been associated with aggression (Manuck et al., 1999) and risk for attempting suicide (Nielsen et al., 1998). The DRD2 gene, associated with smoking and alcohol use, is also a risk marker for a variety of neuropsychiatric conditions (Noble, 2000). These are but a few examples of the pleiotropic nature of these variants. Thus, assessments of the burden of genetic testing for addiction susceptibility must take into account not only the effects of testing for substance use susceptibility but also the effects of learning about susceptibility to other associated conditions. This is particularly true for potentially stigmatizing psychiatric conditions that may arise from perturbations in some of the same biological pathways implicated in substance abuse.

Psychosocial Risks

Assuming that addiction susceptibility tests of acceptable validity and specificity become available in the future, issues surrounding the psychosocial risks of genetic testing will emerge. The potential for adverse psychological consequences of disclosure of genetic information for individuals and families is a particular concern (Biesecker et al., 1993; Lerman & Croyle, 1994). One example relevant to adolescent genetic testing is Sweden's nationwide experimental newborn screening for alpha-antitrypsin deficiency, a genetic enzyme deficiency associated with a high risk of adult-onset emphysema. In a follow-up study of a cohort of children tested for this condition, more than half the families of children who tested positive for the trait suffered severe negative psychological consequences, resulting in a curtailing of the program only 2 years after it was implemented (McNeil, Sveger, & Thelin, 1988). The impact of genetic risk communication at different stages of development must also be considered in this context. In a study of predictive testing for Huntington's disease in the Netherlands, those who became aware of their risk for future disease in adolescence had worse psychological and social outcomes than those who had learned of their genetic status in adulthood (van der Steenstraten, Tibben, Roos, Kamp, & Niermeijer, 1994).

The potential for labeling or discrimination of those testing positive is also a serious concern (Jones, 1996; King, 1992; Reilly, Boshar, & Holtzman, 1997; U.S. Department of Labor, 1998). As early as 1967, researchers noted the negative emotional consequences of labeling children with a mild condition (benign cardiac murmur) as sick (Bergman & Stamm, 1967). Identification of addiction susceptibility in an adolescent may be even more stigmatizing than being at increased risk for a disease or medical condition. In this context, genetic testing generates concerns similar to those addressed in HIV testing (CDC, 2000b; Chapman, 1996; Herek & Capitanio, 1993).

Potential for Racial Discrimination

Racial differences in risk-conferring variants for substance abuse have been found (Lerman et al., 1999), raising concerns that such data may be seized on by media and others (Sherman et al., 1997) and used in destructive ways. Given serious concerns about the potential use of genetic information to stigmatize groups and communities (Proctor, 1988; Reilly & Page, 1998; Wexler, 1980), the use of racial categories within genetics research and practice is currently a topic of debate (Schwartz, 2001; Wilson et al., 2001). The potential for harm to individuals identified with these subpopulations may be particularly onerous for genetic variants associated with increased risk of addiction and related traits. Resulting stigmatization could exacerbate existing discrimination and limit opportunities for members of groups at increased risk.

Privacy Issues

Given this potential for stigmatization and discrimination, the strength of privacy protections and bans on genetic discrimination must also be considered. Despite some modest protections provided by the Health Insurance Portability and Accountability Act of 1996 and new privacy regulations adopted in April 2001 (U.S. Department of Health and Human Services [DHHS], 2000a), current privacy law appears inadequate to the task of protecting patients from possible misuses of information generated by genetic testing. The proposed modifications to the privacy regulations, issued in March 2002, would not improve the protections afforded to genetic information (DHHS, 2002). The 1990 Americans with Disabilities Act prohibits certain uses of genetic information, and a 2000 Executive Order prohibits discrimination of *federal* employees based on genetic information (Clinton, 2000). However, there is no federal law in place in the United States that bans genetic discrimination in the general population. Genetic information relating to behaviors such as nicotine addiction, substance abuse, and psychiatric disorders may be particularly damaging to individuals due to the costs associated with treating such conditions (Garnick, Hendricks, Comstock, & Horgan, 1997).

Informed Consent Issues

Informed consent is an overarching concern when considering the integration of genetic testing into clinical or public health practice (Geller et al., 1995; Geller et al., 1997; Holtzman & Watson, 1999). With regard to genetic testing of adolescents, an additional challenge is to determine the appropriate locus of decision making and the age at which adolescents might be seen to have the capacity for consent. This issue remains a matter of public debate (American Society of Human Genetics, 1995; Geller,

Tambor, Bernhardt, Wissow, & Fraser, 2000; Hoffmann & Wulfsberg, 1995). In the United States, the courts have generally regarded 15 years as the age at which minors can consent independently to necessary medical treatment without parental permission (Wertz, Fanos, & Reilly, 1994). Some states also allow children to obtain substance abuse treatment without parental notification (Wertz et al., 1994). There is some evidence to suggest that, given the option, adolescents may be more apt to seek information about their own health risks. For example, data on HIV testing show that, when Connecticut changed its laws from requiring consent by parents to consent by adolescents alone, the number of adolescents seeking HIV testing increased by 44% (Hein, 1997). Perhaps the most difficult challenge to informed consent in the present context is the lack of empirical information about the potential benefits and harms associated with testing of adolescents for genetic susceptibility to addiction.

CONCLUSION

Ongoing research is elucidating the genetic basis of substance use and dependence.

However, these scientific advances must be viewed in perspective. Biology offers less than half the answer for those seeking to reduce substance abuse among our nation's youth, with social and environmental factors playing an equal or larger role. Thus, genetics remains only one strand in the complicated web of addiction.

Although genetic testing of adolescents for the purposes of risk assessment or intervention targeting is fraught with ethical and practical challenges, genetic discoveries can be used to design more effective prevention approaches. Improved knowledge about the mediating role of sensation seeking and impulsivity can inform the development of broad-based approaches that target the informational and behavioral needs of these high-risk subgroups of adolescents. However, although such approaches can augment decades of progress made in the field of substance abuse prevention, they will clearly not provide the ultimate solution to an extraordinarily complex public health problem. Rather, the expertise of multiple disciplines and methodological approaches is needed to meet the needs of our nation's most vulnerable adolescents.

CHAPTER 19

Health Risk Takers and Prevention

LEWIS DONOHEW
PHILIP PALMGREEN
RICK ZIMMERMAN
NANCY HARRINGTON
DEREK LANE

Much of our research on communication and health over the past two decades has dealt with strategies for helping prevent a number of the problems addressed in this volume, particularly those involving alcohol, drug abuse, and sexual risk taking. One of the central concerns of this work has been how to effectively reach what Caspi and associates (1997) call a "risky personality type" more likely to engage in health risk behaviors. In this chapter, we review some of the evidence to support a recommendation for targeting these individuals in prevention interventions and describe procedures involved in our research.

The research has established that by designing interventions that meet their higher needs for *novelty* and *sensation,* we can considerably advance our ability to capture the attention of these target individuals who begin having sex earlier, have more partners, begin drug use earlier, and take many other

health-related risks. Such interventions have been shown to enhance information processing and motivate attitude and behavior change (Donohew, Helm, Lawrence, & Shatzer, 1990; Donohew, Lorch, & Palmgreen, 1991; Donohew, Palmgreen, & Duncan, 1980; Donohew, Sypher, & Higgins, 1988; Donohew et al., 2000; Lorch et al., 1994; Palmgreen & Donohew, in press; Palmgreen, Donohew, Lorch, Hoyle, & Stephenson, 2001; Palmgreen et al., 1991).

What we have been doing is consistent with the recommendations of a team of investigators conducting a longitudinal study in New Zealand over the past 20-plus years on a cohort of young males and females—from age 3 into adulthood—on a wide range of behavioral characteristics, including health and risk behaviors (Caspi et al., 1997).

The investigators described the emergence of a risky personality type in health behaviors and emphasized the importance of designing means to reach these individuals on the basis of their different needs. The authors noted that the origins of a personality type at risk for health risk behaviors may be found early in life and that individual differences in personality may change receptivity to steps in the persuasion process. They added that if we know the psychological characteristics that motivate persons to engage in health risk behaviors, "It may be possible to tailor campaigns to zero-in on the characteristic motivations, attitudes, and feelings of the audience . . . and motivate risk takers to minimize harm" (Caspi et al., 1997, p. 1061).

In our research, we have drawn on the concept of sensation seeking[1] (Zuckerman, 1979, 1988, 1991, 1994) as a surrogate for the social and biological forces operating to generate such behaviors in a substantial portion of adolescents (a trait that continues throughout one's lifetime, although waning somewhat in both men and women with aging). We (Hoyle, Stephenson, Palmgreen, Lorch, & Donohew, 2002) have also found positive correlations between measures of the concept and every risk factor measured (such as deviance, perceived peer use of marijuana, and perceived family use of marijuana), and negative correlations with all protective factors measured (such as absence of depression, quality of home life, religiosity, and perceived sanctions against marijuana use).[2]

Not only do members of the group we are describing here engage in the activities that increase their health risks, but they also tend to choose peers who are very much like them and thus who either point them toward or reinforce their choices to engage in these activities (Donohew et al., 1999). We have proposed that an individual-level intrapersonal trait and social influences reinforce each other and are complementary rather than contradictory explanations of such behaviors.

Although, clearly, one's environment can include risk factors, this does not remove the effects of sensation seeking. We have found, for example, that white and African American students in an inner-city urban high school who were higher on sensation seeking were substantially more likely than their low sensation seeking counterparts to have used alcohol and marijuana, become sexually active, and had unwanted sex under pressure or when drunk (Donohew et al., 2000).

Thus, there is considerable support, both from behavioral studies and from studies in which biological indicators are used, for sensation seeking as an index of risky personality types to be targeted in prevention campaigns. Sensation seeking is a biologically based personality trait characterized by Zuckerman (1994) as "the seeking of varied, novel, complex, and intense sensations and experiences, and the willingness to take physical, social, legal, and financial risks for the sake of such experience" (p. 27). High sensation seekers (HSS) are receptive to stimuli that are intense, novel, and arousing; stimuli producing lower levels of arousal may be considered "boring" and cause the HSS to seek alternative sources of stimulation. Low sensation seekers (LSS) tend to reject stimuli that are highly intense, preferring the familiar and less complex.[3]

According to Zuckerman (1991), sensation seeking and sensation avoidance may represent adaptation to a dangerous environment in which novel stimuli can be either sources of reward or threats to survival. It has been proposed that the search for novelty (Cloninger, Adolfson, & Svrakic, 1996; Zuckerman, 1994) is a fundamental survival behavior, in which detection of novel stimuli leads to alerting the system for fight or flight (Franklin, Donohew, Dhoundiyal, & Lawrence, 1988).

Because those we call high sensation seekers will go to great lengths to achieve novelty and sensation, the obvious approach to attracting and holding their attention and persuading them to avoid these behaviors is offering them these same types of stimulation in the prevention messages themselves. This is what we have done, drawing on an activation model of information exposure (Donohew, Lorch, & Palmgreen, 1998; Donohew et al., 1980) for theoretical support.

The model assumes that need for stimulation is a function of the catecholamine system (Zuckerman, 1979, 1994) and that the reader or viewer of a mediated or interpersonal message may be largely unaware of the affective inducements to continue or discontinue exposure. The central assumption of the theory is that human beings have individual levels of need for stimulation at which they are most comfortable and that attention is a function primarily of an individual's level of need for stimulation and the level of stimulation provided by a stimulus. From this, it is deduced that if individuals do not achieve or maintain this state on exposure to a message, it is very likely that they will turn away and seek another source of stimulation that helps them achieve the desired state. If activation remains within some acceptable range, however, individuals are more likely to continue exposure to the information. The theory has guided a series of experiments and field studies on improving the effectiveness of public health campaigns (Donohew et al., 1990; Donohew et al., 1991; Donohew, Palmgreen, & Lorch, 1994; Lorch et al., 1994; Palmgreen et al., 1991; Zimmerman & Donohew, 1996).

The result of these studies is a coherent and parsimonious theoretical framework (Donohew et al., 1998; Donohew & Palmgreen, 2003) that guides intervention strategies from inception to delivery and meshes well with a number of other theoretical approaches to prevention. It has proven effective in drug abuse prevention campaigns and also has potential for the prevention of unprotected sex, drinking, smoking, and a variety of other risk-related behaviors that

the individual has the option to engage in or avoid.

The research has focused on identification of simple indices of audiences most likely to be at risk and on developing and testing messages to affect their behavior. We have found that sensation seeking applies across age, sex, and socioeconomic status and across a wide range of health behaviors.

Messages and activities that attract and hold the attention of high sensation seekers are those possessing greater sensation value. In practice, focus groups reveal that these messages have higher levels of the following attributes: (a) novel, creative, or unusual; (b) complex; (c) intense, emotionally powerful or physically arousing; (d) graphic or explicit; (e) somewhat ambiguous; (f) unconventional; (g) fast paced; or (h) suspenseful. Support for the effectiveness of this approach has been found in a number of subsequent studies (Donohew et al., 1998; Donohew et al., 1994; Donohew et al., 2000; Lorch et al., 1994). In one, for example, involving a television campaign featuring high sensation-value messages embedded in like programs, 72% of callers to a hot line were found to be high sensation seekers (Palmgreen et al., 1995).

Early in the program, we studied message sensation value and other intervention stimuli that appeal to those most likely to take risks. We found that high sensation seekers are receptive to stimuli that are intense, novel, and arousing, whereas stimuli producing lower levels of arousal may be considered boring and caused the HSS to seek alternative sources of stimulation. On the other hand, low sensation seekers tend to reject stimuli that are highly intense, preferring the familiar and less complex, but nonetheless, they watch televised messages that reach close to the maximum watched by HSS. *This points to a parsimonious conclusion: Interventions should be designed to reach HSS—the prime target audience—because that will reach both HSS and the secondary audience, LSS.* In our studies, we have found that campaigns that deliver messages aimed at LSS or at the middle ground between HSS and LSS are not well received by HSS (Lorch et al., 1994).

Other research involving prevention of alcohol abuse, risky sex, and HIV has indicated that although high sensation seekers are more likely to become involved in risky situations (e.g., Donohew et al., 1990; Donohew et al., 1998), it may be those who are also *impulsive decision makers* (Langer, Zimmerman, Warheit, & Duncan, 1993) who are more likely to actually engage in the risky behaviors (Donohew & Zimmerman, 1996; Zimmerman & Donohew, 1996). We have operationally defined impulsivity, or an impulsive decision-making style, not as a trait, but as one end of a continuum that varies from those styles that can be considered very rational to those that are consistently impulsive.

Several personality researchers have viewed impulsivity and sensation seeking as related personality traits (Buss & Plomin, 1975; Eysenck & Eysenck, 1977, 1978; Zuckerman, Kuhlman, Joireman, Teta, & Kraft, 1993). In what he has described as the biological foundations of a basic dimension of personality, Zuckerman (1993) has combined impulsivity and sensation seeking into a single dimension of a personality scale, which he and others have examined as part of an alternative model of personality (Ball, 1995; Zuckerman et al., 1993). Zuckerman (1994) concludes that impulsivity is highly related to sensation seeking, particularly in nonplanning and risk-taking aspects.

We have proposed, based on the research to date, that sensation seeking and impulsive decision making are complementary components of a decision-making process that may or may not be "rational." They thus may have interactive effects on risky sexual behaviors, including alcohol use in the context of sexual decision making. Therefore, the combination of these two characteristics could be expected to place individuals at substantially greater risk of HIV infection, sexually transmitted diseases, and pregnancy, making them a prime target group for health interventions.

The most substantial finding to date emerges from a recent study (Palmgreen et al., 2001) employing antimarijuana public service announcements in a 32-month controlled interrupted time-series research design with switching replications. The first campaign was conducted in Fayette County (Lexington), Kentucky, from January through mid-April of 1997, and the second was conducted simultaneously in both Fayette County and Knox County (Knoxville), Tennessee. The two cities were matched because of similarities in a number of characteristics. During the length of the study, beginning 8 months before the first campaign in either city and continuing through 8 months following the second in both cities, extensive in-home interviews were conducted in both Fayette and Knox Counties each month with random samples of 100 members of a cohort beginning with 7th through 10th graders and continuing with the cohort through subsequent grades to the end of the study.

In both counties, marijuana use was increasing among those in the half of the sample with the higher sensation seeking scores, although the rate of increase was greater in Fayette County. After the first campaign, the rate in the county without a media intervention (Knox) continued to go up, but the rate in the county with the intervention (Fayette) went down and continued a downward trend until there was what we have called a "wearout" effect about 10 months later, at which time it started back up. At the point of the second campaign, conducted in both Fayette and Knox Counties, use among the cohort started down in both counties and continued in a downward direction to the end of the study 8 months later. Meanwhile, in both counties, low sensation seekers bounced along at the bottom of the chart with little use. Overall, the campaigns decreased marijuana use among the high sensation seekers by about one fourth ($p < .001$).

This has been followed by a study employing similar methodology in the same two cities focusing on effects of the ONDCP (Office of National Drug Control Policy) national media campaign. The study is intended to provide a more detailed assessment of the campaign than could be carried out at a national level. Here, a cohort starting 1 year younger than those in the original campaign is being studied in the same two cities, and the intervention is the ONDCP's national campaign rather than a local campaign

Given findings from this substantial body of research, it is appropriate to recommend that risky personality types be targeted in prevention campaigns across a wide range of health risk behaviors. In this chapter, we have described characteristics—especially novelty—that have been successfully employed to attract the attention of prime target groups and hold their attention long enough for persuasive information to be presented.

The four principles of what we (Palmgreen & Donohew, in press) have called the SENTAR (sensation seeking targeting) approach are these: (a) use sensation seeking as a targeting variable, (b) conduct formative research with target audience members, (c) design high sensation-value prevention messages, and (d) place messages in high sensation-value contexts (e.g., television programs exciting to the target audience, as determined by formative research). These principles have been adapted for use in classroom interventions, with greater student involvement as an added factor.

NOTES

1. Sensation seeking has been connected with the mesolimbic dopamine pathway in work by Zuckerman and associates (1979, 1988, 1994), which found that sensation seeking is associated with levels of monoamine oxidase (MAO-B), the brain-specific enzyme that breaks down dopamine and other neurotransmitters, and with the male hormone testosterone. According to Bardo, Donohew, and Harrington (1996), the mesolimbic dopamine reward pathway presumably has evolved because it subserves behaviors that are vital to survival, and particularly because it is posited to be responsible for producing reinforcement (Glickman & Schiff, 1967; Vaccarino, Schiff, & Glickman, 1989). Work reported recently by teams conducting research at the National Institutes of Health and in Israel (Benjamin et al., 1996; Cloninger, Adolfson, & Svrakic, 1996; Ebstein, Novick, Umansky, Priel, Osher, Blaine, Bennett, Nemanov, Katz, & Belmaker, 1996) has connected novelty seeking and the D4 dopamine receptor gene (see Vandenbergh, Zonderman, Wang, Uhl, & Costa, 1997). A substantial body of psychopharmacological and genetic research has implicated the mesolimbic dopamine reward pathway as a critical link mediating drug reward (e.g., Koob, Le, & Creese, 1987). Bardo and associates (e.g., Bardo et al., 1993) have studied responses to novelty and selected drugs and their relationship to dopamine D1 and D2 receptors in animals. They have suggested that novelty-seeking and drug-seeking behaviors may involve activation of a common neural substrate (in the mesolimbic dopamine system), supporting the possibility that novel or high-sensation stimulation may substitute for drug reward. Clearly, then, stimuli possessing stimulation-generating characteristics are likely to be sought over those that do not, especially by individuals with higher need for sensation (Bardo et al., 1996).

2. Since at least the 1970s, sensation seeking has been shown to be positively correlated with alcohol and other drug use in numerous studies (Carrol & Zuckerman, 1977; Segal, 1976). A recent review of the literature found 62 published articles examining the relationship between alcohol use and sensation seeking for the 7.5-year period from 1986 to 1994. Zuckerman, Neary, and Brustman (1970) found that 74% of college undergraduates scoring high on the Sensation Seeking Scale had used one or more drugs (including alcohol) as opposed to 23% of those scoring low on the scale. Subsequent studies have replicated the finding of a strong positive correlation between Sensation Seeking Scale scores and alcohol and other drug use. Finally, research indicates differences in sensation seeking are directly associated with differences in drug use (Donohew, Helm, Lawrence, & Shatzer, 1990). In studies of junior and senior high school students (Donohew et al., 1990), high sensation seekers were twice as likely as low sensation seekers to report use of beer and liquor during the past 30 days and up to 7 times as likely to report use of other drugs. The investigators consistently found highly significant differences in use of marijuana, cocaine, uppers, downers, and other drugs between high and low sensation seekers beginning with the onset of puberty and continuing through young adulthood. Donohew, Zimmerman, and others also have found that adolescents who are higher sensation seekers are considerably more likely to engage in behaviors such as initiating sex at an early age, having multiple sexual partners, not using condoms, and having sex following substance use (Donohew et al., 2000). Thus, sensation seeking is appropriate as a targeting variable not only for studies of drug abuse prevention but also for those involving risky sex.

3. The trait is measured by a self-report inventory, the Sensation Seeking Scale (Zuckerman, 1979) which is divided into four factorially derived subscales plus an overall total score. The factor structure has been replicated in other countries. There also are short forms of the scale (e.g., Hoyle et al., 2002). In the longer (40-item) Form V, which has been most often used in prevention studies, the Thrill and Adventure Seeking (TAS) subscale reflects a desire to engage in risky and adventurous sports and activities providing unusual sensations. The Experience Seeking (ES) subscale represents the pursuit of new sensations through music, art, travel, and psychedelic drugs. The Disinhibition subscale (Dis) reflects a pattern of nonconformity to social mores. Items on the Dis subscale express a need to seek stimulation through an extraverted pattern of partying, drinking, and seeking variety in sexual partners. The Boredom Susceptibility (BS) subscale reflects an aversion to repetitive experience.

CHAPTER 20

Cognitive Vulnerability to Depression

Implications for Adolescent Risk Behavior in General

Lauren B. Alloy

Lin Zhu

Lyn Y. Abramson

For many young people, adolescence is a stressful period of transition into adulthood characterized by hormonal, physical, emotional, and cognitive changes. In addition, adolescents face the challenge of coping with many complex issues, such as identity, self-image, independence, and intimacy. They are also at an important juncture in life in which the decisions they make can have a long-term impact on their adult health and well-being. Although this transition is smooth and relatively uneventful for the majority, some experience great difficulties, emotionally or behaviorally.

One of the more prevalent problems faced by many adolescents is depression. In contrast to the belief that it could not occur in childhood or adolescence, researchers now have come to realize that depression is a major mental health problem in adolescence

(Compas, Connor, & Hinden, 1998; Kessler, Avenevoli, & Reis Merikangas, 2001; Weissman et al., 1999). Epidemiological findings have revealed an alarming trend of increased rates of depressive disorders combined with an earlier age of onset in adolescents of recent birth cohorts (Kessler & Walters, 1998). Studies using diagnostic interviews and *Diagnostic and Statistical Manual of Mental Disorders (DSM)* criteria have found the 12-month prevalence rate for major depressive disorder to vary from 3.4% to 16.8% (Haarasilta, Marttunen, Kaprio, & Aro, 2001; Newman et al., 1996; Oldenhinkel, Wittchen, & Schuster, 1999). Of adolescents between the ages of 15 and 18, 25% are expected to suffer from a diagnosable depression in their lifetime (Kessler et al., 1994). However, if self-report measures were used, the rate of children and adolescents reporting significant levels of depressive symptoms jumps to between 20% and 50% (Kessler et al., 2001).

Not only is depression itself a major health problem for adolescents, it also contributes significantly to a wide range of other adolescent risk behaviors and maladaptive outcomes. In this chapter, we briefly review data indicating that depression contributes to a variety of adolescent risky behaviors and negative outcomes. Given the important role that depression plays in many adolescent risk behaviors, we argue that an identification of some of the significant vulnerability factors for depression has broader implications for understanding vulnerability to these other adolescent risk behaviors as well. Consequently, we review evidence, primarily from the Temple-Wisconsin Cognitive Vulnerability to Depression (CVD) Project (Alloy & Abramson, 1999), that cognitive factors, such as hopelessness and negative thinking patterns, and the developmental antecedents of these cognitive styles, such as negative parenting practices and childhood maltreatment, increase vulnerability to depression and suicidality. We end with a brief discussion of the implications of the work on cognitive vulnerability to depression for prevention of depression and other adolescent risk behaviors associated with depression.

DEPRESSION AS A CONTRIBUTOR TO ADOLESCENT RISK BEHAVIORS AND MALADAPTIVE OUTCOMES

Depression in adolescence frequently causes significant impairment in school behavior, academic performance, and family and social relationships (e.g., Gotlib, Lewinsohn, & Seeley, 1995). In addition, there is a pervasive tendency for adolescent depression to co-occur with other psychiatric conditions (e.g., Angold, Costello, & Erkanli, 1999).

Anxiety disorders have the highest frequency of co-occurrence with depression; up to 75% of adolescent depression cases also include at least one anxiety disorder diagnosis, such as generalized anxiety disorder and panic disorder (Birmaher et al., 1996). In addition, depression has been found to be the most common comorbid diagnosis with attention deficit hyperactivity disorder (ADHD; e.g., Cuffe et al., 2001). Adolescent depression also significantly increases risks for antisocial, histrionic, dependent, and passive-aggressive personality disorders in early adulthood, even after controlling for adolescent personality disorders and other confounding factors (Kasen et al., 2001).

Depressive disorders are also prevalent in adolescents struggling with body image and eating disorders. Some researchers found that adolescents with chronic depressive symptoms are at increased risk for the development of bulimia or binge eating disorder (Zaider, Johnson, & Cockell, 2002). Depression is one of the most commonly observed psychiatric problems in patients with eating disorders, even those who have recovered from eating disorders. In a recent literature review of 108 studies of anorexia, Steinhausen (1999) found that the rate of depression was as high as 67% (mean rate 22%). Based on 24 studies, rates of depression in bulimic individuals range from 9% to 37% (mean rate 24.9%). These rates were obtained after the patients had received treatment, including those who had recovered from their bulimia. Other researchers have found that depression tends to develop before eating disorder (e.g., Toner, Garfinkel, & Garner, 1988) and that comorbid depression is associated with more severe eating disorder symptoms and predicts to worse outcome (e.g., Herpertz-Dahlmann, Wewetzer, Schulz, & Remschmidt, 1996). In addition, adolescent onset anorexia was more likely to persist into adulthood if the patients also suffered from comorbid depression (Herpertz-Dahlmann, Wewetzer, & Remschmidt, 1995).

Aside from its psychiatric comorbidity, adolescent depression also has alarming associations with a number of risky behaviors. Research has demonstrated a clear link between depression and suicidal behavior in adults (Compas et al., 1998). This relationship appears to hold true in the adolescent population as well. For example, Lewinsohn, Rohde, and Seeley (1996) reported findings from the Oregon Longitudinal Study indicating a high frequency of suicide attempts among adolescents with major depression. Compared with the frequencies in adolescents with a single diagnosis of substance abuse or conduct disorder, rates of suicide attempts increased dramatically when the diagnosed disorder was comorbid with major depression or depressive symptoms, suggesting that depression significantly elevated the risk for suicide attempts in the already vulnerable young people. Sadly, some adolescents succeed in taking their own lives. In a longitudinal study, Fombonne and colleagues (2001b) reported that compared with nondepressed adolescents, depressed adolescents had a 6-fold increase of death by suicide (2.45%) during the follow-up period. Even higher rates (7.7%) were reported by Weissman et al. (1999).

Other risky behavior also can lead to negative consequences. Nationwide, substance use among adolescents has become the norm rather than the exception (e.g., Johnston, O'Malley, & Bachman, 1995). In addition to a number of predictive factors such as peer pressure and disregard of social norms, depression has been identified as a main correlate of teenage substance use (Loeber et al., 1998). Depressed young people reported using more marijuana and cocaine (Field, Diego, & Sanders, 2001). Another large-scale survey of 16,464 high school students showed that 37% of those who drink weekly and 65% of those who have tried illicit drugs

were depressed (Torikka, Kaltiala-Heino, Rimpelae, Rimpelae, & Rantanen, 2001). Depression comorbid with heavy alcohol use predicted the lowest functioning and the most pervasive impairment compared with adolescents with either problem alone (Windle & Davies, 1999). Others found that among boys without a history of cigarette smoking, those with higher depressive symptoms were more likely to have initiated smoking during the study interval (Killen et al., 1997). In fact, some researchers have suggested that depression serves a primary etiological role in the development of alcohol, tobacco, and drug-related problems (e.g., Rohde, Lewinsohn, & Seeley, 1991; Zucker, Fitzgerald, & Moses, 1995).

Depression also appears to play a role in teenage pregnancy and parenthood. Kessler and colleagues (1997), in a report based on the National Comorbidity Survey, indicated that adolescent depression and other affective disorders were significant predictors of teenage pregnancy and parenthood. In addition, the presence of a mood disorder was also associated with having multiple sexual partners in teenage girls. Having concurrent depression and suicidal ideation significantly predicted infrequent condom use (Rohde, Noell, Ochs, & Seeley, 2001). Such risky behavior could lead to many undesirable consequences, including unwanted pregnancy and sexually transmitted diseases. Often caught unprepared to deal with the stress of early parenthood, teenage mothers are more likely to become welfare recipients and to remain dependent on the welfare system (Moore & Burt, 1982).

Aside from being concurrently associated with other adolescent psychiatric conditions and risk-taking behaviors, adolescent depression also has devastating longer-term impact, predicting adult depression, suicide attempts, and poor overall functioning (Rao et al., 1995; Weissman et al., 1999). In a series of articles, Fombonne and colleagues (2001a,

2001b; Knapp, McCrone, Fombonne, Beecham, & Worster, 2002) reported the long-term impact of childhood and adolescent depression. Their results indicated that the recurrence of a depressive disorder in adulthood was as high as 75.2% for adolescents diagnosed with major depression. Nearly half the depressed adolescents made a suicide gesture or attempt as adults. Weissman et al. (1999) found that 22% of depressed young people made multiple suicide attempts in adulthood. These adolescents also had more social dysfunction; they were less likely to be employed, and had less educational achievement, less income, less stable housing, and fewer rewarding interpersonal relationships. Furthermore, they generated higher health care costs both in adolescence and adulthood (Knapp et al., 2002; Weissman et al., 1999).

In sum, adolescent depression is comorbid with and, in many cases, appears to contribute to, a wide variety of other adolescent and adult maladaptive outcomes and risk behaviors. If depression is a key mediator of many mental health outcomes and risk behaviors, then a greater understanding of some of the important risk factors for depression may also have implications for understanding vulnerability to this wider array of adolescent risk behaviors. Consequently, we next briefly review evidence documenting the role of several cognitive and developmental vulnerabilities to depression with implications for prevention.

COGNITIVE VULNERABILITY THEORIES OF DEPRESSION

From a cognitive perspective, the meaning or interpretation that individuals give to the life events they experience influences whether or not they become depressed. Two major cognitive theories of depression, the hopelessness theory (Abramson, Metalsky, & Alloy, 1989) and

Beck's (1967) theory are vulnerability-stress models, in which variability in people's susceptibility to depression following stressful life events is understood in terms of differences in cognitive styles that affect how those events are interpreted.

According to the hopelessness theory (Abramson et al., 1989), a negative inferential style is characterized by tendencies to attribute negative life events to stable (likely to persist over time) and global (likely to affect many areas of life) causes, to infer that negative consequences will follow from a current negative event, and to infer that the occurrence of a negative event in one's life means that one is flawed or worthless. Individuals who exhibit such an inferential style should be more likely than those who do not to make negative inferences regarding the causes, consequences, and self-implications of any stressful event they encounter, thereby increasing the likelihood that they will develop hopelessness, the proximal cause of the symptoms of depression (particularly, the hypothesized subtype of hopelessness depression).

In Beck's (1967) theory, negative self-schemata revolving around themes of failure, inadequacy, worthlessness, and loss are hypothesized to contribute vulnerability to depression. These negative self-schemata are often represented as a set of dysfunctional attitudes in which one's happiness and self-worth are believed to be contingent on being perfect or on others' approval. When people who hold such dysfunctional attitudes experience negative life events, they are hypothesized to develop negatively biased perceptions of their self (low self-esteem), personal world, and future (hopelessness), which then lead to depressive symptoms. Although hopelessness theory and Beck's theory differ in terms of some of their specifics, both hypothesize that cognitive vulnerability increases risk for depression through its effects on appraisals of personally relevant life events.

A particularly powerful strategy for testing these cognitive-vulnerability hypotheses is the "behavioral high-risk design" (e.g., Alloy, Lipman, & Abramson, 1992). The behavioral high-risk design involves studying individuals who do not currently have the disorder of interest but who are hypothesized as being at high versus low risk for developing the disorder based on the presence versus absence of the behavioral risk factor. For example, in testing the cognitive-vulnerability hypotheses of depression, one would want to select nondepressed individuals who either exhibit or do not exhibit the hypothesized negative cognitive styles. These groups of cognitively high-risk (HR) and low-risk (LR) individuals can then be compared on their likelihood of having had past episodes of depression (retrospective design) or developing future episodes of depression (prospective design). Recent studies using or approximating a behavioral high-risk design have provided substantial support for the cognitive-vulnerability hypotheses as applied to depressive mood or symptoms (see Alloy, Abramson, Safford, & Gibb, in press, for a review). However, the Temple-Wisconsin CVD Project (Alloy & Abramson, 1999), employing a prospective behavioral high-risk design, provides the best evidence to date that negative cognitive styles act as vulnerability factors for clinically significant depressive disorders.

COGNITIVE VULNERABILITY TO DEPRESSION (CVD) PROJECT

In the CVD Project, university freshmen who had no current Axis I psychiatric disorders at the outset of the study, but who were hypothesized to be at high risk (HR) or low risk (LR) for depression based on their cognitive styles, were followed prospectively every 6 weeks for 2.5 years and then every 16 weeks for an additional 3 years with self-report and structured interview assessments of stressful life events, cognitions, and symptoms and diagnosable episodes of depression and other disorders. Participants were selected for the CVD Project based on a two-phase screening procedure. In Phase 1, the Dysfunctional Attitudes Scale (DAS; Weissman & Beck, 1978) and Cognitive Style Questionnaire (CSQ; Alloy et al., 2000), which assesses people's inferential styles regarding the causes, consequences, and self-implications of negative life events, were administered to 5,378 freshmen at Temple University and the University of Wisconsin–Madison. Those participants who scored in the highest (most negative) quartile of the screening sample on both the DAS and CSQ composite for negative events formed a pool of potential HR participants, whereas those who scored in the lowest (most positive) quartile on both instruments formed a pool of potential LR participants. In Phase 2, the Schedule for Affective Disorders and Schizophrenia-Lifetime interview (SADS-L), expanded to permit both Research Diagnostic Criteria (RDC; Spitzer, Endicott, & Robins, 1978) and *DSM-III-R* diagnoses, was administered to a random subsample of participants who met the Phase 1 criteria. Participants who met RDC or *DSM-III-R* criteria for any current Axis I disorder at the time of the Phase I screening were excluded from the study. Participants who had a past unipolar mood disorder but had remitted for a minimum of 2 months were retained so as not to result in an unrepresentative sample of HR participants (see Alloy & Abramson, 1999, and Alloy et al., 2000, for rationale). The final CVD Project sample included 173 HR and 176 LR ethnically and socioeconomically diverse participants across the two sites (see Alloy et al., 2000, for sample demographic characteristics and representativeness).

NEGATIVE COGNITIVE STYLES AS VULNERABILITIES FOR DEPRESSION, SUICIDALITY, AND POOR ACHIEVEMENT

Do negative cognitive styles confer vulnerability to clinically significant depressive disorder? Using a retrospective version of the behavioral high-risk design in the CVD Project, Alloy et al. (2000) compared the likelihood of a past history of depression in the HR and LR participants. Controlling for current levels of depressive symptoms, HR participants did indeed exhibit higher lifetime rates than did LR participants of *DSM-III-R* and RDC major depressive disorder (38.7% vs. 17.0%) and the subtype of hopelessness depression (39.9% vs. 11.9%), as well as marginally higher lifetime rates of RDC Minor Depressive Disorder (22.9% vs. 11.9%). The risk group differences in lifetime prevalence of major depression and hopelessness depression were maintained when other hypothesized risk factors for depression (i.e., inferential style for positive events, sociotropy, autonomy, self-consciousness, stress-reactive rumination) were controlled. These findings were replicated and extended in a study by Haeffel et al. (in press). In a separate sample of 887 undergraduates, Haeffel and colleagues found that negative cognitive styles as measured by the CSQ (featured as vulnerabilities in hopelessness theory) were more strongly and consistently associated with lifetime history of RDC major depression and hopelessness depression than were dysfunctional attitudes measured by the DAS (featured as vulnerabilities in Beck's theory). Interestingly, negative cognitive styles were also significantly associated with a past history of an RDC anxiety disorder among participants.

Although these retrospective findings are suggestive, alone they do not adequately address whether negative cognitive styles confer vulnerability to depression, because the findings are equally consistent with an alternative hypothesis that negative cognitive styles are a consequence of the past experience of depression (the "scar hypothesis"; Lewinsohn, Steinmetz, Larson, & Franklin, 1981). Thus, data from the prospective portion of the CVD Project are needed to decide among the vulnerability and scar hypotheses. Results from the first 2.5 years of follow up in the CVD Project indicate that negative cognitive styles did indeed predict prospectively both first onsets and recurrences of depressive disorders (Alloy et al., in press). Among participants with no prior history of depression, HR individuals were more likely than LR individuals to experience a first lifetime onset of major depression (16.2% vs. 2.7%), minor depression (45.9% vs. 14.4%), and hopelessness depression (35.1% vs. 3.6%), and marginally ($p < .08$) more likely to experience an onset of any anxiety disorder (6.8% vs. 0.9%). These findings provide especially strong support for the cognitive-vulnerability hypothesis because they are based on a truly prospective test, uncontaminated by prior history of depression. Given that depression is a highly recurrent disorder, it is also important to determine whether negative cognitive styles provide risk for recurrences of depression. Among participants with a past history of depression, HR participants also were more likely than LR participants to have a recurrence of major depression (28.6% vs. 9.4%), minor depression (56.1% vs. 32.8%), and hopelessness depression (50.0% vs. 18.8%), and marginally ($p < .10$) more likely to experience an anxiety disorder (10.2% vs. 4.7%), in the first 2.5 years of follow up. All these findings were maintained even after statistically controlling for individuals' initial depressive symptoms at the outset of the study.

According to the cognitive theories of depression, negative cognitive styles should also confer vulnerability to suicidality, ranging from suicidal ideation to completed suicides. Inasmuch as hopelessness has been found to be the best single psychological predictor of suicidal ideation, attempts, and completions (e.g., Abramson et al., 2000; Beck, Brown, Berchick, Stewart, & Steer, 1990), and negative cognitive styles are hypothesized to increase risk for depression and suicidality by increasing the likelihood of becoming hopeless (Abramson et al., 1989), levels of hopelessness should mediate the predictive association between negative cognitive styles and suicidality. Consistent with this hypothesis, Abramson et al. (1998) reported that HR participants in the CVD Project were more likely than LR participants to have had a past history of suicidality, as well as higher levels of suicidality across the first 2.5 years of prospective follow-up, and this relationship was mediated by participants' mean levels of hopelessness across the 2.5-year follow-up. Moreover, the predictive association between cognitive-risk status and prospective levels of suicidality was maintained even after statistically controlling for participants' prior history of suicidality and for other risk factors for suicidality (i.e., prior history of major and minor depression, borderline and antisocial personality dysfunction, and parental history of depression).

In the CVD Project, negative cognitive styles not only increased vulnerability to clinically significant depressive disorders and suicidality but also conferred risk for poor academic achievement, depending on students' ability levels. Specifically, Gibb, Zhu, Alloy, and Abramson (2002) found that freshmen who both exhibited negative attributional styles (internal and stable attributions for negative life events) and had low levels of academic ability (i.e., low SAT scores) received lower cumulative GPAs across their entire college career than freshmen with negative attributional styles and high levels of academic ability (i.e., high SAT scores) or freshmen with positive attributional styles (external and unstable attributions for negative life events), regardless of academic ability. Some, but not all, other investigators have also observed an association between negative attributional styles and subsequent poor achievement in school, work, and sports (see Gibb et al., 2002, for a review).

According to the cognitive theories of depression, people with negative cognitive styles are vulnerable to depression and suicidality, in part, because they tend to engage in negatively biased information processing about themselves when they encounter stressful events. Data from the CVD Project are consistent with the hypothesis that cognitively HR individuals engage in negative self-referent information processing. Participants in the CVD Project were administered a Self-Referent Information Processing Task Battery (SRIP) at Time 1 of the study. Alloy, Abramson, Murray, Whitehouse, and Hogan (1997) found that compared with LR participants, HR participants showed preferential processing of negative depression-relevant stimuli (e.g., words such as *failure*, *unmotivated*, and *useless*) as evidenced by relatively greater endorsement, faster response times, greater accessibility, better recall, and higher predictive certainty of this material. In addition, HR participants were less likely than LR participants to process positive depression-relevant stimuli (e.g., words such as *resourceful*, *competent*, and *energetic*). All the risk group differences in self-referent information processing were maintained when participants' levels of concurrent depressive symptoms were controlled. These findings demonstrate that information-processing biases previously observed in currently depressed individuals also occur in nondepressed individuals who are cognitively vulnerable to depression.

RUMINATION AS AN ADDITIONAL COGNITIVE VULNERABILITY FOR DEPRESSION

According to another cognitive theory of depression, the response styles theory (Nolen-Hoeksema, 1991), individuals who tend to ruminate in response to depressed mood are at greater risk for experiencing prolonged and severe depressive episodes than are individuals who tend to distract themselves from dysphoria. Rumination is an emotion-regulation strategy involving perseverative self-focus that is recursive and persistent. Nolen-Hoeksema (1991) defined depressive rumination as "repetitively focusing on the fact that one is depressed; on one's symptoms of depression; and on the causes, meanings, and consequences of depressive symptoms" (p. 569). Several laboratory and field studies have found that depressive rumination is indeed associated with longer and more severe episodes of depression (see Spasojevic, Alloy, Abramson, MacCoon, & Robinson, in press, for a review). In addition, prospective studies, including the CVD Project, have found that depressive rumination predicts onsets of clinically significant major depression (Nolen-Hoeksema, 2000; Spasojevic & Alloy, 2001). Moreover, using CVD Project data, Spasojevic and Alloy (2001) found that a tendency to ruminate about one's dysphoria served as a proximal mechanism (mediator) linking several more general depressive risk factors (negative cognitive styles, dependency, self-criticism, neediness, and past history of depression) to onsets of major depressive episodes. Indeed, Abramson and colleagues (2002) argued that negative cognitive styles, by their very nature, should increase the likelihood of rumination because cognitively vulnerable individuals have difficulty disengaging their attention from the self-implications of negative life events.

Expanding on the response styles theory, Robinson and Alloy (in press) hypothesized that individuals who exhibit negative cognitive styles and who also tend to ruminate about these negative cognitions in response to the occurrence of stressful life events ("stress-reactive rumination" as opposed to "emotion-focused rumination") may be more likely to develop episodes of depression in the first place. They reasoned that negative cognitive styles provide the negative content but that this negative content may be more likely to lead to depression when it is "on one's mind" and recursively rehearsed than when it is not. Thus, Robinson and Alloy hypothesized that stress-reactive rumination would exacerbate the association between negative cognitive styles and onsets of depressive episodes. Consistent with this hypothesis, they found that cognitive-risk status and stress-reactive rumination measured at Time 1 of the CVD Project did indeed interact to predict onsets of major depression and hopelessness depression. Among HR participants, those who were also high in stress-reactive rumination evidenced higher lifetime prevalence (Alloy et al., 2000) and prospective incidence (Robinson & Alloy, in press) of major depression and hopelessness depression than those who did not tend to ruminate in response to stressors. LR participants exhibited lower rates of past and future depression, regardless of their levels of stress-reactive rumination.

Future studies need to clarify the relationship between stress-reactive rumination, which occurs prior to the onset of depressed mood, and emotion-focused rumination (as described by Nolen-Hoeksema, 1991), which occurs in response to depressed mood. Spasojevic et al. (in press) suggested that insofar as both kinds of rumination appear to act as risk factors for clinically significant depression, there may be a latent depressive rumination style that captures a general tendency to ruminate at various stages of a depressogenic cycle.

DEVELOPMENTAL ANTECEDENTS OF COGNITIVE VULNERABILITY TO DEPRESSION

Inasmuch as negative cognitive styles and the tendency to ruminate act as vulnerabilities for depression, it is important to begin to understand some of the factors that may contribute to the development of these cognitive vulnerabilities. Such understanding may suggest relevant directions for research on potential preventive interventions. Toward this end, as part of the CVD Project, the cognitive styles and lifetime history of psychopathology of 335 of the HR and LR participants' parents (217 mothers and 118 fathers) were assessed. In addition, both participants and their parents reported on the parents' inferential feedback styles and parenting styles. Finally, the parents reported on their children's early childhood life events and the HR and LR participants reported on their own histories of childhood maltreatment.

Modeling and Parental Inferential Feedback

Children's cognitive styles may develop in part through modeling of their parents' cognitive styles or through parental inferential feedback regarding the causes and consequences of negative events in the child's life. In the CVD Project, mothers of HR individuals had more dysfunctional attitudes, but not more negative inferential styles, than mothers of LR individuals, even after controlling for the mothers' levels of depressive symptoms (Alloy et al., 2001). Fathers' cognitive styles did not differ for HR and LR participants. Similarly, other studies have obtained only limited support for the modeling hypothesis (see Alloy et al., 2001, for a review).

In contrast, studies have provided more consistent support for the hypothesis that negative inferential feedback from parents and others (e.g., teachers) may contribute to children's development of negative cognitive styles (Garber & Flynn, 2001; Turk & Bry, 1992). For example, in the CVD Project, Alloy and colleagues (2001) found that according to both participants' and parents' reports, both mothers and fathers of HR individuals provided more negative (stable, global) attributional feedback for negative events in their child's life than did mothers and fathers of LR individuals. In addition, mothers of HR participants also provided more negative-consequence feedback for negative events in their child's life than did mothers of LR participants according to both respondents' reports, as did fathers according to the participants' reports. Moreover, mothers' inferential feedback predicted average hopelessness levels and the likelihood of their child developing an episode of major, minor, or hopelessness depression over the 2.5-year prospective follow up, mediated in part by the child's cognitive-risk status (Alloy et al., 2001). Also using CVD Project data, Crossfield, Alloy, Abramson, and Gibb (in press) found that parental inferential feedback moderated the relationship between negative childhood life events and cognitive-risk status. Specifically, high levels of negative childhood events in interaction with negative maternal inferential feedback were associated with participants' HR status. Thus, there is some evidence that parents might contribute to the development of negative cognitive styles and vulnerability to depression in their children, not so much by modeling negative inferences for events in their own lives, but by providing negative attributional and consequence feedback to their children for negative events in the children's lives.

Parenting Styles

In addition to parental inferential feedback, negative parenting practices may also contribute to the development of cognitive vulnerability to depression. In particular, a parenting style involving lack of emotional warmth or the presence of rejection and negative psychological control (criticism, intrusiveness, and guilt induction), a pattern referred to as "affectionless control" by Parker (1983), has been most consistently implicated in the association between children's risk for depression and parent-child relations (see Alloy et al., 2001, for a review). Consistent with the lack of emotional warmth part of the affectionless control pattern, Alloy et al. (2001) found that the fathers of HR participants exhibited less warmth and acceptance than did fathers of LR participants, as reported by both the participants and their fathers. There were no risk group differences, however, for fathers' levels of psychological control or for mothers' parenting. In addition, low warmth or acceptance from fathers predicted prospective onsets of major, minor, and hopelessness depression in their children during the 2.5-year follow up, but only the prediction of hopelessness depression episodes was mediated by the children's cognitive-risk status. Interestingly, negative parenting practices also predicted a ruminative response style among CVD Project participants, but it was negative psychological control rather than lack of emotional warmth that was related to depressive rumination (Spasojevic & Alloy, in press). Specifically, Spasojevic and Alloy (in press) reported that psychologically overcontrolling parenting (by both mothers and fathers) was associated with a greater tendency to ruminate by their children, whereas emotional warmth/acceptance was unrelated to rumination in their children. In addition, rumination mediated the relationship between the overcontrolling parenting and prospective onsets of major depression in the college-aged offspring. Thus, both lack of emotional warmth and overcontrolling parenting were related to

offspring's cognitive vulnerability to depression, through the alternative mechanisms of negative cognitive styles and a ruminative response style, respectively.

Childhood Maltreatment

Rose and Abramson (1992) proposed a developmental pathway by which childhood negative life events, especially childhood maltreatment, may lead to the development of a negative cognitive style. They suggested that whereas a child may initially explain being beaten or verbally abused by his or her father by saying, "He was just in a bad mood today" (an external, unstable, specific attribution), repeated occurrences of abuse will lead to disconfirmation of these more benign attributions, prompting the child to begin making hopelessness-inducing attributions about the maltreatment (e.g., "I'm a terrible person who deserves all the bad things that happen to me"; an internal, stable, global attribution). Over time, the child's negative attributions may generalize until a negative cognitive style develops. Rose and Abramson (1992) hypothesized that emotional maltreatment may be even more likely than either physical or sexual maltreatment to contribute to the development of negative cognitive styles, because with emotional maltreatment, the abuser directly supplies the negative cognitions to the child (i.e., "You're so stupid; you'll never amount to anything").

In a qualitative and quantitative review of studies examining the relationship between childhood maltreatment and cognitive vulnerability to depression, Gibb (2002) found that a history of both sexual and emotional maltreatment, but not physical abuse, were associated with negative cognitive styles. In the CVD Project, controlling for participants' levels of depressive symptoms, HR participants reported significantly higher levels of childhood emotional, but not physical or sexual, maltreatment than did LR participants (Gibb,

Alloy, Abramson, Rose, Whitehouse, Donovan, et al., 2001). And this was true for emotional maltreatment by nonrelatives (e.g., teachers, peers, etc.) as well as for emotional maltreatment by parents (Gibb, Abramson, & Alloy, 2002). In addition, participants' cognitive-risk status fully or partially mediated the relationship between reported levels of emotional maltreatment and prospective onsets of major depression and hopelessness depression episodes (Gibb, Alloy, Abramson, Rose, Whitehouse, Donovan, et al., 2001) and levels of suicidality (Gibb, Alloy, Abramson, Rose, Whitehouse, & Hogan, 2001) during the first 2.5 years of follow up. Childhood history of maltreatment was also related to a ruminative response style in the CVD Project. Specifically, Spasojevic and Alloy (in press) found that a reported history of childhood emotional maltreatment and, for women, of childhood sexual maltreatment were related to a ruminative response style and that the tendency to ruminate fully or partially mediated the predictive association between emotional and sexual maltreatment (for women) history and prospective onsets of major depression episodes.

It is important to emphasize that the findings from the CVD Project regarding developmental antecedents of negative cognitive styles were retrospective. Thus, they should be viewed as tentative. However, they provide an empirical rationale for more powerful prospective tests of the role that negative parenting practices, maladaptive inferential feedback regarding the causes and consequences of children's negative life events, and maltreatment may play in contributing to the development of negative cognitive styles and attendant vulnerability to depression and suicidality.

IMPLICATIONS FOR PREVENTION

Insofar as the findings from the CVD Project and other studies indicate that negative cognitive styles and a tendency to ruminate are

vulnerabilities for depression and suicidality, modifying these vulnerabilities should be an important goal for prevention of initial onsets and recurrences of depression and, by extension, other maladaptive outcomes and risky behaviors that may be mediated in part by depression. Recent therapy outcome studies suggest that cognitive-behavioral therapy (CBT) may reduce individuals' depressive symptoms as well as the risk for relapse and recurrence of depression in part by reducing the negativity of individuals' attributional styles (Hollon, Thase, & Markowitz, 2002). Modifications of CBT specifically designed to prevent depression in college students are being tested currently with initial success (DeRubeis, Seligman, Schulman, Reivich, & Hollon, 1998). It may be beneficial to teach cognitively vulnerable individuals with a childhood history of maltreatment to reinterpret their abusive histories. The reframing might posit that they were raised by caretakers who, for whatever reason, did not have the psychological competence to raise them in a less abusive way rather than that they were inherently bad and deserving of the abuse. Because negative cognitive styles may be especially likely to confer vulnerability to depression when exacerbated by rumination, depressogenic cognitive styles may also be altered indirectly by training individuals in more effective emotion regulation strategies, such as effective problem solving or active distraction, when appropriate. Alternatively, given the hopelessness theory's (Abramson et al., 1989) recognition of the importance of "hopelessness-inducing environments," it may be possible to help cognitively vulnerable individuals decrease the stressfulness of the environments in which they live.

Furthermore, the findings on some of the potential developmental origins of depressogenic cognitive styles suggest that primary prevention efforts might be aimed at building positive cognitive styles in children. This could be accomplished by educating parents and teachers to model and provide feedback about more benign inferences for stressful events in children's lives, as well as through direct training of children in schools in generating more positive interpretations of stressful events. The Penn Optimism Program is such a school-based program designed precisely to prevent depression through attribution training of children and has shown initial success (see Shatte, Gillham, & Reivich, 2000, for a review). In addition, parenting classes that teach parents less abusive ways of dealing with their children's misbehavior may be beneficial in preventing the development of negative cognitive styles (Rose & Abramson, 1992).

All these prevention proposals require extensive investigation if we are to more fully understand and use what has been learned from research on cognitive vulnerability to depression. Moreover, in addition to testing any prophylactic benefit derived from such interventions for preventing depression itself, the applicability of such prevention strategies to adolescent maladaptive outcomes and risk behaviors more generally must be directly evaluated.

Part II

Section C

Peers and Parents

CHAPTER 21

EMOSA Sexuality Models, Memes, and the Tipping Point

Policy and Program Implications

JOSEPH LEE RODGERS

EMOSA is the acronym for a mathematical modeling approach called "epidemic modeling of the onset of social activities." EMOSA modeling uses the same mathematical models that epidemiologists use to account for the spread of biological organisms (viruses, bacteria, etc.) and adapts those to model the spread of behaviors. The behaviors to which EMOSA modeling has been applied are primarily transition behaviors that threaten adolescents' health.

The development of EMOSA models has been a 15-year collaborative project between me and David Rowe from the University of Arizona. The first EMOSA model was proposed by Rowe, Rodgers, and Meseck-Bushey (1989) to model transition from virginity to nonvirginity, using adolescent data from intact school settings in North Carolina and Florida. Other EMOSA sexuality models have expanded the original to include between-age interactions and national data (Rowe & Rodgers, 1991b), noncoital sexual transitions such as kissing and heavy petting (Rodgers & Rowe, 1993), explanation of race differences in sexual behavior prevalence (Rowe & Rodgers, 1994), and the transition to pregnancy and the acquisition of sexually transmitted disease (STD) (Rodgers, Rowe, & Buster, 1998). EMOSA models have also been developed to explain the spread through adolescent networks of smoking cigarettes (Rowe & Rodgers, 1991a; Rowe, Chassin, Presson, & Sherman, 1996; Rowe, Rodgers, & Gilson, 1999) and drinking alcohol (Rowe & Rodgers, 1991a). In addition, an unpublished EMOSA model was developed to model the spread of crime (Rowe & Rodgers, 2002).

EMOSA models posit an intact interacting network of adolescents. Within the network are some who have performed the behavior of interest (e.g., ever smoking a cigarette, ever having had sexual intercourse), and the rest have not. During a time unit (e.g., a month or a year, depending on how finely the empirical data are specified), the model pairs individuals into dyads (pairing occurs either randomly or reflects correlated mixing). Within these dyads, the model assumes that social influence passes from the person who has performed the behavior to the one who has not. With some transition probability (estimated by fitting the model to real data), the adolescent who has not performed the behavior does so and moves into the "having performed" category. The model applies this process across multiple time intervals, and the proportion that has ever performed the behavior increases toward some eventual asymptote. If the empirical data show a gradual entry into the "having performed" category, then the estimated transition probabilities will be relatively small; if the entry is rapid, they will be closer to 1.

This process is captured in a set of EMOSA equations, which are similar in form to the May-Anderson equations from epidemiology (Anderson & May, 1991). The transition probabilities can be specified globally or can be conditioned on relevant external features. All our models condition on the partner's status on the behavior (which is what drives the potential for social influence); "epidemic" transmission of the behavior occurs if an experienced adolescent influences a nonexperienced adolescent, or "nonepidemic" transmission occurs if two inexperienced adolescents perform the behavior together spontaneously. EMOSA models can also condition on age, gender, race, or other characteristics (Rodgers et al., 1998). The EMOSA sexual development models also condition on the pubertal status of female respondents.

Each version of the model makes simplifying assumptions. An actual adolescent network is more complex than the one described in the model. In reality, adolescents are influenced by more than one "partner." No adolescent network truly exists as intact (and networks overlap). Some important

conditioning properties are ignored by some models (e.g., religious categories, parental influence categories, etc.). These assumptions have been investigated in our own research and also in previous mathematical treatment of social contagion and epidemiological theory (e.g., Burt, 1987; Crane, 1991).

Although the work described in past EMOSA articles is highly methodological, the driving feature of EMOSA modeling is the concept of *social contagion*. The process of social contagion implies social influence that passes from one adolescent to another (Rodgers & Rowe, 1993). Adolescents encounter a range of newly available behaviors to which most have not been previously exposed. This expanded behavioral repertoire—which comprises the so-called transition behaviors (Ensminger, 1987; Rodgers & Rowe, 1993)—includes risk-taking behaviors that can potentially compromise an adolescent's health. Many of these are spread, at least in part, through social contagion. For example, when an adolescent girl tries to convince her friend to smoke a cigarette, there is the potential for her friend to move from the category of "nonsmoker" to "experimental smoker" because of that influence process. These processes are ones that immediately suggest the analogy between biological and social contagion—adolescents may be "spreading" new behaviors to their friends.

Our primary interest has been in the way social contagion contributes to risk-taking behaviors that put adolescent health at actual or potential risk—in particular, smoking, drinking, and unprotected or precocious sexual behavior. Obviously, many behaviors that respond to social contagion processes are healthy and positive. For example, an adolescent boy encouraging his friend to play in the school band or to spend more time on homework would exemplify this side of the process. Ultimately, our interest is in moving research on social contagion from the modeling and research arena into the policy arena

We have believed for a long time that EMOSA modeling results have the potential to bridge the gap between the research and policy arenas (e.g., Rodgers, 2000). We must expect different critiques from each arena. In the following treatment, I'll use what we've learned from past settings in which that bridging has occurred to illustrate how our model works and to suggest policy implications. I will do that by using two popularized accounts of the idea of social contagion. The first comes from a well-known scientist, Richard Dawkins (1989), writing for an intellectual but popular audience in *The Selfish Gene*. The second comes from a recent bestseller, *The Tipping Point*, by Malcolm Gladwell (2000). Both have potential to help deliver the ideas that underlie EMOSA modeling and the policy-relevant findings from this approach to an audience that may not be comfortable with the methodology of fit statistics or nonlinear systems (or, for that matter, the language of epidemiology transported into behavioral domains).

DAWKINS'S "MEME"

The idea of social contagion, as captured in EMOSA modeling, is not new, is not unique, and is certainly not unusual. The methodology of "innovation diffusion" has been in development in the research arena for some time (e.g., Mahajan & Peterson, 1985). It has been used in archeology, marketing, social psychology, leadership studies, and any number of other disciplines. In popular scientific writing, the belief that ideas and behaviors powerful enough to spread through a culture are worthy of study (and deserve a term to describe them) has been around for some time. Dawkins (1989) called such a cultural unit of interest, powerful enough to travel from person to person

(i.e., from "brain to brain"), a "meme" (the "idea equivalent" of a "gene"): "We need a name for the new replicator, a noun that conveys the idea of a unit of cultural transmission, or a unit of *imitation*" (p. 192). He followed with a list of examples of memes: tunes, ideas, catchphrases, clothes fashions, ways of making pots or of building arches. In fact, the idea of a meme itself is so intriguing as to pass through the "cultural soup" to which Dawkins refers. As he noted in a later edition of *The Selfish Gene*, "The word meme seems to be turning out to be a good meme" (Dawkins, 1989, p. 322). He develops the power of a good meme:

> So memes propagate themselves in the meme pool by leaping from brain to brain via a process which, in the broad sense, can be called imitation. When you plant a fertile meme in my mind you literally parasitize my brain, turning it into a vehicle for the meme's propagation in just the way that a virus may parasitize the genetic mechanism of a host cell. (Dawkins, 1989, p. 192)

To adolescents, smoking, drinking, delinquent behaviors, and sexual behaviors are all potential memes. When one adolescent convinces another to try a behavior for the first time, the potential is realized. Exactly this process—the transmission of a behavior from one adolescent to another—is the basis of EMOSA modeling. Furthermore, EMOSA modeling focuses on the beginning of the process, the "onset of social" behaviors. To elaborate the biological analogy, humans go to great effort to prevent infection with a pathogen, knowing that once infected, the threat to health begins in earnest. Similarly, we focus on the first cigarette, the first drink of alcohol, and the first intercourse experience. In no sense is the contest for good health finished with the contraction of a virus, nor is a life of smoking mandated by the first cigarette. The transitional process is the focus of EMOSA modeling, however. In some cases, we have treated further development of these processes by using multiple-transition models in an EMOSA context (see Rodgers & Rowe, 1993, for sexual behavior, and Rowe et al., 1996, for smoking).

To slightly elaborate Dawkins's language, we propose here special types of memes. His list of examples included both ideas and behaviors. Our focus is on behaviors, and for that special case of memes, we propose the name "be-memes" (pronounced with long *es*). Our more specific focus is on the onset of behaviors, and for that more special case, we propose the name "beo-memes," where the extra *o* refers to "onset," as in "behavioral-onset-memes" (and pronounced as in Beowulf). "Beo" is a Gaelic word meaning "living" or "alive." In this context, it is both an abbreviation for "behavior onset" and also a reference to the fact that when a behavior is performed for the first time by a new individual, the behavior has "come to life" within that individual.

What Dawkins has done is exactly what EMOSA modeling has attempted as well. He has developed the concept that ideas, tunes, catchphrases, and so on pass through "thought space," from brain to brain. Although the analogy itself does not automatically imply pathology, if a meme passing from brain to brain is problematic, there are obvious health implications. Nonvirginity is an obvious beo-meme in our culture. Its propriety and health are highly age dependent, and also depend on other conditioning factors (e.g., marital status, STD status of the partner, whether the sex is protected from pregnancy, etc.).

GLADWELL'S TIPPING POINT

Malcolm Gladwell popularized the idea of social contagion. Others began the process before Gladwell's (2000) book (see, e.g., Lynch, 1996, as well as earlier writing by ourselves and others). Gladwell helped the idea of social contagion itself to become a successful (self-referential) meme within U.S. culture by producing a best-selling book on the topic. I will use several of Gladwell's taxonomies to further develop the idea of social contagion. Following, I will apply those to further develop policy implications that emerge from EMOSA modeling. Gladwell defined three "rules of epidemics." The Law of the Few suggests that "some people matter more than others" (p. 19). The Stickiness Factor suggests that "there are specific ways of making a contagious message memorable" (p. 25). The Power of Context suggests that "the key to getting people to change their behavior . . . sometimes lies with the smallest details of their immediate situation" (p. 29).

Gladwell noted that three types of people are required to spread social contagion. Connectors know a lot of other people who happen to be the right people to help spread ideas or behaviors. But Connectors receive their information from Mavens, who are collectors of important information and who are inclined to pass that information along. And both Connectors and Mavens depend on Salesmen to actually spread the beo-meme. As Gladwell (2000) notes, "Mavens are data banks. They provide the message. Connectors are social glue: they spread it. But . . . Salesmen . . . persuade us when we are unconvinced of what we are hearing" (p. 70).

Gladwell discussed extensively one of the topics to which EMOSA models have been applied: smoking. He suggested that there are two ways to stop the spread of smoking—either to stop the adolescents who first begin to smoke or to dampen the influence that they have on other adolescents (p. 238). He also emphasized individual differences caused by "different innate tolerances for nicotine" (p. 243). Furthermore, he suggested two different treatment-oriented approaches to helping reduce smoking. One is to treat depression, which is strongly linked to smoking and may make it much tougher to quit smoking. This approach is probably not relevant, however, to the beo-meme of smoking, the influence that causes adolescents to start smoking in the first place. His second suggestion is that tobacco companies be required to lower the levels of nicotine so that people would be "capable of smoking up to five cigarettes a day without getting addicted" (p. 249; this idea is attributable to Benowitz & Henningfield, 1994), which would reduce the almost immediate dependence that those with high nicotine addiction begin to show on beginning to smoke.

POLICY RECOMMENDATIONS BASED ON EMOSA MODELING

In Rodgers (2000), I presented three policy recommendations that emerge from EMOSA modeling. I will review these recommendations and then reconsider them in light of the meme (and beo-meme) concept and the taxonomies and suggestions presented in Gladwell's (2000) book.

I began the discussion of policy implications by distinguishing between two features of EMOSA models on sexual behavior. One feature is the "probability of transition" to nonvirginity—that is, the likelihood that the beo-meme of nonvirginity is powerful enough to result in an adolescent male or female influencing his or her partner to engage in sexual intercourse for the first time. The second feature is the "social contagion process itself." I noted that most programs directed toward reducing sexuality, pregnancy, or STDs among adolescents focus on the transition probability. Attempting to influence this probability is the basis of "abstinence only" and "just say no" programs. Such programs will naturally have tremendous selection bias: Many adolescents

willing to sign virginity pledges are likely those who would not be influenced to non-virginity in the first place; the behavioral result may be virtually the same with or without the program. Another approach to reducing the transition probability of pregnancy is one in which adolescent girls are paid to not get pregnant. In Rodgers (2000), I noted that "the EMOSA modeling approach suggests that instead of delivering programs that treat individuals and that attempt to reduce likelihood of certain individual behaviors, educators and policymakers would be better advised to consider the *whole process of the spread of behavior itself*" (p. 269).

The three policy recommendations I presented were the following:

1. The individual adolescents who are likely to be sexually precocious (or who are already sexually active) should be targeted for particular attention.

2. Program efforts need to begin sooner, at a younger age, with the important goal of postponing nonvirginity even for only a very few adolescents within the social network.

3. More attention should be given to the role of physical/pubertal development.

My first recommendation sounds, on the surface, to be attractive. However, Gladwell (2000) felt that this is "the most difficult path of all: the most independent, precocious, rebellious teens are hardly likely to be the most susceptible to rational health advice" (p. 238). I agree that traditional "don't-do-it" types of approaches will not (and have not) worked with this group. Such teens are unlikely to be impressed by any of Gladwell's three words: *rationality*, *health*, or *advice*. I don't agree, however, that creative "outside-the-box" types of approaches wouldn't be effective.

I will develop some basic principles of such a program, using Gladwell's (2000) taxonomy that distinguishes between individuals who are likely to spread such a beo-meme. The "independent, precocious, rebellious teens" to whom Gladwell refers are often natural leaders. Empowering them to assist in or to lead, for example, anti-smoking programs might harness some of their talents for influence. Some would be natural Mavens, adolescents who know facts about their friends—who's tried what, who's thinking about trying what, and what each individual's parents, siblings, and other friends would think about them trying new behaviors. Others would be natural Connectors, adolescents who are naturally aware of the social intricacies of the adolescent network: Who might be interested in leading an "internal" antismoking campaign? Which of their friends would immediately jump on board? Who would be oblivious to such a campaign? Finally, the Salesmen would be the adolescents who would naturally implement the campaign among their peers. Although an adult preaching the health hazards would not likely influence a teen considering smoking, and neither would the well-known class moralizer, one of the class leaders might well succeed. Conceptualizing this type of effort is, obviously, much easier than implementing it. Clearly, assigning these roles would not work. Empowering the class to develop such an effort, with targeted support for each type of role, might have a better chance.

Sexual behavior, pregnancy prevention, and STD prevention programs are in many ways more difficult to develop, because of potentially conflicting goals. If the goal is to reduce pregnancy or STDs, then reducing sexual behavior is only one means toward that end; efficacious use of condoms is another that may work better. Substitution of other sexual behaviors (e.g., oral sex or mutual masturbation) for intercourse would also reduce risk of pregnancy (and some STDs). But many policymakers (and parents) simultaneously want to achieve additional health and ethical goals, through reduction of sexual behavior itself.

One of the difficulties in intervening in sexual behavior becomes apparent in evolutionary context. A desire for a cigarette, or for alcohol, has little evolutionary basis. But every human is descended from ancestors who had sex, and many of whom had sex at very young ages. A strong sex drive has obvious adaptive advantages. There are many social control mechanisms that channel sexuality into societally approved settings (e.g., religion, marriage, etc.). But the health-risking features of sex are not equivalent to those associated with smoking and drinking. Careful and protected intercourse does not have high likelihood of damage to long-term health; but one single mistake can lead to pregnancy, which can immediately change the young person's life, or to STDs, which can be devastating or even deadly. Several suggestions for sexual programs seem relevant. Identifying the children of sexually precocious parents would be a possible starting point for identifying those at risk of early pregnancy (a research literature exists to support this suggestion; e.g., Newcomer & Udry, 1987). Identifying those children who go through puberty early would be another (a research literature also exists to support this assertion; e.g., Udry, Billy, Morris, Groff, & Raj, 1985; Udry, Talbert, & Morris, 1986). Second, the "stickiness factor" to which Gladwell (2000) refers is critical. Third, Gladwell's Power of Context suggests that little things often matter, depending on the context. For example, social support for responsible sexual behavior from a single influential classmate (e.g., a Salesman) could have substantial effects. Fourth, timing is undoubtedly one of the contextual factors. Starting pregnancy prevention programs at the time when pregnancy apparently becomes a problem (around age 14) is many years too late; the social contagion process that spreads sexual behavior that eventually leads to pregnancy began much earlier, before teachers and parents were probably even aware that there was a risk.

ADDITIONAL RESEARCH

Intervention programs have seldom been informed by the principles that emerge from the theory of social contagion (or innovation diffusion or tipping point theory, etc.). This theoretical perspective has an obvious advantage over most other methodological research in this area: EMOSA models are actual models of a behavioral process. Many statistical studies attempt to predict behavior, but they use models that are not in any sense descriptive of the processes being modeled (see Rodgers et al., 1998, for elaboration).

There are at least two advantages of this explanatory feature of EMOSA models. First, they can be used to simulate behavior under the simplified assumptions on which the model is based (and, furthermore, can be used to evaluate the legitimacy and importance of those assumptions; Rowe & Rodgers, 1994.) Second, given the assumptions of the model, EMOSA models are both predictive and descriptive tools. This implies that features of EMOSA models could be evaluated in actual settings, as well as the other way around. Past EMOSA research has shown a number of interesting—and occasionally surprising—features of the simplified world that those models describe. The implications of the models could be formally evaluated in intervention settings. Simultaneously, a theoretically driven intervention program would be under evaluation as well.

I offer two examples of such an evaluation process. Others could easily be constructed. One result that has emerged from EMOSA modeling is that nonepidemic transmission occurs only very occasionally (see the original EMOSA article—Rowe et al., 1989). In other words, in EMOSA models, a virgin male or female seldom has a first experience of sexual intercourse with another virgin female or male. In Rodgers (1992), I presented data that addressed this issue directly (by asking adolescents their perceived virginity status of their first partner) rather than indirectly through the model; the two domains matched fairly closely (although not exactly). The implication of this finding for program development is obvious: Little time need be spent intervening to delay virgin-virgin first intercourse experiences. Second, in Rodgers et al. (1998), we found the best-fitting model to be one that contained a fairly constant probability of pregnancy, regardless of age of the female. This appeared counterintuitive, because sexually active adolescents who are older presumably have intercourse more often than those who are younger. But we proposed an approximately compensatory process, where frequency was balanced by efficacy of contraceptive use. This suggestion is speculative but could be tested with direct evidence in intervention settings.

GENERAL PRINCIPLES

I have attempted to let the taxonomies developed by Gladwell (2000) blend and influence my earlier suggestions about policy implications of EMOSA modeling. Several general principles emerge from this discussion.

The first is the importance of treating different individuals differently. A girl who is pubertally mature at age 10 who had parents who began childbearing at age 14 is obviously at different risk of sexually related health problems than a slow-maturing boy whose parents began childbearing in their 30s. Although a separate program cannot be developed for each child, a particular program can differentiate levels of risk. Second, using adolescents themselves as active participants in the program appears efficacious. In other words, the adolescents themselves can spread many different types of behaviors. An anti-smoking beo-meme or an abstinence-only beo-meme is much more likely to be effective when passed through an adolescent network than when an adult mandates or encourages healthy behaviors. Third, recognizing the time dynamic context of the spread of social influence is critical; just like a biological epidemic, a social epidemic is much easier to prevent than to eliminate once it reaches the level of an epidemic. Finally, the idea that health-risking adolescent behaviors are memes (or beo-memes) is an important stimulus to our understanding. The health risks of smoking, drinking, and precocious or unprotected sexual behavior are patently obvious to adults. Why aren't they obvious to teens? Perhaps to teens they are beo-memes that become memes. These are behaviors whose ability to spread through adolescent networks has been demonstrated time after time. Breaking this cycle may require be-memes and beo-memes that are even more powerful and attractive to adolescents than the behaviors that we have been studying.

The onset and continued spread of adolescent transition behaviors in a social network through social influence is, in its own way, just as sure and relentless as the spread of biological organisms such as viruses. If colds were mysterious maladies without known cause, little could be done to prevent them. But recognizing that the cold virus is transmitted from human to human, and building models of the mechanism of spread, is a good starting point for both prevention and treatment. Analogously, understanding the social dynamics of health-risking processes that spread, at least in part, through social contagion, is also a good starting point for both prevention and treatment.

CHAPTER 22

Sustaining and Broadening Intervention Effect

Social Norms, Core Values, and Parents

BONITA F. STANTON

JAMES BURNS

The question of sustaining and broadening the impact of risk reduction intervention is important and complex. Sexual risk, substance use, delinquency, and other risk behaviors are multifactorial in origin and associated with myriad rewards—physical, psychological, and cultural (National Research Council, 1990). Indeed, even the definition of "risky" behavior is both relative and temporal. Effecting a temporary change is difficult; effecting a sustained change is even more difficult: (a) Although models of behavior and behavioral change posit a series of factors that influence risk and protective behaviors, the relationship of these factors to risk and protective behaviors is inconsistent, at times difficult to adequately describe or capture, and appears to vary (although not necessarily in any predictable fashion) by gender, age, socioeconomic class, and locale. (b) Different modes of intervention delivery may be variably effective with different specific target audiences or differing target factors.

Although complex in any population, effecting sustained change is particularly so among adolescents: (a) It is almost uniquely during adolescence that individuals begin to engage in high-risk behaviors. (b) The entrance of adolescents into risky behaviors is not absolute, not uniform, and does not follow a particular set pattern; it varies by gender, ethnicity, socioeconomic status, geographic location, and temporal factors. (c) The relationship between adolescent cognitive abilities and their emotional and cognitive faculties varies throughout adolescence and between adolescents. (d) Biologically, adolescents are more vulnerable to sexually transmitted diseases than are those of other ages. Clearly, then, one should not assume that a single intervention, however delivered, would have a lasting effect, would generalize across multiple-risk behaviors, or both.

Formats used for intervention delivery targeting adolescents have included direct interventions (e.g., face-to-face) to small groups (both investigator formed and "natural-friendship formed"), classrooms, and individuals (e.g., in clinic settings); media-based interventions (stand-alone posters, movies, brochures, and larger, more integrated campaigns); and indirect interventions (e.g., interventions targeting physicians, parents, peers—"opinion leaders" and other potentially influential adults). These approaches have resulted in a range of outcomes, including no change; selected changes in behavior, intentions, perceptions, or some combination of these; and occasionally, substantial changes. As our knowledge of components of successful interventions has increased, so too have the reported rates of successful intervention effect (Kim, Stanton, Li, Dickersin, & Galbraith, 1997; Kirby et al., 1994; Stanton, Kim, Galbraith, & Parrott, 1996).

But despite these considerable successes, sustainability (and its companion, "breadth") remain a major concern (see National Institutes of Health, 1997, consensus statement). Options that have been suggested or explored have included "boosters," including but not limited to repeated classroom exposure, mass media campaigns, and interventions among those with influence (parents, physicians, etc.).

SIGNIFICANT INTERMEDIARIES OF BEHAVIOR AND BEHAVIORAL CHANGE

The research on sustainability and breadth offers comparatively little guidance to interventionists in contrast to that available to inform interventions whose outcomes are short term or content focused. Although there is an abundance of research to change a specific behavior for the short term, the foundation relevant to sustained change across many behaviors is substantially less informed.

Nevertheless, even if directed toward bringing about (rather than sustaining) behavioral change in a single behavior (rather than in multiple risk behaviors), it is intuitively appealing to seek some guidance from this literature. In the past decade, an increasing percentage of the adolescent risk reduction research has been theory based, with social cognitive models dominating the field (Kim et al., 1997; Stanton et al., 1996). A large number of studies exploring intervention impact have posited a relationship between the "constructs" of this model and behavioral outcomes. Although some of the constructs (e.g., the putative intermediaries in behavioral change) have a less consistent relationship with risk and protective behaviors and with intervention effect, others seem to be more dependable and consistent. It seemed plausible to us to explore whether these more "consistent" intermediaries might be more amenable to one or more of the potential options for sustaining and broadening intervention effect. For example, if it turns out that perceived severity and vulnerability are consistent predictors of risk and protective behaviors and that there is good reason to believe that these perceptions are particularly amenable to advertisements through radio and television, then we might anticipate that a mass media campaign would likely represent an effective means of sustaining and broadening intervention effects.

Among the several social cognitive theories employed to guide intervention development and evaluation, for convenience and because of our own familiarity with it, we selected protection motivation theory (PMT) (Rogers, 1983) to guide our search for robust intermediaries. PMT postulates that the decision to engage in a risky or protective behavior represents a balance between (a) perceptions of severity, (b) perceptions of vulnerability, (c) perceptions of *extrinsic* rewards (peer and parental norms) for participating in the risk behavior and perceived *intrinsic* rewards (value system) for participating in the risk behavior versus perceptions of the costs of participating in the protective behavior, (d) perceptions of the effectiveness of the protective behavior, and (e) perceptions of one's ability to conduct the protective behavior.

Both as part of cross-sectional or exploratory studies and as part of intervention evaluations, a substantial literature exists regarding the association of these intermediary variables and their relationship to risk and protective behaviors. A superficial exploration of the literature regarding HIV risk and risk reduction offers a good example of the associations explored and found. The following observations by no means represent an exhaustive review (although a more comprehensive search may be indicated) but, rather, are illustrative—and, we believe, reflective of the wider research experience.

Of the intermediary variables posited as potentially important by PMT, all have been associated in at least a few studies with risk or protective behaviors (*vide infra*). However, for several of the variables, these associations are relatively inconsistent or weak. The evidence regarding the overall importance of perceived vulnerability and severity is mixed, with some studies finding an association between protected behaviors and increased perceived severity (HIV/STDs are serious, drug addiction is a significant problem, etc.) or vulnerability (Cerwonka, Isbell, & Hansen, 2000; MacPhail & Campbell, 2001; Polacsek, Clentano, O'Campo, & Santelli, 1999), but others finding no such association (Brown, O'Grady, Farrell, Flechner, & Nurco, 2001; Morrison-Beedy, Carey, & Lewis, 2002). Likewise, although there is considerable literature supporting the importance of self-efficacy (ability to correctly use condoms, to talk to

partners, to say "no," etc.) and efficacy (condoms are effective in preventing HIV/STDs, nicotine patches do help with tobacco cessation, etc.), many studies have found no such association (Buunk, Bakker, Siero, van den Eijnden, & Yzer, 1998; Cerwonka et al., 2000; McMahon, Malow, Jennings, & Gomez, 2001; Meekers & Klein, 2002; Rotheram-Borus, Gwadz, Fernandez, & Srinivasan, 1998).

By contrast, the evidence for the importance of extrinsic rewards and intrinsic rewards—including peer norms, peer approval, perceived parental actions and approval (and the reciprocal, "response cost" or loss of peer and parental approval, etc.)—is considerably stronger. Research supporting the roles of peer norms and parental norms and approval has been robust across several decades in multiple ethnic niches regarding numerous risk and protective behaviors (Alexander & Campbell, 1967; Billy & Udry, 1985; Booth-Kewley, Minagawa, Shaffer, & Brodine, 2002; Buunk et al., 1998; Cerwonka et al., 2000; DeLamater & MacCorquodale, 1979; Dinges & Oetting, 1993; Dornbusch, Ritter, Leiderman, Roberts, & Fraleigh, 1987; Ennett & Bauman, 1994; Giordano, Cernkovick, & Pugh, 1986; Ianazu & Fox, 1980; Jaccard & Dittus, 1991; Jessor, Costa, Jessor, & Donovan, 1983; Jessor, Graves, Hanson, & Jessor, 1968; Jessor & Jessor, 1974; MacPhail & Campbell, 2001; Morrison-Beedy et al., 2002; Polacsek et al., 1999; Rodgers, Billy, & Udry, 1984; Romer et al., 1994; Stanton et al., 2000; Steinberg, Dornbusch, & Brown, 1992; Steinberg, Fletcher, & Darling, 1994; Steinberg, Mounts, & Lamborn, 1991; Walsh, Ferrell, & Tolone, 1976). In our own work conducted in Baltimore, perceived peer behavior is one of the stronger predictors and correlates of risk and protective behavior (Romer et al., 1994; Stanton et al., in press). Intrinsic rewards or values are more difficult to gauge, although, arguably, parental approval may be considered a reasonable proxy for an internal value system. The importance of perceived parental views and actions is consistent with social learning theory and strong predictors of adolescent risk and protective behaviors (Meekers & Klein, 2002; Jessor & Jessor, 1974; Romer et al., 1999). Of particular importance for behavioral change among adolescents is that the data appear to indicate the importance of intrinsic and extrinsic rewards for adolescents of all ages (Romer, 1994; Romer et al., 1994; Stanton 1994).

SOCIAL NORMS, CORE VALUES, AND INTERVENTION OPTIONS

Taken at face value, these findings, if indeed indicative of the wider literature, might suggest that interventions that influence both extrinsic and intrinsic rewards in particular would be most likely to effect behavioral change. Returning to the intervention options mentioned earlier (face-to-face boosters, mass media, and parental monitoring), all may be reasonable candidates in this regard, but one in particular—parental monitoring—seems to be a particularly strong contender for sustaining and broadening intervention impact among adolescents. Before turning in more detail to the parental monitoring option, it is perhaps useful to briefly explore the other options.

Face-to-face "boosters" offer the opportunity to reinforce old messages; to present new, developmentally and historically correct information; to potentially build on the social interactions established in the earlier face-to-face sessions (if the same subjects are involved); and to enable interactive question-and-answer exchange. This format is probably most supportive of changing or reinforcing perceptions of self-efficacy and efficacy. Practice in condom use and in negotiating

with a sex partner, achievable through the face-to-face format, can be reinforced through boosters. Face-to-face boosters may also be a useful forum in which to discuss facts that might lead to changes in perceptions of vulnerability and disease severity. With regard to the two outcomes of particular interest in this discussion—extrinsic and intrinsic rewards—there is good reason to assume that a face-to-face booster can, through discussion, alter perceptions of peer norms.

Some investigators, including ourselves, have experimented with boosters and have found mixed results. In work we conducted in the mid-1990s, we followed an eight-session, face-to-face HIV risk reduction intervention with boosters at 15 and 27 months. The original intervention effect on unprotected sex, apparent at 6 months (39% of control youth compared with 15% of intervention youth), had waned by 12 months. However, an intervention effect on sexual risk behavior was again apparent at 18 months (39% vs. 19%); in addition, drug use was higher among control compared with intervention youth (21% vs. 11%; Stanton et al., 1997). But the booster at 27 months was not associated with any increase in intervention effect at the next follow-up assessment (36 months; Li, Stanton, & Feigelman, in press). These findings suggested that boosters might both sustain and broaden intervention effect. Recently, in a study conducted among more than 800 youth randomized to one of three conditions (the basic adolescent risk reductions: face-to-face intervention, the same intervention augmented by a parental monitoring intervention [*vide infra*], and a version additionally embellished with boosters at 7 and 10 months), we again found weak evidence for a minor booster effect. Two risk behaviors, use of crack/cocaine and drug selling, were significantly lower among the youth who received the additional boosters compared with youth without the boosters.

The rates of the other risk behaviors and intentions did not differ significantly (Wu et al., 2003).

Mass media may be a particularly effective vehicle for changing perceptions of peer norms. Communication campaigns have been widely used against cigarettes, alcohol, and illicit drugs and have relied on strategies designed to increase social disapproval as well as strategies to increase the perception of severity and vulnerability to the risks associated with these practices (Romer, 1994). Research conducted by the Partnership for a Drug-Free America suggests that the campaigns have been responsible at least in part for the increasing rates of disapproval of illegal drugs in recent years (Black, DiPasquale, Bayer, Koch, & Padgett, 1993). At the same time, there is little reason to believe that a mass media campaign can substantially increase perceptions of self-efficacy and, of particular interest in this discussion, of intrinsic reward or core values.

PARENTS AS AN INTERVENTION OPTION

In contrast to these other options, we would argue, for several reasons, that parents can both sustain and broaden the intervention impact. First, parents are authority figures; there is some evidence that authority figures may influence health-seeking behaviors and that parents are a major source of information regarding sexual and contraceptive behavior (Jaccard & Dittus, 1991; Spanier, 1977). Second, parents serve as role models; intervention efforts that influence parental risk and protective behaviors may be expected to influence youths' behaviors (Jaccard, & Dittus, 1991). Third, parents exert a role in the selection of friends, both directly and indirectly, thereby influencing the child's perceptions of social norms. Finally, and of great importance to the

present discussion, parents "instill values and moral structures within their children, and such moral systems impact on the child's tendency to engage in potentially problematic behavior" (Jaccard & Dittus, 1991, p. 3). Therefore, we have reason to believe that interventions invoking parents by affecting both extrinsic and intrinsic rewards, might well serve to both sustain and broaden intervention impact.

The literature on parenting and adolescent behaviors is rich, with findings that are robust across decades, ethnic groups, and socioeconomic status. This literature has coalesced into the concept of "parental monitoring," including both communication and supervision. Particularly, communication about values has a strong influence on adolescent risk behavior. For example, in a longitudinal study of 10,000 7th to 11th graders selected from the Add-Health Study, teens were over sixfold less likely to engage in sexual activity if they felt that their mothers disapproved of sexual activity compared with those who felt that their mothers did not disapprove. However, youths' perceptions of maternal attitude and actual maternal attitude were only poorly correlated. The authors therefore concluded that parents must be careful to clearly articulate their feelings about risk behaviors to their teens (Dittus & Jaccard, 2000). Consistent with this study were findings from our work over 4 years with 383 African American youth among whom perceptions of parental monitoring were inversely associated with unprotected sex, drug use, and drug trafficking (Li, Stanton, & Feigelman, 2002). Particularly striking about these results, the effects of baseline perceptions of parental monitoring were enduring, extending in some cases through 4 years of follow up (Stanton, 2002; Li, 2002).

These findings are consistent with Baumrind's work extending over four decades in which she determined that close supervision and high demands from parents did not lead to reduced autonomy or creativity. To the contrary, her review of the literature revealed that permissiveness increased aggression. Although she did not advocate physical punishment (also associated with aggression; Baumrind, 1991) or intrusive psychological controls such as withdrawal of love, shaming, or inflicting guilt (associated with dependency), she did advocate direct parental influence through the use of reason, verbal exchange, and affirmation of the child's qualities. She described parenting styles based on *responsiveness* (affectionate, accepting, comforting, reliable, supportive, recognition of achievement, loving, nurturing, and caring) and *control* (active monitoring, setting and enforcing clear standards of behavior, demanding, disciplined, and maintaining structure and regimen in child's daily life; Baumrind, 1965, 1991). On the basis of this work, Macoby and Martin (1983) postulated the existence of four parenting styles: *authoritative* (high responsiveness and high control), *authoritarian* (high control, but low responsiveness), *permissive* (high responsiveness, but low control) and *neglectful* (low responsiveness and low control). Baumrind (1991) then conducted a 10-year longitudinal analysis of 139 Caucasian families, studying the children at ages 4, 10, and 15 years. This work demonstrated that authoritative parenting was associated with the highest degree of adolescent competence and the lowest rates of problem behaviors. Adolescent development was impeded by authoritarian, permissive, and neglectful parents. Since this work, numerous studies have been conducted across ecological, ethnic, temporal, and geographic niches. With few exceptions, the original observations have been substantiated (Dornbusch et al., 1987; Jackson, Bee-Gates, & Henriksen, 1994; Lamborn, Mounts, Steinberg, & Dornbusch, 1991; Radziszewska, Richardson, Dent, & Flay, 1996; Steinberg et al., 1992; Steinberg, Elmen, & Mounta, 1989; Steinberg,

Fletcher, & Darling, 1994; Steinberg, Lamborn, Darling, Mounts, & Dornbusch, 1994; Jackson, 1994; Strage, 1998).

In summary, parents who communicate their expectations clearly, who express their concern for their children, and who monitor their offspring are more likely to raise competent children with less involvement in problem behaviors than parents who practice other communication and child-rearing strategies. That is, the former parents are more likely to transmit a clear set of values (intrinsic rewards) and to influence a child's selection of friends and role models (extrinsic rewards). Thus, there is good reason to expect that a parental monitoring intervention might both broaden and sustain the impact of a face-to-face intervention targeting adolescents. But do we have any evidence that this is so?

Earlier, we alluded to studies in which we have been involved regarding parental monitoring behaviors. In the first of these, conducted among 237 parent-youth (ages 12 to 16 years) dyads, we developed a parental monitoring intervention (Informed Parents and Children Together [ImPACT]) consisting of a 20-minute, culturally appropriate film *(Protect Your Child From AIDS)* followed by two supervised, interactive playacting "vignettes" and a condom demonstration. The intervention was evaluated through a randomized, controlled study. Those dyads assigned to the control condition viewed an educational and job-readiness film *(Goal for It.)* At 2, 6, and 12 months follow-up, agreement between youth reports of risk behaviors and parent assessment of youth risk behaviors was higher among intervention compared with control dyads. There were no reductions in adolescent risk behaviors. We concluded that a culturally appropriate, parental monitoring intervention can increase agreement of youth risk involvement among youth and their parents and provides evidence that this effect endures over time. At the same time, the fact that youth self-reports of risk behaviors were not different between the two groups led us to recommend that parenting interventions be coupled with adolescent-specific (probably face-to-face) interventions (Li et al., 2002; Stanton et al., 2000).

Recently, we conducted such a trial. In this trial among 821 African American parent-youth (ages 12 to 16) dyads residing in 35 urban, low-income communities in Baltimore, all youth received a basic "face-to-face" adolescent risk reduction intervention (Focus on Kids); about two thirds of the youth with their parent(s) also received ImPACT while the others received an attention control. Six months later, approximately one third of the youth (half of those who received ImPACT) received a booster (as they did again at 10 months). Youth received assessments at baseline and 6 and 12 months postintervention. At 6 months follow up, youth in families where both the youth and the parents had received the interventions (the basic face-to-face intervention plus ImPACT) reported significantly lower rates of sexual intercourse without a condom, cigarette use, and alcohol use and marginally lower rates of "risky sexual behavior" compared with youth in families where only the youth had received the basic face-to-face intervention. At 12 months postintervention, rates of alcohol and marijuana use were significantly lower, and cigarette use and overall risk intention were marginally lower among those youth whose families also received ImPACT compared with youth who received only the basic face-to-face intervention. As noted earlier, with regard to the boosters delivered at 7 months and 10 months, two risk behaviors, use of crack/cocaine and drug selling, were significantly lower among the youth who received the additional boosters compared with youth without the boosters. The rates of the other risk behaviors and intentions did not differ significantly. We concluded that the results of this randomized, controlled trial indicate that the inclusion of a parental monitoring intervention affords additional protection from involvement in adolescent risk behaviors 6 and 12 months later compared with the provision of an intervention targeting adolescents only. Although the boosters conferred some additional benefit, the effect was less striking (Wu, 2003).

The evidence we have cited suggests that parental monitoring influences not just one, but multiple risk and protective behaviors. It might be argued that this effect is to be expected given the concept of "problem-prone behavior" (Donovan, Jessor, & Costa, 1988; Jessor et al., 1983). But contrarily, current intervention wisdom and experience argues for a narrow, focused approach (Kim et al., 1997; Kirby et al., 1994; Stanton et al., 1996). We believe that the intrinsic and extrinsic rewards integral to the parent-child relationship transcend the more evanescent extrinsic rewards associated with peer norms and the more content-specific conceptualizations of severity and vulnerability. The parent-child relationship is held hostage anytime a teen acts counter to parental wishes or expectations. As parental expectations are internalized by children, their own sense of self is threatened when they act counter to these expectations. Thus, each time teens go astray, they know it hurts their parents (and their own value system). The specific risk behavior is less important than the act of defiance to parental wishes or expectations.

POTENTIAL EXPERIMENTAL AVENUES

The questions to be addressed in further exploring this intervention approach are legion and can be considered in several broad categories: timing, content, and format. Should such an intervention accompany, precede, follow, or be independent of adolescent face-to-face interventions? Given the hypothesis that these interventions cut across specific risk behaviors, what specific content is necessary to appropriately "arm" parents with regard to each risk behavior? How can we best reach parents with these interventions, and to what extent will these approaches need to vary by age, ethnicity, and culture?

SUMMARY

To summarize, sustaining and broadening intervention effect is a challenge in all populations; there are particular reasons why it is especially difficult among adolescents. We believe that interventions that address core values and perceptions of social norms will be especially effective in achieving the desired goals. There is substantial theoretical reason and some empirical evidence to support the pairing of face-to-face, adolescent-directed interventions with interventions addressing parental supervision and communication.

Part II

Section D
Media Interventions

CHAPTER 23

Adolescent Risk Behavior Research and Media-Based Health Messages

BARBARA DELANEY

I n 1986, a small group of leaders in the advertising industry proposed putting advertising to work to "unsell" drugs to kids. The concept was to look at the ways teens, in particular, approach decisions about using drugs and to try to influence their choices in much the same way that advertising influences purchase decisions. Why not use the creativity of advertising to persuade teens *not* to buy something? This was—and is—the core idea behind the Partnership for a Drug-Free America (PDFA).

UNDERSTANDING THE CORNERSTONE TO EFFECTIVENESS

The key to developing effective communications is to understand the person with whom we are communicating; in marketing terms, that means the consumer and his or her decision to use a drug. Our "consumers" are adolescents and their parents. To be able to effectively educate them, we have to understand them: What makes children want to try drugs? What are their perceptions of and attitudes and beliefs about illegal drugs? Where and how do they gather information about illegal drugs? What role do their parents play in the decision process? What are parents' perceptions of and attitudes and beliefs about drugs?

Our research is an ongoing dialogue with our consumers. But it does not end there, for the most important part of our research is to articulate what we've learned from consumers to the advertising creative professionals who execute our strategies and develop the television commercials and print advertisements. No matter how much we know about illegal drugs, if we cannot translate that knowledge into meaningful insights, then the advertising is unlikely to achieve its aims. Therefore, the research that we conduct must go beyond just the collection of data; it must provide advertising copywriters and art directors with a real understanding of the targets' lives and minds, enabling them to appreciate what makes children, teens, and their parents tick. The PDFA has to make creative teams hear consumers, see them, understand them—to know how to talk to them. We have to turn research into insights that will present solutions rather than problems—solutions that will enthuse and inspire creative thinking.

What makes this even more challenging is that our targets are constantly moving. Although there are developmental similarities between children and teens of the past and those of today and tomorrow, each cohort faces a new environment with new pressures, often accelerated by the pervasive media.

ACADEMIC RESOURCES

The foundation of the PDFA's antidrug educational messages is the University of Michigan's *Monitoring the Future Study* (Johnston, O'Malley, & Bachman, 2001), which shows that when young people perceive a drug as more dangerous or more disapproved of by their peers, they are less likely to use it. "These findings indicate that perceived risks and disapproval are important determinants of marijuana use. Accordingly, prevention efforts should include realistic information about risks and consequences of marijuana use" (Bachman, Johnston, & O'Malley, 1998, p. 887). In recent years, we have also incorporated learning from the University of Kentucky's research on "risky personality types" (Palmgreen, Donohew, Lorch, Hoyle, & Stephenson, 2001). These researchers recommend targeting risky personality types in prevention programs.

Thus, there is considerable support, both from behavioral studies and from studies in which biological indicators are used, for sensation seeking as an index of "risky personality types" to be targeted in prevention

campaigns. Sensation seeking is a biologically based personality trait characterized by Zuckerman (1994) as "the seeking of varied, novel, complex, and intense sensations and experiences, and the willingness to take physical, social, legal, and financial risks for the sake of such experience." High sensation seekers (HSS) are receptive to stimuli that are intense, novel and arousing; stimuli producing lower levels of arousal may be considered "boring" and cause the HSS to seek alternative sources of stimulation. Low sensation seekers (LSS) tend to reject stimuli that are highly intense, preferring the familiar and less complex. (Donohew, 2002, pp. 4-5)

The Partnership also conducts research among its target audiences—quantitative research with adolescents in Grades 6 through 12 and parents with children under 18. In addition, we conduct qualitative research (focus groups, one-on-ones, affinity pairs) with relevant audiences.

The Partnership's Attitude Tracking Study (PATS) surveys adolescents in middle school and high school. Each year, approximately 8,000 students in Grades 6 through 12 are surveyed in schools, and approximately 1,000 parents are surveyed in homes. Both studies are designed to be projectable, with oversampling to allow for detailed analyses of subpopulations. The oversampling is balanced by weighting to yield correct proportions in the final analysis.

The following are examples of the learning that we obtained by incorporating academic research into the Partnership's research.

WHAT WE HAVE LEARNED

Perceptions of Risk

As mentioned above, the foundation of the PDFA's antidrug messages is the

Table 23.1 Examples From the Partnership for a Drug-Free America's Attitude Tracking Studies

What is the risk to a society that legalizes or condones drugs and that doesn't treat its addicts?	*Societal*
If I use drugs, do I risk hurting people I care about?	Relational
If I use drugs, do I risk not achieving my goals?	Aspirational
If I use drugs, do I risk emotional harm?	Emotional
If I use drugs, do I risk death or physical harm?	Physical

Monitoring the Future research, which has identified a strong correlation between adolescents' perceptions of risk and social disapproval of drug use and actual reported use (Bachman et al., 1998). Building on these findings, the Partnership incorporates general risk questions into the PATS. In addition, it augments these essential findings by monitoring the specific risks that have meaning for an adolescent.

To better understand how adolescents perceive the risk of marijuana use, for example, we added questions to the PATS that elicit perceptions of specific physical risks of using marijuana (e.g., going on to harder drugs, getting hooked on marijuana, driving dangerously), specific emotional risks (e.g., becoming a loser, getting depressed, being lonely, becoming boring, becoming lazy), specific aspirational risks (e.g., not getting a job because of pre-employment drug testing, dropping out of school, losing one's driver's license, not getting into a good college), and specific relational risks (e.g., upsetting one's parents, losing friends, not being able to get a girlfriend/boyfriend). These results permit us to measure the risks

that resonate the strongest with adolescents. See Table 23.1 for the risk categories measured in PATS.

In addition, we also need to understand the differences in perceptions of risk among different segments of adolescents: nonusers of a drug, at-risk adolescents, and users of a drug. Our traditional definition of at-risk adolescents has been those youths who do not use a specific drug but who have attitudes and beliefs that are similar to users. To identify those adolescents who are most at risk, we conduct segmentation studies, and after examining attitudes, beliefs, and behaviors, a discriminate function analysis is used to predict the at-risk segment.

A study we conducted in 1996 segmented teens based on their attitudes toward marijuana and lifestyle and behavior (school, social, parental relationships). Three segments were identified:

1. *Anti-use of marijuana teens:* socially well-adjusted; open trusting relationships with parents; "A" and "B" students who rarely miss school; extroverted and friendly; want compliments and approval; seek challenges but prefer careful, more cautious lifestyle

2. *Pro-use of marijuana teens:* attitudes toward marijuana are positive; more likely to be current marijuana users; more likely to feel pressures from external sources to use marijuana; parent less involved; "C," "D," and "F" students; reject cautious approach to life

3. *Teens who were at-risk of becoming users:* attitudes toward marijuana are ambivalent; at risk for marijuana use; have many of the behavioral and attitudinal patterns of the pro-use segment; less supervision from parents; "C" students and grades are falling

The research found that statements that focus on the negative consequences of marijuana use had the greatest potential of

Table 23.2 Comparison of High-Sensation-Seeking (HSS) Versus Low-Sensation-Seeking (LSS) Youths' Recent Use of Drugs

Used in the past 30 days (%)	HSS	LSS	HSS/LSS Ratio
Alcohol	49	22	2.2
Cigarettes	40	16	2.5
Marijuana	30	11	2.7

preventing marijuana use among attitudinally at-risk youths. Statements that focus on the positive consequences or alternatives of not using marijuana were strongest among nonusers.

From the research, we created relevant creative strategies for the advertising copywriters and art directors. These strategies act as "blueprints," detailing the target audience in terms of attitudes, beliefs, and behaviors; outlining the objective of the advertising; and describing the message to be delivered.

Risky Personality Types

Since 1999, the Partnership has, as mentioned earlier, also drawn on the research from the University of Kentucky's study on sensation-seeking youth (Palmgreen et al., 2001). PDFA ads have been part of the University of Kentucky's marijuana research studies in Lexington, Kentucky, and Knoxville, Tennessee. However, we did not incorporate the Sensation Seeking scale into the PATS until 1999. We used four of the identifying statements from the scale, using the methodology for analysis from the University of Kentucky.

Sensation seeking among middle and high school students is generally measured using a 20-item scale developed specifically for adolescents. More recent evidence suggests that an 8-item scale from the original 20 items has levels of reliability and validity sufficient to replace the 20-item scale. Lewis Donohew reports a comparison between the eight-item and reduced four-item scale on a sample of 6,529 seventh through twelfth graders surveyed by the Partnership for a Drug-Free America in 1999. The eight-item scale had an internal reliability of 0.85, while the four-item scale was reduced only slightly to 0.81. The two correlated at 0.94. Although the evidence of these two studies is unpublished, it suggests that the four-item sensation-seeking scale is both a valid and reliable predictor of drug use and intention in middle and high school years. (Hornik et al., 2002, pp. 2-20)

The analysis from the 2001 PATS of adolescents in Grades 7 through 12 found that high-sensation-seeking youths are over twice as likely as low-sensation-seeking youths to be past 30-day users of alcohol, cigarettes, or marijuana. See Table 23.2 for the comparison rates of alcohol, cigarette, and marijuana consumption by level of sensation seeking.

In addition, high-sensation-seeking youths are approximately three times as likely as low-sensation-seeking youths to try other drugs. Table 23.3 shows the lifetime trial rates of inhalants, ecstasy, methamphetamine, LSD, cocaine/crack, ketamine, and GHB by level of sensation seeking.

MOVING TARGET IN A CHANGING ENVIRONMENT

I hope that the previous examples demonstrate how important research is to the PDFA. It is the basis on which we identify our target

Table 23.3 Comparison of High-Sensation-Seeking (HSS) Versus Low-Sensation-Seeking (LSS)
Youth's Ever Use of Drugs

Ever tried (%)	HSS	LSS	HSS/LSS Ratio
Inhalants	26	10	2.6
Ecstasy	18	6	3
Methamphetamine	16	5	3.2
LSD	15	4	3.8
Cocaine/crack	13	5	2.6
Ketamine	7	2	3.5
GHB	4	2	2

Table 23.4 Growth of Marijuana Use in Recent Years

Lifetime prevalence of marijuana—Monitoring the Future	1991 %	1992 %	1993 %	1994 %	1995 %	1996 %
Eighth graders	10.2	11.2	12.6	16.7	19.9	23.1

SOURCE: Johnston, O'Malley, and Bachman (2001).

and develop the creative strategies that advertising agencies use to make antidrug media messages. However, the Partnership has a unique challenge that requires additional research. Our youth target is a moving target in a changing environment. Although there are developmental similarities between children and teens of the past and those of today and tomorrow, each cohort faces a new social environment. To meet this challenge, the PDFA monitors popular culture: What messages do young people receive from movies, music, the Internet, fashion, television, magazines, and societal debates on legalization and medical marijuana, and how might these messages condition adolescents' perceptions of risk and social disapproval?

Popular culture has a profound effect on adolescents. In the early to mid-1990s, music, movies, and fashion propelled marijuana into teens' lives, resembling the appearance of a cultural fad. Although marijuana has been around for years, for this new cohort, there existed what Lloyd Johnston of the University of Michigan's Institute for Social Research calls "generational forgetting"—"the loss of knowledge by the country's youth of the dangers of drugs through the process of generational replacement" (Johnston et al., 2001, p. 35). This means that 8th graders in the early 1990s did not have the familiarity with marijuana that older cohorts had. Because marijuana does not have the immediate and severe effects of a drug such as heroin, these young people's perceptions of the risk in marijuana use was low, especially after trying the drug only once or twice. Marijuana use increased significantly in a very short period of time (as shown in Table 23.4).

Major research studies (*Monitoring the Future*; Johnston et al., 2001, p. 5) and the *National Household Survey on Drug Abuse* (Substance Abuse and Mental Health Services Administration, 2002, p. 44) found that the increase of drug use in the 1990s was specific to adolescents—adults did not show it. According to Lloyd Johnston (Johnston, O'Malley, & Bachman, 1996) there were a number of explanations.

This most recent crop of youngsters grew up in a period in which drug use rates were down substantially from what they had been 10 to 15 years earlier. This gave youngsters less opportunity to learn from others' mistakes. . . . A second likely cause is that in recent years youngsters have heard less about the dangers of drugs from a number of sectors that have paid less attention to the issue, including parents, schools, and the media. Schools are receiving less federal funding for drug abuse prevention; parents appear to be talking less about drugs to their children . . . media news coverage of the drug issues plummeted in the early 90s; and the placement of anti-drug public service ads by the media also declined appreciably. In sum, in the 90s, youngsters have been hearing fewer cautions about drugs from many key sectors of the society. (pp. 6-7)

According to child development experts, the major task of the teen years is achieving an identity. Much of teen behavior, therefore, is an attempt to answer the question, "Who am I really?" Teens create a self through clothing, hair, music, group identification, and not political or social ideas. This self is often fluid and changing. For teens, buying things means surrounding the self with objects that help to define an identity. These objects bolster their confidence almost like a security blanket for a child.

Teens express their need for autonomy through experimentation and risk taking (verbal risk taking: swearing, talking back, challenging, manipulating; behavior risk taking: drugs, dress, not doing what they're told; attitudinal risk taking: adopting provocative beliefs, withdrawal, argumentativeness). They express their need for autonomy through role playing: trying on new identities (handshakes, voices, clothes, hairstyles, handwriting, speech patterns, language) and also through selective identification and incorporation: patterning one's behavior,

appearance and beliefs on role models— selected authority figures, music, TV, movies, sports.

Music, fashion, appearance, and behavior become the outward signs that teens use to assert their unique selves; these signs become their badges of identity. In the early and mid-1990s, drugs, especially marijuana, had a cachet as a badge of identity. There was a growing belief among teens, quantified by the PATS, that "kids who are really cool use drugs," and that "marijuana users are popular." Cultural icons—especially musicians and actors—were seen as purveyors of marijuana or drug "coolness." According to PATS, by 1995, half (54%) of teens in Grades 7 through 12 agreed that "many rock or rap stars make drug use look tempting" and almost half (48%) agreed that "music that kids listen to makes marijuana seem cool."

Recently, we have seen the rapid increase in use of MDMA, popularly called "ecstasy," among youths. This drug was originally used by a niche group of young adults who frequented "raves" (all night parties) and clubs. Since 1999, it has moved out of the "rave" scene and is being used by teens in social settings. *Monitoring the Future* (Johnston et al., 2001, p. 12) found significant increases between 1999 and 2000 among 8th, 10th, and 12th graders. The PATS also indicated that high sensation seekers were especially at risk for experimenting with the drug. High sensation seekers were three times as likely to try the drug, as were low sensation seekers.

To better understand teens' attitudes toward ecstasy and what potential messages could be used to prevent trial, in 2000, the PDFA conducted a strategic study using conjoint, discriminant function and cluster segmentation analysis. The objectives of this study were to identify what claim or statement about the drug and its risks has the most potential to reduce intentions to try ecstasy and to predict those at risk of trying the drug. The results indicated that 77% of youths are unlikely triers of ecstasy, 12% have tried the drug, and 11% are likely to try sometime in the future. The research also identified a potentially strong strategy involving the risks of ecstasy use.

These findings were incorporated into a creative brief that advertising writers and art directors used to create powerful anti-ecstasy messages.

SUMMARY

The Partnership for a Drug-Free America is research based. All the health messages it creates are grounded in research that seeks to understand those adolescents most at risk for drug use and to identify the strategic messages with the greatest potential to prevent drug use.

The Partnership's major survey of adolescents' benefits from research such as *Monitoring the Future* (Bachman et al., 1998) and the *Sensation Seeking* (Palmgreen et al., 2001) research from the University of Kentucky. In addition, the Partnership conducts additional research to gain a greater understanding of our targets in a changing environment. We have questions in the PATS that monitor teens' (a) attitudes toward specific drugs (marijuana, inhalants, ecstasy, methamphetamine, cocaine/crack, LSD, heroin), (b) attitudes toward current issues of legalization and medical marijuana, (c) perceptions of the normalization of drugs, (d) perceptions of the messages coming from popular culture, (e) attitudes toward peer use, (f) perceived availability of drugs, (g) attitudes toward drug treatment, (h) computer and Internet use, (i) sources of information about drugs, (j) awareness of antidrug commercials and ads, and (k) attitudes about those messages and their perceived impact on their attitudes. The PDFA has also conducted strategic studies to segment and predict adolescents most at risk for use of marijuana and ecstasy.

We continue to benefit from the research conducted by the academic community, and we believe that the community would also benefit from in-market research conducted by advertising industry professionals.

CHAPTER 24

Using Beliefs About Positive and Negative Consequences as the Basis for Designing Message Interventions for Lowering Risky Behavior

Joseph N. Cappella

Marco Yzer

Martin Fishbein

One class of intervention aimed at changing adolescents' behavior, intention, knowledge, or belief uses mass-mediated messages as a part of an overall campaign. This chapter focuses on the design of messages for communication campaigns whose goal is to change behavior or, at least, to change intention to behave in a less risky way. Although the problem of message design is very general, we will illustrate an approach to designing messages from our research on adolescent drug use, specifically regular use of marijuana.

THEORIES OF ATTITUDE AND BEHAVIOR CHANGE

Theories of attitude and behavior change are relevant in a general sense to the design of a message strategy for a campaign but are, for the most part, insufficiently specific to be really helpful in the decisions that campaign designers have to make. For example, the elaboration likelihood model of persuasion (Petty & Cacioppo, 1986) is very general with wide applicability. Although it offers clear indications of the conditions under which persuasive messages must be strong or when weaker messages will suffice, it provides little guidance about the constitution of stronger and weaker messages.

Many other theories, both general and specific, have implications for designing messages that modify risky behavior and intention. An extensive and informative review of these theories is available in Petraitis, Flay, and Miller (1995). With the exception of activation theory (Donohew, Lorch, & Palmgreen, 1991, 1998), none is designed specifically to guide the selection of persuasive messages for risky populations. From the point of view of the design of communication campaigns, theories of behavior change are useful when they provide guidance about the content and formatting of persuasive messages. The integrative model of behavior change (Ajzen & Fishbein, 1980; Fishbein, 1980; Fishbein & Ajzen, 1975) offers a structure to guide the content of persuasive messages.

THE INTEGRATIVE MODEL

The integrative theory of behavior change (aka integrative model, or IM) incorporates the central empirical and theoretical components predicting behavior and behavior change from three theories: the health belief model (e.g., Becker, 1974; Rosenstock, Strecher, & Becker, 1994), social cognitive theory (e.g., Bandura, 1986, 1989, 1991), and the theory of reasoned action. The integrative theory holds that a primary determinant of behavior is the person's *intention* to perform it. This intention is itself viewed as a function of three broad factors: (a) the person's *attitude* toward performing the behavior, (b) the person's perception of the *social* (or normative) *pressure* to perform the behavior, and (c) a sense of personal agency, or *self-efficacy,* that he or she has the skills and abilities necessary for performing the behavior under a variety of circumstances (Fishbein, 2000; Fishbein et al., 1992; Fishbein et al., 2002).

The IM posits that attitudes, perceived norms, and self-efficacy are themselves functions of underlying beliefs—about the outcomes of performing the behavior in question (assumed positive and negative consequences), about the normative expectations of specific significant others, and about specific barriers to behavioral performance. For example, the more one believes that performing the behavior in question will lead to "good" outcomes and prevent "bad" ones, the more favorable is one's attitude toward performing the behavior.

The IM has been tested successfully on a wide variety of behaviors and populations. With regard to the intention-behavior relationship, there is substantial evidence to support the use of the IM to predict health behaviors, such as screening (Sheeran, Conner, & Norman, 2001), condom use (Sheeran & Orbell, 1998), healthy eating (Conner, Norman, & Bell, 2002), and exercise (Blue, Wilbur, & Marston-Scott, 2001). Recent research has extended the application of the IM to adolescent marijuana use, showing consequences on intention from attitudes, social norms, and personal efficacy (Fishbein et al., 2002).

To make the discussion of behavioral belief, attitude toward the behavior, and behavioral intention more concrete, let us consider some behavioral beliefs about regular marijuana use among adolescents who are more and less at risk for regular use.

DATA AND MEASUREMENT

Participants and Procedures

The data presented here were gathered in middle and high schools in metropolitan Philadelphia. The sample consisted of 1,175 adolescents, of whom 42% were male. Mean age was 14.83 years ($SD = 1.90$ years, range = 11–19 years). Ethnically, 65% were Caucasian, 22% were African American, and 13% were from other ethnic or racial groups.

Deriving a Measure of Risk

Risk status for regular use was derived from an independent survey administered to 600 adolescents at 22 malls around the United States. A logistic regression of self-reported marijuana use in the past 12 months on eight potential correlates showed that age, the number of times marijuana was offered, the number of friends who use marijuana, and sensation seeking were significant predictors. Ethnicity, spending free time without supervision, peer influence, and parental monitoring were unrelated (or had weak relationships) to marijuana use.

Participants' risk scores were used to categorize people into low- and high-risk groups. To establish the cut-off score, we examined the survey data for the proportion of people who actually had used marijuana in the last 12 months. This proportion was about 25% for 11- to 19-year-old adolescents. Data from another independent, national survey reaffirmed that in a similar age group about 25% had used marijuana in the past 12 months (Hornik et al., 2002). On the basis of these results, we classified the lowest 75% scores on the risk measure as low risk and the highest 25% scores on the risk measure as high risk.

Measured Variables

The target behavior was regular marijuana use—that is, "using marijuana nearly every month in the next 12 months." Measured variables included *intention* to use marijuana, perceived norms of significant others, self-efficacy to say no to marijuana in five specific situations, normative beliefs, and motivation to comply. These are discussed in detail in Yzer, Cappella, Fishbein, Hornik, and Ahern (in press).

Behavioral beliefs are the positive and negative consequences that a person thinks will happen to himself or herself as a result of regular use of marijuana. These beliefs are a part of the reason that adolescents hold the attitudes toward marijuana use that they have. Behavioral beliefs were assessed by asking students to indicate on 5-point scales the extent to which they thought that their regularly using marijuana would lead to 36

outcomes, such as losing one's athletic skills and being more creative (−2 = *very unlikely*, +2 = *very likely*). For each behavioral belief, participants were also asked to evaluate the outcome on a 5-point scale ranging from −2 (*very bad*) to +2 (*very good*).

Results

The results are presented in Table 24.1. The left-hand side of the table focuses on behavioral beliefs. The behavioral beliefs were culled from the previous literature on beliefs associated with marijuana use, focus groups, and the content of antidrug ads that were a part of our archive. They are organized into four groups according to their meaning (and internal reliability). The second and third columns display the mean likelihood that the consequence will happen as judged by high risk and low risk groups. A negative value indicates that the group evaluates the consequence as unlikely; a positive value indicates the outcome is likely. Every belief differs significantly between the high- and low-risk groups, sometimes substantially. Effect sizes are listed in column 4 to represent the magnitude of the difference between groups. The column labeled r_{int} presents the correlation between behavioral belief and intention to use marijuana every month in the next 12 months. All are statistically significant, suggesting that each of the beliefs is a salient predictor of intention, although none exceeds .48 in magnitude.

The right-hand side of the table focuses on differences between high- and low-risk adolescents in terms of the value they place on a behavioral belief. For example, both groups evaluate "damage lungs" as quite bad even though the low-risk group sees this consequence as a worse one in general. The major conclusion from the evaluation section is that, although there are differences between the high- and low-risk groups, they are considerably smaller than those for the

Table 24.1   Mean Differences Between Low-Risk Adolescents (LRA) and High-Risk Adolescents (HRA) on Behavioral Beliefs and Their Evaluations in Regard to Using Marijuana

Behavioral Beliefs Item Description	Likelihood					Evaluation				
	LRA	HRA	F	ES	r_{int}	LRA	HRA	F	ES	r_{int}
Physical and mental costs										
Lose ambition	.92	−.05	113.91*	.10	−.39	−1.45	−1.36	2.79	.00	.22
Become anxious	.67	.05	48.38*	.05	−.27	−.75	−.58	5.21***	.01	.11
Lose athletic skills	1.09	.15	113.07*	.10	−.42	−1.48	−1.25	17.33*	.02	.20
Avoid problems	.65	.16	24.28*	.02	−.27	−.98	−.85	2.83	.00	.14
Damage brains	1.40	.83	46.31*	.04	−.26	−1.84	−1.60	42.02*	.04	.35
Become depressed	1.03	−.05	149.01*	.13	−.44	−1.57	−1.48	3.30	.00	.23
Decreased judgment	1.06	.22	88.00*	.08	−.35	−1.32	−1.19	4.90***	.01	.21
Expressing thoughts	1.05	.08	124.33*	.11	−.41	−1.29	−1.17	5.18***	.01	.18
Become forgetful	1.08	.27	90.93*	.08	−.31	−1.26	−1.14	4.34***	.00	.19
Damage lungs	1.40	1.10	14.12*	.01	−.22	−1.81	−1.52	51.22*	.05	.39
Lose motivation	1.07	.20	96.97*	.09	−.41	−1.50	−1.38	5.93***	.01	.23
Feel tired	1.11	.66	33.96*	.03	−.26	−.87	−.67	9.39**	.01	.17
Use stronger drugs	.59	−.41	83.41*	.08	−.37	−1.76	−1.46	33.22*	.03	.29
Positive outcomes										
Be like coolest kids	−1.20	−.81	21.88*	.02	.19	.68	.39	11.61**	.01	−.06
Fit in with group	−.92	−.29	48.69*	.05	.22	.93	.76	4.14***	.00	−.04
Good time friends	−.79	.37	171.19*	.15	.41	1.19	1.28	1.26	.00	.04
Be like other teens	−.36	.32	57.98*	.05	.15	.01	−.20	8.10**	.01	−.01
Good time	−.86	.39	183.51*	.15	.44	1.26	1.30	.25	.00	.03
Away from problems	−.93	−.48	20.21*	.02	.15	.30	.56	8.25**	.01	.09
More creative	−1.11	−.21	111.08*	.10	.35	1.07	1.10	.12	.00	−.01
Social costs										
Lose friends	.80	−.61	211.50*	.17	−.44	−1.73	−1.60	8.57**	.01	.17
Feel lonely	.77	−.32	139.52*	.12	−.40	−1.43	−1.35	2.15	.00	.17
Lose partner	.85	−.47	189.95*	.16	−.43	−1.41	−1.41	.00	.00	.09
Lose friends' respect	.94	−.40	195.48*	.16	−.44	−1.67	−1.45	21.70*	.02	.24
Destroy relationships	1.13	−.02	157.38*	.14	−.47	−1.79	−1.61	21.37*	.02	.28
Upset parents	1.48	1.06	23.68*	.02	−.24	−1.51	−1.31	14.68*	.01	.26
Self–esteem costs										
Unable to get a job	.98	−.21	162.55*	.14	−.43	−1.55	−1.44	5.05***	.01	.18
In trouble with law	1.15	.31	92.60*	.08	−.33	−1.77	−1.50	33.96*	.03	.35
Mess up life	1.33	.21	151.34*	.13	−.45	−1.68	−1.45	21.84*	.02	.28
Be a bad role model	1.38	.97	22.94*	.02	−.24	−1.62	−1.43	15.11*	.02	.27
Spend much money	1.17	.25	94.82*	.09	−.40	−1.36	−1.33	.17	.00	.14
Act against morals	1.15	.21	107.00*	.10	−.42	−1.49	−1.25	19.34*	.02	.28
Not be good person	.76	−.48	167.22*	.14	−.42	−1.64	−1.40	23.92*	.02	.29
Do worse in school	1.25	.32	102.28*	.09	−.38	−1.67	−1.46	20.83*	.02	.29
Be a loser	1.00	−.34	190.86*	.16	−.48	−1.63	−1.41	17.59*	.02	.22
Look stupid	1.14	.03	154.19*	.13	−.41	−1.45	−1.24	14.47*	.01	.19

NOTE: ES = effect size (eta2)

*$p < .001$; ** $p < .01$; ***$p < .05$

likelihood of consequences. Also there are no "reversals." That is, there are no cases for which the two risk groups evaluate a consequence on the opposite sides of the good-bad value continuum. What the low-risk group sees as a positive (or negative) consequence, the high-risk group sees in the same way.

However, in focusing on the likelihood that a behavioral consequence will happen to the participant, the differences are large, consistent, and revealing. Let us consider two quite different cases that illustrate a general point: "marijuana as a gateway drug" and "regular use affecting performance in school." The high- and low-risk groups differ significantly on how likely these negative consequences are to happen to them. Unsurprisingly, the low-risk group thinks the negative consequence is more likely to happen than does the high-risk group. For the gateway argument, the low-risk group thinks that this is moderately *likely,* whereas the high-risk group thinks it is moderately *unlikely.* Another way to say this is that the low-risk group tends to believe the consequence will happen, and the high-risk group tends to disbelieve it.

"Performance in school" behaves differently. The high-risk group thinks that this outcome is less likely to happen than does the low-risk group, but on average, both groups think that the outcome is more likely than it is unlikely. Both groups believe that this negative consequence will happen if marijuana is used regularly, even though they differ in the strength of their belief.

These two examples point to an important principle. Although the risk groups differ in predictable ways, what the high-risk group finds believable is more important to a campaign strategy than what the low-risk group believes. The high-risk group is the more likely target of the campaign than is the low-risk group, but what that group judges to be believable negative consequences is

very different from what the low-risk group believes. Using the gateway argument with the high-risk group runs against what this group already believes. And although the job of persuasion is to make what is disbelieved believable, that task is more difficult when the topic is one for which the audience already is disposed against accepting the argument. This is sometimes called "biased processing" because the target audience is ready to argue against the claim based on their previous beliefs (Petty & Cacioppo, 1986).

Using the school performance argument with both groups has a better chance at success. Both the high- and low-risk groups believe that regular use of marijuana can affect their performance in school, and because both groups value this ability, persuasive arguments reinforcing the belief are more likely to work. There is less chance of biased processing with this argument because it is not already disbelieved and the argument appeals to both high- and low-risk groups.

One other observation should be made. The school performance belief is strongly believed by the low-risk group ($M = 1.25$ on a scale from -2 to $+2$). There is not much room to change the strength of the low-risk group's belief, although it could be reinforced or made more salient. The high-risk group accepts this consequence less strongly ($M = .32$) so that there is plenty of room to move toward greater acceptance. In effect, the presence of ceiling (or floor) effects might make changing beliefs of the low-risk group difficult, but it is the beliefs of the high-risk group that should be targeted.

Key Persuasion Topics

In Figure 24.1, we present 11 topics for persuasion based on the results of Table 24.1. Four are positive consequences of regular marijuana use that are seen as more

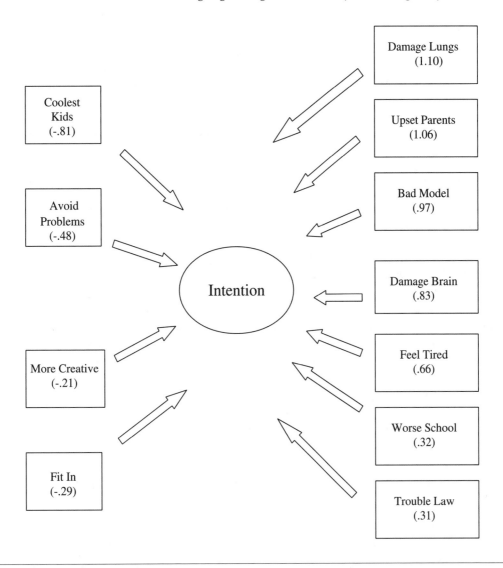

Figure 24.1 Likely Negative Consequence and Unlikely Positive Consequence Beliefs for High-Risk Adolescents: Regular Marijuana Use

unlikely than likely by the high-risk group. Seven are negative consequences rated as more likely than unlikely by the high-risk group. These beliefs represent topics for a persuasion campaign aimed at the high-risk group and at reducing the intention to use marijuana regularly by minimizing the biased processing so typical of high-risk groups who have already heard a great deal about marijuana.

CHALLENGES

Several responses to the strategy we are advocating could be offered: (a) The strategy starts with beliefs (which exist in the minds of participants) but concludes with persuasive arguments. It seems to confuse beliefs (held by the audience) and arguments (existing in the message). (b) The high-risk group already accepts the negative consequences (or rejects the positive ones) listed in Figure 24.1. Why not focus on beliefs that have a strong correlation to intention, are not accepted by the high-risk group, and try to change those? (c) Likely negative consequences (and unlikely positive consequences) cannot be changed easily, so why direct expensive communication campaigns at these beliefs?

Let us take up each of these challenges in turn.

Beliefs Versus Persuasive Arguments

The first objection is simply a misunderstanding of the position being presented. Our view is that the behavioral beliefs of the high-risk group are potential *topics* for persuasive messages; they are not the messages themselves. Beliefs are derived from the audience and represent the audience's logic (or "psycho-logic" as it might be called) for holding an attitude toward the behavior. The audience's belief structures offer one route to the design of persuasive messages by locating beliefs that might serve as topics for persuasive messages.

The persuasive messages themselves may be about a focal belief, but the medium of presentation, the format or style of presentation, and the evidence in support of the belief are all components of a persuasive message that must be designed around the topic in order to have the topic reach, inform, and convince the audience. Many theories speak to the question of the components of persuasive messages, but none is comprehensive.

Activation theory (Donohew et al., 1998) holds that high sensation seekers prefer certain message formats. Sensation seekers are also likely to initiate drug use at earlier ages and to experiment with illegal drugs (Palmgreen, Donohew, Lorch, Hoyle, & Stephenson, 2001). Activation theory cannot say what the topics of persuasive messages directed at high sensation seekers should be, although the style and format

have been researched extensively. Other theories highlight different message features for making topics persuasive. A few of the recent developments include using emotion (Nabi, 2002), examples (Zillman & Brosius, 2000), evidence and reason (Kuhn, 1991), and frames (Rothman & Salovey, 1997).

The strategy we are advocating is not about the form, medium, or elaborated content (evidence, reasons) of the messages that make up a communication campaign but rather the topics of such messages.

Changing Beliefs That Are Not Accepted

One significant challenge to the position we have advocated is that important beliefs not accepted by high-risk groups should be the target of health communication campaigns. For example, in regard to the beliefs listed in Table 24.1, high-risk adolescents do not believe that regular marijuana use is a route (or gateway) to use of other harder drugs. Why not try to change a belief like this rather than focusing on beliefs that are already accepted to some degree?

A campaign strategist could select a belief such as the "gateway" belief—one that is disbelieved by the target population—and try to alter its assessment from unlikely to likely. In fact, a number of antidrug and antimarijuana ads employ the gateway argument. However, one must recognize that the target audience of high-risk adolescents already disbelieves this claim. Disbelief implies they are poised to argue against the message. If the persuasive messages are weak, counterargument may produce more contrary thoughts to the message than favorable, undermining the appeal or even creating a boomerang (Petty & Cacioppo, 1986).

In a recent study using ads that make the gateway argument, some high-risk adolescents moved in a direction counter to the message's appeal, increasing their intention to use marijuana on a regular basis

(Yzer et al., in press). Although we do not have direct evidence of counterarguing by the high-risk group, this is a plausible explanation of the findings. An independent sample of high-risk adolescents evaluated the ad as less effective than a low-risk sample did. The experience that high-risk adolescents have with their own use or the testimony of friends who use marijuana may counter the claims of other persuasive messages.

To change an existing belief that the audience is disposed to discount, one must create strong messages that produce favorable thoughts. In some public health contexts, strong arguments can be offered that are novel, salient to the audience, and plausible (Morley & Walker, 1987). The recent Legacy Foundation campaign (Farrelly et al., 2002) aimed at keeping young people from smoking has employed arguments encouraging resistance to the manipulative intent of big tobacco companies. This argumentative strategy is novel in that it avoids the usual beliefs about health, disease, and smoking; it is salient in that adolescents are frequently concerned about being or at least appearing independent; it is plausible in that large tobacco companies have a reputation of being manipulative.

In short, to change an existing belief that is already disbelieved by the target audience is very difficult. In health contexts where the target audience already has a great deal of prior information, either through previous risky experience or through educational campaigns, the challenges of creating a persuasive campaign that seeks to change negative consequences perceived as unlikely or positive consequences seen as likely are very significant.

Even Accepted Beliefs Are Difficult to Change

The strategy of belief selection for a communication campaign assumes that accepted beliefs are targeted—for example, negative consequences judged likely by the target audience. Two related objections to this approach can be raised: (a) Changing accepted beliefs is very difficult even when there is no a priori bias against acceptance, and (b) obtaining greater acceptance of already accepted beliefs may not be possible because the level of acceptance is too high in the target population. As an example, Table 24.1 notes that "smoking marijuana regularly damages lungs" is seen as a likely outcome by the high-risk population ($M = 1.10$), as well as the low. On a -2 to $+2$ scale, there is not much room to move the high-risk group to full acceptance.

In response to these concerns, one must differentiate between persuasion and priming. Public health campaigns are primarily interested in changing behavioral intentions—and ultimately, behaviors—not just in changing beliefs. Persuasion is focused on changing beliefs that underlie attitudes toward a behavior and ultimately intention. Through persuasion, a change in a behavioral belief that has a fixed correlation with intention should have an impact on behavioral intention.

Priming, however, is a different process (Iyengar & Kinder, 1987). When a behavioral belief is primed, then its salience in decision making at the time of intention formation is stronger than for allied beliefs that are not primed (Cappella, Fishbein, Hornik, Ahern, & Sayeed, 2001). A stronger connection for primed beliefs implies that the weight the primed belief receives in predicting intention is enhanced through the priming process. A hypothetical example contrasting persuasion and priming effects is presented in Table 24.2. What the hypothetical demonstrates is that a change in intention can come about through priming without actual persuasion (i.e., without changing the acceptability of the underlying belief).

Table 24.2   A Hypothetical Example of Persuasion and Priming

	Intention	Slope Belief 1 (Parents)	Mean Belief 1	Slope Belief 2 (Judgment)	Mean Belief 2	Constant
Baseline	0.60	−.5	.5	−.3	.50	1.0
Prime Belief 2	0.50	−.5	.5	−.5	.50	1.0
Change Belief 2	0.50	−.5	.5	−.3	.83	1.0
Prime & Change Belief 2	0.33	−.5	.5	−.5	.83	1.0

NOTE: Intention is generated by a prediction equation: Intention = constant + (Slope Belief 1) × (Mean Belief 1) + (Slope Belief 2) × (Mean Belief 2). Intention scaled (−3 to +3, higher being greater intention to use); belief scaled very unlikely (−2) to very likely (+2).

How can priming occur? Our own research on this process is at a relatively early stage. In the previous literature, priming occurs primarily through repetition of the message topic over an extended time. In health contexts, a campaign that focuses on accepted beliefs may not change the number of people accepting the belief but may alter the association of the belief with intention to behave. If the association becomes stronger, even without belief change, the intention could still change in the desired direction (see Table 24.2 for an example).

There is much yet to be learned about priming. Does the audience's prior knowledge or experience moderate the relationship between exposure and priming (Miller & Krosnick, 1996)? Do message characteristics such as vividness enhance the duration of priming effects (Keller & Block, 1997)? Do message features other than frequency of exposure affect the magnitude or duration of priming?

RECOMMENDATIONS

The strategy that we have outlined in this chapter can be summarized as a series of guidelines for selecting topics for persuasive communication campaigns.

1. *Use the IM to test for the acceptability of behavioral beliefs.* Although many theories predict and explain behavioral intention and behavior, the IM gives a prominent place to behavioral beliefs, assessing their relationship to the target outcomes, intention, and behavior. The theory has been widely and successfully applied to different behaviors. The IM employs a consistent system of measurement that focuses on a specific behavior in a specific context and that insists that behavioral beliefs are consequences of the behavior for me rather than for generalized others. In addition, the theory assesses whether behavioral beliefs correlate with intention so that the salience of the belief for projected action is clear.

2. *Be comprehensive in the behavioral beliefs evaluated.* In typical applications of the IM, the number of behavioral beliefs used is limited by their frequency of mention in focus group and other elicitation procedures. However, if behavioral beliefs are considered to be possible topics for persuasive campaigns, they should include items that do not necessarily arise spontaneously in open-ended elicitation tasks. Rather, possible positive and negative consequences should be included, even if not a part of the initial repertoire of participants.

3. *Behavioral beliefs of the group as a whole are less important than those of the high-risk subgroup.* If campaign strategists focus on the whole population rather than on the high-risk subgroup, it will select different topics for persuasion than if the focus is restricted to the high-risk group. The high-risk group is most in need of appeals directed to it than to the group as a whole. Behavioral beliefs accepted by the high-risk group tend to be accepted by the low-risk group as well, so targeting the highs will usually produce a set of beliefs already accepted by the lows.

4. *The beliefs most likely to yield lower levels of biased processing are unlikely positive consequences and likely negative consequences.* The advantage of selecting beliefs that are already accepted is that the biased processing of persuasive appeals that run counter to the audience's attitudinal predispositions is minimized. Selecting a behavioral belief that is rated as a likely negative consequence by the high-risk group cannot ensure successful persuasion, but an unlikely negative consequence almost certainly will activate vigorous counterarguing.

5. *Changes in intention can occur through persuasion and priming.* Change in belief is not necessary for a change in attitude or intention to behave. The activation of beliefs that are accepted and that operate in the direction of the desired behavior may produce the desired change through priming. In fact, priming a belief such as an unlikely negative consequence (e.g., marijuana as a gateway drug) could have the opposite effect to that intended—namely, making salient the undesirable association between the gateway belief and the intention to use marijuana regularly.

LIMITATIONS

Our data and hypotheses are suggestive but certainly not conclusive. Future work will need to show that messages whose topics are based on accepted behavioral beliefs are more effective than their opposites, especially with high-risk subgroups. These same messages should also produce fewer contrary message-relevant thoughts. Our research to date has shown that persuasion attempts using the gateway argument produce some evidence of boomerang effects among high-risk participants (Yzer et al., in press). Messages based on school performance and those about fitting in with the group exhibit some evidence of increasing antidrug attitudes. Although much more needs to be done, these three studies produce findings consistent with the claims of this chapter.

Part III

PERSPECTIVES FROM DIFFERENT RISK RESEARCH TRADITIONS

Section A

Gambling

CHAPTER 25

Adolescent Gambling
Risk Factors and Implications for Prevention, Intervention, and Treatment

MARK GRIFFITHS

For most individuals, gambling is a social activity enjoyed in moderation. However, for a small but significant minority, gambling can have devastating negative consequences. The American Psychiatric Association (1994) defines pathological gambling as persistent and recurrent maladaptive gambling behavior that disrupts personal, family, or vocational pursuits. Problem ("pathological") gambling is characterized by unrealistic optimism on the gambler's part. All bets are made in an effort to recoup their losses (often referred to as "the chase"). The result is that instead of "cutting their losses" gamblers get deeper into debt and preoccupy themselves with gambling, determined that a big win will repay their loans and solve all their problems. Family troubles begin—both marital and with relatives—as well as illegal borrowing and other criminal activities in an effort to get money. At this point in the pathological gambler's career, family, friends, or both may "bail out" the gambler. Alienation from those closest to the pathological gambler, characterizes the appearance of the final desperation phase. In a last-ditch frenzied effort to repay his or her debts, the person engages in illegal behavior. When there are finally no more options left, the gambler may suffer severe depression and have suicidal thoughts (Griffiths, 1996b). However, as we shall see, pathological gambling (or "problem" gambling as many people in the field prefer to call it) is not the sole domain of adults.

This chapter overviews a number of areas. It first examines problem adolescent gambling before looking more closely at three different problematic forms—lotteries, scratchcards, and slot machines. There is then an overview of risk factors in adolescent gambling and a brief examination of some of the problems with research into problem gambling. The chapter ends by examining both adolescent gambling as a public health issue and intervention and prevention for adolescent gamblers.

PROBLEM
ADOLESCENT GAMBLING

Adolescent gambling is a major problem in society today. Not only is it usually illegal, but it appears to be related to high levels of problem gambling and other activities such as illicit drug taking and alcohol abuse (Giacopassi, Stitt, & Vandiver, 1998; Griffiths & Sutherland, 1998; Gupta & Derevensky, 1998a; Stinchfield, Cassuto, Winters, & Latimer, 1997), and delinquency (Winters, Stinchfield, & Fulkerson, 1993a; Yeoman & Griffiths, 1996). A number of studies in Europe, the United States, Canada, and Australia have noted high levels of gambling among adolescents. In some cases, this is legal, such as slot machine gambling in the United Kingdom (Fisher, 1993; Griffiths, 1995a), whereas other forms are illegal for youths, such as casino gambling, video lottery terminals, and in most jurisdictions, lottery purchases (Giacopassi et al., 1998; Jacobs, 1989; Stinchfield et al., 1997; Winters et al., 1993a).

Adolescents may be more susceptible to pathological gambling (Fisher, 1993; Lesieur & Klein, 1987). For instance, Steinberg (1988) found that between 4% and 8% of U.S. high school pupils could be classified as pathological gamblers. Further studies in the United Kingdom, Canada, and the United States have revealed a general pathological gambling rate of 5% to 6% among youths under 18 years of age. This figure is twice that identified in the adult population (Griffiths, 1995a; Shaffer, LaBrie, Scanlon, & Cummings, 1993).

A typical finding of many adolescent gambling studies has been that problem or pathological gambling appears to be a primarily male phenomenon (Griffiths, 1991a, 1991b; Ide-Smith & Lea, 1988; Stinchfield et al., 1997). It also appears that adults may to some extent foster adolescent gambling. For example, a strong correlation has been found

between adolescent gambling and parental gambling (Browne & Brown, 1994; Fisher, 1993; Griffiths, 1995a; Gupta & Derevensky, 1997; Wood & Griffiths, 1998). Several studies in the United Kingdom have found that although not actually purchasing lottery tickets themselves, young people are given lottery tickets or scratchcards by their parents (Fisher & Balding, 1998; Wood & Griffiths 1998). This is particularly worrisome because a number of studies have shown that when people gamble as adolescents, they are more likely to become problem gamblers as adults (Fisher, 1993; Griffiths, 1995a; Gupta & Derevensky, 1998a; Huxley & Carroll, 1992; Winters et al., 1993a).

Similarly, many studies have indicated a strong link between adult problem gamblers and later problem gambling among their children (Dell, Ruzicka, & Palisi, 1981; Fisher, 1993; Griffiths, 1995a; Ide-Smith & Lea, 1988; Lesieur & Klein, 1987; Winters et al., 1993a). Other factors that have been linked with adolescent problem gambling include working-class youth culture, delinquency, alcohol and substance abuse, poor school performance, theft, and truancy (Fisher, 1993; Griffiths, 1994, 1995a; Griffiths & Sutherland, 1998; Gupta & Derevensky, 1997b, 1998a, 1998b; Winters et al., 1993a; Yeoman & Griffiths, 1996). However, many of the research findings have not differentiated among gambling types. There appear to be three main forms of adolescent gambling that have been widely researched (particularly in the United Kingdom). These are lottery gambling, scratchcard gambling, and slot machine gambling.

ADOLESCENT
LOTTERY GAMBLING

Lotteries have traditionally been researched as "low-impact" forms of gambling. However, a growing body of evidence indicates that lottery playing may be part of a first step in learning how to gamble. The social acceptance of lotteries means that they are often not perceived as bona fide forms of gambling. Children and adolescents are often introduced to these activities at an early age as part of their family social entertainment. Lottery gambling has been found to be one of the most popular forms of adolescent gambling in the United States (e.g., Jacobs, 1989; Winters et al., 1993a), Canada (e.g., Ladouceur & Mireault, 1988), and the United Kingdom (e.g., Fisher & Balding, 1996, 1998; Moran, 1995; Wood & Griffiths, 1998). However, there has been little research examining whether lottery gambling in itself may be problematic for adolescents—except in the United Kingdom.

The U.K. National Lottery has been operating only since November 1994 and was the first government-sanctioned form of gambling. It was also backed by television advertising and associated lottery programs. As a result, studies examining the psychological impact of gambling offer a unique insight into the effect on youth. In a recent study, Fisher and Balding (1998) reported that playing the U.K. National Lottery was a popular form of adolescent gambling, with 40% of the sample of 12- to 15-year-olds ($N = 9,774$) playing. The study also found that over half the attempts by underage people to buy National Lottery products were successful (56%). Wood and Griffiths (1998), in a similar study involving 11- to 15-year-olds ($N = 1,195$), found that 48% of their sample regularly took part in the National Lottery. Most of these adolescents (64%) played the lottery occasionally, although 16% played most weeks and 14% played every week. There were no gender differences in frequency of play. A large minority of the participants bought their own lottery tickets illegally (17%). The study also found a strong correlation between parent and child participation in the National Lottery. In fact, of the participants who took part in these activities, most had their lottery tickets purchased for them by their parents (71%).

It appears that television may play a critical role in influencing adolescent lottery play in the United Kingdom. For instance, in the United Kingdom, the Independent Television Commission (1995) reported that the televised lottery draw program was the second most popular program watched by children 10 to 15 years old, with 38% viewing it. More recently, this figure appears to have drastically escalated; Fisher and Balding (1998) found that the televised draw was watched by 84% of their sample of 12- to 15-year-olds on Saturdays and by 62% on Wednesdays. The explanations center on the early schedule of the programs (before the 9 p.m. "watershed" or prime-time slot) and the combination of celebrities and pop stars who contribute to the overall "glitz and glamour" of the shows. Furthermore, advertising for both the National Lottery and scratchcards is fast persuading viewers that gambling is normal and widely acceptable (Griffiths, 1997a, 1997b). This remains an important area in need of further empirical work.

ADOLESCENT SCRATCHCARD GAMBLING

The rapid event frequency of scratchcards and the instant payout define scratchcards as a "hard" form of gambling. They have been compared with slot machines (Griffiths, 1997a) and appear to carry similar risks. In an American study carried out in Minnesota, Winters et al. (1993a) found that 37% of adolescents had bought scratch tabs, and that 35% had done so in the last year. These figures more than doubled the lottery participation rates. Of the 61 problem gamblers identified, 30% played scratch tabs on a weekly basis. The higher rate for scratch tabs suggests further evidence that this type of gambling is a "harder" form of gambling when compared with lotteries. Scratch tabs and scratchcards have a high event frequency coupled with a fast payout. This is unlike weekly or biweekly lotteries where the gambler must wait until the draw is performed and hence these factors are not as prominent.

In the United Kingdom, Fisher and Balding (1996) studied 12- to 15-year-old boys and girls ($N = 7,200$) from eight southern regions in the United Kingdom and found that 37% of the participants had played scratchcards during the last year. Regular scratchcard players were found to be significantly more likely to be male, have a weekly income of at least £5 ($7.50), and to come from an ethnic minority group. Three percent ($N = 189$) of the adolescents reported playing lottery scratchcards at least twice a week. Regular scratchcard players were more likely to smoke cigarettes, drink alcohol, take illegal drugs, and play fruit machines regularly. In a further study, Fisher and Balding (1998) noted that National Lottery scratchcards were played by 47% of youth. Using the diagnostic screening tool *DSM-IV-J-R* (revised junior version of the *DSM-IV* criteria; Fisher, 1999) to identify problem gamblers, the results suggest a 1% level of possible problem gambling for National Lottery scratchcards. Problem gamblers were identified as predominantly male and found to have a weekly income of £5 ($7.50) or more per week. The parents of the problem gamblers were more than twice as likely to have gambled on each of nine different forms of commercial gambling activities compared with the parents of nonproblem gamblers. Problem gamblers were more than three times as likely as the other adolescents to report that they thought their parents gambled too much. The problem gamblers' parents appeared less likely to disapprove of adolescent gambling than the

other parents. The most common companions overall for lottery and scratchcard gambling were the adolescents' parents, although problem gamblers were more likely to play on their own or with friends.

The study by Wood and Griffiths (1998) showed that 30% of adolescents played scratchcards. Most of the adolescents who played scratchcards played once a month (44%), although 27% played a few times a month, 12% once a week, 13% a few times a week, and 4% played every day. There were no gender differences in frequency of play. A large minority of the participants bought their own scratchcards illegally (26%). Wood and Griffiths (1998) identified 6% adolescent problem scratchcard gambling among players. Furthermore, a large minority of the participants answered that they were in fact worried about how much they spent on scratchcards (17%).

ADOLESCENT SLOT MACHINE GAMBLING

There is widespread, worldwide agreement that slot machines are potentially addictive (see Griffiths, 1995a, 2002, for comprehensive overviews). In the past 10 years, slot machines have been the predominant form of gambling by pathological gamblers treated in self-help groups and professional treatment centers across Europe (see Griffiths & Wood, 1999, for a comprehensive review of the European literature). There are many reasons why this is the case. Slot machines are fast, aurally and visually stimulating and rewarding, require a low initial stake, provide frequent wins, require no preknowledge to commence play, and may be played alone. Clearly, decisions to play slot machines and to continue playing them to excess are contingent on the player's biological and psychological constitution and situational variables. However, structural characteristics of slot machines are designed to induce the player to play, to continue playing, or both. It has further been argued (Griffiths, 1991b, 1993c, 1995a) that a combination of the technological aspects of structural characteristics (event frequency, the near miss, symbol-ratio proportions, light and sound effects, the suspension of judgment, etc.) may contribute habitual and repetitive play in some individuals.

Most research on slot machine gambling by youths has been undertaken in the United Kingdom where they are legally available to children of any age. The most recent U.K. study by Fisher and Balding (1998) found that slot machines were the most popular form of adolescent gambling, with 75% of their sample ($N = 9,774$) participating. A more thorough examination of the literature (Fisher, 1992; Fisher & Balding, 1998; Griffiths, 1995a, 2002) indicates the following:

- At least two thirds of adolescents play slot machines at some point in their lives.
- One third of adolescents will have played slot machines in the last month.
- That 10% to 20% of adolescents are regular slot machine players (playing at least once a week).
- That 0.5% to 6% of adolescents are probable pathological gamblers or have severe gambling-related difficulties.

All studies have reported that boys play slot machines more than girls and that as slot machine playing becomes more regular, it is more likely to be a predominantly male activity. Research has indicated that very few female adolescents have gambling problems on slot machines.

So why do adolescents play slot machines? This again is not easy to answer; there are a host of possible reasons. However, research does suggest that irregular ("social") gamblers play for different reasons than do excessive ("pathological") gamblers (see Griffiths, 1995a, 2002, for detailed overviews). Social gamblers usually play for fun, because their friends or parents do, to win money, for excitement, or for some combination of these reasons. Pathological gamblers appear to play for other reasons, such as mood modification and as a means of escape. As already highlighted, young males seem to be particularly susceptible to slot machine addiction, with up to 6% of adolescents in the United Kingdom experiencing problems with their slot machine playing at any one time using *DSM* criteria (Fisher, 1993; Griffiths, 1995a). This does not mean that everyone who plays slot machines will become addicted (in the same way that not everyone who drinks alcohol will become an alcoholic). What it does mean is that given a cluster of factors (genetic and/or biological predisposition, social upbringing, psychological constitution, situational and structural characteristics), a small proportion of people will, unfortunately, experience severe problems.

Like other potentially addictive behaviors, slot machine addiction causes the individual to engage in negative behaviors such as truancy in order to play the machines (Fisher & Balding, 1998; Griffiths, 1990a, 1990b, 1995a); stealing to fund machine playing (Fisher & Balding, 1998; Griffiths, 1990a, 1993a, 1993b; Yeoman & Griffiths, 1996); getting into trouble with teachers, parents, or both over their machine playing (Griffiths, 1990a, 1993a, 1995a); borrowing money or using lunch money to play the machines (Fisher & Balding, 1998; Griffiths, 1990a, 1995a,); poor schoolwork (Griffiths, 1990a 1995a); and in some cases, aggressive behavior (Griffiths, 1990a, 1995a). These behaviors are not much different from those experienced by other types of adolescent problem gambling.

As has been extensively pointed out elsewhere (e.g. Griffiths, 1993d, 1995a, 1995b, 1996b), slot machine addicts also display bona fide signs of addiction, including withdrawal effects, tolerance, salience, mood modification, conflict, and relapse. It is also worth noting that these types of negative consequences associated with slot machine addiction have also been identified in other more general studies on adolescent gambling addiction in the United States, Canada, and Australia (e.g., Giacopassi et al., 1998; Gupta & Derevensky, 1997, 1998a, 1998b; Langewisch & Frisch, 1998; Lesieur et al., 1991; Moore & Ohtsuka, 1997; Stinchfield et al., 1993).

RISK FACTORS IN ADOLESCENT GAMBLING

Addictions always result from an interaction and interplay between many factors, including the person's biological or genetic predisposition, their psychological constitution, their social environment, and the nature of the activity itself. However, in the case of gambling, it could be argued that technology and technological advance itself can be an important contributory factor. Griffiths (1999) has noted that there is no precise frequency level of a gambling game at which people become addicted because addiction will be an integrated mix of factors in which frequency is just one factor in the overall equation. Other factors and dimensions (external to the person themselves) that have been reported in the general gambling literature and summarized by Griffiths (1999) include the following:

- Stake size (including issues around affordability, perceived value for money)
- Event frequency (time gap between each gamble)
- Amount of money lost in a given time period (important in chasing)
- Prize structures (number and value of prizes)
- Probability of winning (e.g., 1 in 14 million on the lottery)
- Size of jackpot (e.g., over £1 million on the lottery)

- Skill and pseudoskill elements (actual or perceived)
- "Near-miss" opportunities (number of near-winning situations)
- Light and color effects (e.g., use of red lights on slot machines)
- Sound effects (e.g., use of buzzers or musical tunes to indicate winning)
- Social or asocial nature of the game (individual and/or group activity)
- Accessibility (e.g., opening times, membership rules)
- Accessibility (e.g., number of outlets)
- Location of gambling establishment (out of town, next to workplace, etc.)
- Type of gambling establishment (e.g., betting shop, amusement arcade, etc.)
- Advertising (e.g., television commercials)
- The rules of the game

Each of these differences may have implications for the gambler's motivations and as a consequence the social impact of gambling. Although many of these gambling-inducing characteristics depend on individual psychological factors (e.g., reinforcement), they are a direct result of the structural characteristics and could not have influenced gambling behavior independently. It is for this reason, above all others, that a structural approach could be potentially useful.

One consequence of the recent upsurge in research into adolescent gambling is that we can now start to put together a "risk factor model" of those individuals who might be at the most risk of developing pathological gambling tendencies. Based on the preceding overview and previous summaries of the empirical research literature (Griffiths, 1991a, 1995a, 1995c, 2002; Stinchfield & Winters, 1998), a number of clear risk factors in the development of problem adolescent gambling emerge. Adolescent problem gamblers are more likely to

- be male (16-25 years)
- have begun gambling at an early age (as young as 8 years of age)

- have had a big win earlier in their gambling careers
- consistently chase losses
- have begun gambling with their parents or alone
- be depressed before gambling
- to be excited and aroused during gambling
- be irrational (i.e., have erroneous perceptions) during gambling
- have bad grades at school
- engage in other addictive behaviors (smoking, drinking alcohol, illegal drug use)
- come from the lower social classes
- have parents who have a gambling (or other addiction) problem
- have a history of delinquency
- have low self-esteem
- have suffered abuse (physical, emotional sexual, or any combination of these)
- steal money to fund their gambling
- be truant from school to go gambling

This list is probably not exhaustive but incorporates what is known empirically and anecdotally about adolescent problem gambling. Furthermore, Stinchfield and Winters (1998) assert that many risk factors implicated in adolescent problem gambling are very similar to risk factors implicated in adolescent drug abuse (i.e., family history, low self-esteem, depression, history of abuse, etc.). As research into the area grows, new items to such a list will be added, and factors, signs, and symptoms already on these lists will be adapted and modified.

There is, of course, a problem identifying adolescent problem gamblers in that unlike other addictions such as alcoholism or heroin addiction, there is no observable sign or symptom. Although there have been some reports of a personality change in young gamblers (e.g., Griffiths, 1989), many parents may attribute the change to adolescence itself (i.e., evasive behavior, mood swings, and the like are commonly associated with adolescence). It is quite often the case that many parents do not even realize that a problem

exists until their son or daughter is in trouble with the police. Griffiths (1995a) reports a number of possible warning signs, although individually many of these signs could be put down to adolescence. However, if several apply to a child or adolescent, it could be that he or she will have a gambling problem. The signs include the following:

- A sudden drop in the standard of schoolwork
- Going out each evening and being evasive about where he or she has been
- Personality changes such as becoming sullen, moody, or constantly on the defensive
- Money missing from home
- Selling expensive possessions and not being able to account for the money
- Loss of interest in activities he or she used to enjoy
- Lack of concentration
- A "couldn't care less" attitude
- Not taking care of their appearance or hygiene

However, many of these "warning signs" are not necessarily unique to gambling addictions and can also be indicative of other addictions (e.g., to alcohol and other drugs).

RESEARCH INTO PROBLEM GAMBLING: SOME PROBLEMS

Before going on to examine issues surrounding prevention, intervention, and treatment of adolescent problem gambling, a brief overview of some of the major problems in the field is necessary. Evaluation of the literature in the field cannot be attempted without taking into account the many problems (definitional, methodological, conceptual) that characterize the area. Many obvious questions in the field need definitive answers: What characterizes the syndrome of pathological gambling? What characterizes pathological gamblers? How do we identify problem and pathological gambling? What is psychologically peculiar to problem and pathological gamblers? Before any attempt can be made to answer such fundamental questions, it needs to be pointed out that there are many problems in trying to do this. These problems will be outlined briefly below. It is also worth noting that in addition to those outlined below, many methodological problems have been outlined elsewhere (e.g., Shaffer & Korn, 2002).

• Gambling is multifaceted and not a unitary phenomenon. Treating all forms of gambling as equivalent in terms of underlying motivations may cloud the issue rather than clarify it. For instance, can we really say that the buyer of a weekly lottery ticket has a similar underlying psychology to a slot machine player? This may also have implications for intervention, prevention, and treatment.

• Problem gambling is also multifaceted. Evidence suggests it is more a syndrome than a single disorder. Shaffer and Korn (2002) suggest that syndromes have both common and unique components. A syndrome's common components (e.g., depression, anxiety, impulsivity) are shared with other disorders (e.g., drug abuse), whereas its unique components (e.g., chasing, betting increased amounts of money) are specific to problem gambling. Again, this may also have implications for intervention, prevention, and treatment.

• Gambling is one of any number of behaviors that a person may engage in concurrently, and therefore, the gambling behavior has to be viewed as part of that behavior cluster rather than in isolation. For instance, a pathological gambler who is also an alcoholic may be very different in motivational terms from someone whose only problem is gambling. Comorbidity clearly will have implications for intervention, prevention, and treatment.

• Demographic differences may produce very different findings in motivation to gamble. For instance, there may be significant differences due to age (an adult pathological horse race gambler cannot be easily compared with an adolescent slot machine addict), gender (a male pathological horse race gambler cannot be easily compared with a female bingo player), and culture (slot machine playing in the United Kingdom cannot necessarily be compared with slot machine playing in the United States).

• Each individual gambling activity has its own unique structural differences. For instance, gambling can be differentiated in terms of stake size, time gap between each gamble, prize structures, size of jackpot, and so on. Each of these differences may have implications for the gambler's motivations.

• Gambling—like most other behaviors—has definitional problems. What are the boundaries of gambling? Some definitions of gambling would include gambling on the stock market and even the taking out of insurance! Even bigger problems arise when concepts such as "social" and "normal" gambling are defined; these are necessarily on a continuum, and there is always an arbitrary cut off point. The definition of problem gambling suffers from the fact that many words are used interchangeably throughout the literature (e.g., *pathological, compulsive, addictive, habitual, impulsive, excessive*).

• Research into problematic gambling suffers because so many different screening instruments—SOGS (South Oaks Gambling Screen), *DSM*, ICD-10 (International Statistical Classification of Diseases and Related Health Problems, 10th revision), GA (Gamblers Anonymous) 20 Questions—are used that findings on problem gambling in one study cannot be easily compared with results from another study if a different measurement tool was used. Furthermore, screening instruments for assessing problematic gambling may not be appropriate, valid, or reliable for adolescents.

- Gambling behavior has a temporal dimension and is therefore not fixed or static, which has implications for prevention, intervention, and treatment. This may also affect research findings that examine gamblers at different stages of their gambling career.

- Almost every branch of psychology has a perspective (e.g., psychobiological, cognitive, behavioral, psychodynamic, psychosexual, personality) that tends to narrow the focus of gambling research. The same argument can be made about other disciplinary perspectives (genetic, sociological, economic, etc.). All these insular perspectives have implications for both research and treatment in the gambling field.

ADOLESCENT GAMBLING AS A PUBLIC HEALTH ISSUE

The way you define a problem will determine what you do about it.

—Dr. Jonathan Mann, World Health Organization (quoted in Korn, 2002)

Traditionally, gambling has not been viewed as a public health matter (Griffiths, 1996b; Korn, 2000). Consequently, research into the health, social, and economic impacts of gambling are still at an early stage. In August 1995, the *British Medical Journal* published an editorial titled *"Gambling With the Nation's Health?,"* which argued that gambling was a health issue both because it widened the inequalities of income and because there was an association between inequality of income in industrialized countries and lower life expectancy. There are many other more specific reasons why gambling should be viewed as a public health issue— particularly given the massive expansion of gambling opportunities across the world.

It is clear that the social and health costs of problem gambling are large on both an individual and societal level. For adults, personal costs can include irritability, extreme moodiness, problems with personal relationships (including divorce), absenteeism from work, family neglect, and bankruptcy. There can also be adverse health consequences for both the gambler and his or her partner, including depression, insomnia, intestinal disorders, migraines, and other stress-related disorders (Lorenz & Yaffee, 1986, 1988). Many similar effects have been found in adolescents, although in the younger years, education rather than work is compromised.

Health-related problems can also result from gambling withdrawal effects. Rosenthal and Lesieur (1992) found that at least 65% of pathological gamblers reported at least one physical side effect during withdrawal, including insomnia, headaches, upset stomach, loss of appetite, physical weakness, heart racing, muscle aches, breathing difficulty, and chills. Their results were also compared with the withdrawal effects from a substance-dependent control group. They concluded that pathological gamblers experienced more physical withdrawal effects when attempting to stop than did the substance-dependent group. Preliminary analysis of the calls to the United Kingdom's gambling help line also indicate that a significant minority of the callers report health-related consequences as a result of their problem gambling. These include depression, anxiety, stomach problems, other stress-related disorders, and suicidal ideation (Griffiths, Scarfe, & Bellringer, 1999).

Problem gambling is very much the "hidden" addiction. Unlike, say, alcoholism, there is no slurred speech and no stumbling into work. Furthermore, overt signs of problems often do not occur until late in the pathological gambler's career. When it is considered that problem and pathological gambling can be an addiction that destroys families and has medical consequences, it becomes clear that health professionals should be aware of the effects of gambling in just the same way they are aware of other potentially addictive activities such as drinking (alcohol) and smoking (nicotine). As a consequence, problem gambling is a public health issue that needs to be taken seriously by all within the health profession. General practitioners routinely ask patients about smoking and drinking, but gambling is not generally discussed (Setness, 1997). Problem gambling may be perceived as a somewhat "grey" area in the field of health, and it is therefore very easy to deny that health professionals should be playing a role. If the main aim of practitioners is to ensure the health of their clients, it is quite clear that an awareness of gambling and the issues surrounding it should be an important part of basic knowledge.

There is no doubt that opportunities and accessibility to gamble will increase because of deregulation. What has been demonstrated from research evidence in other countries is that where accessibility to gambling increases, *there is an increase not only in the number of regular gamblers but also an increase in the number of problem gamblers* (Griffiths, 1999). Obviously this does not mean that everyone is susceptible to developing gambling addictions, but it does mean that at a societal (rather than individual) level, the more gambling opportunities, the more problems.

There is an urgent need to enhance awareness within the medical and health professions about gambling-related problems and to develop effective strategies to prevent and treat problem gambling (Griffiths & Wood, 2000; Korn, 2000). The rapid expansion of gambling represents a significant public concern, and health practitioners also need to study the impact of gambling on vulnerable, at-risk, and special populations. It is inevitable that a small minority of people will become casualties of gambling directly due to the deregulation of gambling, and therefore, help should be provided for the problem gamblers. Because gambling is here to stay and is effectively state sponsored, governments should consider giving priority funding (from taxes raised from gambling revenue) to organizations and health practitioners who provide advice, counseling, and treatment for people with severe gambling problems.

INTERVENTION AND PREVENTION FOR ADOLESCENT GAMBLERS

According to Korn (2002), the goals of youth gambling intervention are to (a) prevent gambling-related problems; (b) promote informed, balanced attitudes and choices; and (c) protect vulnerable groups. The guiding principles for action on youth gambling are prevention, health promotion, harm reduction, and personal and social responsibility. If the goal is to prevent the development of problem gambling in young people, Ferland, Ladouceur, and Vitaro (2002) claim that an important first step in prevention may be simply giving adolescents the facts about gambling. At present, adolescent attitudes and views about gambling may be predominantly formed by the advertisements for gambling depicted in the mass media that present gambling as exciting and alluring. Such media portrayals may lead adolescents to believe that gambling is fun and exciting and that gambling is an easy way to make money. By providing adolescents with a more realistic view about gambling, it may be possible to limit their interest in gambling and restrict their participation.

Evans and Getz (in press) claim that substance abuse prevention research suggests some useful frameworks that could be applied to adolescent gambling prevention programs. However, there have been very few developed or evaluated. To date, there have been (to my knowledge) only three prevention studies published in the academic literature. Gaboury and Ladouceur (1993) implemented a prevention program with 289 high school students. Their program mostly involved delivering information about gambling in the same way a teacher would. The study showed that the intervention improved students' knowledge and gave them a more realistic attitude toward gambling. It also demonstrated that gambling severity was lower for adolescents who received the intervention. Another study by Ladouceur and his colleagues (Ladouceur, Vezina, Jacques, & Ferland, 2000) demonstrated that among 115 participants chosen at random in a shopping mall, a brochure about gambling could provide new information about problem gambling, at-risk behaviors, and the availability of specialized gambling help.

However, studies outside the gambling arena dealing with adolescents suggest that simply giving information is not enough to create positive effects (Donaldson, Graham, Piccinin, & Hansen, 1997; Edmundson, McAlister, Murray, Perry, & Lichtenstein, 1991; van der Pligt, 1998). Research on prevention programs outside the gambling field has shown that regardless of delivery mode (didactic lecture, videotapes, posters, pamphlets, guest speakers, etc.), the information-only approach has little effect on behavioral change relative to control group behavior (Evans & Getz, in press). Furthermore, information in the form of a teaching session may not be the optimum method for giving information to adolescents. As a consequence of these shortcomings, Ferland et al. (2002) designed a study to correct misconceptions and increase knowledge about gambling in 424 adolescents using a video format. The study found that the video-based intervention had a positive effect in increasing knowledge and in modifying misconceptions about gambling. However, these studies were cross-sectional in design, and there is no way of knowing if the positive benefits reported had any long-lasting effect or changed gambling behavior permanently.

Because research has generally shown that "fear induction" and information-only techniques are unsuccessful, Evans and colleagues (Evans, 1989, 2001; Evans & Getz, in press) have explored how psychosocial models and constructs can be applied to the prevention of health-threatening behaviors in adolescents. At the heart of these approaches is the concept of "social inoculation." The social inoculation model involves "inoculating" adolescents with the knowledge and social skills (i.e., resistance skills) necessary to resist various social pressures to engage in risky behaviors to which they may be exposed (including in this case, gambling).

Evans and Getz (in press) highlight five distinct (yet overlapping) theoretical paradigms that have been central to understanding health and illness-related behavior. These are social cognitive theory, the health belief model, the theory of reasoned action, self-regulation/self-control theory, and the subjective culture and interpersonal relations approach. These perspectives converge on a set of eight conditions necessary for the performance of any volitional behavior. The first three conditions are essential for the action to be performed—in this case, gambling:

1. Strong intention or commitment to engage (or not engage) in gambling

2. Absence of environmental barriers that would make gambling impossible

3. Possession of the skills necessary to engage in gambling

The final five conditions either directly influence the strength of intention or the strength of the action, or moderate the relationship between intention and action:

4. A positive attitude toward gambling (its benefits are perceived to outweigh its costs)

5. A perception of gambling as being consistent with social norms

6. A perception of gambling as being consistent with one's self-image

7. A positive emotional reaction to performing gambling

8. A realistic perception of having the capability to gamble (i.e., self-efficacy)

As Evans and Getz point out, these eight conditions embody a model of semivolitional behavior in general and health behavior in particular. From a prevention standpoint, the social inoculation approach can be understood as an effort to manipulate each of the variables in this model to facilitate health behavior and inhibit health-risking behavior. This may be the way forward in future adolescent gambling prevention schemes.

Historically, there has been no consensus about how to define pathological gambling in adolescents. Shaffer and Hall (1996) proposed the level system (see Table 25.1). The level system is the only classification scheme that directly links various degrees of problem gambling with levels of intervention. Thus, the level system not only provides a straightforward approach to classifying gambling behavior but also links various levels of gambling with appropriate intervention. Shaffer and Hall argue that youths experience a wide range of problems associated with gambling and that it is not useful to simply describe young gamblers as "problem gamblers" or "nonproblem gamblers." The level system therefore classifies young gamblers in terms of the degree of problems associated with gambling. Level 1 gambling is "social gambling," or gambling not associated with any problems. Level 2 gambling, or in-transition gambling, refers to gambling behavior that does not meet the diagnostic criteria for pathological gambling but that does,

nonetheless, appear to be somewhat problematic. Level 3 gambling refers to problem gambling. Adolescents described as Level 3 gamblers report heavy gambling in the face of adverse consequences. This population is the target population for which treatment for pathological gambling may be necessary.

At the moment, there are perhaps more questions than answers when it comes to designing and developing prevention programs. Evans and Getz (in press) assert that it is necessary to systematically determine from target populations (both gambling and nongambling adolescents) what they perceive to be the influences that would lead them to begin or to continue gambling (e.g., media portrayals, friends, parents, etc.).

CONCLUSIONS

Excessive involvement with gambling may bring problems to the individual concerned. These problems appear to be intensified when the individual is an adolescent. The technologies involved in gambling are slowly merging, and adolescents already living and interacting in a multimedia world are discovering that leisure opportunities are becoming more easily accessible and widespread. The risk factors involved in problem adolescent gambling are beginning to be established. Jacobs (1997) has made the point that without early and appropriate prevention, intervention, and treatment, adolescents will become high-risk candidates for developing a variety of dysfunctional behaviors, including a range of addictive behavior patterns.

Through analysis of both the situational and structural characteristics in gambling, Griffiths (1999) has argued that situational characteristics most affect acquisition of the behavior and that structural characteristics have the greatest effect on development and maintenance of it. Furthermore, the most important of these factors appears to be

Table 25.1   Classification of Adolescent Gambling

Level of Gambling Involvement/Definition	Possible Education-Prevention Treatment Interventions	SOGS-RA[a] Score
Level 0: Nongambling. Has never gambled.	Educational awareness–primary prevention	0
Level 1: Nonproblem gambling. Gambles recreationally and does not experience any signs or symptoms of gambling-related disorder.	Secondary prevention	1
Level 2: In-transition gambling. Gambler who experiences subclinical symptoms or displays signs of gambling problems may be progressing either toward more serious symptoms (i.e., progression) or away from these symptoms (i.e., during recovery)	Tertiary prevention–Early treatment to arrest progression. Relapse prevention activities to facilitate and sustain recovery	2-3
Level 3: Gambling-related disorder with impairment. Gambler who meets diagnostic criteria as assessed by the SOGS-RA as impaired in psychological or sociological domains.	Tertiary prevention–to minimize harm	4
Level 4: Impaired gambler who displays willingness to enter treatment.	Treatment	N/A

SOURCE: Adapted from Shaffer and Hall (1996).
NOTE: *Primary prevention* is defined as those efforts that delay or prevent the onset of activities that can lead to harmful gambling. *Secondary prevention* is defined as efforts aimed at minimizing the likelihood that Level 1 gamblers will develop problems related to gambling. *Tertiary prevention* is then defined as those efforts taken with youth to minimize problems that exist with Level 2 and Level 3 gambling. This level of prevention could be associated with early treatment for Level 2 and treatment for Level 3 gamblers and defined as *relapse prevention*. *Treatment* would be defined as those activities associated with arresting the problem gambling behavior and minimizing the harm caused by that behavior. The diagnosis is not made if the gambling behavior is better accounted for by a manic episode.
a. SOGS-RA = South Oaks Gambling Screen revised for adolescents.

accessibility of the activity and event frequency (both of which are critical to the success of gambling). When these two characteristics combine, the greatest problems could occur. This is well demonstrated by the worldwide proliferation in slot machines (and the associated problems that go with them). As Griffiths (1999) points out, it could be that slot machine gambling has more "gambling inducing" structural characteristics (as a result of the inherent technology) than other forms of gambling and could be why a relatively large minority of gamblers in the United Kingdom are "addicted" to slot machines (many of whom are adolescents). With their integrated mix of conditioning effects, rapid event frequency, short payout intervals, and psychological rewards, it is not hard to see how slot machine gambling (and psychologically similar activities such as scratchcard gambling) can become a habit. It may also give us an insight to the possible problems created by the spread of Internet gambling because interactive gaming has many of the characteristics of slot machine gambling.

Steps need to be taken to minimize problem gambling activities because research has shown that the younger a child starts to gamble, the more likely he or she is to develop problems. Possible measures include the following:

- Immediately raising the minimum age of all forms of commercial gambling to at least 18 years
- Imposition of much stricter penalties for shopkeepers and gaming operators who sell scratchcards or lottery tickets to children or allow children to gamble illegally
- Restriction or prohibition of television gambling advertising until after the 9 p.m. watershed or prime-time slot (including the screening of lottery-related programs—in themselves a form of advertising)
- Geographically locating gambling establishments (e.g., amusement arcades, bookmakers) away from sites where more vulnerable members of the population are found (e.g., schools, colleges)
- Capping of lottery jackpots and no rollover jackpots
- Creation of gambling tax levies (out of taxes raised from gambling revenue) given to charities and organizations who provide advice, counseling, treatment, and rehabilitation for people with gambling problems
- Creation of single government departments to oversee all gambling legislation and to provide a coherent and comprehensive framework for gambling activities
- Significant strengthening of the powers of the gambling regulatory authorities

The single most important measure in the United States would be to enforce the legal age of gambling—for example, the purchase of lottery tickets. This would significantly reduce the age at which children start to gamble and would also encourage gaming operators and shopkeepers to prevent under-age gambling. At present, many adolescents as young as 15 and 16 years of age can pass for 18. Enforcing age restrictions would stop many very young adolescents from gambling in the first place.

Furthermore, Griffiths (1995a) asserts that knowledge about structural characteristics also provides information that may help in decreasing "addictiveness" potential of gambling activities. For instance, with slot machines, possible a priori steps include the following:

- Limited use of arousing lighting on the machine
- Plastic payout trays instead of metal ones
- Notices on the machine that clearly state the payout rate and the win probability and a statement indicating that the machine is on the whole chance determined
- A monitoring device that lets gamblers have a running total of how much they have put into the machine (actual amount rather than turnover)
- Equal numbers of winning symbols on each machine reel
- All payouts to be in money rather than tokens
- "Neutral" names for machines and less choice in initial gambling stakes

This list is by no means exhaustive and suggests only possible mechanisms for decreasing the number of people who experience problems with gambling by correcting cognitive distortions, false beliefs, and false expectations.

Further work is needed in a number of areas relating to risk factors. Following the recommendations of (and building on) the U.S. National Research Council (1999, pp. 142-143), these could potentially include the following:

- Longitudinal research that explores the changing nature of risk factors from childhood to adolescence and into adulthood
- Research that controls for important sociodemographic variables in the study of the acquisition, development, and maintenance of risk factors
- Family and twin studies to determine familial risk factors for problem gambling and game playing
- Studies that use adequate and diverse samples (racial or ethnic minorities, females, rural/urban, etc.)
- Further research among individuals and communities that examines the effect of access and availability on gambling and gaming behaviors
- Studies on comorbid gambling and gaming disorders (substance abuse disorders, mood disorders, antisocial personality disorders, etc.)
- Studies to identify both the similarities and differences between traditional forms of gambling/gaming and technologically sophisticated forms
- Research on risk taking and other dimensions of impulse control among gamblers and gamers—using adequate controls
- Studies to determine whether factors are risk factors or consequences of gambling
- Studies that examine people's perceptions of different gambling and gaming activities (because these may affect acquisition, development, and maintenance of the behavior)
- Further research to examine which structural characteristics are more likely to affect "addictiveness" potential in particular forms of gambling. For instance, it may be that light, color, and sound effects are integral to increasing baseline levels of gambling among slot machine gamblers but not in other gambling forms (e.g., lotteries, horse racing, etc.)
- Research that identifies whether certain games may be gateways to subsequent gambling problems, just as previous research indicates there are gateway drugs (e.g., marijuana) that precede the use of hard drugs (e.g., heroin)

- Research that encompasses multiple techniques obtaining data from the same participant (e.g., face-to-face interviews, genetic/neurobiological testing, ethnographic methods, etc.)

Finally, it is worth summarizing some of the recommendations for public health policy and practice made by Shaffer and Korn (2002). They suggest the following:

1. *Adoption of strategic goals* for gambling to provide a focus for public health action and accountability. These goals include
   - preventing gambling-related problems among individuals and groups at risk for gambling addiction,
   - promoting balanced and informed attitudes, behaviors, and policies toward gambling and gamblers by both individuals and communities, and
   - protecting vulnerable groups from gambling-related harm.

2. *Endorsement of public health principles* consisting of three primary principles that can guide and inform decision making to reduce gambling-related problems. These are
   - ensuring that prevention is a community priority, with the appropriate allocation of resources to primary, secondary, and tertiary prevention initiatives,
   - incorporating a mental health promotion approach that builds community capacity, incorporates a holistic view of mental health, and addresses the needs and aspirations of gamblers, individuals at risk of gambling problems, or those affected by them, and
   - fostering personal and social responsibility for gambling policies and practices.

3. *Adoption of harm reduction strategies* directed at minimizing the adverse health, social, and economic consequences of gambling behavior for individuals, families, and communities. These initiatives should include
   - healthy-gambling guidelines for the general public (similar to low-risk drinking guidelines),

- vehicles for the early identification of gambling problems,
- nonjudgmental moderation and abstinence goals for problem gamblers, and
- surveillance and reporting systems to monitor trends in gambling-related participation and the incidence and burden of gambling-related illnesses.

CHAPTER 26

Understanding Youth Gambling Problems

A Conceptual Framework

Jeffrey L. Derevensky
Rina Gupta
Laurie Dickson
Karen Hardoon
Anne-Elyse Deguire

The history of gambling on an international level has passed through a number of cycles from prohibition to widespread proliferation. Gambling has gone from being associated with sin, crime, vice, and degradation to its current position as a socially acceptable form of entertainment, with many governments not only regulating gambling but retaining partial or sole ownership of gambling activities. The prevailing attitudes of governmental legislators and the public at large suggest that new gaming venues (e.g., casinos and new technologies in the form of interactive lotteries and Internet gambling) will continue to expand rapidly. That Harvard, Yale, Princeton, William and Mary, Dartmouth, Rutgers, and the University of Pennsylvania have historically all gained operating funds through lotteries attests to the potential good derived from the proceeds of gambling (Preston, Bernhard, Hunter, & Bybee, 1998). This tradition continues, with many state lotteries actively promoting their products by reporting that a proportion of the proceeds are used for educational initiatives and programs and religious groups using gambling revenues for charitable causes.

Gambling remains a contentious social policy issue in many countries throughout the world.[1] The National Research Council's (1999) seminal review of the scientific literature for the National Gambling Impact Study Commission has noted a trend toward the proliferation of gambling venues, increased individual expenditures, and the seriousness of the adverse consequences for those individuals with a gambling problem. Although the perspective that gambling is not a harmless, innocuous behavior with few negative consequences is slowly changing, most adults strongly support their continued opportunity to gamble and view it as much less harmful than other potentially addictive behaviors and harmful social activities.

Once perceived as an activity primarily relegated to adults, gambling has become popular among adolescents. Although legislative statutes and age regulations generally prohibit children and adolescents from participating in legalized forms of gambling (statutes and gambling activities differ according to their jurisdiction), their resourcefulness enables many youth to engage in both legal and illegal forms of gambling. Research has revealed that upward of 80% of adolescents engage in some form of gambling (see the reviews by Jacobs, 2000; National Research Council, 1999), with most best described as social gamblers. However, current prevalence rates of adolescent problem gamblers are estimated to be between 4% and 8% of the adolescent population (Jacobs, 2000; National Research Council, 1999). In addition, it has been estimated that another 10% to 15% of youth gamble excessively and are at risk for developing a serious gambling problem (National Research Council, 1999).

The rapid movement from social gambler to problem gambler (Gupta & Derevensky, 2000) and the induction of gambling as a rite of initiation into adulthood (Svendsen, 1998) points to the possibility that adolescents may be more susceptible to developing gambling-related problems. Acknowledging difficulties in comparisons of data sets, the National Research Council (1999) report concluded that "the proportion of pathological gamblers among adolescents in the United States could be more than three times that of adults (5.0% versus 1.5%)" (p. 89). Extrapolating from these data, approximately 15.3 million, 12- to 17-year-olds in the United States and Canada have been gambling, and 2.2 million are reported to be experiencing serious gambling-related problems. Trends between 1984 and 1999 indicate a significant increase in the proportion of youth who report gambling during the past year and those who report gambling-related problems (Jacobs, 2000).

It appears that gambling behavior is established early and begins earlier than other potentially addictive behaviors, including tobacco, alcohol, and drug use (Gupta & Derevensky, 1996). Because there are few observable signs of gambling dependence among children, these problems have not been as readily noticed compared with other addictions (e.g., alcohol or substance abuse) (Arcuri, Lester, & Smith, 1985; Hardoon & Derevensky, 2002).

Gambling is advertised widely, easily accessible to youth, and often located in places perceived to be glamorous and exciting (e.g., bars, casinos). Gambling also provides opportunities for socializing, be it positive or negative (Stinchfield & Winters, 1998). Although wagering in casinos, on lotteries, and with electronic gaming, in general, is illegal for adolescents (statutes differ between countries, states, and provinces), the enforcement of such laws, as with underage drinking, is becoming increasingly difficult.

RISK FACTORS FOR YOUTH WITH SERIOUS GAMBLING PROBLEMS

Although our current state of empirical knowledge of adolescent problem gambling has been limited (Dickson, Derevensky, & Gupta, 2002; Griffiths & Wood, 2000; Hardoon & Derevensky, 2002), a brief overview of these findings provides a necessary foundation for our conceptual understanding of this growing problem.

Familial Factors

Results from several studies suggest that the majority of youth tend to gamble with family members (40% to 68%) (Derevensky, Gupta, & Émond, 1995; Gupta & Derevensky, 1997), with most parents not appearing to be concerned with their children's gambling behavior. In several studies, 80% to 90% of parents report knowing that their children gamble for money and have no objection to this behavior (Arcuri et al., 1985). Research has also revealed that 78% of children gamble in their own homes (Gupta & Derevensky, 1997). As well, a strong correlation has been found between adolescent gambling and parental gambling involvement (Wood & Griffiths, 1998). Retrospective studies indicate that 25% to 40% of adult pathological gamblers' parents were problem gamblers (Custer, 1982; Jacobs, Marston, & Singer, 1985) with a large number of adolescents having severe gambling problems reporting that their fathers have similar gambling problems.

Peer Influences

Griffiths (1990a) has reported that 44% of adolescents participated in gambling activities because their friends were engaged in similar practices. As children get older, they tend to gamble less with family members and more with friends in their homes (Gupta & Derevensky, 1996, 1997; Ide-Smith & Lea, 1988). This trend reinforces the notion that for many youth gambling is perceived as a socially acceptable and entertaining pastime. Findings suggesting a strong social learning and peer-modeling component involved in the acquisition of gambling behaviors have also been reported (Gupta & Derevensky, 1997; Hardoon & Derevensky, 2001). Quality friendships and relationships are often lost and replaced by newly acquired friends who may be best viewed as gambling associates (Derevensky & Gupta, 2000b).

Gender Differences

Gambling has been found to be a more popular activity among adolescent males than among females (Jacobs, 2000; National Research Council, 1999). Pathological gambling among adolescent males has been found to be 3 to 4 times that of females (Lesieur et al., 1991; Stinchfield & Winters, 1998; Volberg, 1994; Volberg & Steadman, 1988). Males have also been found to make higher gross wagers and exhibit greater risk-taking behaviors, report initiating gambling at earlier ages, gamble on a larger number and variety of games, gamble more often, spend more time and money when gambling, and experience significantly more gambling-related problems than do female youth (Jacobs, 2000).

Although youth have been found to engage in all forms of legalized and illegal forms of gambling (Jacobs, 2000), female adolescents seem to prefer scratch tickets, lotteries, and bingo, whereas males prefer sports betting and card games (Felsher, Gupta, & Derevensky, 2001; Griffiths, 1989; Jacobs, 2000; NORC, 1999; National Research Council, 1999; Volberg, 1994).

Age of Onset

Adolescents experiencing severe gambling problems report beginning gambling at 9 or 10 years of age (Jacobs, 2000); adult problem gamblers report that their pathological behaviors began in late childhood and adolescence, often between 10 and 19 years of age (Custer, 1982; Dell, Ruzicka, & Palisi, 1981). In the United Kingdom, children are reported to have begun playing fruit machines, legalized low-wage slot machines, as early as 8 to 10 years of age (Griffiths, 1990a).

Personality Factors and Emotional States

Youth with serious gambling problems have been found to be greater risk takers

(Arnett, 1994; Powell, Hardoon, Derevensky, & Gupta, 1999; Zuckerman, 1994), and adolescent problem and pathological gamblers score higher on measures of impulsivity (Zimmerman, Meeland, & Krug, 1985), excitability, extroversion, and anxiety and lower on conformity and self-discipline (Gupta & Derevensky, in press; Vitaro, Ferland, Jacques, & Ladouceur, 1998). Problem and pathological gamblers have been found to be more self-blaming, guilt prone, and anxious and to be less emotionally stable (Gupta & Derevensky, 2000).

Adolescents with gambling problems have been found to have lower self-esteem (Gupta & Derevensky, 1998b), to have higher rates of depression (Gupta & Derevensky, 1998a), and to report greater suicide ideation and suicide attempts compared with other adolescents (Lesieur et al., 1991). They have also been found to have poor or maladaptive general coping skills and tend to use more emotion and avoidant coping styles (Gupta & Derevensky, 2000).

Problem Behaviors Associated With Pathological Gambling

Youth with gambling problems are prone to engage in multiple, comorbid addictive behaviors (smoking, drinking, drug use/abuse) (Gupta & Derevensky, 1998b; Hardoon, Gupta, & Derevensky, 2002; Maden, Swinton, & Gunn, 1992; Winters & Anderson, 2000). They are also more likely to have difficulty in school, including increased truancy and poor school performance (Hardoon et al., 2002; Ladouceur, Boudreault, Jacques, & Vitaro, 1999; Lesieur et al., 1991). Although adolescents with gambling problems report having a peer support group, their old friends are often replaced by *gambling associates* (Gupta & Derevensky, 2000). Problem and pathological gambling has been shown to result in increased delinquency and crime, disruption of familial

relationships, conduct disorders, and decreased academic performance (Hardoon et al., 2002). Those youth with gambling problems appear preoccupied with gambling, planning their next gambling activity, and lying to their family and friends; they are focused on obtaining money with which to gamble (Gupta & Derevensky 2000).

A CONCEPTUAL FRAMEWORK: RESILIENCE RESEARCH

The resiliency literature is predicated on the findings that some individuals appear more immune to adversity, deprivation, and stress than others. For example, one child raised in a family with parental conflict and substance abuse may do well, whereas a sibling may go on to develop an addiction, suicidal ideation, or suicidal behavior. It remains inevitable that all individuals face stressful life events, and children, similar to adults, have different adaptive behaviors and, often, unique ways of coping. A child living with a parent who has a gambling problem may ultimately develop similar gambling behaviors, other psychological problems, delinquent behaviors, or some combination of all of these. Yet we know that certain individuals who have been exposed to excessive and pathological gambling by a parent appear to be resilient. These youth may become community-involved citizens, excel academically, and enter healthy mentoring relationships with another adult. Such youth, who do well despite experiences of multiple stressors, are perceived to be "resilient" (Garmezy, Masten, & Tellegen, 1984; Werner & Smith, 1982).

There is evidence that resiliency is related to biological, self-righting dispositions in human development (Waddington, 1957) and to the protective mechanisms that work in the presence of stressors (Rutter, 1987). Resilient youth seem to more effectively cope with stressful situations and emotional distress in ways that enable them to engage in appropriate adaptive behaviors and to develop in a healthy manner.

Resilient Youth

Empirical research, in general, supports a positive profile that includes efficient problem-solving skills (the ability to think abstractly and to generate and implement solutions to cognitive and social problems), social competence (encompassing the qualities of flexibility, communication skills, concern for others, and prosocial behaviors), autonomy (self-efficacy and self-control), and a sense of purpose and future (exhibited in success orientation, motivation, and optimism) (Brown, D'Emidio-Caston, & Benard, 2001).

A Resilience Focus in the Field of Tobacco, Alcohol, and Drug Abuse Prevention

It is generally acknowledged that it is essential for prevention efforts to be science based. The history of drug and substance use prevention efforts has stimulated the field toward refinement of efforts through theoretical reformulations, evolution of research goals, and refinement of research methodology and program evaluations. Despite findings that the majority of meta-analyses evaluations and comprehensive studies of prevention efforts have generally revealed limited effects on modifying alcohol and illicit drug use among adolescents (Gorman, 1995; Hansen, 1992), the evolution of addiction prevention research has resulted in efforts that progressively have yielded better outcomes. Although early prevention efforts were largely not theory driven, had ill-defined target populations, and lacked specification of outcome measurement variables, more recent science-based programs, such as the Center for Substance Abuse and Prevention

Eight Model Programs (Brounstein & Zweig, 1999), are based on the empirical evidence of their effectiveness.

Theoretical and empirical research that has identified commonalities between problem adolescent gambling and other addictions suggests that prevention efforts arrived at for other addictions may be unique and rich sources of information for those working toward the prevention of problem gambling. Jacobs's (1986) "General Theory of Addictions" provides a useful theoretical framework from which to consider commonalities among addictions. His general theory of addiction construes it as a dependent state acquired over a period of time by a predisposed person in efforts to relieve a chronic stress condition (Jacobs, 1986). Accordingly, physiological and psychological predisposing factors must coexist and come into operation in a stressful environment. Jacobs's theory further posits that addictive behaviors fulfill a need to escape from stressful realities. Multiple addictions are common among chemical dependencies (Winters & Anderson, 2000), and it has been found that severity in one addiction likely increases the severity in others (Hardoon et al., 2002). Empirical and clinical evidence that adolescent problem gambling fits within Jacobs's "General Theory of Addictions" (Gupta & Derevensky, 1998b, 2000) points to the need to examine similarities and differences among the addictions, analyze various risk and protective factors, and understand the coping mechanisms of those youth dealing with an addiction.

Risk and Protective Factors Across Addictions

In an effort to examine current prevention efforts in the fields of alcohol and drug abuse, the concepts of risk and protective factors and their interaction have played a crucial role (Brounstein et al., 1999; Dickson et al., 2002). These prevention efforts seek to prevent or limit the effects of risk factors (those variables associated with a high probability of onset, greater severity, and longer duration of major mental health problems) and increase protective factors (conditions that improve an individual's resistance to risk factors and disorders). By limiting the risk factors through the development of protective factors, it is believed that children will become more resilient. Because children are not necessarily born resilient, acquiring resiliency through multiple opportunities and situations to which they are exposed remains important.

Risk factors constitute those factors that are precursors to unsuccessful coping, maladaptive behaviors, or poor outcomes. Current etiological models have emphasized complex interactions between genetic, biomedical, and psychosocial risk and protective factors (Coie et al., 1993). As a result, successful risk-focused prevention programs have focused on eliminating, reducing, or minimizing risk factors associated with particular outcomes, be it problem gambling, alcohol, or drug addiction. Evidence of resiliency in children (e.g., Garmezy, 1985; Rutter, 1987; Werner, 1986) has evolved from a risk prevention framework to one that includes both risk prevention and the fostering of protective factors. Protective factors can serve to mediate or buffer the effects of individual vulnerabilities or environmental adversity so that the adaptational trajectory is more positive than if the protective factors were not at work. However, protective factors, in and of themselves, do not necessarily promote resiliency. If the strength or number of risk factors outweigh the impact of protective factors, the chance that poor outcomes will ensue increases.

Several studies have examined the effects of a large number of risk and protective factors associated with excessive alcohol and substance abuse (see Dickson et al., 2002, for a comprehensive review). Protective and risk factors have been shown to interact with each other such that protective factors reduce the strength of the stressor for particular negative outcomes. There are numerous positive examples as to how protective factors influence positive outcomes and limit negative behaviors. For example, the effects of positive school experiences have been shown to moderate the effects of family conflict, which in turn decreases the association between family conflict and several adolescent problem behaviors (e.g., pathological gambling, alcohol and substance abuse, suicide, and delinquency) (Jessor, Van Den Bos, Vanderryn, Costa, & Turbin, 1995).

It should be noted that specific forms of dysfunction are typically associated with a number of different risk factors rather than a single, unitary factor. Similarly, a particular risk factor is rarely related to a specific disorder. Exposure to risk likely occurs in diverse ways and in multiple settings. Coie and his colleagues (1993) concluded that (a) risk factors have complex relations to clinical disorders, (b) the salience of risk factors may fluctuate developmentally, (c) exposure to multiple risk factors appears to have cumulative effects, and (d) diverse disorders can share similar fundamental risk factors.

The multiple risk and protective factors that operate on the level of the individual include physiological factors (e.g., biochemical and genetic), personality variables, values and attitudes, early and persistent problem behaviors, and substance use. These risk and protective factors have been found to operate in the family domain through family management practices, parental modeling, familial structure (single-parent families), and family climate (including conflict resolution and socioemotional parent-child bonding). The peer domain has also been particularly relevant in the prevention of adolescent risk behaviors. Such risk and protective factors have been found to operate through peer associations, social expectancies in regard to substance use, and through school performance. The school context also carries with it factors that affect an adolescent's attitudes and behavior. Academic performance, school bonding (perceived connectedness with school), and school policies have also been found either to buffer risk factors of substance abuse or to be precursors to unsuccessful coping and the development of substance abuse. On a community level, risk and protective factors affect adolescent risk behavior via accessibility to substances (a particular problem as related to youth gambling because of its widespread availability and accessibility) and the influence of societal laws, attitudes, and norms.

A Model for Understanding Adolescent Gambling Problems and Adolescent Risky Behaviors

The examination of the commonalities of risk factors for problem gambling and other addictions provides sufficient evidence to suggest that gambling can similarly be incorporated into more general addiction and adolescent risk behavior models. Current research efforts (e.g., Battistich, Schaps, Watson, & Solomon, 1996; Galambos & Tilton-Weaver, 1998; Loeber, Farrington, Stouthamer-Loeber, & Van Kammen, 1998) may suggest a general mental health approach that addresses a number of adolescent risky behaviors (e.g., substance abuse, gambling, risky driving, truancy, and risky sexual activity).

Dickson et al. (2002) have adapted Jessor's (1998) model to view problem gambling within a risky-behavior paradigm. This conceptual framework is predicated on a theoretical foundation for general mental health and prevention programs that foster resiliency. Risk and protective factors operate *interactively*, in and across a number of domains (biology, social environment, perceived environment, personality, and behavior).

One of the most ominous aspects of gambling is the impact it has on the lives of not only a problem gambler but those of family members, peers, friends, and employers. The long-term implications for a society with an increase in the number of problem gamblers may well rest on our prevention initiatives directed for youth. Our current empirical knowledge of youth problem gambling reflects the serious nature of gambling-related problems for youth (Derevensky & Gupta, 2000; Gupta & Derevensky, 2000). Thus, as both a mental and a public health issue (see Korn & Shaffer, 1999, for a comprehensive review), the perspective of problem gambling within the context of a risky lifestyle for many youth beckons the need for additional research in this area.

The effectiveness of future prevention programs can be measured by the extent to which program goals and components decrease risk factors and buttress protective factors, thereby successfully altering life trajectories toward the onset or maintenance of problematic risky behavior *and* enhancing resiliency (Coie et al., 1993). Despite the complexities of using the risk-protective factor model (see Coie et al., 1993), this model remains promising because of (a) its empirical validity in understanding current trends in adolescent risk behavior theory (Jessor, 1998); (b) its role in empirically supported theory of intentional behavioral change (DiClemente, 1999), which has been used to understand the *initiation* of health-protective behaviors and health-risk behaviors such as gambling; and (c) its potential to *modify* problem behaviors such as excessive alcohol use and problem gambling.

CONCLUDING REMARKS

Current trends in research on adolescent problem behavior have also begun to conceptualize risky behavior on a continuum, drawing important distinctions between substance use per se and use-related problems (Baer, MacLean, & Marlatt, 1998). Only recently have health professionals, educators, and public policymakers acknowledged adolescent problem gambling. In light of the scarcity of empirical knowledge about the relationship between adolescent problem gambling and other risk behaviors, particularly alcohol and substance abuse, longitudinal research is imperative. It is important to note that although some of these risk factors are consistent with individuals with delinquent and anti-social behaviors and that delinquents have a higher risk for problem gambling, further empirical research is necessary before definitive conclusions can be drawn concerning the comparability of these groups.

NOTE

1. See the reports from the U.S. National Gambling Study Impact Commission (National Opinion Research Center [NORC], 1999), Canadian Tax Foundation Report (Vaillancourt & Roy, 2000), the U.K. Gambling Review Report (Department for Culture, Media and Sport Gambling Review Body, 2001), the Australian Productivity Commission Report (Australian Productivity Commission, 1999), the National Centre for the Study of Gambling, South Africa Report (Collins & Barr, 2001), and studies conducted in New Zealand (Abbott, 2001).

CHAPTER 27

A Perspective on Adolescent Gambling

Relationship to Other Risk Behaviors and Implications for Prevention Strategies

Marc N. Potenza

Social attitudes toward gambling have shifted dramatically throughout time. Historically, there have been periods during which gambling was commonly viewed as a sin, vice, or personal weakness (Talmadge, 1888). Concurrent with these attitudes, there has been significant societal involvement in gambling at multiple levels, including personal (Long, 1882), public and private institutional (Talmadge, 1888), and governmental (at both state and federal levels). Over the past several decades in the United States, there has been an unprecedented increase in the availability of legalized gambling for adults. Concurrently, there appears to be a growing acceptance of and engagement in gambling activities (Potenza, Kosten, & Rounsaville, 2001). Gambling has been proposed to represent a behavior with addictive potential and possible health correlates (Potenza, Fiellin, Heninger, Rounsaville, & Mazure, 2002). However, the relative paucity of research, particularly of investigations into the health associations of different patterns of gambling behaviors, significantly compromises the ability to make informed policy recommendations (Korn & Shaffer, 1999; National Research Council, 1999).

Adolescents represent a unique population with regard to a variety of risk behaviors, including gambling. As a group transitioning from childhood to adulthood, adolescents frequently engage in novel and potentially dangerous activities. Adultlike cognitive styles emerge as adolescents learn about and from risk experiences. This chapter

AUTHOR'S NOTE: Acknowledgments: This work was supported by a Young Investigator Award from the National Alliance for Research in Schizophrenia and Depression, a Drug Abuse Research Scholar Program in Psychiatry Award from the American Psychiatric Association and the National Institute on Drug Abuse (K12-DA00366), Women's Health Research at Yale, and the National Center for Responsible Gaming.

Table 27.1   Gambling Patterns of Adolescents and Adults in the United States (in percentages)

Type of Gambling	Adolescents (Ages 16-17 Years)		Adults (Ages 18 Years and Older)	
	Lifetime	Past Year	Lifetime	Past Year
Casino	1.9	1.1	56.7	25.5
Track	6.6	2.2	36.6	7.0
Lottery	21.7	13.5	71.8	51.3
Bingo	18.2	6.2	28.1	6.1
Charitable	5.8	2.4	14.3	5.4
Card room	3.4	1.7	7.0	2.3
Private	46.3	28.5	30.6	11.0
Store/bar/restaurant	6.6	3.7	16.9	6.7
Unlicensed	13.3	9.6	21.1	9.2
Internet	0.7	0.2	0.5	0.4
Tribal facility	0.9	0.9	16.0	9.1

SOURCE: Data were derived from the Youth and Adult Surveys of the 1999 *Gambling Impact and Behavior Study* (Gerstein et al., 1999).

will present a brief perspective on (a) the current gambling environment (focusing on the United States and North America), (b) gambling behaviors of adolescents, (c) the relationship of gambling to other risk behaviors of adolescence and (d) current and future efforts and needs in adolescent gambling prevention.

GAMBLING IN THE UNITED STATES

Traditional forms of gambling include lotteries, sports and card gambling, pari-mutuels, and casino gambling (slot machines, table games), among others. Legalized gambling in the United States currently grosses over 50 billion dollars annually, more than the movie, theme park, and music industries combined (Potenza et al., 2001). Internet gambling represents a growing industry currently grossing over a billion dollars annually. With younger generations' increasing disposition to engage in computerized activities and a growing adeptness at using Internet-based resources, adolescent gambling on the Internet poses a growing

concern (Federal Trade Commission, 2002; Mitka, 2001).

ADOLESCENT GAMBLING

High rates of gambling have been reported in adolescents, comparable to those observed in adults. For example, a meta-analysis of prevalence estimate studies performed in North America found that 77% to 83% of adolescents are thought to have gambled within the past year (Shaffer & Hall, 1996), whereas a rate of past-year gambling participation in U.S. adults was estimated from a national survey to be 68% (Gerstein et al., 1999). However, patterns of adolescent and adult gambling differ; for example, adolescents and adults participate with differing frequencies in specific forms of gambling (see Table 27.1) (Gerstein et al., 1999). Because youth gambling is illegal for minors (Federal Trade Commission, 2002), the relatively high rates of gambling (particularly in government-sponsored forms such as the lottery) highlight the need for a more careful analysis of the risks and benefits associated with different levels and types of gambling participation by adolescents.

As with adult prevalence estimates (Shaffer, Hall, & Vander Bilt, 1999), some more recently performed studies of adolescent cohorts have yielded higher estimates (Jacobs, 2000). For example, a review of North American studies performed from 1984 to 1988 found a median rate of 45%, and those from 1998 to 1999 a median rate of 66% (Jacobs, 2000). Although causality is difficult to determine, there has been a concurrent increase in the availability of legalized gambling opportunities for adults (e.g., lotteries and casinos—see below), suggesting a need for careful examination of the impact of adult gambling attitudes and behavior on adolescent gambling participation.

A consistent finding over time has been the high rates of problem and pathological gambling in youth populations. For example, a meta-analysis of prevalence estimate studies performed in North America over the past 30 years found past-year rates of problem and pathological gambling of 3.8% and 1.1%, respectively, in adults and 14.8% and 5.8%, respectively, in youths (Shaffer et al., 1999). As in adults, problem and pathological gambling have been found to be associated with adverse measures of health and well-being. For example, problem and pathological gambling in adults has been associated with high rates of divorce, poor general health, mental health problems, job loss and lost wages, bankruptcy, arrest, and incarceration (Gerstein et al., 1999c). In youths, similar and different problems, reflective of adolescent life, have been found in association with problem and pathological gambling, including high rates of illegal behaviors and legal problems, school delinquency and poor academic performance, family conflicts, and mental health symptoms or disorders (e.g., anxiety, depression, and substance use problems) (Wynne, Smith, & Jacobs, 1996). However, many of the adolescent studies performed to date have been regional investigations using a variety of different measures of problem and pathological gambling behaviors. As such, there has been not only debate regarding the precise meaning of the findings (Stinchfield, 2002) but also a call for more rigorous investigation of youth problem and pathological gambling (National Research Council, 1999). Taken together, the data indicate that problem and pathological gambling in youth populations represent a significant public health concern and warrant additional attention from researchers, clinicians, families, school officials, and policymakers.

GAMBLING AND OTHER RISK BEHAVIORS

Adolescent gambling has been found to be associated with a variety of risk behaviors. One study of 21,297 Vermont high school students incorporated gambling questions into the Centers for Disease Control Youth Risk Behavior Survey (CDC YRBS). Compared with nongambling youths, youths who gamble were found to have higher rates of substance use (alcohol, tobacco, marijuana, cocaine, inhalants, steroids, and illegal drugs), drunk driving, seatbelt nonuse, sexual behavior, and violence (including being threatened, carrying weapons, and fighting) (Proimos, DuRant, Pierce, & Goodman, 1998). The same study found that of the adolescent gamblers, problem gamblers were more likely than the nonproblem gamblers to have participated in these risk behaviors (Proimos et al., 1998). Studies of adolescent gambling in other states have found similar results. For example, in a survey of 75,582 Minnesota public high school students, gambling was found by multiple regression analysis to be associated with antisocial behavior, male gender, feeling bad about gambling, alcohol use, use of chewing tobacco, age, and a desire to stop gambling (Stinchfield, 2000).

The precise nature of the relationship between gambling and other risk behaviors in adolescents has not been rigorously studied.

The high rates of problem and pathological gambling in adolescence and early adulthood are similar to those observed for substance use and substance use disorders (Wagner & Anthony, 2002). Given that individuals with these disorders share common elements (e.g., increased propensity for engaging in risky behaviors), common factors (e.g., impulsiveness) have been proposed as leading to their development (Chambers & Potenza, 2003; Vitaro, Brendgen, Ladouceur, & Tremblay, 2001). Additional research is needed to identify common biological factors leading to adolescent risk behaviors as have been described in adults (Slutske et al., 2000).

AN INFORMED APPROACH TO YOUTH GAMBLING PREVENTION STRATEGIES

Given the significant and apparently growing problems represented by youth gambling, a structured strategy for gambling (and most significantly problem and pathological gambling) prevention is needed presently. Ideally, such an approach would be based on empirically derived data from large-scale studies investigating the effectiveness over time of programs targeting specific populations (Dickson, Derevensky, & Gupta, 2002). However, to date, few studies have been performed in the area of adolescent gambling prevention, none have been longitudinal, and all have been performed in one geographic location, limiting the generalizability of the findings (Ferland, Ladouceur, & Vitaro, 2002; Gaboury & Ladouceur, 1993). As such, there is a distinct need for increased efforts at multiple levels in the development, implementation, and testing of effective prevention strategies.

Public Health Models of Gambling

Recently, there has been a growing movement to conceptualize gambling behaviors in general within a public health model (Korn & Shaffer, 1999; Shaffer & Korn, 2002). Public health models have been successfully employed in conceptualizing and generating health guidelines for nongambling behaviors. Alcohol use represents one behavior for which there exist healthy consumption parameters that are periodically revised given current epidemiological and public health research findings (U.S. Department of Agriculture, 2000). Gambling behaviors seem similarly well suited for consideration of the development of public health guidelines. There exist many similarities between alcohol use and gambling—for example, prohibition in underage populations, correlation of quantity and frequency measures between gambling and alcohol consumption (Welte, Barnes, Wieczorek, Tidwell, & Parker, 2001), shared genetic factors underlying development of problems with excessive alcohol consumption and gambling (Slutske et al., 2000), developmental patterns of excessive engagement (Chambers & Potenza, 2003; Wagner & Anthony, 2002), and possible health risks and benefits of moderate gambling or alcohol consumption (Korn & Shaffer, 1999; Potenza, Fiellin, et al., 2002). There has been a significant amount of research performed in the prevention of underage drinking (Dowdall & Wechsler, 2002). As such, modification of a framework used in youth alcohol prevention might serve as one meaningful starting point for development, testing, and implementation of prevention programs targeting youth gambling behaviors. In addition to similarities, there are also significant differences between gambling and alcohol use (e.g., lack or presence of intoxication and subsequent changes in behavior secondary to intoxication) (Giancola, 2002), and these differences must also be incorporated in the conceptualization of a proposed strategic model for youth gambling prevention.

A Prevention Framework

A preliminary structure is proposed for prevention strategies of gambling, problem gambling, and pathological gambling in adolescents and young adults based on approaches used for prevention work in the public arena (DeJong & Langford, 2002; Stokols, 1996). The proposed framework incorporates contributions from domains recognized as affecting health-related behaviors: intrapersonal (individual) factors, interpersonal (group) processes, institutional factors, community factors, and public policy (DeJong & Langford, 2002; Stokols, 1996). Specific targets of intervention within each domain are described below.

Knowledge, Attitudes, and Intentions

Data suggest that youths often do not completely understand the risks associated with gambling or the odds underlying specific forms of gambling (Ferland et al., 2002; Wood, Griffiths, Derevensky, & Gupta, 2002). On an individual level, increasing knowledge regarding the risks of gambling or teaching the mathematics relating to odds of winning and losing in specific forms of gambling (e.g., lottery, forms of casino gambling) could provide a foundation for adolescents to make better informed decisions regarding participation in gambling (Ferland et al., 2002). Fact-based information regarding gambling behaviors could be conveyed through multiple groups or forums, including peer groups, families, schools, communities, and public policies (Dickson et al., 2002). Interventions involving multiple domains (e.g., family, community, public policy) could include coordinated activities during regional awareness campaigns; for example, Connecticut recently organized a problem gambling awareness prevention week involving mental health agencies and media promotion. Incorporation of gambling awareness education programs into school curricula for various age groups seems particularly attractive (Ferland et al., 2002; Korn & Shaffer, 1999).

Environmental Change

Environmental changes could be enacted in multiple domains. For example, an individual's participation in risk behaviors has been shown to be influenced by peers not only for adolescent substance use (Donohew et al., 1999) but also childhood gambling (Hardoon & Derevensky, 2001). As such, influencing the behaviors of adolescents prone to risk-raking behaviors might be expected to have a diffusion effect. To plan and enact environmental changes, arguably the greatest need is for more high-quality, long-term research into the specific risks and benefits (health, academic, etc.) associated with varying levels of participation in youth gambling.

One important, cost-effective method for obtaining data involves incorporating gambling questions into existing national surveys that regularly study youth risk behaviors. The National Gambling Impact Study Commission recommended to Congress that gambling measures be incorporated into ongoing studies of risk and addictive behaviors (e.g., the National Household Drug Abuse Survey [NHDAS]), and the National Research Council recommended integrating gambling measures into appropriate large-scale studies (National Research Council, 1999). Routine incorporation of gambling measures in the NHDAS, Monitoring the Future, and CDC YRBS studies would provide valuable information annually on the gambling behaviors of young people. Although youth gambling has been found to be associated with a variety of adverse effects in the rare circumstances when modest gambling questions were introduced into one of these surveys (Proimos et al., 1998), a much richer understanding of youth gambling attitudes and behaviors and their relationship to other risk behaviors could be gained from the routine, coordinated introduction of more extensive, structured gambling measures into the surveys.

Normative Behavior

Despite the association between adolescent gambling and negative measures of well-being (e.g., delinquency, substance abuse), relatively little concern exists for the problems posed by youth gambling (Dickson et al., 2002). Many consider youth gambling a "normal" part of growing up; for example, many parents buy their children lottery tickets or see no harm in youth gambling (Ladouceur, Vitaro, & Cote, 2001). Specific strategies that could lead to a social environment in which adolescent gambling was considered less normative involve peers, family members, school administrators, civic leaders, and policymakers. Some of these groups have reported limited involvement in or knowledge of problem gambling prevention efforts. For example, in a survey of high school and college administrators in Massachusetts, only 9% of high school and community college administrators were aware of gambling problems among their students; few (including none of the high school administrators) reported an awareness of state gambling prevention initiatives for student athletes, and only 33% reported an interest in incorporating gambling-related issues into their curricula (Shaffer, Forman, Scanlan, & Smith, 2000). A separate study of parental attitudes toward youth gambling found over a 5-year interval improved understanding in some areas but constancy or deterioration in others (Ladouceur et al., 2001). The results from additional research into the health associations of youth gambling would likely influence a shift in the normative attitudes about the gambling behaviors of young people.

Gambling Availability

Some forms of gambling are easily accessible; for example, lottery gambling is widely accessible and currently legal in the majority of jurisdictions in North America (North American Association of State and Provincial Lotteries, 2002b). Availability is presently restricted via public policy that makes sale of lottery tickets illegal to minors. However, data indicate that many minors have gambled on the lottery (see Table 27.1) (Gerstein et al., 1999; Ladouceur et al., 2001; Wood et al., 2002), and several "sting" operations have found that selling lottery tickets to minors is a recurrent behavior of retailers, suggesting the need for greater enforcement of laws surrounding underage gambling (Viva Consulting, 2001). Alcohol-related policy has been effective in youth prevention efforts; for example, raising the legal drinking age has been found to reduce alcohol-related morbidity and mortality. A similar raising of age limits restricting underage gambling could be considered; that is, raising the legal gambling age to 21 years in all jurisdictions (all states currently have laws prohibiting gambling by minors, but the age limit currently varies from state to state).

Concurrent with implementation of policy interventions, it is important to monitor over time to evaluate systematically their effects. Gambling ventures have become increasingly popular as an event commencing adulthood (e.g., going to the casino for an 18th or 21st birthday), and as such, there exists a need to monitor the effects of making gambling a "forbidden fruit" only to be sampled by adults (e.g., by raising age limits for legal gambling). The potential dangers of a form of gambling with ready accessibility for many youths, Internet gambling, has been the target of federal policy (Federal Trade Commission statement on youth Internet gambling) and medical organizations (the American Psychiatric Association statement on youth Internet gambling; Mitka, 2001). Coordination of efforts across group levels (from individual through policy) seems important in limiting gambling during adolescence.

Gambling Promotion

Gambling promotion represents another area for prevention. Alcohol advertisement in the United States has been restricted in some media—for example, no portrayal of alcohol drinking or hard liquor advertising on television. Although data suggest that alcohol-related advertising increases alcohol consumption, limited bans appear to lead to advertising in other manners—that is, switching of media (Saffer, 2002). It has been suggested, therefore, that in the absence of comprehensive banning of all forms of advertising and promotion, counteradvertising represents a viable prevention strategy (Saffer, 2002). Because gambling advertising and promotion are presently less limited than those for alcohol (Heberling, 2002), more research is needed to investigate the relationship between the type and extent of gambling advertisement and promotion and gambling behaviors in specific populations, particularly youths, and the effects of specific strategies aimed at reducing youth gambling behaviors through limiting or counteradvertising methods. Specific attention should be focused on examining the effects of advertisements or promotions (or restrictions thereof) accessed by potentially vulnerable populations—for example, advertising on video games, Gamblers Anonymous Internet sites, and gambling Web sites with online links (Federal Trade Commission, 2002; Mitka, 2001).

Another strategy whose efficacy and cost-effectiveness have been suggested in the prevention of drunk driving involves media coverage (Yanovitzky, 2002). The effectiveness of similar media campaigns targeting youth gambling behaviors warrants investigation. Prevention can also actively be promoted through the regular inclusion at gambling venues and on gambling items (e.g., lottery tickets) of a listing of resources for help with a gambling problem—for example, the National Council on Problem Gambling's toll-free telephone number (Stevens, Lynm, & Glass, 2001). The extent to which such interventions would be effective for adolescents warrants more direct investigation. Existing data from Texas and Connecticut gambling help lines suggest that adolescents underuse this resource despite statewide advertisement at gambling venues and on gambling items—for example, lottery points of purchase and lottery tickets (Potenza, Steinberg, Wu, Rounsaville, & O'Malley, 2003).

Policy and Law Enforcement

As noted earlier, there have been significant changes over the past several decades in the policies allowing for legalized gambling and in the extent to which the government is involved in legalized gambling. Despite laws prohibiting underage gambling, there exist variations in the age limits defining the restrictions and questions regarding the enforcement of the laws (Viva Consulting, 2001). Additional laws that broadly target underage activities have the potential to reduce multiple youth risk behaviors; for example, the use of distinctive tamper-proof driver's licenses could simultaneously reduce alcohol consumption, drunk driving, and gambling. As with youth alcohol consumption (DeJong & Langford, 2002), until there is a greater call for stricter enforcement of laws meant to target underage gambling, there likely will remain a significant amount of gambling performed by minors. To effect such changes in a timely manner, alterations in societal conceptualization of normative gambling behaviors and the influence of advocacy groups (e.g., similar to Mothers Against Drunk Driving [MADD] in the alcohol field) likely will be required (DeJong & Langford, 2002).

Health Protection, Interventions, and Treatment

Although existing data suggest considerable negative health associations with problem and pathological gambling in adults (Gerstein et al., 1999), less is known about recreational gambling behaviors (Korn & Shaffer, 1999; Potenza, Fiellin, et al., 2002). In particular, the relationship in youths between recreational gambling and health and well-being measures requires more direct examination. Nonetheless, the high rates of problem and pathological gambling in adolescents and the association of these gambling behaviors with other risk behaviors (delinquency, substance use and abuse, and risky sexual behaviors) suggest the need for increased intervention (Petry & Zeena, 2001; Proimos et al., 1998). Active screening for gambling problems in family, school and medical settings warrants consideration. For example, screening for gambling by youths could be accomplished during annual visits to pediatricians. As is the case for adults (Potenza, 2002; Potenza, Fiellin, et al., 2002), this process would be greatly facilitated by the generation of sensitive and specific brief problem gambling screening instruments akin to the CAGE for alcohol use problems (Fiellin, Reid, & O'Connor, 2000). Direct examination of the effectiveness of screening instruments in youth populations is needed to determine their utility in specific settings. Moreover, introduction of formal training for individuals interacting with youths (school teachers, pediatricians, internists, counselors, etc.) regarding the potential dangers of youth gambling, early identification of problem and pathological gambling, and available intervention options are needed (Korn & Shaffer, 1999; Potenza, 2002).

Safe and effective pharmacological and behavioral treatments for pathological gambling in adults are only beginning to emerge (Grant, Kim, & Potenza, 2003; Petry & Roll, 2001; Potenza et al., 2001). Examination of these treatments will require investigations of children, adolescents, and young adults to determine their applicability to younger age groups. Despite reports suggesting high rates of discontinuation and incomplete data on outcome, self-help programs, particularly Gamblers Anonymous and Gam-Anon (Stewart & Brown, 1988), have been used by many problem gamblers and their family members, respectively. Because differences have been observed in the patterns of self-help group participation in 12-step programs (Kelley, Myers, & Brown, 2002), direct examination in youth populations of the patterns of gambling self-help participation and outcome are needed.

SUMMARY AND FUTURE DIRECTIONS

We are currently at a unique and important historical juncture with regard to gambling. Over the past several decades, there has been a growing acceptance of gambling as a normative behavior. Never before in our history has gambling been such a big industry with governments obtaining large revenues through operation or taxation of gambling ventures (North American Association of State and Provincial Lotteries, 2002a). Advances in computer technology and the growing number of individuals using the Internet suggest that Internet gambling will continue to grow in the near future (National Telecommunication and Information

Administration and Economics and Statistics Administration, 2002). To increase our knowledge regarding gambling behaviors, more funding needs to be directed toward well-designed investigations with specific populations into the etiology, prevention, and treatment of problem and pathological gambling and the health benefits and detriments of recreational gambling (Potenza, 2002).

CHAPTER 28

Why Pay Attention to Adolescent Gambling?

RACHEL A. VOLBERG

Why is it that gambling is not even on the "radar" when we consider the array of risks that adolescents must confront as they move toward adulthood? Although few people regard gambling as a serious issue for adolescents, gambling researchers have noted, in the wake of the rapid legalization of lottery and casino gambling in the final decades of the 20th century, that an entire generation of adolescents and young adults has grown up in a society that not only condones, but encourages, gambling (Gupta & Derevensky, 2000; Jacobs, 2000; Shaffer & Hall, 1996; Stinchfield & Winters, 1998). Concern among gambling researchers and clinicians who treat people with gambling problems is that increased availability and decreased stigma has led to increases in adolescent gambling and to increases in the prevalence and severity of gambling problems among adolescents and young adults.

DEFINING OUR TERMS

Gambling is a broad concept that includes diverse activities, undertaken in a wide variety of settings, appealing to different sorts of people and perceived in various ways by participants and observers. People take part in gambling activities—including bingo, lotteries, casino games, horse race and sports wagering, and private wagering on cards, dice, and games of skill—because they enjoy them and obtain benefits from their participation. For most people, gambling is generally a positive experience. However, for a minority, gambling is associated with difficulties of varying severity and duration. Some regular gamblers develop significant, debilitating problems that also typically result in harm to people close to them and to the wider community (Abbott & Volberg, 1999).

A variety of terms have been used to refer to difficulties caused by an individual's gambling. The term *pathological gambling* is generally limited to the far end of a continuum of gambling problems. Pathological gambling was first recognized as a psychiatric disorder by the medical profession in 1980 (American Psychiatric Association, 1980) The disorder is presently viewed as "a continuous or periodic loss of *control* over gambling, accompanied by a *progression,* in gambling frequency and amounts wagered, in preoccupation with gambling and in obtaining money with which to gamble, and a *continuation* of gambling despite adverse consequences" (Cox, Lesieur, Rosenthal & Volberg, 1997, p. 4).

Research on adult problem gambling suggests that pathological gambling has strong antecedents in youthful gambling involvement (Custer & Milt, 1985; Volberg, 1994). However, since pathological gambling is defined as a progressive condition that can take many years to develop, some have argued that problem gambling among adolescents is best viewed as a preclinical state (Volberg & Moore, 1999; Winters, Stinchfield, & Fulkerson, 1993b). In considering adolescents, the term *problem gambling* is often used to refer to the most severe end of a continuum of gambling involvement that stretches from no gambling at all to extremely serious difficulties. "Problem" gamblers are those adolescents who show clear evidence of gambling involvement that has compromised, disrupted, or damaged other important areas in their lives. "At-risk" gamblers are adolescents whose difficulties are less severe but who nonetheless appear to have substantial difficulties related to their gambling.

WHY IS ADOLESCENT GAMBLING RISKY?

There are many reasons to pay attention to adolescents who gamble. As noted above, research with adults has shown that individuals with severe gambling-related difficulties begin gambling much earlier in life than people who gamble without problems. Another reason for concern is that children are most often introduced to gambling activities by members of their immediate family, few of whom are likely to recognize the risks associated with excessive gambling. A third

reason for concern is that adolescents often begin gambling before they begin experimenting with other risky behaviors, including the use of tobacco, alcohol, and drugs, as well as sexual behavior. A fourth concern is that gambling often co-occurs with other risky behaviors and mental health problems and, if unaddressed, may affect adolescents' success in overcoming other difficulties in their lives. Finally, although access to most legal forms of gambling is restricted by age, there is a great deal of evidence suggesting that large numbers of high school and underage college students are able to gamble in casinos, buy lottery tickets, and place bets on horse races.

WHAT DO WE KNOW ABOUT ADOLESCENT GAMBLING?

There is no doubt that adolescents gamble and that some adolescents experience difficulties related to their gambling involvement. Although rates vary from one jurisdiction to another, studies show that up to 80% of youth aged 12 to 17 have gambled in the last 12 months (Gupta & Derevensky, 2000). The most popular types of gambling among adolescents in North America are (a) cards, dice, and board games played with family and friends; (b) private wagers on games of personal skill with friends; (c) sports betting, with peers as well as bookmakers; and (d) bingo.

All the available research shows that male adolescents tend to gamble earlier, gamble on more games, gamble more often, spend more time and money on gambling, and experience more gambling-related problems than do female adolescents. Male adolescents are more likely to participate in skill-based games, whereas female adolescents are more likely to participate in gambling activities with a large "luck" component. In a recent review of the literature, Stinchfield and

Winters (1998) make several additional points about youth gambling. They note that (a) most youth have gambled at some time and many have played a game that is legal for adults; (b) boys, older adolescents, and minority youth are more involved in gambling than their counterparts in the population; (c) many youth start gambling at a remarkably early age; and (d) youth gambling is related to parental gambling.

Youth consistently show elevated rates of problem gambling compared with adults in the general population. Derevensky and Gupta (2000a) estimate that between 4% and 8% of adolescents report very serious gambling problems and another 10% to 15% of adolescents are at risk for developing serious gambling problems. Other estimates of the prevalence of adolescent problem or pathological gambling rates range between 1% and 9%, with a median of 6% (National Research Council, 1999; Shaffer, Hall, & Vander Bilt, 1999).

As with adults, there is solid evidence that problem gambling among adolescents is correlated with a range of "fellow travelers" (Jacobs, 2000). These include high rates of tobacco, alcohol, and marijuana use; high levels of parental gambling and parental gambling problems; illegal activities; poor school performance; truancy; and deep feelings of unhappiness, anxiety, and depression. Although there is little evidence showing a link between *adolescent* gambling and suicidality, several studies have shown that the rate of suicide attempts among adult pathological gamblers in treatment is second only to rates for depressive disorders, schizophrenia, and a few hereditary neurological disorders (Cox et al., 1997).

WHAT ARE THE MAJOR UNANSWERED QUESTIONS?

There are at least two enormous gaps in the research on adolescent gambling and problem gambling. The first is the lack of theoretical models of adolescent (or adult) gambling and problem gambling. The second is the almost complete lack of longitudinal research looking at how gambling involvement changes over the life course, how individuals develop problematic styles of gambling, the risk and protective factors for developing pathological gambling, and how individuals tend to resolve their gambling-related difficulties— whether naturally or with professional help.

To date, most research on adolescent gambling and problem gambling has been descriptive. However, researchers are using increasingly sophisticated analytic techniques to identify the relationships between adolescent demographics, psychosocial variables, and other risky behaviors with gambling and gambling problems. For example, in a large study of Minnesota public school students in 1992 and 1995, multivariate analyses were used to determine that frequent gambling among adolescents was part of a constellation of risk-taking behaviors, including frequent alcohol use and antisocial behaviors such as physical violence, vandalism, shoplifting, and truancy (Stinchfield, Cassuto, Winters, & Latimer, 1997). In a survey of high school students in Montreal, Gupta and Derevensky (1998a) used multivariate techniques to show that depression, dissociation, excitability, disinhibition, and tobacco, alcohol, and drug use were closely correlated with problem gambling severity. Interestingly, these researchers concluded that the predictors of problem gambling are different for boys and girls. For boys, excitability and dissociation were the best predictors of problem gambling, whereas for girls, depression, dissociation, and drug use were the best predictors.

Although research on adolescent gambling remains nascent, there is emerging evidence that the relationship between gambling availability and the prevalence of problem gambling may be mediated by a variety of factors. One recent effort points to the importance of improving our understanding of the possible protective effects of adolescent exposure to heavily age-restricted legal gambling (Volberg, 2002a).

The publication of several extensive reviews just as the first survey of adolescent gambling and problem gambling was fielded in Nevada provided an opportunity to test numerous hypotheses about youth gambling and problem gambling in the most mature casino economy in North America. Surprisingly, several key hypotheses about gambling participation and problem gambling prevalence were *not* supported in the Nevada adolescent study. For example, it was assumed that gambling participation among adolescents in Nevada would be higher than among adolescents in other jurisdictions. Instead, the rate of past-year gambling among adolescents in Nevada (49%) was much lower than the median past-year gambling rate of 66% for studies of adolescents conducted between 1989 and 1999 (Jacobs, 2000). Similarly, studies have consistently shown that significant numbers of underage individuals are able to play lottery games and gamble at casinos in jurisdictions where these activities are legal for adults. It was hypothesized that substantial numbers of Nevada adolescents would have gambled at a casino. Instead, only 3% of the respondents aged 13 to 17 acknowledged ever gambling at a casino.[1] Finally, it was assumed that the prevalence of problem gambling among adolescents in Nevada would be substantially higher than among adolescents in other jurisdictions where legal gambling is both less visible and less available. Instead, the prevalence of problem and at-risk gambling among adolescents in Nevada was significantly *lower* than in other jurisdictions.

There are several possible explanations for the surprising finding that youth in Nevada gamble less than youth in other states and are less likely to have gambling-related problems. One possibility is that there is an "exposure effect" similar to effects noted in relation to illicit drug use where usage decreases over time as perceptions of the risks of use increase. "Perceived harm" has been shown to be an important deterrent to young people's use of illicit drugs. Lifelong exposure may lead adolescents to perceive gambling as something done by their "uncool" parents and therefore not terribly exciting or interesting. Lifelong exposure also means that adolescents in Nevada are more likely than adolescents in other jurisdictions to have parents, adult relatives, or older friends who have gotten into difficulties with gambling. Another possibility is that the well-publicized sanctions applied to youth caught gambling as well as to operators who permit underage individuals to gamble have a deterrent effect on Nevada adolescents. A third possibility is that the focus of problem-gambling services in Nevada on youth is affecting the likelihood that these adolescents will gamble. Youth-focused problem-gambling services in Nevada include an annual scholarship competition; training for school counselors, teachers, and administrators; and prevention programs tied to alcohol, drug, and teen pregnancy curricula in the schools. Yet another possibility is that advertising and news coverage in Nevada has affected underlying beliefs and attitudes toward gambling among Nevada adolescents. Although research is needed to test these hypotheses and explore other possibilities, the results of the Nevada adolescent study suggest that there is much that can be done to protect youth from developing gambling-related problems in spite of the widespread availability of legal opportunities for adults to gamble.

Certainly, the results of the Nevada adolescent survey raise important questions about how and where different types of gambling should be made available. The results of this survey also raise issues related to advertising and the effectiveness of messages about the adult nature of some risky activities. Finally, the results of this survey point to the importance of developing a better understanding of the roles played by family, peers, and communities in fostering or prohibiting adolescent gambling.

Another critical concern in gambling studies parallels challenges in the tobacco, alcohol, and drug fields where product differentiation—including the emergence of new "club" drugs, "smokeless" tobacco products, and "introductory" alcoholic beverages—have created moving targets for researchers. In the gambling field, the recent explosion of Internet gambling has created concern among regulators, researchers, and advocacy groups as evidenced by the recent Federal Trade Commission consumer alert regarding children and online gambling (Federal Trade Commission, 2002).

In the six years since its inception, online gambling has become one of the most popular facets of Internet activity. Although base rates are still low, gambling on the Internet is increasing. For example, a survey of adults aged 18 and over in Oregon found that lifetime Internet gambling increased from 0.3% in 1997 to 1.1% in 2000—an increase that corresponds to an estimated annual growth rate of about 54% (Volberg, 2001). Adolescents are more than twice as likely as adults to acknowledge gambling on the Internet. In the recent Nevada survey, 2.7% of the adolescent respondents had ever gambled on the Internet, compared with 1.5% of adult Nevadans surveyed in a separate study (Volberg, 2002a, 2002b). Nearly one fifth (18%) of the Nevada adolescents with severe gambling problems had gambled on the Internet.

The strong links between online gambling and nongambling games, fantasy games, role-playing games, board games, and card games are an additional cause for concern as adolescents playing nongambling games are bombarded with links to Internet gambling sites. Greenfield Online, a major online survey firm, estimates that 25% of Internet users at any time are adolescents playing on nongambling gaming sites. These activities share common elements with online gambling and, in the aggregate, attract significantly larger numbers of participants. Migration of gamers to online gambling sites is likely to create substantial negative impacts in the future. Without research, however, it will be difficult to determine the extent of such impacts or identify steps likely to mitigate those impacts.

WHAT ARE THE CHALLENGES?

Without a doubt, the greatest challenge facing the gambling research field today is the lack of attention to this issue by researchers in other disciplines as well as by funding agencies and policymakers. Lack of attention has limited the funding available for adolescent gambling research with consequences both for the quantity and quality of the work that has been done to date. Although long-term specialized research on gambling is badly needed, an intermediate and highly cost-effective step would be to add short gambling modules to existing longitudinal studies of adolescents in the United States.

Work is needed to identify the most efficient subset of items from existing adolescent problem-gambling screens. In addition, work is needed to educate researchers investigating topics such as adolescent suicidality, depression, alcohol and drug use, and sexuality about the importance of including gambling items in their studies. Without a broad recognition of the relationship between gambling and other risks to adolescent health in the larger youth research community, however, it is unlikely that this approach will be successful. Finally, although adding a gambling module to existing or newly funded longitudinal studies is highly cost-effective, it is essential to include one or more gambling specialists as integral members of the research teams carrying out such studies. Such an approach prevents new teams from making costly mistakes and ensures that these efforts build on the knowledge base that already exists.

Adolescent gamblers are a particularly vulnerable group in terms of the future development of pathological gambling. Their propensity to display the full clinical disorder is likely to be affected by a variety of risk factors and by the offsetting influence of protective factors as well as efforts at prevention and treatment. It remains to be seen whether youth gambling will garner the attention it deserves as one of an array of behaviors with which adolescents experiment as they grow toward adulthood.

NOTE

1. A separate study of adults in Nevada found that 19% of respondents aged 18 to 20 had been able to gamble in a casino in the past year (Volberg, 2002b). The legal gambling age in Nevada is 21.

Part III

Section B
Sexual Behavior

Risk and Protective Factors Affecting Teen Pregnancy and the Effectiveness of Programs Designed to Address Them

DOUGLAS KIRBY

lthough the U.S. teenage pregnancy rate has declined during recent years, teenage pregnancy nevertheless remains a significant problem in this country. In 1997, the most recent year for which data are currently available, among all females aged 15 to 19, almost 900,000 teens (9.4%) became pregnant (Ventura, Mosher, Curtin, Abma, & Henshaw, 2001). An estimated 78% of these teen pregnancies were unintended (Henshaw, 1998). In addition, more than 40% of teenage females in the United States became pregnant before they reached 20 years of age, and many became pregnant a second time before their 20th birthday (National Campaign to Prevent Teen Pregnancy, 1997). As a result, the teen pregnancy rate in the United States is much higher than that in other Western industrialized countries. For example, it is many times higher than in France (2.3%), Germany (1.9%), and in Italy, Spain, and the Netherlands (1.4%) (Singh & Darroch, 2000).

This chapter will summarize adolescent sexual activity and contraceptive use and the risk and protective factors associated with age of sexual debut, contraceptive use, and pregnancy. It will then summarize the research on the effectiveness of different types of programs designed to address these risk and protective factors. Although it will focus more on those types of programs that have been demonstrated to be effective, it will also review research on types of programs that have not been effective.

AUTHOR'S NOTE: This article is adapted from D. Kirby (2001, May). *Emerging answers: Research findings on programs to reduce teen pregnancy.* Washington DC: National Campaign to Prevent Teen Pregnancy; and from D. Kirby (2002). The antecedents of adolescent initiation of sex, contraceptive use and pregnancy. *American Journal of Health Behavior, 26*(6), 473-485.

ADOLESCENT SEXUAL ACTIVITY AND CONTRACEPTIVE USE

Although youth in the United States do not initiate sex markedly earlier than in other Western industrialized countries, the proportion of teenagers who report that they have had sexual intercourse increases with age. In the United States in 2001, slightly less than half of all high school students (46%) reported ever having had sex, but this ranged from 34% among 9th graders to 61% among 12th graders (Grunbaum et al., 2002). On average across the country, much smaller percentages of youth have had sex during their middle school years, but in some communities, the percentage of middle school students who have had sex is much higher.

Among male and female teenagers who have ever had sex, many do so only sporadically. Among high school students in 2001, 46% had ever had sex, but only 33% had sex during the previous 3 months (Grunbaum et al., 2002). Because their sexual activity is sporadic, adolescents often do not plan to have sex on a particular occasion, but sometimes have unplanned or unintended sex anyway.

Most sexually experienced teenagers do not have sexual intercourse with more than one sexual partner during any given period of time. About 70% of sexually experienced teen females and 54% of sexually experienced teen males have either zero or one sexual partner each year (Moore, Driscoll, & Lindberg, 1998). Nevertheless, for most sexually active teenagers, the numbers of partners accumulate over time, so if they initiate intercourse at early ages, they have a greater number of sexual partners before marriage.

Most sexually experienced teenagers use contraception—typically condoms or oral contraceptives—*some* of the times they have sex. And indeed, use of better contraception, especially long-term hormonal contraceptives

such as Depo-Provera or Norplant, is one of the reasons pregnancy rates declined during the 1990s (Flanigan, 2001).

However, many sexually active teens do not always use contraception consistently and correctly. Because teen sexual activity is often sporadic and unplanned, consistent use of contraceptives is more difficult for teenagers to achieve. In fact, when teenagers are asked why they failed to use contraception, one of their more frequent responses is that they were not expecting or planning to have sex and therefore failed to obtain and use contraception (Kirby et al., 1999). This reason is cited more frequently than other explanations, such as being unable to afford birth control, not knowing where to get it, being embarrassed about purchasing or obtaining it, or not knowing how to use it properly.

RISK AND PROTECTIVE FACTORS

In efforts to reduce teen pregnancy, identifying the important risk and protective factors associated with adolescent sexual behavior, contraceptive use, and pregnancy is important for at least two reasons. First, knowing the critical risk and protective factors can lead to the development of more effective programs. Specifically, if interventions target those factors that (a) have the greatest causal impact on sexual behaviors and (b) can actually be changed by the interventions, then logically, the chances of those interventions having an impact on the sexual behaviors is greatly increased. Second, these risk and protective factors can also be used to identify those youth who are at greatest risk of unintended pregnancy so that they can be targeted by more intensive and effective programs.

Literally hundreds of studies have examined the impact of a wide variety of risk and protective factors on adolescent sexual and contraceptive behavior and pregnancy. Indeed, Emerging Answers alone reviewed more than 250 studies of risk and protective factors (Kirby, 2001a). These studies, in combination, have revealed that there is not a small number of factors that affects adolescent sexual behavior and contraceptive use. Thus, they paint a very complex picture. These risk and protective factors describe not only individual teens themselves (both their biological and psychosocial attributes) but also important people and institutions within their environment—their partners, peers, families, schools, religious affiliations, communities, and even states—as well as the teens' relationships to them.

The communities that teens live in influence teens' sexual behavior. When teens live in poor communities with less advantage and opportunity and more disorganization, they are more likely to engage in sex at an earlier age and to become pregnant or cause a pregnancy. More specifically, when the adults in their communities have lower levels of education, are less likely to be employed, have lower incomes, and engage in higher rates of crime, then these teens are more likely to engage in sex and become pregnant or cause a pregnancy than teens in communities with higher levels of education and income and lower rates of unemployment and crime. In communities with higher levels of education, employment, and income, adults may place greater emphasis on obtaining a higher education, pursuing careers, and avoiding early childbearing; they may also provide role models for these behaviors, and the communities more generally may provide opportunities for education and careers. This does not mean that teens in communities with high levels of education, high employment, high income, and little crime never engage in unprotected sex. It simply means they either are less likely to do so, or do so less frequently.

Similarly, the characteristics of a teen's family are also important in determining risk. When teens have parents with low levels of education and income, they are more likely to engage in sex at an earlier age, to fail to use contraception consistently, and to become pregnant or cause a pregnancy than teens in families with high levels of education and income. This may be due, in part, to the greater emphasis that more educated and wealthier parents place on obtaining an education, pursuing a career, and avoiding early childbearing, an emphasis due in part to the greater resources they may have to support the teens' education and career planning and, in part, to other reasons.

When teens live with both parents and have close relationships with them, they are less likely to engage in unprotected sex and become pregnant. More specifically, when teens live with both parents (instead of only one parent or neither parent), they are less likely to engage in sex, more likely to use contraception if they have sex, and less likely to become pregnant or cause a pregnancy. Furthermore, if teens believe they have considerable parental support, feel connected to their parents, and are appropriately supervised or monitored by their parents, they become less likely to have unprotected sex and become pregnant or cause a pregnancy.

If family members, especially parents, either express values or model behavior consistent with sexual risk taking or early childbearing, then teens are more likely to engage in unprotected sex and become pregnant or cause a pregnancy. Parents can do this in a variety of ways, including having permissive attitudes about premarital sex or teen sex, having negative attitudes about contraception, having sex outside of marriage themselves, cohabitating, giving birth outside of marriage, or having given birth at an early age. In contrast, if parents express clear values about not engaging in sex at an early age and about always using contraception, and if teens hear and understand these values, then these teens are less likely to initiate sex at an early age and more likely to use contraception when sexually active. Similarly, if the siblings of teens model early childbearing by giving birth at an early age, then the teens themselves are more likely to engage in unprotected sex and become pregnant.

Not surprisingly, peers also influence the sexual behavior of teens. When a teen's peers get poor grades, are unattached to school, and engage in a variety of negative behaviors, then the teen is more likely to engage in sex. When a teen's peers get good grades, are more attached to school, and engage in fewer negative behaviors, then that teen is less likely to become pregnant or cause a pregnancy. Furthermore, when teens believe that their peers are having sex, they become more likely to have sex themselves, and when they believe their peers support condom or contraceptive use, they become more likely to use condoms or other contraceptives.

Turning to the teens themselves, as everyone knows, the older teens become, the more likely they are to have sex and to become pregnant, reflecting many important changes that come with increasing age. Some are biological, including physical maturity and higher hormone levels, which may lead to a greater desire for love, intimacy, and sex or to greater sexual attractiveness. Other changes are social—for instance, more pressure from others to have sex, changes in perceived norms about sexual and contraceptive behavior, and the increased opportunity to have sex that comes with greater freedom and independence more generally. Although these biological antecedents associated with older age cannot be changed by programmatic interventions, they can be used to identify higher-risk youth. Furthermore, some of the social factors associated with being older (e.g., greater pressure to have sex) may be amenable to change.

African American and Hispanic youth have sex at an earlier age than do non-Hispanic whites and are also more likely to become pregnant or cause a pregnancy. This reflects, in large part, differences in community levels of education, poverty, and opportunity rather than race or ethnicity per se. When family and community characteristics associated with race and ethnicity are held constant, the impact of race and ethnicity diminishes considerably, but not entirely, in these studies. Cultural values help explain their residual difference. For example, Hispanic families may give greater importance to family and may be more accepting of early childbearing than non-Hispanic white families.

Schools, and the relationships that teens have with them, also influence teens' sexual behavior. Attachment to school and success in school reduce the chances that teens will engage in unprotected sex and become pregnant or cause a pregnancy. When teens feel close to their schools, believe that academic achievement is important, get good grades, do not drop out, or have plans for higher education beyond high school, they initiate sex later, use contraception more effectively, and are less likely to become pregnant or cause a pregnancy. In short, such positive feelings increase motivation to avoid risky sexual behavior.

Attachment to faith communities may also reduce the chances that teens will engage in sex, although the evidence supporting this relationship is less strong. Teens who describe themselves as more religious, who attend religious services more frequently, and have a stronger religious affiliation are less likely to initiate sex by any given age. However, the direction of causality is not entirely clear, for just as attachment to faith communities may affect sexual behavior, sexual behavior may also affect attachment to faith communities. For example, teens who have had sex may feel less comfortable in their churches, synagogues, or mosques and be less likely to attend services.

Using alcohol and drugs, engaging in other problem or risk-taking behaviors, and suffering from emotional distress (including depression) all increase teens' chances of engaging in unprotected sex and becoming pregnant. These antecedents are significantly related to one another and may represent either more general personality traits or exposure to higher-risk environments. There are at least two common interpretations for the relationship between substance use and risky sexual behavior: (a) Both are part of a general inclination to take risks and of an environment that supports such behavior, and (b) drug and alcohol use diminishes both inhibitions and rational decision making, thereby actually increasing the incidence of unprotected sex. Both interpretations are probably valid.

Not surprisingly, early romantic involvement increases the chances of early sexual activity. When teens begin dating at an early age, date frequently, have a greater number of romantic partners, and go steady at an early age, they become more likely to initiate sex at an earlier age. In part, these early romantic relationships may provide both greater opportunity and greater pressure to have sex. Furthermore, sex within a romantic relationship may be more consistent with teens' values and perceived norms than sex in casual relationships. When the romantic partner of a teen is 2 or more years older, then the teen is especially likely to engage in sex. The impact of this factor is quite large, especially among middle school youth.

Prior sexual abuse is also an important risk factor for early voluntary initiation of sex, poor contraceptive use, pregnancy, and childbearing. Youth who have been sexually abused undoubtedly have been exposed to a variety of risk factors. In addition, the past sexual abuse may warp what teens understand as appropriate sexual and contraceptive behavior and may reduce their ability to refrain from sex or to use contraception.

Finally, teens' own sexual beliefs, attitudes, and skills affect their sexual behavior, of course. In fact, these antecedents in general are the most strongly related of all the antecedents to sexual behavior. When teens have permissive attitudes toward premarital sex, perceive personal and social benefits and few costs to having sex, do not care if their friends know they have had sex, lack the confidence in their own ability to avoid sex, have less concern about pregnancy or sexually transmitted diseases (STDs), and intend to have sex, then, not surprisingly, they are more likely to engage in sex. When sexually active teens do not accept the fact that they have had sex and are likely to have sex again, do not perceive they are at risk of pregnancy, do not perceive that pregnancy would have a negative effect on their lives, are less knowledgeable about contraception, and have more negative attitudes toward contraception, then they are less likely to use contraception. Similarly, when teens initiate sex earlier, have more sexual partners, are ambivalent about pregnancy and childbearing, are less motivated to use contraception, and do not always use contraception, then they are more likely to become pregnant or cause a pregnancy. These sexual beliefs, attitudes, and skills can together be called the "sexual psychosocial" antecedents of teen sexual risk-taking behavior.

In part because so many risk and protective factors are related to teens' sexual behavior, few factors are very highly related to behavior. Rather, most of the factors are weakly or, in some instances, moderately related to behavior. And some of these factors are undoubtedly causally related to each other. In particular, some of the more distal factors affect the more proximal sexual factors. For example, community levels of education, employment, and opportunity may affect individual teens' educational goals, perceived costs of early childbearing, and motivation to avoid early childbearing. Similarly, the sexual beliefs and behaviors of family members, peers, and partners undoubtedly affect teens' sexual beliefs and behavior.

These antecedents support a wide variety of theories about adolescent sexual risk-taking behavior—for instance, theories involving economic disadvantage and opportunity (Billy, Brewster, & Grady, 1994), theories involving parent child-rearing practices and parent values about adolescent sexuality (Jaccard, Dittus, & Litardo, 1999), biological theories (Miller et al., 1999), theories suggesting that sexual risking taking is part of a larger syndrome of risk-taking or deviant behavior (Costa, Jessor, Donovan, & Fortenberry, 1995), and social psychological theories of rational behavior (Fishbein et al., 1991). However, the antecedents summarized in these studies clearly demonstrate that no single theoretical perspective is sufficient; the total picture is much more complex.

Summary Themes

At least three overarching observations can be made about all these clusters of antecedents. First, a substantial proportion of all the risk factors involve some form of disadvantage, disorganization, or dysfunction—disadvantaged communities with high unemployment, low income, and high crime rates; poorly educated, low-income families with only one parent; parents who provide insufficient support for and monitoring of their teens; friends who do poorly in school, use drugs, and engage in unprotected sex; and teens themselves who are not attached to family, school, or church and are emotionally distressed, use drugs, and have been sexually coerced or abused.

Second, teens, like all people, are strongly influenced by their physical and social environments—by their families (especially their parents), their peers and friends, their romantic partners (if they have any), their schools and faith communities, and

their communities more generally. All these groups influence teens by emphasizing particular beliefs and norms, modeling certain behaviors, providing opportunities for particular behaviors, and sometimes directly applying pressure to engage or not engage in specific behaviors.

Third, attachment to people or groups who express protective values and model positive behaviors reduces sexual risk taking. When youth are more strongly attached to their parents, to their schools, or to their faith communities, they are less likely to engage in unprotected sex. In general, parents, schools, and faith communities discourage youth from engaging in sex in the first place and then also discourage unprotected sex. Consequently, when youth are more strongly attached to their parents, schools, or faith communities, they are more likely to behave consistently with these values. In addition, teens who belong to either Catholic or fundamentalist Protestant churches, which have strong norms against premarital sex, are less likely to engage in sex than youth who belong to other Protestant churches that have less strict norms. Nonetheless, attachment is not *always* a good thing. Being very popular with peers (who often have less conservative attitudes about sex than parents, schools, or faith communities) and having high-risk peers are both associated with earlier initiation of sex. Therefore, it is attachment to individuals or groups of people who express and model low-risk norms that is protective, not attachment per se.

The identification of these risk and protective factors has several important implications for programs designed to reduce teen pregnancy. First, if programs focus on only one factor, they are not likely to have a large impact. Second, if programs are to markedly reduce teen pregnancy, in combination, they will need to address both sexual and non-sexual risk and protective factors, and they will need to address factors in multiple domains.

Box 29.1   A Typology for Grouping Programs

Programs that focus on the sexual antecedents of teen pregnancy

- Curricula-based education programs

  - Abstinence-only programs
  - Sex and HIV education programs

- Clinic or school-based programs designed to provide reproductive health care or to improve access to condoms or other contraceptives

  - Family planning clinics and services
  - Protocols for clinic appointments and supportive activities
  - School-based and school-linked clinics
  - School condom-availability programs

- Multicomponent, community-wide initiatives

Programs that focus on nonsexual antecedents

- Service learning programs
- Vocational education and employment programs
- Other youth development programs

Programs that focus on both sexual and nonsexual antecedents

- Programs with both sexuality and youth development components

---

It should also be noted that many of the nonsexual risk and protective factors are the same ones associated with other problem behaviors (Flay, 2002). This has important implications for programs. In particular, it means that if programs can effectively address these nonsexual factors, they may be able to reduce teen pregnancy and other problem behaviors.

PROGRAMS DESIGNED TO ADDRESS THESE RISK AND PROTECTIVE FACTORS

People concerned with teen pregnancy, or youth more generally, have developed a great variety of programs to reduce sexual risk taking and pregnancy. No reasonably simple typology can capture all the potentially important ways that programs can be defined. Nevertheless, with the distinction between sexual and nonsexual risk and protective factors in mind, one can divide programs to prevent teen pregnancy into three types: those that focus on sexual factors, those that focus on nonsexual factors, and those that do both. These three broad categories can be further divided into several subcategories. Box 29.1 provides a typology of programs summarized in this review.

Programs That Focus on the Sexual Antecedents of Teen Pregnancy

Programs that focus on the sexual antecedents of teen pregnancy have traditionally been divided into educational programs that focus primarily on improving the knowledge, beliefs, values, attitudes, and skills regarding teen sexual activity and use of contraception (e.g., abstinence, sex and HIV education programs) and those programs that focus primarily on access to contraception (e.g., reproductive health clinics or school-based clinics providing reproductive health care). However, some multicomponent community-wide initiatives attempt to do both.

Curricula-Based Education Programs

According to recent national surveys, nearly every teenager in this country receives some form of abstinence or sex education, but the curricula vary widely in both focus and intensity. This review places curricula into two categories: abstinence-only education and sex or HIV education (sometimes called abstinence-plus). There has been a great growth in the former category since the 1996 welfare reform law made $85 million in federal and state funding available per year for abstinence-until-marriage interventions. However, in practice, curricula-based programs don't divide neatly into these two groups; instead they exist along a continuum.

Abstinence-Only Programs. Very little rigorous evaluation of abstinence-only programs has been completed; in fact, only three studies met the criteria for this review. The primary conclusion that can be drawn from these three studies is that the evidence is not conclusive about abstinence-only programs. None of the three programs evaluated showed an overall positive effect on sexual behavior, nor on contraceptive use among sexually active participants. However, given the paucity of the research and the great diversity of abstinence-only programs (not reflected in these three studies), one should be very cautious about drawing any conclusions about the impact of abstinence-only programs in general.

Sex and HIV Education Programs. Sex and HIV education programs typically emphasize that abstinence is the safest method for preventing STDs and pregnancy, and that condoms and other methods of contraception provide protection against STDs and pregnancy and accordingly are safer than unprotected sex. In this review, "sex" education programs will refer to programs that cover protection against both pregnancy and STDs (and possibly other, broader, sexuality topics), and "HIV" education programs will refer to programs that focus primarily on HIV (and sometimes other STDs). Both groups include a wide variety of programs, ranging from those taught during regular school classes to those taught on school campuses after school to others taught in homeless shelters and detention centers.

Evaluations strongly support the conclusion that sexuality and HIV education curricula do not increase sexual intercourse, either by hastening the onset of intercourse, increasing the frequency of intercourse, or increasing the number of sexual partners. Twenty-eight studies meeting the criteria discussed earlier have examined the impact of middle school-, high school-, or community-based sexuality or HIV education programs on the initiation of intercourse. Nine of them (or about one third) found that the programs delayed the initiation of sex (Aarons et al., 2000; Blake et al., 2000; Coyle, Kirby, Marin, Gomez, & Gregorich, 2000; Ekstrand et al., 1996; Howard & McCabe, 1990; Hubbard, Giese, & Rainey, 1998; Jemmott, Jemmott, & Fong, 1998; Kirby, Barth, Leland, & Fetro, 1991; Klaus et al., 1987; St. Lawrence et al., 1995). Eighteen found no significant impact (Coyle et al., 1999; Eisen, Zellman, & McAlister, 1990; Gottsegen & Philliber, 2000; Jemmott, Jemmott, & Fong, 1992; Jemmott et al., 1998; Kirby, 1985; Kirby, Korpi, Adiri, & Weissman, 1997; Levy et al., 1995; Lieberman, Gray, Wier, Fiorentino, &

Maloney, 2000; Little & Rankin, 2001; Main et al., 1994; Nicholson & Postrado, 1991; Thomas et al., 1992; Walter & Vaughn, 1993; Warren & King, 1994). Only 1 study of 28 found that a sex or HIV education program hastened the initiation of sex (Moberg & Piper, 1998). (It should be noted that this particular program did not focus primarily on sexual behavior but was a comprehensive program that addressed nutrition and use of tobacco, alcohol, and marijuana, as well as sexual behavior.) Overall, these studies provide very strong evidence that sex and HIV education programs do not hasten sex and that some of them actually delay sex.

Nineteen studies examined the impact of sexuality and HIV education programs on the frequency of intercourse. Five found that they reduced the frequency of sex (Coyle et al., 2001; Howard & McCabe, 1990; Jemmott et al., 1992, 1998; St. Lawrence et al., 1995). Thirteen found no significant impact (Blake et al., 2000; Coyle et al., 1999; Jemmott et al., 1998; Kirby, 1985; Kirby et al., 1991; Kirby, Korpi, et al., 1997; Levy et al., 1995; Little & Rankin, 2001; Main et al., 1994; Moberg & Piper, 1990; Rotheram-Borus, Koopman, Haigners, & Davies, 1991). Only 1 of 19 studies found a significant increase in frequency (Moberg & Piper, 1998). Again, this is strong evidence that sex and HIV education programs do not increase the frequency of sex and that some of them reduce it.

Finally, of the 10 studies that examined impact on *number of sexual partners,* 3 found a significant decrease in partners (Jemmott et al., 1992; Main et al., 1994; St. Lawrence et al., 1995), 7 found no impact (Coyle et al., 1999; Gillmore et al., 1997; Kirby et al., 1991; Kirby, Korpi, et al., 1997; Levy et al., 1995; Little & Rankin, 2001; Magura, Kang, & Shapiro, 1994), and none found a significant increase. Once more, this is strong evidence that these programs do not increase the number of sexual partners.

In sum, these data strongly indicate that sex and HIV education programs do not significantly increase any measure of sexual activity, as some people have feared, and that to the contrary, many delay or reduce sexual intercourse among teens. These results are also consistent with reviews of programs evaluated in other countries that have also found that sex and HIV education programs do not increase any measure of sexual activity (Grunseit, Kippax, Aggleton, Baldo, & Slutkin, 1997).

These studies also demonstrate that some programs increased condom use or contraceptive use more generally. Of the 18 programs for which impact on condom use was evaluated, 10 programs (or more than half) significantly increased some measure of condom use (Coyle et al., 1999; Hubbard et al., 1998; Jemmott et al., 1992, 1998; Magura et al., 1994; Main et al., 1994; Rotheram-Borus et al., 1991; St. Lawrence et al., 1995; Walter & Vaughn, 1993). Similarly, 4 of 11 programs that measured contraceptive use more generally significantly increased its use (Aarons et al., 2000; Coyle et al., 1999; Gottsegen & Philliber, 2000; Kirby et al., 1991). None of the programs reduced either condom or contraceptive use. Taken together, these results are quite positive.

The data also suggest that these sex and HIV education programs may be more effective with higher-risk youth than with lower-risk youth. This may be partly due to the behavioral characteristics of high-risk youth—that is, when youth engage in a large amount of unprotected sex, there is greater room for improvement than if they engage in little unprotected sex to begin with. In addition, these findings may be due, in part, to methodological and statistical factors. If a program reduces the proportion of lower-risk youth who initiate sex from 6% to 4%, that impact is more difficult to measure than is the impact of a program that reduces the proportion of higher-risk youth who initiate sex from 12% to 8%, even though the proportional reductions are the same.

The strength of the evidence for the effectiveness of some sex and HIV education programs has improved considerably during recent years. There are now three studies with random assignment, large sample sizes, long-term follow up, measurement of behavior, and proper statistical analyses that have shown statistically significant and programmatically important reductions in adolescent sexual risk taking (Coyle et al., 1999; Jemmott et al., 1998; St. Lawrence et al., 1995). These three studies clearly indicate that certain school-based and community-based sex and HIV education programs can delay sex, decrease the frequency of sex, increase condom or contraceptive use, or decrease unprotected sex. In addition, several studies have found lasting effects for 1 year, some have found effects for about 18 months, and one found effects that lasted at least 31 months after the intervention (Coyle et al., 2001).

The strength of this evidence has also been increased by replications of earlier studies. After the first studies of two curricula, *Be Proud, Be Responsible* (Jemmott, Jemmott, & McCaffree, 1994) and *Reducing the Risk* (Barth, 1996) demonstrated that they were effective, subsequent studies of either the same curricula or slightly different versions have also found them to be effective at delaying sex or increasing condom or contraceptive use. Such confirmation of positive behavioral findings is most encouraging, providing greater evidence that programs found effective in one study and one group of communities can be effective in subsequent communities.

When curricula that are effective at reducing unprotected sex are compared with curricula that are not effective, the effective curricula have 10 distinguishing characteristics. These characteristics reflect different aspects of effective pedagogy. In addition, they are similar to the characteristics of educational programs found to be effective at reducing substance abuse (Dusenbury & Falco, 1995). Effective curricula did the following:

1. Focused on reducing one or more sexual behaviors that lead to unintended pregnancy or HIV/STD infection

2. Were based on theoretical approaches that have been demonstrated to be effective in influencing other health-related risk-taking behavior and on research that identified the important determinants of selected sexual and condom or contraceptive behaviors

3. Gave a clear message about sexual activity and condom or contraceptive use and continually reinforced that message

4. Provided basic, accurate information about the risks of teen sexual activity and about methods of avoiding intercourse or using protection against pregnancy and STDs

5. Included activities that address social pressures that influence sexual behavior

6. Provided modeling and practice of communication, negotiation, and refusal skills

7. Employed a variety of teaching methods designed to involve the participants and have them personalize the information

8. Incorporated behavioral goals, teaching methods, and materials that were appropriate to the age, sexual experience, and culture of the students

9. Lasted a sufficient length of time to complete important activities adequately

10. Selected teachers or peers who believed in the program they were implementing and then provided them with training

Clinic or School-Based Programs Designed to Provide Reproductive Health Care or to Improve Access to Condoms or Other Contraceptives

Although studies have not revealed that the availability of contraception or reproductive health services more generally is related to adolescent initiation of sex or use of contraception, it is nevertheless logical that if youth do not have adequate access to contraception, then they are less likely to use it. Accordingly, many health services have striven to make contraceptives more available to sexually active youth.

Family Planning Clinics and Services. The primary objective of family planning clinics or family planning services offered within other health settings is to provide clients with contraception and other reproductive health services and also to provide clients with the knowledge and skills to use contraception and services. According to a 1992 national survey of family planning clinics, many clinics have special facilities for teenagers, three fourths encourage their counselors to spend extra time with clients under age 18, four fifths have outreach programs for teenagers, many have programs for teenage parents as well as for the parents of these teenagers, and many have sex education training programs for adults and teens (Henshaw & Torres, 1994).

Adolescents do not immediately begin using organized family planning services when they first have sex. Instead, they are far more likely to use a condom the first time they have sex (66%) than oral contraceptives (which require the help of health care providers), and 60% of teen girls wait a year or more after initiating intercourse before visiting a doctor or clinic for contraception (Alan Guttmacher Institute, 1994). However, many sexually active female teenagers do receive family planning services. According to the 1995 National Survey of Family Growth, an estimated 2.6 million 15- to 19-year-old females (or nearly one third of all females in that age group) made one or more visits to a clinic, private medical source, or counselor for family planning; of those, almost two thirds visited a clinic (Abma,

Chandra, Mosher, Peterson, & Piccinino, 1997). Many of these young women received oral contraceptives and other contraceptives that are more effective at preventing pregnancy than condoms or other nonprescription methods that can be purchased without the requirement of a clinic visit or prescription. Accordingly, these family planning services presumably prevented many adolescent pregnancies that would have occurred if these services did not exist or were significantly curtailed.

Unfortunately, there is remarkably little research about the impact of family planning services generally. Although there have been several studies of the effects of family planning clinics on pregnancy or birth rates (Anderson & Cope, 1987; Brewster, Billy, & Grady, 1993; Forrest, Hermalin, & Henshaw, 1981; Lundberg & Plotnick, 1990; Olsen & Weed, 1986; Singh, 1986; Weed & Olsen, 1986), the strength of their conclusions is greatly weakened by conflicting results among studies and by several severe methodological limitations. Thus, the actual impact on adolescent pregnancy rates of either family planning services generally or subsidized family planning clinics specifically has not been accurately estimated.

Protocols for Clinic Appointments and Supportive Activities. Six studies have examined what happens during a clinic visit: the counseling and instruction that takes place between a medical provider and a teen patient and the other materials and activities that can support and reinforce that counseling. Four found positive effects on condom or contraceptive behavior.

The first of the four studies evaluated a very modest intervention for female patients with chlamydia (Orr, Langefeld, Katz, & Caine, 1996). A nurse spent 10 to 20 minutes discussing chlamydia with the aid of a pamphlet, demonstrated how to put a condom on a banana (and got the patient to practice), and engaged the patient in a brief role play involving a woman getting her partner to use a condom. An experimental design measuring the impact at 6 months found that those youth who received the special instruction were substantially more likely to use condoms than those who received the standard intervention.

The second study evaluated a program for males that included two parts: (a) a slide-tape program that focused on anatomy, STDs, contraception, couple communication, and access to health services and (b) a visit with a health care practitioner who focused on contraception, reproductive health goals, health risks, and the patient's related interests. Both parts emphasized abstinence and the use of contraception if sexually active. A strong experimental design and questionnaire data collected a year later indicated that the program did not significantly affect sexual activity but did increase use of contraception, especially by the males' partners and by program participants who were not sexually experienced at baseline (Danielson, Marcy, Plunkett, Wiest, & Greenlick, 1990).

The third effective program focused on HIV/STD prevention and served equal percentages of males and females (Boekeloo et al., 1999). It included a 15-minute audio-taped risk assessment and education program, a discussion icebreaker, two brochures on skills and ways to avoid unprotected sex, a brochure on community resources, and parent brochures. On a one-to-one basis, the patient's physician then reviewed the risk assessment with the patient and discussed concerns and methods of avoiding unprotected sex. An experimental design indicated that the program increased use of condoms during the 3 months after the intervention.

In the fourth study, a family planning clinic substantially improved its clinic protocol for adolescents by placing greater focus on non-medical problems, providing more information and more counseling, delaying the medical

examination until the second visit, and giving more attention to partner and parent involvement (Winter & Breckenmaker, 1991). It also designated one staff person as a teen counselor. The study did not have a strong evaluation design, but its results indicate that it did increase contraceptive use.

The fact that four of these six studies found positive effects on behavior with such brief, modest interventions is quite encouraging. It should be noted that all four of the effective interventions focused on sexual and contraceptive behavior, gave clear messages about appropriate sexual and contraceptive behavior, and included one-to-one consultation about the client's own behavior. At the very least, these studies suggest that such approaches should be further developed and rigorously evaluated. These results should also encourage medical providers to review their instructional protocols with youth and to spend more time talking with individual adolescent patients about their sexual and contraceptive activity.

School-Based and School-Linked Clinics. Many studies of schools with health clinics and schools with condom availability programs have consistently shown that the provision of condoms or other contraceptives through schools does not increase sexual activity (Blake et al., 2000; Furstenberg, Geitz, Teitler, & Weiss, 1997; Guttmacher et al., 1997; Kirby, 1991; Kirby & Brown, 1996; Kirby, Waszak, & Ziegler, 1991; Kisker, Brown, & Hill, 1994). Studies also show that substantial proportions of sexually experienced students have obtained contraceptives from these programs (Kirby & Brown, 1996; Kirby, Waszak, et al., 1991). However, given the relatively wide availability of contraceptives in most communities, most school-based clinics, especially those that did not focus on pregnancy or STD prevention, did not appear to markedly increase the schoolwide use of contraceptives—that is, there appeared to be a substitution effect, meaning that teens merely switched from getting contraception from a source outside of school to getting it in school (Kirby, 1991; Kirby & Brown, 1996; Kirby, Waszak, et al., 1991; Kisker et al., 1994).

By contrast, two studies suggested that school-based or school-linked clinics did increase use of contraception when they focused much more on contraception, gave clear messages about abstinence and contraception, and provided or prescribed contraceptives (Kirby, Waszak, et al., 1991; Zabin, Hirsch, Smith, Streett, & Hardy, 1986). In addition, multiple studies have revealed that a school-based clinic in South Carolina, in combination with other community-wide activities, actually reduced pregnancy rates for many years (Koo, Dunteman, George, Green, & Vincent, 1994; Vincent, Clearie, & Schluchter, 1987). Notably, that clinic gave students a clear message about avoiding unprotected sex, counseled students individually, provided male students with condoms, and took female students needing contraception to a nearby family planning clinic.

Although studies of school condom availability programs consistently demonstrated that the programs did not increase sexual activity, they provided conflicting results about their impact on schoolwide use of condoms. These differences may reflect methodological limitations, differences in the availability of condoms in the community, or differences in the programs themselves.

Multicomponent, Community-Wide Initiatives

In the past two decades, recognizing the complexity of the problem of teen pregnancy and STD, researchers have implemented more multicomponent efforts to change the communities in which teens live—in the hope that healthier environments might reduce rates of teen pregnancy. These initiatives often combine interventions such as media campaigns, increased access to family planning and contraception services, sex education classes for teens, and training in parent-child communication.

The evidence on these initiatives is mixed (Alstead et al., 1999; Donner et al., 2001; Grossman & Pepper, 1999; Hughes, Furstenberg, & Teitler, 1995; Kennedy, Mizuno, Seals, Myllyuoma, & Weeks-Norton, 2000; Koo et al., 1994; Paine-Andrews et al., 1999; Polen & Freeborn, 1995; Prausnitz & Goldbaum, 1998; Sellers, McGraw, & McKinlay, 1994; Vincent et al., 1987). Each study measured effects on teens throughout the community, not just on those teens directly served by programs. Of the 10 studies, 4 found positive effects.

The first effective community initiative, the most intensive, was designed to reduce teen pregnancy in a small, rural South Carolina community. The program included the following components: teachers, administrators, and community leaders were given training in sexuality education; sex education was integrated into all grades in the schools; peer counselors were trained; the school nurse counseled students, provided male students with condoms, and took female students to a nearby family planning clinic; and local media, churches, and other community organizations highlighted special events and reinforced the message of avoiding unintended pregnancy (Koo et al., 1994; Vincent et al., 1987). After the program was put in place, the pregnancy rate for 14- to 17-year-olds promptly declined and, in general, continued to decline for many years. When this program was implemented much less intensively in Kansas and without the school-based clinic services, it failed to have a measurable impact on pregnancy (Paine-Andrews et al., 1999).

The second effective intervention included a large, comprehensive social marketing campaign called *Project* ACTION (Polen & Freeborn, 1995). Three public service announcements were aired multiple times on television, condom vending machines were installed in locations recommended by youth, and teenagers were trained to facilitate small-group workshops that focused on decision-making and assertiveness skills. Results indicated that the campaign did not increase the proportion of higher-risk youth who had ever had intercourse, nor did it increase their acquisition of condoms or their use of condoms with their main partners. However, after the campaign began, there was a significant increase in their use of condoms with casual sexual partners; after the campaign ended, this use returned to baseline levels.

The third program with positive effects was similar to Project ACTION (Kennedy et al., 2000). The Teens Stopping AIDS program in Sacramento included 2,000 30-second public service radio announcements, posters and small promotional materials, skills-building workshops to about 900 youth, peer outreach and, a telephone information line. Analyses of multiple cross-sectional telephone surveys indicated that the proportion of youth exposed to the program increased over time and that the amount of exposure to the components was related to condom use at last sex with main partner, as well as to some of the theoretical determinants of such use.

Less encouraging are the results from three studies of similar programs in Seattle and Boston. When Project ACTION was implemented a second time in Seattle, it significantly increased condom use during the first few months of the program, but not during later months (Prausnitz & Goldbaum, 1998), and when similar campaigns were implemented in different parts of Seattle (Alstead et al., 1999) and Boston (Sellers et al., 1994), they also failed to significantly increase condom use.

The fourth program with positive results was an abstinence-oriented program directed toward preteens and young teens. The *Not Me, Not Now* program (Doniger, Riley, Utter, & Adams, 2001) was a mass communications program to promote abstinence through paid advertising on TV and radio, billboards, posters distributed in schools, educational materials for parents, an interactive Web site, and educational sessions in school and community settings. (These educational sessions reached only 3% of middle school-aged youth in the county.) After the campaign was initiated, the countywide rates of sexual activity among youth 15 and younger declined (but those among youth 17 and younger did not decline significantly), and the pregnancy rates among 15- to 17-year-old teens declined faster in the county than in other geographical regions. These results are encouraging, but it cannot be known with any certainty that these particular program activities, as opposed to other factors, caused the countywide rates of sexual activity and pregnancy to decline.

In sum, about half the community-wide initiatives were found to have some positive effects on behavior. Clearly, the very intensive community-wide initiative in South Carolina that included community-wide education, one-to-one counseling with adolescents, and improved access to reproductive health services had the strongest impact, even a long-term impact on pregnancy rate. In comparison, the community-wide initiatives that relied strongly on media, provided skill-building education to limited numbers of youth, and either provided a telephone hot line or increased the number of condom vending machines had significant community-wide effects in three of five studies, but in two of them the improvement was only for the short term. These results suggest that to be effective for lengthy periods of time, community-wide initiatives need to be intensive and must be sustained.

Programs That Focus on Nonsexual Antecedents

Programs in this category focus on broader reasons behind why teens get pregnant or cause a pregnancy, including disadvantaged families and communities, detachment from school, work, or other important social institutions, and lack of relationships with parents and other caring adults. As noted earlier, research suggests that teens who are doing well in school and have educational and career plans for the future are less likely to get pregnant or cause a pregnancy. Increasingly, programs to prevent teen pregnancy focus on helping young people develop skills and confidence, focus on education, and take advantage of job opportunities and mentoring relationships with adults—thereby helping them create reasons to make responsible decisions about sex. These efforts include service learning, vocational education and employment programs, and youth development programs, broadly defined.

Service Learning Programs

By definition, service learning programs include (a) voluntary or unpaid service in the community (e.g., tutoring, working as a teacher's aide, working in nursing or retirement homes, helping out in day care centers, or helping fix up parks and recreation areas) and (b) structured time for preparation and reflection before, during, and after service (e.g., group discussions, journal writing, or papers). Often the service is voluntary, but sometimes it is prearranged as part of a class. And often, but not always, the service is linked to academic instruction in the classroom.

Service learning programs may have stronger evidence that they reduce actual teen pregnancy rates while youth are in the programs than any other type of intervention. Four different studies, three of which evaluated programs in multiple locations, have consistently indicated that service learning reduces either sexual activity or teen pregnancy (Allen, Philliber, Herrling, & Kuperminc, 1997; Melchior, 1998; O'Donnell et al., 1999; O'Donnell et al., 2000; Philliber & Allen, 1992).

The most rigorous of the studies used an experimental design and evaluated multiple sites around the country that were using the Teen Outreach Program (TOP). On the average, the TOP participants spent about 46 hours doing service. Results revealed that TOP participants reported lower pregnancy rates during the school year in which they participated in TOP than did the control group; they also had lower rates of school failure than the control group (Allen et al., 1997).

Similar results were found in a study of Learn and Serve programs throughout the country (Melchior, 1998). Students in these programs spent an average of 77 hours providing service. This study did not employ an experimental design with random assignment, but it did identify similar students in other school classes or other schools as a comparison group. Its results tended to confirm the TOP results in that participants in the Learn and Serve programs reported lower pregnancy rates during the school year in which they participated. However, the results were only marginally significant ($p = .10$). Notably, this study also evaluated the longer-term impact of participation in Learn and Serve and found that the impact on pregnancy (and also on most other outcomes) did not last through the school year following the year of participation. This suggests that participation in service learning programs may reduce teen pregnancy rates only during the semesters in which youth actually participate.

Finally, a pair of studies measured the impact of a health education curriculum alone and the combined impact of the same health education curriculum and service learning (O'Donnell et al., 1999; O'Donnell et al., 2000). Results indicated that the health education curriculum alone did not significantly decrease recent sexual activity, but the addition of service learning did significantly reduce sexual activity. In the short term, it delayed the onset of sex, and in the long term (more than 3 years later) it both delayed the onset of sex and reduced the percentage of students who had sex the previous month. These studies suggest that service learning may reduce teen pregnancy rates in part by reducing sexual activity.

It is not known for sure why service learning has positive effects on pregnancy, but several explanations have been suggested—participants developed ongoing relationships with caring program facilitators, some may have developed greater autonomy and felt more competent in their relationships with peers and adults, some may have been heartened by the realization that they could make a difference in the lives of others—all of which might have increased motivation to avoid pregnancy. The volunteer experiences may also have encouraged youth to think more about their futures. It may also be that both supervision and alternative activities simply reduced the opportunity for participants to engage in problem behaviors, including unprotected sex. After all, these programs were time intensive—the average number of hours that youth spent in TOP and Learn and Serve programs during the academic year were 46 hours and 77 hours, respectively. The study of TOP found that the kinds of volunteer service varied considerably from site to site, but TOP appeared to be most effective when young people had some control over where they volunteered (Allen et al., 1997). The effectiveness of TOP was not dependent on the fidelity of the implementation of the TOP curriculum (Allen, Philliber, & Hoggson, 1990), which suggests that the service itself is the most important component of the programs.

Vocational Education and Employment Programs

Vocational education programs provide young people with remedial, academic, and vocational education, sometimes coupled with assistance in getting jobs and other health education and health services. Four studies have evaluated the effect of such programs on teen sexual risk taking, pregnancy, and childbearing. A strong study of the Summer Training and Education Program (STEP) revealed that the program did not have a consistent and significant impact on either sexual activity or use of contraception (Grossman & Sipe, 1992; Walker & Vilella-Velez, 1992). Similarly, evaluations of three programs, the Conservation and Youth Service Corps, the Job Corps, and JOB-START, revealed that they did not affect overall teen pregnancy or birth rates at 15- to 48-month follow up (Cave, Bos, Doolittle, & Toussaint, 1993; Jastrzab, Masker, Blomquist, & Orr, 1997; Schochet, Burghardt, & Glazerman, 2000). Thus, these studies provide rather strong evidence that programs such as these four, which offer academic and vocation education and a few support services and are quite intensive, will not decrease pregnancy or birth rates among disadvantaged teens.

At this point, it is simply not clear why some youth development programs (i.e., service learning) reduce teen pregnancy and others with some similar characteristics (i.e., vocational education programs) do not. This is an important area for further research.

Other Youth Development Programs

The *Seattle Social Development Program* (Hawkins, Catalano, Kosterman, Abbott, & Hill, 1999) was designed to increase children's attachment to school and family by improving teaching strategies (e.g., cooperative learning) and parenting skills. To improve the quality of teaching in schools, the program provided 5 days of in-service training for teachers of Grades 1 through 6 each year. Many teachers participated in this. To improve parenting skills, the program offered parenting classes for parents of children in Grades 1 through 3 and Grades 5 and 6; relatively few parents attended. The program also implemented a curriculum unit in schools to increase students' social skills (e.g., decision-making and refusal skills). When these grade school students were followed to age 18, those receiving the intervention were less likely to report a pregnancy than the comparison group. They were also more attached to school, got higher grades, and engaged in fewer delinquent acts.

Programs That Focus on Both Sexual and Nonsexual Antecedents

Three studies have examined programs that address both reproductive health and youth development simultaneously. The first study evaluated three programs in Washington state that provided teens with small-group and individualized education and skill-building sessions, as well as other individual services, including counseling, mentoring, referrals, and advocacy. Results indicated that the programs did not delay sex or increase contraceptive use, but they did decrease the frequency of sex (McBride & Gienapp, 2000). The second study evaluated different programs in 44 sites in California targeted to the sisters of teen girls who had become pregnant—an interesting strategy based on the well-known fact that having an older sister become pregnant increases the chances that the younger sister will do the same. The programs sought to delay sex, increase contraceptive use, and decrease other associated risk behaviors (e.g., drinking and drug use) through individual case management and group activities (mainly recreation) and services. The evaluation showed that the interventions delayed sex and decreased reported pregnancy 9 months later (East & Kiernan, 2000).

Finally, a very rigorous study of the comprehensive Children's Aid Society (CAS)-Carrera Program has demonstrated that, among girls, it significantly delayed the onset of sex, increased the use of condoms and other effective methods of contraception, and reduced pregnancy (Philliber, Kaye, Herring, & West, 2002). The program did not reduce sexual risk taking among boys. The CAS-Carrera Program, which is long-term, intensive, and expensive, includes these components: (a) family life and sex education; (b) individual academic assessment, tutoring, help with homework, preparation for standardized exams, and assistance with college entrance; (c) a work-related intervention that includes a job club, stipends, individual bank accounts, employment, and career awareness; (d) self-expression through the arts; (e) sports activities and (f) comprehensive health care, including mental health and reproductive health services and contraception. This is the first and only study to date that includes random assignment, multiple sites, and a large sample size and that found a positive impact on sexual and contraceptive behavior, and pregnancy, among girls for as long as 3 years.

DISCUSSION AND CONCLUSIONS

The findings from this multitude of studies paint a remarkably consistent picture in a variety of ways. First, the large number of risk and protective factors affecting initiation of sex, use of contraception, and pregnancy among teens suggests that it should be difficult to markedly reduce sexual risk taking and pregnancy. Consistent with this, many programs were not effective at either delaying sex, increasing contraceptive use, or decreasing pregnancy.

Second, the risk and protective factors included both sexual and nonsexual factors, suggesting that if programs addressed either of these two groups, they could be effective. Indeed, some programs, such as selected sex and HIV education programs and clinic protocols, that focus on sexual behavior and contraceptive use, do delay sex or increase contraceptive use, and some programs, such as service learning programs, that focus on nonsexual factors can delay sex and decrease pregnancy.

Third, given that both sexual and nonsexual factors affect sexual risk taking, programs that (a) focus on both groups of factors and (b) focus on multiple factors within each group should be the most effective. Consistent with this, the one program, the CAS-Carrera program, that does focus intensively on both groups of factors, does have the strongest evidence that among teen females it actually reduces sexual risk taking and pregnancy by about half for as long as 3 years.

The patterns among the risk and protective factors and the patterns among the results of impact studies are also consistent with a remarkably simple conceptual framework that involves social norms and connectedness to those expressing those norms. For purposes of illustration, consider an example in a different health area. If an adolescent is around people who express norms favoring smoking, that adolescent is more likely to also smoke; if the adolescent is around people who express norms opposed to smoking, that adolescent is less likely to smoke. Simply put, the norms of this group may affect the adolescent's smoking behavior. In addition, if the adolescent is closely connected to this group, the norms of that group will have a much greater impact on the adolescent's behavior; if the adolescent is not connected to that group, the norms of this group will have much less, if any, impact on the adolescent's smoking. Thus, both the norms of the group and the individual adolescent's connectedness to that group are important, and there is an interaction between these two constructs. There is nothing new about this conceptual framework. Indeed, innumerable other theories recognize

the importance of group norms, and other theories recognize the importance of connectedness to family or other groups. However, this framework seems to have remarkable explanatory power.

The review of risk and protective factors reveals that when youth are more attached to those groups or institutions with conservative norms regarding sexual risk taking (e.g., parents, schools, or faith communities), they are less likely to engage in sexual risk taking. Similarly, when programs increase attachment to parents, schools, or other adults (e.g., service learning programs, the CAS-Carrera Program, and the Seattle Social Development Program), they decrease pregnancy rates. The review of risk and protective factors reveals that when individuals or groups to which youth may be attached express clear norms against sexual risk taking or model positive behavior, then youth are less likely to engage in sexual risk taking or to become pregnant or cause a pregnancy. For example, if parents and siblings model delayed sexual activity or delayed childbearing or if peers abstain from sex, teens are less likely to have sex or to become pregnant or cause a pregnancy. Similarly, when programs, either sex or HIV education programs or clinic protocols, focus on sex, give a clear message about avoiding unprotected sex, and change perceived norms about unprotected sex, youth are less likely to engage in sex or unprotected sex.

Despite the development of multiple groups of programs that reduce sexual risk taking and a more clear understanding why some of them are effective, there remain many important unanswered questions. These include the following:

- Among the numerous risk and protective factors that have been found to be related to sexual risk taking, which have the greatest causal impact on different sexual risk behaviors? How does their impact vary across different groups?

- How can sex and HIV education programs and clinic protocols be made more effective so that they have larger and longer-term effects? Can effective sex and HIV education programs be shortened in some way so that they can be implemented more widely without losing their effectiveness?
- Why do service learning programs decrease reported pregnancy? What are the mediating variables that they affect? Why are service learning programs apparently effective when vocational education programs are not?
- What is the impact on sexual risk taking of other types of programs (e.g., male involvement programs, mentoring programs, or school programs designed to improve success in school)?
- What characteristics of youth development programs are critical to reducing sexual risk

taking? Which important mediating variables do they affect?
- How can effective programs be replicated with fidelity and implemented more widely?

These and many other questions should be addressed by researchers in the coming years.

In sum, very diverse programs can reduce unprotected sex and teen pregnancy. Some effective programs address sexual risk and protective factors, and others address nonsexual, more distal factors. Both types of programs can be effective, and programs that address both appear to be even more effective. Most effective programs either give a clear message about avoiding sex or consistently using condoms or contraception, or they have the potential for increasing attachment to or association with people, often adults, who hold such values.

CHAPTER 30

Healthy Sexual Development

Notes on Programs That Reduce the Risk of Early Sexual Initiation and Adolescent Pregnancy

MIGNON R. MOORE
JEANNE BROOKS-GUNN

Adolescent pregnancy has been understood as problematic behavior inconsistent with appropriate developmental transitions, particularly when it occurs outside of committed, marital relationships (Moore & Brooks-Gunn, 2002; Roth & Brooks-Gunn, in press-b).[1] Consistent political and public concern continues to highlight the problematic social and economic outcomes associated with teenage childbearing. In the past decade, teen pregnancy has captured the attention of federal leaders and policymakers, fueling the 1996 adoption of a national program to combat it, despite the steady decline in adolescent pregnancy rates since in 1991.[2] One result is the significant growth in the numbers of teenage pregnancy prevention programs, with fewer empirical evaluations of those programs,

leaving some concern about their effectiveness in reducing the occurrence or delaying the onset of sexual initiation and pregnancy for youth. Because there are several recently published extensive reviews of pregnancy prevention programs (Franklin, Grant, Corcoran, O'Dell Miller, & Bultman, 1997; Frost & Forrest, 1995; Kirby, 1997; Moore, Sugland, Blumenthal, Glei, & Snyder, 1995) we have chosen in this chapter to focus on four types of programs: media campaigns, abstinence-only programs, contraceptive and sexuality education programs, and comprehensive approaches that combine several intervention strategies. In each case, we either highlight components of each type of program that contribute to its success or bring attention to important issues that may contribute to its ineffectiveness in reducing adolescent sexual activity.

AUTHORS' NOTE: We thank Elaine Harley and Alexandra Murphy for excellent research assistance.

GENERAL PROGRAM CHARACTERISTICS

Most programs are relatively short-lived and directed toward specific groups of youth perceived to be at risk for early sexual activity because of race, family socioeconomic status, neighborhood, or other background characteristics (Moore et al., 1995). Due to difficulties measuring program impact as well as the multiple risks faced by many program participants, few programs are able to demonstrate sustained, large effects on delay of sexual initiation, increase in contraceptive use or delay in pregnancy. Those that have met with some success have tended to adopt a comprehensive approach that affects adolescent sexual decision making by teaching through more than one method how to think critically about problems. These programs also provide education and life skills training that may affect decision making and risk behaviors in other domains. This chapter identifies key program elements in successful and/or popular programs believed to have made a significant contribution to their success or lack thereof.

MEDIA CAMPAIGNS

Most media campaigns are usually one component of a larger multistrategy prevention program that provides information on sexuality education and life skills training through more than one venue. The primary focus of some public awareness campaigns is to disseminate information about teenage pregnancy prevention through various media outlets. These tend to be state or community based and work collaboratively with other community partners to create smaller, locality-based campaigns and to develop and implement interventions consistent with the larger theoretical or ideological perspective of state policymakers or other organizing groups (e.g., National Organization on Adolescent Pregnancy, Parenting, and Prevention). One national media campaign in particular has received attention in recent years for its work on pregnancy prevention: the National Campaign to Prevent Teen Pregnancy.

The National Campaign to Prevent Teen Pregnancy is perhaps the most thorough and far-reaching of all of the current national media campaigns. It has a stated goal of reducing the national rate of teen pregnancy by one third between 1996 and 2005; it provides assistance to state and community groups in the form of fact sheets with information for advocates to present to state legislators, county-by-county data on pregnancy rates, brochures for doctors, pamphlets for clergy, and various other needs assessment manuals.[3] The Campaign's most visible projects involve the use of various media outlets, rather than teen pregnancy organizations, to influence youth behavior. The Campaign has had some success in persuading television programmers and movie producers to examine teenage pregnancy, its effects on families, and its consequences for adolescents and their children. It has also worked with magazines and other print media to encourage publication of teen pregnancy-related articles and public service announcements in English and Spanish and has included popular celebrities in advertisements relating to adolescent pregnancy and parenthood as well. One of the more controversial components of the Campaign's promotion involves a series of public service advertisements in poster and postcard form that use frank, eye-catching images and language to call attention to the consequences of unprotected and teenage sex and to discourage adolescent pregnancy. The advertisements are carefully planned to speak to teenagers directly.

The National Campaign to Prevent Teen Pregnancy is important because it is one of the few media campaigns that has successfully reached broad audiences. One major issue with this and other media campaigns is the difficulty in measuring their impact or success at changing adolescent behavior. Instead, the focus of the organization shifts to efforts to increase exposure and expand its audience by involving as many media outlets as possible.

ABSTINENCE-ONLY PROGRAMS

In 1996, the Department of Health and Human Services was told to create and implement a national strategy to reduce teen pregnancy rates, and this provision was authorized and implemented by Title V of the Personal Responsibility and Work Responsibility Reconciliation Act of 1996. It established a policy designed to encourage the development of national abstinence-only education programs. Beginning in 1998, a program was added to the Maternal and Child Health Block Grant requiring that $50 million be allocated annually to states for the implementation of state-operated abstinence education programs for the fiscal years 1998–2002. As a result, the past decade has seen a dramatic increase in the percentage of school districts that teach abstinence as the only way to prevent pregnancy and STD transmission, per the Title V provision requiring programs receiving abstinence education funds to teach an "unambiguous abstinence message" and prohibiting these programs from endorsing or promoting contraceptive use (Darroch, Landry, & Singh, 2000; Maynard & Johnson, 2001).

Abstinence-only programs focus on changing community values, norms, and behaviors toward adolescent sexual activity, pregnancy, and childbearing to support the delay of these behaviors until adulthood or marriage. Many programs have as their foundation an abstinence-only curriculum supplemented with other services and youth development programs to strengthen parent-child communication and teach life skills and strategies that youth can use to negotiate their way out of problematic situations dealing with sex and other risk behaviors. These programs also help youth improve peer communication about delaying sexual intercourse, offer adult and peer mentors after school and during other critical hours that may be unsupervised, and, in general, promote an ideological framework to combat images and messages in the media and other outlets that might be perceived as supporting nonmarital or adolescent sexual activity (Maynard & Johnson, 2001; Moore et al., 1995).

A few school- and community-based abstinence-only programs have reported lower pregnancy rates at program exit for their participants relative to students in the same school or community who did not participate (e.g., Allen, Philliber, & Herrling, 1997; Vincent, Clearie & Schluchter, 1987). However, many of these types of evaluations have tended not to be empirically rigorous. Few scientifically thorough evaluations have been conducted to measure the influence of abstinence-only programs on delay of sexual initiation and pregnancy, so there is little empirical research identifying the components of these programs that might have the strongest impact on these behaviors (Kirby, 1997; Maynard & Johnson, 2001; Moore et al., 1995; Scott, 1995). This issue is particularly important when comparing comprehensive abstinence-only programs with sexuality and contraceptive education programs that are also comprehensive but whose message both supports abstinence and educates youth about contraception. Currently, the Mathematica Policy Research, Inc., is under contract to the U.S. Department of

Health and Human Services to conduct a national evaluation of Title V abstinence education programs. The evaluations are scheduled to be completed in 2005.

Abstinence Pledges

Part of the impetus behind the federal government's support of Title V abstinence education programs as a nationwide strategy for pregnancy prevention is the consistency of its message with the morality and norms also supported by many religious organizations in the United States. This perspective is reflected in an organized religious social movement to delay sexual initiation among teenagers that began in the early 1990s and has grown since that time. Since 1993, over 2.5 million adolescents have taken public "virginity" pledges, in which they promise to abstain from sexual intercourse until marriage, as part of a program first sponsored by the Southern Baptist Church and later adopted in various forms by hundreds of church, school, and college chapters, as well as other religious organizations.

Comparing virginity pledgers with others in the National Longitudinal Study of Adolescent Health, Bearman and Bruckner (2001) found that adolescents who made the pledge were much less likely to have intercourse than adolescents who did not pledge. However, pledging reduced the likelihood of sexual intercourse for teens in early and middle adolescence (between 12 and 17 years old) only and did not affect the sexual behavior of older teens. Pledging also worked only in schools where there were a limited number of pledgers (maximum 30%), because in these contexts the pledgers as a group were able to distinguish themselves from non-pledgers in a way that established a unique community of identity to be preserved. If there were too many pledgers in the same context, or when individuals moved into late adolescence, virginity pledges were no longer successful at delaying sexual onset.

CONTRACEPTIVE AND SEXUALITY EDUCATION PROGRAMS

There are several types of contraceptive and sexuality education programs to combat adolescent sexual activity. Contraceptive education programs provide access to family planning services in community-based and school-based clinics, as well as other health centers. These programs have at their core a curriculum discussing methods of contraception and the use and effectiveness of those methods in preventing pregnancy and sexual disease transmission. They may also provide contraceptive access or information on where adolescents can obtain contraceptives (Frost & Forrest, 1995). Many programs have an additional educational component that offers information on a broad range of related reproductive health topics, including STD and HIV transmission. The outcomes of interest for programs involving contraceptive and sexuality education are delay of sexual onset, increased contraceptive use, and reduced nonmarital pregnancy and childbearing for adolescents.

Sexual Initiation. Several adolescent pregnancy prevention programs have reported a delay in sexual onset for a significant proportion of their participants compared with individuals in comparison or control groups (Frost & Forrest, 1995; Hardy & Zabin, 1991). All of these programs are comprehensive and provide a range of social services, parenting education, life skills, and medical care, as well as contraceptive services. One issue to keep in mind when evaluating programs whose intended outcome is delayed sexual initiation is the age-graded nature of sexual intercourse. Sexual initiation becomes increasingly normative with age, so the goal of many sexuality education programs is to reduce the proportionate increase in the number of teenagers initiating sex. Programs are most successful when they target those who are younger as well as those who have little sexual experience.

Contraceptive Education. The most important measures of contraception use for adolescents are use at first intercourse, use at most recent intercourse, and consistency of use for the sexually active. Manlove et al. (2000) summarized recent trends in adolescent contraceptive use by reviewing previous studies and by analyzing data from several waves of the National Survey of Family Growth, the National Survey of Adolescent Males, and the Youth Risk Behavior Survey. They found that the number of adolescent women who reported having used contraceptives at first intercourse increased from 48% in 1982 to 76% in 1995, due largely to increases in condom use. The increase was characteristic of women in all racial groups, although it was smallest for Hispanic women. Despite this increase in reporting of contraception use at first intercourse, there has been a decline in contraceptive use at most recent intercourse. This decline is largely due to a decrease in Caucasian and Hispanic teenagers' use of methods other than condoms, since the proportion of teens reporting condom use at most recent intercourse has remained relatively stable from 1988 to 1995 and the proportion of African American teens reporting contraception use did not decline during this same time period. In terms of consistency of contraception use among the sexually active, age was the most important predictor: 74% of sexually active women aged 18 to 19 reported consistent

use, while the corresponding figure for 15- to 17-year-olds was 58%.

Contraceptive and sexuality education programs discuss abstinence as well as methods of contraception as ways to prevent pregnancy and STD/HIV transmission. They range from sexuality education programs taught in school classes to programs taught in community-based centers and organizations or health clinics. In a survey of pregnancy prevention program reviews and the effectiveness of these programs in increasing contraceptive use, Moore et al. (1995) reported that community-based programs had more success over school-based programs in increasing adolescent contraceptive use.

This finding is supported by the Franklin et al. 1997 meta-analysis, as well as the Kirby 1997 report on effective pregnancy prevention programs and research. In thinking about the differences in these two approaches, we see that school-based clinics specifically target the needs of adolescents and are usually in closer proximity to these populations. As a result, they presumably provide greater accessibility. In contrast, most school-based clinics are actually comprehensive health centers whose primary focus does not involve contraceptive distribution (Moore et al., 1995). Many do not even dispense contraceptives or offer prenatal care services, two programs found to relate to teen contraceptive use. Family planning clinics or family planning services in clinical settings emphasize contraception and other reproductive health services, and teach patients how to use contraception. The significant variation in emphasis might explain the differences in program effectiveness by location.

Moore et al. (1995) also found that programs that emphasized contraceptive distribution and knowledge building were more effective than programs solely emphasizing sex education. This finding is consistent with the literature emphasizing the success of comprehensive approaches to sexuality education and life skills building mentioned earlier. The Kirby (1997) review found that sexuality education programs were most effective when they went beyond a dissemination of basic information on sexual disease transmission and pregnancy prevention to also incorporate behavioral goals, teaching methods, and materials that fit well with the age, sexual experience, and culture of the students. The most successful comprehensive approaches also focused on more than one sexual behavior that could potentially lead to pregnancy or STD/HIV transmission, employed a variety of teaching methods to involve more participants, and included activities and skill-building exercises to promote better methods of communication, negotiation, and refusal skills that could be used to address other potential risk behaviors. A major limitation of these findings is the lack of evaluation evidence on which of these factors or combinations makes the greatest contribution to program success.

Finally, Moore et al. (1995) found that older adolescents (16 and older) were more likely than younger adolescents to use contraceptives. Most of the literature on contraceptive use reports a similar finding, that frequency and consistency of contraceptive use increases with age (Alan Guttmacher Institute, 1994; Kahn, Brindis, Claire, & Glei, 1999; O'Donnell, O'Donnell, & Steve, 2001). We would therefore expect to find a relationship between age and effectiveness of prevention programs that incorporate information and expectations of contraceptive use for future sexual intercourse among non-sexually active participants.

The goal of many programs is to increase the proportion of sexually active teenagers using contraceptives consistently during intercourse. One study found the most impressive effects over time for teenagers who were virgins when the study first began (Frost & Forrest, 1995), suggesting that the most effective contraceptive use programs are ones that target younger teenagers who have not yet initiated sex. However, both the meta-analyses by Franklin et al. (1997) and Frost and Forrest (1995) also found that pregnancy prevention programs increased the contraceptive use of sexually active teens. The Franklin et al. (1997) review reported certain programmatic characteristics to have a significant impact on pregnancy rates: Programs emphasizing contraceptive use and distribution performed better than abstinence-based programs and sex education programs without contraceptive knowledge building.

COMPREHENSIVE, MULTICOMPONENT PROGRAMS AND YOUTH DEVELOPMENT PROGRAMS

The available evaluation literature suggests that multicomponent pregnancy prevention programs with a contraception education and access component have had the most success in delaying sexual onset or reducing the proportion of youth engaged in sexual activity, increasing the rates of contraceptive use, and in some instances, decreasing the proportion of adolescents who experienced a pregnancy. We have not seen strong empirical evidence regarding the effectiveness of abstinence-only multicomponent programs in reducing teen sexual activity. However, both types of comprehensive programs are based on a framework that provides information and services that are developmentally appropriate while enhancing social development and providing education and services to reduce the likelihood of problem behavior. These program goals are consistent with the youth development philosophy that focuses on how to facilitate the healthy emotional, psychological, and social development of youth. The similarity in emphasis and organizing structure between the most successful comprehensive pregnancy prevention programs and traditional youth development programs warrants further attention. Of interest are ways that a youth development framework might be incorporated into other prevention programs to improve nonsexual outcomes as well as sexual initiation, contraceptive use, and pregnancy.

The youth development framework emphasizes preparation and development rather than problem prevention and deterrence (Pittman & Cahill, 1991). Youth development programs provide developmentally rich contexts where relationships form, opportunities for growth in multiple areas proliferate, and development occurs (Roth & Brooks-Gunn, 2000). These programs help participants develop "competencies that will enable them to grow, develop their skills and become healthy, responsible and caring youth and adults" (p. 3). Roth and Brooks-Gunn (2000) outline a set of defining characteristics for youth development programs:

1. Program goals that promote positive development rather than focusing solely on the prevention of problem behaviors

2. A program atmosphere of hope, support, and adult belief in youth and their successful development into competent, caring, and well-adjusted adults

3. Program activities that provide opportunities for personal growth, a nurturance of individual interests and talents, and education in ways that are different from the bounded, structured school-learning environment

Many abstinence-only as well as contraceptive and sexuality education programs that are multicomponent and comprehensive appear to have program agendas consistent with the description of successful youth programs provided by Roth and Brooks-Gunn (2000). Although they have not been evaluated as youth development programs and have as their larger goal the prevention of problem behavior, their additional programmatic components make them consistent with the broader goals of more traditional development programs. They provide factual information on sex, sexual activity, and sometimes contraception, and complement this information with life skills training that individuals can use to deal with other issues that accompany adolescence, including ways to improve decision making and communication, build healthy self-esteem, and set life goals.

The goal of youth development programs is to "enhance not only adolescents' skills, but also their confidence in themselves and their future, their character, and their connections to other people and institutions by creating environments, both at and away from the program, where youth can feel supported and empowered" (Roth, Brooks-Gunn, Murray, & Foster, 1998. p. 425). This is a message similar to that of the multipronged pregnancy prevention programs, which determine whether or not this goal has been met through the reduction of sex-related outcomes. Evaluations of development programs that are not focused on adolescent sexual activity and pregnancy have shown concrete reductions in problem behaviors such as school misconduct and truancy (Tierney, Grossman, & Resch, 1995), drug and alcohol use (Johnson et al., 1996), involvement with the criminal justice system, and greater fertility control (Hahn, 1994). In an exhaustive review of youth development program evaluations, Roth et al. (1998) found three elements that were critical to the success of these programs: (a) strong and supportive relationships between adolescents and an unrelated adult, (b) the involvement of family members as well as the adolescent, and (c) a framework that stresses personal as well as academic skill development. There are promising connections to be made in linking traditional development programs with programs that focus on adolescent sexual behavior to create an effective, developmentally sound approach to preventing adolescent pregnancy and at the same time promote healthy adjustment.

SUMMARY

Three considerations emerge from evaluations of pregnancy prevention programs: background factors, outcomes examined, and appropriateness of prevention strategy.

Background Factors. Individual, family, and socioeconomic background factors may have a significant effect on the success of any program and may play an important role in its successful replication across different neighborhood and family contexts. For example, several programs that showed both significant reductions in the proportion of teens initiating sex and significant increases in contraceptive use were based on African American youth in low-income, urban neighborhoods recruited from environments located in or near cities of major research institutions. We know little about how well these programs would work on racial or cultural groups that reside in other impoverished environments but that are more difficult to enroll in studies—for example, low-income rural Caucasian youth. Age and sexual experience at the start of the intervention are also important and related considerations. Most successful interventions contained individuals who were not sexually experienced at baseline; these teenagers not only delayed intercourse for longer periods of time but were more consistent contraceptive users after initiation.

Outcomes Examined. Program effectiveness is also contingent on the sexual outcomes examined. Most programs and program evaluations reported their most significant findings around delay of sexual onset and increase in contraceptive use. Few have been able to show significantly lower rates of pregnancy or childbirth because the follow-up period in the study design is too short or because of high dropout rates among the pregnant teens.

Appropriateness of Prevention Strategy. Finally, we must consider the appropriateness of the prevention strategy for the targeted population. The proliferation of abstinence-only education programs stems from federal and state support that funds only programs that do not provide information or access to contraceptives. However, we know from the existing research that contraceptive-based programs have the greatest success at reducing sexual activity and pregnancy. Because such funding restrictions are based on ideological or moral considerations rather than on effectiveness of intervention strategies, adolescents may not be receiving all of the support and information needed to make the best decisions about their futures.

NOTES

1. The proportion of nonmarital births to teenagers has continued to rise from 67% in 1990 to 79% in 2000 (Henshaw & Feivelson, 2000; Ventura & Bachrach, 2000; Ventura, Mathews, & Hamilton, 2001).

2. The rate of pregnancy for women aged 15 to 19 declined 17% between 1990 and 1996 and 22% between 1991 and 2000 (Henshaw & Feivelson, 2000; Ventura, Mathews, & Hamilton, 2001; Ventura, Mosher, Curtin, Abma, & Henshaw, 2001).

3. See the National Campaign to Prevent Teen Pregnancy Web site at www.teenpregnancy.org.

CHAPTER 31

Adolescent Sex and the Rhetoric of Risk

J. Dennis Fortenberry

From a clinical or public health perspective, the visible tracks of adolescent sex are its untoward consequences marking an otherwise obscure trail of sexuality running through young people's lives. Some consequent sexual infections such as those due to human immunodeficiency virus (HIV) cause a treatable but fatal chronic illness, and all the sexually transmitted diseases may have sequelae that reverberate through the life span. Pregnancy—that most beatified evidence of the biological *Homo sapiens* of the seminal blessings of the divine—is framed as an epidemic scourge threatening ruin to our society. Despite conflicting evidence, pregnancy among teens is causally linked by many to poor birth outcomes, child abuse and neglect, poverty, and multigenerational welfare dependence. The language and images of epidemiological risk pervade both lay and professional discourse surrounding adolescent sex. The content and meaning of adolescent sexual health are diminished by research perspectives that implicitly endorse virginity until heterosexual married monogamy as a public health goal.

The primary purpose of this chapter is to briefly review a few of the implications of exclusive focus on epidemiological risk as a framework for understanding adolescent sexuality. A research orientation will then be outlined that attempts to reframe the rather narrow issues of sexually transmitted diseases and pregnancy within a broader understanding of the phenomenology of adolescent sex. The goal is not to discount the significant contributions drawn from the risk and risk-taking perspectives. Rather, the limitations of this perspective are presented by way of defining a path toward additional ways of enhancing our understanding of adolescent sex and learning how to help youth achieve a healthy sexuality.

RISK AND RISK TAKING

Confusion of the terms *risk* and *risk taking* has led to a great deal of conceptual mischief that mixes epidemiological observation with biological and psychological theory. In epidemiology, *risk* expresses the probability of a specified health outcome. Although risk is often taken as shorthand for adverse or undesirable outcomes, outcomes are technically either harms or benefits. Beneficial outcomes are taken as absence of harms. In a more restricted sense, risk refers to the likelihood of an outcome (usually but not necessarily a disease and usually in a specified time frame), given the presence of specific conditions (*risk factors*). Risk factors—especially those associated with high-visibility public health campaigns—often become synonymous with the adverse outcome. The absence of a risk factor is equated with protection. This language of risk and protection aligns closely to traditional sexual proscriptions: no sex until marriage.

Because traditional epidemiology assumes that a risk factor operates within a set of more-or-less complex causal linkages, so understanding of risk and risk factors obviously offers a useful starting place for intervention. Ideally, risk is probabilistic, objective, and morally neutral. However, the language of risk—as applied to adolescent sex—can be striking in its starkness. This is most clearly epitomized by writings about the various epidemics of HIV infections among adolescents. For example,

> A healthy, productive generation of adolescents in the 1990s will ensure that America has the healthy generation of adults needed to support the growing elderly population in the 21st century. The AIDS epidemic threatens the viability, perhaps the very existence, of this next generation. The social and economic well-being of this first "AIDS generation" may well predict the future well-being of this nation as a whole in the next century. (Hein, 1992, p. 3)

This is an apocalyptic vision of a nation brought to ruin by the infectious consequences of voluntary behaviors. It is quite a burden to attach to a single age group.

Recognition of the magnitude of the HIV epidemic clearly contributed to the increased emphasis on the health risks of adolescent sex. Despite the relative rarity of HIV disease among adolescents, adolescent sex is linked to the HIV-related diseases of adults. Research related to adolescent sexual behavior is now commonly introduced by some variation of the following:

> Many of the new AIDS cases are diagnosed in the 20–29-year-old population. Since the average time from HIV infection to the development of AIDS may be as long as 10 years, many of these young adults are believed to have contracted HIV during adolescence. (Klein et al., 2001, p. 193)

Linking adolescent behavior to adult disease means that almost any aspect of adolescent sexual behavior is problematic. This formulation is difficult to criticize. Stoic acceptance of preventable casualties is immoral, either as personal philosophy or as public health policy. However, research and policy perspectives grounded only in sex-as-risk cannot see adolescent sex as a vehicle for advanced knowledge, expanded experience, and perfected skills.

The shorthand rhetoric of adolescent sex-as-risk also treats specific sexual risk behaviors as inherent attributes of adolescent sexuality. Sex with multiple partners, relatively frequent intercourse, and inconsistent use of barrier contraception (i.e., condoms) are often cited as characteristics of adolescent sexual behavior associated with increased risk of sexually transmitted infections. Although seldom included in recent scientific literature, an assumption that adolescent sex is inherently *promiscuous* lies not far beneath the surface. As risk factors, condom nonuse and number of sex partners increase risk of adverse consequences. As presumed characteristics of adolescent sex, however, these are alarmist phrases used to characterize all adolescent sexual behavior, excluding consideration of those adolescents who regularly attempt prevention of sexually transmitted diseases (STDs) or those for whom sexual experiences with more than one person are potentially useful as a developmental phase.

For most health conditions, persons without risk factors still have some risk of the adverse outcome but at a lower level compared with those with a specified risk factor. For example, coronary artery disease occurs among persons with normal cholesterol levels, albeit at lower rates compared with those with higher cholesterol levels. By contrast, sexual behaviors are a relatively less common class of risk factor (for the outcomes of sexually transmitted diseases and pregnancy) where the absence of a risk factor (e.g., coitus or other sexual contact) completely removes risk of the adverse health outcome. Much of the history of efforts to control sexually transmitted diseases in this century has revolved around efforts—often cloaked in the language and professional stature of medicine—to remove sex as a risk factor for sexually transmitted disease. Implementation of virginity as public health policy (exemplified by recent federal legislation) is only the most recent example of a recurrent effort that has failed in most of the decades of this century.

Of course, abstinence is not the only solution proposed to meet the perceived threats of STD and pregnancy. During the past decade, condom use has become the sine qua non of responsible sex: Each coitus is latex protected, and unprotected opportunity is rejected on principle. In many respects, the change of attitudes about condoms and the dramatic increase in condom use during the past decade reflect the success of public education and behavior change. Condom use by sexually active teenagers is reasonably described as a social norm. Even now, however, the great ambivalence about adolescent sex continues to require emphasis on the risks of sex and inadequacies, even the dangers, of condoms.

For adolescents, the lingering interest in risk elimination (i.e., by removing sex as a risk factor) dominates most discussion about condom use. Abstinence is offered as the preferred choice. Condoms are a begrudged second alternative for those failing abstinence. Here, both public and professional discourse identifies the physical and behavioral deficiencies of condom use, especially for STD prophylaxis. For example, critics responding to recommendations for school-based condom availability programs cited the following data:

> Condoms have a poor track record as contraceptives (30% failure for youngsters), offer no protection against chlamydia or HPV, and have a 17% rate of tearing, breakage, and slipping. With regard to HIV, they are not impermeable. There are no long-term controlled studies demonstrating efficacy. A meta-analysis calculates a 30% failure rate. (Friedman & Trivelli, 1996, p. 285)

The STD prevention effectiveness of condoms is an issue of real concern, although the data for specific STDs are surprisingly unclear. The point of interest, however, is that a prevention effectiveness of less than 100% is defined as ineffective when the topic is sex and the subjects are adolescents. From the sex-as-danger perspective, the risks of sex are great and condoms inadequately effective. The logic of the risk perspective of adolescent sex thus leads once more to abstinence. Curiously, similar standards of effectiveness don't seem to apply in other aspects of adolescents' lives. Rigorous application of the absolute protection rule would require banning high school football because helmets don't prevent all head injury. Teens would also need to "abstain" from contact with motor vehicles because traffic regulations, advanced safety engineering, seatbelts, and airbags do not prevent all collision-related injuries and deaths.

Even when condom effectiveness is not an issue, the risk perspective shapes both research paradigms and public health interventions. As mentioned earlier, condom use is implicitly inconsistent if it falls short of 100% of exposures, and self-reported "Always" use of condoms has become a standard definition of consistent condom use in some adolescent health research (DiClemente, Lodico, et al., 1996). Condom use is often measured by a single item, typically asking the subject to indicate how often a condom was used during sexual intercourse. Various time periods (usually 3 to 12 months) are used, and the subjects are provided with alternatives such as "Never," "Rarely," "About half the time," "Most of the time," and "Always." Only those endorsing "Always" are counted as condom users; all others—despite their obvious behavioral differences as well as their differences in risk of STD—are singly grouped as "nonusers." This approach has been justified because "effectiveness [of condoms] as a risk reduction strategy is dependent on consistent use" (DiClemente, Lodico, et al., 1996, p. 270).

From the perspective that all adolescent sex is dangerous (risky), this approach to condom use measurement is logical. However, other conceptual and methodological issues arise. For starters, substantial variability in behavior is hidden among adolescents who choose the "Always" option on questionnaires. For example, our research group has demonstrated major differences in subjects' interpretations of the meaning of "Always," and we have shown—in a comparison of survey reports of condom use with diary records of sexual activity among adolescent women—that those reporting "Always" condom use recorded condom use for between 0% and 100% of coital events (Fortenberry, Cecil, Zimet, & Orr, 1997). The finding that "Always" does not mean 100% raises very serious questions about the appropriateness of this rather restrictive measurement philosophy. Furthermore, some subjects in our study identified their condom use as "Most of the time" but then indicated condom use for every coital event. From the "all-or-none"

perspective, these highly consistent users would be grouped with those who never used condoms at all.

The problems caused by this purposeful misclassification of subjects' responses are serious enough. When translated to the actual message given to teens, the effects of a 100% condom use standard are potentially quite dangerous. Many teens who fail in this very demanding task believe that a point-of-no-return has been crossed and that additional condom use is now futile. Perhaps more important, a standard of 100% condom use suggests that negotiation within a sexual relationship is not acceptable or that a given relationship may be accurately appraised as having relatively low STD risk. Despite warnings that such demands for absolutism are dangerous (Cates & Hinman, 1992), the risk perspective of adolescent sex leaves no other logical alternative.

The "sex-as-risk" perspective has been taken up for political purposes as well, and it intersects surprisingly well with current public health approaches. In defense of positions advocating "abstinence," some writers argue that failure rates for condoms are so high as to make it hazardous either as public health policy or as a standard for personal behavior. These commentators suggest that condoms promote adolescent sexual activity by removing inhibitions (presumably due to fear of disease); higher levels of sexual activity combined with low levels of efficacy (either for STD/HIV or pregnancy prevention) make abstinence the only feasible health standard for policy or behavior. Several studies demonstrate no effect on levels of sexual activity when condoms are made available, for example, in schools (Kirby, 2002). For the most part, however, this argument has been resistant to data, in part, because of fairly widespread willingness to ignore evidence in favor of ideology.

The risk perspective generates an even more insidious set of problems. Not only is coitus itself dangerous, but noncoital sexual behaviors such as mutual masturbation is suggested as a risk because it is said to cause unanticipated emotional reactions (for which teens may be unprepared) and presumably may lead to coitus. Exactly what the "unanticipated emotional reactions" might be, and the ways in which they might be harmful, is unclear. Recent concern about an "epidemic" of oral sex among adolescents—concern justified because of poorly documented risks of HIV and other sexually transmitted organisms associated with oral sex—additionally suggests that adolescent sexual expression itself (rather than adverse outcomes) is the source of public anxiety (Edwards & Carne, 1998b; Remez, 2000). The idea that mutual masturbation or oral sex experiences may be educating, pleasurable, and self-affirming is alien to the risk perspective. Developmentally, however, such experiences are exactly the point of adolescence. Anke Ehrhardt (1996) points out that the sex-as-risk perspective completely negates those aspects of adolescents' sexual learning that require experience and information if competency is to be achieved. Dr. Ehrhardt suggests that our narrow focus on fear of consequences may lead to increased rates of sexual dysfunction and interpersonal problems.

To this point, issues related to the widely used if not predominant paradigm of adolescent sex as risk have been presented. Adolescent risk taking is a distinct but conceptually related issue that is widely used in discussions of adolescent sexual behavior.

ADOLESCENT SEX AS RISK TAKING

The epidemiological risk associated with adolescent behaviors (including sexual behaviors) led to the development of a peculiar perspective during the 1980s. Volitional behaviors associated with substantial morbidity (i.e., risk) were labeled as *risk taking* in an effort to simultaneously explain epidemiological patterns of morbidity (due to disease, injury, and pregnancy) and the developmental biological, social, and psychological antecedents of these behaviors. One widely cited definition of risk taking noted,

> Our definition of risk taking includes only volitional behaviors in which the outcomes remain uncertain with the possibility of an identifiable negative health outcome. Young people with limited or no experience engage in behaviors with anticipation of benefit and without understanding the immediate or long-term consequences of their actions. (Irwin, 1993, p. 11)

The model seems most directly derived from observations about recreational and motor vehicle injury patterns among adolescents. For example, risky use of bicycles or skateboards (among younger adolescents) and various patterns of risky motor vehicle operation (among older adolescents) are often cited as justification for the risk-taking perspective. The facts that younger drivers tend to drive at higher rates of speed and change lanes without signals and have more single vehicle accidents are usually cited.

Sexual behavior then becomes risk taking because of its inherent risks and because adolescents engage in risk taking while riding bicycles or driving cars. The motor vehicle accident metaphor has been extended even further with the "sex under the influence" paradigm that equates substance use to impaired judgment, loss of control, and subsequent sexual "accidents." This metaphor is so appealing that it has resisted substantial evidence to the contrary.

Risk taking has been applied to a full range of adolescent sexual behaviors. Coitus is risk taking, of course. Having more than one partner during a given time interval (even if these are sequential partners) is risk taking. Failure to use condoms or contraceptives is risk taking. Inconsistent condom use is risk taking. Penile-anal intercourse is risk taking. There is no provision within the risk-taking model for sex that is not risk taking. Sex that would take place because of mutual desire, reciprocated liking, or out of desire for intimate companionship is not considered. Or such considerations would be irrelevant. The risk-taking perspective suggests that adolescent sex is risk taking because the behaviors entail social and physical risks and because many adolescents have sex. Thus, risk taking (including sexual risk taking) becomes a defining characteristic of adolescence. Those who are not risk takers might even be considered abnormal from this perspective. Adolescence—with all its intimations of exploration and change—is reduced by this model to a disease (Baizerman & Erickson, 1988).

Limitations of the Risk Perspective

The focus on adolescent sex as a risky (or risk-taking) behavior has clearly contributed greatly to understanding of adolescent sexuality. As with many ideas that were quite serviceable in their time, the limitations of risk and risk-taking perspectives are increasingly obvious. Here is a partial listing of a few of the more important limitations of these perspectives.

The Negation of the Experiential, Developmental, and Maturational Aspects of Sex. Some writers note that risk and risk-taking aspects of adolescent sex are part of the experimental, tentative nature of adolescent development. For the most part, however, the risk/risk-taking perspective ignores the fact that it is exactly these types of experiences that may stimulate development of adult competencies. A hint of this perspective even seems to have lingered in an otherwise excellent vision of the National Commission on Adolescent Sexual Health: "Society should encourage adolescents to delay sexual behaviors until they are ready physically, cognitively, and emotionally for mature sexual relationships and their consequences" (Sexuality Information and Education Council of the United States, 1995, n.p.).

Neither is this report, or the literature in general, entirely clear about the qualities of "mature sexual relationships," nor is a rationale provided for insisting on the maturity of an interpersonal relationship that by definition is based on relative lack of experience and skill.

The Negation of Important Intra- and Interpersonal Aspects of Sexuality. The risk/risk-taking perspectives seldom address the apparently substantive personal and interpersonal reasons that adolescents might have for having sex. In consequence, we are left with an exclusive—almost pornographic—focus on relative physical proximities of genitals (nearly always the penis and vagina). Our understanding of adolescents' sexualities is so rudimentary that most discussions collapse to the percentage of adolescents who have ever put/received a body appendage in an orifice, with how many people, and to what consequence. So one can say with a fair degree of precision how many teens get gonorrhea or HIV or have an elective abortion but have almost no idea about the relative importance that adolescent boys attach to touching or the frequency of orgasm in adolescent girls.

Lack of Attention to Larger Issues of Social Control of Sexuality. As noted earlier, the risk/risk-taking perspectives—with epidemiologically justified emphasis on abstinence—become powerful tools for reinforcing traditional gendered sex roles and predominant social-cultural themes of nonmarital chastity. Safer sex discussions for adolescents often emphasize the certainty of STD/HIV prevention by abstinence, simultaneously emphasizing the fallibility of condoms. Marriage is reasserted as the defining condition of coital behavior, as a solution to the epidemiological and other social perils of unregulated sex. Legislative insistence on abstinence-only education and provision of federal dollars to encourage marriage among the poor are policies consistent with data provided by risk/risk-taking research perspectives.

BEYOND RISK/RISK TAKING: A RESEARCH AGENDA

Two important points are evident. First, the risk and risk-taking perspectives of adolescent sex create such a narrow focus on the genital specifics of sex that abstinence and mandated virginity are logical outcomes. Second, this view is untenable, not because abstinence is good or bad or because intercourse is good or bad but because the genital specifics are—in a larger sense—irrelevant. The risk/risk-taking perspectives draw focus away from the development of sexuality and its importance in an adolescent's life to the brief conjunction of a few square centimeters of epithelium.

Finally, an additional research orientation is needed to expand understanding of adolescent sexuality and its important personal and public health consequences. Although not exhaustive, several key elements of this expanded research perspective are listed.

Development of the Gendered Aspects of Sexuality Throughout Adolescence. The extension of feminist perspectives to the understanding of sexuality among adolescent girls has increased attention to developmental conflicts between adolescents' sexual knowledge and desire and cultural scripts available from the surrounding culture (Tolman, 2000). Our understanding of adolescent male sexuality could benefit from similarly nuanced analyses.

Place and Geography. Unequal distribution of some sexually transmitted organisms means that risk of infection differs among adolescents with similar sexual behaviors. Social resources, community standards, access to care, and collective efficacy are issues of increasingly recognized importance in the epidemiology of sexually transmitted infections (Ellen, Hessol, Kohn, & Bolan, 1997). Fullilove (2001) and others point out the consequences of destruction of urban communities in the name of "urban renewal." These sorts of influences are typically excluded from risk/risk-taking research perspectives.

Social and Sexual Networks. A recent report found that many adolescent females with bacterial sexually transmitted infections had few behaviors associated with high risk for infection (Bunnell et al., 1999). Infections were presumably "imported" by sex partners with links to higher-risk sexual networks. Selection of sex partners with markedly different levels of sexual activity may be associated with increased levels of risk in some groups (Laumann & Youm, 1999).

Relational Contexts of Sexual Behaviors. Relatively little research addresses adolescent sexual behavior within the context of sexual dyads. Within-dyad communication, conflict, power, and influence are receiving increased attention in terms of adolescent romantic relationships. To date, however, this research gives less attention to issues of sexuality and sexual behavior within these relationships. We have shown, for example, that adolescent dyads with noncongruent levels of involvement in health-harming behaviors such as alcohol and marijuana use are less consistent condom users than dyads congruent for low levels of alcohol/marijuana use but more consistent than dyads congruent for high levels of substance use (Fortenberry, in press).

Phenomenology of Adolescent Sexual Behavior. Variable, day-to-day factors such as opportunity, mood, and partner support may influence the occurrence of sexual activity and related behaviors. For example, we found increased levels of positive mood were associated with increased probability of coitus on any given day but were not associated with condom use when coitus did occur (Fortenberry, Temkit, Harezlak, Tu, & Orr, 2001). Other day-to-day factors such as school difficulties and conflict with parents could also be productively examined as factors surrounding and perhaps influencing adolescent sexual behaviors.

CONCLUSION

The epidemiological consequences of adolescent sexual behavior are an important focus of social and behavioral research. Nearly exclusive focus on risk, however, has created a limited research paradigm with uneasy correspondences to a social and political agenda that excludes sex from adolescent sexual health. With an eye on outcomes, a more balanced research perspective may better inform our understanding of adolescent sexuality and improve efforts to reduce harmful consequences.

Part III

Section C

Suicide

CHAPTER 32

Suicide Risk Among Adolescents

MADELYN S. GOULD

A range of risk behaviors threatens an adolescent's successful transition into adulthood, including problem- and health-related behaviors, such as drug and alcohol abuse, violence, and unprotected sexual intercourse. "Adolescents at risk" do not merely consign their futures to marginal roles in adult society (Ginzberg, 1991); many will be victims of premature deaths due to suicide, homicide, contracting human immunodeficieny (HIV) infection, and other self-injurious behaviors. This chapter focuses on the risk factors for suicide and suicide attempts among youth and examines the extent to which suicide risk covaries with other risk behaviors in adolescence.

The main risk factors for youth suicide to be reviewed here were identified by a review of official mortality statistics (e.g., Centers for Disease Control [CDC], 2002c; National Center for Health Statistics [NCHS], 1999; World Health Organization [WHO], 2001), psychological autopsy studies that employed direct interviews of family, peer informants,

or both (Appleby, Cooper, Amos, & Faragher, 1999; Brent, Baugher, Bridge, Chen, & Chiappetta, 1999; Brent, Bridge, Johnson, & Connolly, 1996; Brent et al., 1988; Brent, Perper, Moritz, Allman, et al., 1993; Groholt, Ekeberg, Wichstrom, & Haldorsen, 1998; Ho, Hung, Lee, Chung, & Chung, 1995; Houston, Hawton, & Shepperd, 2001; Lesage et al., 1994; Marttunen, Aro, Henriksson, & Lonnqvist, 1991; Rich, Young, & Fowler, 1986; Runeson, 1989; Shaffer et al., 1996; Shafii, Carrigan, Whittinghill, & Derrick, 1985), and general population epidemiological surveys and longitudinal studies of nonlethal suicidal behavior (e.g., Andrews & Lewinsohn, 1992; CDC, 2000c; Fergusson & Lynskey, 1995; Garrison, McKeown, Valois, & Vincent, 1993; Gould et al., 1998; Grunbaum et al., 2002; Joffe, Offord, & Boyle, 1988; Kaltiala-Heino, Rimpela, Marttunen, Rimpela, & Rantanen, 1999; Kandel, Raveis, & Davies, 1991; Kashani, Goddard, & Reid, 1989; McKeown et al., 1998; Reifman & Windle,

AUTHOR'S NOTE: The author gratefully acknowledges Margaret Lamm and J. Graham Thomas for their support in compiling review materials.

1995; Reinherz et al., 1995; Roberts & Chen, 1995; Swanson, Linskey, Quintero-Salinas, Pumariega, & Holzer 1992; Velez & Cohen, 1988; Windle, Miller-Tutzauer, & Domenico, 1992; Wunderlich, Bronisch, & Wittchen, 1998). With the exception of a few illustrative studies, this chapter does not include a review of the literature on clinical samples of suicide attempters. Clinical studies can provide information regarding the course of suicidal behavior, and, obviously, they are an important source for treatment trials to reduce suicidal behavior; however, clinical samples do not include the vast majority of suicide attempters in the community, limiting their generalizability (Smith & Crawford, 1986; Velez & Cohen, 1988), and they overestimate the association between problem behaviors due to differentially higher referral rates for people with multiple problems (McConaughy & Achenbach, 1994). The current report is based on a comprehensive, but not exhaustive, review of the most relevant English-language publications listed in PSYCInfo and Medline.

SUICIDE RISK

Overall Rates and Patterns

Suicide was the fourth leading cause of death among 10- to 14-year-olds and the third leading cause of death among 15- to 19-year-olds and 20- to 24-year-olds in 1999 (NCHS, 1999). The rankings vary by gender and ethnicity: Suicide accounts for more deaths among males and whites. Age, gender, and ethnic differences in incidence will be discussed further later in the chapter.

There is no surveillance system for nonlethal suicidal behavior in the United States, with the exception of Oregon, which has mandated the reporting of all attempted suicides among persons younger than 18 years who are treated at a hospital or a hospital emergency department (Andrus et al., 1991). Nevertheless, the surge of general population studies of suicide attempters and ideators in the past decade has yielded reliable estimates of the rates of suicidal behavior (e.g., Andrews & Lewinsohn, 1992; CDC, 1998c; Fergusson & Lynskey, 1995; Garrison et al., 1993; Grunbaum et al., 2002; Gould et al., 1998; Joffe et al., 1988; Kashani et al., 1989; Roberts & Chen, 1995; Swanson et al., 1992; Velez & Cohen, 1988; Windle et al., 1992). Of these studies, the largest and the most representative is the Youth Risk Behavior Survey (YRBS) (Grunbaum et al., 2002), conducted by the Centers for Disease Control and Prevention. The following estimates of suicidal ideation and attempts from this survey of students in Grades 9 through 12 during February through December 2001 are consistent with those cited in the epidemiological literature (e.g., Fergusson & Lynskey, 1995; Garrison et al., 1993; Gould et al., 1998; Lewinsohn, Rohde, & Seeley, 1996; Velez & Cohen, 1988). The YRBS indicated that 19% of high school students "seriously considered attempting suicide" during the past year. Nearly 15% of students made a specific plan to attempt suicide, 8.8% reported any suicide attempt during the past year, and 2.6% of students made a medically serious suicide attempt that required medical attention.

Age

Suicide is uncommon in childhood and early adolescence. Within the 10- to 14-year-old group, most of those who die by suicides are between 12 and 14 years old. Suicide incidence increases markedly in the late teens and continues to rise until the early 20s, reaching a level that is maintained throughout adulthood, until the beginning of the sixth decade when the rates increase markedly among men (NCHS, 1998).

In 1999, 192 boys and 50 girls aged between 10 and 14 committed suicide in the

United States, accounting for 5.8% (242 of 4,121) of all deaths occurring in this age group. The age-specific mortality rate from suicide was 1.2 per 100,000. Although 10- to 14-year-olds represented 7.2% of the U.S. population, the 242 child suicides represented only 0.8% (242 of 29,199) of all suicides. Only 2 children under the age of 10 committed suicide in 1999. Among 15- to 19-year-olds, 1,347 boys and 268 girls committed suicide, yielding a suicide mortality rate of 8.2 per 100,000. This is nearly 7 times as common as in the younger age group. The percentage of all suicides represented by 15- to 19-year-olds (5.5%) is nearly equal to the percentage of 15- to 19-year-olds in the total population (7.2%). Among 20- to 24-year-olds, 1,979 males and 307 females between the ages of 20 and 24 committed suicide, yielding an overall mortality rate of 12.7 per 100,000. This age group represents 6.6% of the total of the population; the suicides in this age group represent 7.2% of all suicides.

The age difference in completed suicide rates is a universal phenomenon (WHO, 2001). The similar age pattern in the international data suggest that cultural factors are unlikely to explain the rarity of suicide before puberty (Shaffer & Hicks, 1994). Shaffer et al. (1996) suggest that the most likely reason underlying the age of onset of suicide appears to be the age of onset for depression or exposure to drugs and alcohol. These two significant risk factors for suicide in adults (e.g., Barraclough, Bunch, Nelson, & Sainsbury, 1974; Robins, Murphy, Wilkinson, Gassner, & Kayes, 1959) and in adolescents (to be discussed later in the chapter) are rare in very young children and become prevalent only in later adolescence.

The developmental trends for completed and attempted suicide vary somewhat. Suicide attempts, like completed suicides, are relatively rare among prepubertal children, and they increase in frequency through adolescence. Suicide attempts reach a peak between 16 and 18 years of age, after which there is a marked decline in frequency as adolescents enter early adulthood (Kessler, Borges, & Walters, 1999; Lewinsohn, Rohde, Seeley, & Baldwin, 2001). This significant drop in frequency is evident only for young women (Lewinsohn et al., 2001).

Gender

A gender paradox in suicide exists in the United States in that completed suicide is more common among males, yet suicidal ideation and attempts are more common among females (CDC, 2000c; Garrison et al., 1993; Gould et al., 1998; Lewinsohn et al., 1996). Nearly 6 times more 15- to 19-year-old boys than girls commit suicide in the United States. The ratio of boys to girls steadily increases from prepuberty to young adulthood (NCHS, 1998). Yet the YRBS (Grunbaum et al., 2002) indicated that female students were significantly more likely to have seriously considered attempting suicide (23.6%), made a specific plan (17.7%), and attempted suicide (11.2%) than male students (14.2%, 11.8%, 6.2%, respectively). A possible explanation for the elevated rates of suicide attempts among teenage girls is their elevated rate of depression (Lewinsohn et al., 1996; Lewinsohn et al., 2001). The YRBS, however, found no significant difference by gender in the prevalence of *medically serious* attempts requiring medical attention (3.1% females, 2.1% males).

The same pattern of sex differences among 15- to 24-year-olds does not exist in all countries (WHO, 2001). Although suicide is more common in males than in females in North America, Western Europe, Australia, and New Zealand, in some countries in Asia (e.g., Singapore), sex rates are equal, and the majority of suicides are committed by females in others (e.g., China).

Both psychopathologic factors and sex-related method preferences are considered to contribute to the pattern of sex differences

(Shaffer & Hicks, 1994). Suicide is often associated with aggressive behavior and alcohol abuse (see discussion below), and both are more common in males. The role of gender-related method preference is more complex. Methods favored by women for suicidal behavior, such as overdoses, tend to be less lethal than the methods favored by men, such as hanging (Moscicki, 1995). These gender-related method preferences have been postulated to explain the different gender ratio in completed versus attempted suicides in the United States. However, an overdose may have quite different implications for lethality in different societies. Where treatment resources are not readily available or when the chosen ingestant is untreatable, overdoses are more likely to be lethal than in countries with well-developed treatment facilities (Shaffer & Hicks, 1994). Thus, in the United States in 1999, only 11% of completed suicides resulted from an ingestion (see section below on Methods), whereas in some South Asian and South Pacific countries, the majority of suicides are due to ingestions of herbicides such as paraquat, for which no effective treatment is available (Haynes, 1987; Shaffer & Hicks, 1994). A further discussion of method preference by age, gender, and ethnicity in the United States is given below.

Ethnicity

Youth suicide has generally been more common in whites than African Americans in the United States (NCHS, 1999), although the highest rates are found among Native American males (Wallace, Calhoun, Powell, O'Neil, & James, 1996). The historically lower suicide rate among African Americans has been hypothesized to be due to differences in religiosity, dissimilar degrees of social integration, and differences in "outwardly" rather than "inwardly" directed aggression (Gibbs, 1997; Shaffer, Gould, &

Hicks 1994). However, the difference in the suicide rates between whites and African Americans has been decreasing during the past 15 years. There was a marked increase in the suicide rate among African American males between 1986 and 1994, a period in which the rates for white males and African American males started to converge. This was followed by declining rates since the mid-1990s among all ethnic groups. The postulated reasons for this secular change will be discussed in a later section. Regrettably, U.S. rates of completed suicide are not readily available for most ethnic minorities, such as Latino and Chinese youth.

The YRBS (Grunbaum et al., 2002) found that African American students were significantly less likely (13.3%) than white or Latino students (19.7% and 19.4%, respectively) to have considered suicide or to have made a specific plan (African Americans: 10.3%; whites: 15.3%; Latinos: 14.1%). Latino students (12.1%) were significantly more likely than either African American or white students to have made a suicide attempt (8.8% and 7.9%, respectively); however, there was no preponderance of medically serious attempts among Latinos (3.4%), compared with whites (2.3%) or African Americans (3.4%). Although some studies have found higher rates of suicidal ideation and attempts among Latino youth (Roberts & Chen, 1995; Roberts, Chen, & Roberts, 1997), Grunbaum et al. (1998) and Walter et al. (1995) did not find a higher prevalence of either among Latinos. These equivocal findings highlight the need for further research in this area.

Geography

In the United States, youth suicide rates, uncorrected for ethnicity, are highest among the Western states and Alaska and lowest in the Northeastern states (NCHS, 2000). The reasons underlying this pattern are unclear. It may reflect different ethnic mixes or the varying availability of firearms (Shaffer, 1988). There is no apparent differential pattern by age or gender. The ratio of white to African American rates is greatest in the South, consistent with earlier reports (Shaffer et al., 1994).

Methods

Firearms are the most common method, and hanging is the second most prevalent method of suicide in the United States, regardless of age or ethnicity (NCHS, 2000). These two methods were the only ones used by 10- to 14-year-olds or by African American youth in 1999. There is some variability of method by gender: Ingestions are the second most prevalent method of suicide for females overall, accounting for 30% of all female suicides, whereas only 6.7% of all male suicides are due to this method. Among 15- to 19-year-olds, ingestions account for 15.7% of female suicides in contrast to 2% of male suicides, and among 20- to 24-year-olds, this method accounts for 18.9 % of female suicides compared with 3.2% of male suicides.

Secular Trends

Over the past three decades, there has been little change in the suicide rate among 10- to 14-year-olds; however, there have been dramatic changes among 15- to 19-year-olds. From the 1960s until 1988, there was a threefold increase in suicides among males aged 15 to 19. The rates then started to plateau until the mid-1990s, when the rates started to steadily decline among all gender and ethnic groups. Suicide rates among 20- to 24-year-olds remained relatively steady from 1980 until the mid-1990s at a level that was a twofold increase compared with 1964 rates. Since the mid-1990s, the declining rate noted among 15- to

19-year-olds has also occurred among 20- to 24 year-olds.

A considerable number of causal explanations, involving diagnostic, social, or familial factors, have been posited for the dramatic secular trends in youth suicidal behavior (Berman & Jobes, 1995; Diekstra, Kienhorst, & de Wilde, 1995). The reasons posited for the increase included changes in the prevalence of substance abuse (Shaffer et al., 1996) and increased availability of firearms (Boyd, 1983; Boyd & Moscicki, 1986; Brent, Perper, & Allman, 1987; Brent, Perper, Allman, Moritz, Wartella, et al., 1991). There was evidence (a) that the rate of suicide by firearms rose faster than the suicide rate by other methods (Boyd, 1983; Boyd & Moscicki, 1986; Brent et al., 1987), (b) that guns were twice as likely to be found in the home of suicide victims as in the homes of attempters or psychiatric controls (Brent et al., 1991), and (c) that an interaction of substance use and firearm use existed, as indicated by the findings of Brent and his colleagues (1991), who reported that suicide victims who used firearms were 5 times more likely to have been drinking than were those who used other methods of suicide.

Similar factors are posited for the recent declines in teenage suicide rates. The restriction of the availability of lethal methods (e.g., firearms) at first seems a possible explanation (Brent et al., 1999) because the decrease in the youth suicide rates largely reflects a decrease in firearm suicides. Legislation restricting access to firearms was passed in 1994 (Ludwig & Cook, 2000), at the time that the decrease became more marked and the rate of handling firearms among high school students has declined (CDC, 1995, 1996, 1998c, 2000c; Grunbaum et al., 2002). However, there are a number of reasons to question this explanation: (a) It is unclear if access to firearms has been reduced: The proportion of suicides by firearms, a plausible proxy for method availability (Cutright & Fernquist

2000), has not changed between 1988 and 1999; (b) there has been a decline ranging from 20% to 30% in the youth suicide rates in England, Finland, Germany, and Sweden where firearms account for very few suicides (WHO, 2001); (c) a systematic examination of the proportion of suicides committed by firearms over a long period of time has shown that the proportion is only weakly related to overall changes in the rate (Cutright & Fernquist, 2000). The decline in youth suicide also does not seem to be due to a decrease in substance use: Repeat benchmark studies that use similar measures and sampling methods such as the YRBS (CDC, 1995, 1996, 1998c, 2000c) give no indication of a decline in alcohol or cocaine use during this time. Better treatment of depression is a likely factor underlying the decrease in suicide rates, supported by the parallel increase in the number of prescriptions for antidepressants for youth during the same time period (Lonnqvist, 2000; Shaffer & Craft, 1999). The delay in the onset of the suicide decline in African American suicides is compatible with a treatment effect because of their greater difficulty in accessing treatment resources (Goodwin, Gould, Blanco, & Olfson, 2001). However, firm conclusions are not possible given the ecological nature of the supporting data. Randomized clinical trials will be necessary before the decline in rates can be confidently attributed to treatment with antidepressants.

Personal Characteristics

Psychopathology

There is overwhelming evidence that psychopathology is the most significant risk factor for suicidal behavior. Psychological autopsy studies have determined that a majority of those who completed suicide had significant psychiatric problems, including previous suicidal behavior, depressive disorder, substance abuse, and conduct disorder.

Generally, at least 90% of youth suicides have had at least one major psychiatric disorder. Depressive disorders are consistently the most prevalent ones: 61% in the New York study (Shaffer et al., 1996), 64% in the Finnish national study (Marttunen et al., 1991), and 49% in the Pittsburgh study (Brent, Perper, Moritz, Allman, et al., 1993). Female victims are more likely than males to have had an affective disorder. The increased risk of suicide (odds ratios [ORs]) for those with an affective disorder ranged from 11 to 27 (Brent et al., 1988; Brent, Perper, Moritz, Allman, et al., 1993; Groholt et al., 1998; Shafii, Steltz-Lenarsky, Derrick, Becker, & Whittinghill, 1988; Shaffer et al., 1996).

Substance abuse has been found to be a significant risk factor, with the exception of the Israeli study of male military conscripts (Apter et al., 1993). Substance abuse is more prevalent in older adolescent male suicide victims (Marttunen et al., 1991; Shaffer et al., 1996). A high prevalence of comorbidity between affective and substance abuse disorder has been found consistently. Disruptive disorders (including conduct disorder, oppositional defiant, and antisocial personality disorder) are also common in male teenage suicide victims (Brent, Perper, Moritz, Allman, et al., 1993; Shaffer et al., 1996). Approximately one third of the males who killed themselves had evidence of a conduct disorder, often comorbid with a mood, anxiety, or substance abuse disorder. Discrepant results have been reported for bipolar disorder, with the Pittsburgh study reporting relatively high rates (Brent et al., 1988; Brent, Perper, Moritz, Allman, et al., 1993), whereas other studies reported no or few bipolar cases (Marttunen et al., 1991; Runeson, 1989; Shaffer et al., 1994). Despite the generally high risk of suicide among people with schizophrenia, schizophrenia accounts for very few of all youth suicides (Brent, Perper, Moritz, Allman, et al., 1993; Shaffer et al., 1996).

Between one quarter to one third of youth suicide victims have made a prior suicide attempt (Brent, 1995; Brent, Perper, Moritz, Allman, et al., 1993; Shaffer et al., 1996). Prior suicidal behavior confers a particularly high risk for boys (i.e., a 30-fold increase); for girls, the risk is also elevated (i.e., approximately 3-fold), but it is not as potent a risk factor as major depression (Shaffer et al., 1996). Similarly strong associations between a history of suicidal behaviors and future attempts have been reported in general population epidemiological surveys and longitudinal studies of nonlethal suicidal behavior (e.g., Lewinsohn, Rohde, & Seeley, 1994; Reinherz et al., 1995).

The psychiatric problems of suicide *attempters* are quite similar to those of adolescents who *complete* suicide, and the gender-specific diagnostic profiles of suicide attempters parallel those of suicide victims (e.g., Andrews & Lewinsohn, 1992; Beautrais, Joyce, & Mulder, 1996; Gould et al., 1998). However, despite the overlap between suicidal *attempts* and *ideation* (Andrews & Lewinsohn, 1992; Reinherz et al., 1995) and the significant prediction of future attempts from ideation (Lewinsohn et al., 1994; Reinherz et al., 1995), the diagnostic profiles of attempters and ideators are somewhat distinct (Gould et al., 1998). In particular, substance abuse and dependence are more strongly associated with suicide attempts than with suicidal ideation (Garrison et al., 1993; Gould et al., 1998; Kandel, 1988).

Recent studies (Giaconia et al., 1995; Mazza, 2000; Wunderlich et al., 1998) have found an association between posttraumatic stress disorder (PTSD) and suicidal behavior among adolescents. In a community study of German adolescents and young adults that examined the associations between suicide attempts and a number of *DSM-IV* (*Diagnostic and Statistical Manual of Mental Disorders*, 4th ed; American Psychiatric Association, 1994) diagnoses, Wunderlich et al. (1998) found that PTSD was among the strongest risk factors for suicide attempt in a univariate analysis; however, the association was no longer significant after adjusting for the presence of other *DSM-IV* diagnoses. In contrast, Mazza (2000) reported that PTSD symptomatology was significantly related to suicidal ideation and showed a trend toward suicide attempt history, even after controlling for depression and gender. In another community study, Giaconia et al. (1995) found that youth with a diagnosis of PTSD had elevated rates of suicide attempts compared with youth who had not experienced trauma, but interestingly, the rate of suicide among youth who had experienced trauma but did not meet the criteria for a diagnosis of PTSD was similar to that of the youth with PTSD. These results suggest that the experience of trauma, rather than PTSD, is the significant risk factor for suicide.

Cognitive and Personality Factors

Hopelessness has been repeatedly found to be associated with suicidality (Howard-Pitney, LaFramboise, Basil, September, & Johnson, 1992; Marcenko, Fishman, & Friedman, 1999; Overholser, Adams, Lehnert, & Brinkman, 1995; Rubenstein, Heeren, Housman, Rubin, & Stechler, 1989; Russell & Joyner, 2001; Shaffer et al., 1996), but it is still unclear whether it is independent of depression. The vast majority of the victims who expressed hopelessness before their deaths had met criteria for a mood disorder; thus, it is unclear whether hopelessness per se or depression accounted for the association. Within clinical (Rotheram-Borus & Trautman, 1988) and nonclinical samples of youth (Cole, 1988; Howard-Pitney et al., 1992; Lewinsohn et al., 1994; Reifman & Windle, 1995), hopelessness has not consistently proven to be an independent predictor of suicidality, once depression is taken into account.

Other dysfunctional cognitive styles have been reported to differentiate suicidal from nonsuicidal youth (Asarnow, Carlson, & Guthrie, 1987; Rotheram-Borus, Trautman, Dopkins, & Shrout, 1990). Poor interpersonal problem-solving ability has been found to be associated with suicidality within clinical samples of adolescents (Asarnow et al., 1987; Rotheram-Borus et al., 1990). Rotheram-Borus and colleagues (1990) reported that minority female attempters generated fewer alternatives to solving stressful problems than both consecutive series of nonsuicidal adolescent outpatients and community controls. Depression did not account for these cognitive differences.

Aggressive-impulsive behavior has been reported to be associated with an increased risk of suicidal behavior (Apter, Plutchik, & van Praag, 1993; McKeown et al., 1998). Brent et al. (1986) characterized two groups of attempters: a dysphoric, hopeless group that plans attempts and an impulsive group that makes attempts without plans or serious intent. The relationships between impulsivity, suicidal behavior, and low levels of cerebrospinal fluid 5-hyroxyindoleacetic acid (CSF 5-HIAA) will be expanded on in a later section.

Sexual Orientation

The New York Study (Shaffer, Fisher, Hicks, Parides, & Gould, 1995) is the only psychological autopsy study of youth suicide, to date, to examine the association of sexual orientation and suicide. Homosexuality was defined in this study as having had homosexual experiences or having declared a homosexual orientation. Three suicide victims and no controls met these criteria. This difference was not statistically significant. All three suicide victims demonstrated evidence of significant psychiatric disorder before death, and in no instance did the suicide directly follow an episode of stigmatization. Given the opportunities for underreporting by informants, the psychological autopsy paradigm is somewhat limited in its capacity to assess the role of sexual orientation.

Recent epidemiological studies suggest a significant association between sexual orientation and nonlethal suicidal behavior. In a survey of Minnesota high school students, Remafedi, French, Story, Resnick, and Blum, (1998) reported a significantly higher rate of suicide attempts among gay and bisexual males compared with heterosexual males. No significant differences by sexual orientation were found for girls. Using the YRBS in Massachusetts, Faulkner and Cranston (1998) and Garofalo and colleagues (1998) found higher rates of suicide attempts among homosexual and bisexual adolescents. Youth who identified as gay, lesbian, or bisexual were 3 times more likely than their peers to have attempted suicide in the past year. In a 21-year longitudinal study of a birth cohort of 1,265 children born in Christchurch, New Zealand, gay, lesbian, and bisexual youth were at increased risks of suicidal ideation and suicide attempts (Fergusson, Horwood, & Beautrais, 1999). Van Heeringen and Vincke (2000) reported that lesbian youth in a Belgian school sample were at 6.2 greater risk for suicide attempts. Russell and Joyner's (2001) study of a nationally representative sample of nearly 12,000 adolescents in the National Longitudinal Study of Adolescent Health (Add Health Study) also provided evidence for an elevated risk of suicidality among sexual minority youth. Youth with same-sex orientation were more than 2 times more likely than their peers to attempt suicide. Adolescents who reported same-sex sexual orientation also exhibited significantly more suicide risk factors, including more alcohol abuse and depression. Moreover, a family history of suicide attempts was more common among boys with same-sex sexual orientation than among heterosexual boys, and girls with same-sex orientation were more likely than heterosexual girls to report victimization and to have friends who attempted suicide. When Russell and Joyner (2001) examined whether youth who report same-sex sexual orientation were still at greater risk than their peers after the other suicide risk factors were taken into account, they found that the effects of same-sex sexual orientation on suicidal ideation or attempts remained but were substantially mediated by depression, alcohol abuse, family history of attempts, and victimization. Russell and Joyner emphasized that although adolescents who report same-sex sexual orientation are at more than 2 times the risk for suicide attempts, the overwhelming majority of sexual minority youth, 84.6% of males and 71.7% of females with same-sex sexual orientation, report no suicidality at all.

Biological Factors

There is evidence that dysregulation of the serotonergic system is associated with suicide, impulsivity, and aggression (e.g., Blumenthal, 1990; Mann & Stoff, 1997). The dysregulation is exhibited by low levels of serotonin metabolites in cerebrospinal fluids, low concentrations of presynaptic serotonergic receptors, and dense concentrations at postsynaptic receptors. These serotonin abnormalities have been localized to the ventrolateral prefrontal cortex and brainstem of suicide victims and attempters (Arango, Underwood, & Mann, 1997). Because the ventrolateral prefrontal cortex plays a role in behavioral inhibition, serotonergic irregularities in this area could make a suicidal individual less able to control his or her suicidal impulses (Arango et al., 1997). Low levels of serotonin among suicide attempters have been found to be predictive of future completed suicide (Asberg, Nordstrom, & Traskman-Bendz, 1986). This dysregulation in the serotonergic system appears to occur in a range of psychiatric disorders. The

examination of biological factors associated with suicide has largely been limited to studies of adults (see Mann & Stoff, 1997, for a comprehensive review of these studies). The few studies examining children and adolescents suggest a similar association between serotonin abnormalities and suicidal behavior. Pfeffer et al. (1998) reported that whole-blood tryptophan levels were significantly lower in prepubertal children with a recent history of a suicide attempt. Greenhill et al. (1995) found a relationship between serotonin measures and medically serious attempts within a small sample of adolescent suicide attempter inpatients with major depressive disorder. Further research is needed to determine whether serotonin-related measures could be predictive of youth suicidal behavior.

Genetic factors may play a role in suicidal behavior, as suggested by adoption and twin studies, and the higher rates of suicidal behavior in the families of suicidal youth. This will be discussed further in the next section, which describes the family history of suicidal behavior.

Family Characteristics

Family History of Suicidal Behavior

A family history of suicidal behavior greatly increases the risk of completed suicide, as reported in several studies (Brent et al., 1988; Brent, Perper, et al., 1994; Gould, Fisher, Parides, Flory, & Shaffer, 1996; Shaffer, 1974; Shafii et al., 1985). The reasons for this familial aggregation are not yet known. It may reflect a genetic factor rather than a general index of family chaos and psychopathology; a family history has been shown to increase suicide risk even when studies have controlled for poor parent-child relationships and parental psychopathology (Brent et al., 1996; Gould et al., 1996). Furthermore, familial aggregation seems more likely to be due to genetic factors than imitation, based on Schulsinger's (1980) adoption study that reported a greater concordance of suicidal behavior with biological relatives than adoptive relatives and the higher rates of suicidal behaviors in monozygotic twins compared with dizygotic twins (Roy, Segal, Centerwall, & Robinette, 1991).

Parental Psychopathology

Studies have also found high rates of parental psychopathology, particularly depression and substance abuse, to be associated with completed suicide in adolescence (Brent et al., 1988; Brent, Perper, et al., 1994; Gould et al., 1996), as well as with suicidal ideation and attempts (e.g., Fergusson & Lynskey, 1995; Joffe et al., 1988; Kashani et al., 1989). Brent, Perper, and colleagues (1994) reported that a family history of depression and substance abuse significantly increased the risk of completed suicide, even after controlling for the victim's psychopathology. They concluded that familial psychopathology adds to suicide risk by mechanisms other than merely increasing the liability for similar psychopathology in an adolescent. In contrast, Gould and her colleagues (1996) found that the impact of parental psychopathology no longer contributed to the youth's suicide risk after the study controlled for the youth's psychopathology. To date, it is unclear precisely how familial psychopathology increases the risk for completed suicide.

Parental Divorce

Two large-scale psychological autopsy studies with general population controls (Brent, Perper, Mortiz, Allman, et al., 1993; Brent, Perper, et al., 1994; Gould et al., 1996) have found that suicide victims are more likely to come from nonintact families of origin, although the overall impact of

separation or divorce on suicide risk is small. In the New York Study (Gould et al., 1996), the association between separation/divorce and suicide decreased when accounting for parental psychopathology. This is consistent with the reported association of divorce and parental depression (Weissman, Fendrich, Warner, & Wickramaratne, 1992). Brent, Perper, et al. (1994) also showed a trend toward higher rates of mental disorder in the parents of both suicide victims and community controls in nonintact families of origin and reported that a nonintact family of origin was not associated with increased suicide risk after controlling for family history of psychopathology (Brent, Perper, et al., 1994).

Population-based studies have reported inconsistent results with regard to the import of divorce as a risk for suicide attempts. Several studies have reported an association of parental separation or divorce and suicide attempts (e.g., Andrews & Lewinsohn, 1992; Beautrais et al., 1996; Fergusson & Lynskey, 1995; Wunderlich et al., 1998); however, McKeown and colleagues (1998) did not find an association between suicidal behavior and the youth's not living with both parents, and Tousignant, Bastien, and Hamel (1993) found that the effects of divorce may be short term if there is adequate parental care. Overall, the impact of divorce on suicide risk appears to be small from both the psychological autopsy studies and community epidemiological studies.

Parent–Child Relationships

There are consistent findings that impaired parent-child relationships are associated with increased risk of suicide and suicide attempts (Beautrais et al., 1996; Brent, Perper, et al., 1994; Fergusson & Lynskey, 1995; Gould et al., 1996; Lewinsohn, Rohde, & Seeley, 1993; Lewinsohn et al., 1994; Tousignant et al., 1993). The New York and Pittsburgh studies, which are the two large controlled studies conducted to date, both report problematic parent-child relationships. The New York Study (Gould et al., 1996) found that suicide victims had significantly less frequent and less satisfying communication with their mothers and fathers. There was no evidence of more negative interactions between victims and their parents, nor was there evidence of a greater history of severe physical punishment. The Pittsburgh study (Brent, Perper, et al., 1994) reported that suicide victims were more likely to be exposed to parent-child discord and physical abuse. The reason for the discrepancies regarding parent-child conflict and physical abuse in the New York and Pittsburgh studies is unclear; the studies used a similar methodology with demographically matched community controls and comparable informants. Family aggression has been noted to be prevalent in suicidal children identified in the general community (Beautrais et al., 1996), as well as in suicidal children seen in clinical settings (see Spirito, Brown, Overholser, & Fritz, 1989, for a review.) A lack of family cohesion, high levels of conflict or dysfunction are consistently reported as increasing the risk of suicidal behaviors among teenagers (Adams, Overholser, & Lehnert, 1994; Asarnow et al., 1987; McKeown et al., 1998; Tousignant et al., 1993).

Adverse Life Circumstances

Stressful Life Events

The psychological autopsy research generally supports the association of life stressors, such as interpersonal losses (e.g., breaking up with a girlfriend or boyfriend) and legal or disciplinary problems, with suicide (Brent, Perper, Moritz, Baugher, Roth, et al., 1993; Gould et al., 1996; Marttunen, Aro, & Lonnqvist, 1993; Rich, Fowler, Fogarty, & Young, 1988; Runeson, 1990). The prevalence of specific stressors have been reported to vary depending on the psychiatric disorder of the

suicide victim (Brent, Perper, Moritz, Baugher, Roth, et al., 1993; Gould et al., 1996; Marttunen, Aro, Henrikksson, & Lonnqvist, 1994; Rich et al., 1988; Runeson, 1990). Interpersonal losses are consistently reported to be more common among suicide victims with substance abuse disorders (Brent, Perper, Moritz, Baugher, Roth et al., 1993; Gould et al., 1996; Marttunen et al., 1994; Rich et al., 1988). Legal or disciplinary crises were more common in victims with disruptive disorders (Brent, Perper, Moritz, Baugher, Roth, et al., 1993; Gould et al., 1996) or substance abuse disorders (Brent, Perper, Moritz, Baugher, Roth, et al., 1993). Despite these associations, specific stressors, such as legal and disciplinary problems, are still associated with an increased risk of suicide, even after adjusting for psychopathology (Brent, Perper, Moritz, Baugher, Roth et al., 1993; Gould et al., 1996).

Similar stressful life events have been reported to be risk factors for suicide attempts among adolescents (Beautrais, Joyce, & Mulder, 1997; Lewinsohn et al., 1996). Beautrais and her colleagues (1997) reported that interpersonal losses and conflicts and legal problems remained significant risk factors for serious suicide attempts after controlling for antecedent social, family, and personality factors. Another adverse experience that has recently been found to increase the risk for suicidal ideation is having been bullied or having bullied someone. Kaltiala-Heino and colleagues (1999) found in their study of 16,410 students aged 14 to 16 years in Finland that depression and severe suicidal ideation were more common among those students who were being bullied or who were bullies. Among girls, severe suicidal ideation was associated with frequently being bullied or being a bully, and for boys it was associated with being a bully. The highest risk of severe suicidal ideation, after adjusting for age, sex, and depression, was seen among students who were bullies (OR = 4.4); the next highest risk was among those who were both bullied and were also bullies (OR = 3.1). The odds ratio for those who were bullied was 2.5. The authors concluded that the need for psychiatric intervention should be considered not only for victims of bullying but also for bullies.

Sexual Abuse

Several community studies have found self-reported child sexual abuse (CSA) to be significantly associated with an increased risk of suicidal behavior (Davidson et al., 1996; Dube et al., 2001; Fergusson, Horwood, & Lynskey, 1996; Fergusson, Lynskey, & Horwood, 1996; Mullen, Martin, Anderson, Romans, & Herbison, 1996; Nelson et al., 2002; Paolucci, Genuis, & Violato, 2001), but only one study specifically focused on adolescent suicidal behavior (Fergusson, Horwood, & Lynskey, 1996; Fergusson, Lynskey, & Horwood, 1996). Fergusson, Horwood, and Lynskey (1996) found a relationship between the severity of reported CSA and rates of suicide attempts in adolescence, with the risk of suicide attempt increasing for increasing severity of CSA (OR for suicide attempt = 11.8 for CSA involving intercourse compared with OR = 2.9 for contact abuse not involving intercourse). In a psychological autopsy study comparing 67 adolescent suicide victims with 67 demographically matched living controls, Brent, Perper, et al. (1994) did not find a significant association between CSA and suicide (but the number determined to have been sexually abused was small, so it would have been hard to find an association; 2 suicide completers vs. 0 controls were sexually abused in the past year; 5 completers vs. 2 controls abused before the past year).

Because of methodological issues, it is difficult to determine whether the association between CSA and suicidal behavior is due to family background factors associated with the presence of CSA or whether CSA acts on its own to increase suicidality. In several studies (Fergusson, Horwood, & Lynskey, 1996; Mullen et al., 1996; Nelson et al., 2002), controlling for potentially confounding factors (e.g., family socioeconomic status, ethnicity, maternal overprotection, parental attachment, parental use of illicit drugs, parental separation in the individual's childhood, violence in the parental relationship) greatly reduced but did not eliminate the association between CSA and suicidality, suggesting that the increased risk of suicide may be partly but not entirely accounted for by factors associated with the presence of CSA. Nelson et al. (2002) attempted to separate the impact of CSA from the impact of family background factors associated with CSA by comparing adverse psychosocial outcomes, including suicidality, in members of twin pairs in which one twin reported CSA but the other did not. His results suggest that although family background risk factors associated with CSA do increase the risk of suicidality, CSA also acts independently as a risk factor for suicidality (Nelson et al., 2002). Mullen et al. (1996) and Fergusson, Horwood, and Lynskey (1996) caution that the direct contribution of CSA to suicidal behavior appears to be more modest than is often claimed and suggest that CSA is but one of many potential causal agents that create vulnerability for later suicidal behavior.

Socioenvironmental and Contextual Factors

Socioeconomic Status

Little information is available in the psychological autopsy literature on the association of socioeconomic status (SES) and suicide. Psychological autopsy studies either matched the cases and controls on this factor (e.g., Brent, Perper, Moritz, Allman, et al., 1993) or did not report it. Among the two studies with available information, Brent and his colleagues (1988) reported no difference between suicide victims and suicidal inpatients in socioeconomic status, and Gould et al. (1996) reported a differential ethnic effect in a comparison between suicide victims and community controls. Only African American, but neither white nor Latino, suicide victims had a significantly higher SES than their general population counterparts. Specifically, there was an overrepresentation of the middle class and an underrepresentation of the poorest strata among the African American suicides.

Higher rates of sociodemographic disadvantage have been found among youth making serious suicide attempts compared with community controls (Beautrais et al., 1996). Specifically, an increased risk of suicide attempts was found among youth who lacked formal educational qualifications, had low annual incomes, and had changed residence within the previous 6 months. Wunderlich et al., (1998) also reported that low SES was moderately associated with suicide attempts in a community sample of 14- to 24-year-olds in Munich, Germany.

School and Work Problems

Difficulties in school, not working or not being in school, and not going to college pose significant suicide risks (Gould et al., 1996). Youngsters who are unaffiliated with either a school or work institution appear to be at substantial risk for completing suicide. Shaffer (1974) noted that many suicides among children under the age of 15 took place after a period of absence from school and that a similar phenomenon had been reported for children who had attempted suicide (Teicher & Jacobs, 1966), suggesting that social isolation associated with absence from school may facilitate suicidal behavior.

Individuals who have made suicide attempts also appear more likely to have difficulties in school. Beautrais et al. (1996)

reported that serious suicide attempters were more likely to have "no formal educational qualification," which is roughly equivalent to dropping out of high school or not going to college. Lewis, Johnson, Cohen, Garcia, and Velez (1988) found that suicide attempters in a community-based sample had significantly lower school achievement than nonattempters. However, the relationship between attempted suicide and low school achievement was explained by the effects of depression. Wunderlich and colleagues (1998) reported that among a random sample of 3,021 young adults aged 14 to 24 years in Germany, school dropouts were 37 times more likely to attempt suicide, even after adjusting for other diagnostic and social risk factors.

Contagion and Imitation

Suicide Clusters

Research has indicated that "outbreaks" or clusters of completed suicides in the United States occur primarily among teenagers and young adults, with only sporadic and minimal effects beyond 24 years of age (Gould, Wallenstein, & Kleinman, 1990; Gould, Wallenstein, Kleinman, O'Carroll, & Mercy, 1990). Similar age-specific patterns have been reported for clusters of *attempted* suicides (Gould, Petrie, Kleinman, & Wallenstein, 1994). Estimates of the percentage of teenage suicides that occurs in clusters average between 1% and 2%, with considerable variation by state and year, yielding estimates from less than 1% to 13% (Gould, Wallenstein, & Kleinman, 1990). These estimates reflect only mortality data and, thus, do not include clusters of attempted suicides (Gould et al., 1994). Although most of the research on clustering of youth suicide has reported significant clustering (Brent et al., 1989; Gould et al., 1994; Gould, Wallenstein, & Kleinman, 1990; Gould, Wallenstein,

Kleinman, O'Carroll, et al., 1990), one study has found no clustering of adolescent suicides within a particular locale for a specified time frame (Gibbons et al., 1990). Given the relative rarity of suicide clusters, the examination of one location does not yield enough statistical power to clearly detect clustering. Case-control psychological autopsies of suicide clusters are attempting to identify the mechanisms underlying youth suicide clusters (Davidson et al., 1989; Gould, Forman, Kleinman, & Wallenstein, 1995). An ongoing psychological autopsy study funded by the National Institute of Mental Health, examining 53 suicide clusters that occurred in the United States between 1988 through 1996, should soon be able to identify the factors that initiate a suicide "outbreak" (Gould, 1999).

Media Influences

There is considerable evidence that suicide stories in the mass media, including newspaper articles (e.g., Barraclough, Shepherd, & Jennings, 1977; Blumenthal & Bergner, 1973; Etzersdorfer, Sonneck, & Nagel-Kuess, 1992; Ganzeboom & de Haan, 1982; Ishii, 1991; Jonas, 1992; Motto, 1970; Phillips, 1974, 1979, 1980; Stack, 1989, 1990a, 1990b, 1992, 1996; Wasserman, 1984), television news reports (e.g., Bollen & Phillips, 1982; Phillips & Carstensen, 1986; Stack, 1990a, 1991, 1993), and fictional dramatizations (e.g., Fowler, 1986; Gould, Shaffer, & Kleinman, 1988; Gould & Shaffer, 1986; Hawton, Simkin, et al., 1999; Holding, 1974, 1975; Schmidtke & Hafner, 1988), are followed by a significant increase in the number of suicides. Prior to 1990, most of the studies focused on U.S. populations, raising the question of whether the findings would generalize to other countries. Since 1990, the effect of media coverage on suicide rates has been documented in many other countries besides the United States, ranging

from Western countries including Austria (e.g., Etzersdorfer et al., 1992), Germany (e.g., Jonas, 1992), and Hungary (e.g., Fekete Mascai, 1990) to Australia (e.g., Hassan, 1995) and to East Asian countries, such as Japan (Ishii, 1991; Stack, 1996). The magnitude of the increase is proportional to the amount, duration, and prominence of media coverage (see Gould, 2001 for review). The impact of suicide stories on subsequent completed suicides has been reported to be greatest for teenagers (Phillips & Carstensen, 1986). Despite this ample body of literature supportive of the hypothesis that suicides dramatized in the media encourage imitation, a few studies did not report an association between media reports and subsequent suicides (Berman, 1988; Phillips & Paight, 1987) or found only an association among adolescent, not adult, suicides (Kessler, Downey, Stipp, & Milavsky, 1989). Stack's (2000) review of 293 findings from 42 studies indicated that methodological differences among studies were strong predictors of differences in their findings. Gould (2001) has summarized interactive factors that may moderate the impact of media stories, including characteristics of the stories, individual reader or viewer attributes, and social context of the stories.

Recently, alternative research strategies have been introduced to study media influences. In contrast to the ecological designs that use death certificate data to study differential community suicide rates, the newer paradigms include experimental designs that examine youths' reactions to media dramatizations or written vignettes about suicide (e.g., Biblarz, Brown, Biblarz, Pilgrim, & Baldree, 1991; Gibson & Range, 1991), content-analytic studies that assess the impact of specific display and content characteristics of media stories (Fekete & Schmidtke, 1995), and studies that directly assess suicide attempters following media displays (Hawton, Simkin, et al., 1999).

PROTECTIVE FACTORS

Protective factors are considered to be influences that buffer the impact of risk factors (Garmezy, 1985; Rutter, 1990). Although sometimes conceptualized as merely the opposite or low end of risk factors, protective factors are generally recognized to be different factors that actively promote positive behavior, which insulates against the consequence of risk factors (Jessor, 1991). Despite the burgeoning research literature during the past two decades on risk factors for youth suicide, there remains a paucity of empirical information on protective factors.

Family Cohesion

Family cohesion has been one focus of inquiry as a protective factor for suicidal behavior (e.g., McKeown et al., 1998; Rubenstein et al., 1989, 1998; Zhang & Jin, 1996). Increasing family cohesion was protective for suicide attempts in a longitudinal study of middle school students (McKeown et al., 1998). Similarly, Rubenstein et al. (1989, 1998) confirmed the role of family cohesion as a protective factor against adolescent suicidal behavior. Students who described family life in terms of a high degree of mutual involvement, shared interests, and emotional support were 3.5 to 5.5 times less likely to be suicidal than were adolescents from less cohesive families who had the same levels of depression or life stress.

Religiosity

The protective role of religiosity on suicide has been a focus of scientific investigation since Durkheim's formulation of a social integration model (Durkheim, 1966), yielding myriad ecological studies of aggregated populations (e.g., Lester, 1992; Neeleman, 1998; Neeleman & Lewis, 1999; Stack, 1983) as well as research among individuals (Hovey, 1999; Sorri, Henriksson, & Lonnqvist, 1996;

Stack, 1998; Stack & Lester, 1991). However, only recently has the protective value of religiosity against suicide, suicidal ideation, and perceived acceptability of suicide been documented in adolescents and young adults (Hilton, Fellingham, & Lyon, 2002; Siegrist, 1996; Zhang & Jin, 1996). Hilton and colleagues (2002) found that young men aged 15 to 34 who were active in the Church of Jesus Christ of Latter-Day Saints (LDS) were at lower risk of suicide than those who were less active or those who were not affiliated with the church. However, the results could be confounded with substance abuse because abstinence from both alcohol and illicit drugs is required of those who are "active" in the church. Siegrist's study (1996) of 2,034 German 15- to 30-year-olds' suicide attitudes found that frequent churchgoers approved of suicide less often than respondents who almost never attended church. Zhang and Jin (1996) found an inverse relationship between religiosity and suicide ideation among American college students, but among their Chinese sample from four universities in Beijing there was a positive correlation between religiosity and suicide ideation, perhaps reflecting the disparate role of religion in different cultures. Only a very small percentage (approximately 1%) of the population in China engages in religious rituals on a regular basis (Zhang & Jin, 1996). Miller and colleagues' (Miller, Warner, Wickramaratne, & Weissman, 1997) finding that maternal religiosity is a protective factor against offspring depression, independent of maternal bonding, social functioning, and demographics implies that maternal religiosity might also protect against suicide.

Means Restriction

In the United States, the most common method for committing suicide is by firearm, as previously discussed. Accordingly, restricting access to firearms may be a protective factor and a recommended prevention measure (Berman & Jobes, 1995; Garland & Zigler, 1993). This strategy is supported by the research finding that the presence of firearms in the home is a significant risk factor for youth suicide (Brent et al., 1991; Brent et al., 1988; Brent, Perper, Moritz, Baugher, Schweers, et al., 1993), as well as for adult suicides (Kellermann et al., 1992). Numerous studies have examined the relationship between firearms legislation and firearm suicides (see Miller & Hemenway, 1999, for a recent comprehensive review). Evidence provided by the studies suggests that gun legislation may have an impact on suicide mortality (Gould & Kramer, 2001). Unfortunately, recent legislative initiatives such as the 1994 Brady Bill, which imposes a delay in purchasing a handgun, did not yield promising results: A comparison of states that did and did not pass Brady Bill statutes showed no impact on the proportion of suicides attributable to firearms except in elderly males (Ludwig & Cook, 2000).

A concern often raised with regard to the effectiveness of means restriction is the likelihood that method substitution will occur. Some evidence of method substitution exists (Lester & Leenaars, 1993; Lester & Murrell, 1982; Rich, Young, Fowler, Wagner, & Black, 1990). However, method substitution does not appear to be an inevitable reaction to firearms restriction (Cantor & Slater, 1995; Carrington & Moyer, 1994; Lester & Murrell, 1986; Loftin, McDowall, Wiersema, & Cottey, 1991). Moreover, even if some individuals do substitute other methods, the chances of survival may be greater if the new methods are less lethal (Cantor & Baume, 1998).

Although firearm restriction may be a protective factor and a plausible approach to suicide prevention, the cultural belief in the individual's right to "keep and bear arms" probably makes it an unpalatable strategy for segments of American society. Less controversial prevention measures involve education about means restriction to parents of high-risk youth. For example, Kruesi and colleagues (1999) demonstrated that injury prevention education in emergency rooms led parents to take new action to limit access to lethal means, such as locking up their firearms. Furthermore, firearm education programs could be directed to parents of youth with alcohol and other substance problems. This strategy is supported by the finding that suicidal teenagers are more likely to use firearms when intoxicated (Brent et al., 1991).

Means restriction strategies also need to be considered for methods of suicide preferred by women, such as overdoses. Although overdoses may be less lethal than firearms, they have quite different implications for lethality depending on the agent. The selective serotonin reuptake inhibitors (SSRIs) and other newer antidepressants are considerably safer in overdose than tricyclics (Kapur, Mieczkowski, & Mann, 1992). However, the differential action among SSRIs (e.g., sedating or disinhibiting) must be considered when prescribing for suicidal individuals. Consequently, education programs for health practitioners regarding safer prescribing practices for high-risk patients is a recommended suicide prevention strategy.

Restricting access to lethal methods may prevent suicides; however, moves to restrict access must consider a number of complexities. Both physical availability and sociocultural acceptability are important determinants of choice of suicide method (Cantor & Baume, 1998), bringing about variation in method preference by gender and nationality (Gould & Kramer, 2001). The means restriction strategies with the greatest potential impact on reducing suicide will be those that target the more commonly preferred methods within a specific population (Cantor & Baume, 1998). Thus, restrictions of specific methods of suicide are likely to have different effects in different population subgroups and locales.

ASSOCIATION OF YOUTH SUICIDE WITH OTHER RISK BEHAVIORS

There is ample evidence that problem risk behaviors, such as drug use, delinquency, alcohol and sexual precocity are interrelated (Jessor, 1991). The interrelationships between suicidal ideation and behavior and other risk behaviors in adolescence has also been documented (Flisher et al., 2000; Garrison et al., 1993; King et al., 2001; Orpinas, Basen-Engquist, Grunbaum, & Parcel, 1995; Walter et al., 1995; Windle et al., 1992; Woods et al., 1997). In their evaluation of the 1993 Massachusetts YBRS from a representative sample of students in Grades 9 though 12, Woods et al. (1997) reported that ever attempting suicide was significantly associated with physical fights in the past 12 months, regular cigarette use in the past 30 days, substance use before the last sexual activity, lack of seat belt use, gun carrying in the past 30 days, and lifetime use of other drugs. Similarly, Garrison et al.'s (1993) sample from the South Carolina YRBS exhibited higher suicide risk given aggressive behavior, cigarette use, and substance use. The Texas YRBS (Orpinas et al., 1995) also showed that violence-related behaviors were associated with health risk behaviors, including suicidal ideation. In a similar pattern, Walter et al., (1995) reported that sexual, assaultive, and suicidal behavior significantly coexist among urban minority junior high school students, and secondary data analyses from the National Adolescent Student Health Survey (Windle et al., 1992) indicated that sex, alcohol use, and risky behaviors (such as swimming alone and taking someone else's medication) were significant predictors of suicidal ideation and attempts. In a community sample of 9- to 17-year-old youth, interviewed in the Methods for the Epidemiology of Child and Adolescent Mental Disorders (MECA) study, Flisher et al. (2000) reported that the risk of suicidal ideation and attempts increased 2.8-, 3.4-, 4.3-, 4.4-, and 6.6-fold when an individual engaged in the following risk behaviors: violence, intercourse, alcohol use, marijuana use, cigarette use, respectively. Similarly, King et al. (2001), studying the same population, found that the increased likelihood for suicidality with the risk behaviors remained even after adjusting for demographics and the youth's psychiatric diagnoses. However, the associations were greatly diminished after controlling for family environmental factors. King et al. (2001) concluded that the

> association between the risk behaviors and suicidal ideation or attempt may not be attributable to the direct deleterious effects of substance use or the other risk behaviors, but rather to possible shared psychosocial or psychopathological risk factors that underlie a propensity both for risk behaviors and for suicidal feelings or action. (p. 844)

CONCLUSIONS

This review has underscored mental illness, family characteristics, and stressful life events as key risk factors for youth suicide. A suicide risk model, adapted from Shaffer and colleagues (Shaffer, Garland, Gould, Fisher, & Trautman, 1988), highlights a constellation of predisposing and vulnerability characteristics in the young that combine with proximal factors within a social milieu to increase suicide risk. Predisposing and vulnerability characteristics include psychiatric disorder, particularly depression and substance abuse, and character and personality traits, including aggressive-impulsive behavior and biological and genetic factors. Proximal factors consist of stressful life events, and social milieu includes community suicide rates, cultural attitudes, and media displays. The presence of the underlying vulnerability predisposes an individual to suicidal behavior. This vulnerability reduces the capacity of the youth to respond adequately to stressors (Hurrelmann, 1989), while also precipitating stressors, such as getting into trouble at school (Gould et al., 1996). Other facilitating factors, such as exposure to a suicide, increase the risk burden. Protective factors, such as family cohesiveness, religiosity, and restriction of lethal means, may mitigate the impact of the accumulating suicide risk. Future research needs to increasingly identify factors that protect against suicidal behavior so that they may be enhanced.

Suicidal behavior and other risk behaviors in adolescence are interrelated, such that an adolescent who engages in one risk behavior is likely to have another problem behavior, including suicidal ideation and attempts. Furthermore, some risk behaviors, such as substance abuse, are antecedent risk factors for suicidal behavior. As such, optimal prevention and intervention strategies should target multiple risk behaviors to maximize their impact. Case-finding prevention strategies, which identify and refer suicidal youth (Gould & Kramer, 2001), should be comprehensive to identify multiple risk behavior, and risk reduction strategies can both minimize risks and increase protective factors for a range of risk behaviors. The next generation of evidence-based prevention practices should include a focus on multiple risk factors, because it is generally recognized that risk behaviors have many common causes that are probably interactive.

CHAPTER 33

Some Strategies to Prevent Youth Suicide

David A. Brent

One challenge of prevention is to find an intervention that is efficient as well as effective. Because youth suicide results from the convergence of multiple risk factors, prevention of youth suicide can be most effectively and efficiently achieved by developing and applying interventions that affect multiple risk factors. In this chapter, I briefly review studies of adolescent suicide that identify the most salient risk factors for suicide, try to sift the evidence in terms of a hierarchy of importance for those risk factors, and, finally, recommend some lines of intervention that may target multiple risk factors.

Shaffer et al. (1996) conducted a large, controlled psychological autopsy study of adolescent suicide. In males, the most salient psychiatric risk factors for adolescent suicide were past attempt, mood disorder, and substance abuse. In females, mood disorder and past attempt were both significant risk factors.

Additional psychosocial risk factors were parental psychiatric illness and suicide attempt, and "drifting"—that is, not being connected to school, work, or family (Gould, Fisher, Parides, Flory, & Shaffer, 1996).

Beautrais, Joyce, and Mulder (1997), in controlled studies of serious suicide attempters under the age of 30, identified mood disorder as having the largest population attributable risk (PAR), followed by substance abuse in both males and females (see Table 33.1). Comorbid conditions greatly increased the risk above that of single conditions. In analyses focusing on 13- to 24-year-old serious suicide attempters, sociodemographic disadvantage, adverse family circumstances, and psychiatric disorder all made significant contributions to risk (Beautrais et al., 1997).

Brent, Baugher, Bridge, Chen, and Chiappetta (1999), in pooling across several studies of adolescent suicide, found that in males, the most significant risk factors were

AUTHOR'S NOTE: From Western Psychiatric Institute and Clinic, 3811 O'Hara Street, Pittsburgh, PA 15213. This work was supported by NIMH grants MH55123, MH56612, MH61835, and Services for Teens at Risk (STAR), an appropriation from the Commonwealth of Pennsylvania.

Table 33.1 Population Atributable Risk (PAR, in percentages) in Youth Suicide/Serious Attempts

Variable	Transformed Regression	Grouped	Logistic Regression
Males			
Mood disorder	37.5	39.3	64.3
Substance abuse	28.2	31.5	26.1
Conduct/antisocial	28.3	31.0	34.1
Anxiety disorder	—	—	16.6
Past attempts	—	36.0	—
Gun in the home	59.8	69.2	—
Family history of psychiatric disorder	51.4	59.9	—
Females			
Mood disorder	69.3	64.5	79.2
Substance abuse	23.2	—	22.4
Conduct/antisocial	—	—	21.5
Anxiety disorder	—	—	7.0
Eating disorder	—	—	14.8
Handgun in the home	57.8	55.0	—
Past suicide attempt	—	62.9	—

SOURCE: Brent, Baugher, Bridge, Chen, and Chiappetta (1999), ages 10 to 19; Beautrais, Joyce, and Mulder (1997), ages < 30.

mood disorder, substance abuse, conduct disorder, gun in the home, family history of psychiatric disorder, and a past attempt (see Table 33.1). In females, mood disorder, past attempt, and a handgun in the home were the most significant risk factors.

In a study of familial transmission of suicide attempt, it was found that offspring of adult mood-disordered suicide attempters were highly likely to eventually make an attempt (Brent et al., 2002). This is important because the rate of parental suicide attempt and psychopathology is very high in samples of adolescent attempters and completers (Brent et al., 1999; Brent, Perper, et al., 1994; Gould et al., 1996). A subgroup that was highly likely to transmit suicidal behavior to their offspring was those who had a history of sexual abuse themselves. This group was likely to have children who also were sexually abused and, thus, had higher rates of mood disorder, substance abuse, and impulsive aggression. Familial

transmission was also more likely with greater family loading for suicidal behavior and increased impulsive aggression in parents and offspring (Brent et al., 2002).

Several patterns emerge from studies examining subsets of intersecting risk factors. First, the combination of mood disorder and past attempt puts youth at extraordinarily high risk for completion of suicide (Brent et al., 1999; Shaffer et al., 1996). Second, the combination of mood and substance abuse disorders poses at least a 50-fold increased risk for completed suicide (Beautrais et al., 1997; Brent et al., 1999; Shaffer et al., 1996). Third, the combination of mood disorder and impulsive aggression appears to increase the risk for attempt and completion (Brent et al., 2002; Brent, Johnson, et al., 1993; Brent, Johnson, et al., 1994). Fourth, parental mood disorder and attempt, particularly in the context of past parental sexual abuse, are strong risk factors for attempts in offspring (Brent et al., 2002). Finally, youth who are disconnected from major support systems (school, work, and family) appear to be at very high risk for completion, particularly in the context of other risk factors that are likely to contribute to their "drifting" status. It is likely that these 5 risk factors overlap substantially.

One approach to prevention is to develop multimodal interventions that target individuals who are likely to have combinations of risk factors. For example, treatment of depressed suicide attempters might involve a combination of state-of-the-art treatment of depression with antidepressants, as well as psychotherapy to deal with common antecedents of suicide attempts, related to interpersonal ineffectiveness, anger control, poor social problem solving, and family conflict. Initial treatment studies suggest that interpersonal and cognitive treatments may be helpful in reducing these psychosocial defects (Wood, Trainor, Rothwell, Moore, & Harrington, 2001). Adolescents with comorbid mood and substance abuse problems could be treated with selective serotonin reuptake inhibitors (SSRIs), which may, in addition to treating depressed mood, also decrease drive for substance use (Cornelius et al., 2000; Cornelius et al., 1997). Motivation interviewing may be used to enhance the likelihood of abstinence or, at least, to result in a reduction of the amount of substance use.

A fairly high proportion of suicide attempters have a parent with a mood disorder who has also attempted suicide. A multimodal approach to prevent the familial transmission of suicidal behavior could include (a) treatment of the parent's mood disorder, (b) prevention of transmission of mood disorders by cognitive behavioral treatment of youths with subsyndromal depression (Clarke et al., 2002), (c) identification of a history of sexual abuse in the parent and teaching the parent with an abuse history the importance of careful supervision

and monitoring to protect his or her child from being abused, and (d) detection and treatment of mood disorders, substance abuse, and impulsive aggression in the offspring.

As noted earlier—"drifting," that is, being disconnected from major social support systems—is strongly associated with completed suicide (Gould et al., 1996). Prevention demonstration projects in school settings have shown that adolescents on the verge of dropping out have many indicators of suicidal risk (Eggert, Thompson, Herting, & Nicholas, 1995; Thompson & Eggert, 1999; Thompson, Eggert, & Herting, 2000). Furthermore, intervention studies have shown that such marginal youths can be "reconnected," with subsequent improvement in school and family functioning. This approach, in combination with targeting of mood and substance abuse disorders, might be helpful for reducing suicide risk in youths who may present as dropouts, as runaways, or as referrals to juvenile justice or child welfare but who otherwise would not come to the attention of mental health specialists who could provide the required treatment.

Most of these interventions assume the ability to link the at-risk youth with some kind of intervention services. The approach I outlined might help to engage youths who otherwise might not connect with any services. For these disconnected, drifting youths who cannot be engaged, the intervention study of Motto and Bostrom (2001) may serve as a useful template. In this study, adult psychiatric patients who refused follow-up treatment were randomized to treatment as usual or to an experimental intervention, which consisted of a letter sent on a quarterly basis inquiring about the patient's welfare. The patients assigned to the experimental group had a lower suicide rate over a 5-year period. Some similar type of intervention may be useful for younger patients.

Finally, an intervention that focuses on firearms may be in order. Firearm availability accounts for a higher PAR than psychopathology for suicides under the age of 16 (Brent et al., 1999). A loaded gun in the home is one of the sole risk factors for suicide in adolescents with no apparent psychopathology (Brent, Perper, Moritz, Baugher, Roth, et al., 1993; Brent, Perper, Moritz, Baugher, Schweers, et al., 1993). Therefore, an intervention to reduce access to guns may lower the suicide rate.

Simply asking parents of patients to remove guns from the home is not very effective. In one study of depressed adolescents participating in a clinical psychotherapy trail, only 27% of parents with guns in the home removed them when asked (Brent, Baugher, Birmaher, Kolko, & Bridge, 2000). People who were less likely to remove guns when asked were married with some degree of marital dissatisfaction and had a handgun or a loaded gun. Parents were more likely to remove the gun if the patient had made a recent suicide attempt and the parent was a single parent. What can be inferred from the data is that if the parent is not the gun owner, and particularly if the relationship with the spouse is discordant, talking with the non-gun-owning parent about removal is quite ineffective. Probably, parents whose guns are stored loaded keep the gun for protection, and consistent with other data, they are less likely to want to remove guns (Webster, Wilson, Duggan, & Pakula, 1992). Finally, if the child has made a recent attempt, parents were more likely to comply with the request to remove firearms, presumably because they concurred with the clinician's assessment of high suicidal risk. Therefore, more effective approaches to securing firearms would include (a) talking directly with the gun-owning parent, (b) asking the parent to secure rather then remove the gun, and (c) making sure that parents understand the increased risk for suicide associated with having firearms in the home.

CHAPTER 34

Implications of Focusing on Black Youth Self-Destructive Behaviors Instead of Suicide When Designing Preventive Interventions

Sean Joe

Reacting to reports of a precipitous rise from the 1980s to the early 1990s in the rate of suicide among African American youths, the U.S. Surgeon General declared in 1999 that suicide among this population was an emergent public health problem (Centers for Disease Control and Prevention [CDC], 1998b; Griffith & Bell, 1989; Shaffer, Gould, & Hicks, 1994; U.S. Public Health Service, 2000). Uncommon in the past, suicide among African American adolescents has increased sharply since 1985 and is now the third leading cause of death among 15- to 24-year-old African Americans (Miniño, Arias, Kochanek, Murphy, & Smith, 2002). From 1980 to 1995, the suicide rate increased 114% for 10- to 19-year-old African Americans, stemming mostly from the rise in completed suicides among males (Goldsmith, Pellmar, Kleinman, & Bunney, 2002). Among African American men, Joe

and Kaplan (2001) found the steepest increase in the rate of suicide was for adolescent males aged 15 to 19 years: During the period of 1979 to 1997, the suicide rate increased by 70% (from 6.7 to 11.4 per 100,000 individuals) among these young men. Joe and Kaplan (2002) attribute this increase to a growing use of firearms to complete suicides among African American adolescent males; for suicides among the 15- to 19-year-old group alone, firearms accounted for 70% of all suicides among African American males. From 1979 to 1997, firearm suicide rates among African American males increased by 132% for those aged 15 to 19 and by 24% for those aged 20 to 24 (Joe & Kaplan, 2002). Despite these alarming statistics and increased attention from the public health community, very little is known about what has caused the rise in suicidal behavior itself among young African American males.

EXPLAINING THE INCREASED RISK

Frameworks for understanding the more recent patterns of suicide completion and the use of firearms among younger African Americans remain speculative. Scholars have pointed to several psychosocial risk factors, including frustration, rage, despair, alienation, fatalistic behavior, social deprivation, and immense social stress associated with unemployment, racism, and poverty (Bell & Clark, 1998; Seiden, 1970); family disorganization (Davis, 1980b; Hendin, 1969); external restraint and status integration (Davis, 1980a; Gibbs & Martin, 1964; Henry & Short, 1954; Maris, 1969); the breakdown in traditional social institutions, such as the church, family, and schools (Davis, 1980a, 1982; Gibbs, 1988; Smith & Carter, 1986); migration (Davis, 1980a; Prudhomme, 1938); and living in northern or urban areas, substance abuse, mental disorders, homosexuality (Rotheram-Borus, Hunter, & Rosario, 1994), and delinquency (Gibbs, 1997). Status integration theories—namely, assimilation and acculturation into mainstream culture frameworks, based on the work of Durkheim (1951)—are the most prominent explanations for changes in the rates of suicide completion among African Americans (Gibbs, 1988; Henry & Short, 1954; Maris, 1969; Prudhomme, 1938). There is moderate, yet inconclusive, evidence to support this hypothesis for young African American male suicidal behavior (Burr, Hartman, & Matteson, 1999; Gould, Fisher, Parides, Flory, & Shaffer, 1996).

Despite the breadth of explanations, empirical evidence has insufficiently explained the rise in suicide completion, particularly in firearm-related suicide among young African American males. Moreover, changes in the patterns of African Americans' suicidality cannot be accounted for by a single sociological, pharmacological, or psychological explanation; rather, a multitheoretical approach may prove more effective. Single theoretical approaches are not comprehensively adequate to account for the complex relationship between suicide and African American social or cultural beliefs about suicide, phenomenological and historical experiences with physical and psychological strain, unique expression of depressive symptomology, mental health service use history, or involvement in other high-risk behaviors (Davis, 1982; Gibbs, 1988; Poussaint & Alexander, 2000).

Instead, the recent increase in suicide risk for young African Americans is best explained from a historical, phenomenological, gendered, and multitheoretical perspective. Using an intergenerational strain framework, the author extends the prominent status integration hypothesis, originally proposed by Prudhomme (1938), to explain recent changes in the patterns of African American suicidality. Prudhomme contended that, as African Americans further integrated into American society, successive generations could not bear the strains that earlier generations could withstand. The extended intergenerational strain framework used in this analysis advances Prudhomme's conclusion using two primary hypotheses.

First, recent changes in the pattern of suicide among young African Americans may reflect their experience of a new form of social deprivation. For instance, they grow up in more extreme and concentrated poverty, at a time in which the protection provided by parents, the church, and other community institutions has been considerably weakened (Wilson, 1996). Equally ominous, the ecological landscape—marked by unprecedented underemployment and ineffective social institutions—has led to profound hopelessness, despair, demoralization, loneliness, depression, and violence among many young African Americans (Gibbs, 1997; Holinger et al., 1994; Vega, Gil, Warheit, Apospori, & Zimmerman, 1993; Wilson, 1996). New generations of these children have been raised amid extreme firearm-related violence and within segregated communities that lack the symbols of hope , which helped earlier generations face the challenges of adverse life circumstances (Polednak, 1997). Tragically, far too many young African Americans, males in particular, escape these conditions today by adopting self-destructive lifestyles (Spencer, Dupree, & Hartmann, 1997).

The second component, the hypothesis of transmissible psychological strain, contends that, with each succeeding generation, there is a change in the coping mechanisms and psychological armor used by African Americans, particularly their normative understanding and interpretation of the impact of racism or discrimination on preventing individual merit from resulting in individual success. These changes make younger African Americans more susceptible to suicidal forces. One reason is that there has been a change in the normative beliefs and expectations, personal efficacy, and attributional orientation of succeeding generations of younger African Americans (Veroff, Douvan, & Kulka, 1981), who may be more likely to accept suicidal behavior than older adults. These psychosocial changes represent an unexpected outcome of American civil and social rights movements, which have been crucial in raising the expectations, achievement opportunity, and aspirations of African Americans. However, these movements have also led to a belief among many African American youths that their opportunities are limited only by their skills and motivation. Many become frustrated, angry, and depressed when those expectations do not materialize, because as much as normative achievement expectations have changed, many of the institutional barriers associated with the legacy of racism continue to thwart individual effort and ability. Younger African Americans of today, therefore, are more likely than previous generations to believe that their life events are solely dependent on their actions, which means they are more susceptible to depression and other risk factors for suicide.

Understanding changes in the attributional orientation of African Americans is central to the hypothesis of transmissible strain. Several researchers have used attributional orientation to explain African American mental health (Jackson et al., 1996; LaVeist, Sellers, & Neighbors, 2001). At one time, an external attributional orientation (which refers to system blaming) among African Americans buffered this group from internalizing limited individual success dictated by a raced society; more recently, this mindset has been exchanged for a more internal orientation (which refers to self-blaming). Traditionally, African Americans have been able to maintain a healthy psychological outlook in the face of racial discrimination by viewing personal setbacks in the context of external realities of racial social structure endemic to life in America. An external attributional style helps them to cope, through enhanced personal efficacy and increased self-esteem, with personal disappointments resulting from interpersonal or institutional factors. Thus, an external attributional orientation protects from the negative consequences of exposure to various types of discrimination.

These social, ecological, and psychological changes in the life of African Americans in the United States may explain changes in the pattern of suicide among males, but not females. African American female adolescents do not complete suicide at a rate comparable to males. The lower rate of suicide completion among females may be attributed to their being more likely to seek and receive emotional support (Gibbs, 1988), having different achievement expectations and experiences with strain, having less access to firearms, or having stronger religious affiliations than males (Gibbs & Hines, 1989).

The proposed intergenerational strain framework clearly provides a more complex and comprehensive multihypotheses explanation of the recent changes in the patterns of suicide completion and suicidal behavior among young African American males. Although over 90% of suicide victims have a significant, often undiagnosed and untreated psychiatric illness at the time of death (Brent, Perper, Moritz, Allman, et al., 1993; Shaffer et al., 1996), historical and cultural factors moderate the effects of social conditions and psychiatric illness on changes in the patterns of suicidal behavior among African Americans. The hypotheses proposed by this perspective should be researched and considered when designing suicide awareness and preventive interventions for African American youths. Furthermore, the significant historical and cultural factors highlighted in this theoretical framework must also be addressed when designing suicide preventive initiatives for young African American males.

FOCUS ON SELF-DESTRUCTIVE BEHAVIORS

The first hypothesis in the intergenerational strain framework highlights the many macro-level environmental changes fostering maladaptive coping strategies among African American males, which are often expressed as multiple forms of self-destructive behaviors, including suicide, interpersonal violence, and substance abuse. A self-destructive behavior perspective reflects a shift away from studying single problem behaviors toward focusing on multiple problem behaviors linked together by common risk factors. Furthermore, it highlights the importance of examining the interplay between individual, social, environmental, cultural, and psychological factors commonly associated with influencing multiple forms of negative health risk behaviors among African American youths. Indeed, a self-destructive behavior perspective may be more accurate in describing the prevalence of suicide among this population or the many problem behaviors that share similar self-injurious risk and precipitating factors as suicide. For example, scholars argue that the actual number of suicides among African Americans may be considerably higher if the number of deaths that were technically misclassified as homicides or accidents were included (Satcher, 1998; Seiden, 1970; Wolfgang, 1959). One study also found that more misclassifications for cause of death occur for African Americans (14.92%) (Phillips & Ruth, 1993) than for other groups.

The concept "self-destructive behavior" as used in this discussion refers to externalizing behaviors displayed by adolescents in which the resultant fatal physical harm to them is a priori—an expected, accepted, or intentional outcome. Self-destructive behaviors differ from thrill-seeking behaviors; in the latter case, adolescents accept the possibility that physical harm could result from their actions rather than intend or expect such an outcome. Behaviors that could be considered self-destructive range from those for which the risk of fatality tend to be distal, such as substance use, to behaviors that pose a more immediate and lethal health threat, such as suicidal behavior.

An emphasis on the self-destructive nature of young African Americans' risky externalizing behaviors allows for an examination of shared risk association between multiple unhealthy behaviors among this population. Researchers have argued that effective prevention programs must consider the multiplicity and interrelatedness that exists among various maladaptive behaviors predicated by common risk factors (Seifer, Sameroff, Dickstein, Keitner, & Miller, 1996). To date, researchers have paid only limited attention to the shared association of multiple risky health behaviors at the individual level and to the testing of strategies to prevent or reduce multiple problem behaviors among African American youths. In addition, a focus on self-destructive behaviors is a potentially more effective perspective for designing interventions that target culturally taboo behaviors and health outcomes, such as suicide.

The pervasive social stigma associated with suicide and psychiatric illness in African American communities is a significant barrier to designing effective preventive interventions for this population (Poussaint & Alexander, 2000) and to engaging the black community in efforts to increase suicide awareness. Although the stigma of suicide is not unique to African Americans, it is extremely powerful among this group, primarily for religious reasons. A recent study reports that African Americans are less accepting of suicide than European Americans, a finding attributed to their more orthodox religious beliefs (Neeleman, Wessely, & Lewis, 1998). Early's (1992) unique study of religion and suicide found that African Americans express a combined religious condemnatory belief and secular attitude about suicide as a mortal sin and define it as a "white thing" that is foreign to African American culture. The same normative and religious belief that African Americans hold about suicide, which could serve as a possible protective factor, is also a potential barrier, given the clear descriptive evidence that suicide does occur more frequently than previously considered. Of concern is the potentially adverse effect of promoting or normalizing suicidal behavior among this population given its unprecedented and epic resiliency in the face of continued social and psychological oppression.

Shifting the rhetoric around suicide prevention toward a focus on self-destructive behaviors could avoid many of the religious and cultural stigmas of suicide and may find greater support within the African American community, thus making it easier to engage the community in discussions about suicide prevention and in preventive interventions. In addition, African Americans tend to draw a fine, yet important, distinction between suicide and other self-destructive behaviors, such as drug abuse and drinking (Early 1992; Poussaint & Alexander, 2000), and tend to be more forgiving of self-destructive behaviors other than suicide. Thus, preventive interventions focused more on self-destructive behaviors are also more likely to find support among the African American community and to be successful in reducing the risk for African American adolescents of suicide as well as other forms of self-destructive behaviors.

IMPLICATIONS FOR PREVENTION

Specific recommendations for preventive interventions are limited by the lack of scientifically tested interventions for African Americans. Nevertheless, when considered in light of the trends and patterns presented above and within the context of an intergenerational strain framework, suicide prevention programs targeting young African American males appear to be warranted. To overcome a major barrier to prevention efforts—specifically, the belief that suicide does not occur among this population—the public health community must adopt a more palatable approach to suicide prevention by focusing on self-destructive behaviors. This perspective suggests that greater emphasis should be placed on targeting multiple forms of self-destructive behaviors while encouraging families and communities to engage in mental wellness promotion, prevention, and increased mental health services.

Prevention efforts should also focus on the sociocultural and gendered differences in the expression of depression and or suicidal intent among this population—for example, youths who are verbally abusive, report somatic symptoms, have conflict relations with peers, and act out in school. These behaviors may signal feelings of alienation, hopelessness, and despair among African American youths, which often result in confrontations with the police and entry into the juvenile justice system. Interventions focusing on family attachment (such as child-parent bonding) and the development of more nurturing psychosocial environments for African American youths may also prove valuable in reducing the risks associated with suicidal behavior (Stack, 1996; Summerville, Kaslow, Abbate, & Cronan, 1994). In addition, interventionists must also consider macro-level strategies to combat the strain many young African American adolescents experience when structural barriers limit opportunities for individual success. Effort must be initiated to reduce maladaptive coping strategies and the internal blaming that occurs among African American adolescents that result from the low presence of effective developmental institutions. For example, borrowing from an intervention approach used by child abuse advocates, having an adult say, "It is not your fault," and identifying what is beyond individual control may be an effective strategy for helping young African Americans make sense of their stressful developmental experiences.

Religious institutions and other community-based organizations, as well as institutions developed by the African American community, may be more acceptable resources than municipal agencies for conducting preventive interventions, including psychological screening for illness associated with suicide and for depression and substance abuse, in particular. Resources must be made available through joint public health and community initiatives that focus on reducing the stigma of psychiatric services among African Americans while increasing access to mental health services in poor communities. I would suggest the development of targeted preventive efforts to increase the level of awareness regarding suicide in the juvenile justice system, in schools, in youth service and recreational centers (e.g., Boys and Girls Club), in churches and local organizations, and among other community members who are frequently in contact with young African American men. Furthermore, the training of natural supports in the community to recognize the signs and symptoms of suicide risk, particularly depression, is recommended.

In addition, it is essential to address the availability of firearms as a pivotal risk factor among suicidal African American male adolescents. Although it is not possible to draw more definitive causal links from the current research on African American firearm suicide, the connection between firearm possession and suicides is well documented (see, e.g., Kaplan & Geling, 1998; Kellermann et al., 1992). Therefore, health professionals need to conduct probing histories of the availability of firearms with their depressed and suicidal African American adolescent patients. For prevention purposes, parents and caring adults should be encouraged to remove firearms from the home. As a sound public health practice, it is easier to remove the physical agent of potential self-inflicted injury than to modify risk-taking behavior (Boyd & Moscicki, 1986).

Early preventive interventions with young children must also become an integral part of more coordinated suicide prevention efforts. For example, children can benefit from stress management techniques that seek to impart more traditional African American religious values and increase a child's sense of ethnic identification and social connectedness. Preventive efforts must target boys who are at the greatest risk, particularly those who are in dysfunctional families or abusive circumstances, who are sexual and gender minorities, and who have histories of mental illness. Early prevention initiatives for young African Americans must also incorporate youth development activities that mitigate the adverse effect of poverty and assist their healthy transition from childhood to adulthood.

In summary, suicide prevention efforts targeted at African Americans should be tested with the most rigorous scientific approaches appropriate and should be comprehensive enough to address the complex dynamics of African American suicidal behaviors. In addition, prevention trials should be developed to monitor closely the potentially adverse effects of interventions and the increased awareness among African Americans of suicidal behaviors.

FUTURE RESEARCH

The empirical literature on African American suicide or suicidal behaviors is inadequate for designing primary or secondary interventions. Why were previous generations of African Americans able to endure centuries of epic cruelty and manage to avoid succumbing to hopelessness and depression, whereas recent generations experience higher rates of suicide among the young? Beyond age and gender, researchers are unable to provide a more detailed profile of the African American adolescent males most at risk for suicide completion, which limits efforts to design preventative interventions.

Nonetheless, researchers have identified important risk and protective factors. The few studies that have examined suicidality among African American adolescents have identified depression, delinquent behavior, lack of family support, history of abuse, and, in a few cases, substance abuse as risk factors (Hernandez, Lodico, & DiClemente, 1993; Juon & Ensminger, 1997; King, Raskin, Gdowski, Butkus, & Opipari, 1990; Morano, Cisler, & Lemerond, 1993; Negron, Piacentini, Graae, Davies, & Shaffer, 1997; Summerville, Abbate, Siegel, Serravezza, & Kaslow, 1992). However, most of this research has focused on female suicide attempters, and none has looked at the risk factors for African American male adolescents who attempt or complete suicide.

Regarding protective factors for African American youths, Gibbs (1988) cited strong kinship ties and social support. Others have found that family support and cohesive families protected African American college students from suicidal ideation and depression (Kimbrough, Molock, & Walton, 1996). Although no one has examined the role of cultural identity in preventing suicidal behaviors in African Americans, several have found that adolescents with positive ethnic identity are less prone to dysphoric affect and academic problems and are less likely to be sexually active (Charlot-Swilley, 1998). If behavioral scientists want to reduce the incidence of suicide in the African American community, it is as important to focus on those factors that may serve as buffers against suicide, not just on the risks these youths face.

Furthermore, given the views regarding suicide in the African American community, priority should be given to rigorous qualitative and ethnographic studies. Ethnographic methods may be more effective for documenting the complex experiences of African Americans and could provide greater understanding of what has caused the recent increases in African American suicidal behavior.

More specific data (e.g., segmented by race, age, socioeconomic status, sex, and geography) are needed to disentangle the relative effects of race and class on suicidal outcomes. Furthermore, psychological autopsy studies and further examination of the role and availability of firearms as a potential vector for suicide must be conducted (Joe & Kaplan, 2002). In addition, future research is needed to further our understanding of the factors outlined in the intergenerational strain framework, including the following:

- The roles of racism and segregation on attribution orientation
- The effect on short- and long-term suicide trends of socioeconomic status, changes in the neighborhood context, availability of firearms, and adverse psychosocial and developmental experiences of African American males over the last three decades
- The shared etiological roots of substance abuse and other self-destructive behaviors (unprotected sexual behavior, suicidal behavior) in the African American community
- The protective factors (e.g., the role of religious activity, spirituality, extended family, and perceptions of neighborhoods) and, in particular, how risk and protective factors vary with gender

Finally, research on suicidal behavior among African American youths may make significant contributions to the suicide prevention field as a whole. For example, an increased understanding of the social, economic, historical, and cultural context in which the suicidal behavior of African American youths occurs may enhance clinical awareness, research designs, and policy response to self-destructive behaviors in other minority populations. Moreover, given the projected doubling of the African American population in the United States by 2050 and the social conditions experienced by African American youths, the creation of evidence-based preventive interventions capable of keeping succeeding cohorts of young African American males from engaging in multiple forms of self-destructive behaviors would be a significant public health accomplishment.

Part III

Section D

Alcohol, Tobacco, and Drugs

CHAPTER 35

Alcohol, Tobacco, and Marijuana Use Among Youth

Same-Time and Lagged and Simultaneous-Change Associations in a Nationally Representative Sample of 9- to 18-Year-Olds

ROBERT HORNIK

Adolescent alcohol, tobacco, and marijuana use are substantially associated in all cross-sectional surveys. A smaller number of studies shows a sequence of initiation of these three (and other illicit) substances (Kandel, 2002). The general conclusion in the literature is that alcohol or cigarette use precede marijuana use and that these three precede harder drug use, although there are some exceptions, particularly when intensity of use is included.

The sequence of drug involvement from use of alcohol or cigarettes or both to use of marijuana and then to other illicit drugs is well documented (e.g., Duncan, Duncan, & Hops, 1998; Kandel, 1975; Kandel & Yamaguchi, 1993; Merrill, 1999). A number

of cross-sectional and longitudinal studies have outlined the progression from licit (for adults) to illicit drugs among adolescents and young adults. This phenomenon has been found in different ethnic groups and in different countries (Barnes, Welte, & Hoffman, 2002; Blaze-Temple & Lo, 1993; Manning et al., 2001; Sullivan & Farrell 1999). In this "gateway" theory, individuals progress from a lower-stage drug to the next higher-stage drug; an individual is unlikely to proceed to a high-level drug without first having tried a substance at a lower stage (Labouvie & White, 2002).

In general, increasing use of a substance is a precursor for progressing to the next stage. Lewinsohn et al. (1999) found that daily smoking was associated with increased risk of

AUTHOR'S NOTE: The author is grateful to Vani Henderson for research assistance in preparing this chapter. The data were collected by Westat, under contract to the National Institute on Drug Abuse on Contract Number N01DA-8-5063 as part of the evaluation of the National Youth Anti-Drug Media Campaign. The author and Dr. David Maklan of Westat are coprincipal investigators for that evaluation.

future marijuana, hard-drug, and multiple-drug use disorders. Bailey (1992) found that increasing frequencies of drug and cigarette use may be markers for more usage of illicit substances. Kandel, Yamaguchi, and Chen (1992) also found that frequency of use at a lower stage of drug use is a strong predictor of further progression. However, although the gateway effect seems to hold true among drug "experimenters," it may not be appropriate for heavy or drug-dependent users. Some studies (Golub & Johnson, 1994; Mackesy-Amiti, Fendrich, & Goldstein, 1997) have found that serious drug users were less likely to follow the typical sequence identified in previous studies (alcohol, then marijuana, followed by other illicit drugs).

Although a developmental sequence in drug involvement has been identified, the use of a drug at one stage does not inevitably lead to the use of drugs higher up in the sequence (Golub & Johnson, 1994) or mean that current use will extend indefinitely (Chen & Kandel, 1995).

A new national longitudinal survey of youth confirms many of those results and extends them in one important way. Prior research either depended on restricted or national cross-sectional surveys (cf. Kandel & Yamaguchi, 2002) or made use of longitudinal surveys of a restricted population (Bailey, 1992; Duncan et al., 1998; Kandel & Yamaguchi, 1999). In contrast, this survey follows a U.S. nationally representative sample of 9- to 18-year-olds for an 18-month period. This report focuses on transitions from nonuse to any use of each of the three substances. The study makes it clear for a national population that marijuana use is rarely found and rarely initiated absent tobacco and alcohol use, but the reverse is not true.

The data are drawn from a set of national surveys (the National Survey of Parents and Youth) sponsored by the National Institute on Drug Abuse for the purpose of evaluating the National Youth Anti-Drug Media Campaign. The evaluation is being undertaken by Westat and the Annenberg School for Communication of the University of Pennsylvania. The survey reported here includes a nationally representative sample of youth initially interviewed in the first half of 2000 and then reinterviewed in the last half of 2001, on average about 18 months later. The total sample size was 2,435 youth between the ages of 9 and 17 at the first interview and between 10 and 18 at the second interview. The response rate for the baseline survey was 64%, and 81% of those first interviewed were reinterviewed at the follow-up wave. The questionnaires were administered in-home on laptop computers, with all questions and answers appearing on the screen and read to the respondents and all answers given by touching the computer screen. The respondents were promised confidentiality. These youth have been reinterviewed for a third time in the last half of 2002, but those data are not yet available.

The questions used for the analyses presented here appear in Table 35.1. Additional questions were also asked about frequency and recency of all these behaviors, but the analysis in this chapter addresses only the information about whether the substance was ever used.

All three behaviors were highly associated with the age of the respondent.

About 25% of all youth in the sample reported some prior use of alcohol, 17% reported prior use of cigarettes, and 8% reported prior use of marijuana. Each of these behaviors was closely associated with the age of the respondent (see Figure 35.1).

These three behaviors are highly associated in the population.

At the baseline measurement wave, the gamma between any marijuana use and any alcohol use was .96, the gamma between any marijuana use and any cigarette use was .97, and the gamma between any alcohol use and any cigarette use was .90. All three relationships are presented in Table 35.2.

Marijuana use is rarely found absent tobacco and cigarette use.

Table 35.1   Questions Used to Measure Ever Use of Tobacco, Alcohol, and Marijuana

Have you ever smoked part or all of a cigarette?

Never	0
Once or twice, but not in the last 30 days	1
Occasionally in the past, but not in the last 30 days	1
Regularly in the past, but not in the last 30 days	1
I have smoked in the last 30 days	1
REFUSED	
DON'T KNOW	

Have you ever, even once, had a drink of any alcoholic beverage, that is, more than a few sips?

Yes	1
No	0
REFUSED	
DON'T KNOW	

The next questions are about marijuana and hashish. Marijuana is sometimes called pot, grass, or weed. Marijuana is usually smoked, either in cigarettes, called joints, or in a pipe. Hashish is a form of marijuana that is also called hash. From now on, when marijuana is mentioned, it means marijuana or hashish.

Have you ever, even once, used *marijuana?*

Yes	1
No	0
REFUSED	
DON'T KNOW	

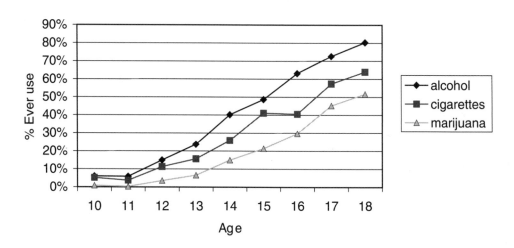

Figure 35.1

Barely 1% of youth who had never used cigarettes or never used alcohol claimed they had used marijuana (in contrast, about 12% and 19% of those who had never used marijuana claimed to have used cigarettes and alcohol respectively).

Table 35.2 Cross-Sectional Associations of Marijuana Use, Cigarette Use, and Alcohol Use

	Cigarette Use		Alcohol Use	
	No	Yes	No	Yes
Marijuana Use				
No	99%	60%	99%	71%
Yes	1%	40%	1%	29%
N	1,990	429	1,818	602
Alcohol Use				
No	86%	25%		
Yes	14%	75%		
N	1,992	430		

Table 35.3 Comparison of Marijuana Use at Baseline and 18-Month Follow Up

Marijuana Use Follow-Up	Marijuana Use Baseline		
	No	Yes	N
No	1,997 (83%)[a]	23 (1%)	2,020
Yes	231 (10%)	170 (7%)	401
N	2,228	193	2,421

a. Number of Cases (% of total).

The relationship between any use of alcohol and cigarettes was not so clear-cut, although it did favor alcohol as the prior behavior. Of those who had never used cigarettes, 14% had used alcohol, and of those who had never used alcohol, 6% claimed to have used cigarettes. These sets of relationships suggest some ordering between the three behaviors, with alcohol trial first, tobacco use second much of the time, and marijuana use third. However, because all these data are cross-sectional, it is difficult to be certain about temporal implications.

Youth provide consistent answers over time to these questions about ever having used each of these three substances. Youth were reinterviewed an average of 18 months after their first interview. Their reports about substance use were highly consistent. Three patterns of responses were considered credible: never use both times, some use both times, or never use the first time and some use the second time. An inconsistent report would have been a claim of some use the first time but never use the second time. In practice, these inconsistent reports were very rare for marijuana (1%) and tobacco use (2%) and rare for alcohol use (4%). The relative odds of subsequent report of use, given prior use versus prior nonuse, was 17 times for alcohol, 49 times for cigarettes, and 64 times for marijuana. The gammas for the three substance uses over time were .89, .96, and .97 for alcohol, cigarettes, and marijuana, respectively. Tables 35.3, 35.4, and 35.5 display these over-time associations.

Prior use predicts subsequent initiation of other substance use among nonusers at baseline.

For each of the three substances, it is possible to see which youth who were nonusers of a substance at baseline were more likely to initiate use in the next 18 months as a function of other substance use. For all three substances, prior use of another substance was predictive of initiation. As previously noted, about 75% of the respondents had never used alcohol when they were first interviewed. Most had never used cigarettes either. But those who had already used cigarettes at baseline were almost 6 times as

Table 35.4 Comparison of Cigarette Use at Baseline and 18-Month Follow Up

	Cigarette Use Baseline		
Cigarette Use Follow Up	No	Yes	N
No	1,730 (71%)[a]	50 (2%)	1,780
Yes	267 (11%)	381 (16%)	648
N	1,997	431	2,428

a. Number of cases (% of total).

Table 35.5 Comparison of Alcohol Use at Baseline and 18-Month Follow Up

	Alcohol Use Baseline		
Alcohol Use Follow Up	No	Yes	N
No	1,428 (59%)[a]	108 (4%)	1,536
Yes	393 (16%)	496 (20%)	889
N	1,821	604	2,425

a. Number of cases (% of total).

Table 35.6 Prediction of Follow Up Alcohol Use, by Baseline Cigarette and Marijuana Use Among Youth Who Had Not Used Alcohol at Baseline

	Cigarette Use Baseline		Marijuana Use Baseline	
Alcohol Use Follow Up	No	Yes	No	Yes
No	81%	43%	79%	25%
Yes	19%	58%	21%	75%
N	1,714	106	1,801	16
Gamma	.70		.84	

likely as those who had not smoked at baseline to initiate alcohol use in the succeeding 18 months, as shown in Table 35.6.

That table also shows that marijuana use at baseline was highly predictive of alcohol initiation. Prior marijuana users were 11 times as likely to initiate alcohol use as were nonusers. But because there were few youth who had not used alcohol who had used marijuana (only 16 of 1,817), this association is trivial.

Most youth had not initiated cigarette use at baseline (83%). Subsequent initiation was somewhat associated with both marijuana use and with alcohol use as shown in Table 35.7. However, as with the previous analysis for alcohol, there were very few youth who had not used cigarettes who had used marijuana (*n* of 23, 1% of the sample). So once again, the significant prediction by marijuana use at baseline of initiation of cigarette use (despite a relative odds of 3.5) is not worth much attention. The alcohol effects were similar in predictive power (relative odds of 2.9), but because there were more youth who had initiated alcohol use but not cigarettes (14% of the sample), this result has more importance.

Table 35.7 Prediction of Follow-Up Cigarette Use, by Baseline Alcohol and Marijuana Use Among Youth Who Had Not Used Cigarettes at Baseline

Cigarettes Use Follow Up	Marijuana Use Baseline		Alcohol Use Baseline	
	No	Yes	No	Yes
No	87%	65%	89%	73%
Yes	13%	35%	11%	27%
N	1,967	23	1,715	277
Gamma		.56		.49

Table 35.8 Prediction of Follow-Up Marijuana Use, by Baseline Alcohol and Cigarette Use Among Youth Who Had Not Used Marijuana at Baseline

Marijuana Use Follow Up	Cigarette Use Baseline		Alcohol Use Baseline	
	No	Yes	No	Yes
No	94%	59%	94%	71%
Yes	6%	41%	6%	29%
N	1,963	259	1,798	426
Gamma		.83		.73

The most interesting results concern the ability of cigarette and alcohol use at baseline to predict subsequent initiation of marijuana use among nonusers at baseline. Table 35.8 shows that cigarette users at baseline were nearly 11 times as likely as nonusers to initiate marijuana use. Indeed, although prior cigarette users make up only 12% of the entire sample of marijuana nonusers, they are close to half of all of those who initiate use. Alcohol use at baseline also predicts marijuana initiation well, with relative odds of 6.4. Although this is less of an association than for cigarette use, alcohol use is no less useful in locating youth who will initiate marijuana use. Although alcohol users make up 19% of the sample who were not using marijuana at baseline, they are more than half of those who initiate marijuana use by the second interview wave.

If a youth reported prior use of both alcohol and tobacco, he or she was at particular risk

of initiating use of marijuana. Whereas about 4% of those with no use of alcohol or cigarettes initiated marijuana use, 24% with only one type of prior use and 44% of those who had previous experience with both alcohol and cigarettes initiated marijuana use in the subsequent 18 months.

One might be concerned that this finding is merely an artifact of age—older youth were more likely to be users of all three substances. However, it turns out that this association remains strong even when age is statistically controlled. The results hold for every age but can be seen most clearly in Figure 35.2, which displays the association of prior use and marijuana initiation for each of three age groups. The patterns at each age are remarkably similar. The major difference at each age is the number of people who are in each prior use category. There are many more in the higher categories of prior substance use in the older age groups. Whereas

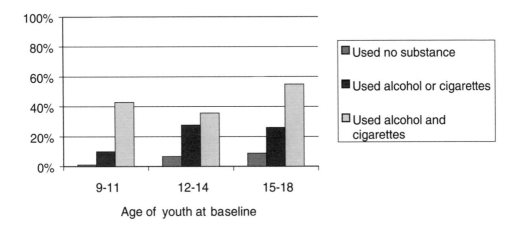

Figure 35.2 Percent Initiating Marijuana Use by Use of Tobacco and Alcohol Among Nonusers of All three Substances at Baseline

less than 1% of the 9- to 11-year-olds were prior users of both alcohol and cigarettes, more than 50% of the 14- to 18-year-olds were in that high-prior-use group. However, this does not reduce the actual association of prior use and marijuana initiation.

In sum, all prior use of any of the three substances predicts initiation of the other two. Marijuana use rarely precedes either cigarette or alcohol use, so it is the least important precursor behavior. Cigarette use is a better predictor of subsequent alcohol use than alcohol use is of subsequent cigarette use, but each is an important predictor of the other. Thus, neither is always the gateway to the other. The most informative results come from the analysis of initiation of marijuana use. Both prior alcohol use and prior tobacco use predict initiation of marijuana to such a degree that in the absence of such prior use, the risk of subsequent marijuana initiation is low. In the presence of prior use of both substances, marijuana initiation becomes much more probable, reaching 44%.

Youth who initiated any of the three substances were more likely to initiate use of the others as well.

Table 35.9 Association of the Initiation of Alcohol and Marijuana Use Over the 18 Months of Follow Up, Among Nonusers of Alcohol and Marijuana at Baseline

Initiated Marijuana Use	Initiated Alcohol Use		
	No	Yes	N
No	99%	77%	1,690
Yes	1%	23%	107
N	1,418	379	
Gamma		.92	

Finally, the chapter looks at the likelihood that a youth who initiated use of one of the three substances would initiate use of the others. Tables 35.9, 35.10, and 35.11 present those associations.

Initiation of marijuana was associated strongly with both cigarette initiation and alcohol initiation. Very few youth initiated marijuana use unless they also initiated alcohol and cigarette use. The complete picture of this association is presented in Figure 35.3. Essentially, no youth initiated marijuana use unless he or she also initiated cigarette and

Table 35.10   Association of the Initiation of Cigarette and Marijuana Use Over the 18 Months of Follow Up, Among Nonusers of Cigarettes and Marijuana at Baseline

Initiated Marijuana Use	Initiated Cigarette Use		
	No	Yes	N
No	98%	69%	1,841
Yes	2%	31%	122
N	1,705	258	
Gamma		.92	

Table 35.11   Association of the Initiation of Alcohol and Cigarette Use Over the 18 Months of Follow Up, Among Nonusers of Alcohol and Cigarettes at Baseline

Initiated Cigarette Use	Initiated Alcohol Use		
	No	Yes	N
No	95%	64%	1,522
Yes	5%	36%	192
N	1,382	332	
Gamma		.82	

alcohol use.

Alcohol initiation and cigarette initiation were a little less closely associated, but initiation of one of those behaviors was much more likely if the other was initiated as well.

CONCLUSIONS AND DISCUSSION

All three behaviors—tobacco, cigarette, and alcohol use—are closely associated with one another. They covary with age, but that isn't the whole explanation for their association. The association remains even when age is held constant. The most striking results in this chapter involve the prediction of marijuana

initiation. If youth do not use alcohol and they do not use cigarettes, they are at low risk to initiate marijuana use. At baseline, it was rare for a youth to have claimed use of marijuana if he or she did not also claim tobacco use, alcohol use, or both. Initiation of marijuana is predicted from baseline use of alcohol and cigarettes. Finally, among those who did not previously use tobacco or alcohol, initiation of marijuana use is very well predicted from simultaneous initiation of those other substance use behaviors. Virtually no one initiated marijuana use if he or she did not also initiate tobacco and alcohol use.

Consistent with the existing literature, these findings establish, for a national sample of youth, that marijuana is a behavior taken up after tobacco and alcohol use, and only if those behaviors are present as well. In addition, it is clear that there is no consistent causal order for the initiation of alcohol and tobacco, although the level of alcohol use is higher at every age after 12 than is the level of tobacco use. Prior alcohol use predicts subsequent cigarette initiation, and prior cigarette use predicts subsequent alcohol initiation.

These analyses focus only on ever use of each substance. It is possible that analyses that considered the frequency and recency of each behavior might show somewhat different patterns of association and prediction. Also, the only confounding variable controlled in these analyses is age. It is possible that other risk factors—for example, the personality characteristic, sensation seeking—would account for some of the cross-sectional and predictive association among these substance use behaviors.

Are there implications of these findings for intervention development? Two arguments derive from these results. First, these behaviors go together—they are not alternative ways of taking risks. There is no result here that suggests that curtailing one of these behaviors risks an increase in another. Second,

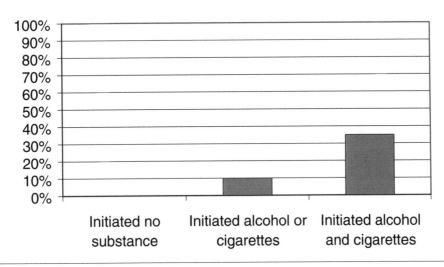

Figure 35.3   Percent Initiating Marijuana Use by Use of Tobacco and Alcohol Among Nonusers of All Three Substances at Baseline

these results reinforce efforts to reduce cigarette and alcohol use. Use of those substances is dangerous in its own right, and youth are more likely to initiate use of one or both substances than to initiate use of marijuana. In addition, use of cigarettes, alcohol, or both clearly precedes marijuana use. Indeed, their use seems to be a necessary condition for initiation of marijuana use. The results documenting the strong predictive relationship between prior tobacco and alcohol use and subsequent marijuana initiation are consistent with a gateway hypothesis. If a youth avoids initiation of the first two substances, he or she is virtually assured of avoiding the third, at least in the period of time examined in these analyses. Nonetheless, it is a separate matter to infer that an intervention that succeeded in curtailing tobacco

and alcohol use would succeed in reducing marijuana use. It might be that whatever drives some youth to early initiation of alcohol and tobacco would also drive them to marijuana initiation, regardless of whether they had resisted the prior substances. Also, this analysis focused on ever use of each substance. That behavior is of public health concern only because it is associated with subsequent abuse. This analysis does not address whether the reduced marijuana initiation that might come from a successful intervention to reduce precursor behaviors would also reduce abuse of marijuana and other drugs. Only if that proposition were credible would this analysis increase the justification for an early focus on tobacco and alcohol for their own sakes and as routes for reducing marijuana initiation.

Part IV

OVERARCHING APPROACHES AND RECOMMENDATIONS FOR FUTURE RESEARCH

CHAPTER 36

Positive Youth Development Is Necessary and Possible

Brian R. Flay

POSITIVE YOUTH DEVELOPMENT REQUIRES COMPREHENSIVE BEHAVIORAL AND EDUCATIONAL PROGRAMS

To date, most prevention, health promotion, character education, and social-emotional learning programs (and research) neglect the obvious link with academic achievement. We need to link prevention and health promotion with success in school and life. All good education needs to include content and programs to develop positive and successful youth. This need is urgent in our society today as the public and politicians demand more accountability.

Most education dollars today are targeted to improving basic reading, writing, and math skills and conducting testing to determine if learning is actually occurring. Although the demands on schools are ever increasing, there are also increasing demands for family, community, and after-school programs. Communities are also in crisis, with adolescent behavior getting worse, and the opportunities for positive youth development decreasing.

Risky behaviors, unhealthy behaviors, antisocial behavior, poor mental health, and poor academic achievement remain highly prevalent and continue to pose critical dilemmas for parents and educators. I argue and present evidence that these problems are highly correlated, predict and are predicted by each other, have many of the same risk and protective factors, and severely limit success and happiness in life. The logical conclusion of all this is that we need to prevent problem behaviors by promoting positive behaviors in a comprehensive, coherent, and

AUTHOR'S NOTE: Preparation of this chapter and some of the work reported herein was supported by grants from the National Institute on Drug Abuse (DA10306, DA11019, DA13474), the National Institute on Alcohol Abuse and Alcoholism (AA11266), the National Cancer Institute (CA 80266, CA86273), the Centers for Disease Control (CCU509661), and the Robert Wood Johnson Foundation. This chapter is adapted from Flay, B. R. (2002). Positive Youth Development Requires Comprehensive Health Promotion Programs. *American Journal of Health Behavior,* 26(6), 407-424.

integrated approach rather than by the disjointed approach to prevention and promotion taken by education today. I present preliminary evidence that such an approach can effectively prevent multiple problem behaviors and increase multiple positive behaviors and achievement.

MANY KINDS OF BEHAVIORS ARE RELATED

Evidence

The idea that different adolescent problem behaviors cluster and have the same underlying causes has been evident for many years and is evident in several theories (Jessor & Jessor, 1977). There is less clear evidence supporting the idea of a health-enhancing lifestyle, although it is clear that all health-enhancing behaviors tend to correlate negatively with health-compromising behaviors among adults and younger adolescents (Donovan, Jessor, & Costa, 1993).

Increasingly, studies are also documenting the relationships between problem behaviors of many kinds and academic achievement (Bryant, Schulenberg, Bachman, O'Malley, & Johnston, 2000; Durlak, 1998; Radziszewska, Richardson, Dent, & Flay, 1996). Studies also show that self-concept and self-esteem are correlated with both problem behaviors and academic performance (Hansford & Hattie, 1982; Hoge, Smit, & Crist, 1995; Jones & Heaven, 1998; Purkey, 1970; Skaalvik & Valas, 1999; Symons, Cinelli, James, & Groff, 1997). Data also suggest a relationship between problem behaviors and poor mental health (e.g., affective disorders, anxiety disorders), especially in clinical samples, but also in population samples (Breslau, Kilbey, & Andreski, 1991; Radziszewska et al., 1996). Psychological well-being has been reported as a mediator between learning of personal competence skills and

reduced substance use (Griffin, Scheier, & Botvin, 2001).

Although evidence for relationships between behaviors is strong, the direction of the relationships is often unclear. Does poor academic achievement lead to increased disruptive behavior, violence, and/or substance use, or vice versa? Modern theories of behavioral development would suggest that these relationships are, in fact, bidirectional, with one causal direction being dominant at some developmental stages and the other direction at other developmental stages. Thus, I consider all the relationships between problem behaviors, mental health, healthy behaviors, and conventional social behaviors to be bidirectional. Furthermore, I consider positive development in all areas to be the primary determinants of a successful and happy life.

Implications of the Correlation of Behaviors

Because all adolescent behaviors are interrelated, future prevention and health promotion programs should address all youth behavioral development in a comprehensive and coherent way.

BEHAVIORS HAVE COMMON ETIOLOGY

Empirical Evidence

The empirical literature on predictors and causes of adolescent behaviors is vast (Durlak, 1998). To understand the mass of findings, reviewers have proposed various groupings of predictors, and in contrast to many other empirical literature, there is an emerging agreement about the major predictors of youth behavior across domains (Conrad, Flay, & Hill, 1992; Dahlberg, 1998; Hawkins, Catalano, & Miller, 1992; Mrazek & Haggerty, 1994; Petraitis, Flay, &

Miller, 1995). Three generally agreed-upon categories consist of (a) *individual/person* (biological makeup, personality, character traits, and prior behaviors), (b) *social situation/context* (including family, school, peers, and neighborhood), and (c) *broader sociocultural environmental* influences (economic, political, religious, etc).

The more proximal the cause to a behavior, the more likely it is to be specific to that behavior. For example, attitudes toward violence will be predictive of violence but less predictive of substance use or mental health.

More distal influences, on the other hand, are likely to have more generalizable effects. Thus, school and home environment and parental involvement are associated with various factors affecting children's mental and physical well-being. A positive school environment both reduces the risk of substance use and delinquency (Battistich & Hom, 1997; Durlak, 1998) and improves academic achievement (Bulach, Malone, & Castleman, 1995). Parental involvement is also very important to a child's overall behavior in school, motivation to learn, grades and test scores, and long-term success (Zellman & Waterman, 1998).

A special case of distal influences concerns social disadvantage (education, income). Health-compromising behaviors seem to be a "patterned response" to disadvantaged social environments, with those from disadvantaged situations being less likely than those who are more advantaged to "mature out" of problem behaviors as they approach adulthood (Elliott, 1993). To the degree that low parental education and subsequent family poverty serves to place children at disadvantage, poor children may grow up with compromised social and economic skills.

Effects of poverty on academic achievement and children's risk for school dropout are well documented (Dubow & Ippolito, 1994). This is especially true for minorities, who represent one third of all work-age youths (U.S. Bureau of the Census, 1994). Dropouts can expect a life of chronic unemployment or low-status, low-paying employment and disenfranchisement from society and its institutions (Steinberg, Blinde, & Chan, 1984). The resulting depressed self-esteem, dissatisfaction, and alienation experienced by many dropouts can escalate to disordered, aggressive behaviors and a greater probability of crime (Levin, 1972).

Theoretical Support

Many theories of youth risky behaviors have been proposed over the years (see Petraitis et al., 1995, for an extensive review). If research on youth problem and positive behavior is to advance, our theories need to be integrated with each other. Fortunately, a rapprochement among multivariate theories is possible because they are largely complementary, and where one theory is weak, another is usually strong. For instance, bonding theories can describe why adolescents become involved with deviant peers, social learning theories can describe how involvement with deviant peers affects an adolescent's beliefs about a particular behavior, and cognitive-affective theories describe how attitudes toward the specific behavior can affect the likelihood of the behavior. The one theory that comes closest to integrating all of the above theories, and that comprehensively accounts for the multiple empirical findings reviewed above, is the theory of triadic influence (TTI; Flay & Petraitis, 1994).

In its simplest form, TTI asserts that the various causes of behavior fall into three distinct "streams" of influence: (a) *intrapersonal factors* that affect behavior-specific *self-efficacy* or related approach and avoidance skills, (b) *social and interpersonal situations* that affect the social pressure adolescents feel to engage in problem behavior and their *social normative beliefs*, and

(c) *sociocultural-environmental contexts* that affect attitudes toward problem behavior (see Figure 36.1). Note the parallelism with the three classes of predictors of behavior noted earlier. Within each stream of influence, there are two substreams, representing control and affective factors (e.g., values and evaluations, bonding and motivation to comply, self-determination) and identity and cognitive factors (e.g., expectancies, normative beliefs, social skills). TTI then asserts that each stream flows through seven tiers of influence, ranging from a variety of *ultimate* and *distal* variables that might affect problem behavior only indirectly (e.g., parental divorce) to a few *proximal* variables that affect problem behavior fairly directly (e.g., smoking-related intentions). Consistent with cognitive-social theories, in TTI all predictors of behavior are ultimately mediated by the cognitive-affective construct of intentions (or decisions).

TTI further posits that each instance of a behavior has a feedback influence on its predictors (not shown in Figure 36.1). Thus, adolescents' experimentation with smoking might change their relationships with peers and family, their own perceptions of the physiological effects of smoking, and their "knowledge" about the personal and social effects of use. These changes might occur toward the top of streams of influence and then filter down just as original causes did. However, they might also occur at the proximal level—that is, smoking alters one's expectancies about and attitudes toward smoking, one's expectations of reinforcement from others, and one's self-efficacy for refusing offers to smoke.

TTI is one of the most comprehensive models of behavior to date, in that it provides a single, unifying framework that organizes the constructs from many other theories, including theories of social control and social bonding (Elliott, 1993), social development (Hawkins & Weis, 1985), peer

clustering (Oetting & Beauvais, 1986), personality (Kaplan, 1975), cognitive-affective predictors (Fishbein & Ajzen, 1975), social learning (Akers, Krohn, Lanza-Kaduce, Radosevich, 1979), social cognitive theory (Bandura, 1986), biological vulnerability (Sher, 1991), and other integrative theories (Jessor & Jessor, 1977). Furthermore, TTI also provides dozens of testable hypotheses about causal processes, including mediation, moderation, and reciprocal effects. Thus, TTI provides the framework for generating hypotheses and integrating results concerning direct and indirect effects, interactions between predictors, and feedback effects that represent the immediate and long-term consequences of prior behavior, including ongoing changes in problem behavior and its predictors. Indeed, the theory can be applied to all of the behaviors under consideration in this chapter. Note, however, that the more distal or ultimate the predictors, the more commonality they have with the multiple behaviors, and the more proximal the predictors, the more specific to the behavior they must be (Flay & Petraitis, 1994).

Implications of Common Etiology

All behaviors have many of the same causes, especially at the ultimate or distal levels. Social influences—families, schools, peers, neighborhoods, and communities—are particularly important during adolescence. All are amenable to health promotion and educational efforts. Thus, future prevention and health promotion programs need to involve whole schools, families, and communities in an integrated and coherent way. Classroom curriculum can teach content and social skills. To be most effective, curricula must be schoolwide, encompassing every grade level in a carefully scoped and sequenced (developmentally appropriate) way. Cultural appropriateness may also be important (Pasick, Otero-Sabogal, & D'Onofrio, 1996).

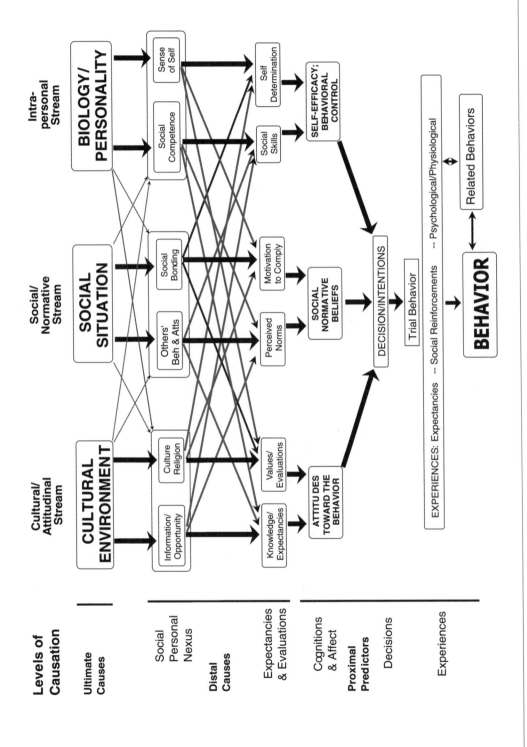

Figure 36.1. Theory of Triadic Influence

351

Schoolwide climate change can provide a safe learning environment and provide a common language and consistent reinforcement of positive behaviors, as can integrated family and community programs. Family programs can also teach improved parenting skills in a way consistent with a coherent program, and community components can strengthen school and community links and provide opportunities for students to observe and engage in community service.

COMPREHENSIVE YOUTH DEVELOPMENT IS NECESSARY AND POSSIBLE

What Does Comprehensiveness Entail?

Multiple reviews and commentaries during recent years indicate that prevention science is advancing our knowledge of what is efficacious for the prevention of problem behaviors. Social influence and social skills programs, especially interactive programs with 18+ program hours that include skills development and changing of normative beliefs, are effective for all kinds of behavior change (Durlak, 1998), including the prevention of substance use (Tobler & Stratton, 1997), violence (Derzon, Wilson, & Cunningham, 1999), unsafe sexual behaviors (Kirby, 2001a, 2001b; Moore, Sugland, & Blumenthal, 1995), character education (Berkowitz, 2002; Licona, Schaps, & Lewis, n.d.), and mental health promotion (Durlak & Wells, 1997; Mrazek & Haggerty, 1994).

However, emerging programs, even those meeting all the above conditions, still appear to be only somewhat effective, and not consistently so. In addition, the effects decay rather quickly. For optimum effectiveness, programs need to meet all the following conditions (Hechinger, 1992). They must be (a) comprehensive—covering multiple health-compromising and health-enhancing (positive) behaviors; (b) developmentally appropriate; (c) continuous and longitudinal—over several grades, with carefully designed review, reinforcement, and extension; (d) culturally sensitive; and (e) school and classroom focused, although not limited to the school. They should also (f) use peers, where appropriate, to demonstrate skills and alter norms; (g) include proper training of teachers and other school personnel involved in delivery; (h) involve parents actively in homework exercises and other activities; (i) be adapted to local conditions with input from students, parents, school leaders, and community leaders; (j) include school improvement and reorganization components; and (k) include ongoing evaluation at all stages of development, implementation, and institutionalization.

Selected Programs With Comprehensive Effects

There is already a trend toward more comprehensive and multimodal programs that address multiple behaviors and that involve families and community. This appears to be contrary to early views of behavior change. Relying on theories of behavior that considered only the more proximal predictors, researchers often claimed that programs had to target specific behaviors to be effective. The assumption was that programs that targeted multiple behaviors would be less effective because teaching of skills had to be specific to the behaviors being prevented. However, with recognition that many of the social skills being taught were also relevant to multiple behaviors, researchers started to address multiple behaviors.

Several research groups have reported comprehensive schoolwide programs that both reduce multiple problem behaviors and enhance achievement. In the earliest of such reports (Elias, Gara, Schuyler, & Branden-Muller, 1991), a social-emotional learning program both reduced problem behaviors and enhanced achievement. Durlak and Wells (1997) found that some mental health programs that reduced subsequent maladaptation also improved school performance. Evaluation of the Child Development Project found that students in program schools where program implementation was high were less likely than students in matched comparison schools to use alcohol or marijuana, carry a weapon, steal a car, skip school, or threaten another with harm up to 2 years after (Battistich, Schaps, Watson, & Solomon, 1996). The Seattle Social Development Group has reported program effects on behavior, school bonding, and achievement (Abbott et al., 1998). Results from the Aban Aya Youth Project (Flay, Graumlich, Segawa, et al., 2002) confirm that a comprehensive program that is culturally specific (African American), developmentally appropriate, long-lasting (approximately 20 scoped and sequenced sessions per grade for Grades 5–8), and involves parents and community can reduce multiple problem behaviors—substance use, violence, and unsafe sexual behavior. A version of the program that included higher parent and community involvement was more effective than a version that was classroom based only.

Perhaps the most impressive of the programs having effects on multiple behaviors and academic achievement is the Positive Action (PA) Program (Allred, 1995). PA is grounded in a broad theory of self-concept (Purkey & Novak, 1970) that posits that people determine their self-concepts by what they do; that actions, more than thoughts or feelings, determine self-concept; and that making positive and healthy behavioral choices results in feelings of self-worth. The program consists of integrated classroom curriculum materials for K–12, school preparation and teacher training, schoolwide climate change, a family program with student-parent interaction, and community components. It uses proven strategies and methods, such as active learning, positive classroom management, a detailed curriculum with almost daily lessons, a schoolwide climate program, parental support and involvement, and community involvement. The program teaches children what actions are positive, that they feel good when they do positive actions, and that they then have more positive thoughts and future actions. This approach is consistent with the new positive psychology movement (Seligman & Csikszentmihalyi, 2000). The program also trains teachers and parents to identify and reinforce positive feelings, thoughts, and actions by students, leading to continual reinforcement of positive actions and enhanced student bonding with parents and school.

Data from various comparison group designs involving about 300 elementary schools delivering the PA program demonstrate consistent positive effects of the program on student self-concept (using various measures), school performance (attendance, achievement), school behavior (discipline, suspensions), and other behavior (crime, violence, substance use) (Flay & Allred, in press; Flay, Allred, & Ordway, 2001). These results were obtained from all sorts of schools with varying minority representation, mobility rates, and poverty levels, in different states, at different times (late 1970s through 2001). Several thousand other schools have reported similar results of PA from individual case studies. All effects were equally positive or better in schools with high versus low minority representation and different levels of poverty. This pattern of results is very compelling, because most other evaluated programs do not work as well in schools with high proportions of minority students or students living in poverty.

Implications of Comprehensive Programming

Comprehensive, long-term, schoolwide interventions that involve families and communities but that are not too difficult to implement, can successfully reduce multiple problem, risky, unhealthy, and antisocial behaviors and increase multiple positive, healthy, and prosocial behaviors, improve mental health and self-concept, and enhance academic performance.

SUMMARY

In this chapter, I have provided evidence that multiple positive and negative behaviors are highly correlated and are predictive of each other. One conclusion from this is that youth behavioral development should be addressed by a comprehensive, coherent, and integrated approach rather than the disjointed approaches to prevention and promotion taken by education today. We must link problem behavior prevention, health promotion, mental health development, and character development, not only with each other, but also with academic achievement.

I also argued that all forms of youth behavior have many of the same causes. This is especially true of causes at the distal and ultimate levels. A person's genetic predispositions, family social circumstances, cultural background, and learning environment all have profound influences on the development of his or her behavioral patterns—directly, in interaction with each other, and indirectly through other variables. Much empirical etiological data and many theories of behavioral development support this. The clear conclusion from this knowledge is that prevention and health promotion programs that address those distal and ultimate influences that are amenable to change should affect multiple behaviors and outcomes.

I presented several examples of comprehensive approaches to prevention and health promotion that appear to prevent multiple problem behaviors and to increase multiple positive behaviors and outcomes at the same time. Curricula can address multiple behaviors effectively. Schools that actively respond to problem behaviors and cultivate a positive, healthy environment can have lasting effects on students' long-term behaviors in adolescence and beyond. Providing an environment that is prochild and that responds to a child's needs will increase a child's positive behavior and academic performance.

My analysis also suggests that programs that also alter social contexts, such as school climate, families, and communities, can have larger and longer-lasting effects on a broader array of behaviors. Findings from multiple studies suggest that comprehensive programs that involve curriculum, teacher training, schoolwide climate change, and involvement of parents and community can affect multiple outcomes, including academic achievement. Although such programs hold great promise for producing more young adults headed into a productive and happy life, we have much more work to do before we can develop these programs with confidence in their effectiveness. The need for such programs is urgent in our schools, homes, and society today; the public and politicians demand more accountability, not only for enhanced student learning, but also for improved student behavior. The ultimate success and happiness of future generations, and their ultimate contribution to a civil society, depends on our being able to develop comprehensive, coherent, and integrated prevention and health promotion programs that are effective across multiple domains.

CHAPTER 37

Youth Development
Programs and Healthy Development
A Review and Next Steps

JODIE L. ROTH
JEANNE BROOKS-GUNN

The notion of adolescence as a time of great risk and opportunity has taken hold in the American consciousness. A time of bodily changes, expanding independence, and growing self-discovery, adolescence can be characterized as a series of challenges. Each challenge carries the possibility of risk, opportunity, or both. These challenges, or developmental transitions, present critical junctures along the path that connects children to their transformed physical, mental, and social adult selves (Graber & Brooks-Gunn, 1996; Schulenberg, Maggs, & Hurrelmann, 1997). Most individuals navigate transitions equipped with the competencies and supports they need to meet new challenges and take on new roles while further developing the cognitive, emotional, social, or physical skills necessary for these new roles (Graber & Brooks-Gunn, 1996). Many, however, do not. Individual differences in the negotiation of a transition are associated with development prior to the

transition, the timing of the transition, the individual's experience of the transition, and the context in which the transition occurs (Rutter, 1989). A varied collection of efforts, including after-school programs, targeted interventions, school policies, community development, and federal agencies exist to assist adolescents through these transitions on their way to healthy, self-sufficient adulthoods.

Over the past decade, the efforts of the youth development movement to shift the paradigm for helping youth from deterrence to development, captured by the phrase *problem free is not fully prepared,* has led to an increase in the acceptance of youth preparation and development, not just problem prevention and deterrence, as desirable goals requiring strategic action (Pittman, Irby, & Ferber, 2000). Programs incorporating this philosophy view youth as resources to be developed rather than as problems to be managed; they strive to influence adolescents' developmental transitions toward healthy (positive) outcomes by increasing their exposure to developmental opportunities and supports (Roth, Brooks-Gunn, Murray, & Foster, 1998). Rooted, in part, in the research showing the common antecedents and comorbidity of many health-compromising behaviors (e.g., drug use, early childbearing) that limit adolescents' preparation for and success at the developmental transitions to adulthood, the youth development approach offers insight into programmatic elements that build adolescents' capacities for success, which includes, but is not limited to, curbing health-compromising behaviors. Youth development programs, then, square perfectly with the goals of this volume, exploring ways to reduce more than one risk to healthy development.

In this chapter, we use the youth development paradigm to frame and support our ideas for how to intervene in the lives of today's youth to enhance their chances of healthy development, including reducing their health-compromising behaviors. In the next section, we define briefly the goal for youth—healthy development. We then provide support for our suggested pathway to improving youths' lives—youth development programs. In the last section, we discuss needed next research steps for advancing the goal of healthy development by increasing the supply and appropriateness of programs offering a positive youth development setting.

THE GOAL: HEALTHY DEVELOPMENT

Generally speaking, healthy development encompasses all our hopes and aspirations for a nation of healthy, happy, and competent adolescents on their way to productive and satisfying adulthoods (Roth & Brooks-Gunn, 2000). Differences arise when we look at what specifically constitutes "healthy, happy, and competent" adolescents as well as "productive and satisfying" adulthoods.

The meaning of healthy adulthood, the goal of healthy adolescent development, fluctuates depending on the purpose and audience. To some, economic self-sufficiency is the primary requirement: A gainfully employed individual, not reliant on public funds or services, is considered a "successful" adult. To others, psychological stability and well-being are critical. One model of adult well-being lists six essential features: (a) self-acceptance, (b) positive relationships with others, (c) autonomy, (d) environmental mastery, (e) purpose in life, and (f) personal growth (Ryff, 1996). *Healthy People 2010*, the federal Office of Disease Prevention and Healthy Promotion's blueprint for how to increase the number of Americans who achieve a longer and healthier life, offers a different perspective on healthy adulthood (U.S. Department of Health and Human Services, 2001). This effort has 10 leading health indicators, 7 pertaining to individuals and 3 concerning communities and policy. The 7 individual behaviors related to healthy adulthood include (a) physical activity, (b) maintaining appropriate weight, (c) tobacco avoidance, (d) avoiding substance abuse, (e) responsible sexual behavior, (f) mental health, and (g) avoiding injury and violence. Regardless of which criteria for successful (or healthy) adulthood one chooses, the foundation for these behaviors begins during childhood and adolescence.

What to include on lists of healthy or successful adolescent development differs as well. The differences, however, are mostly in organization and terminology. Typically, successful adolescent development is discussed in terms of skills and competence in the physical, intellectual, psychological, emotional, and social arenas (see National Research Council, 2002). Sometimes these areas are extended to emphasize other qualities, such as the moral and spiritual, civic, and cultural aspects of one's life (e.g., see Pittman, Irby, Tolman, Yohalem, & Ferber, 2001).

Or alternatively, they are shortened to succinctly express the desired outcomes for the nation's youth: the ability to be productive, connect, and navigate (Connell, Gambone, & Smith, 2000). Lerner, Fisher, and Weinberg (2000) categorize the desired outcomes into five Cs: (a) competence in academic, social, and vocational areas; (b) confidence or a positive self-identity; (c) connections to community, family, and peers; (d) character or positive values, integrity, and moral commitment; and (e) caring and compassion. Pittman et al. (2001) add one more C—contribution.

Researchers produce similar lists when discussing the inputs, ingredients, or assets necessary to help youth develop into healthy adolescents on their way to healthy adulthoods. These lists typically include people, experiences, and opportunities in the varying contexts that influence development, including the family, school, peers, neighborhoods, and larger social context (Roth & Brooks-Gunn, 2000). Theory, empirical research, and practical wisdom converge to suggest important personal and social assets for healthy development (National Research Council, 2002; Roth & Brooks-Gunn, 2000). For example, Benson (1997) describes 40 internal and external assets believed to be the universal building blocks of positive (healthy) development. The 20 external assets envelop youth with familial and extra-familial networks that provide support, empowerment, boundaries and expectations, and constructive use of time. The 20 internal assets serve to nurture, within individuals, positive commitments, values, and identities, as well as social competencies. The external assets describe the necessary ingredients in youths' environment (home, school, community) for positive development. The internal assets illustrate personal qualities that facilitate positive development.

Put another way, adolescents need access to safe places, challenging experiences, and caring people on a daily basis (Zeldin, 1995). In their extensive review of developmental theory and empirical research, the National Research Council's Committee on Community-Level Programs for Youth suggests a provisional list of eight features of positive developmental settings. Whether at home, school, among friends, in an after-school program, or in the community, positive developmental settings provide (a) physical and psychological safety, (b) appropriate structure, (c) supportive relationships, (d) opportunities to belong, (e) positive social norms, (f) support for efficacy and mattering, (g) opportunities for skill building, and (h) integration of family, school, and community efforts (National Research Council, 2002). When circumstances prevent both economically affluent and disadvantaged families, schools, and communities from providing their youth with these fundamental resources, youth development programs offer *one* avenue for increasing youths' exposure to positive developmental settings.

ONE PATHWAY: YOUTH DEVELOPMENT PROGRAMS

This shift in thinking about what adolescents need for successful adulthood, coupled with the risks associated with unsupervised time during the after-school hours, has spurred growing public support, both ideologically and financially, for more structured activities during after-school hours (e.g., the expansive growth in funding for the federal government's 21st Century Community Learning Centers). In some communities, an array of school-based extracurricular activities—sports, music, art, community service—as well as community-based youth programs provide youth with ample choices for positive developmental settings outside of school or family. This is far from the norm. Availability, cost, transportation, and interest limit many youths' choices during nonschool hours. In a recent opinion poll, 62% of 14- to 17-year-olds agreed with the statement, "Adults criticize teens for wasting time, but adults don't realize there's not much for teens to do after school." Over half wished for more after-school activities in their neighborhood or community (YMCA of the USA, 2001).

Youth development programs can provide developmentally rich contexts, where relationships form, opportunities for growth in multiple areas proliferate, and development occurs. Programs incorporating, at least to some degree, the youth development philosophy come in all shapes and sizes, from small, single-focus programs, such as sports teams or youth newspapers, to affiliates of national youth-serving organizations, such as Big Brothers/Big Sisters and Boys and Girls Clubs. They are located in or sponsored by local schools, civic organizations, parks, museums, libraries, community organizations, and religious institutions (Roth & Brooks-Gunn, 2003a). Approximately 500 national and 17,000 state and local organizations classify themselves as youth development programs (Erickson, 1998).

Although we believe youth development programs hold great promise for improving the lives and futures of American youth, we caution against unrealistic expectations. One program, even an extraordinarily good program, cannot do it all. Young people do not grow up in programs, but in families, schools, and neighborhoods. Our best chance of positively influencing adolescent development through programs lies in increasing the web of options available to all youth in all communities and ensuring that those options take an approach consistent with the youth development framework. In trying to further this goal, we focus on *one* category of options—those offered by youth development programs.

At a general level, youth development programs help participants develop "competencies that will enable them to grow, develop their skills and become healthy, responsible, and caring youth and adults" (Networks for Youth Development, 1998, p. 4). More specifically, we have identified three characteristics that theory and ethnographic research suggest differentiates youth development programs from other types of programs for adolescents (see Roth & Brooks-Gunn, 2003c, for more details). The three characteristics are (a) program goals, (b) program atmosphere, and (c) program activities.

The *goals* of youth development programs promote positive development, even when seeking to prevent problem behaviors. Youth development programs help young people navigate adolescence in healthy ways and prepare them for their future by fostering their positive development. They recognize that activities focused solely on the prevention of problem behaviors, such as violence or substance abuse, do not necessarily equip adolescents with the tools for a responsible and productive adulthood. Youth development programs can be distinguished from ameliorative services by their emphasis on promoting normal development and recognizing youths' need for both ongoing support and challenging opportunities.

Leaders and staff members at youth development programs create and nourish an atmosphere of hope. The positive, youth-centered atmosphere, or tone, conveys the adults' belief in adolescents as resources to be developed rather than problems to be managed. This guiding principle allows them to create not just a space, but a place, for youth. Individual attention, cultural appropriateness, and the choice and responsibility given to adolescents set a positive tone for youth development. The atmosphere in these programs resembles that in a caring family, where knowledgeable and supportive adults empower adolescents to develop their competencies. Like successful families, these programs create physically and psychologically safe places with a strong sense of membership, commitment, explicit rules and responsibilities, and expectations for adolescents' success. Sustained involvement over time also characterizes a commitment to creating an environment that nourishes youths' potential for positive development.

Program activities provide formal and informal opportunities for adolescents to nurture their interests and talents, practice new skills, and gain a sense of personal or group recognition. Regardless of the specific activity, the emphasis lies in providing real challenges and active participation. Program activities also broaden youths' exposure to new worlds. Activities can have both direct (i.e., homework sessions and tutoring) and indirect (i.e., encourage adolescents to stay in school and try harder) links to education, but they present information and learning opportunities in a way that is different from school. The activities at many youth development programs offer leadership development opportunities, academic supports, and health education information.

Although still sparse, the growing available evidence supports the efficacy of youth development programs. In our previous work, we set out to determine if programs with more of a youth development bent— loosely defined as programs promoting positive behaviors by attempting to enhance competencies—led to better outcomes for participants (Roth et al., 1998). Our efforts met with a number of methodological challenges, including the paucity of experimental or quasi-experimental evaluations of such programs and few measures other than beliefs and academic-related behaviors and involvement to tap positive outcomes. For the most part, positive outcomes were measured as the absence of negative outcomes. Despite these obstacles, we concluded that the available limited evidence pointed to the effectiveness of the youth development framework. These obstacles, however, led us to warn that although the basis of the youth

development movement rests on sound and compelling theoretical thinking, the enthusiasm for youth development programs far outstrips the empirical evidence of their effectiveness.

In the years since then, a number of reports have been released that employ rigorous standards of evidence to identify programs successful in reducing specific negative outcomes, such as substance abuse (Brounstein & Zweig, 1999), violence prevention (Elliot, 1998), and mental disorders (Greenberg, Domitrovich, & Bumbarger, 1999), or promoting positive development (Catalano, Berglund, Ryan, Lonczak, & Hawkins, 1999; National Research Council, 2002). Overlap exists in the model programs identified in each report, despite their focus on different outcomes. These reviews identify 48 soundly evaluated programs that succeed in producing positive outcomes for their nonadjudicated teenage participants (ages 10–18). Adolescents who participated in the programs fared better than those who did not on at least one measure of development. We use these 48 effective programs as our database for investigating how programs create positive developmental settings for young people.

The evaluations varied not only in which outcomes they measured but also in how they assessed those outcomes. That is, the studies differed in both the specific measures and the number of measures used to assess the same construct. To take these discrepancies in measurement into account, we assigned a rating of success to programs when participants scored significantly ($p < .05$) better on at least one measure of the construct than adolescents who did not attend the program. The evaluations also differed in the depth of their analyses; some investigated outcomes for specific subgroups of participants, such as males and females or more and less at-risk participants, whereas others did not. To compensate for these differences in detail, we assigned a rating of success when participation in the program led to positive outcomes for at least some subgroup of the participants.

We examined the programs' effectiveness in reducing four specific risk behaviors: (a) a reduction in use of substances, including cigarettes, alcohol, and/or other drugs; (b) behavior that decreases the risk of early childbearing, including the postponement of sexual activity, fewer sexual partners, and contraceptive use; (c) a reduction in delinquent or aggressive behavior, home or school behavior problems, and/or mental illness; and (d) improved school performance, in terms of either grades, test scores, or attendance. The majority of the programs (73%) successfully altered only one of these four risk behaviors. Only 11 (23%) of the programs succeeded in altering two or more of these risk behaviors. Our ability to determine the successfulness of these programs in altering risk behavior is hindered, however, by the program evaluators' methodology; many more measured attitudes and/or knowledge of risk behaviors than measured the behaviors themselves.

Our goal in this chapter is to move beyond the question of whether or not programs can reduce risk-taking behaviors to the question of *how* they do. Thus, we use this database of programs to test our belief that programs incorporating a youth development philosophy achieve greater success not only in reducing risky, health-compromising behaviors but in promoting other aspects of positive development as well. As part of this test, we endeavor to determine which elements of the youth development approach are critical for their success.

Ideally, synthesizing the findings from these empirical evaluations would allow us to identify which programmatic elements work best for improving the lives of young people. Then we could provide a blueprint of sorts of the necessary and optional elements for a successful program. Such a list would be an invaluable tool for program designers and those interested in increasing the web of positive developmental settings available to adolescents.

As a field, however, we are far from this ideal. Few studies systematically varied elements of program design to determine which, or what mix, are critical to program success (Roth et al., 1998). In addition, the general lack of theory predicting expected outcomes based on specific programmatic approaches and activities limits our ability to draw conclusions about *why* the program did or did not alter adolescents' development. Similarly, measures of program implementation and fidelity, rarely available, would help untangle the black box of programmatic effects. The limited types of outcome measures employed to judge program success prohibit a full understanding of what programs can do. Too often, due to demands for accountability and insufficient measures of positive behaviors, success is measured only in terms of a reduction in health-compromising behaviors, even when this is beyond what we may realistically expect from the program.

The program evaluations we used to create the database of programs can be viewed as the best of the available research. Even among them, there are considerable methodological flaws, particularly pertaining to group comparability and attrition issues. Their findings of how the programs enhance youth development are constrained by few measures of adolescent development other than engagement in problem behaviors, attitudes toward risky behaviors, and knowledge of risk-avoiding strategies.

We categorized the program outcomes by Lerner et al.'s (2000) five Cs of healthy adolescent development: competence, confidence, connections, character, and caring. To do so, we drew on our efforts to develop national indicators of confidence, character, and caring (Roth, Borbely, & Brooks-Gunn, 2001) and adapted the operational definitions of the youth development objectives developed by Catalano et al. (1999) to arrive at the following operational definitions for the five Cs (Roth & Brooks-Gunn, 2003b). The *promotion of competence,* the first C, includes enhancing participants' social, academic, cognitive, and vocational competencies. Social competence refers to interpersonal skills such as communication, assertiveness, refusal and resistance, and conflict resolution skills. Cognitive competence describes cognitive abilities, including logical and analytic thinking, problem-solving, decision-making, planning and goal-setting skills. School grades, attendance, test scores, and graduation rates are included under academic competence. Vocational competence pertains to work habits and career choice explorations.

Promoting adolescents' confidence, the second C, consists of outcomes relating to improving adolescents' self-esteem, self-concept, self-efficacy, identity, and belief in the future. *Encouraging connections,* the third C, involves building and strengthening adolescents' relationship with other people and institutions, such as school. The fourth C, *character,* is perhaps the most difficult to define. Increasing self-control, decreasing engagement in health-compromising (problem) behaviors, developing respect for cultural or societal rules and standards and a sense of right and wrong (morality), and spirituality describe character-building outcomes. *Developing caring and compassion,* the fifth C, implies improving youths' empathy and identification with others.

Two things become apparent when we look at the outcomes organized by the five Cs of healthy development. First, more programs demonstrated success at improving participants' character (75%) than their competence (63%), confidence (44%), connections (40%), or caring (19%). Second, when we compare the 11 programs that succeeded in altering two or more of the risk behaviors with the other 37 programs, we found differences that suggest *how* these programs achieved their success. A larger percentage of these programs also improved adolescents' confidence, connections, and character. Programs altering multiple risk behaviors also succeeded in improving more of the five Cs than did programs altering fewer risk behaviors: (3.0 vs. 2.2), $F(1, 47) = 4.1, p = .048$. Thus, consistent with the youth development philosophy, programs that viewed adolescents as resources to be developed led to better outcomes in all areas of adolescents' healthy development.

Further support for the effectiveness of this approach in programming for adolescents comes from program goals. Using the same operational definitions described above for the five Cs, we looked at how many aspects of healthy development each program sought to address. Overall, the programs altering multiple risk behaviors endorsed significantly more goals than the other programs: (4.1 vs. 3.2), $F(1, 47) = 6.03, p = .018$. Table 37.1 shows the differences between the two types of programs. The largest difference was in the connections goal. All 11 programs altering multiple risk behaviors sought to improve participants' connections with other people or institutions, but only 65% of the other programs embraced this goal. More of the multiple-risk-altering programs also addressed participants' confidence.

We looked more closely at other elements of the youth development approach to programs to see if we could uncover other differences that contributed to program success. As described earlier, positive developmental settings provide young people with a supportive, caring environment where they feel valued. The atmosphere of youth programs was somewhat difficult to assess from the information provided in the program evaluations. Written program descriptions paint an incomplete picture of staff members' approach to participants. Many of the qualities that

Table 37.1   Comparison of Programs Positively Altering Two or More Risk Behaviors With Programs Positively Altering Fewer Risk Behaviors

	Programs Improving Multiple Risk Behaviors (N = 11)		Programs Improving Fewer Risk Behaviors (N = 37)	
	Number	Percentage	Number	Percentage
Outcomes				
Competence	7	64	23	62
Confidence	6	55	15	40
Connections	7	64	12	32
Character	11	100	25	68
Caring	2	18	7	19
Program Elements				
Goals				
Competence	11	100	37	100
Confidence	9	82	23	62
Connections	11	100	24	65
Character	10	91	29	78
Caring	4	36	5	14
Atmosphere				
Supportive	10	91	12	32
Empowering	5	45	13	35
Expecting	8	73	36	97
Rewarding	9	82	23	62
Lasted at least 9 months	8	73	13	35
Activities				
Build skills	10	91	36	97
Authentic activities	4	44	12	32
Broaden horizons	5	45	10	27
Other contexts	5	45	18	48

distinguish a positive, caring, youth-centered tone depend on the staff's demeanor and attitude toward the adolescent participants as well as the quality of relationships. Unfortunately, few studies measure the attitudes of staff members or the quality of relationships. Although the measures are imperfect, we distinguish five dimensions of program atmosphere referred to in the literature from the program descriptions. Programs in which the structure, activities, and staff members encourage the development of supportive relationships with adults and among peers, empower adolescents, communicate expectations for positive behavior, and provide opportunities for recognition convey a positive view of youth. Program duration also relates to program atmosphere. Longer-term programs recognize that development is ongoing; as a result, they offer more enduring support and greater opportunities for meaningful relationships (Roth & Brooks-Gunn, 2003b).

We drew on the definitions provided by Catalano et al. (1999) and the National Research Council (2002) to develop the operational definitions of the first four indicators of program atmosphere. Programs classified as providing a supportive atmosphere encourage participants to develop a supportive relationship with adults and/or peers through participating in the program. Because we were interested in capturing the atmosphere that participants experience when attending the program, we did not consider programs that provided parent training to improve parent-youth relationships as providing a supportive program atmosphere unless they also directly encouraged supportive relationships with program staff members, mentors, or peers. Similarly, programs that worked to improve youths' social skills but that did not specifically encourage a sense of belonging or bonding with other program participants were not judged as offering a supportive program environment. An empowering atmosphere existed when program staff members and activities encouraged adolescents to engage in useful roles, practice self-determination, and develop or clarify their goals for the future. Programs conveyed a belief in adolescents as capable individuals when they communicated expectations for positive behavior by defining clear rules for behavior and consequences for infractions, fostering prosocial norms, and encouraging youth to practice healthy behaviors. They could provide opportunities for recognition by rewarding positive behaviors within the program or by structuring opportunities for public recognition of skills.

Table 37.1 shows the differences between the two groups of programs. All but one of the programs altering multiple risk behaviors encouraged the development of a supportive relationship within the program, but less

than one third of the other programs did the same. Fewer, however, conveyed expectations for positive behavior. Recognition for positive behaviors was a part of more of the multiple-risk-altering programs than of the programs improving fewer risk behaviors. A larger percentage of the multiple-risk-altering programs lasted at least 9 months. Thus, programs altering multiple risk behaviors provided participants with more of the elements of a supportive environment than did programs altering fewer risk behaviors: (3.6 vs. 2.6), $F(1, 47) = 6.35$, $p = .015$.

Program activities, the third way programs can implement the positive youth development philosophy, are the vehicle through which most programs attract and engage participants. As noted earlier, the specific focus of the activity (e.g., sports, literacy) does not matter as much as the opportunities provided through participation. Consistent with this view, we depict the types of opportunities afforded by the array of program activities and components. We identified three features of program activities that capture the youth development philosophy: opportunities for adolescents to build skills, engage in real and challenging activities, and broaden their horizons. We also included a fourth dimension—increasing developmental supports in other contexts of adolescents' worlds, such as family, school, or community (Roth & Brooks-Gunn, 2003b).

To classify the programs according to these features, we inferred opportunities from the components and activities described in the program descriptions. Some activities, such as community service, afford participants multiple opportunities—to build skills, engage in real and challenging activities, and broaden their horizons. Other types of activities provide more limited opportunities. For example, academic instruction or homework help components primarily build (school-related) skills. We judged programs that included a competency-building curriculum, life skills training, direct academic instruction, homework help, or community service to offer participants the opportunity to build skills.

Activities that allow adolescents to engage in real and challenging activities were harder to infer from the program descriptions without more information about the quality of the activities. For example, activities described as "educational" can be real, challenging, and authentic, such as designing, writing, and producing a newspaper, or disconnected, mechanical, or rote, such as practicing spelling and grammar. Therefore, we included only employment, leadership opportunities (such as tutoring or peer mediation), and community service as activities that provide the opportunity to engage in an authentic, real, and challenging activity.

The literature describes youth development programs as places where young people can expand their horizons by providing them with opportunities they might otherwise not have, such as visiting a museum or engaging in a recreational activity requiring equipment not readily available. We considered programs that arrange for field trips, cultural activities, community service, employment opportunities, recreation, and mentors to expand participants' horizons by exposing them to new people, places, and situations.

There is a question within the youth development literature of whether the primary focus of youth development programs should be preparing adolescents for the world by ensuring that they possess the five Cs or by shaping a better world for youth by also increasing the supports available to them at home, school, and in their community. The fourth feature addresses this question by indicating if the program activities attempted to improve at least one context—family, school, or community—through parent activities (e.g., parenting classes), teacher training, modifying school climate or structure, or changing community

attitudes or norms. Table 37.1 shows the characteristics of the program activities for both types of programs. None of the opportunities offered by the different program activities differed between the two types of programs.

It appears that the atmosphere, rather than the opportunities provided by program activities, differentiates successful programs that alter multiple risk behaviors from other successful programs for youth. In particular, these programs provide adolescents with a supportive and less demanding environment. The findings also support the assertion that programs combining youth development with risk reduction are more likely to achieve their goals.

MANY BARRIERS: NEEDED RESEARCH

The operational definitions we created to determine program goals, atmosphere, and activities can serve as the basis for the development of survey or observational measures for use in program evaluations. Program descriptions only tell us so much about *how* the program works. Our understanding, as a field, of why some programs are better at promoting youth development than others would be vastly improved by the development and inclusion in evaluation studies of measures of the quality of the atmosphere that programs create and the types of opportunities they provide. Too often, this process information is not collected or reported in outcome studies.

We also need to measure a broader array of program outcomes to fully understand the impact of youth development programs. Current evaluation efforts fail to capture the broader view of youth development held by many programs. Measures of the ingredients of youth development (competence, confidence, connections, character, and caring) need to be included in evaluation efforts in addition to the more traditional measures of risky behaviors. We are encouraged by recent, although still preliminary, efforts to create such measures (Moore, Evans, Brooks-Gunn, & Roth, 2001; Roth et al., 2001).

We are hopeful that the recent burgeoning in attention to the after-school hours, and with it a general acceptance of the principles of the youth development movement, will be met with an increase in funding and willpower to create and include these new measures as part of program evaluation efforts. Without these improvements, we are limited in our ability to provide guidance to program developers on how best to create programs that provide positive developmental opportunities by encouraging positive development in all areas, including (but not limited to) decreasing risky behaviors.

CHAPTER 38

A Contextual Perspective for Understanding and Preventing STD/HIV Among Adolescents

RALPH J. DICLEMENTE
GINA M. WINGOOD
RICHARD A. CROSBY

A dolescence is a developmental period characterized by rapid physical, psychological, social, cultural, and cognitive changes. Although many adolescents navigate the sometimes turbulent course from childhood to adulthood to become productive and healthy adults, there is growing concern that far too many others may not achieve their full potential. Adolescence, unfortunately, is also a period fraught with many threats to the health and well-being of adolescents, and a time when many suffer substantial impairment and disability (DiClemente, Hansen & Ponton, 1996a).

adolescents today, and perhaps increasing numbers in the years to come, are at risk for adverse health outcomes stemming from their behavior. Contemporary threats to adolescent health are primarily the consequence of risk behaviors and related outcomes such as substance use, violence, risky sexual behavior, teenage pregnancy, and sexually transmitted diseases, to name but a few (DiClemente, Hansen, & Ponton, 1996b; Dryfoos, 1990; Jessor, Turbin, & Costa, 1998). One of the most significant and immediate risks to the health and well-being of adolescents is the risk of acquiring sexually transmitted diseases (STDs), including human immunodeficiency virus (HIV) infection.

TEMPORAL TRENDS IN ADOLESCENT MORBIDITY

Over the past few decades, there has been a marked change in the causes of morbidity among adolescents (Sells & Blum, 1996). Many

THE BURDEN OF STDS AND HIV AMONG ADOLESCENTS

The risk of acquiring a sexually transmitted disease (STD) is one of the more significant and immediate risks to the health and well-being of adolescents. In the United States, more than 15 million new cases of STDs occur each year (American Social Health Association, 1998); as many as two thirds of these infections may occur among people under 25 years of age (Eng & Butler, 1997). By age 24, at least one in three sexually active young adults is estimated to have contracted an STD (Centers for Disease Control and Prevention, 1993). These infections are a prominent source of personal loss among adolescents and exact an economic toll on society. Costs can be measured in terms of bacterial infections, such as chlamydia, and in terms of health outcomes, such as the number of ectopic pregnancies and the rate of infertility cases associated with STD infection (Chow, Darling, & Greenbert, 1987; Eng & Butler, 1997; Washington, Johnson, & Sanders, 1987; Westrom et al. 1980). Viral infections are also important. Infection with human papillomavirus clearly contributes to subsequent cervical carcinoma (Koutsky & Kiviat, 1999). Although infection with genital herpes has not been linked to significant long-term physical sequelae, recent evidence suggests that considerable psychosocial morbidity may occur as a consequence of genital herpes infection (Corey & Wald, 1999; Melville et al., in press; Smith et al. 2000).

Perhaps of greatest concern, STDs significantly increase adolescents' risk of acquiring HIV infection (CDC, 1998a; Fleming & Wasserheit, 1999). In the United States, adolescents and young adults are a population at increased risk of HIV infection (Rosenberg & Biggar, 1998). Recent estimates suggest that 50% of new HIV infections occur among people younger than 25 years of age and 25% of new HIV infections occur among adolescents younger than 22 years of age (Office of National AIDS Policy, 1996). Given the possibility that many adolescents infected with HIV may remain unaware of their serostatus for many years—creating

substantial opportunity for transmission and decreasing the odds of effective responses to therapy—the primary prevention of HIV infection among adolescents is a public health priority.

PREVENTION

Understanding the complex web of influences that affects adolescents' STD/HIV-associated risk behavior is critically important to the design and implementation of risk reduction interventions and public health and prevention education policy, as well as for informing clinical practice and counseling guidelines. Two in-depth reports, from the National Academy of Sciences (1986) and the National Commission on AIDS (1993), have recommended research to understand the factors that influence adolescents' use of HIV/STD-prevention strategies. However, understanding the antecedents of both risk and protective behaviors is a formidable challenge due to competing influences (individual, familial, relational, community, and societal) that interact to shape adolescents' sexual behavior. Historically, adolescents' HIV/STD-associated risk behavior was largely viewed as an individual-level phenomenon. Recently, however, research has begun to recognize the importance of a contextual perspective that expands investigational and intervention efforts beyond the individual level.

A Contextual Perspective

From a contextual perspective, competing factors represent a reciprocal web of causality that influences adolescents' risk taking. In essence, adolescents' sexual behavior represents the behavioral endpoint of converging influences. Individual, interpersonal, social, economic, and other influences are embedded within a cultural context superimposed over traditions, values, and patterns of social organization. Of great importance, from a prevention perspective, many of these factors are modifiable.

We can think of the different levels of influence as representing five concentric spheres, with the individual at the center and successive rings representing the family, peers and other relational influences, the community, and, finally, society. The innermost sphere, representing the individual (i.e., adolescents), includes psychological characteristics and behaviors (e.g., self-esteem, sensation seeking, substance abuse). The family, relational, and community spheres suggest that interactions among adolescents and family members, intimate partners, and peers, have a strong influence on adolescents' behaviors and provide the context for those behaviors. The outermost sphere indicates that characteristics of the society at large (e.g., socioeconomic status, health care policies, media exposures, gender and racial/ethnic discrimination) provide a broader context in which adolescents, institutions, and communities are embedded. Each sphere, singularly, exerts an influence on adolescents' behavior; however, it is the interaction among spheres that ultimately shapes adolescents' sexual risk behavior.

THE BASIS FOR PREVENTION INTERVENTIONS

The risk and protective behaviors for STD/HIV infection have been well articulated elsewhere (Aral & Holmes, 1999; Eng & Butler, 1997; Rosenberg et al., 1999). A primary and formidable challenge confronting public health researchers and practitioners has been understanding the psychosocial antecedents of these behaviors. The task is particularly complex because empirical investigation of such a personal, and often nonpublic and nondisclosed behavior, is

logistically complicated. Yet human and financial resources have been mobilized to identify and understand these antecedents because this process is widely considered essential to the development of effective behavioral intervention programs. In essence, behavioral interventions seek to minimize antecedents of adolescents' sexual risk behavior and maximize the antecedents of their sexual-protective behaviors.

Initially, individual-level interventions were designed to target adolescents' STD/HIV-associated risk behaviors. Interventions at this level are designed to enhance adolescents' HIV/STD-preventive knowledge, attitudes, and beliefs; foster the development of perceived peer norms as supportive of HIV/STD-preventive practices; promote mastery of risk reduction skills; and, finally, motivate adolescents to adopt these preventive practices. In many cases, these interventions are offered in a small-group format over multiple sessions. Several individual-level interventions have reduced adolescents' HIV-associated risk behaviors (Kirby, 2000, 2001b).

In a recent comprehensive review of published behavioral intervention studies designed to reduce adolescents' sexual risk behaviors, the strategies and content of the intervention approaches were largely geared toward (a) increasing awareness of STD/HIV, (b) increasing favorable attitudes and motivations for practicing safer sex (i.e., avoiding sex, using condoms, using contraception), and (c) providing adolescents with skills that enhance their ability to practice safer sex (e.g., communication and negotiation skills, condom use skills, and refusal skills). Exceptions were characterized by a few studies that included condom distribution programs and components including parental involvement (Robin et al., in press). One important observation of this review is that intervention approaches have predominately targeted the individual level rather than adopting a contextual approach.

While effective at motivating behavior change, individual-level interventions may not be of sufficient intensity to sustain behavior changes over protracted periods of time, particularly in the face of pervasive countervailing pressures, such as negative peer pressure or media pressure, that promote or reinforce sexual risk behavior. Furthermore, addressing behavior change at the individual level lacks sufficient breadth to reach large segments of the at-risk adolescent population. Thus, to enhance their clinical and public health impact there is a need to expand the scope of STD/HIV behavioral interventions for adolescents (DiClemente, 2000, 2001; DiClemente & Wingood, 2000). To promote the development of interventions that use a contextual approach, potentially addressing but often transcending the individual level, we review here selected studies that confirm the profound effects of the diversity of influences captured in the different levels of influence on adolescents' STD/HIV-associated risk behavior.

The Familial Level

Emerging empirical evidence suggests that parent-adolescent communication is an important determinant of adolescents' sexual risk-taking behavior. Greater communication has been associated with (a) reduced likelihood of early sexual initiation (DiIorio, Kelley, & Hockenberry-Eaton, 1999; Jaccard, Dittus, & Gordon, 1996), (b) less frequent intercourse (Dutra, Miller, & Forehand, 1999; Holtzman & Rubinson, 1995; Jaccard et al., 1996), (c) increased use of condoms and other contraceptives (DiClemente, Wingood, Crosby, Cobb, et al. 2001; Dutra et al., 1999; Jaccard et al., 1996; Miller, Levin, Whitaker, & Xiaohe, 1998), and (d) having fewer sex partners (Dutra et al., 1999; Holtzman & Rubinson, 1995).

Accumulating evidence also suggests that parental monitoring may be an important determinant of risk behavior. Lack of parental monitoring has been associated with adolescents' participation in (a) unprotected sexual behaviors (Biglan et al., 1990; DiClemente, Wingood, Crosby, Sionean, et al., 2001; Li, Feigelman, & Stanton, 2000; Li, Stanton, & Feigelman, 2002; Small & Luster, 1994), (b) earlier initiation of sexual activity (Romer et al., 1999), and (c) sex with nonmonogamous male partners as well as sex with multiple male partners among adolescent females (DiClemente, Wingood, Crosby, Sionean, et al., 2001). In recent studies among African American adolescent females, we found that infrequent parental monitoring was associated with multiple behavioral outcomes (e.g., risky sex, multiple partners, and selection of nonmonogamous partners) as well as biologically confirmed adverse outcomes (e.g., STD infection and pregnancy) assessed over relatively brief periods of follow up (Crosby, DiClemente, Wingood, Harrington, Davies, Hook, et al., 2002b; Crosby, DiClemente, Wingood, Lang, & Harrington, 2003; DiClemente, Wingood, Crosby, Sionean, et al., 2001).

Recent studies suggest that family-level interventions may effectively lower adolescents' sexual risk behavior (Pequegnat & Szapocznik, 2000). A primary goal of family-level STD/HIV intervention programs is to facilitate more frequent discussion between adolescents and their parents about sex-related issues, potentially opening the door for an ongoing dialogue that can provide adolescents with a "lifeline" during times when they are making critical sexual decisions. Simons-Morton and Hartos (2002) have offered an important theoretical framework for achieving increased parental monitoring. A recent intervention trial for parents of low-income African American adolescents suggested that programs may facilitate parental monitoring (Stanton et al., 2000). Furthermore, a recent program that involved parents in the school-based sex education found beneficial effects. For example, a youth development program that provided training to parents as well as their elementary school-aged children, decreased the odds of risky sexual behavior among these children as they progressed through adolescence (Hawkins, Catalano, Kosterman, Abbott, & Hill, 1999). Favorable outcomes included a lower likelihood of sexual experience, multiple sex partners, and pregnancy.

The Relational Level

Recent evidence suggests that relationship dynamics between adolescents and their sex partners may be an important intervention point. For example, studies suggest that more frequent sexual communication between partners may lead to increased protective behaviors (Crosby et al., 2001; Lindberg, Ku, & Sonenstein, 1998; Whitaker, Miller, May, & Levin, 1999). Relationship length and the amount of time spent with partners may also be strong determinants of protective behavior; as each increases, condom use becomes less likely (Crosby et al., 2000). For adolescent females, having a sex partner who is 2 to 3 years older may be a substantial risk factor for engaging in risky sex (DiClemente et al., 2002; Miller, Clark, & Moore, 1997). Older partners may also serve as a "bridge" between sexual networks—importing STDs from networks of young adults to networks of teens. In a recent study of pregnant teens, our research team found that those involved with partners 2 years or more their senior were 4 times more likely to acquire chlamydia over a 6-month period of observation (Begley, Crosby, DiClemente, et al., in press).

Other relational factors that also may predispose adolescents to sexual risk include low resistance to partner's request for condom use (Plichta, Weisman, Nathanson, Ensminger, & Robinson, 1992), perceptions of partner control over STD acquisition (Rosenthal et al., 1999), perception of low partner support of condoms (Weisman, Plichta, Nathanson, Ensminger, & Robinson, 1991), being a date rape victim (Valois, Oeltmann, Waller, & Hussey, 1999), and being a victim of dating violence (Silverman, Raj, Mucci, & Hathaway, 2001; Valois et al., 1999; Wingood, DiClemente, McCree, Harrington, & Davies, 2001). The number and magnitude of the identified relational factors suggests that addressing STD/HIV prevention in a dyadic intervention rather than focusing entirely on one of the partners may be more advantageous in achieving sexual risk reduction.

The Community Level

Examples of community-level influences include community norms regarding safer sex, neighborhood and community cohesion, and the extent of community involvement in safer-sex programs for adolescents. Peer norms surrounding sexual behaviors and condom use are robust influences on risky sexual behavior. Perceiving that friends and similar-aged teens are engaging in risky sex may foster personal adoption of the same behaviors. In contrast, perceived peer norms supportive of sexual-protective behaviors may influence the adoption and maintenance of safer-sex practices (Boyer et al., 2000; Crosby et al., 2000; Doljanac & Zimmerman, 1998). An extreme form of negative peer pressure may be gang involvement. Our research team found that African American adolescent females involved in a gang, relative to those who were not gang involved, were more likely to test positive for common sexually transmitted disease such as *Trichomonas vaginalis* and *Neisseria gonnorrhoeae* (Wingood et al., 2002).

Community characteristics can also influence adolescents' adoption of STD/HIV-protective behaviors. Affiliations with social organizations (Crosby, DiClemente, Wingood, Harrington, Davies, & Malow, 2002;

Crosby et al., 2002), perceiving high levels of social support (St. Lawrence, Brasfield, Jefferson, & Allyene, 1994), and positive school environments may foster safer-sex behaviors among adolescents. For example, Resnick et al. (1997) found that when adolescents feel a positive connection to peers, teachers, and other members of the school, they were more likely to delay sexual initiation. An emerging line of inquiry suggests that factors such as neighborhood cohesion (i.e., social capital) may also influence adolescents' sexual risk behaviors. Social capital is an index composed of trust, reciprocity, and cooperation among members of a social network (Putnam, 2000). A recent study demonstrated that social capital was inversely correlated with AIDS case rates as well as with the incidence of chlamydia, gonorrhea, and syphilis among adults (Holtgrave & Crosby, 2003). More recent research has shown that adolescents with greater levels of social capital were less likely to engage in selected sexual risk behaviors (Crosby, Holtgrave, DiClemente, Wingood, & Gayle, under review).

Community commitment to sexual risk reduction among adolescents may also be vital. Adolescents with better accessibility to and availability of condoms tend to have higher rates of condom use, without an increase in overall rates of sexual activity (Furstenberg, Geitz, Teitler, & Weiss, 1997; Guttmacher et al., 1997; Sellers, McGraw, & McKinlay, 1994). The theoretical assumption underlying school condom availability programs is that program effectiveness may be achieved by affecting several mediating variables, such as peer norms about condom use, self-efficacy in obtaining condoms, barriers to condom use, and social context (DiClemente & Peterson, 1994).

The Societal Level

Societal characteristics play distinct roles in shaping adolescents' sexual behaviors. For example, music, television, movies, the Internet, and magazines may all substantially contribute to adolescents' socialization (Thornburgh & Lin, 2002), thereby influencing the adoption of sexually risky or protective behaviors. Media portraying violence and aggression toward females serve as an important illustration of this point. To investigate this question, Wingood and colleagues (2002) examined exposure to rap music videos among African American adolescent females over a 12-month time period. They found that adolescents reporting greater exposure to rap music videos were significantly more likely to have multiple sex partners, to use drugs, and to have a laboratory-confirmed positive test for STDs. Furthermore, they also investigated exposure to X-rated movies among the same sample and found that adolescents who reported viewing X-rated movies in the 3-months prior to assessment were more likely to report negative condom attitudes, to have had multiple sex partners, and to have had more frequent sexual intercourse; were less likely to use contraception during last intercourse; and more likely to test positive for chlamydia (Wingood, DiClemente, Harrington, et al., 2001).

Societal conditions characteristic of the context of poverty may also be an important barrier to adolescents' adoption of safer-sex practices. Low educational achievement and pessimism about future academic success have been linked to early debut and risky sex (Harvey & Spigner, 1995; Small & Luster, 1994). Among some impoverished adolescent populations, sex may be bartered for money, drugs, or both (Lown, Winkler, Fullilove, & Fullilove, 1995). Adolescents living in stressful environments are generally more likely to take sexual risks. Homeless adolescents, for example, are more likely than their same-age peers to experience an early sexual debut, to report multiple sex partners who have a high-risk of STD infection, and to report sexual abuse (Eng & Butler,

1997; Ennett, Federman, Bailey, Ringwalt, & Hubbard, 1999).

Finally, the prevalence of STD/HIV among adults clearly reflects a risk for adolescents. STD/HIV screening and treatment infrastructures may be less developed in communities experiencing poverty, social disruption, or both. Thus, again, societal conditions may well inflate adolescents' odds of contacting and becoming infected by a sexually transmitted disease (Aral & Wasserheit, 1995).

Adolescents from low-income families are also likely to experience financial barriers to receiving health care. For example, the Institute of Medicine recently estimated that one quarter of adolescents and young adults at high risk of STD infection do not have health insurance. Thus, adolescents who do not seek STD care remain likely to infect their sex partners, creating higher risk of STD infection within the sexual network.

CONTEXTUAL PROGRAMS TO PREVENT STD/HIV AMONG ADOLESCENTS

In the broadest conceptualization, contextual interventions are focused on individuals, communities, families, social networks, and social institutions in which adolescents congregate (i.e., schools, youth centers, churches) and are designed to counter media influences that cultivate or reinforce risky sexual behavior, attitudes, and beliefs. Contextual interventions are designed to promote STD/HIV-protective behavior by providing adolescents with information and skills to change behavior through naturally occurring channels of influence (i.e. social/ friendship networks) and social institutions in the community (i.e., Boys & Girl Clubs). Simultaneously, they also attempt to provide a supportive environment that encourages STD/HIV-preventive behavior (Crosby,

DiClemente, Wingood, Harrington, Davies, Hook, et al., 2002a; Crosby, DiClemente, Wingood, Harrington, Davies, & Malow, 2002). Socioenvironmental interventions also have the capacity to enhance access to community resources (i.e., STD and HIV screening and treatment, drug treatment, access to condoms), mobilize community support for STD/HIV prevention efforts, and modify norms that reinforce and maintain STD/HIV-preventive practices.

One example of a social/environmental intervention tailored to young gay men is that of Kegeles, Hays, and Coates (1996). This project involved the use of opinion leaders who recruited other opinion leaders and so on, thus setting up a self-perpetuating process for changing community norms. They also used an enhanced publicity campaign, using small media (pamphlets, flyers, and brochures) to spread awareness of the program and establish its legitimacy, invite young men to become involved, and provide a continuing reminder that safe sex is the norm. In addition, to attract younger gay men, they hosted a wide variety of social events at a project facility. The approach successfully increased condom use and decreased the proportion of men with more than one partner.

Another contextual approach that holds promise is the use of social marketing or media interventions to motivate adolescents' adoption of STD/HIV-preventive behaviors, reinforce prevention messages, and sustain behavior change. Social marketing and media-based interventions remain an understudied intervention mode in the United States. However, there is evidence that media may help to create an environment conducive to HIV prevention. In particular, mass media can help increase awareness of the twin epidemics of STDs and HIV and their impact and encourage public funding for prevention, treatment, and social services. In a number of European countries, as well as in Canada,

New Zealand, and Australia, the media have been instrumental in creating a social climate that makes a wide spectrum of prevention strategies more acceptable. In addition, messages about STD/HIV disseminated through the mass media may facilitate more open discussion of sexuality in circumstances where heretofore this was not possible. The widespread promotion of condoms, for example, which is commonplace now in most countries of Western Europe, may reflect, to some extent, the attention given to the HIV epidemic by mass media.

Evidence for the efficacy of media interventions can be gleaned from the campaigns undertaken in Switzerland. Trend analyses of ongoing evaluations of media-based interventions in Switzerland have observed marked reductions in risk behaviors. For example, between 1987 and 1991, an aggressive marketing campaign aimed at 21- to 30-year-olds observed an increase in condom use with casual sex partners from 8% to 50%. Among a younger subgroup, 17- to 20-year-olds, effects were even more marked; condom use increased from 19% to 73%. Equally important from a health policy perspective, the Swiss study found that rates of sexual activity remained unchanged during implementation of the media campaign. More recently, evidence from an evaluation of HIV prevention messages diffused through a radio soap opera in Tanzania supported the efficacy of media for promoting behavior change. Evaluation of HIV-associated risk behaviors among people residing in the broadcast area and those in the control area indicates that condom use markedly increased in the intervention areas. Although media-based interventions may be effective at promoting the adoption of preventive behaviors, they need not be limited to PSA-type announcements but may be integrated into mainstream media shows.

Social marketing and media interventions are not a panacea. Whether such media campaigns would enjoy support and success in the United States is arguable. However, media programs, even those that may be less candid or innovative, may still serve to create a social climate conducive to open discussion about sex, STDs, and HIV. Media messages may also reinforce prevention messages for individuals exposed to other, more intensive interventions conducted at different levels (i.e., individual level, relational level, or family level). In this way, media campaigns may directly affect individuals' behavior and may indirectly influence behavior by affecting social norms to help sustain newly adopted STD/HIV-preventive behaviors or reinforce maintenance of low-risk behaviors in the face of countervailing social pressures.

CONCLUSION

This chapter has argued for a broader contextual perspective in examining the diverse array and sources of influences that may affect adolescents' risk for STD/HIV. Interventions that use a contextual approach can create preventive synergy within a community by targeting different sources or levels of influence simultaneously. Developing contextual interventions may effectively promote and reinforce the adoption and long-term maintenance of STD/HIV-preventive behaviors among adolescents.

CHAPTER 39

Findings and Future Directions

KATHLEEN HALL JAMIESON
DANIEL ROMER

In this final chapter, we summarize the major findings of the Reducing Adolescent Risk Conference. Underlying the conference was the assumption that the well-being of young people could be improved if the research community shared findings, identified common interventions, and ensured that campaigns designed to address one risk did not exacerbate another. The conference was convened to open channels of communication within the research communities that study adolescent health risks. The following conclusions and recommendations are a step toward an integrated framework for the study of adolescent risk.

We divide the recommendations into four categories that address (a) universal programs for all young people, (b) targeted programs for those most at risk, (c) strategies to counteract societal influences that promote risky behavior, and (d) the need for more research to understand the links between risky behaviors. Although the findings are derived from the chapters included in this volume, many significant presentations at the conference are not represented here. In addition, the final session of the conference was devoted to

synthesizing what was learned and to implications for future research. We include these sources as we summarize the recommendations of the conference.

UNIVERSAL INTERVENTIONS THAT PROMOTE HEALTHY DEVELOPMENT HAVE GREAT PROMISE

In the Preface to this volume, it was noted that neither the states nor the federal government has a comprehensive youth development strategy for schools and communities. Most strategies focus on specific risk behaviors and identify separate programs for each. However, several findings from the conference point the way toward universal programs that can promote healthy development and help reduce a range of risk behaviors for all youth.

Several presenters made the point that adolescents are naturally drawn to new behaviors, many of which are risky. However, learning to evaluate risks is part of the job of adolescence (see Byrnes, chap. 2;

Lapsley, chap. 4). Hence, the universal programs we identify have the potential to give young people the skills they need and the environments in which to practice those skills so that they can make good decisions about the risky choices they will inevitably face. Furthermore, because popular peers are seen as models of risk behavior (see findings presented in Chapter 1), simply telling youth that certain behaviors are risky will not be a successful strategy on its own. However, in a context of early and continuous universal programs that encourage mature decision making and healthy choices, youth may be more willing to consider messages that provide them with risk information (see Gerrard, Gibbons, & Gano, chap. 9). It is with this expectation that we offer the following recommendations.

Adolescents can be taught to become better decision makers. Adolescents are sensitive to risk information (Fishbein, chap. 7; Johnston, chap. 8; Gerrard et al., chap. 9). However, they differ in decision-making and problem-solving skills (Steinberg, chap. 3; Shure, chap. 10; Parker & Fischhoff, chap., 12) and in their capacity and disposition to effectively use risk information (Millstein, chap. 5). Like adults, adolescents are subject to affect biases (Slovic, chap. 6) and unrealistic optimism (Lapsley, chap. 4). Yet a long line of research has identified interventions to help pre- and early adolescents become better decision makers (Shure, chap. 10; Griffin, chap. 11). These skills include abilities such as generating alternative solutions to problems, recognizing the perspectives of others in reaching solutions, and appreciating the need for planning to reach goals. In addition, adolescents can be sensitized to long-term and not just the short-term effects of risk and protective behavior (Fong & Hall, chap. 13). All these skills can help youth evaluate risks, recognize unhealthy influence from peers and the media, and solve social and life problems

in constructive ways. We need additional research to determine the optimum ages at which to deliver these educational interventions and to determine the duration of their effects.

Programs to help youth make better decisions should be integrated into the school curriculum at all ages. Considerable discussion at the conference focused on the need to find better ways to integrate health promotion into the schools. Decision-making skills and other related competencies could be initiated as part of the elementary school curriculum and elaborated as children age. Such competencies could be incorporated into a number of different subject areas, including reading and mathematics. Information about specific risks (e.g., tobacco and drugs) could be introduced as part of these programs to illustrate the principles of effective problem solving (Griffin, chap. 11). Research is needed to develop and test such curricula.

Attachment to adults and institutions in the community is protective for youth. School and after-school environments (Kirby, chap. 29; Brent, chap. 33; Flay, chap. 36; Roth & Brooks-Gunn, chap. 37) can be designed to increase attachment both to school and to adults and peers who support healthy norms of behavior. Research is needed to identify the best means of creating environments in which youth feel valued and part of a community (LaRusso & Selman, chap. 14; Joe, chap. 34). Such environments encourage respect for adolescent viewpoints, increase mature decision making, and reduce cynicism about health messages. These challenges are even greater in poor nonwhite communities where attachments to healthy environments have been strained (Joe, chap. 34). The findings we reported in Chapter 1 indicate that prosocial activities, such as community service, can have broad effects in reducing risky behavior. In addition, integrating healthy norms into youth environments may be effective in encouraging youth both to stay in school and to make good decisions about risky behavior. Further testing of such programs in both school and after-school settings is needed to refine the interventions and to identify program components that are effective.

Multilevel interventions are more likely to be successful than programs that rely on only one modality or setting. Research is needed to test multilevel interventions that involve parents, schools, and the larger community (Stanton & Burns, chap. 22; Flay, chap. 36; DiClemente, Wingood, & Crosby, chap. 38). Parents are especially important in helping to monitor their children and encourage good decision-making skills. Research to identify ways of engaging parental participation in the creation of healthier schools and community programs is needed.

Consensus is lacking on the best strategy to prevent sexual risks. Sexual risk behavior creates major dilemmas for universal programs because it varies by cultural and by income (Kirby, chap. 29; Moore & Brooks-Gunn, chap. 30). What fits some cultures may not fit others, and approaches that focus exclusively on the risks of sex may stigmatize sex altogether (Fortenberry, chap. 31). Major national evaluations are underway to assess the effects of the abstinence-first programs funded by welfare reform legislation (Maynard, 2002). Research also is needed to determine the appropriate ages at which different types of programs may be most effective. Abstinence may be more effective in early adolescence. As youth age, greater information and access to contraception and condoms may be more likely to produce positive outcomes, if provided in a context that includes norms for healthy development and for youth who have learned effective problem-solving skills (Kirby, chap. 29; Moore & Brooks-Gunn, chap. 30).

SOME YOUTH WILL NEED TARGETED INTERVENTIONS

Despite the promise of universal programs, there still will be a need for targeted interventions. Some major directions for these programs were also identified at the conference.

Early identification and treatment of multiple-problem youth is feasible. Multiple-problem youth account for a large proportion of risky behavior among adolescents (Biglan & Cody, chap. 15; Severson, Andrews, & Walker, chap. 16). Many of these youth can be identified in elementary school (Severson et al., chap. 16) and if necessary assigned to special programs (Winters, August, & Leitten, chap. 17). Teachers can help to identify multiple-problem youth (Severson et al., chap. 16). Research also is needed to determine ways to collect teacher diagnostic ratings that protect the privacy of the information so that it is does not lead to stigmatization of multiple-problem youth. Further research is needed to refine ways to help multiple-problem youth redirect their risky developmental paths while their behavior is amenable to change.

Impulsiveness and sensation seeking underlie many risk behaviors. Personality differences in these characteristics may be genetically based (Lerman, Patterson, & Shields, chap. 18) and will require interventions that can help those with impulsive decision-making styles and high needs for stimulation. Research is needed to determine if decision-making skills can be taught to high-risk youth to minimize impulsive and ill-considered decisions. Other strategies that may be effective should also be explored, such as channeling needs for stimulation into less risky activities (e.g., exercise and sports).

Depression and other affective disorders place youth at risk for a range of hazardous outcomes. Depression is prevalent among adolescents (Alloy, Zhu, & Abramson, chap. 20) and is a major risk factor for suicide (Gould, chap. 32). Research is needed to identify ways to encourage youth to seek help for mental disorders. This proposed program intersects with the agenda to create school environments that encourage students to feel part of an accepting community (Brent, chap. 33). Research is also needed to understand the role of depression in addictive behavior and to determine if treatment of depression can help to reduce reliance on these behaviors.

Despite the important role of individual differences, macro-trends in risk behavior have great influence. Assessment of risk behavior over time in the Monitoring the Future research program indicates great variation in rates of risk behavior despite the likely presence of the same personality predispositions (Johnston, chap. 8). Hence, we should not lose track of the role of environmental influences. Diffusion of risk behavior in peer networks needs to be studied, both as a source of risk (Rodgers, chap. 21) and as a potential avenue of intervention to promote safer behavior (Kinsman, 2002).

OUR CULTURE PROMOTES RISKY BEHAVIOR IN YOUTH

Many risky behaviors are promoted by powerful forces in our culture, including marketing (e.g., of tobacco and alcohol) and the government (e.g., the lottery). Some ways to reduce the effects of these forces were also considered.

Advertising of many risky products reaches adolescents. Many risks facing adolescents involve behaviors that are legal for adults but proscribed for youth (e.g., alcohol, gambling, cigarettes). Advertising of these products creates dilemmas for social policy.

Research-based guidelines should be developed to help advertisers avoid appealing to young people as much as possible. Monitoring of advertising designed to target the young should be a research priority.

Media campaigns to encourage safer behavior and counteradvertising programs can benefit from careful message development strategies. Considerable discussion at the conference focused on the role of the media in both encouraging and discouraging risk behavior. Presenters (Donohew, chap. 19; Delaney, chap. 23; Cappella, Yzer, & Fishbein, chap. 24; Pechmann, 2002) described methods for creating better messages. There is also a need to screen health-promoting messages for possible effects on other risk behaviors. Countermarketing should be used to blunt the appeal of images employed by advertising for tobacco and alcohol and for gambling (Slovic, chap. 6).

Gambling is an attractive activity to young people. Rates of gambling among youth are high, and youth are more susceptible to problem gambling than are adults (Griffiths, chap. 25; Derevensky, Gupta, Dickson, Hardoon, & Deguire, chap. 26). Gambling shares many characteristics with other addictive behaviors (Griffiths, chap. 25; Derevensky et al., chap. 26; Potenza, chap. 27). As gambling becomes more prevalent, its influence on youth will increase. Research is needed to understand both how the young become exposed to gambling and to identify potential interventions that can shield them from gambling addiction (Potenza, chap. 27; Volberg, chap. 28).

Access to firearms is a major risk for violence, including suicide. Developing parental interventions to reduce access to guns is a high research priority (Brent, chap. 33; Joe, chap. 34). Research to test the effectiveness of potential government restrictions on access to firearms, such as fingerprint activated trigger locks, is also needed.

Use of some illicit drugs, such as marijuana, may be reduced by preventing the use of tobacco and encouraging responsible use of alcohol. It has long been known that tobacco and alcohol use usually precede marijuana use. Current practices among youth appear to follow the same pattern (Hornik, chap. 35). Programs that reduce use of tobacco and alcohol as a strategy to reduce subsequent marijuana use should be tested.

MORE RESEARCH IS NEEDED TO UNDERSTAND THE CAUSAL CONNECTIONS AMONG RISK BEHAVIORS

The central conclusion of the conference was that we need a greater understanding of the developmental pathways that lead to comorbidity in risk behavior. It has long been known that risk behaviors covary. What is less well understood are the reasons for these connections. Interventions designed to influence one or more risk behaviors should assess effects on other behaviors. Studies of the effects of potential influences on risk behavior (see example in Chapter 1 of this volume) should also examine effects on common factors that underlie and mediate comorbidity. Interventions able to minimize more than one risk behavior will be cost-effective and more easily adopted by schools and communities.

SUMMARY

The research community is on the verge of fashioning a new approach to healthy adolescent development. Research on adolescent risk behaviors has generated a wealth of understanding of the causes and developmental pathways that lead to risky behavior. This research has also identified educational and community approaches that have the potential not only to avert many of these outcomes but also to help the young make a stronger transition to adulthood. Although these approaches will need further research to identify effective methods of implementation, the agenda is clear. It is now a matter of will and dedication to make these approaches a reality.

Appendix A
Reducing Adolescent Risk:
Conference Schedule
June 27-30, 2002

THURSDAY, JUNE 27, 2002

Session 1: General Risk Perception and Behavior

Session Leader: Susan Millstein, University of California, San Francisco

James Byrnes, University of Maryland

Meg Gerrard, Iowa State University

Bonnie Halpern-Felsher, University of California, San Francisco

Daniel Lapsley, Ball State University

Andrew Parker, Virginia Tech University

Robert Selman, Harvard University

Myrna B. Shure, Drexel University

Laurence Steinberg, Temple University

Session 2: Suicide

Session Leader: Madelyn Gould, Columbia University

Lauren Alloy, Temple University

Aaron T. Beck, University of Pennsylvania

Alan L. Berman, American Association of Suicidology

David Brent, Western Psychiatric Institute

Jane Gillham, University of Pennsylvania

Ian Gotlib, Stanford University

Lawrence Greenhill, Columbia University

Sean Joe, School of Social Work, University of Pennsylvania

Steve Stack, Wayne State University

FRIDAY, JUNE 28, 2002

Breakfast

Invited Speaker: Caryn Lerman, Director, Tobacco Research Program at the Leonard & Madlyn Abramson Family Cancer Research Institute, University of Pennsylvania

Session 3: Gambling

Session Leader: Mark Griffiths, Nottingham University, United Kingdom

Jeffrey Derevensky, McGill University

Richard I. Evans, University of Houston

Marc Potenza, Yale University School of Medicine

Rachel Volberg, University of Massachusetts

Ken C. Winters, University of Minnesota

Lunch

Invited Speaker: Aaron T. Beck, Professor Emeritus, University of Pennsylvania

Session 4: Tobacco

Session Leader: Paul Slovic, University of Oregon

Brian Flay, University of Illinois, Chicago

Geoffrey Fong, University of Waterloo

Lyndon Haviland, The American Legacy Foundation

Caryn Lerman, University of Pennsylvania

Daniel McGoldrick, Tobacco Free Kids

Connie Pechmann, University of California, Irvine

Herbert Severson, Oregon Research Institute

Neil Weinstein, Rutgers University

Session 5: Pregnancy

Session Leader: Douglas Kirby, Education Training Research Associates

Jane Brown, University of North Carolina

Jacqueline Darroch, Alan Guttmacher Institute

James Jaccard, SUNY Albany

Rebecca Maynard, University of Pennsylvania

Mignon Moore, Columbia University

Marisa Nightingale, The National Campaign To Prevent Teen Pregnancy

Joseph Rodgers, University of Oklahoma

Diane Scott-Jones, Boston College

SATURDAY, JUNE 29, 2002

Session 6: HIV/STD

Session Leader: John Jemmott, The Annenberg School for Communication

Ralph DiClemente, Emory University

Martin Fishbein, The Annenberg School for Communication

Dennis Fortenberry, Indiana University

Loretta Jemmott, University of Pennsylvania

Robert Johnson, New Jersey Medical School

Sara Kinsman, Children's Hospital of Pennsylvania

Freya Sonenstein, Urban Institute

Bonita Stanton, West Virginia University

Antonia Villarruel, University of Michigan

Gina Wingood, Emory University

Lunch

Invited Speaker: David Shaffer, Irving Phillips Professor of Child Psychology, Columbia University

Session 7: Alcohol/Drugs

Session Leader: Lloyd Johnston, University of Michigan

Anthony Biglan, Oregon Research Institute

Joseph Cappella, The Annenberg School for Communication

Barbara Delaney, Partnership for a Drug-Free America

Lewis Donohew, University of Kentucky

Kenneth Griffin, Cornell Medical School

George Hacker, The Center for Science in the Public Interest

Robert Hornik, The Annenberg School for Communication

Michael Windle, University of Alabama at Birmingham

Appendix B
Conference Attendees,
June 27 – June 30, 2002

CARMEN ANDERSON
Program Officer, Children,
    Youth & Families
The Heinz Endowment

ELIJAH ANDERSON
Board of Directors
American Academy of Political
    and Social Science

JANET AUDRAIN
Assistant Professor
Psychiatry, University of Pennsylvania

DAN BARRETT
The Annenberg School for
    Communication
University of Pennsylvania

COURTNEY BENNETT
Program Officer
The David and Lucile Packard
    Foundation

TYRONE BENTLEY
Developmental Pediatric Fellow
Children's Seashore House/C.H.O.P.

ALAN L. BERMAN
Executive Director
American Association of Suicidology

LINDA BLOCK
Health Communication Specialist
Centers for Disease Control

LISA BOLTON
Associate Professor of Marketing
Wharton, University of Pennsylvania

NICOLETTE BOREK
Division of Mental Disorders,
Behavior Research and AIDS
National Institute of Mental Health

RHONDA BOYD
Instructor
University of Pennsylvania
    School of Medicine

GREG BROWN
Assistant Professor
Department of Psychiatry
University of Pennsylvania

ELAINE CASEY
Program Officer
The Pew Charitable Trusts

ROSE CHENEY
Executive Director
Firearm Injury Center at Penn
University of Pennsylvania

MIKE CODY
Professor
Annenberg School
University of Southern California

LINDA CROSSETT
Acting Chief of Research Application
    Branch
Centers for Disease Control

MAURA DUNFEY
Research & Communications
    Coordinator
Firearm Injury Center at Penn
University of Pennsylvania

JEANETTE FRIEDMAN
Caron Foundation

LYNNE HAVERKOS
Program Director
National Institute of Child Health and
    Human Development

FREDERICK HELDRING
Executive Director
American Academy of Political and
    Social Science

GREGG HENRIQUES
Assistant Professor
Department of Psychiatry
University of Pennsylvania

JUDY HERRMAN
University of Delaware
Center for Community
    Development & Family Policy

NICOLE HEWITT
Center for Health Behavior and
    Communication Research
The Annenberg Public Policy Center
University of Pennsylvania

JANET HSU
Center for Health Behavior and
    Communication Research
The Annenberg Public Policy Center
University of Pennsylvania

JOAH IANNOTTA
National Academy of Science

CAROLE JOHNSON
Program Officer
The Pew Charitable Trusts

LINDA KOENIG
Assistant Chief for Behavioral Science
Division of HIV/AIDS Prevention
Centers for Disease Control

KITTY KOLBERT
The Annenberg School for Communication
University of Pennsylvania

DEMIE KURZ
Codirector, Women's Studies Program
University of Pennsylvania

MARIA LARUSSO
Graduate School of Education
Harvard University

RAY LORION
Chair & Professor of Psychology
    in Education
Graduate School of Education
University of Pennsylvania

JANE MACHIN
Wharton, University of Pennsylvania

JOE MCLLHANEY
Director
The Medical Institute, Austin, TX

MARY ANN MEYERS
Board of Directors
American Academy of Political and
    Social Science

LYNN MILLER
Professor
Annenberg School
University of Southern California

KLAUS NAUDÉ
Board of Directors
American Academy of Political and
    Social Science

SUSAN NEWCOMER
Demographic & Behavioral Sciences
    Branch
National Institute of Child Health and
    Human Development

JAMES NONNEMAKER
Research Economist
RTI International

FREDA PATTERSON
Project Manager
Tobacco Use Research Center

JANE LESLIE PEARSON
Chief, Preventive Interventions Programs
National Institute of Mental Health

ROBERT W. PEARSON
Executive Director
American Academy of Political and
    Social Science

JAROSLAV PELIKAN
Board of Directors
American Academy of Political and
    Social Science

WILLO PEQUEGNAT
Chief, Prevention Translational
    Research Program
National Institute of Mental Health

LOUIS H. POLLAK
Board of Directors
American Academy of Political and
    Social Science

LESHAWNDRA PRICE
National Institute of Mental Health

JANE PRITZL
Division of Adolescent and School Health
Centers for Disease Control

KAREN REIVICH
University of Pennsylvania

KELLY SCHMITT
Assistant Director, Education
    and Research
Sesame Street Research

DON SCHWARZ
Associate Professor & Vice Chair
    of Pediatrics
Children's Hospital of Pennsylvania

MELISSA SEIDE
Program Manager
Firearm Injury Center at Penn
University of Pennsylvania

BELINDA SIMS
Chief, Preventive Interventions Program
National Institute of Mental Health

JANET ST. LAWRENCE
Chief of Behavioral Interventions &
    Research Branch
Division of STD Prevention
Centers for Disease Control

GLADYS THOMAS
Center Administrator, Center
    for Health Behavior and
    Communication Research
Annenberg Public Policy Center
University of Pennsylvania

MARCO YZER
The Amsterdam School of
    Communication Research
University of Amsterdam

References

Aarons, S. J., Jenkins, R. R., Raine, T. R., El-Khorazaty, M. N., Woodward, K. M., Williams, R. L., et al. (2000). Postponing sexual intercourse among urban junior high school students: A randomized controlled evaluation. *Journal of Adolescent Health, 27*(4), 236-247.

Abbott, M. W. (2001). *What do we know about gambling and problem gambling in New Zealand?* (Report No. 7 of the New Zealand Gaming Survey). Wellington, New Zealand: Department of Internal Affairs.

Abbott, M. W., & Volberg, R. A. (1999). *Gambling and problem gambling in the community: An international overview and critique.* Wellington, New Zealand: Department of Internal Affairs. Retrieved December 13, 2002, www.dia.govt.nz/Pubforms.nsf/URL/report1.pdf/$file/report1.pdf

Abbott, R. D., O'Donnell J., Hawkins J. D., Hill, K. G., Kosterman, R., & Catalano, R. F. (1998). Changing teaching practices to promote achievement and bonding to school. *American Journal of Orthopsychiatry, 68*(4), 542-552.

Aberson, B., & Shure, M. B. (2002). Problem solving training as a form of crisis prevention. In S. E. Brock & P. J. Lazurus (Eds.), *Best practices in crisis prevention and intervention in the schools* Bethesda, MD: National Association of School Psychologists.

Abma, J., Chandra, A., Mosher, W., Peterson, L., & Piccinino, L. (1997). Fertility, family planning, and women's health: New data from the 1995 National Survey of Family Growth. *Vital and Health Statistics, 23*(19), 1-114.

Abramson, L. Y., Alloy, L. B., Hankin, B. L., Haeffel, G. J., MacCoon, D. G., & Gibb, B. E. (2002). Cognitive vulnerability-stress models of depression in a self-regulatory and psychobiological context. In I. H. Gotlib & C. L. Hammen (Eds.), *Handbook of depression* (pp. 268-294). New York: Guilford.

Abramson, L. Y., Alloy, L. B., Hogan, M. E., Whitehouse, W. G., Cornette, M., Akhavan, S., et al. (1998). Suicidality and cognitive vulnerability to depression among college students: A prospective study. *Journal of Adolescence, 21,* 473-487.

Abramson, L. Y., Alloy, L. B., Hogan, M. E., Whitehouse, W. G., Gibb, B. E., & Hankin, B. L., et al. (2000). The hopelessness theory of suicidality. In T. E. Joiner & M. D. Rudd (Eds.), *Suicide science: Expanding boundaries* (pp. 17-32). Boston: Kluwer Academic.

Abramson, L. Y., Metalsky, G. I., & Alloy, L. B. (1989). Hopelessness depression: A theory-based subtype of depression. *Psychological Review, 96,* 358-372.

Achenbach, T. M. (1991). *Manual for the Teacher's Report Form and 1991 profile.* Burlington: University of Vermont.

Achenbach, T. M., & Edelbrock, C. (1983). *Manual for the child behavior checklist and revised child behavior profile.* Burlington: University of Vermont, Department of Psychiatry.

Adams, D. M., Overholser, J. C., & Lehnert, K. L. (1994). Perceived family functioning and adolescent suicidal behavior. *Journal of the American Academy of Child and Adolescent Psychiatry, 33,* 498-507.

Aiken, L.S., Gerend, M.A., & Jackson, K.M. (2001). Subjective risk and health protective behavior: Cancer screening and cancer prevention. In A. Baum, T. A. Revenson, & J. E. Singer (Eds.), *Handbook of health psychology* (pp. 727-746). Mahwah, NJ: Lawrence Erlbaum.

Ainslie, G. (1975). Specious reward: A behavioral theory of impulsiveness and impulse control. *Psychological Bulletin, 82*, 463-509.

Ainslie, G., & Haslam, N. (1992). Self-control. In G. F. Loewenstein & J. Elster (Eds.), *Choice over time* (pp. 177-209). New York: Russell Sage.

Ajzen, I. (1985). From intentions to actions. In J. Kuhl & J. Beckman (Eds.), *Action control from cognition to behavior*. New York: Springer-Verlag.

Ajzen, I., & Fishbein, M. (1980). *Understanding attitudes and predicting social behavior*. Englewood Cliffs, NJ: Prentice Hall.

Akers, R. L. (1984). Delinquent behavior, drugs, and alcohol: What is the relationship? *Today's Delinquency, 3*(1), 19-47.

Akers, R. L., Krohn, M. D., Lanza-Kaduce, L., & Radosevich, M. (1979). Social learning and deviant behavior: A specific test of a general theory. *American Sociological Review, 44*, 636-655.

Alan Guttmacher Institute. (1994). *Sex and America's teenagers*. New York: Author.

Alexander, C. N., & Campbell, E. Q. (1967). Peer influences on adolescent drinking. *Quarterly Journal of Studies on Alcohol, 28*, 444-453.

Allen, J. P., Philliber, S., & Herrling, S. (1997). Preventing teen pregnancy and academic failure: Experimental evaluation of a developmentally based approach. *Child Development, 68*, 729-742.

Allen, J. P., Philliber, S., Herrling, S., & Kuperminc, G. P. (1997). Preventing teen pregnancy and academic failure: Experimental evaluation of a developmentally-based approach. *Child Development, 64*(4), 729-742.

Allen, J. P., Philliber, S., & Hoggson, N. (1990). School-based prevention of teen-age pregnancy and school dropout: Process evaluation of the national replication of the Teen Outreach Program. *American Journal of Community Psychology, 18*(4), 505-524.

Alloy, L. B., & Abramson, L. Y. (1999). The Temple-Wisconsin Cognitive Vulnerability to Depression (CVD) Project: Conceptual background, design, and methods. *Journal of Cognitive Psychotherapy: An International Quarterly, 13*, 227-262.

Alloy, L. B., Abramson, L. Y., Hogan, M. E., Whitehouse, W. G., Rose, D. T., Robinson, M. S., et al. (2000). The Temple-Wisconsin CVD Project: Lifetime history of Axis I psychopathology in individuals at high and low cognitive risk for depression. *Journal of Abnormal Psychology, 109*, 403-418.

Alloy, L. B., Abramson, L. Y., Murray, L. A., Whitehouse, W. G., & Hogan, M. E. (1997). Self-referent information processing in individuals at high and low cognitive risk for depression. *Cognition and Emotion, 11*, 539-568.

Alloy, L. B., Abramson, L. Y., Safford, S. M., & Gibb, B. E. (in press). The Cognitive Vulnerability to Depression (CVD) Project: Current findings and future directions. In L. B. Alloy & J. H. Riskind (Eds.), *Cognitive vulnerability to emotional disorders*. Mahwah, NJ: Lawrence Erlbaum.

Alloy, L. B., Abramson, L. Y., Tashman, N. A., Berrebbi, D. S., Hogan, M. E., Whitehouse, W. G., et al. (2001). Developmental origins of cognitive vulnerability to depression: Parenting, cognitive, and inferential feedback styles of the parents of individuals at high and low cognitive risk for depression. *Cognitive Therapy and Research, 25*, 397-423.

Alloy, L. B., & Clements, C. (1992). Illusion of control: Invulnerability to negative affect and depressive symptoms after laboratory and natural stressors. *Journal of Abnormal Psychology, 101*, 234-243.

Alloy, L. B., Lipman, A., & Abramson, L. Y. (1992). Attributional style as a vulnerability factor for depression: Validation by past history of mood disorders. *Cognitive Therapy and Research, 16*, 391-407.

Allred, C. G. (1995). *Positive actions for living*. Twin Falls, ID: Positive Actions.

Alstead, M., Campsmith, M., Halley, C. S., Hartfield, K., Goldbaum, G., & Wood, R. W. (1999). Developing, implementing, and evaluating a condom promotion program targeting sexually active adolescents. *AIDS Education and Prevention, 11*(6), 497-512.

American Psychiatric Association. (1980). *Diagnostic and statistical manual of mental disorders* (3rd ed.). Washington, DC: Author.

American Psychiatric Association. (1994). *Diagnostic and statistical manual of mental disorders* (4th ed.). Washington, DC: Author.

American Social Health Association. (1998). *STDs in America: How many cases and at what cost?* Menlo Park, CA: Author.

American Society of Human Genetics Board of Directors and the American College of Medical Genetics Board of Directors. (1995). ASHG/ACMG Report. Points to consider: Ethical, legal, and psychosocial implications of genetic testing in children and adolescents. *American Journal of Human Genetics, 57*, 1233-1241.

Americans with Disabilities Act of 1990, 42 U.S.C. § 12101 *et seq.* (West (1993).

Anderson, J. E., & Cope, L. G. (1987). The impact of family planning program activity on fertility. *Family Planning Perspectives, 19*(4), 152-157.

Anderson, R. M., & May, R. M. (1991). *Infectious diseases of humans: Dynamics and control.* Oxford, UK: Oxford University Press.

Andrews, J. A., & Lewinsohn, P. M. (1992). Suicidal attempts among older adolescents: Prevalence and co-occurrence with psychiatric disorders. *Journal of the American Academy of Child and Adolescent Psychiatry, 31*, 655-662.

Andrus, J. K., Fleming, D. W., Heumann, M. A., Wassell, J. T., Hopkins, D. D., & Gordon, J. (1991). Surveillance of attempted suicide among adolescents in Oregon, 1988. *American Journal of Public Health, 81*, 1067-1069.

Angold, A., Costello, E. J., & Erkanli, A. (1999). Comorbidity. *Journal of Child Psychology and Psychiatry and Allied Disciplines, 40*, 57-87.

Aos, S., Phipps, P., Barnoski, R., & Lieb R. (2001). *The comparative costs and benefits of programs to reduce crime.* Olympia: Washington State Institute for Public Policy.

Appleby, L., Cooper, J., Amos, T., & Faragher, B. (1999). Psychological autopsy study of suicides by people aged under 35. *British Journal of Psychiatry, 175*, 168-174.

Apter, A., Bleich, A., King, R., Kron, S., Fluch, A., Kotler, M., & Cohen, D. J. (1993). Death without warning? A clinical postmortem study of suicide in 43 Israeli adolescent males. *Archives of General Psychiatry, 50*, 138-142.

Apter, A., Plutchik, R., & van Praag, H. M. (1993). Anxiety, impulsivity, and depressed mood in relation to suicidal and violent behavior. *Acta Psychiatrica Scandinavica, 87*, 1-5.

Aral, S. O., & Holmes, K. K. (1999). Social and behavioral determinants of the epidemiology of STDs: Industrialized and developing countries. In K. K. Holmes, P. F. Sparling, P. Mardh, et al. (Eds.), *Sexually transmitted diseases* (pp. 39-76). New York: McGraw-Hill.

Aral, S. O., & Wasserheit, J. N. (1995). Interactions among HIV, other sexually transmitted diseases, socioeconomic status, and poverty in women. In A. O'Leary & L. S. Jemmott (Eds.), *Women at risk: Issues in the primary prevention of AIDS* (pp. 13-42). New York: Plenum.

Arango, V., Underwood, M. D., & Mann, J. J. (1997). Biologic alterations in the brainstem of suicides. *Psychiatric Clinics of North America, 20*, 581-593.

Arcuri, A. F., Lester, D., & Smith, F. O. (1985). Shaping adolescent gambling behavior. *Adolescence, 20*, 935-938.

Arend, R., Gove, F. L., & Sroufe, A. L. (1979). Continuity of individual adaptation from infancy to kindergarten: A predictive study of ego-resiliency and curiosity in preschoolers. *Child Development, 50*, 950-959.

Arnett, J. (1990a). Contraceptive use, sensation seeking and adolescent egocentrism. *Journal of Youth and Adolescence, 19*, 171-180.

Arnett, J. (1990b). Drunk driving, sensation seeking and egocentrism among adolescents. *Personality and Individual Differences, 11*, 541-546.

Arnett, J. (1992). Reckless behavior in adolescence: A developmental perspective. *Developmental Review, 12*, 339-373.

Arnett, J. (1994). Sensation seeking: A new conceptualization and a new scale. *Personality and Individual Differences, 16*, 289-296.

Asarnow, J., Carlson, G., & Guthrie, D. (1987). Coping strategies, self perceptions, hopelessness, and perceived family environments in depressed and suicidal children. *Journal of Consulting and Clinical Psychology, 55*, 361-366.

Asberg, M., Nordstrom, P., & Traskman-Bendz, L. (1986). Biological factor in suicide. In A. Roy (Ed.), *Suicide.* (pp. 47-71). Baltimore, MD: Williams & Wilkins.

Audrain, J., Tercyak, K., Shields, A., Bush, A., Espinel, C., & Lerman, C. (in press). Which adolescents are most receptive to tobacco industry marketing? Implications for counter-advertising campaigns. *Health Communication.*

Australian Productivity Commission. (1999). *Australia's gambling industries.* Melbourne, Australia: Author.

Ayers, W., Dohrn, B., & Ayers, R. (Eds.). (2001). *Zero tolerance: Resisting the drive for punishment in our schools.* New York: New Press.

Bachman, J. G., Johnston, L. D., & O'Malley, P. M. (1984). *Monitoring the Future: Questionnaire responses from the nation's high school seniors, 1982.* Ann Arbor, MI: Institute for Social Research.

Bachman, J. G., Johnston, L. D., & O'Malley, P. M. (1990). Explaining the recent decline in cocaine use among young adults: Further evidence that perceived risks and disapproval lead to reduced drug use. *Journal of Health and Social Behavior, 31*, 173-184.

Bachman, J. G., Johnston, L. D., & O'Malley, P. M. (1998). Explaining the recent increases in students' marijuana use: The impacts of perceived risks and disapproval from 1976 through 1996. *American Journal of Public Health, 88*, 887-892.

Bachman, J. G., Johnston, L. D., O'Malley, P. M., & Humphrey, R. H. (1988). Explaining the recent decline in marijuana use: Differentiating the effects of perceived risks, disapproval, and general lifestyle factors. *Journal of Health and Social Behavior, 29*, 92-112.

Baer, J. S., MacLean, M. G., & Marlatt, G. A. (1998). Linking etiology and treatment for adolescent substance abuse: Toward a better match. In R. Jessor (Ed.), *New perspectives on adolescent risk behavior.* New York: Cambridge University Press.

Bailey, S. L. (1992). Adolescents' multisubstance use patterns: The role of heavy alcohol and cigarette use. *American Journal of Public Health, 82*, 1220-1224.

Baizerman, M. L., & Erickson, J. B. (1988). Adolescence is not a medical condition: On life as illness and the misuse of medical metaphors. *Minnesota Medicine, 71*, 131-133.

Ball, S. A. (1995). The validity of an alternative five-factor measure of personality in cocaine users. *Psychological Assessment, 7*, 148-154.

Bandura, A. (1986*). Social foundations of thought and action: A social cognitive theory.* Englewood Cliffs, NJ: Prentice Hall.

Bandura, A. (1989). Perceived self-efficacy in the exercise of control over AIDS infection. In V. M. Mays, G. W. Albee & S. F. Schneider (Eds.), *Primary prevention of AIDS: Psychological approaches. Primary prevention of psychopathology* (Vol. 13, pp. 128-141). Newbury Park, CA: Sage.

Bandura, A. (1991). Social cognitive theory of moral thought and action. In W. M. Kurtines & J. L. Gewirtz (Eds.), *Handbook of moral behavior and development* (pp. 45-103). Hillsdale, NJ: Lawrence Erlbaum.

Bandura, A. (1994). Social cognitive theory and exercise of control over HIV infection. In R. J. Clemente & J. L. Peterson (Eds.), *Preventing AIDS: Theories and methods of behavioral interventions* (pp. 25-29). New York: Plenum.

Bandura, A. (1997). *Self-efficacy: The exercise of control.* New York: W. H. Freeman.

Bangert-Drowns, R. L. (1988). The effects of school based substance abuse education: A meta-analysis. *Journal of Drug Education, 18*, 243-265.

Bardo, M., Bowling, S. L., Robinet, P. M., Rowlett, J. K., Lacy, J. K., & Mattingly, M. (1993). Role of dopamine D1 and D2 receptors in novelty-maintained place preference. *Experimental Clinical Pharmacology, 1,* 101-109.

Bardo, M., Donohew, L., & Harrington, N. G. (1996). Psychobiology of novelty-seeking and drug-seeking behavior. *Brain and Behavior, 77*(1-2), 23-43.

Barnes, G. M., Welte, J. W., & Hoffman, J. H. (2002). Relationship of alcohol use to delinquency and illicit drug use in adolescents: Gender, age, and racial/ethnic differences. *Journal of Drug Issues, 32,* 153-178.

Barraclough, B. M., Bunch, J., Nelson, B., & Sainsbury, P. (1974). A hundred cases of suicide: Clinical aspects. *British Journal of Psychiatry, 125,* 355-373.

Barraclough, B. M., Shepherd, D., & Jennings, C. (1977). Do newspaper reports of coroners' inquests incite people to commit suicide? *British Journal of Psychiatry, 131,* 258-532.

Barrish, H. H., Saunders, M., & Wolf, M. M. (1969). Good behavior game: Effects of individual contingencies for group consequences on disruptive behavior in a classroom. *Journal of Applied Behavior Analysis, 2,* 119-124.

Barth, R. P. (1996). *Reducing the risk: Building skills to prevent pregnancy, STD & HIV* (3rd ed.). Santa Cruz, CA: Education Training Research.

Barton, J., Chassin, L., Presson, C. C., & Sherman, S. J. (1982). Social image factors as motivators of smoking initiation in early and middle adolescence. *Child Development, 53,* 1499-1511.

Battistich, V., & Hom, A. (1997). The relationship between student's sense of their school as a community and their involvement in problem behavior. *American Journal of Public Health, 87*(12), 1997-2001.

Battistich, V., Schaps, E., Watson, M., & Solomon, D. (1996). Prevention effects of the child development project: Early findings from an ongoing multi-site demonstration trial. *Journal of Adolescent Research, 11*(1), 12-35.

Baumrind, D. (1965). Parental control and parental love. *Children, 12,* 230-234.

Baumrind, D. (1991). The influence of parenting style on adolescent competence and substance use. *Journal of Early Adolescence, 1,* 56-95.

Bearman, P., & Bruckner, H. 2001. Promising the future: Virginity pledges and first intercourse. *American Journal of Sociology, 106*(4), 859-912.

Beautrais, A. L., Joyce, P. R., & Mulder, R. T. (1996). Risk factors for serious suicide attempts among youths aged 13 through 24 years. *Journal of the American Academy of Child and Adolescent Psychiatry, 35*(9), 1174-1182.

Beautrais, A. L., Joyce, P. R., & Mulder, R. T. (1997). Precipitating factors and life events in serious suicide attempts among youths aged 13 through 24 years. *Journal of the American Academy of Child and Adolescent Psychiatry, 36*(11), 1543-1551.

Beck, A. T. (1967). *Depression: Clinical, experimental, and theoretical aspects.* New York: Harper & Row.

Beck, A. T., Brown, G., Berchick, R. J., Stewart, B. L., & Steer, R. A. (1990). Relationship between hopelessness and ultimate suicide: A replication with psychiatric patients. *American Journal of Psychiatry, 147,* 190-195.

Becker, M. H. (1974). The health belief model and personal health behavior. *Health Education Monographs, 2,* 324-473.

Begley, E., Crosby, R. A., DiClemente, R. J., Wingood, G. M., & Rose, E. (in press). Older partners and STD prevalence among pregnant African American teens. *Sexually Transmitted Diseases.*

Belk, R., Mayer, R., & Driscoll, A. (1984). Children's recognition of consumption symbolism in children's products. *Journal of Consumer Research, 10,* 386-397.

Bell, C. C., & Clark, D. C. (1998). Adolescent suicide. *Pediatric Clinics of North America, 45,* 365-380.

Benjamin, J., Li, L., Patterson, C., Greenberg, B., Murphy, D., & Hamer, D. (1996). Population and familial association between the D4 dopamine receptor gene and measures of novelty seeking. *Nature Genetics, 12,* 81-84.

Bennett, K. J., Lipman, E. L., Brown, S., Racine, Y., Boyle, M. H., & Offord, D. R. (1999). Predicting conduct problems: Can high-risk children be identified in kindergarten and Grade 1? *Journal of Consulting and Clinical Psychology, 67*(4), 470-480.

Benowitz, N., & Henningfield, J. (1994). Establishing a nicotine threshold for addiction. *New England Journal of Medicine, 331,* 123-125.

Benowitz, N. L. (2001). The nature of nicotine addiction. In P. Slovic (Ed.), *Smoking: Risk, perception, & policy* (pp. 159-187). Thousand Oaks, CA: Sage.

Benowitz, N. L., Perez-Stable, E. J., Herrera, B., & Jacob, P., III. (2002). Slower metabolism and reduced intake of nicotine from cigarette smoking in Chinese-Americans. *Journal of the National Cancer Institute, 94*(2), 108-115.

Benson, P. (1997). *All kids are our kids: What communities must do to raise caring and responsible children and adolescents.* San Francisco, CA: Jossey-Bass.

Benthin, A., Slovic, P., & Severson, H. (1993). A psychometric study of adolescent risk perception. *Journal of Adolescence, 16,* 153-168.

Bergen, A. W., Korczak, J. F., Weissbecker, K. A., & Goldstein, A. M. (1999). A genome-wide search for loci contributing to smoking and alcoholism. *Genetic Epidemiology, 17*(Suppl 1), S55-S60.

Bergman, A., & Stamm, S. (1967). The morbidity of cardiac nondisease in schoolchildren. *New England Journal of Medicine, 276*(18), 1008-1013.

Berkowitz, M. W. (2002). The science of character education. In W. Damon (Ed.), *Bringing in a new era in character education* (pp. 43-63). Stanford: Hoover Institution Press.

Berman, A. L. (1988). Fictional depiction of suicide in television films and imitation effects. *American Journal of Psychiatry, 145,* 982-986.

Berman, A. L., & Jobes, D. (1995). A population perspective: Suicide prevention in adolescents (age 12-18). *Suicide and Life-Threatening Behavior, 25,*143-154.

Berry, D. C., & Broadbent, D. E. (1988). Interactive tasks and the implicit-explicit distinction. *British Journal of Psychology, 79,* 251-272.

Beyth-Marom, R., Austin, L., Fischhoff, B., Palmgren, C., & Jacobs-Quadrel, M. (1993). Perceived consequences of risky behaviors: Adults and adolescents. *Developmental Psychology, 29,* 549-563.

Beyth-Marom, R., & Fischhoff, B. (1997). Adolescents' decisions about risks: A cognitive perspective. In J. Schulenberg, J. L. Maggs, & K. Hurrelmann (Eds.), *Health risks and developmental transitions during adolescence* (pp. 110-135). New York: Cambridge University Press.

Beyth-Marom, R., Fischhoff, B., Quadrel, M. J., & Furby, L. (1991). Teaching adolescents decision-making. In J. Baron & R. V. Brown (Eds.), *Teaching decision-making to adolescents* (pp. 19-60). Mahwah, NJ: Lawrence Erlbaum

Biblarz, A., Brown, R. M., Biblarz, D. N., Pilgrim, M., & Baldree, B. F. (1991). Media influence on attitudes toward suicide. *Suicide and Life-Threatening Behavior, 21,* 374-384.

Bierut, L., Rice, J., Edenberg, H., Goate, A., Foroud, T., & Cloninger, C. (2000). Family-based study of the association of the dopamine D2 receptor gene (DRD2) with habitual smoking. *American Journal of Medical Genetics, 90,* 299-302.

Biesecker, B. B., Boehnke, M., Calzone, K., Markel, D., Garber, J., Collins, F., et al. (1993). Genetic counseling for families with inherited susceptibility to breast and ovarian cancer. *JAMA, 269*(15), 1970-1974.

Biglan A. (2001). [Expert report in the case of *United States of America vs. Philip Morris, Incorporated et al.*]. Civil Action No. 99-CV-2496 (GK).

Biglan, A., Ary, D. V., Duncan, T. E., Black, C., & Smolkowski, K. (2000). A randomized control trial of a community intervention to prevent adolescent tobacco use. *Tobacco Control, 9,* 24-32.

Biglan, A., Brennan, P., Foster, S. L., Holder, H., Cunningham, P., Derzon, J., et al. (in press). *The prevention of multiple problems of youth.* New York: Guilford Press.

Biglan, A., Metzler, C. A., Wirt, R., Ary, D., Noell, J., Ochs, L., et al. (1990). Social and behavioral factor associated with high-risk sexual behavior among adolescents. *Journal of Behavioral Medicine, 13*(3), 245-261.

Billy, J. O. G., Brewster, K. L., & Grady, W. R. (1994). Contextual effects on the sexual behavior of adolescent women. *Journal of Marriage and the Family 1994, 56*(2), 387-404.

Billy, J. O. G., & Udry, J. R. (1985). The influence of male and female best friends on adolescent sexual behavior. *Adolescence, 20,* 21-32.

Birmaher, B., Ryan, N. D., Williamson, D. E., Brent, D. A., Kauffman, J., Dahl, R. E., et al. (1996). Childhood and adolescent depression: A review of the past 10 years: Part I. *Journal of the American Academy of Child and Adolescent Psychiatry, 35,* 1427-1439.

Bjorklund, D. F., & Green, B. L. (1992). The adaptive nature of cognitive immaturity. *American Psychologist, 47,* 46-54.

Black, G. S., DiPasquale, S., Bayer, L., Koch, G. G., & Padgett, C. A. (1993). *The Partnership for a Drug-Free America: Secondary school students, college students, and young adults 1975-1992: Vol 1. Secondary school students.* Rockville, MD: National Institute on Drug Abuse.

Blanton, H., Gibbons, F. X., Gerrard, M., Conger, K. J., & Smith, G. E. (1997). Development of health risk prototypes during adolescence: Family and peer influence. *Journal of Family Psychology, 11,* 271-288.

Blasi, A., & Hoeffel, E. C. (1974). Adolescence and formal operations. *Human Development, 17,* 344-363.

Blaze-Temple, D., & Lo, S. K. (1992). Stages of drug use: A community survey of Perth teenagers. *British Journal of Addiction, 87,* 215-225.

Blos, P. (1962). *On adolescence.* New York: Free Press.

Blue, C., Wilbur, J., & Marston-Scott, M. (2001). Exercise among blue-collar workers: Application of the theory of planned behavior. *Research Nursing Health, 24,* 481-493.

Blum, K., Noble, E. P., Sheridan, P. J., Montgomery, A., Ritchie, T., Jagadeeswaran, P., et al. (1990). Allelic association of human dopamine D2 receptor gene in alcoholism. *JAMA, 263*(15), 2055-2060.

Blumenthal, S. J. (1990). Youth suicide: Risk factors assessment, and treatment of adolescent and young adult suicidal patients. *Psychiatric Clinics of North America, 13,* 511-556.

Blumenthal, S., & Bergner, L. (1973). Suicide and newspapers: A replicated study. *American Journal of Psychiatry, 130,* 468-471.

Boekeloo, B. O., Schamus, L. A., Simmens, S. J., Cheng, T. L., O'Connor, K., & D'Angelo, L. J. (1999). A STD/HIV prevention trial among adolescents in managed care. *Pediatrics, 103*(1), 107-115.

Bollen, K. A., & Phillips, D. P. (1982). Imitative suicides: A national study of the effect of television news stories. *American Sociological Review, 47,* 802-809.

Bolos, A. M., Dean, M., Lucas-Derse, S., Ramsburg, M., Brown, G. L., & Goldman, D. (1990). Population and pedigree studies reveal a lack of association between the dopamine D2 receptor gene and alcoholism. *JAMA, 264*(24), 3156-3160.

Booth-Kewley, S., Minagawa, R. Y., Shaffer, R. A., & Brodine, S. K. (2002). A behavioral intervention to prevent sexually transmitted diseases/human immunodeficiency virus in a Marine Corps sample. *Military Medicine, 167*(2), 145-150.

Bornstein, R. F. (1989). Exposure and affect: Overview and meta-analysis of research, 1968-1987. *Psychological Bulletin, 106,* 265-289.

Borras, E., Coutelle, C., Rosell, A., Fernandez-Muixi, F., Broch, M., Crosas, B., et al. (2000). Genetic polymorphism of alcohol dehydrogenase in Europeans: The ADH2*2 allele decreases the risk for alcoholism and is associated with ADH3*1. *Hepatology, 31*(4), 984-989.

Botvin, G. J. (2000). Preventing drug abuse in schools: Social and competence enhancement approaches targeting individual-level etiologic factors. *Addictive Behaviors, 25,* 887-897.

Botvin, G. J., Baker, E., Dusenbury, L., Botvin, E. M., & Diaz, T. (1995). Long-term follow-up results of a randomized drug abuse prevention trial in a white middle-class population. *JAMA, 273,* 1106-1112.

Botvin, G. J., Baker, E., Dusenbury, L., Tortu, S., & Botvin, E. M. (1990). Preventing adolescent drug abuse through a multi-modal cognitive-behavioral approach: Results of a 3-year study. *Journal of Consulting & Clinical Psychology, 58*(4), 437-446.

Botvin, G. J., & Griffin, K. W. (1999). Preventing drug abuse. In A. J. Reynolds, R. P. Weissberg, & H. J. Walberg (Eds.), *Positive outcomes in children and youth: Promotion and evaluation* (pp. 197-228). Thousand Oaks, CA: Sage.

Botvin, G. J., Malgady, R. G., Griffin, K. W., Scheier, L. M., & Epstein, J. A. (1998). Alcohol and marijuana use among rural youth: Interaction of social and intrapersonal influences. *Addictive Behaviors, 23,* 379-387.

Boverie, P. E., Scheuffele, D. J., & Raymond, E. L. (1994). Multimethodological approach to examining risk-taking. *Current Psychology: Developmental, Learning, Personality, Social, 13,* 289-302.

Boyd, J. H. (1983). The increasing rate of suicide by firearms. *New England Journal of Medicine, 308,* 872-874.

Boyd, J. H., & Moscicki, E. K. (1986). Firearm and youth suicide. *American Journal of Public Health, 76,* 1240-1242.

Boyer, C. B., Shafer, M., Wibbelsman, C. J., Seeberg, D., Teitle, E., & Lovell, N. (2000). Associations of sociodemographic, psychosocial, and behavioral factors with sexual risk and sexually transmitted diseases in teen clinic patients. *Journal of Adolescent Health, 27*(2), 102-111.

Brandt, A. (1985). *No magic bullet: A social history of venereal disease in the United States since 1880.* New York: Oxford University Press.

Brener, N. D., & Collins, J. L. (1998). Co-occurrence of health-risk behaviors among adolescents in the United States. *Journal of Adolescent Health, 22,* 209-213.

Brennan, P. A., Grekin, E. R., & Mednick, S. A. (1999). Maternal smoking during pregnancy and adult male criminal outcomes. *Archives of General Psychiatry, 56*(3), 215-219.

Brent, D. A. (1995). Risk factors for adolescent suicide and suicidal behavior: Mental and substance abuse disorders, family environmental factors, and life stress. *Suicide and Life-Threatening Behavior, 25,* 52-63.

Brent, D. A., Baugher, M., Birmaher, B., Kolko, D., & Bridge, J. (2000). Compliance with recommendations to remove firearms by families participating in a clinical trial for adolescent depression. *Journal of the American Academy of Child and Adolescent Psychiatry, 39,* 1220-1226.

Brent, D. A., Baugher, M., Bridge, J., Chen, T., & Chiappetta, L. (1999). Age- and sex-related risk factors for adolescent suicide. *Journal of the American Academy of Child and Adolescent Psychiatry, 38,* 1497-1505.

Brent, D. A., Bridge, J., Johnson, B. A., & Connolly, J. (1996). Suicidal behavior runs in families: A controlled family study of adolescent suicide victims. *Archives of General Psychiatry, 53,* 1145-1152.

Brent, D. A., Johnson, B. A., Perper, J., Connolly, J., Bridge, J., Bartle, S., & Rather, C. (1994). Personality disorder, personality traits, impulsive violence, and completed suicide in adolescents. *Journal of the American Academy of Child and Adolescent Psychiatry, 33,* 1080-1086.

Brent, D. A., Kalas, R., Edelbrock, C., Costello, A. J., Dulcan, M. K., & Conover, N. (1986). Psychopathology and its relationship to suicidal ideation in childhood and adolescence. *Journal of the American Academy of Child and Adolescent Psychiatry, 25,* 666-673.

Brent, D. A., Kerr, M. M., Goldstein, C., Boxigar, J., Wartella, M., & Allan, M. J. (1989). An outbreak of suicide and suicidal behavior in a high school. *Journal of the American Academy of Child and Adolescent Psychiatry, 28*(6), 918-924.

Brent, D. A., Oquendo, M.A., Birmaher, B., Greenhill, L., Kolko, D. J., Stanley, B., et al. (2002). Familial pathways to early-onset suicide attempts: A high-risk study. *Archives of General Psychiatry, 59*(9), 801-807.

Brent, D. A., Perper, J. A., & Allman, C. J. (1987). Alcohol, firearms, and suicide among youth: Temporal trends in Allegheny County, PA, 1960-1983. *Journal of the American Medical Association, 257,* 3369-3372.

Brent, D. A., Perper, J. A., Allman, C. J., Moritz, G. M., Wartella, M. E., & Zelenak, J. P. (1991). The presence and accessibility of firearms in the homes of adolescent suicides: A case-control study. *JAMA, 266,* 2989-2995.

Brent, D. A., Perper, J. A., Goldstein, C. E., Kilko, D. J., Allan, M. J., Allman, C. J., & Zelenak, J. P. (1988). Risk factors for adolescent suicide: A comparison of adolescent suicide victims with suicidal inpatients. *Archives of General Psychiatry, 45,* 581-588.

Brent, D. A., Perper, J. A., Moritz, G., Allman, C., Friend, A., Roth, B. S., et al. (1993). Psychiatric risk factors for adolescent suicide: A case control study. *Journal of the American Academy of Child and Adolescent Psychiatry, 32*(3), 521-529.

Brent, D. A., Perper, J. A., Moritz, G., Baugher, M., Roth, C., Balach, L., & Schweers, J. (1993). Stressful life events, psychopathology and adolescent suicide: A case control study. *Suicide and Life-Threatening Behavior, 23*(3), 179-187.

Brent, D. A., Perper, J. A., Moritz, G., Baugher, M., Schweers, J., & Ross, C. (1993). Firearms and adolescent suicide: A community case control study. *American Journal of Diseases of Children, 147,* 1066-1071.

Brent, D. A., Perper, J. A., Moritz, G., Liotus, L., Schweers, J., Balach, L., et al. (1994). Familial risk factors for adolescent suicide: A case-control study. *Acta Psychiatrica Scandinavica, 89,* 52-58.

Breslau, N., Kilbey, M., & Andreski, P. (1991). Nicotine dependence, major depression, and anxiety in young adults. *Archive of General Psychiatry, 48,* 1069-1074.

Brewster, K. L., Billy, J. O. G., & Grady, W. R. (1993). Social context and adolescent behavior: The impact of community on the transition to sexual activity. *Social Forces, 71,* 713-740.

Brody, G. H., Ge, X., Conger, R., Gibbons, F. X., Murry, V. M., Gerrard, M., & Simmons, R. L. (2001). The influence of neighborhood disadvantage, collective socialization, and parenting on African American children's affiliation with deviant peers. *Child Development, 72,* 1231-1246.

Brounstein, P. J., & Zweig, J. M. (1999). *Understanding substance abuse prevention: Toward the 21st Century, a primer on effective programs.* Rockville, MD: U.S. Department of Health and Human Services, Substance Abuse and Mental Health Services Administration, Center for Substance Abuse Prevention.

Brown, B. S., O'Grady, K. E., Farrell, E. V., Flechner, I. S., & Nurco, D. N. (2001). Factors associated with frequent and infrequent HIV testing. *Substance Use & Misuse, 36*(12), 1593-1609.

Brown, J. H., D'Emidio-Caston, M., & Benard, B. (2001). *Resilience education.* Thousand Oaks, CA: Corwin.

Brown, T. N., Schulenberg, J., Bachman, J. G., O'Malley, P. M., & Johnston, L. D. (2001). *Consistency and change in correlates of youth substance use, 1976-1997* (Monitoring the future occasional paper No. 49). Ann Arbor, MI: Institute for Social Research. (Available at www.monitoringthefuture.org)

Browne, B. A., & Brown, D. J. (1994). Predictors of lottery gambling among American college students. *Journal of Social Psychology, 134,* 339-347.

Brownell, K. D., Marlatt, G. A., Lichtenstein, E., & Wilson, G. T. (1986). Understanding and preventing relapse. *American Psychologist, 41,* 765-782.

Bry, B. H., McKeon, P., & Padina, R. J. (1982). Extent of drug use as a function of number of risk factors. *Journal of Abnormal Psychology, 91,* 237-279.

Bryant, A. L., Schulenberg, J., Bachman, J. G., O'Malley, P. M., & Johnston, L. D. (2000). Understanding the links among school misbehavior, academic achievement, and cigarette use: A national panel study of adolescents. *Prevention Science, 1*(2), 71-87.

Bryk, A., & Schneider, B. (2002). *Trust in schools: A core resource for improvement.* New York: Russell Sage.

Bulach, C., Malone, B., & Castleman, C. (1995). Investigation of variables related to student achievement. *Mid-Western Educational Researcher, 8*(2), 23-29.

Bunnell, R. E., Dahlberg, L., Rolfs, R., Ransom, R., Gershman, K., Farshy, C., et al. (1999). High prevalence and incidence of sexually transmitted diseases in urban adolescent females despite moderate risk behaviors. *Journal of Infectious Diseases, 180,* 1624-1631.

Burr, J. A., Hartman, J. T., & Matteson, D. W. (1999). Black suicide in U.S. metropolitan areas: An examination of the racial inequality and social integration-regulation hypotheses. *Social Forces, 77,* 1049-1081.

Burt, R. S. (1987). Social contagion and innovation: Cohesion versus structural equivalence. *American Journal of Sociology, 92*, 1287-1335.

Burton, L. M., Obeidallah, D., & Allison, K. (1996). Ethnographic insights on social context and adolescent development among inner city African-American teens. In R. Jessor, A. Colby, & R. Schweder (Eds.), *Ethnography and human development*. Chicago: University of Chicago Press.

Buss, A. H., & Plomin, R. (1975). *A temperament theory of personality development*. New York: John Wiley.

Buunk, B. P., Bakker, A. B., Siero, F. W., van den Eijnden, R. J., & Yzer, M. C. (1998). Predictors of AIDS-preventive behavioral intentions among adult heterosexuals at risk for HIV-infection: Extending current model measures. *AIDS Education and Prevention, 10*(2), 149-172.

Byrnes, J. P. (1998). *The nature and development of decision-making: A self-regulation model*. Mahwah, NJ: Lawrence Erlbaum.

Byrnes, J. P. (2001). *Cognitive development in instructional contexts* (2nd ed.). Needham Heights, MA: Allyn & Bacon.

Byrnes, J. P. (in press). The development of self-regulated decision-making. In J. E. Jacobs & P. A. Klaczynski (Eds.), *The development of judgment and decision-making in children and adolescents*. Mahwah, NJ: Lawrence Erlbaum.

Byrnes, J. P., & Miller, D. C. (1997). The role of contextual and personal factors in children's risk-taking. *Developmental Psychology, 33*, 814-823.

Byrnes, J. P., Miller, D. C., & Reynolds, M. (1999). Learning to make good decisions: A self-regulation perspective. *Child Development, 70*, 1121-1140.

Byrnes, J. P., Miller, D. C., & Schafer, W. D. (1999). Gender differences in risk-taking: A meta-analysis. *Psychological Bulletin, 125*, 367-383.

Campbell, S. (1995). Behavior problems in preschool children: A review of recent research. *Journal of Child Psychology and Psychiatry, 36*, 113-149.

Cantor, C. H., & Baume, P. J. (1998). Access to methods of suicide: What impact? *Australian and New Zealand Journal of Psychiatry, 31*, 8-14.

Cantor, C. H., & Slater, P. J. (1995). The impact of firearm control legislation on suicide in Queensland: Preliminary findings. *Medical Journal of Australia, 162*, 583-585.

Caplan, M., Weissberg, R. P., Grober, J. S., Sivo, P., Grady, K., & Jacoby, C. (1992). Social competence promotion with inner-city and suburban young adolescents: Effects of social adjustment and alcohol use. *Journal of Consulting & Clinical Psychology, 60*, 56-63.

Cappella, J. N., Fishbein, M., Hornik, R., Ahern, R. K., & Sayeed, S. (2001). Using theory to select messages in antidrug media campaigns: Reasoned action and media priming. In R. Rice & C. K. Atkins (Eds.), *Public communication campaigns* (pp. 214-230). Thousand Oaks, CA: Sage

Carrington, P. J., & Moyer, S. (1994). Gun control and suicide in Ontario. *Journal of Psychiatry, 151*, 606-608.

Carrol, E. N., & Zuckerman, M. (1977). Psychopathology and sensation seeking in "downers," "speeders," and "trippers": A study of the relationship between personality and drug choice. *International Journal of the Addictions, 12*(4), 591-601.

Caspi, A., Harrington, H., Moffitt, T. E., Begg, D., Dickson, N., Langley, J., et al. (1997). Personality differences predict health-risk behaviors in young adulthood: Evidence from a longitudinal study. *Journal of Personality and Social Psychology, 73*, 1052-1063.

Caspi, R. F., Elder, G. H., & Bem, D. J. (1987). "Moving against the world": Life course patterns of explosive children. *Developmental Psychology, 23*, 308-313.

Catalano, R. F., Berglund, M. L., Ryan, J. A. M., Lonczak, H. S., & Hawkins, J. D. (1999). *Positive youth development in the United States: Research findings on evaluations of positive youth development programs*. Seattle: University of Washington, School of Social Work, Social Development Research Group.

Cates, W., Jr., & Hinman, A. R. (1992). AIDS and absolutism: The demand for perfection in prevention. *New England Journal of Medicine, 327*, 492-493.

Cauffman, E., & Steinberg, L. (2000a). (Im)maturity of judgment in adolescence: Why adolescents may be less culpable than adults. *Behavioral Sciences and the Law, 18,* 1-21.

Cauffman, E., & Steinberg, L. (2000b). Researching adolescents' judgment and culpability. In T. G. Grisso & R. G. Swartz (Eds.), *Youth on trial: A developmental perspective on juvenile justice* (pp. 325-343). Chicago: University of Chicago Press.

Cauffman, E., Steinberg, L., & Woolard, J. (2002, April). *Age differences in psychosocial capacities underlying competence to stand trial.* Paper presented at the biennial meetings of the Society for Research on Adolescence, New Orleans, LA.

Cave, G., Bos, H., Doolittle, F., & Toussaint, C. (1993). *JOBSTART: Final report on a program for school dropouts.* New York: Manpower Demonstration Research Corporation.

CDC AIDS Community Demonstration Projects Research Group. (1999). Community-level HIV intervention motivates behavior change in five cities. *American Journal of Public Health, 89*(3), 336-345.

Centers for Disease Control and Prevention. (1993). *Division of STD/HIV Prevention Annual Report, 1992.* Atlanta, GA: U.S. Department of Health and Human Services.

Centers for Disease Control and Prevention. (1995). Youth risk behavior surveillance—United States, 1993. *Morbidity and Mortality Weekly Report, 44*(SS01), 1-56.

Centers for Disease Control and Prevention. (1996). Youth Risk Behavior Surveillance—United States, 1995. *Morbidity and Mortality Weekly Report, 45*(SS04), 1-84.

Centers for Disease Control and Prevention. (1998a). HIV prevention through early detection and treatment of other sexually transmitted diseases—United States. Recommendations of the advisory committee for HIV and STD prevention. *Morbidity and Mortality Weekly Report, 47,* 1-24.

Centers for Disease Control and Prevention. (1998b). Suicide among African-American youths—United States, 1980–1995. *Morbidity and Mortality Weekly Report, 47,* 193-196.

Centers for Disease Control and Prevention. (1998c). Youth risk behavior surveillance—United States, 1997. *Morbidity and Mortality Weekly Report, 47*(SS03), 1-89.

Centers for Disease Control and Prevention. (2000a). CDC Surveillance Summaries. *Morbidity and Mortality Weekly Report 2000, 49*(SS05).

Centers for Disease Control and Prevention. (2000b). HIV-related knowledge and stigma—United States, 2000. *JAMA, 284*(24), 3118-3119.

Centers for Disease Control and Prevention. (2000c). Youth risk behavior surveillance—United States, 1999. *Morbidity and Mortality Weekly Report, 49*(SS05), 1-96.

Centers for Disease Control and Prevention. (2002a). Annual smoking-attributable mortality: Years of potential life lost, and economic costs—United States, 1995-1999. *Morbidity and Mortality Weekly Report, 51*(14), 300-303.

Centers for Disease Control and Prevention. (2002b). CDC surveillance summaries: Youth risk behavior survey, 2001. *Morbidity and Mortality Weekly Report, 51*(SS04).

Centers for Disease Control and Prevention. (2002c). *CDC wonder mortality data request screen.* Office of Statistics and Programming. Retrieved April 10, 2002, from http://wonder.cdc.gov/mortsql.hgtml

Centers for Disease Control and Prevention. (2002d). Trends and cigarette smoking among high school students—United States, 1991-2001. *Morbidity and Mortality Weekly Report, 51*(19), 409-412.

Cerwonka, E. R., Isbell, T. R., & Hansen, C. E. (2000). Psychosocial factors as predictors of unsafe sexual practices among young adults. *AIDS Education and Prevention, 112*(2), 141-153.

Chaloupka, F. J., Grossman, M., & Tauras, J. A. (1997). Public policy and youth smokeless tobacco use. *Southern Economic Journal, 64*(2), 503–516.

Chamberlain, P. (1994). *Family connections: Treatment foster care for adolescents with delinquency.* Eugene, OR: Castalia.

Chamberlain, P., & Reid, J. B. (1998). Comparison of two community alternatives to incarceration for chronic juvenile offenders. *Journal of Consulting & Clinical Psychology, 66*(4), 624-633.

Chambers, R. A., & Potenza, M. N. (2003). Neurodevelopment, impulsivity and adolescent gambling. *Journal of Gambling Studies, 19*(1), 55-89.

Chapman, S. (1996). Legal issues in HIV medicine. *Medical Journal of Australia, 165*(3), 147-149.

Charlot-Swilley, D. (1998, August). *Improving the socio-emotional functioning of African American girls: An investigation based on culturally and gender specific intervention programs.* Paper presented at the annual conference of the Association of Black Psychologists. Atlanta, GA.

Chen, C. C., Lu, R. B., Chen, Y. C., Wang, M. F., Chang, Y. C., Li, T. K., et al. (1999). Interaction between the functional polymorphisms of the alcohol-metabolism genes in protection against alcoholism. *American Journal of Human Genetics, 65*(3), 795-807.

Chen, K., & Kandel, D. (1995). The natural history of drug use from adolescence to the mid-thirties in a general population sample. *American Journal of Public Health, 85,* 41-47.

Choi, W., Ahluwalia, J., Harris, K., & Okuyemi, K. (2002). Progression to established smoking: The influence of tobacco marketing. *American Journal of Preventive Medicine, 22*(4), 228-233.

Chow, W. H., Darling, J. R., & Greenbert, R. S. (1987). The epidemiology of ectopic pregnancy. *Epidemiology Review, 9,* 70-94.

Christenson, S. L., Hurley, C. M., Sheridan, S. M., & Fenstermacher, K. (1997). Parents' and school psychologists' perspectives on parent involvement activities. *School Psychology Review, 26,* 111-130.

Christiansen, B., Smith, G. T., Roehling, P. V., Goldman, M. S. (1989). Using alcohol expectancies to predict adolescent drinking behavior after one year. *Journal of Consulting and Clinical Psychology, 57*(1), 93-99.

Chung, T., Martin, C. S., Armstrong, T. D., & Labouvie, E. W. (2002). Prevalence of DSM-IV alcohol diagnoses and symptoms in adolescent community and clinical samples. *Journal of American Academy of Children and Adolescent Psychiatry, 41*(5), 546-554.

Cigler, T., LaForge, K., McHugh, P., Kapadia, S., Leal, S., & Kreek, M. (2001). Novel and previously reported single-nucleotide polymorphisms in the human 5-HT(1B) receptor gene: No association with cocaine or alcohol abuse or dependence. *American Journal of Medicine and Genetics, 105*(6), 489-497.

Clark, A. (1995). Population screening for genetic susceptibility. *British Medical Journal, 311,* 35-38.

Clark, D., & Winters, K. C. (in press). Measuring risks and outcomes in substance use disorders prevention research. *Journal of Consulting and Clinical Psychology.*

Clarke, G. N., Hornbrook, M., Lynch, F., Polen, M., Gale, J., O'Connor, E., et al. (2002). Group cognitive-behavioral treatment for depressed adolescent offspring of depressed parents in a health eminence organization. *Journal of the American Academy of Child Psychiatry, 41,* 305-313.

Clarke, S. H., & Campbell, F. A. (1998). Can intervention early prevent crime later? The Abecedarian project compared with other programs. *Early Childhood Research Quarterly, 13*(2), 319-343.

Cleveland, M. J., Gibbons, F. X., Gerrard, M., & Pomery, E. A. (under review). *The impact of parenting on African American adolescents' risk cognitions and risk behavior: A study of moderation and mediation.* Manuscript submitted for publication.

Clinton, P. W. (2000). *Executive order to prohibit discrimination in federal employment based in genetic information.* Retrieved February 12, 2001, from www.nhgri.nih.gov/NEWS/Executive_order

Cloninger, C. R., Adolfson, R., & Svrakic, N. M. (1996). Mapping genes for human personality. *Nature Genetics, 13,* 3-4.

Cohn, L.D., MacFarlane, S., Imai, W. K., & Yanez, C. (1995). Risk perception: Differences between adolescents and adults. *Health Psychology,14*, 217-222.

Coie, J. (1996). Prevention of violence and antisocial behaviour. In R. D. Peters & R. J. McMahon (Eds.), *Preventing childhood disorders, substance abuse, and delinquency* (pp. 1-18). Thousand Oaks, CA: Sage.

Coie, J., Watt, N., West, S., Hawkins, J., Asarnow, J., Markman, H., et al. (1993). The science of prevention. *American Psychologist, 48*(10), 1013-1022.

Colby, S. M., Tiffany, S. T., Shiffman, S., & Niaura, R. S. (2000). Are adolescent smokers dependent on nicotine? A review of the evidence. *Drug and Alcohol Dependence, 59*(Suppl. 1), S83-S95.

Cole, D. A. (1988). Hopelessness, social desirability, depression, and parasuicide in two college student samples. *Journal of Consulting and Clinical Psychology, 56*, 131-136.

Collins, F. S. (1999). Shattuck Lecture: Medical and societal consequences of the Human Genome Project. *New England Journal of Medicine, 341*(1), 28-37.

Collins, P., & Barr, G. (2001). *Gambling and problem gambling in South Africa: A national study.* Cape Town, South Africa: University of Cape Town, National Centre for the Study of Gambling.

Comings, D., Ferry, L., Bradshaw-Robinson, S., Burchette, R., Chiu, C., & Muhleman, D. (1996). The dopamine D2 receptor (DRD2) gene: A genetic risk factor in smoking. *Pharmacogenetics, 6*, 73-79.

Comings, D., Gonzalez, N., Wu, S., Saucier, G., Johnson, P., Verde, R., & MacMurray, J. (1999). Homozygosity at the dopamine DRD3 receptor gene in cocaine dependence. *Molecular Psychiatry, 4*(5), 484-487.

Comings, D., Muhleman, D., Gade, R., Johnson, P., Verde, R., Saucier, G., & MacMurray, J. (1997). Cannabinoid receptor gene (CNR1): Association with i. v. drug use. *Molecular Psychology, 5*(2), 128-130.

Comings, D. E., Gade-Andavolu, R., Gonzalez, N., Wu, S., Muhleman, D., Chen, C. C., et al. (2001). The additive effect of neurotransmitter genes in pathological gambling. *Clinical Genetics, 60*(2), 107-116.

Committee for Children. (1992). *Second Step: Violence prevention curriculum for preschool-grade 9.* Seattle, WA: Author.

Compas, B. E., Connor, J. K., & Hinden, B. R. (1998). New perspectives on depression during adolescence. In R. Jessor (Ed.), *New perspectives on adolescent risk behavior* (pp. 319-364). Cambridge, UK: Cambridge University Press.

Connell, J. P., Gambone, M. A., & Smith, T. J. (2000). Youth development in community settings. In Public/Private Ventures (Ed.), *Youth development: Issues, challenges and directions* (pp. 281-324). Philadelphia, PA: Public/Private Ventures.

Conner, M., Norman, P., & Bell, R. (2002). The theory of planned behavior and healthy eating. *Health Psychology, 21*, 194-201.

Conner, M. T., & Norman, P. (1996). The role of social cognitions in health behaviours. In M. Conner & P. Norman (Eds.), *Predicting health behaviour: Research and practice with social cognition models* (pp. 1-22). London: Open University Press.

Conrad, K. M., Flay, B. R., & Hill, D. (1992). Why children start smoking cigarettes: Predictors of onset. *British Journal of Addiction, 87*, 1711-1724.

Cook, C., Palsson, G., Turner, A., Holmes, D., Brett, P., Curtis, D., et al. (1996). A genetic linkage study of the D2 dopamine receptor locus in heavy drinking and alcoholism. *British Journal of Psychiatry, 169*(2), 243-248.

Cooper, M. L., Agocha, V. B., & Sheldon, M. S. (2000). A motivational perspective on risky behaviors: The role of personality and affect regulatory processes. *Journal of Personality, 68*, 1059-1088.

Corey, L., & Wald, A. (1999). Genital herpes. In K. K. Holmes, P. F. Sparling, P. Mardh, et al. (Eds.), *Sexually transmitted diseases* (3rd ed., pp. 285-312). New York: McGraw-Hill.

Cornelius, J. R., Bukstein, O., Birmaher, B., Salloum, I. M., Lynch, K., Pollock, N., et al. (2000). Fluoxetine in adolescents with major depression and an alcohol use disorder: An open-label trial. *Addictive Behaviors, 25,* 1-6.

Cornelius, J. R., Salloum, I. M., Ehler, J. G., Jarrett, P. J., Cornelius, M. D., Perel, J. M., et al. (1997). Fluoxetine in depressed alcoholics. *Archives of General Psychiatry, 54,* 700-705.

Costa, F. M., Jessor, R., Donovan, J. E., & Fortenberry, J. D. (1995). Early initiation of sexual intercourse: The influence of psychosocial unconventionality. *Journal of Research on Adolescence, 5*(1), 93-121.

Cox, S., Lesieur, H. R., Rosenthal, R. J., & Volberg, R. A. (1997). *Problem and pathological gambling in America: The national picture.* Columbia, MD: National Council on Problem Gambling.

Coyle, K. K., Basen-Enquist, K. M., Kirby, D. B., Parcel, G. S., Banspach, S. W., Collins, J. L., et al. (2001). Safer choices: Reducing teen pregnancy, HIV and STDs. *Public Health Reports, 116* (Suppl. 1), 82-93.

Coyle, K. K., Basen-Enquist, K. M., Kirby, D. B., Parcel, G. S., Banspach, S. W., Harrist, R. B., et al. (1999). Short-term impact of safer choices: A multi-component school-based HIV, other STD, and pregnancy prevention program. *Journal of School Health, 69*(5), 181-188.

Coyle, K. K., Kirby, D., Marin, B., Gomez, C., & Gregorich, S. (2000). *Effect of Draw the Line/Respect the Line on sexual behavior in middle schools.* Unpublished manuscript, Education Training Research, Santa Cruz, CA.

Crabbe, J. C. (2002). Genetic contributions to addiction. *Annual Review of Psychology, 53,* 435-462.

Crane, J. (1991). The epidemic theory of ghettos and neighborhood effects on dropping out and teenage childbearing. *American Journal of Sociology, 96,* 1226-1259.

Crick, N. R. (1996). The role of overt aggression, relational aggression and prosocial behavior in the prediction of children's future social adjustment. *Child Development, 67,* 2317-2327.

Crosby, R. A., DiClemente, R. J., Wingood, G. M., Cobb, B., Harrington, K., Davies, et al. (2001). Condom use and correlates of African American adolescent females' infrequent communication with sex partners about preventing sexually transmitted diseases and pregnancy. *Health Education and Behavior, 29,* 219-231.

Crosby, R. A., DiClemente, R. J., Wingood, G. M., Harrington, K., Davies, S., Hook, E. W., III, & Oh, M. K. (2002). African American adolescent females' activity in community organizations is associated with STD/HIV-protective behaviors: A prospective analysis. *Journal of Epidemiology and Community Health, 56,* 549-550.

Crosby, R. A., DiClemente, R. J., Wingood, G. M., Harrington, K., Davies, S. L., Hook, E. W., & Oh, M. K. (2002b). Low parental monitoring predicts subsequent pregnancy among African American adolescent females. *Journal of Pediatric and Adolescent Gynecology,15,* 43-46.

Crosby, R. A., DiClemente, R. J., Wingood, G. M., Lang, D., & Harrington, K., (2003). Infrequent parental monitoring predicts STD acquisition among low-income African American adolescent females. *Archives of Pediatrics & Adolescent Medicine 157:* 169-173.

Crosby, R. A., DiClemente, R. J., Wingood. G. M., Lang D., & Harrington, K. F. (in press). Infrequent parental monitoring predicts sexually transmitted infections among low-income African American adolescent females. *Archives of Pediatrics and Adolescent Medicine.*

Crosby, R. A., DiClemente, R. J., Wingood, G. M., Sionean, C., Cobb, B., & Harrington, K. (2000). Correlates of unprotected vaginal sex among African American female teens: The importance of relationship dynamics. *Archives of Pediatrics and Adolescent Medicine,154,* 893-899.

Crosby, R. A., Holtgrave, D. R., DiClemente, R. J., Wingood, G. M., & Gayle, J. A. (2002). *Social capital as a predictor of adolescents' sexual risk behavior: A state-level exploratory study*. Manuscript submitted for publication.

Crossfield, A. G., Alloy, L. B., Abramson, L. Y., & Gibb, B. E. (in press). The development of depressogenic cognitive styles: The role of negative childhood life events and parental inferential feedback. *Journal of Cognitive Psychotherapy: An International Quarterly*.

Crowley, T. J., & Riggs, P. D. (1995). Adolescent substance use disorder with conduct disorder and comorbid conditions. In E. Rahdert & D. Czechowicz (Eds.), *Adolescent drug abuse: Clinical assessment and therapeutic interventions* (Research Monograph 156, pp. 49-111). Rockville, MD: National Institute of Drug Abuse.

Cubells, J., Kranzler, H., McCance-Katz, E., Anderson, G., Malison, R., Price, L., et al. (2000). A haplotype at the DBH locus, associated with low plasma dopamine beta-hydroxylase activity, also associates with cocaine-induced paranoia. *Molecular Psychiatry, 5*(1), 56-63.

Cuffe, S. P., McKeown, R. E., Jackson, K. L., Addy, C. L., Abramson, R., & Garrison, C. Z. (2001). Prevalence of Attention-Deficit/Hyperactivity Disorder in a community sample of older adolescents. *Journal of the American Academy of Child and Adolescent Psychiatry, 40*, 1037-1044.

Custer, R. L. (1982). An overview of compulsive gambling. In P. A. Carone, S. F. Yolles, S. N. Kieffer, & L. W. Krinsky (Eds.), *Addictive disorders update* (pp. 107-124). New York: Human Sciences Press.

Custer, R. L., & Milt, H. (1985). *When luck runs out: Help for compulsive gamblers and their families*. New York: Facts on File.

Cutright, P., & Fernquist, R. M. (2000). Firearms and suicide: The American experience, 1926–1996. *Death Studies, 24*, 705-719.

Dackis, C., & O'Brien, C. (2001). Cocaine dependence: A disease of the brain's reward centers. *Journal of Substance Abuse Treatment, 21*(3), 111-117.

Dahlberg, L. (1998). Youth violence in the United States: major trends, risk factors, and preventive approaches. *American Journal of Preventive Medicine, 14*(4), 259-272.

Dalley, M. B., Bolocofsky, D. N., & Karlin, N. J. (1994). Teacher-ratings and self-ratings of social competency in adolescents with low- and high-depressive symptoms. *Journal of Abnormal Child Psychology, 22*, 477-485.

Daly, E. J., Duhon, G., & Witt, J. (2002). Proactive approaches for identifying and treating children at risk for academic failure. In K. Lane, F. Gresham, & T. O'Shaughnessy (Eds.), *Interventions for children with or at risk for emotional and behavioral disorders*. Boston: Allyn & Bacon.

Damasio, A. (1994). *Descartes' error*. New York: Putnam.

Danielson, R., Marcy, S., Plunkett, A., Wiest, W., & Greenlick, M. R. (1990). Reproductive health counseling for young men: What does it do? *Family Planning Perspectives, 22*(3), 115-121.

Darroch, J. E., Landry, D. J., & Singh, S. (2000). Changing emphases in sexuality education in the U.S. public secondary schools, 1988-1999. *Family Planning Perspectives, 32*(5), 204-211.

Davidson, J. R., Hughes, D. C., George, L. K., & Blazer, D. G. (1996). The association of sexual assault and attempted suicide within the community. *Archives of General Psychiatry, 53*, 550-555.

Davidson, L. E., Rosenberg, M. L., Mercy, J. A., Franklin, J., & Simmons, J. T. (1989). An epidemiologic study of risk factors in two teenage suicide clusters. *JAMA, 262*, 2687-2692.

Davidson, R. (1998). Affective style and affective disorders: Perspectives from affective neuroscience. *Cognition and Emotion, 12*(3), 307-330.

Davis, R. A. (1980a). Black suicide and the relational system: Theoretical and empirical implications of communal and family ties. *Research in Race and Ethnic Relations, 2*, 43-71.

Davis, R. A. (1980b). Suicide among young blacks: Trends and perspectives. *Phylon, 43,* 223-229.

Davis, R. A. (1982). Black suicide and social support system: An overview and some implications for mental health practitioners. *Phylon, 43,* 307-314.

Dawkins, R. (1989). *The selfish gene.* Oxford, UK: Oxford University Press.

DeJong, W., & Langford, L. M. (2002). A typology for campus-based alcohol prevention: Moving toward environmental management strategies. *Journal of Studies on Alcohol, S14,* 140-147.

DeLamater, J., & MacCorquodale, P. (1979). *Premarital sexuality: Attitudes, relationships, behavior.* Madison: University of Wisconsin Press.

Dell, L. J., Ruzicka, M. F., & Palisi, A. T. (1981). Personality and other factors associated with gambling addiction. *International Journal of the Addictions, 16,* 149-156.

Dellu, F., Piazza, P. V., Mayo, W., Le Moal, M., & Simon, H. (1996). Novelty-seeking in rats: Biobehavioral characteristics and possible relationship with the sensation-seeking trait in man. *Neuropsychobiology, 34*(3), 136-145.

Denham, S. A., & Almeida, M. C. (1987). Children's social problem solving skills, behavioral adjustment, and interventions: A meta-analysis evaluating theory and practice. *Journal of Applied Developmental Psychology, 8,* 391-409.

Department for Culture, Media and Sport Gambling Review Body. (2001). *U.K. gambling review report.* Norwich, UK: Stationery Office.

Derevensky, J. L., & Gupta, R. (2000a). Prevalence estimates of adolescent gambling: A comparison of the SOGS-RA, *DSM-IV-J,* and the GA 20 Questions. *Journal of Gambling Studies, 16*(2/3), 227-251.

Derevensky, J. L., & Gupta, R. (2000b). Youth gambling: A clinical and research perspective. *e-Gambling: The Electronic Journal of Gambling Issue, 2,* 1-10.

DeRubeis, R. J., Seligman, M. E. P., Schulman, P., Reivich, K., & Hollon, S. D. (1998, August). *Cognitive behavioral training seminar in prevention of depression and anxiety in college students.* Paper presented at the American Psychological Association Meeting, San Francisco, CA.

Derzon, J. H., Wilson, S. J., & Cunningham, C. A. (1999). *The effectiveness of school-based interventions for preventing and reducing violence.* Center for Evaluation Research and Methodology, Vanderbilt University. Retrieved June 25, 2002, from http://harmfish.org/pub/arss99sd.pdf

Dickson, L., Derevensky, J., & Gupta, R. (2002). The prevention of youth gambling problems: A conceptual model. *Journal of Gambling Studies, 18*(2), 97-160.

DiClemente, C. C. (1999). Prevention and harm reduction for chemical dependency: A process perspective. *Clinical Psychology Review, 19,* 173-186.

DiClemente, R. J. (Ed.). (1992). *Adolescents and AIDS: A generation in jeopardy.* Newbury Park, CA: Sage.

DiClemente, R. J. (2000). Looking forward: Future directions for HIV prevention research. In J. L. Peterson & R. J. DiClemente (Eds.), *Handbook of HIV prevention* (pp. 311-324). New York: Plenum Press.

DiClemente, R. J. (2001). Development of programmes for enhancing sexual health. *Lancet, 358,* 1828-1829.

DiClemente, R. J., Hansen, W., & Ponton, L. E. (1996a). Adolescents at-risk: A generation in jeopardy. In R. J. DiClemente, W. Hansen, & L. E. Ponton, (Eds.), *Handbook of adolescent health risk behavior* (pp. 1-4). New York: Plenum.

DiClemente, R. J., Hansen, W., & Ponton, L. E. (1996b). *Handbook of adolescent health risk behavior.* New York: Plenum.

DiClemente, R. J., Lodico, M., Grinstead, O. A., Harper, G., Rickman, R. L., Evans, P. E., et al. (1996). African-American adolescents residing in high-risk urban environments do use condoms: Correlates and predictors of condom use among adolescents in public housing developments. *Pediatrics, 98,* 269-278.

DiClemente, R. J., & Peterson, J. L. (1994). *Preventing AIDS. Theories and methods of behavioral interventions.* New York: Plenum Press.

DiClemente, R. J., & Wingood, G. M. (2000). Expanding the scope of HIV prevention for adolescents: Beyond individual-level interventions. *Journal of Adolescent Health, 26,* 377-378.

DiClemente, R. J., Wingood, G. M., Crosby, R. A., Cobb, B. K., Harrington, K., Davies S. L., et al. (2001). Parent-adolescent communication about sexuality-related topics and adolescents' risky sexual behaviors, communication with sex partners, and self-efficacy to discuss sexuality-related issues with sex partners. *Journal of Pediatrics, 139,* 407-412.

DiClemente, R. J., Wingood, G. M., Crosby, R. A., Sionean, C., Cobb, B. K., Harrington, K., et al. (2001). Parental monitoring: Association with adolescents' risk behaviors. *Pediatrics, 107*(6), 1363-1368.

DiClemente, R. J., Wingood, G. M., Crosby, R. A., Sionean, C., Cobb, B. K., Harrington, K., et al. (2002). Sexual risk behaviors associated with having older sex partners: A study of African American female adolescents. *Sexually Transmitted Diseases, 29,* 20-24.

Diekstra, R. F., Kienhorst, C. W. M., & de Wilde, E. J. (1995). Suicide and suicidal behavior among adolescents. In M. Rutter & D. Smith (Eds.), *Psychosocial disorders in young people: Time trends and their causes* (pp. 686-761). New York: John Wiley.

DiFranza, J. R., Rigotti, N. A., McNeill, A. D., Ockene, J. K., Savageau, J. A., St. Cyr, D., & Coleman, M. (2000). Initial symptoms of nicotine dependence in adolescents. *Tobacco Control, 9,* 313-319.

DiIorio, C., Kelley, M., & Hockenberry-Eaton, M. (1999). Communication about sexual issues: Mothers, fathers, and friends. *Journal of Adolescent Health, 24,* 181-189.

Dinges, M. M., & Oetting, E. R. (1993). Similarity in drug use patterns between adolescents and their friends. *Adolescence, 28,* 253-266.

Dishion, T. J. (1990). The peer context of troublesome child and adolescent behavior. In P. E. Leone (Eds.), *Understanding troubled and troubling youth* (pp. 128-153). Newbury Park, CA: Sage.

Dishion, T. J., Eddy, J. M., Haas, E., Li, F., & Spracklen, K. M. (1997). Friendships and violent behavior during adolescence. *Social Development, 6*(2), 207-225.

Dishion, T. J., & Patterson, G. R. (1993). Antisocial behavior: Using a multiple gating strategy. In M. I. Singer, L. T. Singer, & T. M. Anglin (Eds.), *Handbook for screening adolescents at psychosocial risk* (pp. 375-399). New York: Lexington.

Dittus, P. J., & Jaccard, J. (2000). Adolescents' perceptions of maternal disapproval of sex: Relationship to sexual outcomes. *Journal of Adolescent Health, 26,* 268-278.

Dobkin, P. L., Tremblay, R. E., Masse, L. C., & Vitaro, F. (1995). Individual and peer characteristics in predicting boys' early onset of substance abuse: A seven-year longitudinal study. *Child Development, 66,* 1198-1214.

Dolan, L. J., Kellam, S. G., Brown, C. H., Werthamer-Larsson, L., Rebok, G. W., Mayer, L. S., et al. (1993). The short-term impact of two classroom-based preventive interventions on aggressive and shy behaviors and poor achievement. *Journal of Applied Developmental Psychology, 14*(3), 317-345.

Dolcini, M. M., Cohn, L. D., Adler, N. E., Millstein, S. G., Irwin, C. E., Kegeles, S. M., & Stone, G. C. (1989). Adolescent egocentrism and feelings of invulnerability: Are they related? *Journal of Early Adolescence, 9,* 409-418.

Doljanac, R. F., Zimmerman, M. A. (1998). Psychosocial factors and high-risk sexual behavior: Race differences among urban adolescents. *Journal of Behavioral Medicine, 21*(5), 451-467.

Doll, R., Peto, R., Wheatley, K., Gray, R., & Sutherland, I. (1994). Mortality in relation to smoking: 40 years' observations on British male doctors. *British Medical Journal, 309,* 901-911.

Donaldson, S. I., Graham, J. W., Piccinin, A. M., & Hansen, W. B. (1997). Resistant-skills training and onset of alcohol use: Evidence for beneficial and potentially harmful effects in public schools and private Catholic schools. In G. A. Marlatt & G. R. Vanden Bos

(Eds.), *Addictive behaviors: Readings on etiology, prevention, and treatment* (pp. 215-238). Washington DC: American Psychological Association.

Donaldson, S. I., Sussman, S., MacKinnon, D. P., Severson, H. H., Glynn, T., Murray, D. M., et al. (1996). Drug abuse prevention programming: Do we know what content works? *American Behavioral Scientist, 39,* 868-883.

Donaldson, S. I., Thomas, C. W., Graham, J. W., Au, J. G., & Hansen, W. B. (2000). Verifying drug abuse prevention program effects using reciprocal best friend reports. *Journal of Behavioral Medicine, 23,* 585-601.

Doniger, A. S., Riley, J. S., Utter, C. A., & Adams, E. (2001). Impact evaluation of the "Not Me, Not Now" abstinence-oriented, adolescent pregnancy prevention communications program, Monroe County, N.Y. *Journal of Health Communication, 6*(1), 45-60.

Donohew, L. (2002, June). *Health risk-takers and prevention.* Prepared for Adolescent Risk Conference, Institute for Adolescent Risk Communication, Annenberg Public Policy Center, University of Pennsylvania.

Donohew, L., Helm, D., Lawrence, P., & Shatzer, M. (1990). Sensation seeking, marijuana use, and responses to drug abuse prevention messages. In R. Watson (Ed.), *Drug and alcohol abuse prevention* (pp. 73-93). Camden, NJ: Humana Press.

Donohew, L., Lorch, E., & Palmgreen, P. (1991). Sensation seeking and targeting of televised anti-drug PSAs. In L. Donohew, H. E. Sypher, & W. J. Bukoski (Eds.), *Persuasive communication and drug abuse prevention* (pp. 209-226). Hillsdale, NJ: Lawrence Erlbaum.

Donohew, L., Lorch, E., & Palmgreen, P. (1998). Applications of a theoretic model of information exposure to health interventions. *Human Communication Research, 24,* 454-468.

Donohew, L., & Palmgreen, P. (2003). Constructing theory. In G. Stempel III, G. C. Wilhoit, & D. Weaver (Eds.), *Mass communication research and theory* (pp. 111-128). Boston: Allyn & Bacon.

Donohew, L., Palmgreen, P., & Duncan, J. (1980). An activation model of information exposure. *Communication Monographs, 47,* 295-303.

Donohew, L., Palmgreen, P., & Lorch, E. (1994). Attention, need for sensation, and health communication campaigns. *American Behavioral Scientist, 38*(2), 310-322.

Donohew, L., Sypher, H. E., & Higgins, E. T. (Eds.), (1988). *Communication, social cognition, and affect.* Hillsdale, NJ: Lawrence Erlbaum.

Donohew, L., & Zimmerman, R. S. (1996). *Sensation seeking, impulsive decision-making, and adolescent risk behaviors.* Unpublished manuscript, American Public Health Association, New York.

Donohew, L., Zimmerman, R., Cupp, P., Novak, S., Colon, S., & Abell, R. (2000). Sensation seeking, impulsive decision-making, and risky sex: Implications for risk-taking and design of interventions. *Personality and Individual Differences, 28,* 1079-1091.

Donohew, R. L., Hoyle, R. H., Clayton, R. R., Skinner, W. F., Colon, S. E., & Rice, R. E. (1999). Sensation seeking and drug use by adolescents and their friends: Models for marijuana and alcohol. *Journal of Studies on Alcohol, 60,* 622-631.

Donohue, B., Van Hasselt, V., Hersen, M., & Perrin, S. (1999). Substance refusal skills in a population of adolescents diagnosed with conduct disorder and substance abuse. *Addictive Behaviors, 24*(1), 37-46.

Donovan, J. E., & Jessor, R. (1978). Adolescent problem drinking: Psychosocial correlates in a national sample study. *Journal of Studies on Alcohol, 39,* 1506-1524.

Donovan, J. E., & Jessor, R. (1985). Structure of problem behavior in adolescence and young adulthood. *Journal of Consulting and Clinical Psychology, 53,* 890-904.

Donovan, J. E., Jessor, R., & Costa, F. M. (1988). Syndrome of problem behavior in adolescence: A replication. *Journal of Consulting and Clinical Psychology, 56,* 762-765.

Donovan, J. E., Jessor, R., & Costa, F. (1993). Structure of health-related behavior in adolescence: A latent variable approach. *Journal of Health and Social Behavior, 34,* 346-362.

Dornbusch, S. M., Ritter, P. L., Leiderman, P. H., Roberts, D. F., & Fraleigh, M. J. (1987). The relation of parenting style to adolescent school performance. *Child Development, 58,* 1244-1257.

Dowdall, G. W., & Wechsler, H. (2002). Studying college alcohol use: Widening the lens, sharpening the focus. *Journal of Studies on Alcohol, S14,* 14-22.

Dryfoos, J. G. (1990). *Adolescents at risk.* New York: Oxford University Press.

D'Silva, M., Harrington, N., Palmgreen, P., Donohew, L., & Lorch, E. (2001). Drug use prevention for the high sensation seeker: The role of alternative activities. *Substance Use & Misuse, 36*(3), 373-385.

Duaux, E., Gorwood, P., Griffon, N., Bourdel, M., Sautel, F., Sokoloff, P., et al. (1998). Homozygosity at the dopamine D3 receptor gene is associated with opiate dependence. *Molecular Psychiatry, 3,* 333-336.

Dube, S. R., Anda, R. F., Felitti, V. J., Chapman, D. P., Williamson, D. F., & Giles, W. H. (2001). Childhood abuse, household dysfunction, and the risk of attempted suicide throughout the life span: Findings from the Adverse Childhood Experiences Study. *JAMA, 286,* 3089-3096.

Dubow, E. F., & Ippolito, M. F. (1994). Effects of poverty and quality of the home environment on changes in the academic and behavioral adjustment of elementary school-age children. *Journal of Clinical Child Psychology, 23*(4), 401-412.

Duggan, P. M., Lapsley, D. K., & Norman, K. (2000, April). *Adolescent invulnerability and personal uniqueness: Scale development and initial construct validation.* Paper presented at the Eighth Biennial Meeting of the Society for Research on Adolescence, Chicago.

Duggirala, R., Almasy, L., & Blangero, J. (1999). Smoking behavior is under the influence of a major quantitative trait locus on human chromosome 5q. *Genetic Epidemiology, 17*(Suppl. 1), S139-S144.

Duncan, S. C., Duncan, T. E., & Hops, H. (1998). Progressions of alcohol, cigarette, and marijuana use in adolescence. *Journal of Behavioral Medicine, 21,* 375-388.

Durkheim, E. (1951). *Suicide* (G. Simpson, Ed.). Glencoe, IL: Free Press. (Original work published 1897)

Durkheim, E. (1966). *Suicide.* New York: Free Press.

Durlak, J. A. (1998). Common risk and protective factors in successful prevention programs. *American Journal of Orthopsychiatry, 68*(4), 512-520.

Durlak, J. A., & Wells, A. M. (1997). Primary prevention mental health programs for children and adolescents: A meta-analytic review. *American Journal of Community Psychology, 25,* 115-152.

Dusenbury, L., & Falco, M. (1995). Eleven components of effective drug abuse prevention curricula. *Journal of School Health, 65*(10), 420-425.

Dutra, R., Miller, K. S., & Forehand, R. (1999). The process and content of sexual communication with adolescents in two-parent families: Associations with sexual risk-taking behavior. *AIDS and Behavior, 3,* 59-66.

Dwyer, K. P., Osher, D., & Warger, C. (1998). *Early warning timely response: A guide to safe schools.* Washington, DC: U.S. Department of Education.

Early, K. E. (1992). *Religion and suicide in the African-American community.* Westport, CT: Greenwood Press.

East, P., & Kiernan, E. (2000). *California's Adolescent Sibling Pregnancy Prevention Program: Evaluating the impact of pregnancy prevention services to the siblings of pregnant and parenting teens.* San Diego: University of California, San Diego Medical Center.

Eaves, L., & Eysenck, H. (1975). The nature of extraversion: A genetical analysis. *Journal of Personality and Social Psychology, 32*(1), 102-112.

Ebbesen, E. B., & Konecni, V. J. (1980). On the external validity of decision-making research: What do we know about decisions in the real world? In T. S. Wallsten (Ed.), *Cognitive processes in choice and decision behavior* (pp. 21-45). Hillsdale, NJ: Lawrence Erlbaum.

Ebstein, R., Novick, O., Umansky, R., Priel, B., Osher, Y., Blaine, D., et al. (1996). Dopamine D4 receptor (D4DR) exon III polymorphism associated with the human personality trait of novelty seeking. *Nature Genetics, 12,* 78-80.

Eddy, J. M., Reid, J. B., & Fetrow, R. A. (2000). An elementary school-based prevention program targeting modifiable antecedents of youth delinquency and violence: Linking interests of families and teachers (LIFT). *Journal of Emotional and Behavioral Disorders, 8*(3), 165-176.

Edmundson, E., McAlister, A., Murray, D., Perry, C., & Lichtenstein, E. (1991). Approaches directed to the individual. In *Strategies to control tobacco use in the United States: A blueprint for public health in the 1990s* (Publication No. 92-3316, pp. 147-199). Washington DC: National Institutes of Health.

Edwards, S., & Carne, C. (1998b). Oral sex and the transmission of viral STIs. *Sexually Transmitted Infections, 74,* 6-10.

Edwards, W. (1954). The theory of decision making. *Psychological Bulletin, 51,* 380-417.

Eggert, L. L., Thompson, E. A., Herting, J. R., & Nicholas, L. J. (1995). Reducing suicide potential among high-risk youth: Tests of a school-based prevention program. *Suicide and Life-Threatening Behavior, 25*(2), 276-296.

Ehrhardt, A. A. (1996). Our view of adolescent sexuality: A focus on risk behavior without the developmental context. *American Journal of Public Health, 86,* 1523-1525.

Eisen, M., Zellman, G. L., & McAlister, A. L. (1990). Evaluating the impact of a theory-based sexuality and contraceptive education program. *Family Planning Perspectives, 22*(6), 261-271.

Eisenberg, N., Fabes, R. A., Shepard, S. A., Murphy, B. C., Guthrie, I. K., Jones, S., Friedman, J., Poulin, R., & Mazsk, P. (1997). Contemporaneous and longitudinal prediction of children's social functioning from regulation and emotionality. *Child Development, 68,* 367-383.

Ekstrand, M. L., Siegel, D. S., Nido, V., Faigeles, B., Cummings, G. A., Battle, R., et al. (1996, July). *Peer-led AIDS prevention delays onset of sexual activity and changes peer norms among urban junior high school students.* Paper presented at the 11th International Conference on AIDS, Vancouver, Canada.

Elias, M. J., Gara, M., Schuyler, T. F., & Branden-Muller, L. R. (1991). The promotion of social competence: Longitudinal study of a preventive school-based program. *American Journal of Orthopsychiatry, 61,* 409-417.

Elkind, D. (1967). Egocentrism in adolescence. *Child Development, 38,* 1025-1034.

Elkind, D. (1978). Understanding the young adolescent. *Adolescence, 19,* 127-134.

Ellen, J. M., Adler, N., Gurvey, J. E., Dunlop, M. B. V., Millstein, S. G., & Tschann, J. (2002). Improving predictions of condom behavioral intentions with partner-specific measures of risk perception. *Journal of Applied Social Psychology, 32*(3), 648-663.

Ellen, J. M., Hessol, N. A., Kohn, R. P., & Bolan, G. A. (1997). An investigation of geographic clustering of repeat cases of gonorrhea and chlamydial infection in San Francisco, 1989-1993: Evidence for core groups. *Journal of Infectious Diseases, 175,* 1519-1522.

Ellickson, P. L., Tucker, J. S., & Klein, D. J. (2001). High risk behaviors associated with early smoking: Results from a 5-year follow-up study. *Journal of Adolescent Health, 28,* 465-473.

Elliott, D. S. (1993). Health enhancing and health compromising lifestyles. In S. G. Millstein, A. C., Petersen, & E. O. Nightingale, (Eds.), *Promoting adolescent health* (pp. 119-145). New York: Oxford University Press.

Elliot, D. S. (1998). *Blueprints for violence prevention and reduction.* Boulder: University of Colorado, Center for the Study of Prevention of Violence.

Elliott, D. S., & Huizinga, D. (1984). *The relationship between delinquent behavior and ADM problems.* Boulder, CO: Behavioral Research Institute.

Elliott, D. S., Huizinga, D., & Menard, S. (1989). *Multiple problem youth: Delinquency, drugs and mental health problems.* New York: Springer-Verlag.

Embry, D. D. (2000). *The PAX Acts Game Solution: Applying replicated research and current evaluation from the Good Behavior Game for achievement and prevention in schools*. A special presentation to the National Crime Prevention Council. Tucson, AZ: PAXIS Institute.

Endicott, J., & Spitzer, R. L. (1978). A diagnostic interview: The schedule for affective disorders and schizophrenia. *Archives of General Psychiatry, 35*, 837-844.

Eng, T. R., & Butler, W. T. (1997). *The hidden epidemic: Confronting sexually transmitted diseases*. Washington, DC: National Academy Press.

Ennett, S. T., & Bauman, K. E. (1994). The contribution of influence and selection to adolescent peer group homogeneity: The case of adolescent cigarette smoking. *Journal of Personality and Social Psychology, 67*, 653-663.

Ennett, S. T., Federman, E. B., Bailey, S. L., Ringwalt, C. L., & Hubbard, M. L. (1999). HIV-risk behaviors associated with homelessness characteristics in youth. *Journal of Adolescent Health, 25*, 344-353.

Ensminger, M. E. (1987). Adolescent sexual behavior as it relates to other transition behaviors in youth. In S. Hofferth & C. D. Hayes (Eds.), *Risking the future: Adolescent sexuality, pregnancy, and childbearing* (Vol. 2, pp. 36-55). Washington, DC: National Academy Press.

Epstein, S. (1994). Integration of the cognitive and psychodynamic unconscious. *American Psychologist, 49*, 709-724.

Epstein, S., & Meier, P. (1989). Constructive thinking: A broad coping variable with specific components. *Journal of Personality and Social Psychology, 57*, 332-350.

Erickson, J. B. (1998). *Directory of American youth organizations* (7th ed.). Minneapolis, MN: Free Spirit.

Eron, L. D., & Huesman, L. R. (1984). The relation of prosocial behavior to the development of aggression and psychopathology. *Aggressive Behavior, 10*, 201-211.

Etzersdorfer, E., Sonneck, G., & Nagel-Kuess, S. (1992). Newspaper reports and suicide. *New England Journal of Medicine, 327*, 502-503.

Evans, J., Reeves, B., Platt, H., Leibenau, A., Goldman, D., Jefferson, K., & Nutt, D. (2000). Impulsiveness, serotonin genes and repetition of deliberate self-harm (DSH). *Psychological Medicine, 30*(6), 1327-1334.

Evans, R. I. (1989). The evolution of challenges to health researchers in health psychology. *Health Psychology, 8*, 631-639.

Evans, R. I. (2001). Social influences in etiology and prevention of smoking and other health threatening behaviors in children and adolescents. In A. Baum, T. A. Revenson & J. E. Singer (Eds.), *Handbook of health psychology* (pp. 459-468). Mahwah, NJ: Lawrence Erlbaum.

Evans, R. I., & Getz, J. G. (in press). Resisting health risk behavior: The social innoculation approach and its extensions. In T. P. Gullotta & M. Bloom (Eds.), *The encyclopedia of primary prevention and health promotion*. New York: Kluwer/Academic.

Everett, M. W., & Palmgreen, P. (1995). Influences of sensation seeking, message sensation value, and program context on effectiveness of anticocaine public service announcements. *Health Communications, 7*(3), 225-248.

Eysenck, H., & Fulker, D. (1983). The components of type A behavior and its genetic determinants. *Personality and Individual Differences, 4*(5), 499-505.

Eysenck, M. (1992). *Anxiety: The cognitive perspective*. Hover, UK: Lawrence Erlbaum.

Eysenck, S. B. G., & Eysenck, H. J. (1977). The place of impulsiveness in a dimensional system of personality description. *British Journal of Social and Clinical Psychology, 16*, 57-68.

Farrelly, M. C., Healton, C. G., Davis, K. C., Messeri, M. P., Hersey, J. C., & Haviland, M. L. (2002). Getting to the truth: Evaluating national tobacco countermarketing campaigns. *American Journal of Public Health, 92*, 901-907.

Faulkner, A. H., & Cranston, K. (1998). Correlates of same-sex behavior in a random sample of Massachusetts high school students. *American Journal of Public Health, 88*, 262-266.

Federal Trade Commission. (2002). *Online gambling and kids: A bad bet*. Retrieved July 26, 2002, from www.ftc.gov/bcp/conline/pubs/alerts/olgamble.htm

Fekete, S., & Macsai, E. (1990). Hungarian suicide models, past and present. In G. Ferrari (Ed.), *Suicidal behavior and risk factors* (pp. 149-156). Bologna, Italy: Monduzzi Editore.

Fekete, S., & Schmidtke, A. (1995). The impact of mass media reports on suicide and attitudes toward self-destruction: Previous studies and some new data from Hungary and Germany. In B. L. Mishara (Ed.), *The impact of suicide* (pp. 142-155). New York: Springer.

Felsher, J., Gupta, R., & Derevensky, J. (2001, June). *An examination of lottery ticket purchases by minors*. Paper presented at the annual meeting of the National Council on Problem Gambling, Seattle, WA.

Fenigstein, A., Scheier, M. F., & Buss, A. H. (1975). Public and private self-consciousness: Assessment and theory. *Journal of Consulting and Clinical Psychology, 43*, 522-527.

Ferber, T., Pittman, K., & Marshall, T. (2002). *State youth policy: Helping all youth to grow up fully prepared and fully engaged*. Takoma Park, MD: Forum for Youth Investment.

Fergusson, D. M., Horwood, L. J., & Beautrais, A. L. (1999). Is sexual orientation related to mental health problems and suicidality in young people? *Archives of General Psychiatry, 56*, 876-880.

Fergusson, D. M., Horwood, L. J., & Lynskey, M. T. (1996). Childhood sexual abuse and psychiatric disorder in young adulthood: II. Psychiatric outcomes of childhood sexual abuse. *Journal of the American Academy of Child and Adolescent Psychiatry, 35*, 1365-1374.

Fergusson, D. M., & Lynskey, M. (1995). Childhood circumstances, adolescent adjustment, and suicide attempts in a New Zealand birth cohort. *Journal of the American Academy of Child and Adolescent Psychiatry, 34*, 612-622.

Fergusson, D. M., Lynskey, M. T., & Horwood, L. J. (1996). Childhood sexual abuse and psychiatric disorder in young adulthood: I. Prevalence of sexual abuse and factors associated with sexual abuse. *Journal of the American Academy of Child and Adolescent Psychiatry, 35*, 1355-1364.

Ferland, F., Ladouceur, R., & Vitaro, F. (2002). Prevention of problem gambling: Modifying misconceptions and increasing knowledge. *Journal of Gambling Studies, 18*, 19-29.

Field, T., Diego, M., & Sanders, C. (2001). Adolescent depression and risk factors. *Adolescence, 36*, 491-498.

Fiellin, D. A., Reid, M. C., & O'Connor, P. G. (2000). Screening for alcohol problems in primary care: A systematic review. *Archives of Internal Medicine, 160*, 1977-1989.

Finnegan, W. (1990, September). Out there, I. *The New Yorker*, 51-86.

Finucane, M. L., Alhakami, A., Slovic, P., & Johnson, S. M. (2000). The affect heuristic in judgments of risks and benefits. *Journal of Behavioral Decision Making, 13*, 1-17.

Fischhoff, B. (1992). Giving advice: Decision theory perspectives on sexual assault. *American Psychologist, 47*, 577-588.

Fischhoff, B., & Beyth-Marom, R. (1983). Hypothesis evaluation from a Bayesian perspective. *Psychological Review, 90*, 239-260.

Fischhoff, B., Parker, A., Bruine de Bruin, W., Downs, J., Palmgren, C., Dawes, R. M., et al. (2000). Teen expectations for significant life events. *Public Opinion Quarterly, 64*, 189-205.

Fishbein, M. (1963). An investigation of the relationships between beliefs about an object and the attitude toward that object. *Human Relations, 16*, 233-240.

Fishbein, M. (1980). A theory of reasoned action: Some applications and implications. In H. Howe & M. Page (Eds.), *Nebraska symposium on motivation* (pp. 65-116). Lincoln: University of Nebraska.

Fishbein, M. (2000). The role of theory in HIV prevention. *AIDS Care, 12*(3), 273-278.

Fishbein, M., & Ajzen, I. (1975). *Belief, attitude, intention, and behavior: An introduction to theory and research*. Reading, MA: Addison-Wesley.

Fishbein, M., Bandura, A., Triandis, H. C., Kanfer, F. H., Becker, M. H., & Middlestadt, S. E. (1992). *Factors influencing behavior and behavior change: Final report—theorist's workshop*. Rockville, MD: National Institute of Mental Health.

Fishbein, M., Cappella, J., Hornik, R., Sayeed, S., Yzer, M., & Ahern, R. K. (2002). The role of theory in developing effective anti-drug public service announcements. In W. Crano & M. Burgoon (Eds.), *Mass media and drug prevention: Classic and contemporary theories and research* (pp. 89-117). Mahwah, NJ: Lawrence Erlbaum.

Fishbein, M., & Jarvis, B. (2000). Failure to find a behavioral surrogate for STD incidence: What does it really mean? *Sexually Transmitted Diseases, 27*(8), 452-455.

Fisher, S. (1999). A prevalence study of gambling and problem gambling in British adolescents. *Addiction Research, 7*, 509-538.

Fisher, S. E. (1992). Measuring pathological gambling in children: The case of fruit machines in the U.K. *Journal of Gambling Studies, 8*, 263-285.

Fisher, S. E. (1993). Gambling and pathological gambling in adolescence. *Journal of Gambling Studies, 9*, 277-287.

Fisher, S. E., & Balding, J. (1996). Under sixteen's find the lottery a good gamble. *Education and Health, 13*(5), 65-68.

Fisher, S. E., & Balding, J. (1998). *Gambling and problem gambling among young people in England and Wales*. London: Office of the National Lottery.

Fiske, S., & Taylor, S. (1984). Attention. In S. T. Fiske & S. Taylor (Eds.), *Social cognition* (pp. 184-212). New York: Random House.

Flaherty, E. W., Marecek, J., Olsen, K., & Wilcove, G. (1983). Preventing adolescent pregnancy: An interpersonal problem-solving approach. *Prevention in Human Services, 2*(3), 49-64.

Flanigan, C. (2001). *What's behind the good news: The decline in teen pregnancy rates during the 1990s*. Washington, DC: National Campaign to Prevent Teen Pregnancy.

Flay, B. R. (2002). Positive youth development requires comprehensive health promotion programs. *American Journal of Health Behavior, 26*(6), 407-424.

Flay, B. R., & Allred, C. G. (in press). Long-term effects of the positive action program: A comprehensive, positive youth development program. *American Journal of Health Behavior*.

Flay, B. R., Allred, C. G., & Ordway, N. (2001). Effects of the positive action program on achievement and discipline: Two matched-control comparisons. *Prevention Science, 2*(2), 71-90.

Flay, B. R., Graumlich, S., Segawa, E., Burns, J. L., Holliday, M. Y., & Aban Aya Investigators. (2002). *Effects of two prevention programs on high-risk behaviors among African-American youth: A randomized trial*. Manuscript submitted for publication.

Flay, B. R., & Petraitis, J. (1994). The theory of triadic influence: A new theory of health behavior with implications for preventive interventions. In G. S. Albrecht (Ed.), *Advances in medical sociology: Vol 4. A reconsideration of models of health behavior change*. Greenwich, CT: JAI Press.

Fleming, D. T., & Wasserheit, J. N. (1999). From epidemiological synergy to public health policy and practice: the contribution of other sexually transmitted diseases to sexual transmission of HIV infection. *Sexually Transmitted Infections, 75*, 3-17.

Fleming, M., Towey, K., & Jarosik, J. (2001). *Healthy Youth 2010: Supporting 21 Critical Adolescent Objectives*. American Medical Association. Retrieved June 4, 2002, from www.ama-assn.org/ama/upload/mm/39/healthy2010.pdf

Flisher, A. J., Kramer, R. A., Hoven, C. W., King, R., Bird, H. R., Davies, M., et al. (2000). Risk behavior in a community sample of children and adolescents. *Journal of the American Academy of Child and Adolescent Psychiatry, 39*, 881-887.

Fombonne, E., Worster, G., Cooper, V., Harrington, R., & Rutter, M. (2001a). The Maudsley long-term follow-up of child and adolescent depression: 1. Psychiatric outcomes in adulthood. *British Journal of Psychiatry, 179*, 210-217.

Fombonne, E., Worster, G., Cooper, V., Harrington, R., & Rutter, M. (2001b). The Maudsley tong-term follow-up of child and adolescent depression: 2. Suicidality, criminality, and social dysfunction in adulthood. *British Journal of Psychiatry, 179,* 218-223.

Fong, G. T., Cameron, R., Brown, K. S., Campbell, H. S., Zanna, M. P., Murnaghan, D., et al. (2002, November). *The psychosocial and behavioral effects of graphic warning labels on youth.* Paper presented at the National Conference on Tobacco or Health, San Francisco.

Forness, S. R., & Kavale, K. A. (1996). Treating social skills deficits and learning disabilities: A meta-analysis. *Learning Disability Quarterly, 19,* 2-13.

Forrest, J. D., Hermalin, A. I., & Henshaw, S. K. (1981). The impact of family planning clinic programs on adolescent pregnancy. *Family Planning Perspectives, 13*(3), 109-116.

Fortenberry, J. D. (in press). Health behaviors and reproductive health risk within adolescent sexual dyads. In P. Florsheim (Ed.), *Adolescent romantic relations and sexual behavior: Theory, research, and practical implications.* Mahwah, NJ: Lawrence Erlbaum.

Fortenberry, J. D., Cecil, H., Zimet, G. D., & Orr, D. P. (1997). Concordance between self-report questionnaires and coital diaries for sexual behaviors of adolescent women with sexually transmitted diseases. In J. Bancroft (Ed.), *Researching sexual behavior* (pp. 237-249). Bloomington: Indiana University Press.

Fortenberry, J. D., Orr, D. P., Katz, B. P., Brizendine, E. J., & Blythe, M. J. (1997). "Sex under the influence": A diary self-report study of substance use and sexual behavior among adolescent women. *Sexually Transmitted Diseases, 24,* 313-319.

Fortenberry, J. D., Temkit, M., Harezlak, J., Tu, W., & Orr, D. P. (2001). Association of daily mood with sexual activity among adolescent girls. *International Journal of STD & AIDS, 12* (Suppl 2), 174.

Fowers, B. J., Lyons, E. M., & Montel, K. H. (1996). Positive mental illusions about marriage: Self-enhancement or relationship enhancement. *Journal of Family Psychology, 10,* 192-208.

Fowler, B. P. (1986). Emotional crisis imitating television. *Lancet, 1,* 1036-1037.

Franke, P., Nothen, M., Wang, T., Knapp, M., Lichtermann, D., Neidt, H., et al. (2000). DRD4 exon III VNTR polymorphism-susceptibility factor for heroin dependence? Results of a case-control and a family-based association approach. *Molecular Psychiatry, 5*(1), 101-104.

Franklin, C., Grant, D., Corcoran, J., O'Dell Miller, P., & Bultman, L. (1997). Effectiveness of prevention programs for adolescent pregnancy: A meta-analysis. *Journal of Marriage and Family, 59*(3), 551-567.

Franklin, J., Donohew, L., Dhoundiyal, V., & Lawrence, P. (1988). Attention and our ancient past: The scaly thumb of the lizard. *American Behavioral Scientist, 31,* 312-326.

Freud, A. (1981). The concept of developmental lines. *Psychoanalytic Study of the Child, 36,* 129-136.

Frey, K. A., Hirschstein, M. K., & Guzzo, B. A. (2000). Second Step: Preventing aggression by promoting social competence. *Journal of Emotional & Behavioral Disorders, 8,* 102-112.

Friedman, L. S., Lichtenstein, E., & Biglan, A. (1985). Smoking onset among teens: An empirical analysis of initial situations. *Addictive Behaviors, 10*(1), 1-13.

Friedman, Z., & Trivelli, L. (1996). Condom availability for youth: A high-risk alternative. *Pediatrics, 97,* 285.

Frost, J. J., & Darroch Forrest, J. (1995). Understanding the impact of effective teenage pregnancy prevention programs. *Family Planning Perspectives, 27*(5), 188-195.

Fulker, D., Eysenck, S., & Zuckerman, M. (1980). A genetic and environmental analysis of sensation seeking. *Journal of Research in Personality, 14,* 261-281.

Fullilove, M. T. (2001). Root shock: The consequences of African American dispossession. *Journal of Urban Health, 78,* 72-80.

Furby, L., & Beyth-Marom, R. (1992). Risk-taking in adolescence: A decision-making perspective. *Developmental Review, 12,* 1-44.

Furstenberg, F. F., Geitz, L. M., Teitler, J. O., & Weiss, C. C. (1997). Does condom availability make a difference? An evaluation of Philadelphia's health resource centers. *Family Planning Perspectives, 29*(3), 123-127.

Gaboury, A., & Ladouceur, R. (1993). Evaluation of a prevention program for pathological gambling among adolescents. *Journal of Primary Prevention, 14*(1), 21-28.

Galambos, N. L., & Tilton-Weaver, L. C. (1998). Multiple risk behavior in adolescents and young adults. *Health Reports, 10*(2), 9-20.

Ganzeboom, H. B. G., & de Haan, D. (1982). Gepubliceerde zelfmoorden en verhoging van sterfte door zelfmoord en ongelukken in Nederland 1972-1980. *Mens en Maatschappij, 57,* 55-69.

Garber, J., & Flynn, C. (2001). Predictors of depressive cognitions in young adolescents. *Cognitive Therapy and Research, 25,* 353-376.

Garber, J., Weiss, B., & Shanley, N. (1993). Cognitions, depressive symptoms and development in adolescence. *Journal of Abnormal Psychology, 102,* 47-57.

Gardner, W., Scherer, D., & Tester, M. (1989). Asserting scientific authority: Cognitive development and adolescent legal rights. *American Psychologist, 44,* 895-902.

Garland, A. F., & Zigler, E. (1993). Adolescent suicide prevention: Current research and social policy implications. *American Psychologist, 48,*169-182.

Garmezy, N. (1985). Stress resistant children: The search for protective factors. In J. Stevenson (Ed.), *Recent research in developmental psychopathology.* Oxford, UK: Pergamon Press.

Garmezy, N. (1985). The NIMH-Israeli high-risk study: Commendations, comments, and cautions. *Schizophrenia Bulletin, 11,* 349-353.

Garmezy, N., Masten, A. S., & Tellegen, A. (1984). The study of stress and competence in children: A building block for developmental psychopathology. *Child Development, 55,* 97-111.

Garnick, D. W., Hendricks, A. M., Comstock, C., & Horgan, C. (1997). Do individuals with substance abuse diagnoses incur higher charges than individuals with other chronic conditions? *Journal of Substance Abuse Treatment, 14*(5), 457-465.

Garofalo, R., Wolf, R., Cameron, M. S., Kessel, S., Palfrey, J., & DuRant, R. H. (1998). The association between health risk behaviors and sexual orientation among a school-based sample of adolescents. *Pediatrics, 101,* 895-902.

Garrison, C. Z., McKeown, R. E., Valois, R. F., & Vincent, M. L. (1993). Aggression, substance use, and suicidal behaviors in high school students. *American Journal of Public Health, 83,* 179-184.

Gelernter, J., Kranzler, H., & Cubells, J. (1999). Genetics of two mu-opioid receptor gene (OPRM1) exon I polymorphisms: Population studies, and allele frequencies in alcohol- and drug-dependent subjects. *Molecular Psychiatry, 4*(5), 476-483.

Gelernter, J., Kranzler, H., Satel, S., & Rao, P. (1994). Genetic association between dopamine transporter protein alleles and cocaine-induced paranoia. *Neuropsychopharmacology, 11*(3), 195-200.

Geller, G., Bernhardt, B., Heizisouer, K., Holtzman, N., Stefanek, M., & Wilcox, P. (1995). Informed consent and BRCA1 testing. *Nature Genetics, 11,* 364.

Geller, G., Botkin, J., Green, M., Press, N., Biesecker, B., & Wilfond, B. (1997). Genetic testing for susceptibility to adult-onset cancer: The process and content of informed consent. *JAMA, 277,* 1467-1474.

Geller, G., Tambor, E., Bernhardt, B., Wissow, L., & Fraser, G. (2000). Mothers and daughters from breast cancer families: A qualitative study of their perceptions of the risks and benefits associated with minors' participation in genetic susceptibility research. *JAMWA, 55,* 280-284.

Gerber, M. M., & Semmel, M. I. (1984). Teacher as imperfect test: Re-conceptualizing the referral process. *Educational Psychologist, 19*(3), 137-148.

Gerrard, M. (1982). Sex, sex guilt, and contraceptive use. *Journal of Personality and Social Psychology, 42,* 153-158.

Gerrard, M. (1987). Sex, sex guilt, and contraceptive use revisited: Trends in the 1980s. *Journal of Personality and Social Psychology, 52*, 975-980.

Gerrard, M., Gibbons, F. X., Benthin, A. C., & Hessling, R. M. (1996). A longitudinal study of the reciprocal nature of risk behaviors and cognitions in adolescents: What you do shapes what you think, and vice versa. *Health Psychology, 15*, 344-354.

Gerrard, M., Gibbons, F. X., & Bushman, B. J. (1996). Relation between perceived vulnerability to HIV and precautionary sexual behavior. *Psychological Bulletin, 119*, 390-409.

Gerrard, M., Gibbons, F. X., Reis-Bergan, M., & Russell, D. W. (2000). Self-esteem, self-serving cognitions, and health risk behavior. *Journal of Personality, 68*, 1177-1201.

Gerrard, M., Gibbons, F. X., Reis-Bergan, M., Trudeau, L., Vande Lune, L., & Buunk, B. P. (2003). Inhibitory effects of drinker and nondrinker prototypes on adolescent alcohol consumption. *Health Psychology, 21*, 601-609.

Gerrard, M., Gibbons, F. X., Vande Lune, L., Pexa, N. A., & Gano, M. L. (2002). Adolescents' substance-related risk perceptions: Antecedents, mediators, and consequences. *Risk, Decision, and Policy, 7*, 175-191.

Gerrard, M., Gibbons, F. X., Zhao, L., Russell, D. W., & Reis-Bergan, M. (1999). The effect of peers' alcohol consumption on parental influence: A cognitive mediational model. *Journal of Studies on Alcohol, 13*, 32-44.

Gerstein, D., Hoffmann, J., Larison, C., Engelman, L., Murphy, S., Palmer, A., et al. (1999). *Gambling impact and behavior study*. University of Chicago, National Opinion Research Center.

Giaconia, R. M., Reinherz, H. Z., Silverman, A. B., Pakiz, B., Frost, A. K., & Cohen, E. (1995). Traumas and posttraumatic stress disorder in a community population of older adolescents. *Journal of the American Academy of Child and Adolescent Psychiatry, 34*, 1369-1380.

Giacopassi, D., Stitt, B. G., & Vandiver, M. (1998). An analysis of the relationship of alcohol to casino gambling among college students. *Journal of Gambling Studies, 14*, 135-149.

Giancola, P. R. (2002). Alcohol-related aggression during the college years: Theories, risk factors and implications. *Journal of Studies on Alcohol, S14*, 129-139.

Giancola, P. R., Martin, C. S., Tarter, R. E., Pelham, W. E., & Moss, H. B. (1996). Executive cognitive functioning and aggressive behavior in preadolescent boys at high risk for substance abuse/dependence. *Journal of Studies on Alcohol, 57*, 352-359.

Gibb, B. E. (2002). Childhood maltreatment and negative cognitive styles: A quantitative and qualitative review. *Clinical Psychology Review, 22*, 223-246.

Gibb, B. E., Abramson, L. Y., & Alloy, L. B. (2002). *Emotional maltreatment and cognitive vulnerability to depression: The influence of maltreatment by non-relatives*. Manuscript submitted for publication.

Gibb, B. E., Alloy, L. B., Abramson, L. Y., Rose, D. T., Whitehouse, W. G., Donovan, P., et al. (2001). History of childhood maltreatment, depressogenic cognitive style, and episodes of depression in adulthood. *Cognitive Therapy and Research, 25*, 425-446.

Gibb, B. E., Alloy, L. B., Abramson, L. Y., Rose, D. T., Whitehouse, W. G., & Hogan, M. E. (2001). Childhood maltreatment and college students' current suicidality: A test of the hopelessness theory. *Suicide and Life-Threatening Behavior, 31*, 405-415.

Gibb, B. E., Zhu, L., Alloy, L. B., & Abramson, L. Y. (2002). Cognitive styles and academic achievement in university students: A longitudinal investigation. *Cognitive Therapy and Research, 26*, 309-315.

Gibbons, F. X., & Gerrard, M. (1995). Predicting young adults' health-risk behavior. *Journal of Personality and Social Psychology, 69*, 505-517.

Gibbons, F. X., & Gerrard, M. (1997). Health images and their effects on health behavior. In B. P. Buunk & F. X. Gibbons (Eds.), *Health, coping and well-being: Perspectives from social comparison theory* (pp. 63-94). Mahwah, NJ: Lawrence Erlbaum.

Gibbons, F. X., Gerrard, M., Blanton, H., & Russell, D. W. (1998). Reasoned action and social reaction: Willingness and intention as independent predictors of health risk. *Journal of Personality and Social Psychology, 74*, 1164-1180.

Gibbons, F. X., Gerrard, M., Cleveland, M. J., Wills, T. A., & Brody, G. H. (2003). *Perceived discrimination and substance use in African American parents and their children: A panel study*. Manuscript under review.

Gibbons, F. X., Gerrard, M., & Lane, D. (in press). A social reaction model of adolescent health risk. In J. M. Suls & K. Wallston (Eds.), *Social psychological foundations of health and illness*. Oxford, UK: Blackwell.

Gibbons, F. X., Gerrard, M., Ouellette, J. A., & Burzette, R. (1998). Cognitive antecedents to adolescent health risk: Discriminating between behavioral intention and behavioral willingness. *Psychology and Health, 13,* 319-339.

Gibbons, F. X., Gerrard, M., & Pomery, E. A. (in press). Reactance or social reaction? Why don't kids just say "no?" In R. Wright, J. Greenberg, & S. Brehm (Eds.), *A festschrift for Jack Brehm*. Mahwah, NJ: Lawrence Erlbaum.

Gibbons, F. X., Lane, D. J., Gerrard, M., Eggleston, T., & Reis-Bergan, M. (2003). *Image manipulation as a means of reducing risk willingness*. Manuscript in preparation.

Gibbons, F. X., Lane, D. J., Gerrard, M., Pomery, E. A., & Lautrup, C. L. (2002). Drinking and driving: A prospective assessment of the relation between risk cognitions and risk behavior. *Risk, Decision, and Policy, 7,* 267-283.

Gibbons, R. D., Clark, D. C., & Fawcett, J. A. (1990). A statistical method for evaluating suicide clusters and implementing cluster surveillance. *American Journal of Epidemiology, 132,* 183-191.

Gibbs, J. P., & Martin, W. T. (1964). *Status integration and suicide*. Eugene: University of Oregon Press.

Gibbs, J. T. (1988). Conceptual, methodological, and structural issues in black youth suicide: Implications of assessment and early intervention. *Suicide and Life-Threatening Behavior, 18,* 73-89.

Gibbs, J. T. (1992). Homicide and suicide among young black males: The Janus face of despair. In C. D. Llewelyn & R. J. Brown (Eds.). *The African-American male: A second emancipation* (pp. 15-26). New York: National Urban League.

Gibbs, J. T. (1997). African-American suicide: A cultural paradox. *Suicide and Life-Threatening Behavior, 27*(1), 68-79.

Gibbs J. T., & Hines, A. M. (1989). Factors related to sex differences in suicidal behavior among black youth: Implications for intervention and research. *Journal of Adolescent Research, 4,* 152-172.

Gibson, C. L., Piquero, A. R., & Tibbetts, S. G. (2000). Assessing the relationship between maternal cigarette smoking during pregnancy and age at first police contact. *Justice Quarterly, 17,* 519-542.

Gibson, J. A. P., & Range, L. M. (1991). Are written reports of suicide and seeking help contagious? High schoolers' perceptions. *Journal of Applied Social Psychology, 21,* 1517-1523.

Gillmore, M. R., Morrison, D. M., Richey, C. A., Balassone, M. L., Gutierrez, L., & Farris, M. (1997). Effects of a skill-based intervention to encourage condom use among high- risk, heterosexually active adolescents. *AIDS Prevention and Education, 9*(Suppl. A), 44-67.

Ginzberg, E. (1991). Adolescents at risk conference: Overview. *Journal of Adolescent Health, 12,* 588-590.

Giordano, P. G., Cernkovick, S. A., & Pugh, M. D. (1986). Friendship and delinquency. *American Journal of Sociology, 91,* 1170-1202.

Gladwell, M. (2000). *The tipping point: How little things can make a big difference*. Boston: Little Brown.

Glickman, S. E., & Schiff, B. B. (1967). A biological theory of reinforcement. *Psychology Review, 74,* 81-109.

Goldberg, J. H., Halpern-Felsher, B. L., & Millstein, S. G. (2002). Beyond invulnerability: The importance of benefits in adolescents' decision to drink alcohol. *Health Psychology, 21,* 477-484.

Goldsmith, S. K., Pellmar, T. C., Kleinman, A. M., & Bunney, W. E. (Eds.). (2002). *Reducing suicide: A national imperative.* Washington, DC: National Academy Press.

Golub, A., & Johnson, B. D. (1994). The shifting importance of alcohol and marijuana as gateway substances among serious drug users. *Journal of Studies on Alcohol, 55,* 607-614.

Goodman, L. A., & Kruskal, W. H. (1979). *Measures of association for cross classification.* New York: Springer-Verlag.

Goodwin, R., Gould, M. S., Blanco, C., & Olfson, M. (2001). Prescription of psychotropic medications to youths in office-based practice. *Psychiatric Services, 52,* 1081-1087.

Goossens, L., Beyers, W., Emmen, M., & van Aken, M. A. G. (2002). The imaginary audience and personal fable: Factor analyses and concurrent validity of the "New Look" measures. *Journal of Research on Adolescence, 12,* 193-215.

Gorman, W. B. (1995). Are school-based resistance skills training programs effective in preventing alcohol misuse? *Journal of Alcohol and Drug Education, 41*(1), 74-98.

Gorwood, P., Philippe, B., Ades, J., Hamon, M., & Boni, C. (2000). Serotonin transporter gene polymorphisms, alcoholism, and suicidal behavior. *Society of Biological Psychiatry,* 259-264.

Gotlib, I. H., Lewinsohn, P. M., & Seeley, J. R. (1995). Symptoms versus a diagnosis of depression: Differences in psychosocial functioning. *Journal of Consulting and Clinical Psychology, 65,* 90-100.

Gottfredson, M. R., & Hirschi, T. (1990). *A general theory of crime.* Stanford, CA: Stanford University Press.

Gottsegen, E., & Philliber, W. W. (2001). Impact of a sexual responsibility program on young males. *Adolescence, 36*(143), 427-433.

Gould, M. S. (1999). *Psychological autopsy of cluster suicides in adolescents* (Grant R01 MH47559-04S2). Washington, DC: National Institute of Mental Health.

Gould, M. S. (2001). Suicide and the media. In H. Hendin & J. J. Mann (Eds.), *Suicide prevention: Clinical and scientific aspects.* New York: Annals of the New York Academy of Sciences.

Gould, M. S., Fisher, P., Parides, M., Flory, M., & Shaffer, D. (1996). Psychosocial risk factors of child and adolescent completed suicide. *Archives of General Psychiatry, 53,* 1155-1162.

Gould, M. S., Forman, J., Kleinman, M., & Wallenstein, S. (1995). *Psychological autopsy of cluster suicides in adolescents.* Paper presented at the 42nd meeting of the American Academy of Child and Adolescent Psychiatry, New Orleans, LA.

Gould, M. S., King, R., Greenwald, S., Fisher, P., Schwab-Stone, M., et al. (1998). Psychopathology associated with suicidal ideation and attempts among children and adolescents. *Journal of the American Academy of Child and Adolescent Psychiatry, 37,* 915-923.

Gould, M. S., & Kramer, R. A. (2001, Spring). Youth suicide prevention. *Suicide and Life-Threatening Behavior, 31*(Suppl.), 6-31.

Gould, M. S., Petrie, K., Kleinman, M., & Wallenstein, S. (1994). Clustering of attempted suicide: New Zealand national data. *International Journal of Epidemiology, 23*(8), 1185-1189.

Gould, M. S., & Shaffer, D. (1986). The impact of suicide in television movies: Evidence of imitation. *New England Journal of Medicine, 315,* 690-694.

Gould, M. S., Shaffer, D., & Kleinman, M. (1988). The impact of suicide in television movies: Replication and commentary. *Suicide and Life-Threatening Behavior, 18,* 90-99.

Gould, M. S., Wallenstein, S., & Kleinman, M. (1990). Time-space clustering of teenage suicide. *American Journal of Epidemiology, 131,* 71-78.

Gould, M. S., Wallenstein, S., Kleinman, M. H., O'Carroll, P., & Mercy, J. (1990). Suicide clusters: An examination of age-specific effects. *American Journal of Public Health, 80,* 211-212.

Graber, J. A., & Brooks-Gunn, J. (1996). Transitions and turning points: Navigating the passage from childhood through adolescence. *Developmental Psychology, 32*, 768-776.

Grant, B. F., & Dawson, D. A. (1997). Age of onset of alcohol use and its association with DSM-IV alcohol abuse and dependence: Results from the national Longitudinal Alcohol Epidemiologic Survey. *Journal of Substance Abuse, 9*, 103-110.

Grant, J. E., Kim, S. W., & Potenza, M. N. (2003). Advances in the pharmacological treatment of pathological gambling disorder. *Journal of Gambling Studies, 19*(1), 85-109.

Greenberg, M. T., Domitrovich, C., & Bumbarger, B. (1999). *Preventing mental disorders in school-age children: A review of the effectiveness of prevention programs.* State College: Pennsylvania State University.

Greenberg, M. T., Kusche, C. A., & Speltz, M. (1990). Emotion regulation, self-control and psychopathology: The role of relationships in early childhood. In D. Cicchetti & S. Toth, (Eds.), *Rochester symposium on developmental psychopathology* (Vol. 2). New York: Cambridge University Press.

Greenberg, M. T., Speltz, M. L., & Deklyen, M. (1993). The role of attachment in the early development of disruptive behavior problems. *Development and Psychopathology, 5*, 191-213.

Greene, K., Kramar, M., Walters, L. H., Rubin, D. L., Hale, J., & Hale, L. (2000). Targeting adolescent risk-taking behaviors: The contributions of egocentrism and sensation-seeking. *Journal of Adolescence, 23*, 439-461.

Greene, K., Rubin, D. L., & Hale, J. L. (1995). Egocentrism, message explicitness and AIDS messages directed towards adolescents: An application of the theory of reasoned action. *Journal of Social Behavior and Personality, 10*, 547-570.

Greene, K., Rubin, D. L., Walters, L. H., & Hale, J. L. (1996). The utility of understanding adolescent egocentrism in designing health promotion messages. *Health Communication, 8*, 131-152.

Greenhill, L., Waslick, B., Parides, M., Fan, B., Shaffer, D., & Mann, J. J. (1995). Biological studies in suicidal adolescent inpatients. *Scientific Proceedings of the Annual Meeting of the American Academy of Child and Adolescent Psychiatry, 11*, 124.

Greenwood, C. R., Walker, H. M., Todd, N. M., & Hops, H. (1979). Preschool teachers' assessment and treatment of socially withdrawn preschool children. *Behavioral Assessment, 4*, 273-297.

Gresham, F. (1986). Conceptual issues in the assessment of social competence in children. In P. S. Strain, M. J. Guralnick, & H. M. Walker (Eds.), *Children's social behavior: Development, assessment, and modification* (pp. 143-179). New York: Academic Press.

Griffin, K. W., Botvin, G. J., Scheier, L. M., & Nichols, T. R. (2002). Factors associated with regular marijuana use among high school students: A long-term follow-up study. *Substance Use & Misuse, 37*, 225-238.

Griffin, K. W., Scheier, L. M., & Botvin, G. J. (2001). Protective role of personal competence skills in adolescent substance use: Psychological well-being as a mediating factor. *Psychology of Addictive Behaviors, 15*(3), 194-203.

Griffith, E., & Bell, C. C. (1989). Recent trends in suicide and homicide among blacks. *JAMA, 262*, 2265-2269.

Griffiths, M. D. (1989). Gambling in children and adolescents. *Journal of Gambling Behavior, 5*, 66-83.

Griffiths, M. D. (1990a). The acquisition, development and maintenance of fruit machine gambling in adolescence. *Journal of Gambling Studies, 6*, 193-204.

Griffiths, M. D. (1990b). The cognitive psychology of gambling. *Journal of Gambling Studies, 6*, 31-42.

Griffiths, M. D. (1991a). Amusement machine playing in childhood and adolescence: A comparative analysis of video games and fruit machines. *Journal of Adolescence, 14*, 53-73.

Griffiths, M. D. (1991b). The psychobiology of the near miss in fruit machine gambling. *Journal of Psychology, 125*, 347-357.

Griffiths, M. D. (1993a). Fruit machine gambling: The importance of structural characteristics. *Journal of Gambling Studies, 9*, 101-120.

Griffiths, M. D. (1993b). Factors in problem adolescent fruit machine gambling: Results of a small postal survey. *Journal of Gambling Studies, 9,* 31-45.

Griffiths, M. D. (1993c). Fruit machine addiction in adolescence: A case study. *Journal of Gambling Studies, 9,* 387-399.

Griffiths, M. D. (1993d). Tolerance in gambling: An objective measure using the psychophysiological analysis of male fruit machine gamblers. *Addictive Behaviors, 18,* 365-372.

Griffiths, M. D. (1994). Co-existent fruit machine addiction and solvent abuse: A cause for concern? *Journal of Adolescence, 17,* 491-498.

Griffiths, M. D. (1995a). *Adolescent gambling.* London: Routledge.

Griffiths, M. D. (1995b). Technological addictions. *Clinical Psychology Forum, 76,* 14-19.

Griffiths, M. D. (1995c). Towards a risk factor model of fruit machine addiction: A brief note. *Journal of Gambling Studies, 11,* 343-346.

Griffiths, M. D. (1996a). Behavioral addictions: An issue for everybody. *Journal of Workplace Learning, 8*(3), 19-25.

Griffiths, M. D. (1996b). Pathological gambling: A review of the literature. *Journal of Psychiatric and Mental Health Nursing, 3,* 347-353.

Griffiths, M. D. (1997a). The national lottery and scratchcards. *The Psychologist: Bulletin of the British Psychological Society, 10,* 23-26.

Griffiths, M. D. (1997b). Selling hope: The psychology of the National Lottery. *Psychology Review, 23,* 26-29.

Griffiths, M. D. (1999). Gambling technologies: Prospects for problem gambling. *Journal of Gambling Studies, 15,* 265-283.

Griffiths, M. D. (2002). *Gambling and gaming addiction in adolescence.* Oxford, UK: British Psychological Society/Blackwell.

Griffiths, M. D., Scarfe, A., & Bellringer, P. (1999). The UK national telephone helpline: Results on the first year of operation. *Journal of Gambling Studies, 15,* 83-90.

Griffiths, M. D., & Sutherland, I. (1998). Adolescent gambling and drug use. *Journal of Community and Applied Social Psychology, 8,* 423-427.

Griffiths, M. D., & Wood, R. T. A. (1999). *Lottery gambling and addiction: An overview of European research.* Lausanne, Switzerland: Association of European Lotteries.

Griffiths, M. D., & Wood, R. T. A. (2000). Risk factors in adolescence: The case of gambling, video-game playing and the internet. *Journal of Gambling Studies, 16,* 199-225.

Groholt, B., Ekeberg, O., Wichstrom, L., & Haldorsen, T. (1998). Suicide among children and younger and older adolescents in Norway: A comparative study. *Journal of the American Academy of Child and Adolescent Psychiatry, 37*(5), 473-481.

Grosenick, J. (1981). Public school and mental health services to severely behavior disordered students. *Behavior Disorders, 6,* 183-190.

Gross, J. (1999). Emotion regulation: Past, present, future. *Cognition and Emotion, 13*(5), 551-573.

Grossman, J., & Pepper, S. (1999). *Plain talk and adolescent sexual behavior.* Philadelphia: Public/Private Ventures.

Grossman, J. B., & Sipe, C. L. (1992). *Summer Training and Education Program (STEP): Report on long-term impacts.* Philadelphia: Public/Private Ventures.

Grunbaum, J. A., Basen-Engquist, K., & Pandey, D. (1998). Association between violent behaviors and substance use among Mexican-American and non-Hispanic white high school students. *Journal of Adolescent Health, 23,* 153-159.

Grunbaum, J. A., Kann, L., Kinchen, S. A., Williams. B., Ross, J. G., Lowry, R., & Kolbe, L. (2002).Youth risk behavior surveillance–United States, 2001. *MMWR Surveillance Summaries, 51*(4), 1-62.

Grunseit, A., Kippax, S., Aggleton, P., Baldo, M., & Slutkin, G. (1997). Sexuality education and young people's sexual behavior: A review of studies. *Journal of Adolescent Research, 12*(4), 421-453.

Gullone, E., Moore, S., Moss, S., & Boyd, C. (2000). The adolescent risk-taking questionnaire: Developmental and psychometric evaluation. *Journal of Adolescent Research, 15,* 231-250.

Gupta, R., & Derevensky, J. (1996). The relationship between gambling and video-playing behavior in children and adolescents. *Journal of Gambling Studies, 12*(4), 375-394.

Gupta, R., & Derevensky, J. (1997). Familial and social influences on juvenile gambling. *Journal of Gambling Studies, 13,* 179-192.

Gupta, R., & Derevensky, J. L. (1998a). Adolescent gambling behavior: A prevalence study and an examination of the correlates associated with problem gambling. *Journal of Gambling Studies, 14,* 319-345.

Gupta, R., & Derevensky, J. (1998b). An empirical examination of Jacob's general theory of addictions: Do adolescent gamblers fit the theory? *Journal of Gambling Studies, 14,* 17-49.

Gupta, R., & Derevensky, J. L. (2000). Adolescents with gambling problems: From research to treatment. *Journal of Gambling Studies, 16*(2/3), 315-342.

Gupta, R., & Derevensky, J. L. (in press). Personality characteristics and risk-taking tendencies among adolescent gamblers. *Journal of Social Psychology.*

Guttmacher, S., Lieberman, L., Ward, D., Freudenberg, N., Radosh, A., & Jarlais, D. D. (1997). Condom availability in New York City public high schools: Relationships to condom use and sexual behavior. *American Journal of Public Health, 87*(9), 1427-1433.

Haapasalo, J., & Tremblay, R. E. (1994). Physically aggressive boys from ages 6 to 12: Family background, parenting behavior, and prediction to delinquency. *Journal of Consulting and Clinical Psychology, 62,* 1044-1052.

Haarasilta, L., Marttunen, M., Kaprio, J., & Aro, H. (2001). The 12-month prevalence and characteristics of major depressive episode in a representative nationwide sample of adolescents and young adults. *Psychological Medicine, 31,* 1169-1179.

Haeffel, G. J., Abramson, L. Y., Voelz, Z. R., Metalsky, G. I., Halberstadt, L., Dykman, B. M., et al. (in press). Cognitive vulnerability to depression and lifetime history of Axis I psychopathology: A comparison of negative cognitive styles (CSQ) and dysfunctional attitudes (DAS). *Journal of Cognitive Psychotherapy: An International Quarterly.*

Haggerty, K., Kosterman, R., Catalano, R. F., & Hawkins, D. (1999). *Preparing for the drug-free years* (Office of Juvenile Justice and Delinquency Prevention Juvenile Justice Bulletin). Washington, DC: Office of Juvenile Justice and Delinquency Prevention.

Hahn, A. (with Leavitt, T., & Aaron, P.). (1994). *Evaluation of the quantum opportunities program. Did the program work? A report on the post secondary outcomes and cost-effectiveness of the QOP Program (1989-1993).* Waltham, MA: Brandeis University, Heller Graduate School, Center for Human Resources.

Hall, P. A., & Fong, G. T. (1997). The health benefits of long-term thinking: A correlational study (Abstract). *Canadian Psychology, 38,* 127.

Hall, P. A., & Fong, G. T. (2001). *The effects of a brief time perspective intervention for increasing exercise behavior among university students: Final report.* Waterloo, Ontario, Canada: National Cancer Institute of Canada, Centre for Behavioral Research and Program Evaluation.

Hall, P. A., & Fong, G. T. (in press). The effects of a brief time perspective intervention for increasing physical activity among young adults. *Psychology and Health.*

Hallikainen, T., Saito, T., Lachman, H. M., Volavka, J., Pohjalainen, T., Ryynänen, O. P., et al. (1999). Association between low activity serotonin transporter promoter genotype and early onset alcoholism with habitual impulsive violent behavior. *Molecular Psychiatry, 4*(4), 385-388.

Hamilton, J. (1983). Development of interest and enjoyment in adolescence: Part I. Attentional capacities. *Journal of Youth and Adolescence, 12*(5), 355-362.

Hammond, J. R., Keeney, R. L., & Raiffa, H. (1998). *Smart decisions.* Cambridge, MA: Harvard Business School.

Hansen, W. B. (1992). School-based substance abuse prevention: A review of the state of the art in curriculum, 1980-1990. *Health Education Research: Theory & Practice, 7,* 403-430.

Hansford, B. C., & Hattie, J. A. (1982). The relationship between self and achievement/performance measures. *Review of Educational Research, 52*(1), 123-142.

Hardoon, K. K., & Derevensky, J. L. (2001). Social influences involved in children's gambling behavior. *Journal of Gambling Studies, 17*, 191-216.

Hardoon, K. K., & Derevensky, J. (2002). Child and adolescent gambling behavior: Our current knowledge. *Clinical Child Psychology and Psychiatry, 7*, 263-281.

Hardoon, K., Gupta, R., & Derevensky, J. (2002, June). *An examination of the influence of emotional and conduct problems upon adolescent gambling problems.* Paper presented at the annual meeting of the National Council on Problem Gambling, Dallas, TX.

Hardy, J. B., & Zabin, L. S. (1991). *Adolescent pregnancy in an urban environment: Issues, programs, and evaluation.* Baltimore: Urgan & Schwarzenberg.

Harter, S. (1990). Self and identity development. In S. S. Feldman & G. R. Elliot (Eds.), *At the threshold: The developing adolescent* (pp. 352-387). Cambridge, MA: Harvard University Press.

Harvey, S. M., & Spigner, C. (1995). Factors associated with sexual behavior among adolescents: A multivariate analysis. *Adolescence, 30*, 253-264.

Hassan, R. (1995). Effects of newspaper stories on the incidence of suicide in Australia: A research note. *Australian and New Zealand Journal of Psychiatry, 29*, 480-483.

Hawkins, J. D., Catalano, R., Kosterman, R., Abbott, R., & Hill, K., (1999). Preventing adolescent health-risk behaviors by strengthening protection during childhood. *Archives of Pediatrics & Adolescent Medicine, 153*, 226-234.

Hawkins, J. D., Catalano, R. K., & Miller, J. Y. (1992). Risk and protective factors for alcohol and other drug problems in adolescence and early adulthood: Implications for substance abuse. *Psychological Bulletin, 112*, 64-105.

Hawkins, J. D., Doveck, H. J., & Lishner, D. M. (1988). Changing teaching practices in mainstream classrooms to reduce discipline practices among low achievers. *American Educational Research Journal, 25*, 31-50.

Hawkins, J. D., von Cleve, E., & Catalano, R. F., Jr. (1991). Reducing early childhood aggression: Results of a primary prevention program. *Journal of the American Academy of Child and Adolescent Psychiatry, 30*(2), 208-217.

Hawkins, J. D., & Weis, J. G. (1985). The social development model: An integrated approach to delinquency prevention. *Journal of Primary Prevention, 6*, 73-97.

Hawton, K., Houston, K., & Shepperd, R. (1999a). Suicide in young people. *British Journal of Psychiatry, 175*, 271-276.

Hawton, K., Simkin, S., Deeks, J. J., O'Connor, S., Keen, A., Altman, D. G, et al. (1999). Effects of a drug overdose in a television drama on presentations to hospital for self poisoning: Time series and questionnaire study. *British Medical Journal, 318*, 972-977.

Haynes, R. H. (1987). Suicide and social response in Fiji: A historical survey. *British Journal of Psychiatry, 151*, 21-26.

Health Insurance Portability and Accountability Act of 1996, Pub. L. No. 104-191, 110 Stat. 1937.

Heath, A. C., Kirk, K., Meyer, J., & Martin, N. (1999). Genetic and social determinants of initiation and age at onset of smoking in Australian twins. *Behavior Genetics, 29*, 395-407.

Heath, A. C., & Martin, N. G. (1988). Teenage alcohol use in the Australian twin register: Genetic and social determinants of starting to drink. *Alcoholism, Clinical and Experimental Research, 12*(6), 735-741.

Heath, A. C., & Martin, N. (1993). Genetic models for the natural history of smoking: Evidence for a genetic influence on smoking persistence. *Addictive Behaviors, 18*, 19-34.

Heberling, M. (2002). State lotteries: Advocating a social ill for the social good. *Independent Review, 6*, 597-606.

Hechinger, F. M. (1992). *Fateful choices.* New York: Carnegie Council.

Heilizer, F., & Cutter, H. S. G. (1971). Generality and correlates of risk taking. *Journal of General Psychology, 85*, 259-283.

Hein, K. (1992). Adolescents at risk for HIV infection. In R. J. DiClemente (Ed.), *Adolescents and AIDS: A generation in jeopardy* (pp. 3-16). Newbury Park, CA: Sage.

Hein, K. (1997). Adolescent HIV testing: Who says who signs? *American Journal of Public Health, 87*(8), 1277-1278.

Heinz, A., Goldman, D., Jones, D., Palmour, R., Hommer, D., Gorey, J., et al. (2000). Genotype influences in vivo dopamine transporter availability in human striatum. *Neuropsychopharmacology, 22*, 133-139.

Hendin, H. (1969). *Black suicide.* New York: Basic Books.

Henry, A. F., & Short, J. F. (1954). *Suicide and homicide.* Glencoe, IL: Free Press.

Henshaw, S. K. (1998). Unintended pregnancy in the United States. *Family Planning Perspectives, 30*(1), 24-29.

Henshaw, S. K., & Feivelson, D. J. (2000). Teenage abortion and pregnancy statistics by state, 1996. *Family Planning Perspectives, 32*(6), 272-280.

Henshaw, S. K., & Torres, A. (1994). Family planning agencies: Services, policies, and funding. *Family Planning Perspectives, 26*, 52-59.

Herek, G., & Capitanio, J. (1993). Public reactions to AIDS in the US: A second decade of stigma. *American Journal of Public Health, 83*(4), 574-577.

Hernandez, J. T., Lodico, M., & DiClemente, R. J. (1993). The effects of child abuse and race on risk-taking in male adolescents. *Journal of the National Medical Association, 85*(8), 593-597.

Herpertz-Dahlmann, B. M., Wewetzer, C., & Remschmidt, H. (1995). The predictive value of depression in anorexia nervosa: Results of a seven-year follow-up study. *Acta Psychiatrica Scandinavica, 91*, 114-119.

Herpertz-Dahlmann, B. M., Wewetzer, C., Schulz, E., & Remschmidt, H. (1996). Course and outcome in adolescent anorexia nervosa. *International Journal of Eating Disorders, 19*, 335-345.

Higgens, J. P., & Thies, A. P. (1981). Problem-solving and social position among emotionally disturbed boys. *American Journal of Orthopsychiatry, 51*, 356-358.

Hill, S., Zezza, N., Wipprecht, G., Xu, J., & Neiswanger, K. (1999). Linkage studies of D2 and D4 receptor genes and alcoholism. *American Journal of Medical Genetics, 88*(6), 676-685.

Hilton, S. C., Fellingham, G. W., & Lyon, J. L. (2002). Suicide rates and religious commitment in young adult males in Utah. *American Journal of Epidemiology, 155*(5), 412-419.

Hingson, R., Heeren, T., & Winter, M. (1996). Lowering state legal blood alcohol limits to 0.08%: The effect on fatal motor vehicle crashes. *American Journal of Public Health, 86*, 1297-1299.

Ho, T. P., Hung, S. F., Lee, C. C., Chung, K. F., & Chung, S. Y. (1995). Characteristics of youth suicide in Hong Kong. *Social Psychiatry and Psychiatric Epidemiology, 30*, 107-112.

Hochbaum, G. (1958). *Public participation in medical screening program: A sociopsychological study* (U.S. Public Health Service Publication No. 572). Washington, DC: Government Printing Office.

Hoffmann, D. E., & Wulfsberg, E. A. (1995). Testing children for genetic predispositions: Is it in their best interest? *Journal of Law, Medicine & Ethics, 23*(4), 331-344.

Hofman, K. L., Tambor, E. S., Chase, G. A., Geller, G., Faden, R., & Holtzman, N. A. (1993). Physicians' knowledge of genetics and genetic tests. *Academic Medicine, 68*(8), 625-632.

Hoge, D., Smit, E., & Crist, J. (1995). Reciprocal effects of self-concept and academic achievement in 6th and 7th grade. *Journal of Youth and Adolescence, 24*(3), 295-314.

Hogue, A., Liddle, H. A., Becker, D., Johnson-Leckrone, J. (2002). Family-based prevention counseling for high-risk young adolescents: Immediate outcomes. *Journal of Community Psychology, 30*, 1-22.

Holden, C. (2001). "Behavioral" addictions: Do they exist? *Science, 294*(2), 980-982.

Holder, H. D., Saltz, R. F., Grube, J. W., Voas, R. B., Gruenewald, P. J., & Treno, A. J. (1997). A community prevention trial to reduce alcohol-involved accidental injury and death: Overview. *Addiction, 92*(Suppl 2), 155-171.

Holding, T. A. (1974). The B.B.C. "Befrienders" series and its effects. *British Journal of Psychiatry, 124*, 470-472.

Holding, T. A. (1975). Suicide and "The Befrienders." *British Medical Journal, 3,* 751-753.

Holinger, P. C., Offer, D., Barter, J. T., & Bell, C. C. (1994). *Suicide and homicide among adolescents.* New York: Guilford Press.

Hollon, S. D., Thase, M. E., & Markowitz, J. C. (2002). Treatment and prevention of depression. *Psychological Science in the Public Interest, 3,* 39-77.

Holtgrave, D. R., & Crosby, R. A. (2003). Social capital, poverty, and income inequality as predictors of gonorrhea, syphilis, chlamydia and AIDS case rates in the United States. *Sexually Transmitted Infections, 79:* 62-64.

Holtzman, D., & Rubinson, R. (1995). Parent and peer communication effects on AIDS-related behavior among U.S. high school students. *Family Planning Perspectives, 27,* 235-240.

Holtzman, N. A., & Watson, M. S. (1999). Promoting safe and effective genetic testing in the United States. Final report of the Task Force on Genetic Testing. *Journal of Child & Family Nursing, 2(5),* 338-390.

Horne, W., & Packard, T. (1985). Early identification of learning problems: A meta-analysis. *Journal of Educational Psychology, 77(5),* 597-607.

Hornik, R. C., Maklan, D., Cadell, D., Prado, A., Barmada, C., Jacobsohn, L., et al. (2002, May). *Evaluation of the National Youth Anti-Drug Media Campaign: Fourth annual report of findings.* Report delivered to National Institute on Drug Abuse, National Institutes of Health.

Houston, K., Hawton, K., & Shepperd, R. (2001). Suicide in young people aged 15-24: A psychological autopsy study. *Journal of Affective Disorders, 63,* 159-170.

Hovey, J. D. (1999). Religion and suicidal ideation in a sample of Latin American immigrants. *Psychological Reports, 85,* 171-177.

Howard, M., & McCabe, J. (1990). Helping teenagers postpone sexual involvement. *Family Planning Perspectives, 22(1),* 21-26.

Howard-Pitney, B., LaFramboise, T. D., Basil., M., September, B., & Johnson, M. (1992). Psychological and social indicators of suicide ideation and suicide attempts in Zuni adolescents. *Journal of Consulting and Clinical Psychology, 60,* 473-476.

Hoyle, R., Stephenson, M., Palmgreen, P., Lorch, E., & Donohew, L. (2002). Reliability and validity of a brief measure of sensation seeking. *Personality and Individual Differences, 32,* 401-414.

Hubbard, B. M., Giese M. L., & Rainey, J. (1998). A replication of Reducing the Risk, a theory-based sexuality curriculum for adolescents. *Journal of School Health, 68(6),* 243-247.

Hudson, L. M., Peyton, E. F., & Brion-Meisels, S. (1976, September). Social reasoning and relating: An analysis of videotaped social interactions. In H. Furth (Chair), *Integrations of development in social cognition and social behavior.* Symposium presented at the meeting of the American Psychological Association, Washington, DC.

Hughes, M. E., Furstenberg, F. F., Jr., & Teitler, J. O. (1995). The impact of an increase in family planning services on the teenage population of Philadelphia. *Family Planning Perspectives, 27(2),* 60-65, 78.

Hundleby, J. D., Carpenter, R. A., Ross, R. A., & Mercer, G. W. (1982). Adolescent drug use and other behaviors. *Journal of Child Psychology and Psychiatry, 23,* 61-68.

Hurrelmann, L. (1989). *Human development and health.* Berlin: Springer-Verger.

Huttenlocher, P. R. (1994). Synaptogenesis, synapse elimination, and neural plasticity in human cerebral cortex. In C. A. Nelson (Ed.), *Threats to optimal development: Integrating biological, psychological, and social risk factors: Vol. 27. Minnesota Symposia on Child Psychology* (pp. 35-54). Hillsdale, NJ: Lawrence Erlbaum.

Huxley, J., & Carroll, D. (1992). A survey of fruit machine gambling in adolescents. *Journal of Gambling Studies, 8,* 167-179.

Ianazu, J., & Fox, G. (1980). Maternal influence on the sexual behavior of teenage daughters. *Journal of Family Issues, 1,* 81-102.

Ide-Smith, S., & Lea, S. E. G. (1988). Gambling in young adolescents. *Journal of Gambling Behavior, 4,* 110-118.

Independent Television Commission. (1995). Child's-eye view. *Spectrum, 17,* 24.

Institute of Medicine. (1987). *Risking the future: Adolescent sexuality, pregnancy, and child-bearing.* Washington, DC: National Academy Press.

Institute of Medicine. (1994). *Reducing risks for mental disorder: Frontiers for preventive intervention research.* Washington, DC: National Academy Press.

Irwin, C. E. (1993). Adolescence and risk taking: How are they related? In N. J. Bell & R. W. Bell (Eds.), *Adolescent risk taking* (pp. 7-28). Newbury Park, CA: Sage.

Isen, A. (2001). An influence of positive affect on decision making in complex situations: Theoretical issues with practical implications. *Journal of Consumer Psychology, 11*(2), 75-85.

Ishiguro, H., Saito, T., Akazawa, S., Mitushio, H., Tada, K., Enomoto, M., et al. (1999). Association between drinking-related antisocial behavior and a polymorphism in the serotonin transporter gene in a Japanese population. *Alcoholism, Clinical and Experimental Research, 23*(7), 1281-1284.

Ishii, K. (1991). Measuring mutual causation: Effect of suicide news on suicides in Japan. *Social Science Research, 20,* 188-195.

Iyengar, S., & Kinder, D. R. (1987). *News that matters.* Chicago: University of Chicago Press.

Jaccard, J., & Dittus, P. (1991). *Parent-teen communication: Toward the prevention of unintended pregnancies.* New York: Springer-Verlag.

Jaccard, J., Dittus, P. J., & Gordon, V. V. (1996). Maternal correlates of adolescent sexual and contraceptive behavior. *Family Planning Perspectives, 28,* 159-165, 185.

Jaccard, J., Dittus, P. J., & Litardo, H. A. (1999). Parent-adolescent communication about sex and birth control: Implications for parent-based interventions to reduce unintended adolescent pregnancy. In W. Miller & L. Severy (Eds.), *Advances in population: Psychological perspectives.* London: Kingsley.

Jackson, C., Bee-Gates, D. J., & Henriksen, L. (1994). Authoritative parenting, child competencies, and initiation of cigarette smoking. *Health Education Quarterly, 21,* 103-106.

Jackson, D. N., Hourany, L., & Vidmar, N. J. (1972). A four-dimensional interpretation of risk taking. *Journal of Personality, 40,* 483-501.

Jackson, J. S., Brown, T. N., Williams, D. R., Torres, M., Sellers, S. L., & Brown, K. (1996). Racism and the physical and mental health status of African Americans: A thirteen year national panel study. *Ethnicity and Disease, 11*(1-2), 132-137.

Jackson, K. M., & Aiken, L. S. (2000). A psychosocial model of sun protection and sunbathing in young women: The impact of health beliefs, attitudes, norms, and self-efficacy for sun protection, *Health Psychology, 19,* 469-478.

Jacobs, D. F. (1986). A general theory of addictions: A new theoretical model. *Journal of Gambling Behavior, 2*(1), 15-31.

Jacobs, D. F. (1989). Illegal and undocumented: A review of teenage gambling and the plight of children of problem gamblers in America. In H. J. Shaffer, S. A. Stein, B. Gambino, T. N. Cummings, & R. L. Custer (Eds.), *Compulsive gambling: Theory, research and practice.* Lexington, MA: Lexington Books.

Jacobs, D. F. (1997, June). *Effects on children of parental excesses in gambling.* Paper presented at the National Conference on Problem Gambling, Orlando, FL.

Jacobs, D. F. (2000). Juvenile gambling in North America: An analysis of long-term trends and future prospects. *Journal of Gambling Studies, 16,* 119-152.

Jacobs, D. F., Marston, A., & Singer, R. (1985). Testing a general theory of addiction: Similarities and differences among alcoholics, pathological gamblers, and overeaters. In J. J. Sanchez-Soza (Ed.), *Health and clinical psychology* (Vol. 4). Amsterdam: Elsevier Science.

Jacobs, J. E., & Potenza, M. (1991). The use of judgment heuristics to make social and object decisions: A developmental perspective. *Child Development, 62,* 166-178.

Jacobs-Quadrel, M., Fischhoff, B., & Davis, W. (1993). Adolescent (in)vulnerability. *American Psychologist, 48,* 102-116.

Jamieson, P., & Romer, D. (2001). What do young people think they know about the risks of smoking? In P. Slovic (Ed.), *Smoking: Risk, perception, and policy*. Thousand Oaks, CA: Sage.

Jarvis, J., McIntyre, D., & Bates, C. (2002). Effectiveness of smoking cessation initiatives [Electronic version]. *British Medical Journal, 324,* 608.

Jastrzab, J., Masker, J., Blomquist, J., & Orr, L. (1997). *Youth corps: Promising strategies for young people and their communities*. Cambridge, MA: Abt Associates.

Jemmott, J. B. III, & Jemmott, L. S. (2000). HIV behavioral interventions for adolescents in community settings. In J. L. Peterson and R. J. DiClemente (Eds.), *Handbook of HIV prevention* (pp. 103-128). New York: Plenum Press.

Jemmott, J. B., III, Jemmott, L. S., & Fong, G. T. (1992). Reductions in HIV risk-associated sexual behaviors among black male adolescents: Effects of an AIDS prevention intervention. *American Journal of Public Health, 82*(3), 372-377.

Jemmott, J. B., III, Jemmott, L. S., & Fong, G. T. (1998). Abstinence and safer sex: A randomized trial of HIV sexual risk-reduction interventions for young African-American adolescents. *JAMA, 279*(19), 1529-1536.

Jemmott, J. B., III, Jemmott, L. S., Fong, G. T., & McCaffree, K. (1999). Reducing HIV risk-associated sexual behavior among African American adolescents: Testing the generality of intervention effects. *American Journal of Community Psychology, 27,* 167-187.

Jemmott, L. S., Jemmott, J. B., III, & McCaffree, K. A. (1994). *Be proud! Be responsible!* New York: Select Media.

Jensen, A. R. (1998). *The g factor*. Westport, CT: Praeger.

Jessor, R. (1991). Risk behavior in adolescence: A psychosocial framework for understanding and action. *Journal of Adolescent Health, 12,* 597-605.

Jessor, R. (1992). Risk behavior in adolescence: A psychosocial framework for understanding and action. *Developmental Review, 12,* 374-390.

Jessor, R. (1998). New perspectives on adolescent risk behavior. In R. Jessor (Ed.), *New perspectives on adolescent risk behavior*. Cambridge, UK: Cambridge University Press.

Jessor, R., Costa, F., Jessor, S. L., & Donovan, J. E. (1983). Time of first intercourse: A prospective study. *Journal of Personality and Social Psychology, 44*(3), 608-626.

Jessor, R., Graves, T. D., Hanson, R. C., & Jessor, S. L. (1968). *Society, personality and deviant behavior: A study of a tri-ethnic community*. New York: Holt, Rinehart & Winston.

Jessor, R., & Jessor, S. L. (1977). *Problem behavior and psychosocial development: A longitudinal study of youth*. New York: Academic Press.

Jessor, R., Turbin, M. S., & Costa, F. M. (1998). Protective factors in adolescent health. *Journal of Personality and Social Psychology, 75,* 788-800.

Jessor, R., Van Den Bos, J., Vanderryn, J., Costa, F. M., & Turbin, M. S. (1995). Protective factors in adolescent problem behavior: Moderator effects and developmental change. *Developmental Psychology, 31,* 923-933.

Jessor, S. L., & Jessor, R. (1974). Maternal ideology and adolescent problem behavior. *Developmental Psychology, 10*(2), 246-254.

Joe, S., & Kaplan, M. S. (2001). Suicide among African American men. *Suicide and Life-Threatening Behavior, 31*(1), 106-121.

Joe, S., & Kaplan, M. S. (2002). Firearm-related suicide among young African-American males. *Psychiatric Services, 53*(3), 332-334.

Joffe, R. T., Offord, D. R., & Boyle, M. H. (1988). Ontario Child Health Study: Suicidal behavior in youth aged 12-16 years. *American Journal of Psychiatry, 145,* 1420-1423.

Johnson, J., Muhleman, D., MacMurray, J., Gade, R., Verde, R., Ask, M., et al. (1997). Association between the cannabinoid receptor gene (CNR1) and the P300 event-related potential. *Molecular Psychiatry, 2*(2), 169-171.

Johnson, K., Strader, T., Berbaum, M., Bryant, D., Bucholtz, G., Collins, D., et al. (1996). Reducing alcohol and other drug use by strengthening community, family, and youth resiliency: An evaluation of the Creating Lasting Connections program. *Journal of Adolescent Research, 11,* 36-67.

Johnston, L. D. (1973). *Drugs and American youth*. Ann Arbor, MI: Institute for Social Research.

Johnston, L. D. (1991a). Contributions of drug epidemiology to the field of drug abuse prevention. In C. Leukefeld & W. Bukoski (Eds.), *Drug abuse prevention research: Methodological issues* (NIDA Research Monograph 107, pp. 57-80). Washington, DC: National Institute on Drug Abuse.

Johnston, L. D. (1991b). Toward a theory of drug epidemics. In R. L. Donohew, H. Sypher, & W. Bukoski (Eds.), *Persuasive communication and drug abuse prevention* (pp. 93-132). Hillsdale, NJ: Lawrence Erlbaum.

Johnston, L. D., O'Malley, P. M., & Bachman, J. G. (1995). *Drug use among American high school seniors, college students, and young adults, 1975-1995* (DHSS Publication No. ADM91-1813). Rockville, MD: National Institute on Drug Abuse.

Johnston, L. D., O'Malley, P. M., & Bachman, J. G. (1996, December 19). *Monitoring the Future national survey results on drug use*. Press Release, National Institute on Drug Abuse.

Johnston, L. D., O'Malley, P. M., & Bachman, J. G. (2000). *Monitoring the Future national survey results on drug use, 1975-1999: Vol. 1. Secondary school students* (NIH Publication No. 00-4802). Rockville, MD: National Institute on Drug Abuse.

Johnston, L. D., O'Malley, P. M., & Bachman, J. G. (2001). *National survey results on drug use from the Monitoring the Future study, 1975-2000. Vol. I: Secondary school students* (NIH Publication No. 01-4924). Bethesda, MD: National Institute on Drug Abuse.

Johnston, L., O'Malley, P., & Bachman, J. (2002). *Monitoring the future national results on adolescent drug use; overview of key findings, 2001*. Bethesda, MD: National Institute on Drug Abuse. (Available on the Web at www.monitoringthefuture.org)

Johnston, L. D., O'Malley, P. M., Bachman, J. G., & Schulenberg, J. (1993). *Aims and objectives of the Monitoring the Future study* (Monitoring the Future Occasional Paper No. 34.). Ann Arbor, MI: Institute for Social Research.

Johnston, L. D., O'Malley, P. M., Schulenberg, J. E., & Bachman, J. G. (2001). *The aims and objectives of the Monitoring the Future study and progress toward fulfilling them as of 2001*. (Monitoring the Future Occasional Paper No. 52). Ann Arbor: Institute for Social Research. (Available on the Web at www.monitoringthefuture.org)

Jonas, K. (1992). Modelling and suicide: A test of the Werther effect. *British Journal of Social Psychology, 31*, 295-306.

Jones, N. L. (1996). *Genetic information: Discrimination and privacy issues* (CRS Report for Congress). Washington, DC: Congressional Research Service the Library of Congress.

Jones, S., & Heaven, P. (1998). Psychosocial correlates of adolescent drug-taking behavior. *Journal of Adolescence, 21*(2), 127-134.

Jorm, A., Henderson, A., Jacomb, P., Christensen, H., Korten, A., Rodgers, B., et al. (2000). Association of smoking and personality with a polymorphism of the dopamine transporter gene: Results from a community survey. *American Journal of Medical Genetics, 96*, 331-334.

Juon, H. S., & Ensminger, M. E. (1997). Childhood, adolescent, and young adult predictors of suicidal behaviors: A prospective study of African Americans. *Journal of Child Psychology and Psychiatry, 38*(5), 553-563.

Kahn, J. G., Brindis, C. D., Claire, D., & Glei, D. A. (1999). Pregnancies averted among U.S. teenagers by the use of contraception. *Family Planning Perspectives, 31*, 29-34.

Kahneman, D., Slovic, P., & Tversky, A. (1982). *Judgment under uncertainty: Heuristics and biases*. New York: Cambridge University Press.

Kaltiala-Heino, R., Rimpela, M., Marttunen, M., Rimpela, A., & Rantanen, P. (1999). Bullying, depression, and suicidal ideation in Finnish adolescents: School survey. *British Medical Journal, 319*, 348-351.

Kandel, D. (1975). Stages in adolescent involvement in drug use. *Science, 190*, 912-914.

Kandel, D. (1988). Substance use, depressive mood, and suicidal ideation in adolescence and young adulthood. In A. R. Stiffman & R. A. Feldman (Eds.), *Advancement in adolescent mental health*. Greenwich, CT: JAI press.

Kandel, D. B. (Ed.). (2002). *Stages and pathways of drug involvement: Examining the gateway hypothesis*. New York: Cambridge University Press.

Kandel, D. B., Raveis, V. H., & Davies, M. (1991). Suicidal ideation in adolescence: Depression, substance abuse, and other risk factors. *Journal of Youth and Adolescence, 20*, 289-309.

Kandel, D. B., & Yamaguchi, K. (1993). From beer to crack: Developmental patterns of drug involvement. *American Journal of Public Health, 83*, 851-855.

Kandel, D. B., & Yamaguchi, K. (1999). Developmental stages of involvement in substance abuse. In P. J. Ott, R. E. Tarter, & R. T. Ammerman (Eds.), *Sourcebook on substance abuse: Etiology, epidemiology, assessment and treatment* (pp. 50-74). New York: Allyn & Bacon.

Kandel, D. B., Yamaguchi, K. (2002). Stages of drug involvement in the U.S. population. In D. B. Kandel (Ed.), *Stages and pathways of drug involvement: Examining the gateway hypothesis* (pp. 65-89). New York: Cambridge University Press.

Kandel, D. B., Yamaguchi, K., & Chen, K. (1992). Stages of progression in drug involvement from adolescence to adulthood: Further evidence for the gateway theory. *Journal of Studies on Alcohol, 52*, 447-457.

Kanfer, F. H. (1970). *Self-regulation: Research, issues and speculations*. New York: Appleton-Century-Crofts.

Kann, L., Kinchen, S. A., Williams, B. I., Ross, J. G., Lowry, R., Grunbaum, J., Kolbe, L. J., & State and Local YRBSS Coordinators. (2000). Youth risk behavior surveillance—United States, 1999. *Morbidity & Mortality Weekly Report, 49*(No. SS-5), 1-95.

Kaplan, H. B. (1975). *Self-attitudes and deviant behavior*. Pacific Palisades, CA: Goodyear.

Kaplan, M. S., & Geling, O. (1998). Firearm suicides and homicides in the United States: Regional variations and patterns of gun ownership. *Social Science and Medicine, 46*, 1227-1233.

Kapur, S., Mieczkowski, M. A., & Mann, J. J. (1992). Antidepressant medication and the relative risk of suicide attempt and suicide. *JAMA, 268*, 3441-3445.

Kasen, S., Cohen, P., Skodol, A., Johnson, I. G., Smailes, E., & Brook, J. S. (2001). Childhood depression and adult personality disorder: Alternative pathways of continuity. *Archives of General Psychiatry, 58*, 231-236.

Kashani, J. H., Goddard, P., & Reid, J. C. (1989). Correlates of suicidal ideation in a community sample of children and adolescents. *Journal of the American Academy of Child and Adolescent Psychiatry, 28*, 912-917.

Kauffman, J. (1999). How we prevent the prevention of emotional and behavioral disorders. *Exceptional Children, 65*(4), 448-468.

Kazdin, A. E. (1987). *Conduct disorders in childhood and adolescence*. London: Sage.

Kegeles, S. M., Hays, R. B., & Coates, T. J. (1996). The Mpowerment project: A community-level HIV prevention intervention for young gay men. *American Journal of Public Health, 86*, 1129-1136.

Kellam, S. G., & Anthony, J. C. (1998). Targeting early antecedents to prevent tobacco smoking: Findings from an epidemiologically based randomized field trial. *American Journal of Public Health, 88*(10), 1490-1495.

Kellam, S. G., Brown, C. H., Rubin, B. R., & Ensminger, M. E. (1983). Paths leading to teenage psychiatric symptoms and substance use: Developmental epidemiological studies in Woodlawn. In S. B. Guze, F. J. Earls, & J. E. Barett (Eds.), *Child psychopathology and development* (pp. 17-75). New York: Raven Press.

Kellam, S. G., Ling, X., Merisca, R., Brown, C. H., & Ialongo, N. (1998). The effect of the level of aggression in the first grade classroom on the course and malleability of aggressive behavior into middle school. *Development & Psychopathology, 10*(2), 165-185.

Kellam, S. G., Mayer, L. S., Rebok, G. W., & Hawkins, W. E. (1998). Effects of improving achievement on aggressive behavior through two preventive interventions: An investigation of causal paths. In B. Dohrenwend (Ed.), *Adversity, stress, & psychopathology* (pp. 486-505). New York: Oxford University Press.

Keller, P. A., & Block, L. G. (1997). Vividness effects: A resource matching perspective. *Journal of consumer Research, 24,* 295-304.

Kellermann, A. L., Rivera, F. P., Somes, G., Reay, D., Francisco, J., Banton, J. G., et al. (1992). Suicide in the home in relation to gun ownership. *New England Journal of Medicine, 327,* 467-472.

Kelley, J. F., Myers, M. G., & Brown, S. A. (2002). Do adolescents affiliate with 12-step groups? A multivariate process model of effects. *Journal of Studies on Alcohol, 63,* 293-304.

Kelly, J., & Kalichman, S. (1998). Reinforcement value of unsafe sex as a predictor of condom use and continued HIV/AIDS risk behavior among gay and bisexual men. *Health Psychology, 17*(4), 328-335.

Kendler, K. (2001). Twin studies of psychiatric illness. *Archives of General Psychiatry, 58,* 1005-1014.

Kendler, K. S., Gardner, C. O., Neale, M. C., & Prescott, C. A. (2001). Genetic risk factors for major depression in men and women: Similar or different heritabilities and same or partly distinct genes? *Psychological Medicine, 31*(4), 605-616.

Kendler, K. S., Neale, M., Sullivan, P., Corey, L., Gardner, C., & Prescott, C. (1999). A population-based twin study in women of smoking initiation and nicotine dependence. *Psychological Medicine, 29,* 299-308.

Kendler, K. S., & Prescott, C. A. (1998). Cannabis use, abuse, and dependence in a population-based sample of female twins. *American Journal of Psychiatry, 155*(8), 1016-1022.

Kennedy, M. G., Mizuno, Y., Seals, B. F., Myllyuoma, J., & Weeks-Norton, K. (2000). Increasing condom use among adolescents with coalition-based social marketing. *AIDS, 14,* 1809-1818.

Keough, K. A., Zimbardo, P. G., & Boyd, J. N. (1999). Who's smoking, drinking, and using drugs? Time perspective as a predictor of substance use. *Basic and Applied Social Psychology, 21,* 149-164.

Kessler, R. C., Avenevoli, S., & Reis Merikangas, K. R. (2001). Mood disorders in children and adolescents: An epidemiological perspective. *Biological Psychiatry, 49,* 1002-1014.

Kessler, R. C., Berglund, P. A., Foster, C. L., Saunders, W. B., Stang, P. E., & Walters, E. E. (1997). Social consequences of psychiatric disorders, II: Teenage parenthood. *American Journal of Psychiatry, 54,* 1405-1411.

Kessler, R. C., Borges, G., & Walters, E. E. (1999). Prevalence of and risk factors for lifetime suicide attempts in the National Comorbidity Survey. *Archives of General Psychiatry, 56,* 617-626.

Kessler, R. C., Downey, G., Stipp, H., & Milavsky, R. (1989). Network television news stories about suicide and short-term changes in total U. S. suicides. *Journal of Nervous and Mental Disorders, 177*(Suppl 9), 551-555.

Kessler, R. C., McGonagle, K. A., Zhao, S., Nelson, C. B., Hughes, M., Eshleman, S., et al. (1994). Lifetime and 12-month prevalence of DSM-III-R major depressive disorder in the general population: Results from the US National Comorbidity Survey. *Archives of General Psychiatry, 51,* 8-19.

Kessler, R. C., & Walters, E. E. (1998). Epidemiology of DSM-III-R major depression and minor depression among adolescents and young adults in the National Comorbidity Survey. *Depression and Anxiety, 7,* 3-14.

Killen, J. D., Robinson, T. N., Haydel, K. F., Hayward, C., Wilson, D. M., Hammer, L. D., et al. (1997). Prospective study of risk factors for the initiation of cigarette smoking. *Journal of Consulting and Clinical Psychology, 65,* 1011-1016.

Kim, N., Stanton, B., Li, X., Dickersin, K., & Galbraith, J. (1997). Effectiveness of 40 adolescent AIDS-risk reduction interventions: A quantitative review. *Journal of Adolescent Health, 20,* 204-215.

Kimbrough, R. M., Molock, S. D., & Walton, K. (1996). Perception of social support, acculturation, depression, and suicidal ideation among African American college students at predominantly black and predominantly white universities. *Journal of Negro Education, 65*(3), 295-307.

King, C. A., Raskin, A., Gdowski, C. L., Butkus, M., & Opipari, L. (1990). Psychosocial factors associated with urban adolescent female suicide attempts. *Journal of the American Academy of Child and Adolescent Psychiatry, 29,* 289-294.

King, P. A. (1992). The past as prologue: Race, class, and gene discrimination. In G. J. Annas & S. Elias (Eds.), *Gene mapping: Using law and ethics as guides* (pp. 94-111). New York: Oxford University Press.

King, R. A., Schwab-Stone, M., Flisher, A. J., Greenwald, S., Kramer, R. A., Goodman, S. H., et al. (2001). Psychosocial and risk behavior correlates of youth suicide attempts and suicidal ideation. *Journal of the American Academy of Child and Adolescent Psychiatry, 40,* 837-846.

Kingsley, G. T. (1998). *Neighborhood indicators: Taking advantage of the new potential.* National Neighborhood Indicators Partnership. Washington, DC: Urban Institute.

Kinsman, S. B. (2002). *Risk initiation among adolescents: Does diffusion exist?* Paper presented at the Reducing Adolescent Risk Conference, Annenberg Public Policy Center, Philadelphia, PA.

Kirby, D. (1985). The effects of selected sexuality education programs: Toward a more realistic view. *Journal of Sex Education and Therapy, 11*(1), 28-37.

Kirby, D. (1991). *An evaluation of the Lake Taylor High School Health Center.* Scotts Valley, CA: ETR Associates.

Kirby, D. (1997). *No easy answers: Research findings on programs to reduce teen pregnancy (summary).* Washington, DC: National Campaign to Prevent Teen Pregnancy.

Kirby, D. (2000). School-based interventions to prevent unprotected sex and HIV among adolescents. In J. L. Peterson & R. J. DiClemente (Eds.), *Handbook of HIV prevention* (pp. 83-101). New York: Plenum Press.

Kirby, D. (2001a). *Emerging answers: Research findings on programs to reduce teen pregnancy.* Washington, DC: National Campaign to Prevent Teen Pregnancy.

Kirby, D. (2001b). Understanding what works and what doesn't in reducing adolescent sexual risk-taking. *Family Planning Perspectives, 33*(6), 276-281.

Kirby, D. (2002). The impact of schools and school programs upon adolescent sexual behavior. *Journal of Sex Research, 39*(1), 27-33.

Kirby, D., Barth, R., Leland, N., & Fetro, J. (1991). Reducing the risk: A new curriculum to prevent sexual risk-taking. *Family Planning Perspectives, 23*(6), 253-263.

Kirby, D., Brener, N. D., Brown, N. L., Peterfreund, N., Hillard, P., & Harrist, R. (1999). The impact of condom distribution in Seattle schools on sexual behavior and condom use. *American Journal of Public Health, 89*(2), 182-187.

Kirby, D., & Brown, N. (1996). School condom availability programs in the United States. *Family Planning Perspectives, 28*(5), 196-202.

Kirby, D., Korpi, M., Adivi, C., & Weissman, J. (1997). An impact evaluation of Project SNAPP: An AIDS and pregnancy prevention middle school program. *AIDS Education and Prevention, 9*(Suppl. A), 44-61.

Kirby, D., Waszak, C., & Ziegler, J. (1991). Six school-based clinics: Their reproductive health services and impact on sexual behavior. *Family Planning Perspectives, 23*(1), 6-16.

Kisker, E. E., Brown, R. S., & Hill, J. (1994). *Health caring: Outcomes of the Robert Wood Johnson Foundation's school-based adolescent health care program.* Princeton, NJ: Robert Wood Johnson Foundation.

Kitzman, H., Olds, D. L., Sidora, K., Henderson, C. R., Hanks, C., et al. (2000). Enduring effects of nurse home visitation on maternal life course: A 3-year follow-up of a randomized trial. *JAMA, 283*(15), 1983-1989.

Klaus, H., Bryan, L. M., Bryant, M. L., Fagan, M. U., Harrigan, M. B., & Kearns, F. (1987). Fertility awareness/natural family planning for adolescents and their families: Report of a multisite pilot project. *International Journal of Adolescent Medicine and Health, 3*(2), 101-119.

Klein, J., Rossbach, C., Nijher, H., Geist, M., Wilson, K., Cohn, S., et al. (2001). Where do adolescents get their condoms? *Journal of Adolescent Health, 29,* 186-193.

Klesges, R. C., Somes, G., Pascale, W., Klesges, L. M., Murphy, M., Brown, K., &Williams, E. (1988). Knowledge of beliefs regarding the consequences of cigarette smoking and their relationships to smoking status in a biracial sample. *Health Psychology, 7*, 387-401.

Knapp, M., McCrone, P., Fombonne, E., Beecham, J., & Worster, G. (2002). The Maudsley long-term follow-up of child and adolescent depression. 3. Impact of comorbid conduct disorder on service use and costs in adulthood. *British Journal of Psychiatry, 180*, 19-23.

Knetsch, J. (1989). The endowment effect and evidence of nonreversible indifference curves. *The American Economic Review, 79*, 1277-1284.

Kolbe, L. J., Kann, L., & Collins, J. L. (1993). Overview of the Youth Risk Behavior Surveillance System. *Public Health Reports, 108*(Suppl. 1), 2-10.

Koo, H. P., Dunteman, G. H., George, C., Green, Y., & Vincent, M. (1994). Reducing adolescent pregnancy through school and community-based education: Denmark, South Carolina, revised 1991. *Family Planning Perspectives, 26*(5), 206-217.

Koob, G. F., Le, H. T., & Creese, I. (1987). The D1 dopamine receptor antagonist SCH 23390 increases cocaine self-administration in the rat. *Neuroscience Letters, 79*, 315-320.

Koop, C. E., & Lundberg, G. D. (1992). Violence in America: A public health emergency. *JAMA, 267*, 3076-3077.

Koopmans, J., Boomsma, D., Heath, A., & van Doornen, L. (1995). A multivariate genetic analysis of sensation seeking. *Behavior Genetics, 25*(4), 349-356.

Kopstein, A., Crum, R., Celentano, D., & Martin, S. (2001). Sensation seeking needs among 8th and 11th graders: Characteristics associated with cigarette and marijuana use. *Drug and Alcohol Dependence, 62*(3), 195-203.

Korn, D. A. (2000). Expansion of gambling in Canada: Implications for health and social policy. *Canadian Medical Association Journal, 163*(1), 61-64.

Korn, D. A., & Shaffer, H. (1999). Gambling and the health of the public: Adopting a public health perspective. *Journal of Gambling Studies, 15*, 289-365.

Kosten, T., Ball, S., & Rounsaville, B. (1994). A sibling study of sensation seeking and opiate addiction. *Journal of Nervous and Mental Disease, 18*(5), 284-289.

Kotler, M., Cohen, H., Segman, R., Gritsenko, I., Nemanov, L., Lerer, B., et al. (1997). Excess dopamine D4 receptor (D4DR) exon III seven repeat allele in opioid-dependent subjects. *Molecular Psychiatry, 2*(3), 251-254.

Koutsky, L. A., & Kiviat, N. B. (1999). Genital human papillomavirus. In K. K. Holmes, P. F. Sparling, P. Mardh, et al (Eds.), *Sexually transmitted diseases* (3rd ed., pp. 361-384). New York: McGraw-Hill.

Kranzler, H. R., Gelernter, J., O'Malley, S., Hernandez-Avila, C. A., & Kaufman, D. (1998). Association of alcohol or other drug dependence with alleles of the mu-opioid receptor gene (OPRM1). *Alcoholism, Clinical and Experimental Research, 22*(6), 1359-1362.

Kruesi, M. J. P., Grossman, J., Pennington, J. M., Woodward, P. J., Duda, D., & Hirsch, J. G. (1999). Suicide and violence prevention: Parent education in the emergency department. *Journal of the American Academy of Child and Adolescent Psychiatry, 38*, 250-255.

Kuhn, D. (1991). *The skills of argument*. New York: Cambridge University Press.

Labouvie, E., & White, H. R. (2002). Drug sequences, age of onset, and use trajectories as predictors of drug use/dependence in young adulthood. In D. Kandel (Ed.), *Stages and pathways of drug involvement* (pp. 19-41). Cambridge, UK: Cambridge University Press.

Ladd, G. W., & Asher, S. R. (1985). Social skill training and children's peer relations. In L. L. Abate & M. Milan (Eds.), *Handbook of social skills training* (pp. 219-244). New York: John Wiley.

Ladouceur, R., Boudreault, N., Jacques, C., & Vitaro, F. (1999). Pathological gambling and related problems among adolescents. *Journal of Child & Adolescent Substance Abuse, 8*(4), 55-68.

Ladouceur, R., & Mireault, C. (1988). Gambling behaviors among high school students in the Quebec area. *Journal of Gambling Behavior, 4*(1), 3-12.

Ladouceur, R., Vezina, L., Jacques, C., & Ferland, F. (2000). Does a brochure about pathological gambling provide new information? *Journal of Gambling Studies, 16*, 103-107.

Ladouceur, R., Vitaro, F., & Cote, M-A. (2001). Parents' attitudes, knowledge and behavior toward youth gambling: A five-year follow-up. *Journal of Gambling Studies, 17*, 101-116.

Lally, J. R., Mangione, P. L., Honig, A. S., & Wittner, D. S. (1988). More pride, less delinquency: Findings from the ten-year follow-up study of the Syracuse University Family Development Research Program. *Zero to Three, 8*(4), 13-18.

Lalonde Commission of Canada. (1974). *A new perspective of the health of Canadians.* Ottawa, Ontario: Ministry of National Health and Welfare.

Lamborn, S. D., Mounts, N. S., Steinberg, L., & Dornbusch, S. M. (1991). Patterns of competence and adjustment among adolescents from authoritative, authoritarian, indulgent and neglectful families. *Child Development, 62*, 1049-1065.

Langer, L., Zimmerman, R., Warheit, G. J., & Duncan, R. C. (1993). An examination of the relationship between adolescent decision-making orientation and AIDS-related knowledge, attitudes, beliefs, behaviors, and skills. *Health Psychology, 12*, 227-234.

Langewisch, M. W. J., & Frisch, G. R. (1998). Gambling behavior and pathology in relation to impulsivity, sensation seeking, and risky behavior in male college students. *Journal of Gambling Studies, 14*, 245-262.

Lapsley, D. (1985). Elkind on egocentrism. *Developmental Review, 5*, 227-236.

Lapsley, D. K. (1993). Toward an integrated theory of adolescent ego development: The "new look" at the imaginary audience and personal fable. *American Journal of Orthopsychiatry, 63*, 562-571.

Lapsley, D. K. (2000, April). Adolescent narcissism: An empirical typology and a new assessment strategy. In D. Lapsley (Chair), *Adolescent narcissism: Interdisciplinary perspectives.* Symposium conducted at the eight biennial meeting of the Society for Research on Adolescence, Chicago.

Lapsley, D. K., FitzGerald, D. P., Rice, K. G., & Jackson, S. (1989). Separation-individuation and the "new look" at the imaginary audience and personal fable: A test of an integrative model. *Journal of Adolescent Research, 4*, 483-505.

Lapsley, D. K., & Flannery, D. (2002). *Personal fables, risk behaviors and adjustment in early and middle adolescence.* Manuscript under review.

Lapsley, D. K., Milstead, M., Quintana, S., Flannery, D., & Buss, R. (1986). Adolescent egocentrism and formal operations: Tests of a theoretical assumption. *Developmental Psychology, 22*, 800-807.

Lapsley, D. K., & Murphy, M. (1985). Another look at the theoretical assumptions of adolescent egocentrism. *Developmental Review, 5*, 201-217.

Lapsley, D. K., & Rice, K. G. (1988). The "new look" at the imaginary audience and personal fable: Towards a general model of adolescent ego development. In D. K. Lapsley & F. C. Power (Eds.), *Self, ego, and identity: Integrative approaches* (pp. 109-129). New York: Springer.

Laumann, E. O., & Youm, Y. (1999). Racial/ethnic group differences in the prevalence of sexually transmitted diseases in the United States: A network explanation. *Sexually Transmitted Diseases, 26*, 250-261.

LaVeist, T. A., Sellers, R., & Neighbors, H. W. (2001). Perceived racism and self and system blame attribution: Consequences for longevity. *Ethnicity and Disease, 11*, 711-721.

Laviola, G., Adriani, W., Terranova, M. L., & Gerra, G. (1999). Psychobiological risk factors for vulnerability to psychostimulants in human adolescents and animal models. *Neuroscience and Biobehavior Reviews, 23*(7), 993-1010.

Leff, S. S., Power, T. J., Manz, P. H., Costigan, T. E., & Nabors, L. A. (2001). School-based aggression prevention programs for young children: Current status and implications for violence prevention. *School Psychology Review, 30*(3), 344-362.

Lerman, C., Audrain, J., Main, D., Boyd, N., Caporaso, N., Bowman, E., et al. (1999). Evidence suggesting the role of specific genetic factors in cigarette smoking. *Health Psychology, 18*(1), 14-20.

Lerman, C., & Berrettini, W. (in press). Elucidating the role of genetic factors in smoking behavior and nicotine dependence. *American Journal of Medical Genetics.*

Lerman, C., Caporaso, N., Audrain, J., Main, D., Boyd, N., & Shields, P. (2000). Interacting effects of the serotonin transporter gene and neuroticism in smoking practices and nicotine dependence. *Molecular Psychiatry, 5,* 189-192.

Lerman, C., Caporaso, N., Bush, A., Zheng, Y., Audrain, J., & Main, D., et al. (2001). Tryptophan hydroxylase gene variant and smoking behavior. *American Journal of Medical Genetics, 105*(6), 518-520.

Lerman, C., & Croyle, R. (1994). Psychological issues in genetic testing for breast cancer susceptibility. *Archives of Internal Medicine, 154*(6), 609-616.

Lerman, C., Gold, K., Audrain, J., Lin, T. H., Boyd, N. R., Orleans, C. T., et al. (1997). Incorporating biomarkers of exposure and genetic susceptibility into smoking cessation treatment: Effects on smoking-related cognitions, emotions, and behavior change. *Health Psychology, 16*(1), 87-99.

Lerman, C., & Niaura, R. (in press). Applying genetic approaches to the treatment of nicotine dependence. *Oncogene.*

Lerman, C., Shields, P., Audrain, J., Main, D., Cobb, B., Boyd, N., et al. (1998). The role of the serotonin transporter gene in cigarette smoking. *Cancer Epidemiology, Biomarkers & Prevention, 7,* 253-255.

Lerner, J. S., & Keltner, D. (2000). Beyond balance: Toward a model of emotion-specific influences on judgment and choice. *Cognition and Emotion, 14*(4), 473-493.

Lerner, R. M., Fisher, C. B., & Weinberg, R. A. (2000). Toward a science for and of the people: Promoting civil society through the application of developmental science. *Child Development, 71,* 11-20.

Lesage, A. D., Boyer, R., Grunberg, F., Vanier, C., Morissette, R., Menard-Buteau, C., & Loyer, M. (1994). Suicide and mental disorders: A case-control study of youth men. *American Journal of Psychiatry, 151*(7), 1063-1068.

Lesch, K. P., & Merschdorf, U. (2000). Impulsivity, aggression, and serotonin: A molecular psychobiological perspective. *Behavioral Sciences & the Law, 18*(5), 581-604.

Lesieur, H. R., Cross, J., Frank, M., Welch, M., White, C. M., Rubenstein, G., et al. (1991). Gambling and pathological gambling among university students. *Addictive Behaviors: An International Journal, 16,* 517-527.

Lesieur, H. R., & Klein, R. (1987). Pathological gambling among high school students. *Addictive Behaviors, 12*(2), 129-135.

Lester, D. (1992). Religiosity, suicide and homicide: A cross-national examination. *Psychological Reports, 71,* 1282.

Lester, D., & Leenars, A. (1993). Suicide rates in Canada before and after tightening firearm control laws. *Psychological Reports, 72,* 787-790.

Lester, D., & Murrell, M. (1986). The influence of gun control laws on personal violence. *Journal of Community Psychology, 14,* 315-318.

Levin, M. (1972). *The costs to the nation of inadequate education* (Report to the Select Committee on Equal Education Opportunity of the U.S. Senate). Washington, DC: Government Printing Office.

Levy, S. R., Perhats, C., Weeks, K., Handler, A., Zhu, C., & Flay, B. R. (1995). Impact of a school-based AIDS prevention program on risk and protective behavior for newly sexually active students. *Journal of School Health, 65*(4), 145-151.

Lewinsohn, P. M., Rohde, P., & Brown, R. A. (1999). Level of current and past adolescent cigarette smoking as predictors of future substance use disorders in young adulthood. *Addiction, 94,* 913-921.

Lewinsohn, P. M., Rohde, P., & Seeley, J. R. (1993). Psychosocial characteristics of adolescents with a history of suicide attempt. *Journal of the American Academy of Child and Adolescent Psychiatry, 32,* 60-68.

Lewinsohn, P. M., Rohde, P., & Seeley, J. R. (1994). Psychosocial risk factors for future adolescent suicide attempts. *Journal of Consulting and Clinical Psychology, 62,* 297-305.

Lewinsohn, P. M., Rohde, P., & Seeley, J. R. (1996). Adolescent psychopathology: III. The clinical consequences of comorbidity. *Journal of the American Academy of Child and Adolescent Psychiatry, 34,* 510-519.

Lewinsohn, P. M., Rohde, P., Seeley, J. R., & Baldwin, C. L. (2001). Gender differences in suicide attempts from adolescence to young adulthood. *Journal of the American Academy of Child and Adolescent Psychiatry, 40*(4), 427- 434.

Lewinsohn, P. M., Steinmetz, J., Larson, D., & Franklin, J. (1981). Depression related cognitions: Antecedents or consequences? *Journal of Abnormal Psychology, 90,* 213-219.

Lewis, S. A., Johnson, J., Cohen, P., Garcia, M., & Velez, C. N. (1988). Attempted suicide in youth: Its relationship to school achievement, educational goals and socioeconomic status. *Journal of Abnormal Child Psychology, 16(4),* 459-471.

Li, T., Zhu, Z. H., Liu, X., Hu, X., Zhao, J., Sham, P. C., et al. (2000). Association analysis of polymorphisms in the DRD4 gene and heroin abuse in Chinese subjects. *American Journal of Medical Genetics, 96*(5), 616-621.

Li, X., Feigelman, S., & Stanton, B. (2000). Perceived parental monitoring and health risk behaviors among urban low-income African-American children and adolescents. *Journal of Adolescent Health, 27,* 43-48.

Li, X., Stanton, B., & Feigelman, S. (2002). Impact of perceived parental monitoring on adolescent risk behavior over 4 years. *Journal of Adolescent Health, 27,* 49-56.

Lichtenstein, S., & Fischhoff, B. (1980). Training for calibration. *Organizational Behavior and Human Performance, 26,* 149-171.

Lichtermann, D., Hranilovic, D., Trixler, M., Franke, P., Jernej, B., Delmo, C. D., et al. (2000). Support for allelic association of a polymorphic site in the promoter region of the serotonin transporter gene with risk for alcohol dependence. *American Journal of Psychiatry, 157*(12), 2045-2047.

Licona, T., Schaps, E., & Lewis, C. (n.d.). *Eleven principles of effective character education.* Washington, DC: Character Education Partnership. Retrieved June 25, 2002, from www.character.org/principles

Lieberman, L. D., Gray, H., Wier, M., Fiorentino, R., & Maloney, P. (2000). Long-term outcomes of an abstinence-based, small-group pregnancy prevention program in New York City schools. *Family Planning Perspectives, 32*(5), 237-245.

Lightfoot, C. (1997). *The culture of adolescent risk-taking.* New York: Guilford Press.

Lindberg, L. D., Ku, L., & Sonenstein, F. L. (1998). Adolescent males' combined use of condoms with partners' use of female contraceptive methods. *Maternal and Child Health Journal, 2*(4), 201-209.

Lipsey, M. W. (1998). Juvenile delinquency treatment: A meta-analytic inquiry into the variability of effects. In T. D. Cook (Ed.), *Meta-analyses for explanation: A casebook* (pp. 83-127). New York: Russell Sage.

Little, C. B., & Rankin, A. (2001). Why do they start it? Explaining reported early-teen sexual activity. *Sociological Forum, 16(4),* 703-729.

Lochman, J. E., & Dodge, K. A. (1994). Social-cognitive processes of severely violent, moderately aggressive and nonaggressive boys. *Journal of Consulting and Clinical Psychology, 62,* 366-374.

Loeber, R. (1991). Antisocial behavior: More enduring than changeable? *Journal of the American Academy of Child and Adolescent Psychiatry, 30,* 393-397.

Loeber, R., & Farrington, D. P. (Eds.). (1998). *Serious and violent juvenile offenders: Risk factors and successful interventions.* Thousand Oaks, CA: Sage.

Loeber, R., Farrington, D., Stouthamer-Loeber, M., & Van Kammen, W. (1998). Multiple risk factors for multiproblem boys: Co-occurrence of delinquency, substance use, attention deficit, conduct problems, physical aggression, covert behavior, depressed mood, and shy/withdrawn behavior. In R. Jessor (Ed.), *New perspectives on adolescent risk behavior.* Cambridge, UK: Cambridge University Press.

Loeber, R., Green, S. M., Lahey, B. B., Frick, P. J., & McBurnett, K. (2000). Findings on disruptive behavior disorders from the first decade of the developmental trends study. *Clinical Child and Family Psychology Review, 3,* 37-59.

Loewenstein, G. (1996). Out of control: Visceral influences on behavior. *Organizational Behavior and Human Decision Processes, 65,* 272-292.

Loewenstein, G. (2001). A visceral account of addiction. In P. Slovic (Ed.), *Smoking: Risk, perception, & policy* (pp. 188-215). Thousand Oaks, CA: Sage.

Loewenstein, G. F., & Elster, J. (Eds.). (1992). *Choice over time.* New York: Russell Sage.

Loewenstein, G. F., Weber, E. U., Hsee, C. K., & Welch, E. S. (2001). Risk as feelings. *Psychological Bulletin, 127,* 267-286.

Loftin, C., McDowall, D., Wiersema, B., & Cottey, T. J. (1991). Effects of restrictive licensing of handguns on homicide and suicide in the District of Columbia. *New England Journal of Medicine, 325,* 1615-1620.

Lonczak, H. S., Abbott, R. D., Hawkins, J. D., Kosterman, R., & Catalano, R. F. (2002). Effects of the Seattle Social Development project on sexual behavior, pregnancy, birth, and sexually transmitted disease outcomes by age 21 years. *Archives of Pediatric and Adolescent Medicine, 156*(5), 438-447.

London, S., Idle, J., Daly, A., & Coetzee, G. (1999). Genetic variation of CYP2A6, smoking, and risk of cancer. *Lancet, 353,* 898-899.

Long M. (1882). *The life of Mason Long, converted gambler* (5th ed.). Fort Wayne, IN: Mason Long.

Lonnqvist, J. (2000). Suicide mortality in Finland declined by 21% from 1990 to 1998. *Psychiatria Fennica, 31,* 5.

Lopes, L. L. (1987). Between hope and fear: The psychology of risk. *Advances in Experimental Social Psychology, 20,* 255-295.

Lorch, E. P., Palmgreen, P., Donohew, L., Helm, D., Baer, S. A., & Dsilva, M. U. (1994). Program context, sensation seeking, and attention to televised anti-drug public service announcements. *Human Communication Research, 20*(3), 390-412.

Lorenz, V. C., & Yaffee, R. A. (1986). Pathological gambling: Psychosomatic, emotional and marital difficulties as reported by the gambler. *Journal of Gambling Behavior, 2,* 40-45.

Lorenz, V. C., & Yaffee, R. A. (1988). Pathological gambling: Psychosomatic, emotional and marital difficulties as reported by the spouse. *Journal of Gambling Behavior, 4,* 13-26.

Lown, E. A., Winkler, K., Fullilove, R. E., & Fullilove, M. T. (1995). Tossin' and tweakin': Women's consciousness in the crack culture. In A. Aauire (Ed.), *Women and AIDS: Psychological perspectives* (pp. 90-106). Thousand Oaks, CA: Sage.

Ludwig, J., & Cook, P. J. (2000). Homicide and suicide rates associated with implementation of the Brady Handgun Violence Prevention Act. *JAMA, 284,* 585-591.

Lueders, K. K., Hu, S., McHugh, L., Myakishev, M. V., Sirota, L. A., & Hamer, D. H. (2002). Genetic and functional analysis of single nucleotide polymorphisms in the beta2-neuronal nicotinic acetylcholine receptor gene. *Nicotine and Tobacco Research, 4*(1), 115-125.

Lundberg, S., & Plotnick, R. D. (1990). Effects of state welfare, abortion, and family planning policies on premarital childbearing among adolescents. *Family Planning Perspectives, 22,* 246-251.

Lynam, D. R. (1996). Early identification of chronic offenders: Who is the fledgling psychopath? *Psychological Bulletin, 120,* 209-234.

Lynch, A. (1996). *Thought contagion: How belief spreads through society.* New York: Basic Books.

Mackesy-Amiti, M. E., Fendrich, M., & Goldstein, P. J. (1997). Sequence of drug use among serious drug users: Typical vs. atypical progression. *Drug and Alcohol Dependence 45,* 185-196.

Macoby, E., & Martin, J. (1983). Socialization in the context of the family: Parent-child interaction. In E. M. Hetberington (Ed.), *Handbook of child psychology: Vol 4. Socialization, personality and social development* (pp. 1-101). New York: John Wiley.

MacPhail, C., & Campbell, C. (2001). "I think condoms are good but, aai, I hate those things." *Social Science & Medicine, 52*(11), 1613-1627.

Madden, P., Heath, A., Pedersen, N., Kaprio, J., Koskenvuo, M., & Martin, N. (1999). The genetics of smoking persistence in men and women: A multicultural study. *Behavior Genetics, 29,* 423-431.

Maddux, J. E., & Rogers, R. W. (1983). Protection motivation and self-efficacy: A revised theory of fear appeals and attitude change. *Journal of Experimental Social Psychology, 19,* 469-479.

Maden, T., Swinton, M., & Gunn, J. (1992). Gambling in young offenders. *Criminal Behavioral and Mental Health, 2,* 300-308.

Magura, S., Kang, S., & Shapiro, J.L. (1994). Outcomes of intensive AIDS education for male adolescent drug users in jail. *Journal of Adolescent Health, 15*(6), 457-463.

Mahajan, V., & Peterson, R. A. (1985). *Models for innovation diffusion.* Beverly Hills, CA: Sage.

Main, D. S., Iverson, D. C., McGloin, J., Banspach, S. W., Collins, K., Rugg, D., et al. (1994). Preventing HIV infection among adolescents: Evaluation of a school-based education program. *Preventive Medicine, 23*(4), 409-417.

Manlove, J., Terry, E., Gitelson, L., Romano, A., Papillo, A., & Russell, S. (2000). Explaining demographic trends in teenage fertility: 1980-1995. *Family Planning Perspectives, 32*(4), 166-175.

Mann, J. J., & Stoff, D. M. (1997). A synthesis of current findings regarding neurobiological correlates and treatment of suicidal behavior. *Annals of the New York Academy of Sciences, 836,* 352-363.

Manning, V., Best, D., Rawaf, S., Rowley, J., Floyd, K., & Strang, J. (2001). Drug use in adolescence: the relationship between opportunity, initial use and continuation of use of four illicit drugs in a cohort of 14-16-year-olds in South London. *Drugs-Education, Prevention and Policy, 8,* 397-405.

Manuck, S., Flory, J., Ferrell, R., Dent, K., Mann, J., & Muldoon, M. (1999). Aggression and anger-related traits associated with a polymorphism of the tryptophan hydroxylase gene. *Biological Psychiatry, 45*(5), 603-614.

Marcenko, M. O., Fishman, G., & Friedman, J. (1999). Reexamining adolescent suicidal ideation: A developmental perspective applied to a diverse population. *Journal of Youth and Adolescence, 28,* 121-138.

Maris, R. W. (1969). *Social forces in urban suicide.* Homewood, IL: Dorsey.

Marteau, T., & Lerman, C. (2001). Genetic risk and behavioural change. *British Medical Journal, 322,* 1056-1059.

Marttunen, M. J., Aro, H. M., Henriksson, M. M., & Lonnqvist, J. K. (1991). Mental disorders in adolescent suicide. *Archives of General Psychiatry, 48,* 834-839.

Marttunen, M. J., Aro, H. M., Henrikksson, M. M., & Lonnqvist, J. K. (1994). Psychosocial stressors more common in adolescent suicides with alcohol abuse compared with depressive adolescent suicides. *Journal of the American Academy of Child and Adolescent Psychiatry, 33*(4), 490-497.

Marttunen, M. J., Aro, H. M., & Lonnqvist, J. K. (1993). Precipitant stressors in adolescent suicide. *Journal of the American Academy of Child and Adolescent Psychiatry, 32*(6), 1178-1183.

Matsushita, S., Yoshino, A., Murayama, M., Kimura, M., Muramatsu, T., & Higuchi, S. (2001). Association study of serotonin transporter gene regulatory region polymorphism and alcoholism. *American Journal of Medical Genetics, 105*(5), 446-450.

Maynard, R. A., & Johnson, A. (2001, November 15). Testimony before the House Ways and Means Subcommittee on Human Resources Hearing on Teen Pregnancy Prevention.

Mazza, J. J. (2000). The relationship between posttraumatic stress symptomatology and suicidal behavior in school-based adolescents. *Suicide and Life-Threatening Behavior, 30*(2), 91-103.

McBride, D., & Gienapp, A. (2000). Using randomized designs to evaluate a client-centered program to prevent adolescent pregnancy. *Family Planning Perspectives, 32*(5), 227-235.

McConaughy, S. H. (1993). Responses to commentaries on advances in empirically-based assessment. *School Psychology Review, 22,* 334-342.

McConaughy, S. H., & Achenbach, T. (1994). Comorbidity of empirically based syndromes in matched general populations and clinical samples. *Journal of Child Psychology and Psychiatry, 35,* 834-839.

McGue, M., Pickens, R. W., & Svikis, D. S. (1992). Sex and age effects on the inheritance of alcohol problems: A twin study. *Journal of Abnormal Psychology, 101*(1), 3-17.

McIntyre, D. (2002). *A picture of misery: The truth about smoking, in smokers' own words: No Smoking Day 2002.* Retrieved January 3, 2003, from http://www.ash.org.uk/html/cessation/nsd2002.html

McKeown, R. E., Garrison, C. Z., Cuffe, S. P., Waller, J. L., Jackson, K. L., & Addy, C. L. (1998). Incidence and predictors of suicidal behaviors in a longitudinal sample of young adolescents. *Journal of the American Academy of Child and Adolescent Psychiatry, 37*(6), 612-619.

McMahon, R. C., Malow, R. M., Jennings, T. E., & Gomez, C. J. (2001). Effects of a cognitive-behavioral HIV prevention intervention: HIV negative male substance abusers in a VA residential treatment. *AIDS Education and Prevention, 12*(1), 91-107.

McNeil, T., Sveger, T., & Thelin, T. (1988). Psychosocial effects of screening for somatic risk: The Swedish alpha 1 antitrypsin experience. *Thorax, 43*(7), 505-507.

Meekers, D., & Klein, M. (2002). Understanding gender differences in condom use self-efficacy: Youth in urban Cameroon. *AIDS Education and Prevention, 13*(1), 62-72.

Meier, D. (2002). *In schools we trust.* Boston: Beacon Press.

Melchior, A. (1998). *National evaluation of Learn and Serve America school and community-based programs.* Waltham, MA: Center for Human Resources, Brandeis University.

Melville, J., Sniffen, S., Crosby, R. A., Salazar, L., DiClemente, R. J., Whittington, W., Dithmer-Schreck, D., & Wald, A. (in press). Psychosocial impact of serologic diagnosis of herpes simplex virus type 2: A qualitative assessment. *Sexually Transmitted Infections.*

Merrill, J. C., Kleber, H. D., Shwartz, M., Liu, H., & Lewis, S. R. (1999). Cigarettes, alcohol, marijuana, other risk behaviors, and American youth. *Drug and Alcohol Dependence, 56,* 205-212.

Miller, J. M., & Krosnick, J. A. (1996). News media impact on the ingredients of presidential evaluations: A program of research on the priming hypothesis. In D. C. Mutz, P. M. Sniderman, & R. A. Brody (Eds.), *Political persuasion and attitude change* (pp. 79-99). Ann Arbor: University of Michigan Press.

Miller, K. S., Clark, L. F., & Moore, J. S. (1997). Sexual initiation with older male partners and subsequent HIV risk behavior among female adolescents. *Family Planning Perspectives, 29,* 212-214.

Miller, K. S., Levin, M. L., Whitaker, D. J., & Xiaohe, X. (1998). Patterns of condom use among adolescents: The impact of mother-adolescent communication. *American Journal of Public Health, 88,* 1542-1544.

Miller, L., Warner, V., Wickramaratne, P., & Weissman, M. (1997). Religiosity and depression: Ten-year follow-up of depressed mothers and offspring. *Journal of the American Academy of Child and Adolescent Psychiatry, 36,* 1416-1425.

Miller, M., & Hemenway, D. (1999). The relationship between firearms and suicide: A review of the literature. *Aggression and Violent Behavior, 4,* 59-75.

Miller, P., Plant, M., Plant, M., & Duffy, J. (1995). Alcohol, tobacco, illicit drugs, and sex: An analysis of risky behaviors among young adults. *International Journal of the Addictions, 30,* 239-258.

Miller, W. B., Pasta, D. J., MacMurray, J., Chiu, C., Wu, H., Comings, D. E. (1999). Dopamine receptor genes are associated with age at first sexual intercourse. *Journal of Biological Science, 31*(part 1), 43-54.

Millstein, S. G. (1993). Perceptual, attributional and affective processes in the perceptions of vulnerability through the life span. In N. J. Bell & R. W. Bell (Eds.), *Adolescent risk taking* (pp. 55-65). Newbury Park, CA: Sage.

Millstein, S. G., & Halpern-Felsher, B. L. (2002a). Age differences in risk judgment among adolescents and adults. *Journal of Research on Adolescence, 12,* 399-422.

Millstein, S. G., & Halpern-Felsher, B. L. (2002b). Perceptions of risk and vulnerability. *Journal of Adolescent Health, 31*, 10-27.

Miniño, A. M., Arias, E., Kochanek, K. D., Murphy, S. L., & Smith, B. L. (2002). Deaths: Final Data for 2000. *National vital statistics reports* (Vol. 50, No. 15). Hyattsville, MD: National Center for Health Statistics.

Mischel, W. (1984). Convergences and challenges in the search for consistency. *American Psychologist, 39*, 351-364.

Mitchell, S. H. (1999). Measures of impulsivity in cigarette smokers and non-smokers. *Psychopharmacology (Berl), 146*(4), 455-464.

Mitka, M. (2001). Win or lose, Internet gambling stakes are high. *JAMA, 285*, 1005.

Moberg, D. P., & Piper, D. L. (1990). An outcome evaluation of project model health: A middle school health promotion program. *Health Education Quarterly, 17*(1), 37-51.

Moberg, D. P., & Piper, D. L. (1998). The Healthy for Life Project: Sexual risk behavior outcomes. *AIDS Education and Prevention, 10*(2), 128-148.

Moffitt, T. E. (1993). Adolescent-limited and life-course persistent antisocial behavior: A developmental taxonomy. *Psychological Review, 100*, 674-701.

Moore, K. A., & Burt, M. R. (1982). *Private crisis, public cost: Policy perspective on teenage childbearing.* Washington, DC: Urban Institute.

Moore, K. A., Driscoll, A. K., & Lindberg, L. D. (1998). *A statistical portrait of adolescent sex, contraception, and childbearing.* Washington, DC: National Campaign to Prevent Teen Pregnancy.

Moore, K. A., Evans, V. J., Brooks-Gunn, J., & Roth, J. (2001). What are good child outcomes? In A. Thornton (Ed.), *The well-being of children and families: Research and data needs* (pp. 59-84). Ann Arbor: University of Michigan Press.

Moore, K. A., Sugland, B., & Blumenthal, C. (1995). *Adolescent pregnancy prevention programs: Interventions and evaluations.* Washington, DC: Child Trends.

Moore, K. A., Sugland, B., Blumenthal, C., Glei, D., & Snyder, N. (1995). *Adolescent pregnancy prevention programs: Interventions and evaluations.* Washington, DC: Child Trends.

Moore, M. R., & Brooks-Gunn, J. (2002). "Adolescent parenthood." In M. Bornstein (Ed.), *Handbook of parenting: Vol. 3. Being and becoming a parent* (pp. 173-215). Mahwah, NJ: Lawrence Erlbaum.

Moore, S. M., & Otshuka, K. (1997). Gambling activities of young Australians: Developing a model of behavior. *Journal of Gambling Studies, 13*, 207-236.

Moran, E. (1995). Majority of secondary school children buy tickets. *British Medical Journal, 311*, 1225-1226.

Morano, C. D., Cisler, R. A., & Lemerond, J. (1993). Risk factors for adolescent suicidal behavior: Loss, insufficient familial support, and hopelessness. *Adolescence, 28*, 851-865.

Morley, D. D., & Walker, K. B. (1987). The role of importance, novelty, and plausibility in producing belief change. *Communication Monographs, 54*(4), 436-442.

Morrison-Beedy, D., Carey, M. P., & Lewis, B. P. (2002). Modeling condom-use stage of change in low-income, single, urban women. *Research in Nursing & Health, 25*(2), 122-134.

Moscicki, E. K. (1995). Epidemiology of suicidal behavior. *Suicide and Life-Threatening Behavior, 25*(1), 22-35.

Motto, J. A. (1970). Newspaper influence on suicide. *Archives of General Psychiatry, 23*, 143-148.

Motto, J. A., & Bostrom, A. G. (2001). A randomized controlled trial of postcrisis suicide prevention. *Psychiatric Services, 52*, 828-833.

Mrazek, P. J., & Biglan, A. (2002). *Creating communities that monitor the well-being of America's youth.* Manuscript in preparation.

Mrazek, P. J., & Haggerty, R. J. (Eds.). (1994). *Reducing risks for mental disorders: Frontiers for preventive intervention research.* Washington, DC: National Academy Press.

Mullen, P. E., Martin, J. L., Anderson, J. C., Romans, S. E., & Herbison, G. P. (1996). The long-term impact of the physical, emotional, and sexual abuse of children: A community study. *Child Abuse and Neglect, 20*, 7-21.

Mulrine, A. (2002, May 27). Risky business. *U.S. News & World Report,* pp. 42-49.

Murray, S. L., Holmes, J. G., & Griffin, D. W. (1996). The benefits of positive illusions: Idealization and the construction of satisfaction in close relationships. *Journal of Personality and Social Psychology, 70,* 79-98.

Nabi, R. (2002). Discrete emotions and persuasion. In J. P. Dillard & M. Pfau (Eds.), *The persuasion handbook: Developments in theory and practice* (pp. 289-308). Thousand Oaks, CA: Sage.

National Academy of Sciences. (1986). *Confronting AIDS.* Washington, DC: National Academy Press.

National Campaign to Prevent Teen Pregnancy. (1997). *Whatever happened to childhood? The problem of teen pregnancy in the United States.* Washington, DC: Author.

National Center for Health Statistics. (1998).*Vital statistics of the United States: Vol. 2. Mortality.* Hyattsville, MD: Author.

National Center for Health Statistics. (1999). *Death rates for 358 selected causes, by 5-year age groups, race, and sex: United States* (Worktable 292a, Worktable GM292A_1,2001). Retrieved January 3, 2003, from www.cdc.gov/nchs/data/statab/VS00199.TABLE292A.pl1.pdf

National Center for Health Statistics. (2000). *Injury mortality reports.* Retrieved January 3, 2003, from webapp.cdc.gov/sasweb/ncipc/nfirates2000.html

National Commission on Acquired Immune Deficiency Syndrome. (1993). *Behavioral and social sciences and the HIV/AIDS epidemic.* Washington, DC: Government Printing Office.

National Health Survey. (2000). *Summary of findings from the 2000 National Household Survey on Drug Abuse.* Rockville, MD: Office of Applied Studies, NHSDA.

National Highway Traffic Safety Administration. (2001). *Traffic safety facts 2000 — Children.* Washington, DC: U.S. Department of Transportation.

National Human Genome Research Institute. (2001, September). *Issue update: Employment discrimination.* Retrieved October, 2000, from www.nhgri.nih.gov/policy_and_public_affairs/legislation/workplace.htm

National Institute on Alcohol Abuse & Alcoholism. (1996). *State trends in alcohol mortality, 1979-1992.* Rockville, MD: Author.

National Institutes of Health. (1997). *Intervention to prevent HIV risk behaviors* (Consensus development panel statement). Bethesda, MD: Author.

National Opinion Research Center. (1999). *Gambling impact and behavior study: Report to the National Gambling Impact Study Commission.* Chicago, IL: National Opinion Research Center at the University of Chicago.

National Research Council. (1990). *AIDS: The second decade.* Washington, DC: National Academy Press.

National Research Council. (1999). *Pathological gambling: A critical review.* Washington, DC: National Academy Press.

National Research Council. (2002). *Community programs to promote youth development.* Washington, DC: National Academy Press.

National Telecommunication and Information Administration and Economics and Statistics Administration. (2002). Falling through the Net: Toward digital inclusion. Retrieved July 31, 2002, from www.ntia.doc.gov/ntiahome/?digitaldivide/?execsumfttn00.htm

Nattiv, A., & Puffer, J. C. (1991). Lifestyles and health risks of collegiate athletes. *Journal of Family Practice, 33*(6), 585-590.

Neeleman, J. (1998). Regional suicide rates in the Netherlands: Does religion still play a role? *International Journal of Epidemiology, 27,* 466-472.

Neeleman, J., & Lewis, J. (1999). Suicide, religion, and socioeconomic conditions. An ecological study in 26 countries, 1990. *Journal of Epidemiological Community Health, 53,* 204-210.

Neeleman, J., Wessely, S., & Lewis, G. (1998). Suicide acceptability in African- and white Americans: The role of religion. *Journal of Nervous & Mental Disease, 186*(1), 12-16.

Negron, R., Piacentini, J., Graae, F., Davies, M., & Shaffer, D. (1997). Microanalysis of adolescent suicide attempters and ideators during the acute suicide episode. *Journal of the American Academy of Child and Adolescent Psychiatry, 36*(11), 1512-1519.

Nelson, E. C., Heath, A. C., Madden, P. A., Cooper, M. L., Dinwiddie, S. H., Bucholz, K. K., et al. (2002). Association between self-reported childhood sexual abuse and adverse psychosocial outcomes: Results from a twin study. *Archives of General Psychiatry, 59,* 139-145.

Networks for Youth Development. (1998). *The handbook of positive youth outcomes.* New York: Fund for the City of New York.

Newcomb, M. D., & Bentler, P. M. (1988). *Consequences of adolescent drug use: Impact on the lives of young adults.* Newbury Park, CA: Sage.

Newcomb, M. D., Maddahian, E., & Bentler, P. M. (1986). Risk factors for drug use among adolescents: Concurrent and longitudinal analyses. *American Journal of Public Health, 76,* 525-531.

Newcomer, S. F., & Udry, J. R. (1984). Mothers' influence on the sexual behavior of their teenage children. *Journal of Marriage and the Family, 49,* 235-240.

Newman, D., Moffitt, T. E., Caspi, A., Magdol, L., Silva, P. A., & Stanton, W. (1996). Psychiatric disorders in a birth cohort of young adults: Prevalence, comorbidity, clinical significance, and new case incidence from ages 11 to 21. *Journal of Consulting and Clinical Psychology, 64,* 552-562.

Nicholson, H. J., & Postrado, L. T. (1991). *Girls Incorporated preventing adolescent pregnancy: A program development and research project.* New York: Girls Incorporated.

Nielsen, D., Virkkunen, M., Lappalainen, J., Eggert, M., Brown, G., Long, J., et al. (1998). A tryptophan hydroxylase gene marker for suicidality and alcoholism. *Archives of General Psychiatry, 55*(7), 593-602.

Noble, E. P. (1993). The D2 dopamine receptor gene: A review of association studies in alcoholism. *Behavior Genetics, 23*(2), 119-129.

Noble, E. P. (2000). The DRD2 gene in psychiatric and neurological disorders and its phenotypes. *Pharmacogenomics, 1*(3), 309-333.

Noble, E. P., Ozkaragoz, T., Ritchie, T., Zhang, X., Belin, T., & Sparkes, R. (1998). D2 and D4 dopamine receptor poplymorphisms and personality. *American Journal of Medical Genetics, 81,* 257-267.

Noble, E. P., St. Jeor, S. T., Ritchie, T., Syndulko, K., St. Jeor, S. C., & Fitch, R., et al. (1994). D2 dopamine receptor gene and cigarette smoking: A reward gene? *Medical Hypotheses, 42,* 257-260.

Noel, M. (1982). Public school programs for the emotionally disturbed: An overview. In M. Noel & N. Haring (Eds.), *Progress of change: Issues in educating the emotionally disturbed* (Vol. 2, pp. 11-28). Seattle: University of Washington Press.

Nolen-Hoeksema, S. (1991). Responses to depression and their effects on the duration of the depressive episode. *Journal of Abnormal Psychology, 100,* 569-582.

Nolen-Hoeksema, S. (2000). Ruminative responses predict depressive disorders. *Journal of Abnormal Psychology, 109,* 504-511.

North American Association of State and Provincial Lotteries. (2002a). *FY00 & FY01 sales and profits.* Retrieved July 31, 2002, from www.naspl.org/sales&profits.html

North American Association of State and Provincial Lotteries. (2002b). *Lottery history.* Retrieved July 26, 2002, from www.naspl.org/history.html

Nygren, T., Isen, A., Taylor, P., & Dulin, J. (1996). The influence of positive affect on the decision rule in risk situations: Focus on outcome (and especially avoidance of loss) rather than probability. *Organizational Behavior and Human Decision Processes, 66,* 59-72.

O'Donnell, L., O'Donnell, C., & Steve, A. (2001). Early sexual initiation and subsequent sex-related risks among urban minority youth: The reach for health study. *Family Planning Perspectives, 33,* 268-275.

O'Donnell, L., Stueve, A., Doval, A. S., Duran, R., Haber, D., Atnafou, R., et al. (1999). The effectiveness of the Reach for Health community youth service learning program in reducing early and unprotected sex among urban middle school students. *American Journal of Public Health, 89*(2), 176-181.

O'Donnell, L., Stueve, A., O'Donnell, C., Duran, R., Doval, A. S., Wilson, R. F., et al. (2002). Long-term reductions in sexual initiation and sexual activity among urban middle schoolers in the Reach for Health service learning program. *Journal of Adolescent Health, 31,* 93-100.

Oetting, E. R., & Beauvais, F. (1986). Peer cluster theory: Drugs and the adolescent. *Journal of Counseling and Development, 65,* 17-22.

Office of National AIDS Policy. (1996). *Youth and HIV/AIDS: An American agenda.* Washington, DC: Author.

Offord, D. R. (1987). Prevention of behavioral and emotional disorders in children. *Journal of Child Psychology and Psychiatry, 28,* 9-19.

Okuyama, Y., Ishiguro, H., Nankai, M., Shibuya, H., Watanabe, A., & Arinami, T. (2000). Identification of a polymorphism in the promoter region of DRD4 associated with the human novelty seeking personality trait. *Molecular Psychiatry, 5*(1), 64-69.

Oldenhinkel, A. J., Wittchen, H. -U., & Schuster, P. (1999). Prevalence, 20-month incidence and outcome of unipolar depressive disorders in a community sample of adolescents. *Psychological Medicine, 29,* 655-668.

Olds, D. L., Henderson, C. R., Jr., Kitzman, H. J., Eckenrode, J., Cole, R. E., & Tatelbaum, R. (1998). The promise of home visitation: Results of two randomized trials. *Journal of Community Psychology, 26*(1), 5-21.

Olsen, J. A., & Weed, S. E. (1986). Effects of family-planning programs for teenagers on adolescent birth and pregnancy rates. *Family Perspective, 20*(3), 153-170.

Olweus, D. (1993). *Bullying at school.* Malden, UK: Blackwell.

Orpinas, K., Basen-Engquist, K., Grunbaum, J., & Parcel, G. S. (1995). The co-morbidity of violence-related behaviors with health-risk behaviors in a population of high school students. *Journal of Adolescent Health, 16,* 216-225.

Orr, D. P., Langefeld, C. D., Katz, B. P., & Caine, V. A. (1996). Behavioral intervention to increase condom use among high-risk female adolescents. *Journal of Pediatrics, 128*(2), 288-295.

Osgood, D. W., Johnston, L. D., O'Malley, P. M., & Bachman, J. G. (1988). The generality of deviance in late adolescence and early adulthood. *American Sociological Review, 53,* 81-93.

Ouellette, J. A., Gerrard, M., Gibbons, F. X., & Reis-Bergan, M. (1999). Parents, peers, and prototypes: Antecedents of adolescent alcohol expectancies, alcohol consumption, and alcohol-related life problems in rural youth. *Psychology of Addictive Behaviors, 13,* 183-197.

Overholser, J. C., Adams, D. M., Lehnert, K. L., & Brinkman, D. C. (1995). Self-esteem deficits and suicidal tendencies among adolescents. *Journal of the American Academy of Child and Adolescent Psychiatry, 34,* 919-928.

Paine-Andrews, A., Harris, K. J., Fisher, J. L., Lewis, R., Williams, E. L., Fawcett, S. B., et al. (1999). Effects of a replication of a multi-component model for preventing adolescent pregnancy in three Kansas communities. *Family Planning Perspectives, 31*(4), 182-189.

Palmgreen, P., & Donohew, L. (in press). Effective mass media strategies for drug abuse prevention campaigns. In W. J. Bukoski & Z. Sloboda (Eds.), *Handbook of drug abuse theory, science and practice.* New York: Plenum.

Palmgreen, P., Donohew, L., Lorch, E. P., Hoyle, R., & Stephenson, M. (2001). Television campaigns and adolescent marijuana use: Tests on sensation-seeking targeting. *American Journal of Public Health, 91,* 291-296.

Palmgreen, P., Donohew, L., Lorch, E. P., Hoyle, R., & Stephenson, M. (2002). Television campaigns and sensation seeking targeting of adolescent marijuana use: A controlled time series approach. In R. C. Hornik (Ed.), *Public health communication: Evidence for behavior change.* Mahwah, NJ: Lawrence Erlbaum.

Palmgreen, P., Donohew, L., Lorch, E., Rogus, M., Helm, D., & Grant, N. (1991). Sensation seeking, message sensation value, and drug use as mediators of PSA effectiveness. *Health Communication, 3,* 217-234.

Palmgreen, P., Lorch, E. P., Donohew, L., Harrington, N. G., Dsilva, M., & Helm, D. (1995). Reaching at-risk populations in a mass media drug abuse prevention campaign: Sensation seeking as a targeting variable. *Drugs and Society, 8*(3/4), 29-45.

Paolucci, E. O., Genuis, M. L., & Violato, C. (2001). A meta-analysis of the published research on the effects of child sexual abuse. *Journal of Psychology, 135,* 17-36.

Parker, A. M., & Fischhoff, B. (2002). *Decision-making competence: An individual-differences approach.* Manuscript in preparation.

Parker, G. (1983). Parental "affectionless control" as an antecedent to adult depression. *Archives of General Psychiatry, 34,* 138-147.

Parker, J. G., & Asher, S. R. (1987). Peer relations and later personal adjustment: Are low-accepted children at risk? *Psychological Bulletin, 102,* 357-389.

Parsian, A., Chakraverty, S., Fisher, L., & Cloninger, C. R. (1997). No association between polymorphisms in the human dopamine D3 and D4 receptors genes and alcoholism. *American Journal of Medical Genetics, 74*(3), 281-285.

Parsons, J., Halkitis, P., Bimbi, D., & Borkowski, T. (2000). Perceptions of the benefits and costs associated with condom use and unprotected sex among late adolescent college students. *Journal of Adolescence, 23,* 377-391.

Pasick, R. J., Otero-Sabogal, R., & D'Onofrio, C. (1996). Similarities and differences across cultures: Questions to inform a third generation for health promotion research. *Health Education Quarterly, 23,* S142-S161.

Patkar, A., Berrettini, W., Hoehe, M., Hill, K., Sterling, R., Gottheil, E., et al. (2001). Serotonin transporter (5-HTT) gene polymorphisms and susceptibility to cocaine dependence among African-American individuals. *Addiction Biology, 6*(4), 337-345.

Patterson, G. R. (1982). *Coercive family process.* Eugene, OR: Castalia.

Patterson, G. R. (1986). Performance models for antisocial boys. *American Psychologist, 41,* 432-444.

Patterson, G. R. (1993). Orderly change in a stable world: The antisocial trait as a chimera. *Journal of Consulting and Clinical Psychology, 61,* 911-919.

Patterson, G. R., DeBaryshe, B. D., & Ramsey, E. (1989). A developmental perspective on antisocial behavior. *American Psychologist, 44*(2), 329-335.

Patterson, G. R., Reid, J. B., & Dishion, T. J. (1992). *Antisocial boys: A social interactional approach* (Vol. 4). Eugene, OR: Castalia.

Pelligrini, A. D. (2001). Sampling instances of victimization in middle school: A methodological comparison. In J. Juvonen & S. Graham (Eds.), *Peer harassment in school: The plight of the vulnerable and victimized* (pp. 125-144). New York: Guilford Press.

Pentz, M. A., Dwyer, J. H., MacKinnon, D. P., Flay, B. R., Hansen, W. B., Wang, E., et al (1989). A multi-community trial for primary prevention of adolescent drug abuse: Effects on drug use prevalence. *JAMA, 261,* 3259-3266.

Pentz, M. A., MacKinnon, D. P., Flay, B. R., Hansen, W. B., Johnson, C. A., & Dwyer, J. H. (1989). Primary prevention of chronic diseases in adolescence: Effects of the Midwestern Prevention Project (MPP) on tobacco use. *American Journal of Epidemiology, 130,* 713-724.

Pequegnat, W., & Szapocznik, J. (2000). *Working with families in the era of HIV/AIDS.* Thousand Oaks, CA: Sage.

Perkins, K., Gerlach, D., Broge, M., Grobe, J., & Wilson, A. (2000). Greater sensitivity to subjective effects of nicotine in nonsmokers high in sensation seeking. *Experimental and Clinical Psychopharmacology, 8*(4), 462-471.

Perloff, L., & Fetzer, B. (1986). Self-other judgments and perceived vulnerability to victimization. *Journal of Personality and Social Psychology, 50*(3), 502-510.

Perry, C. L., Williams, C. L., Forster, J. L., Wolfson, M., Wagenaar, A. C., Finnegan, J. R., et al. (1993). Background, conceptualization, and design of a community-wide research program on adolescent alcohol use: Project Northland. *Health Education Research, 8,* 125-136.

Peterson, L. (1996). Establishing the study of development as a dynamic force in health psychology. *Health Psychology, 15*, 155-157.

Petraitis, J., Flay, B. R., & Miller, T. Q. (1995). Reviewing theories of adolescent substance use: Organizing pieces in the puzzle. *Psychological Bulletin, 117*, 67-86.

Petraitis, J., Flay, B. R., Miller, T. Q., Torpy, E. J., & Greiner, B. (1998). Illicit substance use among adolescents: A matrix of prospective predictors. *Substance Use & Misuse, 33*(13), 2561-2604.

Petry, N. M., & Casarella, T. (1999). Excessive discounting of delayed rewards in substance abusers with gambling problems. *Drug and Alcohol Dependence, 56*(1), 25-32.

Petry, N. M., & Roll, J. M. (2001). A behavioral approach to understanding and treating pathological gambling. *Seminars in Clinical Neuropsychiatry, 6*, 177-183.

Petry, N. M., & Zeena, T. (2001). Comparison of problem-gambling and non-problem-gambling youths seeking treatment for marijuana abuse. *Journal of the American Academy of Child and Adolescent Psychiatry, 40*, 1324-1331.

Petty, R. E., & Cacioppo, J. T. (1986). The elaboration likelihood model of persuasion. In L. Berkowitz (Ed.), *Advances in experimental social psychology* (Vol. 19, pp. 123-205). Orlando, FL: Academic Press.

Pfeffer, C. R., McBride, A., Anderson, G. M., Kakuma, T., Fensterheim, L., & Khait, V. (1998). Peripheral serotonin measures in prepubertal psychiatric inpatients and normal children: Associations with suicidal behavior and its risk factors. *Biological Psychiatry, 44*, 568-577.

Philliber, S., & Allen, J. P. (1992). Life options and community service: Teen Outreach Program. In B. C. Miller, J. J. Card, R. L. Paikoff, & J. L. Peterson (Eds.), *Preventing adolescent pregnancy* (pp. 139-155). Newbury Park, CA: Sage.

Philliber, S., Kaye, J. W., Herring, S., & West, E. (2002). Preventing teen pregnancy: An evaluation of the Children's Aid Society Carrera program. *Perspectives on Sexual and Reproductive Health, 34*(5), 244-251.

Phillips, D. (1974). The influence of suggestions on suicide: Substantive and theoretical implications of the Werther effect. *American Sociological Review, 39*, 340-354.

Phillips, D. (1979). Suicide, motor vehicle fatalities, and the mass media: Evidence toward a theory of suggestion. *American Journal of Sociology, 84*, 1150-1174.

Phillips, D. (1980). Airplane accidents, murder, and the mass media: Towards a theory of imitation and suggestion. *Social Forces, 58*, 1001-1004.

Phillips, D., & Carstensen, L. L. (1986). Clustering of teenage suicides after television news stories about suicide. *New England Journal of Medicine, 315*, 685-689.

Phillips, D., & Paight, D. J. (1987). The impact of televised movies about suicide: A replicative study. *New England Journal of Medicine, 317*, 809-811.

Phillips, D., & Ruth, T. E. (1993). Adequacy of official suicide statistics for scientific research and public policy. *Suicide and Life-Threatening Behavior, 23*(4), 307-319.

Pianezza, M., Sellers, E., & Tyndale, R. (1998). Nicotine metabolism defect reduces smoking. *Nature, 393*, 750.

Pickens, R. W., & Svikis, D. S. (1991). Genetic influences in human substance abuse. *Journal of Addictive Diseases, 10*(1-2), 205-213.

Pickens, R. W., Svikis, D., McGue, M., & LaBuda, M. (1995). Common genetic mechanisms in alcohol, drug, and mental disorder comorbidity. *Drug and Alcohol Dependence, 39*(2), 129-138.

Pierce, J. P., Choi, W. S., Gilpin, E. A., Farkas, A. J., & Merritt, R K. (1996). Validation of susceptibility as a predictor of which adolescents take up smoking in the United States. *Health Psychology, 15*, 355-361.

Pittman, K. J., & Cahill, M. (1991). *A new vision: Promoting youth development.* Washington, DC: Academy for Educational Development.

Pittman, K., Irby, M., & Ferber, T. (2000). Unfinished business: Further reflections on a decade of promoting youth development. In Public/Private Ventures (Ed.), *Youth devel-*

opment: Issues, challenges, and directions (pp. 17-64). Philadelphia, PA: Public/Private Ventures.

Pittman, K. J., Irby, M., Tolman, J., Yohalem, N., & Ferber, T. (2001, September). *Preventing problems, promoting development, encouraging engagement: Competing priorities or inseparable goals?* (Working paper, the Forum for Youth Investment). Retrieved December 18, 2002, from www.forumforyouthinvestment.org/preventproblems.pdf

Plichta, S. B., Weisman, C. S., Nathanson, C. A., Ensminger, M. E., & Robinson, J. C. (1992). Partner-specific condom use among adolescent women clients of a family planning clinic. *Journal of Adolescent Health, 13*(6), 506-511.

Plomin, R. (1990). The role of inheritance in behavior. *Science, 248*(4952), 183-188.

Plomin, R., DeFries, J., & Loehlin, J. (1977). Genotype-environment interaction and correlation in the analysis of human behavior. *Psychological Bulletin, 84*(2), 309-322.

Polacsek, M., Clentano, D. D., O'Campo, P., & Santelli, J. (1999). Correlates of condom use state of change: Implications for intervention. *AIDS Education and Prevention, 11*(1), 38-52.

Polednak, A. P. (1997). *Segregation, poverty, and mortality in urban African Americans.* New York: Oxford University Press.

Polen, M. R., & Freeborn, D. K. (1995). *Outcome evaluation of Project ACTION.* Portland, OR: Kaiser Permanente Center for Health Research.

Ponton, L. E. (1997). *The romance of risk: Why teenagers do the things they do.* New York: Basic Books.

Poppen, P. J., & Reisen, C. A. (1997). Perception of risk and sexual self-protective behavior: A methodological critique. *AIDS Education and Prevention, 9*(4), 373-390.

Potenza, M. N. (2002). A perspective on future directions in the prevention, treatment and research of pathological gambling. *Psychiatric Annals, 32*(3), 203-207.

Potenza, M. N., Fiellin, D. A., Heninger, G. R., Rounsaville, B. J., & Mazure, C. M. (2002). Gambling: An addictive behavior with health and primary care implications. *Journal of General & Internal Medicine, 17*, 721-732.

Potenza, M. N., Kosten, T. R., & Rounsaville, B. J. (2001). Pathological gambling. *JAMA, 286*, 141-144.

Potenza, M. N., Steinberg, M. A., Wu, R., Rounsaville, B. J., & O'Malley, S. S. (2003). *Characteristics of older adult problem gamblers calling a gambling helpline.* Manuscript submitted for publication.

Poussaint, A. F., & Alexander, A. (2000). *Lay my burden down.* Boston: Beacon Press.

Powell, G. J., Hardoon, K., Derevensky, J., & Gupta, R. (1999). Gambling and risk taking behavior of university students. *Substance Use and Misuse, 34*(8), 1167-1184.

Prausnitz, S., & Goldbaum, G. (1998). *Outcome evaluation of Project Action.* Seattle, WA: Northwest AIDS Foundation.

Prescott, C. A., & Kendler, K. S. (1999). Age at first drink and risk for alcoholism: A non-causal association. *Alcoholism, Clinical and Experiment Research, 23*(1), 101-107.

Preston, F., Bernhard, B. J., Hunter, R., & Bybee, S. (1998). Gambling as stigmatized behavior: Regional relabeling and the law. *Annals of the American Academy of Social and Political Science, 556*, 186-196.

Preuss, U., Koller, G., Soyka, M., & Bondy, B. (2001). Association between suicide attempts and 5-HTTLPR-S-allele in alcohol-dependent and control subjects: Further evidence from a German alcohol-dependent inpatient sample. *Biological Psychiatry, 50*(8), 636-639.

Proctor, R. (1988). *Racial hygiene: Medicine under the Nazis.* Cambridge, MA: Harvard University Press.

Proimos, J., DuRant, R. H., Pierce, J. D., & Goodman, E. (1998). Gambling and other risk behaviors among 8th- to12th-grade students. *Pediatrics, 102*, 1-6.

Prudhomme, C. (1938). The problem of suicide in the American Negro. *Psychoanalytic Review, 25,* 187-204, 372-391.

Purkey, W. (1970). *Self-concept and school achievement.* Englewood Cliffs, NJ: Prentice Hall.

Putnam, R. D. (2000). *Bowling alone: The collapse and revival of American community.* New York: Touchstone.

Radziszewska, B., Richardson, J. L., Dent, C. W., & Flay, B. R. (1996). Parenting style and adolescent depressive symptoms, smoking, and academic achievement: Ethnic, gender and SES differences. *Journal of Behavioral Medicine, 19*(3), 289-305.

Raiffa, H. (1968). *Decision analysis.* Reading, MA: Addison-Wesley.

Raine, A., Brennan, P., & Mednik, S. A. (1994). Birth complications combined with early maternal rejection at age 1 year predispose to violent crime at age 18 years. *Archives of General Psychiatry, 51*(12), 984-988.

Rao, U., Ryan, N., Birmaher, B., Dahl, R., Williamson, D., Kaufman, J., et al. (1995). Unipolar depression in adolescents: Clinical outcome in adulthood. *Journal of the American Academy of Child and Adolescent Psychiatry, 34,* 566-578.

Reid, J. B. (1993). Prevention of conduct disorder before and after school entry: Relating interventions to developmental findings. *Development and Psychopathology, 5,* 243-262.

Reid, J. B., Eddy, J. M., Fetrow, R. A., & Stoolmiller, M. (1999). Description and immediate impacts of a preventive intervention for conduct problems. *American Journal of Community Psychology, 27*(4), 483-517.

Reid, J. B., & Patterson, G. R. (1991). Early prevention and intervention with conduct problems: A social interactional model for the integration of research and practice. In G. Stoner, M. R. Shinn, & H. M. Walker (Eds.), *Interventions for achievement and behavior problems* (pp. 715-739). Silver Spring, MD: National Association of School Psychologists.

Reifman, A., & Windle, M. (1995). Adolescent suicidal behaviors as a function of depression, hopelessness, alcohol use, and social support: A longitudinal investigation. *American Journal of Community Psychology, 23,* 329-354.

Reilly, P. R., & Page, D. C. (1998). We're off to see the genome. *Nature Genetics, 20*(1), 15-17.

Reilly, P. R., Boshar, M. F., & Holtzman, S. H. (1997). Ethical issues in genetic research: Disclosure and informed consent. *Nature Genetics, 15,* 16-20.

Reinherz, H. A., Giaconia, R. M., Silverman, A. B., Friedman, A., Pakiz, B., Frost, A. K., & Cohen, E. (1995). Early psychosocial risks for adolescent suicidal ideation and attempts. *Journal of the American Academy of Child and Adolescent Psychiatry, 34,* 599-611.

Reis-Bergan, M., Gibbons, F. X., & Gerrard, M. (2003). *Experience as a moderator of the developmental shift from willingness to intentions.* Manuscript submitted for publication.

Reisen, C. A., & Poppen, P. J. (1999). Partner-specific risk perception: A new conceptualization of perceived vulnerability to STDs. *Journal of Applied Social Psychology, 29*(4), 667-684.

Reiss, D. (with Neiderhiser, J. M., Hetherington, E. M., & Plomin, R.). (2000). *The relationship code: Deciphering genetic and social influences on adolescent development.* Cambridge, MA: Harvard University Press.

Remafedi, G., French, S., Story, M., Resnick, M. D., & Blum, R. (1998). The relationship between suicide risk and sexual orientation: Results of a population-based study. *American Journal of Public Health, 88,* 57-60.

Remez, L. (2000). Oral sex among adolescents: Is it sex or is it abstinence? *Family Planning Perspectives, 32,* 298-304.

Resnick, M., Bearman, P. S., Blum, R.W., Bauman, K. E., Harris, K. M., Jones, J., et al. (1997). Protecting adolescents from harm: Findings from the National Longitudinal Study on Adolescent Health. *JAMA, 278*(10), 823-832.

Reyna, V. F., & Ellis, S. C. (1994). Fuzzy-trace theory and framing effects in children's risky decision making. *American Psychological Society, 5*(5), 275-279.

Rich, C. L., Fowler, R. C., Fogarty, L. A., & Young, D. (1988). San Diego Suicide Study: III. Relationships between diagnoses and stressors. *Archives of General Psychiatry, 45,* 589-592.

Rich, C. L., Young, D., & Fowler, M. D. (1986). San Diego Suicide Study: I. Young vs. old subjects. *Archives of General Psychiatry, 45,* 577-582.

Rich, C. L., Young, J. G., Fowler, R. C., Wagner, J., & Black, N. A. (1990). Guns and suicide: Possible effects of some specific legislation. *American Journal of Psychiatry, 147,* 342-346.

Rippl, S. (2002). Cultural theory and risk perception: A proposal for a better measurement. *Journal of Risk Research, 5*(2), 147-165.

Roberts, R. E., & Chen, Y. (1995). Depressive symptoms and suicidal ideation among Mexican-origin and Anglo adolescents. *Journal of the American Academy of Child and Adolescent Psychiatry, 34,* 81-90.

Roberts, R. E., Chen, Y., & Roberts, C. R. (1997). Ethnocultural differences in prevalence of adolescent suicidal behaviors. *Suicide and Life-Threatening Behavior, 27,* 208-217.

Robin, L., Dittus, P., Whitaker, D., Crosby, R. A., Ethier, K., Mezhoff, J., et al. (in press). Behavioral interventions to reduce incidence of HIV, STD, and pregnancy among adolescents: A decade in review. *Journal of Adolescent Health.*

Robins, E., Murphy, P. I., Wilkinson, R. H., Jr., Gassner, S., & Kayes, J. (1959). Some clinical considerations in the prevention of suicide based on a study of 134 successful suicides. *American Journal of Public Health, 49,* 888-988.

Robins, L. N. (1966). *Deviant children grown up: A sociological and psychiatric study of sociopathic personality.* Baltimore: Williams & Wilkins.

Robins, L. N., & McEvoy, L. (1990). Conduct problems as predictors of substance abuse. In L. N. Robins & M. Rutter (Eds.), *Straight and devious pathways from childhood to adulthood* (pp. 182-204). Cambridge, UK: Cambridge University Press.

Robins, L. N., & Przybeck, T. R. (1985). Age of onset of drug use as a factor in drug and other disorders. In C. I. Jones & R. J. Battjes (Eds.), *Etiology of drug abuse: Implications for prevention* (pp. 178-192). Rockville, MD: National Institute on Drug Abuse.

Robins, R. W., & Beer, J. S. (2001). Positive illusions about the self: Short-term benefits and long-term costs. *Journal of Personality and Social Psychology, 80,* 340-352.

Robinson, M. S., & Alloy, L. B. (in press). Negative cognitive styles and stress-reactive rumination interact to predict depression: A prospective study. *Cognitive Therapy and Research.*

Rodgers, J. L. (1992). The development of sexuality in adolescence. In S. B. Friedman, M. Fisher, & S. K. Schonberg (Eds.), *Comprehensive adolescent health care.* St. Louis, MO: Quality Medical.

Rodgers, J. L. (2000). Social contagion and adolescent sexual behavior: Theoretical and policy implications. In J. Bancroft (Ed.), *The role of theory in sex research* (pp. 258-278). Bloomington, IN: Kinsey Institute.

Rodgers, J. L., Billy, J. O. G., & Udry, J. R. (1984). A model of friendship similarity in mildly deviant behaviors. *Journal of Applied Social Psychology, 14,* 413-425.

Rodgers, J. L., & Rowe, D. C. (1993). Social contagion and adolescent sexual behavior: A developmental EMOSA model. *Psychological Review, 100,* 479-510.

Rodgers, J. L., Rowe, D. C., & Buster, M. (1998). Social contagion, adolescent sexual behavior, and pregnancy: A nonlinear dynamic EMOSA model. *Developmental Psychology, 34,* 1096-1113.

Roesch, S. (1999). Modelling the direct and indirect effects of positive emotional and cognitive traits and states on social judgments. *Cognition and Emotion, 13*(4), 387-418.

Rogers, R. W. (1975). A protection motivation theory of fear appeals and attitude change. *Journal of Psychology, 91,* 93-114.

Rogers, R. W. (1983). Cognitive and physiological processes in fear appeals and attitude change: A revised theory of protection motivation. In J. T. Cacioppo & R. E. Petty (Eds.), *Social psychophysiology: A sourcebook* (pp. 153-176). New York: Guilford Press.

Rohde, P., Lewinsohn, P. M., & Seeley, J. R. (1991). Comorbidity of unipolar depression, II: Comorbidity with other mental disorders in adolescents and adults. *Journal of Abnormal Psychology, 100,* 214-222.

Rohde, P., Noell, J., Ochs, I., & Seeley, J. R. (2001). Depression, suicidal ideation and STD-related risk in homeless older adolescents. *Journal of Adolescence, 24,* 447-460.

Romer, D. (1994). Using mass media to reduce adolescent involvement in drug-trafficking. *Pediatrics, 93,* 1073-1077.

Romer, D., Black, M., Ricardo, I., Figelman, S., Kalijee, L., Galbraith, J., et al. (1994). Social influences on the sexual behavior of youth at risk for HIV exposure. *American Journal of Public Health, 84,* 977-985.

Romer, D., Stanton, B., Galbraith, J., Feigelman, S., Black, M. M., & Li, X. (1999). Parental influence on adolescent sexual behavior in high-poverty settings. *Archives of Pediatrics & Adolescent Medicine, 153,* 1055-1062.

Rose, D. T., & Abramson, L. Y. (1992). Developmental predictors of depressive cognitive style: Research and theory. In D. Cicchetti & S. L. Toth (Eds.), *Rochester symposium on developmental psychopathology* (Vol. 4, pp. 323-349). Hillsdale, NJ: Lawrence Erlbaum.

Rosenberg, M. D., Gurvey, J. E., Adler, N., Dunlop, M. B., & Ellen, J. M. (1999). Concurrent sex partners and risk for sexually transmitted diseases among adolescents. *Sexually Transmitted Diseases, 26,* 208-212.

Rosenberg, P. S., & Biggar, R. J. (1998). Trends in HIV incidence among young adults in the United States. *JAMA, 279*(23), 1894-1899.

Rosenstock, I. M. (1966). Why people use health services. *Milbank Memorial Fund Quarterly, 44,* 94-127.

Rosenstock, I. M. (1974). Historical origins of the health belief model. In M. H. Becker (Ed.), *The health belief model and personal health behavior.* San Francisco: Society for Public Health Education.

Rosenstock, I. M., Strecher, V. J., & Becker, M. H. (1994). The health belief model and HIV risk behavior change. In R. J. DiClemente & J. L. Peterson (Eds.), *Preventing AIDS: Theories and methods of behavioral interventions* (pp. 5-24). New York: Plenum Press.

Rosenthal, R., & Lesieur, H. (1992). Self-reported withdrawal symptoms and pathological gambling. *American Journal of the Addictions, 1,* 150-154.

Rosenthal, S. L., Cohen, S. S., DeVellis, R. F., Biro, F. M., Lewis, L. M., Succop, P. A., et al. (1999). Locus of control for general health and STD acquisition among adolescent girls. *Sexually Transmitted Diseases, 26,* 472-475.

Roth, J. L., Borbely, C. J., & Brooks-Gunn, J. (2001, June). *Developing indicators of confidence, character and caring in adolescents.* Paper presented at the Child Trends conference, Key Indicators of Child and Youth Well-Being: Completing the Picture, Bethesda, MD.

Roth, J. L., & Brooks-Gunn, J. (2000). What do adolescents need for healthy development? Implications for youth policy. *Society for Research in Child Development Social Policy Report, 14*(1).

Roth, J. L., & Brooks-Gunn, J. (2003a). What exactly is a youth development program? Answers from research and practice. *Applied Developmental Science, 7,* 92-109.

Roth, J. L., & Brooks-Gunn, J. (2003b). What is a youth development program? Identifying defining principles. In R. M. Lerner & F. Jacobs & D. Wertlieb (Eds.), *Promoting positive child, adolescent, and family development: A handbook of program and policy innovations* (Vol. 2, pp. 197-224). Thousand Oaks, CA: Sage.

Roth, J. L., & Brooks-Gunn, J. (2003c). Youth development programs: Risk, prevention and policy. *Journal of Adolescent Health, 32,* 170-182.

Roth, J. L., Brooks-Gunn, J., Murray, L., & Foster, W. (1998). Promoting healthy adolescents: Synthesis of youth development program evaluations. *Journal of Research on Adolescence, 8*(4), 423-459.

Rotheram-Borus, M. J., Gwadz, M., Fernandez, M. I., & Srinivasan, S. (1998). Timing of HIV interventions on reductions in sexual risk among adolescents. *American Journal of Community Psychology, 26*(1), 73-76.

Rotheram-Borus, M. J., Hunter, J., & Rosario, M. (1994). Suicidal behavior and gay-related stress among gay and bisexual male adolescents. *Journal of Adolescent Research, 9,* 498-508.

Rotheram-Borus, M. J., Koopman, C., Haigners, C., & Davies, M. (1991). Reducing HIV sexual risk behaviors among runaway adolescents. *JAMA, 266*(9), 1237-1241.

Rotheram-Borus, M. J., & Trautman, P. D. (1988). Hopelessness, depression and suicidal intent among adolescent suicide attempters. *Journal of the American Academy of Child and Adolescent Psychiatry, 27,* 700-704.

Rotheram-Borus, M. J., Trautman, P. D., Dopkins, S. C., & Shrout, P. E. (1990). Cognitive style and pleasant activities among female adolescent suicide attempters. *Journal of Consulting and Clinical Psychology, 58, 554*-561.

Rothman, A. J., & Salovey, P. (1997). Shaping perceptions to motivate healthy behavior: The role of message framing. *Psychological Bulletin, 121*(1), 3-19.

Roussos, S. T., & Fawcett, S. B. (2000). A review of collaborative partnerships as a strategy for improving community health. *Annual Review of Public Health, 21,* 369-402.

Rowe, D. (1985). Sibling interactions and self-report delinquent behavior: A study of 265 twin pairs. *Criminology, 23,* 223-240.

Rowe, D. C., Chassin, L., Presson, C., & Sherman, S. J. (1996). Parental smoking and the epidemic spread of cigarette smoking. *Journal of Applied Social Psychology, 26,* 437-454.

Rowe, D. C., & Rodgers, J. L. (1991a). Adolescent smoking and drinking: Are they "epidemics"? *Journal of Studies in Alcohol, 52,* 110-117.

Rowe, D. C., & Rodgers, J. L. (1991b). An "epidemic" model of adolescent sexual intercourse prevalences: Applications to national survey data. *Journal of Biosocial Science, 23,* 211-219.

Rowe, D. C., & Rodgers, J. L. (1994). A social contagion model of adolescent sexual behavior: Explaining race differences. *Social Biology, 41,* 1-18.

Rowe, D. C., & Rodgers, J. L. (2002). *An epidemic model of the post-war crime wave, 1950–1987.* Unpublished manuscript.

Rowe, D. C., Rodgers, J. L., & Gilson, M. (2000). Epidemics of smoking: Modeling tobacco use among adolescents. In J. S. Rose, L. Chassin, C. C. Presson, & S. J. Sherman (Eds.), *Multivariate applications in substance use research.* Mahwah, NJ: Lawrence Erlbaum.

Rowe, D. C., Rodgers, J. L., & Meseck-Bushey, S. (1989). An "epidemic" model of sexual intercourse prevalences for black and white adolescents. *Social Biology, 36,* 127-145.

Roy, A., Rylander, G., Forslund, K., Asberg, M., Mazzanti, C., Goldman, D., & Nielsen, D. (2001). Excess tryptophan hydroxylase 17 779C allele in surviving cotwins of monozygotic twin suicide victims. *Neuropsychobiology, 43*(4), 233-236.

Roy, A., Segal, N. L., Centerwall, B. S., & Robinette, C. D. (1991). Suicide in twins. *Archives of General Psychiatry, 48,* 29-32.

Rubenstein, J. L., Halton, A., Kasten, L., Rubin, C., & Stechler, G. (1998). Suicidal behavior in adolescents: Stress and protection in different family contexts. *American Journal of Orthopsychiatry, 68,* 274-284.

Rubenstein, J. L., Heeren, T., Housman, D., Rubin, C., & Stechler, G. (1989). Suicidal behavior in "normal" adolescents: Risk and protective factors. *American Journal of Orthopsychiatry, 59*(1), 59-71.

Rubin, K. H., & Mills, R. (1988). The many faces of social isolation in childhood. *Journal of Consulting and Clinical Psychology, 56,* 916-924.

Runeson, B. (1989). Mental disorder in youth suicide: *DSM-III-R* Axes I and II. *Acta Psychiatrica Scandinavica, 79,* 490-497.

Runeson, B. (1990). Psychoactive substance use disorder in youth suicide. *Alcohol & Alcoholism, 25,* 561-568.

Russell, S. T., & Joyner, K. (2001). Adolescent sexual orientation and suicide risk: Evidence from a national study. *American Journal of Public Health, 91,* 1276-1281.

Rutter, M. (1987). Psychosocial resilience and protective mechanism. *American Journal of Orthopsychiatry, 57,* 316-331.

Rutter, M. (1989). Pathways from childhood to adult life. *Journal of Child Psychology and Psychiatry and Applied Disciplines, 30,* 23-51.

Rutter, M. (1990). Psychosocial resilience and protective mechanisms. In J. Rolf, A. S. Masten, D. Cicchetti, et al. (Eds.), *Risk and protective factors in the development of psychopathology*. Cambridge, UK: Cambridge University Press.

Ryff, C. D. (1996). Psychological well-being. In J. E. Birren (Ed.), *Encyclopedia of Gerontology: Age, aging, and the aged* (Vol. 2, pp. 365-369). San Diego, CA: Academic Press.

Saarni, C., Mumme, D., & Campos, J. (1998). Emotional development: Action, communication, and understanding. In N. Eisenberg & W. Damon (Eds.), *Handbook of child psychology* (5th ed., Vol. 3, pp. 237-309). New York: John Wiley.

Sabol, S., & Hamer, D. (1999). An improved assay shows no association between the CYP2A6 gene and cigarette smoking behavior. *Behavioral Genetics, 29*(4), 257-261.

Sabol, S., Nelson, M., Fisher, C., Gunzerath, L., Brody, C., & Hu, S., et al. (1999). A genetic association for cigarette smoking behavior. *Health Psychology, 18*, 7-13.

Saffer, H. (2002). Alcohol advertising and youth. *Journal of Studies on Alcohol, S14*, 173-181.

Sallis, J. F., Calfas, K. J., Nichols, J. F., Sarkin, J. A., Johnson, M. F., Caparosa, S., et al. (1999). Evaluation of a university course to promote physical activity: Project GRAD. *Research Quarterly for Exercise and Sport, 70*, 1-10.

Salovey, P., Rothman, A. J., Rodin, J. (1998). Health behavior. In D. T. Gilbert, S. T. Fiske, & G. Lindzey (Eds.), *The handbook of social psychology* (pp. 633-683). New York: Oxford University Press.

Sampson, R. J., & Laub, J. H. (1994). Urban poverty and the family context of delinquency: A new look at structure and process in a classic study. *Child Development, 65*, 523-540.

Satcher, D. (1998). Bringing the public health approach to the problem of suicide. *Suicide and Life-Threatening Behavior*, 325-327.

Scheier, M. F., & Carver, C. S. (1985). Optimism, coping, and health: Assessment and implications of generalized outcome expectancies. *Health Psychology, 4*, 219-247.

Schinka, J., Town, T., Abdullah, L., Crawford, F., Ordorica, P., Francis, E., et al. (2002). A functional polymorphism within the mu-opioid receptor gene and risk for abuse of alcohol and other substances. *Molecular Psychiatry, 7*(2), 224-228.

Schmidtke, A., & Hafner, A. (1988). The Werther effect after television films: New evidence for an old hypothesis. *Psychological Medicine, 18*, 665-676.

Schochet, P. Z., Burghardt, J., & Glazerman, S. (2000, February 9). *National Job Corps study: The short-term impacts of Job Corps on participants' employment and related outcomes* (Report and Evaluation Report Series 00-A). Washington, DC: U.S. Department of Labor, Employment and Training Administration.

Schulenberg, J., Maggs, J. L., & Hurrelmann, K. (Eds.). (1997). *Health risks and developmental transitions during adolescence*. New York: Cambridge University Press.

Schulsinger, F. (1980). Biological psychopathology. *Annual Review of Psychology, 31*, 583-606.

Schultz, L. H., Barr, D. J., & Selman, R. L. (2001). The value of a developmental approach to evaluating character development programs: An outcomes study of Facing History in Ourselves. *Journal of Moral Education, 30*(1), 3-27.

Schultz, L. H., & Selman, R. L. (2002). *The relationship questionnaire: A method to assess social competence in children and adolescents from a developmental perspective*. Unpublished manuscript, Cambridge.

Schwartz, R. S. (2001). Racial profiling in medical research. *New England Journal of Medicine, 344*(18), 1392-1393.

Scott, C. (1995). Adolescent pregnancy prevention. *Family Relations, 44*(4), 384-401.

Segal, B. (1976). Personality factors related to drug and alcohol use. In D. J. Lettieri (Ed.), *Predicting adolescent drug abuse: A review of issues, methods, and correlates* (Publication No. ADM 77-299). Washington, DC: Department of Health, Education, and Welfare.

Seiden, R. H. (1970). We're driving young blacks to suicide. *Psychology Today, 4*(3), 24-28.

Seifer, R., Sameroff, A., Dickstein, S., Keitner, G., & Miller, I. (1996). Parental psychopathology, multiple contextual risks, and one-year outcomes in children. *Journal of Clinical Child Psychology, 25*(4), 423-435.

Seligman, M. E. P., & Csikszentmihalyi M. (2000). Positive psychology: An introduction. *American Psychologist, 55,* 5-14.

Sellers, D. E., McGraw, S. A., & McKinlay, J. B. (1994). Does the promotion and distribution of condoms increase teen sexual activity? Evidence from an HIV prevention program for Latino youth. *American Journal of Public Health, 84*(12), 1952-1959.

Sells, W. C., Blum, R. W. (1996). Morbidity and mortality among US adolescents: An overview of data and trends. *American Journal of Public Health.* 513-519.

Selman, R. (1980). *The growth of interpersonal understanding: Developmental and clinical analyses.* New York: Academic Press.

Selman, R. (2002). *A developmental approach to the understanding and prevention of adolescent health risks.* Final Report to the Robert Wood Johnson Foundation.

Selman, R. L. (in press). *The promotion of social awareness: Powerful lessons from the partnership of developmental theory and classroom practice.* New York: Russell Sage.

Selman, R. L., & Adalbjarnardottir, S. (2002). A developmental method to analyze the meaning adolescents make of risk and relationship: The case of "drinking." *Applied Developmental Science, 22,* 450-459.

Setness, P. A. (1997). Pathological gambling: When do social issues become medical issues? *Postgraduate Medicine, 102,* 13-18.

Severson, H. H. (1984). Adolescent social drug use: School prevention programs. *School Psychology Review, 13*(2), 150-160.

Severson, H. H., & Walker, H. M. (2002). Pro-active approaches for identifying children at-risk for sociobehavioral problems. In K. L. Lane, F. M. Gresham, & T. E. O'Shaughnessy (Eds.), *Interventions for children with or at risk for emotional and behavioral disorders.* Boston: Allyn & Bacon.

Sexuality Information and Education Council of the United States. (1995). *Consensus statement on adolescent sexual health.* Retrieved January 14, 2003, from www.siecus. org/policy/poli0002.html

Shaffer, D. (1974). Suicide in childhood and early adolescence. *Journal of Child Psychology and Psychiatry, 15,* 275-291.

Shaffer, D. (1988). The epidemiology of teen suicide: An examination of risk factors. *Journal of Clinical Psychiatry, 49*(9), 36-41.

Shaffer, D., & Craft, L. (1999). Methods of adolescent suicide prevention. *Journal of Clinical Psychiatry, 60,* 70-74.

Shaffer, D., Fisher, P., Hicks, R. H., Parides, M., & Gould, M. (1995). Sexual orientation in adolescents who commit suicide. *Suicide and Life-Threatening Behavior, 25,* 64-71.

Shaffer, D., Garland, A., Gould, M., Fisher, P., & Trautman, P. (1988). Preventing teenage suicide: A critical review. *Journal of the American Academy of Child and Adolescent Psychiatry, 27,* 675-687.

Shaffer, D., Gould, M. S., Fisher, P., Trautman, P., Moreau, D., Kleinman, M., et al. (1996). Psychiatric diagnosis in child and adolescent suicide. *Archives of General Psychiatry, 53*(4), 339-348.

Shaffer, D., Gould, M., & Hicks, R. (1994). Worsening suicide rate in black teenagers. *American Journal of Psychiatry, 151*(12), 1810-1812.

Shaffer, D., & Hicks, R. (1994). Suicide. In I. B. Pless (Ed.), *The epidemiology of childhood disorders* (pp. 339-365). New York: Oxford University Press.

Shaffer, H. J. (1996). Understanding the means and objects of addiction: Technology, the Internet and gambling. *Journal of Gambling Studies, 12*(4), 461-469.

Shaffer, H. J., Forman, D. P., Scanlan, K. M., & Smith, F. (2000). Awareness of gambling-related problems, policies and educational programs among high school and college administrators. *Journal of Gambling Studies, 16,* 93-101.

Shaffer, H. J., & Hall, M. N. (1996). Estimating prevalence of adolescent gambling disorders: A quantitative synthesis and guide toward standard gambling nomenclature. *Journal of Gambling Studies, 12,* 193-214.

Shaffer, H. J., Hall, M. N., & Vander Bilt, J. (1999). Estimating the prevalence of disordered gambling behavior in the United States and Canada: A research synthesis. *American Journal of Public Health, 89*(9), 1369-1376.

Shaffer, H. J., & Korn, D. (2002). Gambling and related mental disorders: A public health analysis. *Annual Review of Public Health, 23,* 171-212.

Shaffer, H. J., LaBrie, R., Scanlon, K. M., & Cummings, T. N. (1993). *At risk, problem and pathological gambling among adolescents: Massachusetts Adolescent Gambling Screen (MAGS).* Cambridge, MA: Harvard Medical School.

Shafii, M., Carrigan, S., Whittinghill, J. R., & Derrick, A. (1985). Psychological autopsy of completed suicide in children and adolescents. *American Journal of Psychiatry, 142,* 1061-1064.

Shafii, M., Steltz-Lenarsky, J., Derrick, A. M., Becker, C., & Whittinghill, R. (1988). Comorbidity of mental disorders in the post-mortem diagnosis of completed suicide in children and adolescents. *Journal of Affective Disorders, 14,* 227-233.

Shatte, A. J., Gillham, J. E., & Reivich, K. (2000). Promoting hope in children and adolescents. In J. E. Gillham (Ed.), *The science of optimism and hope: Research essays in honor of Martin E. P. Seligman* (pp. 215-234). Philadelphia: Templeton Foundation Press.

Shaw, D. S., Wagner, E. F., Arnett, J., & Aber, M. S. (1992). The factor structure of the reckless behavior questionnaire. *Journal of Youth and Adolescence, 21,* 305-323.

Shea, S. H., Wall, T. L., Carr, L. G., & Li, T. K. (2001). ADH2 and alcohol-related phenotypes in Ashkenazic Jewish American college students. *Behavior Genetics, 31*(2), 231-239.

Shedler, J., & Block, J. (1990). Adolescent drug use and psychological health: A longitudinal inquiry. *American Psychologist, 45*(5), 612-630.

Sheeran, P., Conner, M., & Norman, P. (2001). Can the theory of planned behavior explain patterns of health behavior change? *Health Psychology, 20,* 12-19.

Sheeran, P., & Orbell, S. (1998). Do intentions predict condom use? Meta-analysis and examination of six moderator variables. *British Journal of Psychology, 37,* 231-250.

Sher, K. J. (1991). *Children of alcoholics.* Chicago: University of Chicago Press.

Sherman, S. L., DeFries, J. C., Gottesman, I. I., Loehlin, J. C., Meyer, J. M., Pelias, M. Z., et al. (1997). Behavioral genetics '97: ASHG STATEMENT Recent developments in human behavioral genetics: Past accomplishments and future directions. *American Journal of Human Genetics, 60,* 1265-1275.

Shi, J., Hui, L., Xu, Y., Wang, F., Huang, W., & Hu, G. (2002). Sequence variations in the mu-opioid receptor gene (OPRM1) associated with human addiction to heroin. *Human Mutation, 19*(4), 459-460.

Shure, M. B. (1982). Interpersonal problem solving: A cog in the wheel of social cognition. In F. C. Serafica (Ed.), *Social-cognitive development in context.* New York: Guilford Press.

Shure, M. B. (1984). *Problem solving and mental health of ten- to twelve-year-olds* (Final Report #MH-35989). Washington, DC: National Institute of Mental Health.

Shure, M. B. (1992a). *I Can Problem Solve (ICPS): An interpersonal cognitive problem solving program for children (preschool).* Champaign, IL: Research Press.

Shure, M. B. (1992b). *I Can Problem Solve (ICPS): An interpersonal cognitive problem solving program for children (kindergarten/primary grades).* Champaign, IL: Research Press.

Shure, M. B. (1992c). *I Can Problem Solve (ICPS): An interpersonal cognitive problem solving program for children (intermediate elementary grades).* Champaign, IL: Research Press.

Shure, M. B. (1996). *Raising a thinking child: Help your young child to resolve everyday conflicts and get along with others.* New York: Pocket Books.

Shure, M. B. (1999). *Preventing violence the problem solving way* (Office of Juvenile Justice and Delinquency Prevention Juvenile Justice Bulletin). Washington, DC: Office of Juvenile Justice and Delinquency Prevention.

Shure, M. B. (2000). *Raising a thinking child workbook*. Champaign, IL: Research Press.

Shure, M. B. (2001). *Raising a thinking preteen: The "I Can Problem Solve" program for 8- to 12-year-olds*. New York: Owl/Holt.

Shure, M. B., & Spivack, G. (1972). Means-ends thinking, adjustment and social class among elementary school-aged children. *Journal of Consulting and Clinical Psychology, 38*, 348-353.

Shure, M. B., & Spivack, G. (1978). *Problem solving techniques in childrearing*. San Francisco: Jossey-Bass.

Shure, M. B., Spivack, G., & Jaeger, M. A. (1971). Problem-solving thinking and adjustment among disadvantaged preschool children. *Child Development, 42*, 1791-1803.

Siegrist, M. (1996). Church attendance, denomination and suicide ideology. *Journal of Social Psychology, 136*(5), 559-566.

Silverman, J. G., Raj, A., Mucci, L. A., & Hathaway, J. E. (2001). Dating violence against adolescent girls and associated substance use, unhealthy weight control, sexual risk behavior, pregnancy, and suicidality. *JAMA, 286*(5), 572-579.

Simons-Morton, B., & Hartos, J. (2002). Application of the authoritative parenting model to adolescent health behavior. In R. J. DiClemente, R. A. Crosby, & M. Kegler (Eds.), *Emerging theories in public health promotion practice and research* (pp. 100-125). San Francisco, CA: Jossey-Bass.

Simpson, H. (Ed.). (1996). *New to the road: Reducing the risks for young motorists*. Los Angeles, CA: UCLA School of Medicine, Youth Enhancement Service.

Singh, S. (1986). Adolescent pregnancy in the United States: An interstate analysis. *Family Planning Perspectives, 18*(5), 210-220.

Singh, S., & Darroch, J. (2000). Adolescent pregnancy and childbearing: Levels and trends in developed countries. *Family Planning Perspectives, 32*(1), 14-23.

Skaalvik, E. M., & Valas, H. (1999). Relations among achievement, self-concept, and motivation in mathematics and language arts: A longitudinal study. *Journal of Experimental Education, 67*(2), 135-149.

Skara, S., Sussman, S., & Dent, C. (2001). Predicting regular cigarette use among continuation high school students. *American Journal of Health Behavior, 25*(2), 147-156.

Skiba, R. J., & Noam, G. G. (Eds.). (2001). *Zero tolerance: Can suspension and expulsion keep schools safe?* San Francisco: Jossey-Bass.

Skinner, H. A. (1982). *Development and validation of lifetime alcohol consumption assessment procedure* (Substudy No. 1284). Toronto, Ontario: Addiction Research Foundation.

Slovic, P. (1987). Perception of risk. *Science, 236*, 280-285.

Slovic, P. (2000). What does it mean to know a cumulative risk? Adolescents' perceptions of short-term and long-term consequences of smoking. *Journal of Behavioral Decision Making, 13*, 259-266.

Slovic, P. (2001). Cigarette smokers: Rational actors or rational fools? In P. Slovic (Ed.), *Smoking: Risk, perception, & policy* (pp. 97-124). Thousand Oaks, CA: Sage.

Slovic, P., Finucane, M. L., Peters, E., & MacGregor, D. G. (2002). The affect heuristic. In T. Gilovich, D. Griffin, & D. Kahneman (Eds.), *Heuristics and biases: The psychology of intuitive judgment* (pp. 397-420). New York: Cambridge University Press.

Slutske, W. S., Eisen, S., True, W. R., Lyons, M. J., Goldberg, J., & Tsuang, M. (2000). Common genetic vulnerability for pathological gambling and alcohol dependence in men. *Archives of General Psychiatry, 57*, 666-674.

Slutske, W. S., True, W. R., Scherrer, J. F., Heath, A. C., Bucholz, K. K., Eisen, S. A., et al. (1999). The heritability of alcoholism symptoms: "Indicators of genetic and environmental influence in alcohol-dependent individuals" revisited. *Alcoholism, Clinical and Experimental Research, 23*(5), 759-769.

Small, S. A., & Luster, T. (1994). Adolescent sexual activity: An ecological, risk-factor approach. *Journal of Marriage and the Family, 56*, 181-192.

Smith, A., Denham, I., Keogh, L., Jacobs, D., McHarg, V., Marceglice, A., et al. (2000). Psychosocial impact of type-specific herpes simplex serological testing on asymptomatic sexual health attendees. *International Journal of STD & AIDS, 11*, 15-20.

Smith, G., Goldman, M., Greenbaum, P., & Christiansen, B. (1995). Expectancy for social facilitation from drinking: The divergent paths of high-expectancy and low-expectancy adolescents. *Journal of Abnormal Psychology, 104*(1), 32-40.

Smith, J. A., & Carter, J. H. (1986). Suicide and black adolescents: A medical dilemma. *Journal of the National Medical Association, 78*, 1061-1064.

Smith, K., & Crawford, S. (1986). Suicidal behavior among "normal" high school students. *Suicide and Life-Threatening Behavior, 16*, 313-325.

Snyder, J. (1991). Discipline as a mediator of the impact of maternal stress and mood on child conduct problems. *Development and Psychopathology, 3*, 263-276.

Snyder, M. (1974). Self-monitoring of expressive behavior. *Journal of Personality and Social Psychology, 30*, 526-537.

Sorri, H., Henriksson, M., & Lonnqvist, J. (1996). Religiosity and suicide: Findings from a nation-wide psychological autopsy study. *Crisis, 17*(3), 123-127.

Spanier, G. B. (1977). Sources of sex information and premarital sexual behavior. *Journal of Sex Research, 13*, 73-88.

Spasojevic, J., & Alloy, L. B. (2001). Rumination as a common mechanism relating depressive risk factors to depression. *Emotion, 1*, 25-37.

Spasojevic, J., & Alloy, L. B. (in press). Who becomes a depressive ruminator? Developmental antecedents of ruminative response style. *Journal of Cognitive Psychotherapy: An International Quarterly.*

Spasojevic, J., Alloy, L. B., Abramson, L. Y., MacCoon, D., & Robinson, M. S. (in press). Reactive rumination: Outcomes, mechanisms, and developmental antecedents. In C. Papageorgiou & A. Wells (Eds.), *Depressive rumination: Nature, theory and treatment.* New York: John Wiley.

Spear, P. (2000). The adolescent brain and age-related behavioral manifestations. *Neuroscience and Biobehavioral Reviews, 24*, 417-463.

Spencer, M. B., Dupree, D., & Hartmann, T. (1997). A phenomenological variant of ecological systems theory (PVEST): A self-organization perspective in context. *Development and Psychopathology, 9*, 817-833.

Spielman, R. S., & Ewens, W. J. (1996). The TDT and other family-based tests for linkage disequilibrium and association. *American Journal of Human Genetics, 59*(5), 983-989.

Spirito, A., Brown, L., Overholser, J., & Fritz, G. (1989). Attempted suicide in adolescence: A review and critique of the literature. *Clinical Psychology Review, 9*, 335-363.

Spitz, M., Shi, H., Yang, F., Hudmon, K., Jiang, H., & Chamberlain, R. (1998). Case-control study of the D2 dopamine receptor gene and smoking status in lung cancer patients. *Journal of the National Cancer Institute, 90*, 358-363.

Spitzer, R. L., Endicott, J., & Robins, E. (1978). Research diagnostic criteria: Rationale and reliability. *Archives of General Psychiatry, 35*, 773-782.

Spivack, G., Cianci, N., Quercetti, L., & Bogaslav, B. (1980). *High-risk early school signs for delinquency, emotional problems, and school failure among urban males and females* (Report #76-JN-990024 to the National Institute of Juvenile Justice and Delinquency). Washington, DC: Law Enforcement Assistance Administration.

Spivack, G., Platt, J. J., & Shure, M. B. (1976). *The problem solving approach to adjustment.* San Francisco: Jossey-Bass.

Spivack, G., & Shure, M. B. (1974). *Social adjustment of young children.* San Francisco: Jossey-Bass.

Spoth, R. L., Redmond, C., & Shin, C. (2000). Reducing adolescents' aggressive and hostile behaviors: Randomized trial effects of a brief family intervention four years past baseline. *Archives of Pediatric & Adolescent Medicine, 154*(12), 1248-1257.

Spoth, R. L., Redmond, C., & Shin, C. (2001). Randomized trial of brief family interventions for general populations: Adolescent substance use outcomes 4 years following baseline. *Journal of Consulting and Clinical Psychology, 69*(4), 627-642.

St. Lawrence, J. S., Brasfield, T. L., Jefferson, K. W., & Allyene, E. (1994). Social support as a factor in African American adolescents' sexual risk behavior. *Journal of Adolescent Research, 9*(3), 292-310.

St. Lawrence, J. S., Jefferson, K. W., Alleyne, E., Brasfield, T. L., O'Bannon, R. E., III, & Shirley, A. (1995). Cognitive-behavioral intervention to reduce African American adolescents' risk for HIV infection. *Journal of Consulting and Clinical Psychology, 63*(2), 221-237.

Stack, S. (1983). The effect of religious commitment on suicide: A cross-national analyses. *Journal of Health and Social Behavior, 24,* 362-374.

Stack, S. (1989). The effect of publicized mass murder and murder-suicides on lethal violence. *Social Psychiatry and Psychiatric Epidemiology, 24,* 202-208.

Stack, S. (1990a). Audience receptiveness, the media, and aged suicide. *Journal of Aging Studies, 4,* 195-209.

Stack, S. (1990b). A reanalysis of the impact of non-celebrity suicides: A research note. *Social Psychiatry and Psychiatric Epidemiology, 25,* 269-273.

Stack, S. (1991). Social correlates of suicide by age: Media impacts. In A. Leenaars et al. (Eds.), *Life span perspectives of suicide: Time-lines in the suicide process* (pp. 187-213). New York: Plenum Press.

Stack, S. (1992). The effect of the media in suicide: The Great Depression. *Suicide and Life-Threatening Behavior, 22,* 255-267.

Stack, S. (1993). The media and suicide: A nonadditive model, 1968-1980. *Suicide and Life-Threatening Behavior, 23,* 63-66.

Stack, S. (1996). The effects of marital integration on African-American suicide. *Suicide and Life-Threatening Behavior, 26,* 405-414.

Stack, S. (1998). Heavy metal, religiosity, and suicide acceptability. *Suicide and Life-Threatening Behavior, 28*(4), 388-394.

Stack, S. (2000). Media impact on suicide: A quantitative review of 293 findings. *Social Science Quarterly, 81*(4), 956-971.

Stack, S., & Lester, D. (1991). The effect of religion on suicide ideation. *Social Psychiatry and Psychiatric Epidemiology, 26,* 168-170.

Stanovich, K. E., & West, R. F. (2000). Individual differences in reasoning: Implications for the rationality debate? *Behavioral and Brain Sciences, 23,* 645-726.

Stanton, B., Fang, X., Li, X., Feigelman, S., Galbraith, J., & Ricardo, I. (1997). Evolution of risk behaviors over 2 years among a cohort of urban African American adolescents. *Archives of Pediatrics & Adolescent Medicine, 151,* 398-406.

Stanton, B., Kim, N., Galbraith, J., & Parrott, M. (1996). Design issues addressed in published evaluations of adolescent HIV-risk reduction interventions: A review. *Journal of Adolescent Health 18,* 387-396.

Stanton, B., Li, X., Galbraith, J., Cornick, G., Feigelman, S., Kaljee, L., et al. (2000). Parental underestimates of adolescent risk behavior: A randomized, controlled trial of parental monitoring intervention. *Journal of Adolescent Health, 26,* 18-26.

Stanton, B., Li, X., Pack, R., Cottrell, L., Harris, C. V., & Burns, J. M. (2002). Longitudinal influences of perceptions of peer and parental factors on African-American adolescent risk involvement. *Journal of Urban Health, 79,* 536-548.

Stanton, W. R. (1995). DSM-III-R tobacco dependence and quitting during late adolescence. *Addictive Behaviors, 20*(5), 595-603.

Steinberg, D. (1998). *Predictors of relapse and recurrence in depression: The scar hypothesis and impact of depressive episodes.* Doctoral dissertation, Temple University.

Steinberg, L. (2002, June). *Is decision making the right framework for research on adolescent risk taking.* Paper presented at the Reducing Adolescent Risk Conference, Annenberg Public Policy Center, Philadelphia, PA.

Steinberg, L., Blinde, P. L., & Chan K. S. (1984). Dropping out among language minority youth. *Review of Educational Research, 54*(1), 113-132.

Steinberg, L., & Cauffman, E. (1996). Maturity of judgment in adolescence: Psychosocial factors in adolescent decisionmaking. *Law and Human Behavior, 20,* 249-272.

Steinberg, L., Dornbusch, S. M., & Brown, B. B. (1992). Ethnic differences in adolescent achievement: An ecological perspective. *American Psychologist, 47,* 723-729.

Steinberg, L., Elmen, J. D., & Mounta, N. S. (1989). Authoritative parenting, psychosocial maturity and academic success among adolescents. *Child Development, 60,* 1424-1436.

Steinberg, L., Fletcher, A., & Darling, N. (1994). Parental monitoring and peer influences on adolescent substance use. *Pediatrics, 93,* 1060-1064.

Steinberg, L., Lamborn, S. D., Darling, N., Mounts, N. S., & Dornbusch, S. M. (1994). Overtime changes in adjustment and competence among adolescents from authoritative, authoritarian, indulgent and neglectful families. *Child Development, 65,* 754-770.

Steinberg, L., Mounts, N. S., & Lamborn, S. (1991). Authoritative parenting and adolescent adjustment across varied ecological niches. *Journal of Research on Adolescence, 1,* 19-36.

Steinhausen, H.-C. (1999). Eating disorders. In H. -C. Steinhausen & F. C. Verhulst (Eds.), *Risks and outcomes in developmental psychopathology* (pp. 210-230). Oxford, UK: Oxford University Press.

Steinlauf, B. (1979). Problem solving skills, locus of control, and the contraceptive effectiveness of young children. *Child Development, 50,* 268-271.

Stevens, L. M., Lynm, C., & Glass, R. M. (2001). When gambling becomes a bad bet. *JAMA, 286,* 260.

Stewart, R. M., & Brown, R. I. (1988). An outcome study of Gamblers Anonymous. *British Journal of Psychiatry, 152,* 284-288.

Stinchfield, R. (2000). Gambling and correlates of gambling among Minnesota public school students. *Journal of Gambling Studies, 16,* 153-174.

Stinchfield, R. (2002). Youth gambling: How big a problem? *Psychiatric Annals, 32,* 197-202.

Stinchfield, R., Cassuto, N., Winters, K., & Latimer, W. (1997). Prevalence of gambling among Minnesota public school students in 1992 and 1995. *Journal of Gambling Studies, 13*(1), 25-48.

Stinchfield, R., & Winters, K. C. (1998). Gambling and problem gambling among youths. *Annals of the American Academy of Political and Social Science, 556,* 172-185.

Stober, J. (1997). Trait anxiety and pessimistic appraisal of risk and chance. *Personality and Individual Differences, 22*(4), 465-476.

Stokols, D. (1996). Translating social ecological theory into guidelines for community health promotion. *American Journal of Health Promotion, 20,* 282-298.

Strage, A. A. (1998). Family context variables and the development of self-regulation in college students. *Adolescence, 33,* 17-31.

Strahan, E. J., White, K., Fong, G. T., Fabrigar, L. R, Zanna, M. P., & Cameron, A. J. R. (2002). Enhancing the effectiveness of message labels on tobacco packaging: A social psychological perspective. *Tobacco Control, 11,* 183-190.

Strathman, A., Gleicher, F., Boninger, D. S., & Edwards, C. S. (1994). The consideration of future consequences: Weighing immediate and distant outcomes of behavior. *Journal of Personality and Social Psychology, 66,* 742-752.

Straub, R., Sullivan, P., Ma, Y., Myakishev, M., Harris-Kerr, C., & Wormley, B. (1999). Susceptibility genes for nicotine dependence: A genome scan and follow-up in an independent sample suggest that regions on chromosomes 2, 4, 10, 16, 17, and 18 merit further study. *Molecular Psychiatry, 4,* 129-144.

Substance Abuse and Mental Health Services Administration. (1999). *The relationship between mental health and substance abuse among adolescents.* Rockville, MD: Author.

Substance Abuse and Mental Health Services Administration. (2001). *Summary of findings from the 2000 National Household Survey on Drug Abuse* (DHHS Publication No. SMA 01-3549). Rockville, MD: U.S. Department of Health and Human Services.

Substance Abuse and Mental Health Services Administration. (2002). *Results from the 2001 National Household Survey on Drug Abuse: Vol. 1. Summary of National Findings* (Office of Applied Studies, NHSDA Series H-17, DHHS Publication No. SMA 02-3758). Rockville, MD: U.S. Department of Health and Human Services.

Sullivan, P. F., Eaves, L. J., Kendler, K. S., & Neale, M. C. (2001). Genetic case-control association studies in neuropsychiatry. *Archives of General Psychiatry, 58*(11), 1015-1024.

Sullivan, P. F., & Kendler, K. (1999). The genetic epidemiology of smoking. *Nicotine and Tobacco Research, 1*(S), 51-57.

Sullivan, T. N., & Farrell, A. D. (1999). Identification and impact of risk and protective factors for drug use among urban African American adolescents. *Journal of Clinical Child Psychology, 28,* 122-136.

Summerville, M. B., Abbate, M. F., Siegel, A. M., Serravezza, J., & Kaslow, N. J. (1992). Psychopathology in urban female minority adolescents with suicide attempts. *Journal of the American Academy of Child and Adolescent Psychiatry, 31,* 663-668.

Summerville, M. B., Kaslow, N. J., Abbate, M. F., & Cronan, S. (1994). Psychopathology, family functioning, cognitive style in urban adolescents with suicide attempts. *Journal of Abnormal Child Psychology, 22,* 221-235.

Swan, G. E., Carmelli, D., & Cardon, L. R. (1996). The consumption of tobacco, alcohol, and coffee in Caucasian male twins: a multivariate genetic analysis. *Journal of Substance Abuse, 8*(1), 19-31.

Swanson, J. W., Linskey, A. O., Quintero-Salinas, R., Pumariega, A. J., & Holzer, C. E., III. (1992). A binational school survey of depressive symptoms, drug use, and suicidal ideation. *Journal of the American Academy of Child and Adolescent Psychiatry, 31,* 669-678.

Symons, C. W., Cinelli, B., James, T. C., & Groff, P. (1997). Bridging student health risks and academic achievement through comprehensive school health programs. *Journal of School Health, 67*(6), 220-227.

Talmadge, T. D. (1888). *Gambling: Social dynamite (or the wickedness of modern society)* (pp. 144-160). Chicago: Standard.

Tarter, R., Vanyukov, M., Giancola, P., Dawes, M., Blackson, T., Mezzich, A., et al. (1999). Epigenetic model of substance use disorder etiology. *Development and Psychopathology, 11,* 657-683.

Taylor, S. E., & Brown, J. D. (1988). Illusion and well-being: A social-psychological perspective on mental health. *Psychological Bulletin, 110,* 193-210.

Taylor, S. E., & Gollwitzer, P. M. (1995). Effects of mindset on positive illusions. *Journal of Personality and Social Psychology, 69,* 213-226.

Taylor, S. E., Kemeny, M. E., Reed, G., Bower, J. E., & Gruenewald, T. L. (2000). Psychological resources, positive illusions and health. *American Psychologist, 55,* 99-109.

Taylor, S. E., Lichtman, R. R., & Wood, J. V. (1984). Attributions, beliefs about control, and adjustment to breast cancer. *Journal of Personality and Social Psychology, 46,* 489-502.

Teicher, J. D., & Jacobs, J. (1966). Adolescents who attempt suicide. *American Journal of Psychiatry, 122,* 1248-1257.

Tester, M., Gardner, W., & Wilfong, E. (1987). Experimental studies of the development of decision-making competence. In *Children, risks, and decisions: Psychological and legal implications.* New York: American Psychological Association.

Thomas, B., Mitchell, A., Devlin, M., Goldsmith, C., Singer, J., & Watters, D. (1992). Small group sex education at school: The McMaster Teen Program. In B. C. Miller, J. J. Card, R. L. Paikoff, & J. L. Peterson (Eds.), *Preventing adolescent pregnancy* (pp. 28-52). Newbury Park, CA: Sage.

Thompson, E. A., & Eggert, L. L. (1999). Using the suicide risk screen to identify suicidal adolescents among potential high school dropouts. *Journal of the American Academy of Child & Adolescent Psychiatry, 38,* 1506-1514.

Thompson, E. A., Eggert, L. L., & Herting, J. R. (2000). Mediating effects of an indicated prevention program for reducing youth depression and suicide risk behaviors. *Suicide & Life-Threatening Behavior, 30,* 252-271.

Thornburgh, D., & Lin, H. S. (Eds.). (2002). *Youth, pornography, and the Internet.* Washington, DC: National Academy Press.

Thornton, B., Gibbons, F. X., & Gerrard, M. (2002). Risk perception and prototype perception: Independent processes predicting risk behavior. *Personality and Social Psychology Bulletin, 38,* 986-999.

Tierney, J. P., Grossman, J. B., & Resch, N. L. (1995). *Making a difference: An impact study of Big Brothers/Big Sisters.* Philadelphia: Public/Private Ventures.

Tobler, N. S., Roona, M. R., Ochshorn, P., Marshall, D. G., et al. (in press). School-based adolescent drug prevention programs: 1998 meta-analysis. *Journal of Primary Prevention.*

Tobler, N. S., & Stratton, H. H. (1997). Effectiveness of school-based drug prevention programs: A meta-analysis of the research. *Journal of Primary Prevention, 18,* 71-128.

Tolan, P. H., Guerra, N. G., & Kendall, P. (1995). A developmental-ecological perspective on antisocial behavior in children and adolescents: Towards a unified risk and intervention framework. *Journal of Consulting and Clinical Psychology, 63,* 579-584.

Tolman, D. L. (2000). Object lessons: Romance, violation and female adolescent sexual desire. *Journal of Sex Education and Therapy, 25,* 70-79.

Toner, B. B., Garfinkel, P. E., & Garner, D. M. (1988). Affective and anxiety disorders in the long-term follow-up of anorexia nervosa. *International Journal of Psychiatry in Medicine, 18,* 357-364.

Torikka, A., Kaltiala-Heino, R., Rimpelae, A., Rimpelae, M., & Rantanen, P. (2001). Depression, drinking, and substance use among 14- to 16-year-old Finnish adolescents. *Nordic Journal of Psychiatry, 55,* 351-357.

Tousignant, M., Bastien, M. F., & Hamel, S. (1993). Suicidal attempts and ideations among adolescents and young adults: The contribution of the father's and mother's care and of parental separation. *Social Psychiatry and Psychiatric Epidemiology, 28,* 256-261.

Tremblay, R. E., Pagani-Kurtz, L., Masse, L. C., Vitaro, F., & Pihl, R. O. (1995). A bi-modal preventive intervention for disruptive kindergarten boys: Its impact through mid-adolescence. *Journal of Consulting & Clinical Psychology, 63*(4), 560-568.

Triandis, H. C. (1977). *Interpersonal behavior.* Monterey, CA: Brooks/Cole.

Tsuang, M. T., Bar, J. L., Harley, R. M., & Lyons, M. J. (2001). The Harvard Twin Study of Substance Abuse: What we have learned. *Harvard Review of Psychiatry, 9*(6), 267-279.

Tsuang, M. T., Lyons, M. J., Harley, R. M., Xian, H., Eisen, S., Goldberg, J., et al. (1999). Genetic and environmental influences on transitions in drug use. *Behavior Genetics, 29*(6), 473-479.

Turk, E., & Bry, B. H. (1992). Adolescents' and parents' explanatory styles and parents' causal explanations about their adolescents. *Cognitive Therapy and Research, 16,* 349-357.

U.S. Bureau of the Census. (1994). *Statistical abstract of the United States* (114th ed.). Washington, DC: Government Printing Office.

U.S. Bureau of the Census. (2001). *Annual demographic survey* (March Suppl.). Retrieved December 16, 2002, from http://ferret.bls.census.gov/macro/032001/faminc/new 06_000.htm

U.S. Department of Agriculture. (2000). *Discussion of proposed changes* (for Dietary Guidelines for Americans, 5th ed.). Retrieved July 25, 2002, from www.ars.usda.gov/dgac/dgac_ration.pdf

U.S. Department of Health and Human Services. (1994). *Preventing tobacco use among young people: A report of the surgeon general.* Washington, DC: Government Printing Office.

U.S. Department of Health and Human Services. (2000a). *Protecting the privacy of patients' health information summary of the final regulation.* Washington, DC: Author.

U.S. Department of Health and Human Services. (2000b). *Tracking healthy people 2010.* Washington DC: Government Printing Office.

U.S. Department of Health & Human Services, Substance Abuse & Mental Health Services Administration. (2000). *National household survey on drug abuse, 1998.* Ann Arbor, MI: Inter-University Consortium for Political and Social Research.

U.S. Department of Health and Human Services. (2001). *Healthy people 2010.* Retrieved December 15, 2003, from www.health.gov/healthypeople/About/hpfact.htm

U.S. Department of Health and Human Services. (2002, March). Standards for privacy of individually identifiable health information. Proposed Rule, 67. *Federal Register,* 14776-14815.

U.S. Department of Labor. (1998). *Genetic information in the workplace.* Washington, DC: Department of Labor, Department of Health and Human Services, Equal Opportunity Commission, Department of Justice.

U.S. Public Health Service. (2000). *The surgeon general's call to action to prevent suicide, 1999.* Washington, DC: Government Printing Office.

U.S. Surgeon General. (1979). *Healthy people: The surgeon general's report on health promotion and disease prevention* (U.S. Department of Health and Welfare Publication No. 79-55071). Washington, DC: Government Printing Office.

Udry, J. R. (1998). *The national longitudinal study of adolescent health (add health), waves I & II, 1994–1996* (Data Sets 48-50, 98, A1-A3, Kelley, M. S., & Peterson J. L.) [machine-readable data file and documentation]. Chapel Hill, NC: University of North Carolina at Chapel Hill, Carolina Population Center.

Udry, J. R., Billy, J. O. G., Morris, N. M., Groff, T. R., & Raj, M. H. (1985). Serum androgenic hormones motivates sexual behavior in adolescent boys. *Fertility and Sterility, 43,* 90-94.

Udry, J. R., Talbert, L. M., & Morris, N. M. (1986). Biosocial foundations for adolescent female sexuality. *Demography, 23,* 217-230.

Uhl, G., Blum, K., Noble, E., & Smith, S. (1993). Substance abuse vulnerability and D2 receptor genes. *Trends in Neurosciences, 16*(3), 83-88.

Uhl, G., Liu, Q., Walther, D., Hess, J., & Naiman, D. (2001). Polysubstance abuse-vulnerability genes: Genome scans for association, using 1,004 subjects and 1,494 single-nucleotide polymorphisms. *American Journal of Human Genetics, 69*(6), 1290-1300.

Ussher, M., Taylor, A., West, R., & McEwen, A. (2000). Does exercise aid smoking cessation? A systematic review. *Addiction, 95*(2), 199-208.

Vaccarino, F. J., Schiff, B. B., & Glickman, S. E. (1989). Biological view of reinforcement. In S. B. Klein & R. R. Mowrer (Eds.), *Contemporary learning theories* (pp. 111-142). Hillsdale, NJ: Lawrence Erlbaum.

Vaillancourt, F., & Roy, A. (2000). *Gambling and governments in Canada, 1969-1998: How much? Who pays? What payoff?* (Special Studies in Taxation and Public Finance, No. 2). Toronto, Ontario: Canadian Tax Foundation.

Valois, R. F., Oeltmann, J. E., Waller, J., & Hussey, J. R. (1999). Relationship between number of sexual intercourse partners and selected health risk behaviors among public high school adolescents. *Journal of Adolescent Health, 25,* 328-335.

van den Bree, M., Johnson, E., Neale, M., & Pickens, R. (1998). Genetic and environmental influences on drug use and abuse/dependence in male and female twins. *Drug and Alcohol Dependence, 52,* 231-241.

van den Bree, M., Johnson, M., Neale, M. C., Svikis, D., McGue, M., & Pickens, R. W. (1998). Genetic analysis of diagnostic systems of alcoholism in males. *Biological Psychiatry, 43,* 139-145.

van der Pligt, J. (1998). Perceived risk and vulnerability as predictors of precautionary behavior. *British Journal of Health Psychology, 3,* 1-14.

van der Steenstraten, I., Tibben, A., Roos, R., Kamp, J. V. D., & Niermeijer, M. (1994). Predictive testing for Huntington disease: Nonparticipants compared with participants in the Dutch program. *American Journal of Human Genetics, 55*(4), 618-625.

Van der Velde, F. W., Hooykaas, C., & van der Plight, J. (1996). Conditional versus unconditional risk estimated in models of AIDS-related risk behavior. *Psychology and Health, 12,* 87-100.

Van Heeringen, C., & Vincke, J. (2000). Suicidal acts and ideation in homosexual and bisexual young people: A study of prevalence and risk factors. *Social Psychiatry and Psychiatric Epidemiology, 35,* 494-499.

van Ommen, G., Bakker, E., & Dunnen, J. D. (1999). The human genome project and the future of diagnostics, treatment, and prevention. *Lancet, 354*(Suppl 1), 5-10.

Vandenbergh, D., Bennett, C., Grant, M., Strasser, A., O'Connor, R., Stauffer, R., et al. (in press). Smoking status and the human dopamine transporter variable number of tandem repeats (VNTR) polymorphism: Failure to replicate and finding that never-smokers may be different. *Nicotine and Tobacco Research.*

Vandenbergh, D., Rodriguez, L., Miller, I., Uhl, G., & Lachman, H. (1997). High activity catechol-o-methyltransferuse allele is more prevalent in polysubstance. American *Journal of Medical Genetics (Neuropsychiatric Genetics), 74,* 439-442.

Vandenbergh, D., Zonderman, A., Wang, J., Uhl, G., & Costa, P. (1997). No association between novelty seeking and dopamine D4 receptor (D4DR) exon III seven repeat alleles in Baltimore Longitudinal Study of Aging participants. *Molecular Psychiatry, 2,* 417-419.

Vega, W., Gil, A. G., Warheit, G. J., Apospori, E., & Zimmerman, R. (1993). The relationship of drug use to suicide ideation and attempts among African American, Hispanic, and white non-Hispanic male adolescents. *Suicide and Life-Threatening Behavior, 23,* 110-119.

Velez, C. N., & Cohen, P. (1988). Suicidal behavior and ideation in a community sample of children: Maternal and youth reports. *Journal of the American Academy of Child and Adolescent Psychiatry, 27,* 349-356.

Ventura, S. J., & Bachrach, C. A. (2000). Nonmarital childbearing in the United States, 1940-1999. In *National vital statistics reports* (Vol. 48, No. 16). Hyattsville, MD: National Center for Health Services.

Ventura, S. J., Mathews, T. J., & Hamilton, B. E. (2001). Births to teenagers in the United States, 1940-2000. In *National vital statistics reports* (Vol. 49, No. 10). Hyattsville, MD: National Center for Health Services.

Ventura, S. J., Mosher, W. D., Curtin, S. C., Abma, J. C., & Henshaw, S. (2001). Trends in pregnancy rates for the United States, 1976-97: An update. In *National vital statistics reports* (Vol. 49, No. 4). Hyattsville, MD: National Center for Health Statistics.

Veroff, J., Douvan, E., & Kulka, R. (1981). *The inner-American: A self-portrait from 1957–1976.* New York: Basic Books.

Viken, R., Rose, R., Kaprio, J., & Koskenvuo, M. (1994). A developmental genetic analysis of adult personality: Extraversion and neuroticism from 18 to 59 years of age. *Journal of Personality and Social Psychology, 66*(4), 722-730.

Vincent, M. A. L., Clearie, A. F., & Schluchter, M. D. (1987). Reducing adolescent pregnancy through school and community based education. *JAMA, 257,* 3382-3386.

Viscusi, W. K. (1992). *Smoking: Making the risky decision.* New York: Oxford University Press.

Viscusi, W. K. (2002). *Smoke-filled rooms: A postmortem on the tobacco deal.* Chicago: University of Chicago Press.

Vitaro, F., Brendgen. M., Ladouceur, R., & Tremblay, R. E. (2001). Gambling, delinquency, and drug use during adolescence: Mutual influences and common risk factors. *Journal of Gambling Studies, 17,* 171-190.

Vitaro, F., Ferland, F., Jacques, C., & Ladouceur, R. (1998). Gambling, substance use, and impulsivity during adolescence. *Psychology of Addictive Behaviors, 12*(3), 185-194.

Viva Consulting. (2001). *Teen gamble a sure bet.* Retrieved July 26, 2002, from www.vivaconsulting.com/advocacy/adolescents1.html

Volberg, R. A. (1994). The prevalence and demographics of pathological gamblers: Implications for public health. *American Journal of Public Health, 84*(2), 237-241.

Volberg, R. A. (2001). *Changes in gambling and problem gambling in Oregon, 1997 to 2000.* Salem: Oregon Gambling Addiction Treatment Foundation. Retrieved December 16, 2002, from www.gamblingaddiction.org/oregonreport/frame.htm

Volberg, R. A. (2002a). *Gambling and problem gambling among adolescents in Nevada.* Carson City, NV: Department of Human Resources. Retrieved December 16, 2002, from http://hr.state.nv.us/directors/GamblingAmongAdolescents_Nevada.pdf

Volberg, R. A. (2002b). *Gambling and problem gambling in Nevada.* Carson City, NV: Department of Human Resources. Retrieved December 18, 2002, from http://hr.state.nv. us/directors/NV_Adult_Report_final.pdf

Volberg, R. A., & Steadman, H. J. (1988). Refining prevalence estimates of pathological gambling. *American Journal of Psychiatry, 145,* 502-505.

Volberg, R. A., & Moore, W. L. (1999). *Gambling and problem gambling among Washington state adolescents: A replication study, 1993 to 1999.* Olympia, WA: Washington State Lottery. Retrieved December 18, 2002, from www.wscpg.org/hpdfs/ 99AdolescentReport.pdf

Waddington, C. H. (1957). *The strategy of genes.* London: Allen & Unwin.

Wagenaar, A. C., & Toomey, T. L. (2000). *Effects of minimum drinking age laws: Review and analyses of the literature.* Paper prepared for Advisory Council Subcommittee, Rockville, MD.

Wagner, F. A., & Anthony, J. C. (2002). From first drug use to drug dependence: Developmental periods of risk for dependence upon marijuana, cocaine, and alcohol. *Neuropsychopharmacology, 26,* 479-488.

Wahlberg, A. (2001). The theoretical features of some current approaches to risk perception. *Journal of Risk Research, 4*(3), 237-250.

Wakschlag, L. S., Lahey, B. B., Loeber, R., Green, S. M., Gordon, R. A., & Leventhal, B. L. (1997). Maternal smoking during pregnancy and the risk of conduct disorder in boys. *Archives of General Psychiatry, 54*(7), 670-676.

Walker, G., & Vilella-Velez, F. (1992). *Anatomy of a demonstration.* Philadelphia, PA: Public/Private Ventures.

Walker, H. M., Colvin, G., & Ramsey, E. (1995). *Antisocial behavior in school: Strategies and best practices.* Pacific Grove, CA: Brooks/Cole.

Walker, H. M., Horner, R., Sugai, G., Bullis, M., Sprague, J., Bricker, D., et al. (1996). Integrated approaches to preventing antisocial behavior patterns among school age children and youth. *Journal of Emotional and Behavioral Disorders, 4,* 193-256.

Walker, H. M., Kavanah, K., Stiller, B., Golly, A., Severson H. H., & Feil E. G. (1998). First step to success: An early intervention approach for preventing school antisocial behavior. *Journal of Emotional and Behavioral Disorders, 6*(2), 66-80.

Walker, H. M., & McConnell, S. R. (1995). *Walker-McConnell scale of social competence and school adjustment.* San Diego, CA: Singular.

Walker, H. M., & Severson, H. H. (1990). *Systematic screening for behavior disorders: User's guide and administration manual.* Longmont, CO: Sopris West.

Walker, H. M., Severson, H. H., & Feil, E. (1995). *The early screening project: A proven child-find process.* Longmont, CO: Sopris West.

Walker, H. M., Severson, H. H., Stiller, B., Williams, G. J., Haring, N., Shinn, M., et al. (1988). Systematic screening of pupils in the elementary age range at risk for behavior disorders: Development and trial testing of a multiple gating model. *RASE: Remedial and Special Education, 9*(3), 8-20.

Wallace, J. D., Calhoun, A. D., Powell, K. E., O'Neil, J., & James, S. P. (1996). *Homicide and suicide among Native Americans, 1979–1992* (Violence Surveillance Series, No. 2). Atlanta, GA: Centers for Disease Control and Prevention,

Walsh, R. H., Ferrell, M. Z., & Tolone, W. L. (1976). Selection of reference group, perceived reference group permissiveness, and personal permissiveness, attitudes and behavior: A study of two consecutive panels (1967-1971; 1970-1974). *Journal of Marriage and the Family, 38,* 495-507.

Walter, H. J., & Vaughn, R. D. (1993). AIDS risk reduction among a multi-ethnic sample of urban high school students. *JAMA, 270*(6), 725-730.

Walter, H. J., Vaughan, R. D., Armstrong, B., Krakoff, R. Y., Maldonado, L. M., Tiezzi, L., et al. (1995). Sexual, assaultive, and suicidal behaviors among urban minority junior high school students. *Journal of the American Academy of Child and Adolescent Psychiatry, 34,* 73-80.

Warren, W. K., & King, A. J. C. (1994). *Development and evaluation of an AIDS/STD/ sexuality program for grade 9 students*. Kingston, Ontario: Social Program Evaluation Group.

Washington, A. E., Johnson, R. E., & Sanders, L. L. (1987). Chlamydia trachomatis infections in the United States: What are they costing us? *JAMA, 257*, 2070-2072.

Wasserman, I. M. (1984). Imitation and suicide: A reexamination of the Werther effect. *American Sociological Review, 49*, 427-436.

Weber, E., & Hsee, C. (2000). Culture and individual judgment and decision making. *Applied Psychology: An International Review, 49*(1), 32-61.

Webster, D. W., Wilson, M. E. H., Duggan, A. K., & Pakula, L. C. (1992). Parents' beliefs about preventing gun injuries to children. *Pediatrics, 89*(5), 908-914.

Wechsler, D. (1972). *Wechsler Intelligence Scale for Children—Revised*. New York: The Psychological Corporation.

Weed, S. E., & Olsen, J. A. (1986). Effects of family planning programs for teenage pregnancy replication and extension. *Family Perspectives, 20*(3), 173-195.

Weinberg, N. Z., Rahdert, E., Colliver, J. D., & Glantz, M. D. (1998). Adolescent substance abuse: A review of the past 10 years. *Journal of the American Academy of Child and Adolescent Psychiatry, 37*(3), 252-261.

Weinstein, N. D. (1980). Unrealistic optimism about future life events. *Journal of Personality and Social Psychology, 39*, 806-820.

Weinstein, N. D. (1987). Unrealistic optimism about susceptibility to health problems: Conclusions from a community-wide sample. *Journal of Behavioral Medicine, 10*, 481-500.

Weinstein, N. D. (1988). The precaution adoption process. *Health Psychology, 7*, 355-386.

Weinstein, N. D. (1993). Testing four competing theories of health protective behavior. *Health Psychology, 12*, 324-333.

Weinstein, N. D., & Nicolich M. (1993). Correct and incorrect interpretations of correlations between risk perceptions and risk behaviors. *Health Psychology, 12*(3), 235-245.

Weinstein, N. D., & Slovic, P. (2001). Unpublished data.

Weisman, C. S., Plichta, S., Nathanson, C. A., Ensminger, M., & Robinson, J. C. (1991). Consistency of condom use for disease prevention among adolescent users of oral contraceptives. *Family Planning Perspectives, 23*(2), 71-74.

Weissberg, R. P., Barton, H. A., & Shriver, T. P. (1997). The social-competence promotion program for young adolescents. In G. W. Albee & T. P. Gullotta (Eds.), *Primary prevention works: Issues in children's and families' lives* (pp. 268-290). Thousand Oaks, CA: Sage.

Weissman, M. M., Fendrich, M., Warner, V., & Wickramaratne, P. (1992). Incidence of psychiatric disorder in offspring at high and low risk for depression. *Journal of the American Academy of Child and Adolescent Psychiatry, 31*, 640-648.

Weissman, M. M., Wolk, S., Goldstein, R., Moreau, D., Adams, P., Greenwald, S., et al. (1999). Depressed adolescents grow up. *JAMA, 281*, 1707-1713.

Welch, H. G., & Burke, W. (1998). Uncertainties in genetic testing for chronic disease. *JAMA, 280*(17), 1525-1527.

Welte, J., Barnes, G., Wieczorek, W., Tidwell, M-C., & Parker, J. (2001). Alcohol and gambling pathology among U.S. adults: Prevalence, demographic patterns and comorbidity. *Journal of Studies on Alcohol, 62*, 706-712.

Werner, E. E. (1986). Resilient offspring of alcoholics: A longitudinal study from birth to age 18. *Journal of Studies on Alcohol, 47*, 34-40.

Werner, E. E., & Smith, R. S. (1982). *Vulnerable but invincible: A study of resilient children*. New York: McGraw-Hill.

Wertz, D. C., Fanos, J. H., & Reilly, P. (1994). Genetic testing for children and adolescents: Who decides? *JAMA, 272*(11), 875-881.

Westrom, L. (1980). Incidence, prevalence, and trends of acute pelvic inflammatory disease and its consequences in industrialized countries. *American Journal of Obstetrics & Gynecology, 238*, 882.

Wexler, N. S. (1980). *Will the circle be broken? Sterilizing the genetically impaired.* New York: Plenum Press.

Whalen, C. K., Henker, B., O'Neil, R., Hollingshead, J., Holman, A., & Moore, B. (1994). Optimism in children's judgments of health and environmental risks. *Health Psychology, 13,* 319-325.

Whitaker, D. J., Miller, K. S., May, D. C., & Levin, M. L (1999). Teenage partner's communication about sexual risk and condom use: The importance of parent-teenager discussion. *Family Planning Perspectives, 31,* 117-121.

Whitfield, J. B., Nightingale, B. N., Bucholz, K. K., Madden, P. A., Heath, A. C., & Martin, N. G. (1998). ADH genotypes and alcohol use and dependence in Europeans. *Alcoholism, Clinical and Experimental Research, 22*(7), 1463-1469.

Wills, T. A., Gibbons, F. X., Gerrard, M., & Brody, G. H. (2000). Test of a model of factors relevant for early onset of substance use among African-American children. *Health Psychology, 19,* 253-263.

Wilson, J. F., Weale, M. E., Smith, A. C., Gratrix, F., Fletcher, B., Thomas, M. G., et al. (2001). Population genetic structure of variable drug response. *Nature Genetics, 29,* 265-269.

Wilson, W. J. (1996). *When work disappears: The new world of the urban poor.* New York: Knopf.

Windle, M., & Davies, P. T. (1999). Depression and heavy alcohol use among adolescents: Concurrent and prospective relations. *Development and Psychopathology, 11,* 823-844.

Windle, M., Miller-Tutzauer, C., & Domenico, D. (1992). Alcohol use, suicidal behavior, and risky activities among adolescents. *Journal of Research on Adolescence, 2,* 317-330.

Windle, M., & Windle, R. C. (1999). Adolescent tobacco, alcohol, and drug use: Current findings. *Adolescent Medicine, 10*(1), 153-163, vii.

Wingood, G. M., DiClemente, R. J., Crosby, R. A., Harrington, K., Davies, S. L., & Hook, E. W. (2002). Gang involvement and the health of African-American female adolescents. *Pediatrics, 110,* 1-5.

Wingood, G. M., DiClemente, R. J., Harrington, K., Davies, S., Hook, E. W. III, & Oh, M. K. (2001). Exposure to X-rated movies and adolescents' sexual and contraceptive-related attitudes and behaviors. *Pediatrics, 107*(5), 1116-1119.

Wingood, G. M., DiClemente, R. J., McCree, D. H., Harrington, K., & Davies, S. L. (2001). Dating violence and the sexual health of black adolescent females. *Pediatrics, 107*(5), E72.

Winkielman, P., Zajonc, R. B., & Schwarz, N. (1997). Subliminal affective priming resists attributional interventions. *Cognition and Emotion, 11*(4), 433-465.

Winter, L., & Breckenmaker, L. C. (1991). Tailoring family planning services to the special needs of adolescents. *Family Planning Perspectives, 23*(1), 24-30.

Winters, K. C., & Anderson, N. (2000). Gambling involvement and drug use among adolescents. *Journal of Gambling Studies, 16*(2-3), 175-198.

Winters, K. C., Stinchfield, R. D., & Fulkerson, J. (1993a). Patterns and characteristics of adolescent gambling. *Journal of Gambling Studies, 9,* 371-386.

Winters, K. C., Stinchfield, R. D., & Fulkerson, J. (1993b). Toward the development of an adolescent gambling problem severity scale. *Journal of Gambling Studies, 9*(1), 63-84.

Wolfgang, M. E. (1959). Suicide by mean of victims-precipitated homicide. *Journal of Clinical and Experimental Psychopathology, 20,* 335-349.

Wood, A., Trainor, G., Rothwell, J., Moore, A., & Harrington, R. (2001). Randomized trial of a group therapy for repeated deliberate self-harm in adolescents. *Journal of the American Academy of Child and Adolescent Psychiatry, 40,* 1246-1253.

Wood, R. T. A., & Griffths, M. D. (1998). The acquisition, development and maintenance of lottery and scratchcard gambling in adolescence. *Journal of Adolescence, 21,* 265-272.

Wood, R. T. A., Griffiths, M. D., Derevensky, J. L., & Gupta, R. (2002). Adolescent accounts of the UK national lottery and scratchcards: An analysis using Q-sorts. *Journal of Gambling Studies, 18,* 161-184.

Woods, E. R., Lin, Y. G., Middleman, A., Beckford, P., Chase, L., & DuRant, R. H. (1997). The association of suicide attempts in adolescents. *Pediatrics, 99,* 791-796.

World Health Organization. (2001). *Suicide rates and absolute numbers of suicide by country.* Retrieved December 8, 2002, from www5.who.int/mental_health/main.cfm?p=0000000021

Wu, Y., Stanton, B., Galbraith, J., Kaljee, L., Cottrell, L., Li, X., Harris, C. V., D'Alessandri, D., & Burns, J. M. (2002). Sustaining and broadening intervention impact: A randomized controlled trial of three adolescent risk reduction intervention approaches. *Pediatrics, 111,* e32-e38.

Wunderlich, U., Bronisch, T., & Wittchen, H. U. (1998). Comorbidity patterns in adolescents and young adults with suicide attempts. *European Archives of Psychiatry and Clinical Neuroscience, 248,* 87-95.

Wynne, H., Smith, G., & Jacobs, D. F. (1996). *Adolescent gambling and problem gambling in Alberta.* Edmonton, Alberta: Alberta Drug and Alcohol Commission.

Yamaguchi, K., & Kandel, D. B. (1984). Patterns of drug use from adolescence to young adulthood: II. Sequences of progression. *American Journal of Public Health, 74,* 673-681.

Yanovitzky, I. (2002). Effect of news coverage on the prevalence of drunk-driving behavior: Evidence from a longitudinal study. *Journal of Studies on Alcohol, 63,* 342-351.

Yeoman, T., & Griffiths, M. D. (1996). Adolescent machine gambling and crime. *Journal of Adolescence, 19,* 183-188.

YMCA of the USA. (2001). *After school for America's teens: A national survey of teen attitudes and behaviors in the hours after school.* Retrieved December 8, 2002, from www.ymca.net/presrm/news/2001/unsupervisedteensinschool.htm

Yoon, P. W., Chen, B., Faucett, A., Clyne, M., Gwinn, M., Lubin, I. M., et al. (2001). Public health impact of genetic tests at the end of the 20th century. *Genetics in Medicine, 3*(6), 405-410.

Yoshikawa, H. (1994). Prevention as cumulative protection: Effects of early family support and education on chronic delinquency and its risks. *Psychological Bulletin, 115,* 28-54.

Yoshikawa, H. (1995). Long-term effects of early childhood programs on social outcomes and delinquency. *The Future of Children, 5*(3), 51-75.

Yzer, M., Cappella, J. N., Fishbein, M., Hornik, R., & Ahern, R. K. (in press). How effective is the message that marijuana is a gateway to hard drugs in anti-marijuana campaigns? *Journal of Health Communication.*

Zabin, L. S., Hirsch, M. B., Smith, E. A., Streett, R., & Hardy, J. B. (1986). Evaluation of a pregnancy prevention program for urban teenagers. *Family Planning Perspectives, 18*(3), 119-126.

Zabin, L. S., Stark, H. A., & Emerson, M. R. (1991). Reasons for delay in contraceptive clinic utilization: Adolescent clinic and non-clinic populations compared. *Journal of Adolescent Health, 12*(3), 225-232.

Zaider, T. I., Johnson, J. G., & Cockell, S. J. (2002). Psychiatric disorders associated with the onset and persistence of bulimia nervosa and binge eating disorder during adolescence. *Journal of Youth & Adolescence, 31,* 319-329.

Zajonc, R. B. (1980). Feeling and thinking: Preferences need no inferences. *American Psychologist, 35,* 151-175.

Zeelenberg, M., van Dijk, W. W., Manstead, A. S. R., & van der Pligt, J. (2000). On bad decisions and disconfirmed expectancies: The psychology of regret and disappointment. *Cognition and Emotion, 14,* 521-541.

Zeldin, S. (1995). *Opportunities and supports for youth development: Lessons from research implications for community leaders and scholars.* Washington, DC: Academy for Educational Development, Center for Youth Development and Policy Research.

Zellman, G. L., & Waterman, J. M. (1998). Understanding the impact of parent school involvement on children's educational outcomes. *Journal of Educational Research, 91*(6), 370-380.

Zhang, J., & Jin, S. (1996). Determinants of suicide ideation: A comparison of Chinese and American college students. *Adolescence, 31,* 451-467.

Zillman, D., & Brosius, H. (2000). *Exemplification in communication: The influence of case reports on the perception of issues.* Mahwah, NJ: Lawrence Erlbaum.

Zimmerman, M. A., Meeland, T., & Krug, S. E. (1985). Measurement and structure of pathological gambling behavior. *Journal of Personality Assessment, 49*(1), 76-81.

Zimmerman, R., & Donohew, L. (1996, November). *Sensation seeking, impulsive decision-making, and adolescent sexual behaviors.* Paper presented at the American Public Health Association, New York.

Zimring, F. (1998). *American youth violence.* New York: Oxford University Press.

Zins, J. E., Elias, M. J., Greenberg, M. T., & Weissberg, R. P. (2000). Promoting social and emotional competence in children. In K. Minke & G. Bear (Eds.), *Preventing school problems—promoting school success: Strategies and programs that work* (pp. 71-99). Bethesda, MD: National Association of School Psychologists.

Zucker, R. A., Fitzgerald, H. E., & Moses, H. D. (1995). Emergence of alcohol problems and the several alcoholisms: A developmental perspective on etiologic theory and life course trajectory. In D. Cicchetti & D. J. Cohen (Eds.), *Developmental psychopathology* (Vol. 2, pp. 677-711). New York: John Wiley.

Zuckerman, M. (1979). *Sensation seeking: Beyond the optimal level of arousal.* Hillsdale, NJ: Lawrence Erlbaum.

Zuckerman, M. (1988). Behavior and biology: Research on sensation seeking and reactions to the media. In L. Donohew, H. E. Sypher, & E. T. Higgins (Eds.), *Communication, social cognition, and affect* (pp. 173-194). Hillsdale, NJ: Lawrence Erlbaum.

Zuckerman, M. (1991). *The psychobiology of personality.* New York: Cambridge University Press.

Zuckerman, M. (1993). Impulsive unsocialized sensation seeking: The biological foundations of a basic dimension of personality. In J. Bates & T. Wachs (Eds.), *Temperament: Individual differences at the interface of biology and behavior* (pp. 219-225). Washington, DC: American Psychological Association.

Zuckerman, M. (1994). *Behavioral expressions and biosocial bases of sensation seeking.* New York: Cambridge University Press.

Zuckerman, M., & Kuhlman, D. M. (2000). Personality and risk-taking: Common biosocial factors. *Journal of Personality, 68,* 999-1029.

Zuckerman, M., Kuhlman, D. M., Joireman, J., Teta, P., & Kraft, M. (1993). A comparison of three structural models for personality: The big three, the big five and the alternative five. *Journal of Personality and Social Psychology, 65,* 757-768.

Zuckerman, M., Neary, R. S., & Brustman, B. A. (1970). Sensation-seeking scale correlates in experience (smoking, drugs, alcohol, "hallucinations" and sex) and preference for complexity (designs). *Proceedings of the 78th Annual Convention of the American Psychological Association.* Washington, DC: American Psychological Association.

Name Index

Baaker, A. B., 195
Bachman, J. G., 14, 58, 62, 63, 64, 67, 68, 71, 72, 93, 132, 149, 150, 161, 204, 205, 207, 208, 209, 348
Bachrach, C. A., 292(n1)
Baer, J. S., 246
Baer, S. A., 165, 167, 168
Bailey, S. L., 336, 372
Baizerman, M. L., 298
Baker, E., 129
Bakker, E., 161
Balach, L., 309, 311, 312, 313, 314, 322, 324
Balassone, M. L., 273
Balding, J., 225, 226, 227
Baldo, M., 273
Baldree, B. F., 316
Baldwin, C. L., 305
Ball, S., 158, 168
Bandura, A, 36, 55, 211, 270, 350
Bangert-Drowns, R. L., 94
Banspach, S. W., 272, 273, 274, 276
Banton, J. G., 330
Bar, J. L., 156
Bardo, M., 151, 158, 160, 169(n1)
Barmada, C., 206
Barnes, G., 250, 335
Barnoski, R., 129, 130
Barr, D. J., 114
Barr, G., 246(n1)
Barraclough, B. M., 305, 316
Barrish, H. H., 128
Barter, J. T., 326
Barth, R., 272, 273, 274
Bartle, S., 322
Barton, H. A., 97, 107
Basen-Enquist, K. M., 272, 273, 274, 306, 319
Basil, M., 309
Bastien, M. F., 312, 313
Bates, C., 45, 161
Battistich, V., 245, 349, 353
Battle, R., 272
Baugher, M., 303, 307, 309, 312, 313, 318, 321, 322, 324
Bauman, K. E., 195, 371
Baume, P. J., 318
Baumrind, D., 198
Bayer, L., 197
Bearman, P., 287, 371
Beautrais, A. L., 309, 310, 312, 313, 315, 321, 322
Beauvais, F., 350
Bechhofer, L., 272, 273, 276
Beck, A. T., 174, 175, 177
Becker, C., 308
Becker, D., 129
Becker, M. H., 49, 52, 211, 270
Beckford, P., 319
Bee-Gates, D. J., 198
Beecham, J., 174
Begg, D., 165, 166

Begley, E., 370
Belin, T., 153, 158, 162
Belk, R., 107
Bell, C. C., 325, 326
Bell, R., 211
Bellringer, P., 231
Bem, D. J., 140
Benard, B., 243
Benjamin, J., 158, 169(n1)
Bennett, C., 154
Bennett, K. J., 134
Benowitz, N., 189
Benowitz, N. E., 45
Benowitz, N. L., 154
Benson, P., 357
Benthin, A. C., 19, 25, 41
Bentler, P. M., 93, 133
Berbaum, M., 290
Berchick, R. J., 177
Bergen, A. W., 154
Berglund, P. A., 173, 359, 361, 363
Bergman, A., 163
Bergner, L., 316
Berkowitz, M. W., 352
Berman, A.L., 307, 316, 318
Bernhard, B. J., 239
Bernhardt, B., 163, 164
Berrebbi, D. S., 179, 180
Berrettini, W., 152, 157
Berry, D. C., 16
Best, D., 335
Beyers, W., 28
Beyth-Marom, R., 16, 25, 26, 36, 41, 100, 104
Biblarz, A., 316
Biblarz, D. N., 316
Bierut, L., 153
Biesecker, B., 163
Biesecker, B. B., 162
Biggar, R. J., 367
Biglan, A., 14, 125, 127, 129, 130, 131, 133, 369
Billy, J. O. G., 190, 195, 270, 275
Bimbi, D., 41
Bird, H. R., 319
Birmaher, B., 172, 173, 303, 322, 323, 324
Bjorklund, D. F., 27
Black, C., 130
Black, G. S., 197
Black, M., 195, 196
Black, M. M., 196, 369
Black, N. A., 318
Blackson, T., 143
Blaine, D., 169(n1)
Blake, S. M., 272, 273, 276
Blanco, C., 308
Blangero, J., 154
Blanton, H., 76, 77, 81
Blasi, A., 27
Blaze-Temple, D., 335
Blazer, D. G., 314

Whalen, C. K., 25, 27
Wheatley, K., 107
Whitaker, D., 368, 369, 370
White, C. M., 228, 241, 242
White, K., 108
Whitehouse, W. G., 175, 176, 177, 178, 179, 180, 181
Whitfield, J. B., 156
Whitmore, C., 125
Whittinghill, J. R., 303, 311
Whittinghill, R., 308
Whittington, W., 367
Wibblesman, C. J., 370
Wichstrom, L., 303, 308
Wickramaratne, P., 312, 317
Wieczorek, W., 250
Wier, M., 272
Wiersema, B., 318
Wiest, W., 276
Wilbur, J., 211
Wilcove, G., 87, 90
Wilcox, P., 163
Wilfond, B., 163
Wilfong, E., 41
Wilkinson, R. H., Jr., 305
Williams, B., 303, 305, 306, 307
Williams, B. I., 93, 266
Williams, C. L., 130
Williams, D. R., 327
Williams, E. L., 277
Williams, G. J., 134
Williams, R. L., 272, 273
Williamson, D., 173
Williamson, D. E., 172
Williamson, D. F., 314
Wills, T. A., 78, 81
Wilson, A., 158
Wilson, G. T., 106
Wilson, J. F., 163
Wilson, K., 294
Wilson, M. E. H., 324
Wilson, S. J., 352
Wilson, W. J., 326
Windle, M., 149, 173, 303, 304, 309, 319
Windle, R. C., 149
Windsor, R., 272, 273, 276
Wingood, G. M., 366, 369, 370, 371, 372
Winkielman, P., 47
Winkler, K., 371
Winter, L., 276
Winter, M., 130
Winters, K., 224, 225, 228, 229, 240, 241, 242, 243, 256, 257, 258
Winters, K. C., 139, 145(n1)
Wipprecht, G., 155
Wirt, R., 125, 133, 369
Wissow, L., 164
Witt, J., 133
Wittchen, H., 171

Wittchen, H. U., 304, 309, 312, 315
Wittner, D. S., 127
Wolf, M. M., 128
Wolf, R., 310
Wolfgang, M. E., 328
Wolfson, M., 130
Wolk, S., 171, 173, 174
Wood, A., 323
Wood, J. V., 40
Wood, R. T. A., 224, 225, 226, 232, 240, 241, 251, 252
Wood, R. W., 277, 278
Woods, E. R., 319
Woodward, K. M., 272, 273
Woodward, P. J., 318
Woolard, J., 18
Wormley, B., 154
Worster, G., 173, 174
Wu, H., 270
Wu, R., 253
Wu, S., 153, 157
Wu, Y., 197, 199
Wulfsberg, E. A., 164
Wunderlich, U., 304, 309, 312, 315
Wynne, H., 249

Xian, H., 156
Xiaohe, X., 369
Xu, J., 155
Xu, Y., 157

Yaffee, R. A., 231
Yamaguchi, K., 58, 335, 336
Yanez, C., 25
Yang, F., 153
Yanovitzky, L., 253
Yoeman, T., 224, 227
Yohalem, N., 356, 357
Yoon, P. W., 162
Yoshikawa, H., 127, 134
Yoshino, A., 155
Youm, Y., 299
Young, D., 303, 313, 318
Yu, S., 87
Yzer, M., 210, 211, 212, 217, 219
Yzer, M. C., 195

Zabin, L. S., 79, 277, 287
Zaider, T. I., 172
Zajonc, R. B., 45, 47
Zanna, M. P., 108, 110
Zeelenberg, M., 42
Zeena, T., 254
Zeldin, S., 357
Zelenak, J. P., 303, 307, 308, 311, 312, 318
Zellman, G. L., 272, 349
Zezza, N., 155
Zhang, J., 317
Zhang, X., 153, 158, 162

Subject Index

About the Editor

Daniel Romer is the Research Director of the Adolescent Risk Communication Institute at the Annenberg Public Policy Center, University of Pennsylvania. He directs research on adolescent risk perception and behavior with particular emphasis on the effects of the media and other social influences.

About the Contributors

Lyn Abramson is Professor of Psychology, University of Wisconsin—Madison. Her study, "The Cognitive Vulnerability to Depression (CVD) Project," is considered a landmark study on how people's thinking patterns—their cognitive styles—contribute to their risk of becoming depressed. Funded by an $11 million National Institute of Mental Health (NIMH) grant, the study followed college freshmen for 5 years at both Temple University and the University of Wisconsin. A second NIMH-funded project extended this investigation to the study of bipolar disorder in young people. Professors Abramson and Alloy have published over 100 articles in the psychopathology and social psychology literature. Dr. Abramson recently was presented the University of Wisconsin's Kellett mid-career award for her research accomplishments. Professors Abramson and Alloy recently presented an American Psychological Association (APA) joint master lecture on cognitive vulnerability to depression and jointly won the 2002 APA Division 12 Distinguished Scientific Contribution Award.

Lauren Alloy is Professor of Psychology, Temple University. Her study, "The Cognitive Vulnerability to Depression (CVD) Project," is considered a landmark study on how people's thinking patterns—their cognitive styles—contribute to their risk of becoming depressed. Funded by an $11 million National Institute of Mental Health (NIMH) grant, the study followed college freshmen for 5 years at both Temple University and the University of Wisconsin. A second NIMH-funded project extended this investigation to the study of bipolar disorder in young people. Professors Alloy and Abramson have published over 100 articles in the psychopathology and social psychology literature. Alloy recently was presented Temple University's Paul W. Eberman Faculty Research Award for her achievements in research. Professors Alloy and Abramson recently presented an American Psychological Association (APA) joint master lecture on cognitive vulnerability to depression and jointly won the 2002 APA Division 12 Distinguished Scientific Contribution Award.

Judy A. Andrews is a Research Scientist at the Oregon Research Institute, where her NIH grants focus on the etiology of substance use from early childhood through young adulthood and the evaluation of tobacco cessation programs, including both smoking and smokeless tobacco cessation. She is an author on over 50 articles in professional journals. She is currently the principal investigator of a

National Institute of Drug Abuse funded study to identify etiological factors and processes predictive of children's attitudes toward and use of substances, including cigarettes, smokeless tobacco, alcohol, marijuana, and inhalants.

Gerald August is Professor of Psychiatry in the Division of Child and Adolescent Psychiatry at the University of Minnesota. He is Clinical Director of the Clinic for Attention-Deficit and Learning Disorders at the Fairview University Medical Center. He specializes in the area of disruptive behavioral disorders, including drug abuse, attention-deficit/hyperactivity (ADHD) and conduct disorder and has published a number of studies over the past 15 years addressing issues of diagnosis and classification, comorbidity, epidemiology, natural history, and treatment. In recent years, he has expanded his scientific inquiry to include the prevention of drug abuse and antisocial behavior, where early childhood behavioral problems, such as ADHD and aggressiveness, are conceptualized as potential risk factors. He recently completed an NIMH-funded, longitudinal-experimental research study that focused on developmental pathways of ADHD and is currently funded to examine the efficacy of the Early Risers Drug Abuse and Violence Prevention Program among high-risk children living in rural and urban communities.

Anthony Biglan is Senior Scientist at the Oregon Research Institute, Eugene, Oregon. He has been conducting research on the development and prevention of child and adolescent problem behavior for the past 23 years. His work has included studies of the risk and protective factors associated with tobacco, alcohol, and other drug use; high-risk sexual behavior; and antisocial behavior. Recently, he led a team of scholars in a review of current research into the development and prevention of youth problem behaviors. A book summarizing the evidence and defining next steps for research and practice is forthcoming.

David Brent is Professor of Psychiatry and Division Chief, Child and Adolescent Psychiatry, Department of Psychiatry, University of Pittsburgh, and Director, Center to Improve Treatments in Youth (CITY). He has extensive experience as an investigator and clinician in the area of adolescent depression and suicidal behavior. He has been continuously funded by NIMH since 1985 and is now leading projects on the treatment of resistant depression in adolescents, the treatment of depressed adolescent suicide attempts, and familial and genetic aspects of early-onset suicidal behavior.

Jeanne Brooks-Gunn is Virginia and Leonard Marx Professor of Child Development and Education, Teachers College, Columbia University. As a developmental psychologist, she serves as consultant to and trainer of in-house researchers, faculty, and students in areas of child development. She provides expertise for writing grant proposals and is expanding her role as a coprincipal investigator on several projects involving early childhood. She is also involved in projects such as Early Head Start National Evaluation Research Project and the Girls Health and Development Project. She is a member of the National Advisory Committee of the Institute for Research on Poverty, an Advisory Board Member of Substance Abuse and Sex of the National Center on Addiction and Substance

Abuse, and a Senior Faculty Affiliate of the Joint Center on Poverty Research, Northwestern University/University of Chicago.

James Burns is Associate Professor of Pediatrics in the Section of Adolescent Medicine at West Virginia University. He is board certified in both pediatrics and adolescent medicine and is currently the program director of the WVU Adolescent Medicine fellowship and director of the Ambulatory Pediatrics Division. He has practiced clinical adolescent medicine for the past 16 years and has lectured extensively on topics pertaining to common adolescent problems. One of his special interests is the effect of parenting style on adolescent behaviors, including substance abuse, tobacco, academic performance, and conduct disorder.

James P. Byrnes is Professor in the Department of Human Development at the University of Maryland. He has authored numerous books and articles on decision making and cognitive development, including *Minds, Brains, and Education: Understanding the Psychological and Educational Relevance of Neuroscientific Research* (2001) and *The Nature and Development of Decision-Making: A Self-Regulation Model* (1998). In 1996, he was nominated for the National Council for the Social Studies' Exemplary Research in Social Studies Award, and in 2001 he was named a Fellow of Division 15 of the American Psychological Association.

Joseph N. Cappella is Professor of Communication and Gerald R. Miller Chair at the Annenberg School for Communication, University of Pennsylvania. His research has resulted in 75 articles and book chapters and three coauthored books. The research has focused on political communication, health, social interaction, nonverbal behavior, media effects, and statistical methods. The articles have appeared in journals in psychology, communication, health, and politics. He has edited special issues of *Journal of Language and Social Psychology* and *Journal of Communication*. His research has been supported by grants from the National Institutes of Mental Health, the National Institute on Drug Abuse, The Twentieth Century Fund, and from the following foundations: Markle, Ford, Carnegie, Pew, and Robert Wood Johnson. He is a Fellow of the International Communication Association and its past president, and recipient of the B. Aubrey Fisher Mentorship Award.

Christine Cody has worked with Anthony Biglan and his associates at Oregon Research Institute (ORI) in Eugene, Oregon, since 1994. She has a background in mass communications and writing. At ORI, she works in the areas of tobacco use cessation and the prevention of adolescent substance use and other problem behaviors. She is the assistant editor of the newsletter for the Society for Research on Nicotine and Tobacco. She has coauthored chapters and edited several manuscripts with Dr. Biglan. She is currently completing an English degree at the University of Oregon, where she will pursue graduate studies in literature and the environment.

Richard Crosby is Assistant Professor in the Department of Behavioral Sciences and Health Education in the Rollins School of Public Health at Emory University. His research interests are focused on HIV/STD prevention among adolescent and young adult populations. Currently affiliated with the Emory Center for AIDS Research, he has published numerous articles that report empirical findings relevant to sexual risk behaviors of adolescents and adults. He received his BA (1981) from the University of Kentucky and his MA (1984) from Central Michigan University. His PhD (1998), from Indiana University, is in health behavior.

Anne-Elyse Deguire currently heads the prevention initiatives at the International Centre for Youth Gambling Problems and High-Risk Behaviors at McGill University after having obtained her master's degree in psycho-education at the Université de Montreal. She has been involved in multiple prevention efforts with both elementary and secondary school students. She remains actively involved in the development, training, implementation, and evaluation of the Centre's prevention initiatives and has presented her work at national and international conferences.

Barbara Delaney is Executive Vice President and Director of Research, Partnership for a Drug-Free America. She joined the Partnership in September 1994 and directs the organization's consumer research programs. She supervises a group in conducting strategic research, understanding trends in drug attitudes and behavior, and ascertaining the impact of media on the drug issue. Previously, she was responsible for research and strategic programs at major advertising agencies. Most recently, she was a Senior Vice President and Strategic Planning Director at J. Walter Thompson.

Jeffrey Derevensky is Professor of School/Applied Child Psychology, Department of Educational and Counseling Psychology, McGill University; Associate Professor, Department of Psychiatry, McGill University; Associate Professor, Department of Community Dentistry, McGill University; Visiting Fellow, Department of Psychology, Institute for Advanced Study, Indiana University; Director, Social Psychology Program, Department of Psychology, University of Houston; Distinguished University Professor, Psychology Department, University of Houston; and Director, Social Psychology/Behavioral Medicine Research Group, University of Houston. He is a child psychologist who has published widely, is on the editorial board of the *Journal of Gambling Studies,* and is associate editor of the *Canadian Journal of School Psychology.* He is a member of the National Centre for Gambling Studies, University of Alberta; National Network on Gambling Issues and Research, Canadian Centre on Substance Abuse; Centre d'Excellence, Université Laval; and is an International Associate of the Centre for the Study of the Social Impact of Gambling, University of Plymouth, England.

Laurie Dickson is a PhD student in School/Applied Child Psychology at McGill University. She has been involved in gambling research at the Center for Addiction and Mental Health in Toronto and McGill University's International Centre for Youth Gambling Problems and High-Risk Behaviors. Her interests include the study of resiliency, risk taking, and prevention of adolescent high-risk behaviors and the development and evaluation of science-based prevention programs for children and adolescents.

Ralph J. DiClemente is Charles Howard Candler Professor of Public Health and Associate Director, Emory/Atlanta Center for AIDS Research, Emory University; Professor, School of Medicine, Department of Medicine, Emory University; and Chair, Department of Behavioral Sciences and Health Education, Rollins School of Public Health, Emory University. He is an internationally recognized expert on the development and evaluation of prevention programs tailored to African American adolescents and young adults. He is particularly well versed in designing programs that use peer-based models of implementation and that are culturally and developmentally appropriate. He has published extensively in the area of HIV/STD prevention—particularly among African American adolescents and young adults—and the area of partner violence. He is the author of more than 120 publications, including the *Handbook of Adolescent Health Risk Behaviors,* which received an award from the British Medical Association.

Lewis Donohew is Professor in the Department of Communication at the University of Kentucky. His areas of interest are attention theory construction, communication and decision-making, and public communication campaigns. He and his associates have been studying strategies for reducing drug use and risky sex among adolescents through the development of television-based campaigns and classroom interventions, funded by agencies of the National Institutes of Health. A major focus is on how to design messages for different levels of sensation seeking, a biologically based personality variable associated with needs for novel, complex, ambiguous, and emotionally intense stimuli and a predictor of drug use. His work includes investigation of personality and drug use, design of communication campaigns for abuse prevention, and evaluation research.

Baruch Fischhoff is Professor, Carnegie Mellon University. His research includes risk communication and management, adolescent and health decision making, and environmental protection. He is a member of the Institute of Medicine of the National Academy of Sciences and has served on some two dozen NAS/NRC/IOM committees. He has coauthored or edited four books, *Acceptable Risk* (1981), *A Two-State Solution in the Middle East* (1993), *Preference Elicitation* (1999), and *Risk Communication: The Mental Models Approach* (2001). He holds a BS in mathematics from Wayne State University and an MA and PhD in psychology from the Hebrew University of Jerusalem.

Martin Fishbein is the Harry C. Coles Jr. Distinguished Professor of Communication and Director of the Health Communication Program in the Annenberg Public Policy Center, Annenberg School for Communication, University of Pennsylvania. Developer of the Theory of Reasoned Action, he studies the relationships among beliefs, attitudes, intentions, and behaviors in both field and laboratory settings. His research interests are in the areas of attitude theory and measurement, communication and persuasion, behavioral prediction and change, and intervention development, implementation, and evaluation. Prior to joining the faculty at Penn, he was a visiting scientist at the Centers for Disease Control and Prevention where he worked in the area of STD and HIV prevention. He has published over 250 articles and chapters and has coauthored or edited 6 books. His current research is supported by NIDA, NIMH, and NICHD.

Brian R. Flay is distinguished Professor, Public Health and Psychology, Health Research and Policy Centers, University of Illinois, Chicago. His research interests include the etiology and prevention of adolescent smoking, drug use, unsafe sex, and violence behaviors and the promotion of positive youth development and enhanced school performance. He is also interested in theories of adolescent behavior development and change and evaluation research methods. He is currently conducting several school-based randomized trials of the Positive Action program, a comprehensive approach to positive youth development.

Geoffrey T. Fong is Associate Professor, Department of Psychology, University of Waterloo. His background is in cognitive, social, and health psychology. He is currently the principal investigator of two large-scale international studies that evaluate the psychosocial and behavioral effects of national-level tobacco control policies—the North American Student Smoking Survey, which is assessing the effects of the graphic Canadian warning labels on tobacco packaging, and the International Tobacco Control Policy Survey, a cohort survey of over 9,000 adult smokers across four countries—Canada, United States, United Kingdom, and Australia—which is designed to evaluate the effects of multiple national-level tobacco control policies. He is also conducting research on the effects of media depictions of smoking in the mass media (especially in movies and TV) on adolescents and young adults. In addition, he is a coinvestigator on several research projects at the University of Pennsylvania designed to formulate, implement, and evaluate the effectiveness of behavioral interventions aimed at reducing HIV sexual risk behavior among adolescents. He is also conducting research on the effects of alcohol on health risk behaviors, including risky sexual behaviors. He received his AB degree from Stanford University and his PhD from the University of Michigan.

J. Dennis Fortenberry is Professor of Pediatrics, Adolescent Medicine, Indiana University, and Associate Director, Division of Adolescent Medicine. His research focuses on adolescent sexuality, care-seeking behaviors related to sexually transmitted infections, and stigma as a barrier to care for sexually transmitted infections.

Michelle L. Gano is a graduate student in Social Psychology at Iowa State University. She is conducting research on social comparison and perceptions of risk associated with unprotected sexual behavior and on the antecedents and consequences of substance-related risk perceptions.

Meg Gerrard is Professor of Psychology, Iowa State University, and Research Scientist, the Institute for Social and Behavioral Sciences. Her research interests include applied social psychology, health, interpersonal processes, sexuality/sexual orientation, social cognition, and social psychological perspectives on health behavior and risk-taking. She has published extensively on these topics in the health and psychology literature, including recent articles such as "Drinking and Driving: A Prospective Assessment of the Relation Between Risk Cognitions and

Risk Behavior," in *Risk, Decision, and Policy,* and "Adolescents' Substance-Related Risk Perceptions: Antecedents, Mediators, and Consequences," also in *Risk, Decision, and Policy.*

Frederick X. Gibbons is a fellow of the American Psychological Society and the Society of Personality and Social Psychology. He has been a pioneer in the application of social comparison theory to understanding health risk behaviors. This work has resulted in the development of a new model of adolescent health behavior that incorporates social, psychological, and cognitive factors—the Prototype/Willingness Model. This research has been supported by grants from the National Science Foundation, the National Cancer Institute, and the National Institutes of Mental Health, Alcoholism and Alcohol Abuse, and Drug Abuse.

Madelyn Gould is Professor in Psychiatry and Public Health (Epidemiology), Columbia University College of Physicians and Surgeons, and Research Scientist, New York State Psychiatric Institute. She has a strong commitment to applying her research to program and policy development. She has received numerous federally funded grants from the National Institutes of Mental Health (NIMH) and the Centers for Disease Control (CDC), including projects to examine risk factors for teenage suicide, various aspects of cluster suicides, the impact of the media on suicide, the effect of suicide on fellow students, and the utility of telephone crisis services for teenagers. She has received funding from the American Foundation for Suicide Prevention to investigate the role of the media in the initiation of suicide clusters and has participated in a number of state and national government commissions. She helped develop a community response plan for suicide clusters and was a member of the Work Group on Contagion and the Reporting of Suicide. As part of the Surgeon General's 1999 National Suicide Prevention Strategy, she authored the chapter on youth suicide prevention, and she has served as a leadership consultant for the Surgeon General's Leadership Working Group for a National Suicide Prevention Strategy. In 1991, she received the Shneidman Award for Research from the American Association of Suicidology.

Kenneth W. Griffin is Assistant Professor, Department of Public Health, Weill Medical College, Cornell University. He conducts research on adolescent risk behaviors, with a primary focus on the etiology and prevention of alcohol, tobacco, and other drug use among youth from different ethnic, cultural, and socioeconomic backgrounds. His research has been supported by the National Institute on Drug Abuse, the National Cancer Institute, and the National Institute on Alcoholism and Alcohol Abuse. He recently received the Early Career Award for outstanding contributions to prevention science from the Society for Prevention Research.

Mark Griffiths is Professor of Gambling Studies, Nottingham Trent University (UK). A chartered psychologist, he has established an international reputation in the area of gambling and gaming addictions that culminated in the award of the John Rosecrance Research Prize for "outstanding scholarly contributions to the field of gambling research." He has published over 100 refereed research papers, books, and book chapters and has over 250 other nonrefereed publications. He has served as a member on a number of national committees and is currently the U.K. National Chair of Gamcare (National Association on Gambling). He has appeared on over 1,000 radio and television programs.

Rina Gupta is a child psychologist and Assistant Professor (part-time) of School/Applied Child Psychology at McGill University. Her research has been focused on youth gambling problems. She is on the editorial board of the *Journal of Gambling Studies* and is Codirector of the McGill University Youth Gambling Research & Treatment Clinic and the International Centre for Youth Gambling Problems and High-Risk Behaviors. She has provided more than 100 clinical and research presentations at national and international conferences and meetings, has published widely, and has provided expert testimony before a number of national and international commissions.

Peter A. Hall is Assistant Professor of Psychology in the Clinical Psychology program at the University of Saskatchewan, Canada. He is also affiliated with the FIT for Active Living rehabilitation program at Saskatoon City Hospital. His research interests include health psychology, social cognition, and behavior change. His ongoing research involves investigating the determinants of health protective behavior performance, and designing interventions to promote healthy behavioral practices among the general population and special medical populations. His laboratory work involves investigating temporal influences on human behavior within the domain of health.

Kathleen Hall Jamieson is Professor of Communication and the Walter H. Annenberg Dean of the Annenberg School for Communication at the University of Pennsylvania. She is also Director of the Annenberg Public Policy Center. She is a Fellow of the American Academy of Arts and Sciences and a member of the American Philosophical Society. She is the author, coauthor, or editor of 12 books, including *The Press Effect* (2003), *Electing the President 2000: The Insiders' View* (2001). and *Everything You Think You Know About Politics . . . and Why You're Wrong* (2000).

Karen Hardoon is a clinician and research coordinator at the International Centre for Youth Gambling Problems and High-Risk Behaviors. She obtained her PhD in School/Applied Child Psychology at McGill University where she was the recipient of an FCAR doctoral fellowship examining the relationship between psychosocial risk factors and youth gambling behaviors. She received the Outstanding Master's Thesis Award from the National Council on Problem Gambling for her work examining the social influences involved in children's gambling behavior. She is the principal author of several papers and has made numerous presentations at national and international conferences.

Nancy Grant Harrington, PhD, is Associate Professor and Chair of the Department of Communication at the University of Kentucky. She is principal investigator or coprincipal investigator on four major research projects dealing with drug abuse prevention, including a laboratory study of need for sensation and need for cognition in a drug abuse prevention context. Her primary areas of interest are in interpersonal communication and in health communication.

Robert Hornik is Wilbur Schramm Professor of Communication and Health Policy at the Annenberg School for Communication, University of Pennsylvania. He has led efforts to design or evaluate more than 24 large-scale public health communication and education programs. These projects include evaluations of national AIDS education programs in four developing countries, and of communication for child survival programs in 10 developing countries, and evaluations of two anti-domestic violence prevention interventions in the United States. He is currently co-principal investigator and scientific director for the evaluation of the National Youth Anti-Drug Media Campaign. He is author of *Development Communication,* coauthor of *Educational Reform With Television: The El Salvador Experience, and editor of Public Health Communication: Evidence for Behavior Change.*

Sean Joe, MSW, PhD, is Research Assistant Professor at the University of Pennsylvania's School of Social Work. His current research, funded by the National Institute of Mental Health, focuses on urban adolescent self-destructive behaviors, black males suicidal behavior, and developing father-focused, family-based interventions to prevent African American adolescent males from engaging in multiple forms of self-destructive behaviors. He has published in the areas of suicide, violence, and firearm-related violence and his work on African American suicide has been used in setting the National Suicide Prevention Strategy of the United States Surgeon General. He also has a significant interest in theoretical and methodological issues regarding community level intervention research, community organizing, and positive youth development which he exercises by engaging in intervention research and social change organizing to positively enhance the transition of urban youth to young adulthood.

Lloyd D. Johnston is a Distinguished Research Scientist at the University of Michigan's Institute for Social Research. A social psychologist by training, he has been the principal investigator of the Monitoring the Future (MTF) study since its inception in 1975 and of the Youth, Education, and Society (YES) study since 1997. Johnston has written and lectured extensively in the areas of substance abuse epidemiology, etiology, policy, and prevention and is the author of nearly 50 books and monographs and over 100 articles and chapters. He has helped to design national surveys in more than a dozen foreign countries. He served as a presidential appointee to the National Commission on Drug-Free Schools and the White House Conference for a Drug-Free America.

Douglas Kirby is a Senior Research Scientist at Education Training Research Associates in Scotts Valley, California. For 25 years, he has directed large studies of adolescent sexual behavior, abstinence-only programs, sexuality and HIV education programs, school-based clinics, school condom availability programs, and youth development programs. He has coauthored research on several effective curricula that significantly reduced unprotected sex. In *Emerging Answers:*

Research Findings on Programs to Reduce Teen Pregnancy, he painted a more comprehensive and detailed picture of the risk and protective factors associated with adolescent sexual behavior and identified important groups of programs that reduce sexual risk taking or pregnancy. Over the years, he has also authored or coauthored more than 100 volumes, articles, and chapters on adolescent sexual behavior and programs designed to change that behavior.

Derek R. Lane, PhD, is Assistant Professor of Communication at the University of Kentucky and specializes in interpersonal and instructional communication. He is coinvestigator on a number of major funded projects, including a laboratory study of need for sensation and need for cognition in a drug abuse prevention context.

Daniel K. Lapsley is Professor and Chairman, Department of Educational Psychology, Ball State University. He is the editor or author of five books and numerous articles and chapters on various features of human development and educational psychology, particularly in the areas of moral psychology, self, ego and identity development, personality, and adjustment and social cognition. His research has won awards from the American Educational Research Association and the National Council for the Social Studies Advisory Committee on Research, and he currently serves on the review boards for the *Journal of Educational Psychology,* the *Journal of Early Adolescence,* and the *Journal of Adolescent Research.*

Maria D. LaRusso is currently completing her doctorate in human development and psychology at the Harvard Graduate School of Education. She also works on various research projects evaluating the effectiveness of interventions and prevention programs for reducing risk behavior and promoting social development in adolescence. Previously, she worked with issues of risk in adolescence as a child and family therapist.

Willa Leitten is Project Manager for the Center of Adolescent Substance Abuse Research, Department of Psychiatry, University of Minnesota. Her areas of research interest are youth with learning problems and indicated and selected prevention programs. She currently runs a brief intervention pilot program for mild drug-abusing teenagers.

Caryn Lerman is Mary W. Calkins Professor and Director of the Tobacco Use Research Center, Department of Psychiatry and the Annenberg Public Policy Center, University of Pennsylvania, and Associate Director, Cancer Control and Population Science, University of Pennsylvania Cancer Center. As the principal investigator of an NCI/NIDA Transdisciplinary Tobacco Use Research Center (P50) Grant, her current projects include investigation of genetic profiles to predict response to bupropion for smoking cessation, bio-behavioral predictors of response to alternate forms of nicotine replacement therapy, and laboratory-based studies of genetic influences on nicotine sensitivity. She is a member of the National Cancer Institute (NCI) Board of Scientific Advisors and has been the recipient of the Society of Behavioral Medicine New Investigator Award (1989) and the American Psychological Association Early Career Award for Outstanding Contributions to Health Psychology (1995).

She has published over 140 articles in the areas of genetics, cancer control, and tobacco use.

Susan G. Millstein is Professor of Pediatrics, Department of Pediatrics, Division of Adolescent Medicine, and Associate Director for Research and Academic Affairs in the Division of Adolescent Medicine, Department of Pediatrics at University of California, San Francisco. She also holds faculty appointments at the Institute for Health Policy Studies at UCSF, in the Postdoctoral Program on Psychology and Medicine UCSF, and at the Center on Adolescence at Stanford University. Her research interests focus on affective and cognitive contributions to health-related decision making, risk perception, and judgment. She has published widely on adolescent health issues ranging from adolescents' health behaviors to the delivery of adolescent health services. Her research has been supported by national foundations, as well as the National Institutes of Child Health and Human Development, and Alcoholism and Alcohol Abuse. She is active in a variety of national activities related to adolescent health promotion and prevention.

Mignon R. Moore is Assistant Professor, Department of Sociology, Columbia University. Her research and teaching interests include sociology of the family, racial and ethnic identity, urban poverty, and adolescent development. She has been awarded grants from the Andrew W. Mellon Foundation, the Ford Foundation, and the Woodrow Wilson National Fellowship Foundation.

Philip Palmgreen, PhD, is Professor of Communication at the University of Kentucky. He is widely known for his work on media campaigns and prevention of risky behavior, especially drug use. He has served as principal or coprincipal investigator on a series of projects supported by the National Institute on Drug Abuse and the National Institute on Mental Health investigating the design and targeting of televised public service announcements for populations at risk for drug abuse or HIV infection. He served for four years as a primary scientific advisor to the Office of National Drug Control Policy's National Youth Anti-Drug Media Campaign. He has authored over 50 research articles and book chapters, edited two books, and presented over 50 scholarly papers.

Andrew M. Parker is Assistant Professor of Marketing, Virginia Polytechnic Institute and State University. His research interests focus on decision processes and risk appraisal in adolescents and adults. He received his BA in 1993 from the University of Michigan, majoring in psychology and statistics. In 1996, he received an MS in statistics from Carnegie Mellon University and in 1997 a second MS, this time in behavioral decision theory, from the same institution. His PhD, also in behavioral decision theory, was awarded by Carnegie Mellon in 2000.

Freda Patterson is a smoking cessation counselor for the Tobacco Use Research Center at the University of Pennsylvania. She holds a master's degree in health education and is currently pursuing a doctoral degree at Temple University's Department of Public Health. Her interests include racial differences in tobacco use and smoking patterns among adolescents and young adults.

Marc N. Potenza is Director, Problem Gambling Clinic; Director, Women and Addictive Disorders Core, Women's Health Research at Yale; and Assistant Professor of Psychiatry, Yale University School of Medicine. His major research interest is in the field of addiction psychiatry. In particular, his work focuses on the relationship between pathological gambling and drug use disorders. He is applying a variety of techniques to investigate the characteristics of pathological gamblers, ranging from clinical investigations into the characteristics, consequences, and treatment of problem and pathological gambling to functional magnetic resonance imaging studies exploring regional brain activities underlying gambling urges in pathological gamblers. Recent awards he has received include a Young Investigator Award from the National Alliance for Research on Schizophrenia and Depression, a Neuroscience Research Award from the National Center for Responsible Gaming, and a Drug Abuse Research Scholar Program in Psychiatry Award from the National Institute on Drug Abuse and the American Psychiatric Association.

Joseph Lee Rodgers is Robert Glenn Rapp Foundation Presidential Professor, Department of Psychology, University of Oklahoma. He is a quantitative psychologist who develops mathematical models of adolescent development. His research has focused on adolescent sexuality, behavior genetics, family structure, fertility decision making, and intellectual development. His recent books include *The Biodemography of Fertility* (2003), *The Ontogeny of Human Bonding Systems* (2001), and *Genetic Influences on Human Fertility and Sexuality* (2000). He has received a number of university awards for teaching statistics and research methods. He has been at OU since 1981 and has held visiting research and teaching appointments at the University of Hawaii, Ohio State University, University of North Carolina, Duke University, and Odense University in Denmark.

Jodie L. Roth is a research scientist at the National Center for Children and Families at Teachers College, Columbia University. She is interested in how programs and institutions affect adolescents' development. Her research currently focuses on how prevention and youth development programs in schools and the community can promote healthy adolescent development. She received her PhD from the Combined Program in Education and Psychology at the University of Michigan in 1995.

Robert L. Selman is Roy Edward Larsen Professor of Human Development and Education, Harvard Graduate School of Education, and Professor of Psychology, Harvard Medical School. His work focuses on promoting social awareness as a way to reduce risks to health and to facilitate educational achievement. He currently does practice-based research on interpersonal and intergroup development and its connection to literacy. He is the author of *The Promotion of Social Awareness* (2003), *Making a Friend in Youth* (with L.H. Schultz, 1990), and *The Growth of Interpersonal Understanding* (1980).

Herbert H. Severson is Senior Research Scientist, Oregon Research Institute, and Professor of Counseling Psychology, University of Oregon. He has been an investigator of NIH grants focused on development and evaluation of tobacco prevention and cessation. He has recently focused his research on evaluating smokeless tobacco cessation programs and school and community prevention programs. He is a contributing author of three Surgeon General Reports, over 100 articles in professional journals, four books, and over 20 video and interactive computer-based programs on tobacco prevention and cessation. He is currently developing Internet-delivered interactive programs for both tobacco cessation and parenting education. He is also evaluating screening and early interventions for preschool primary grade children who exhibit high-risk behaviors.

Alexandra E. Shields is Assistant Professor of Public Policy, Institute for Health Care Research and Policy, Georgetown Public Policy Institute, Georgetown University, and Lecturer in Medicine, Harvard Medical School, Partner's Health Care Institute for Health Policy.

Myrna B. Shure is Developmental Psychologist, Department of Psychology, Drexel University. Her Interpersonal Cognitive Problem Solving (ICPS) programs, now called I Can Problem Solve (also ICPS) and her pioneering research with George Spivack have won national awards and have been recognized by the 1999 President's Report on School Safety; the Center for the Study of Prevention and Violence; Blueprints for Violence Prevention, the Expert Panel; Safe, Disciplined, and Drug Free Schools, U.S. Department of Education; and the Center for Substance Abuse Prevention. She is the author or coauthor of six books: *I Can Problem Solve* curriculum guides for preschool through Grade 6 for use in schools, and numerous book chapters and journal articles. She was a recipient of the 1998 Sarah Award in Education given by the Philadelphia chapter of Women in Communications and the 1999 recipient of the Psychology in the Media Award, Pennsylvania Psychological Association. She writes a weekly parenting column for the *Philadelphia Daily News* and speaks nationwide on issues relating to our nation's youth.

Paul Slovic is President of Decision Research and Professor of Psychology at the University of Oregon. He studies human judgment, decision making, and risk analysis. He is past president of the Society for Risk Analysis and in 1991 received its Distinguished Contribution Award. In 1993, he received the Distinguished Scientific Contribution Award from the American Psychological Association, and in 1995, he received the Outstanding Contribution to Science Award from the Oregon Academy of Science. He received a BA degree from Stanford University, an MA and PhD from the University of Michigan, and an honorary doctorate from the Stockholm School of Economics.

Bonita Stanton is Professor and Chairperson of the Department of Pediatrics at Wayne State University. Formerly Chair, Department of Pediatrics, West Virginia University, she has received funding for over 10 years from the NIH, AHCPR, the Fogarty Foundation, and the World AIDS Foundation regarding adolescent risk and protective behaviors in settings around the world. She is an emeritus member of the Board of Trustees of the Child Health Foundation and has consulted with numerous national and international groups on issues related to urban health, HIV/AIDS transmission in youth, and health services research. Her special interests are pediatric infectious diseases, AIDS, HIV prevention in adolescents and adolescent risk reduction in low-income adolescents, and community health. She has been an author and reviewer of numerous journals and is board certified in pediatrics.

Laurence Steinberg is the Distinguished University Professor and Laura H. Carnell Professor of Psychology at Temple University and is currently Director of the John D. and Catherine T. MacArthur Foundation Research Network on Adolescent Development and Juvenile Justice. His research has focused on a range of topics in the study of contemporary adolescence, including parent-adolescent relationships, adolescent employment, high school reform, and juvenile crime and justice. He is the author or coauthor of more than 200 scholarly articles and several books on growth and development during the teenage years.

Rachel A. Volberg is Senior Research Scientist at the National Opinion Research Center, Washington, D.C.; and Adjunct Associate Professor, Department of Biostatistics & Epidemiology, School of Public Health, University of Massachusetts, Amherst. She is President of Gemini Research, the only international organization that specializes in managing studies of gambling in the general population. She sits on the board of directors of the National Council on Problem Gambling. She has directed or consulted on numerous surveys of gambling and problem gambling among adults and adolescents in the United States and Canada. Internationally, she has directed or consulted on gambling studies in countries as diverse as Australia, New Zealand, Norway, and Sweden. Her publications include numerous government reports, book chapters, and scholarly articles, including the recent book *When the Chips are Down: Problem Gambling in America* (2001).

Hill M. Walker is Codirector of Institute on Violence and Destructive Behavior, and Director of the Center on Human Development at the College of Education, University of Oregon. He is the author of over 200 articles, chapters, and books in the area of children's behavior disorders. He is the coauthor, with Herbert Severson, of *Systematic Screening for Behavior Disorders (SSBD)* (1990); author of *The Acting Out Child: Coping With Classroom Disruption* (2nd ed., 1995); coauthor, with Geoffrey Colvin and Elizabeth Ramsey, of *Antisocial Behavior in School: Strategies and Best Practices* (1995); and senior author of *First Step to Success: Helping Young Children Overcome Antisocial Behavior* (1997), an early intervention program for grades K–3.

Gina M. Wingood is Associate Professor in the Department of Behavioral Sciences and Health Education, and Co-Director, Behavioral and Social Science Core, Emory Center for AIDS Research. Her research interest is in primary and secondary HIV prevention for women. She has published numerous articles on effective HIV prevention interventions for women. She is currently the principal investigator on two NIMH-funded grants both of which focus on reducing African American women's sexual risk. One grant, titled STARS (*Sisters Talking About Responsible Solutions*), is designed to test the efficacy of an HIV prevention program to reduce high-risk sexual behaviors over a 2-year follow-up period. A second grant, titled *EBAN,* is a sexual risk reduction program for African American serodiscordant couples designed to reduce high-risk sexual behaviors and incident STDs over a 1-year follow-up period. She received her MPH in maternal and child health from the University of California, Berkeley, and her ScD from the Harvard University School of Public Health in Health and Social Behavior.

Ken C. Winters is Director of the Center for Adolescent Substance Abuse Research and Associate Professor of Psychiatry at the University of Minnesota. His research interests include adolescent drug abuse and problem gambling. He has published numerous assessment tools and research articles in these areas and has received several research grants. He is on the editorial board of the *Journal of Child and Adolescent Substance Abuse* and is an associate editor for the *Psychology of Addictive Behaviors* and the *Journal of Gambling Studies.* He is a consultant to many organizations, including the Hazelden Foundation, the National Institute on Drug Abuse, the Center for Substance Abuse Treatment, the World Health Organization, and the Mentor Foundation.

Marco Yzer is Assistant Professor at the Department of Communication Science at the Amsterdam School of Communications Research (ASCoR) of the University of Amsterdam. He received his PhD in social psychology from the University of Groningen in 1999. He then joined the Annenberg Public Policy Center of the University of Pennsylvania as a postdoctoral fellow to work on a project that experimentally tested the effectiveness of antidrug messages targeted at adolescents. Yzer's research interests include the evaluation of mass media campaigns, experimental tests of message effectiveness, tests of the validity of theories of behavioral prediction and change, and the applicability of these issues to health communication.

Lin Zhu is a recent graduate from Temple University's clincial psychology program. She has collaborated with Dr. Lauren Alloy on many projects. Most recently, they examined cross-cultural differences in optimism and well-being in Chinese and American college students. Dr. Zhu is currently in charge of student training in a mental health center.

Rick S. Zimmerman, PhD, is Associate Professor of Communication in the Department of Communication, with an adjunct appointment in the Department of Behavioral Science in the College of Medicine, both at the University of Kentucky. He is the developer of the Impulsive Decision-Making Scale and currently holds five major grants on prevention of sexual risk taking in relation to alcohol use and HIV, involving classroom and media approaches. He also conducts a statewide program of research in HIV prevention.